TEXTILES OF THE
EARLY ISLAMIC CALIPHATES

TEXTILES OF THE
EARLY ISLAMIC CALIPHATES

JOCHEN SOKOLY

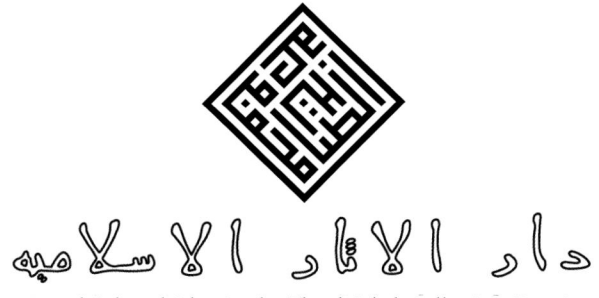

Dar al-Athar al-Islamiyyah   The al-Sabah Collection, Kuwait

FRONTISPIECE: Detail, Cat. 66 (LNS 56 T)
PAGE 6: Detail, Cat. 114 (LNS 75 T)
PAGE 514: Detail, Cat. 55 (LNS 68 T)
PAGES 546–47: Cat. 54 (LNS 57 T)

First published in the United Kingdom in 2025 by
Thames & Hudson Ltd, 6–24 Britannia Street, London WC1X 9JD

First published in the United States of America in 2025 by
Thames & Hudson Inc., 500 Fifth Avenue, New York,
New York 10110

Textiles of the Early Islamic Caliphates
© 2025 Gulf Museum Consultancy Company, WLL, Kuwait
Text © 2025 Jochen Sokoly

Series editor: Salam Kaoukji

Photography: Muhammad Ali, Robert Lorenzo, Michael Tejero

Design: Maggi Smith

EU Authorized Representative: Interart S.A.R.L.
19 rue Charles Auray, 93500 Pantin, Paris, France
productsafety@thameshudson.co.uk
interart.fr

A CIP catalogue record for this book is available from the British
Library

Library of Congress Control Number 2025933328

ISBN 978-0-500-96605-1
01

Printed and bound in China by C & C Offset Printing Co. Ltd

Co-sponsored by
Kuwait Foundation for the Advancement of Sciences
The Kuwait Foundation for the Advancement of Sciences (KFAS) was
established in 1976 by an Amiri Decree under the direction of the late
Amir of Kuwait, H.H. Sheikh Jaber Al-Ahmad Al-Jaber Al-Sabah
with a vision to create and nurture a thriving culture of science,
technology, and innovation (STI) for a sustainable Kuwait. Fully
sponsored by national shareholding companies, KFAS promotes STI
in the community at all age and professional segments.
For more information, visit the website: www.kfas.org

CONTENTS

IN MEMORY OF
SHEIKH NASSER SABAH AL-AHMAD AL-SABAH
(1948–2020)

FOREWORD

When my husband Nasser al-Sabah and I were presented with a selection of inscribed *tiraz* textiles, we immediately felt compelled to purchase them and thence collect as many examples of the type as we could.

As most of these examples were either produced for the court or intended for the general public and probably had been buried with their owners, they thus offered definitive exemplification of styles and titulature favoured over different periods. We were therefore confident that they would contribute significant historical documentation and resources to researchers and art history students who studied the subject.

Hussa Sabah al-Salem al-Sabah
Co-owner and Director of The al-Sabah Collection, Kuwait

ACKNOWLEDGMENTS

In memory of Ralph Pinder-Wilson, who taught me to read inscriptions,
and my parents, Friedrich and Elisabeth Sokoly

My foremost gratitude goes to the late Sheikh Nasser Sabah al-Ahmad al-Sabah and Sheikha Hussa Sabah al-Salim al-Sabah. Both made me feel very welcome every time I visited Kuwait. The al-Sabah Collection became my focal point for many years during which a great many friendships developed with those working there, a number of which have persisted to this day. I am grateful for Sue Kaoukji's wisdom, advice and knowledge as a curator. Manuel Keene, formerly curator, was also a treasure trove of knowledge. Deborah Freeman, assistant curator for many years, and a good friend, has read part of this book at manuscript stage. Aurora Luis was always on top of paperwork and logistics. Layla Moussawi helped to read inscriptions and texts in Arabic, and discussed historical issues. Among the team of conservators at The al-Sabah Collection my thanks go first to Maria Mertzani, who has been a good friend since the beginning. In general the conservators provided a stable presence, while visitors and research scholars would come and go. Lieve Hibler-Vandenbulcke was a model of accuracy and determination in her work. Abdulaziz al-Duweesh became a good friend, and I have seen him grow from a recent university graduate to an expert who now installs exhibitions for The al-Sabah Collection worldwide. My gratitude also goes to conservators Kirsty Norman, Frankie Halahan and Sophie Budden. Among the support staff, Benji Hilario was the one without whom nothing worked. He made all the objects available for study. Muhammad Ali photographed all the pieces and was always a source of interesting stories concerning Kuwait. Mutlaq Juraid helped in all matters relating to the collection in the later years and assisted with travel.

I thank Katie Marsh for initiating my first contact with The al-Sabah Collection. It was Louise Mackie who, during a visit to Kuwait, had suggested to the Collection that I be considered to write a catalogue of their *tiraz* textiles. I am indebted to her, as she was also instrumental in supporting me during my doctoral research on *tiraz* textiles as a Gervers Fellow at the Royal Ontario Museum in Toronto, and later served as external examiner for my DPhil viva at Oxford University. Her wealth of expertise on Islamic textiles and her willingness to share her knowledge have been invaluable.

This book has been in the making for a long time and required many visits to Kuwait which were organised by The al-Sabah Collection. Virginia Commonwealth University awarded me several generous faculty grants over the years that supported work on this book. I am particularly indebted to my VCU colleagues Radha Dalal and Fikria El Kaouakibi. I am very grateful to Harvard PhD candidates Walid Akef for translating all the Arabic inscriptions into English and Sarah Molina who edited my catalogue text. I am grateful to my VCU colleague Tiffany Schureman for assisting in sourcing and ordering many contextual images. My colleagues Burzine Waghmar at SOAS, Martina Rugiardi and Navina Haidar Haykel at the Metropolitan Museum, New York, Mina Moraitou at the Benaki Museum, Athens, Idit Sharoni and Deena Lawi at the Islamic Art Museum, Jerusalem, Nahla Nassar at the Khalili Collection, London, Ina Sandmann and Katherine Vose at the Sarikhani Collection, Regula Schorta and Catherine Depierraz at the Abegg Stiftung, Bern, Tracy Meserve and Molly Megan at the Textile Museum, Washington, DC, Jonathan Bloom, and Bernard O'Kane all deserve my gratitude for supplying contextual images. My colleague Roland-Pierre Gayraud at CNRS, France, provided images from his excavation at Istabl 'Antar in Cairo and provided background concerning the contents of the burials found there, for which I am grateful. I thank Aimée Froom and Chadwick Redmon at the Museum of Fine Arts, Houston, for rephotographing a textile featured in the catalogue. Many thanks also go to Mikel Herran Subiñas, Robert Davies and Rosemary Roberts for their help in editing. At Thames & Hudson I thank Mark Ralph for all his support in seeing this project through to the finished book.

My time in Kuwait was made special by the friends I made there: Aruna and Ghazi Sultan, Lucy Topalian and Paula Al-Sabah. Finally, such a project and the research that underpins it would have never been conceivable without the support and encouragement of my late parents, Friedrich and Elisabeth Sokoly to whom this book is dedicated.

Jochen Sokoly

NOTE TO THE READER

The Islamic calendar begins with year 1 of the *Hijra*. The word *Hijra* ('a severing of ties of kinship or association') describes a journey the Prophet Muhammad and his followers took from Mecca to Medina. It corresponds to the year 622 of the Common Era (CE), which is based on the Julian calendar. Throughout the text, years are given in the Common Era, except where specific *hijri* dates are concerned, for example when a date or year is mentioned in an Arabic text or an inscription. In those cases, both *hijri* and Common Era dates are given in the format 1 AH / 622 CE, where 'AH' stands for *anno Hegirae*, or 'in the year of the *Hijra*'. As the Islamic calendar is based on the lunar year, one *hijri* year corresponds to 354–355 days, as opposed to a solar year of 365 days in the Julian calendar of the Common Era. As a consequence, a year in the Islamic calendar corresponds to two Common Era years, with just a small number of exceptions.

Throughout the book, Arabic names and terms without English equivalent have been transliterated using the system established for the *International Journal of Middle East Studies*. To make the book more accessible to the non-specialist reader, this system has been simplified further by removing all diacriticals and underscores, except for the letter *ayn* (') and the *hamza* ('), a character denoting a glottal stop. This also applies to entries in the *Encyclopaedia of Islam* listed in the bibliography. Furthermore, in the adjectives 'Umayyad' and 'Abbasid', which describe two of the early Islamic caliphates, the initial *ayn* has also been dropped. It has also been decided to follow written Arabic, rather than spoken Arabic, in the transliteration of words that end and begin in a vowel, so that '*wa'l-kitab*' (where one vowel is dropped) becomes '*wa al-kitab*', or 'Abu'l-Hasan' becomes 'Abu al-Hasan'; the one exception to this rule concerns caliphal titles (*laqab*), where '*bi'llah*' becomes '*bi-llah*'. Foreign words and proper nouns that are commonly used in English and have a recognized English form have been anglicized. Place names follow English usage and reflect current national borders. The word *tiraz* is used both as a singular and plural. False English plurals are often used for Arabic nouns (as in '*laqab*s').

PREFACE

The al-Sabah Collection's holdings of early Islamic textiles comprise a variety of different material from diverse geographic origins. The current book focuses on a group of early medieval Islamic textiles, also referred to as *tiraz* textiles, most of which once constituted parts of burial outfits belonging to deceased members of the diverse religious communities in Egypt during the centuries leading up to the twelfth century CE. The collection presented here is a good cross-section of this material and provides a comprehensive overview of the different types of materials and techniques used across the early Islamic world.

In its strictest sense the term *tiraz* implies that these textiles comprise inscriptions that record regulated caliphal protocols similar to those found on coins or official early Islamic papyrus documents reflecting political and administrative hierarchy: invocations to God and a ruling caliph, administrative information relating to a chain of delegation concerning orders by members of the caliph's family or a vizier, often their execution by a bureaucrat, the type of workshop, its location, and the year of manufacture.[1] Indeed, The al-Sabah Collection features many inscribed *tiraz* textiles that are significant historically because they record administrative data hitherto not published. However, for the present work a more liberal definition of *tiraz* has been adopted, rather than the narrow one which focuses on historical data alone. It has allowed for the inclusion of a variety of textiles that are related to *tiraz* in terms of type or aesthetic, but are inscribed with non-historical Quranic verses, benedictory phrases, non-meaningful epigraphic repeats, or sometimes only comprise bands of vegetal or zoomorphic decoration, or patterns. This approach is borne out by the fact that in the historical literary sources the term *tiraz* is often not clearly defined. In the sources relating to the earliest occurrences the term is for one not limited to textiles or clothing, while later texts that mention clothing with *tiraz* bands (*tirazi* or *mutarraz*) are not very descriptive about what they looked like. Furthermore, recent excavations of burials in Egypt have shown that caliphal *tiraz* and non-caliphal *tiraz* were used concurrently, often enshrouding the same body.

The book concentrates on material that dates or can be attributed to before the end of the twelfth century CE. In Egypt this period is marked by the fall of the Fatimid dynasty in 1171. With the rise of the Ayyubids (1171–1250) and later the Mamluks (1250–1517) the *tiraz* practice underwent significant changes in how inscriptions were conceived in terms of content and aesthetic, changes that reflect developments across the Islamic world.

The current book is meant as a resource for both the general reader and the specialist. Its aim is to provide a context for a body of material that often seems hard to understand, and has remained obscure for a long time, because of its fragmentary nature, the nature of the raw materials, production techniques or the difficulty in navigating the various types and styles of inscriptions. It is with this in mind that the Catalogue is preceded by three introductory chapters. Chapter 1 provides a general view into the origins and development of the clothing cultures of the Early Islamic world from the point of view of historical sources, visual representations of clothing and surviving garments. Chapter 2 looks at how inscriptions on tiraz textiles served as political statements and administrative documents, as well as their role as caliphal gifts, in order to understand their archaeological survival as burial shrouds. Chapter 3 provides an investigation into the materials and processes of manufacture of inscribed textiles and proposes new ways to look at the material at large through the lens of textiles in The al-Sabah Collection. The Catalogue provides not only a listing of the textiles, organised chronologically, as well as geographically, but also historical background on the various regions and places of production, as well as detailed narratives concerning the particular historical figures mentioned in some of the inscriptions, as well as technical data, all of which link back to the introductory chapters.

Ultimately, the present book attempts to make the world of early Islamic inscribed textiles more accessible to wider general audience, but also provides an impetus to specialists of early Islamic history, administration, epigraphy, or craft practice to investigate the multiversity of data provided by this body of material and perhaps see these objects in a new light.

Detail, Cat. 189 (LNS 422 T)

BLACK SEA

CASPIAN SEA

Constantinople
(Istanbul)

Caucasus

Rum

MEDITERRANEAN

Bilad al-Sham
(Greater Syria)

☐ Mosul

Ifriqiya

Qasr al-Hayr al-Gharbi ○

Dura Europos ○   Samarra ○

Taq-i Bustan ○

Baghdad (Madinat al-Salam)

☆ Damascus

Alexandria ☐

Khirbat al-Mafjar
Jerusalem ☆○○

○ Tabariyya
Amman

IRAQ

Isfahar

☆ Ctesiphon

Tustar
(Shushtar) ○

Cairo
(Misr al-Fustat Al-Qahira) ☆

○ Qusayr 'Amra

Kufa ○

Wasit ○

Khuzestar

Basra ☐

Kuwait City ☐

THE GUL

Qusayr al-Qadim ○

ARABIAN PENINSULA

Medina ☐

RED SEA   Hijaz

Mecca ☐

Tihama

Dahlak ○

Hadramaw

☆ San'a'
Ma'afir   YEMEN

Nile Delta inset:

Alexandria ☐

Damietta,
Abwan
Bura ○ ○
Shata ○ ○ Tuna
○ ○ Tinnis

Sanhur ○

NILE DELTA   ○ ○
Mahallat al-Dakhil,
Samnud, Dumayra

Biyawrnabara

LOWER EGYPT   ☆ Al-Qahira (Cairo),
Misr al-Fustat

Fayyum   ○ Madinat al-Fayyum
Tuttun ○ ○ Deir al-Naqlun
Qays ○ ○ Bahnasa

○ Ashmunayn

Asyut ○

○ Akhmim

UPPER EGYPT

Thebes ○

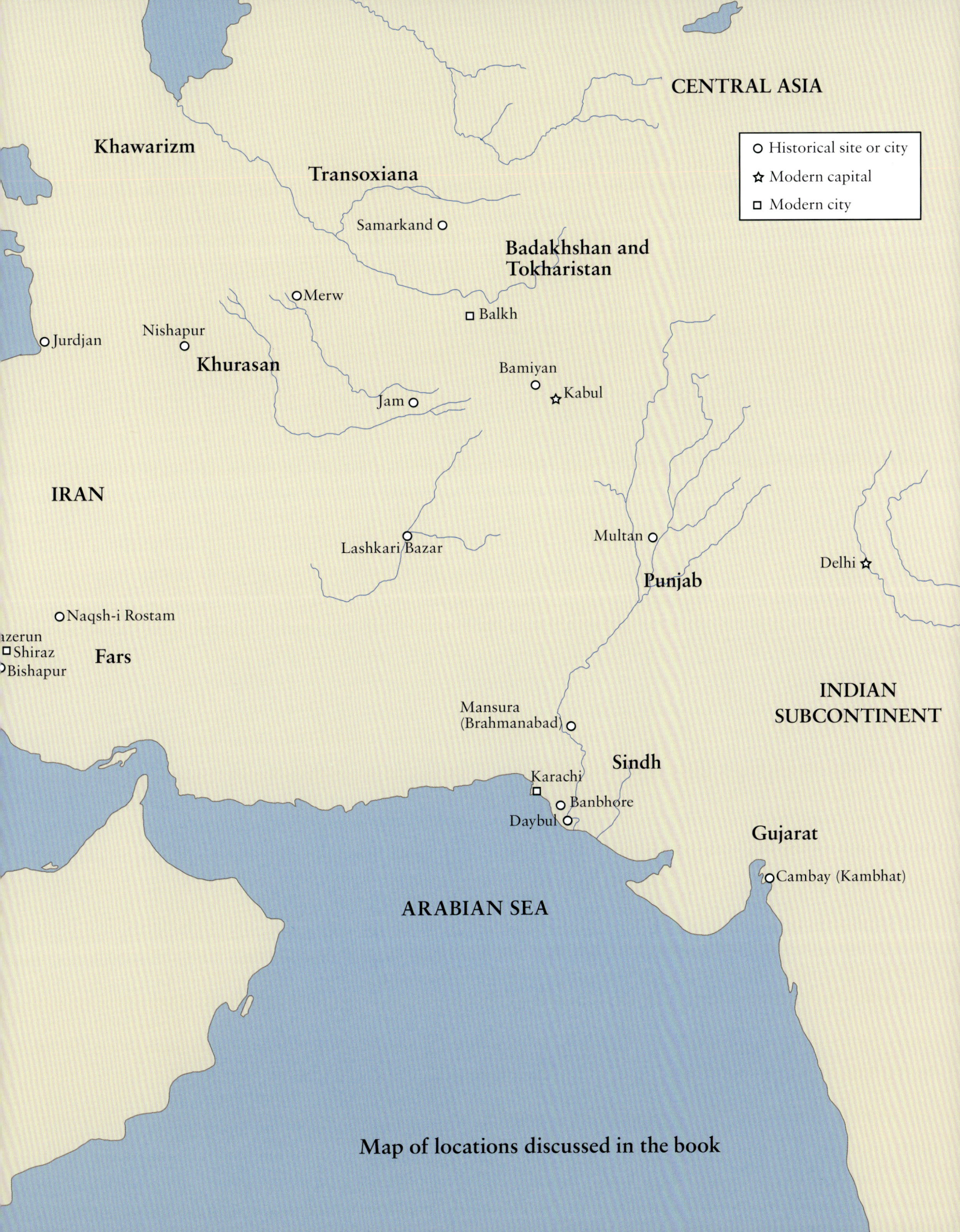

CENTRAL ASIA

○ Historical site or city
☆ Modern capital
□ Modern city

Khawarizm

Transoxiana

Samarkand ○

Badakhshan and
Tokharistan

Merw ○

□ Balkh

○ Jurdjan

Nishapur
○

Khurasan

Bamiyan
○

Jam ○

☆ Kabul

IRAN

Lashkari Bazar ○

Multan ○

Punjab

Delhi ☆

○ Naqsh-i Rostam

azerun
□ Shiraz

Fars

○ Bishapur

INDIAN
SUBCONTINENT

Mansura
(Brahmanabad) ○

Sindh

Karachi
□

○ Banbhore

Daybul ○

Gujarat

ARABIAN SEA

○ Cambay (Kambhat)

Map of locations discussed in the book

THE WORLD OF DRESS DURING THE EARLY ISLAMIC CALIPHATES: FASHION, DIPLOMACY AND TRADE

Textiles and fashion were as important in the early Islamic world as they are today, economically and culturally. When, in the seventh and eighth centuries, the caliphates stepped into the footprints of the late Roman Empire in many parts of the Mediterranean, and the Sasanians did the same in the Iranian world and central Asia, they inherited textile industries and trade networks that had been flourishing for many centuries. In time, the clothing traditions that had existed in Arabia before the advent of Islam merged with these non-Arab traditions to create a new Islamic identity in clothing and fashion that was pluralistic and differentiated by regional variations.[1] Looking at what has survived from the early Islamic world, and considering the evidence of literary sources, what emerges is a society for which textiles, fashion and clothing were paramount. The sheer variety of surviving garments and fabrics is staggering, in terms of their materials, production techniques, colours and range of quality and styles, as well as their modes of decoration. This diversity is mirrored by how historical texts discuss fabrics and clothing, the variations in wording they use to denote minute differences between cloth types and weaves, and the array of names for particular garments – all of this going far beyond what a modern person would be accustomed to.

The inscribed *tiraz* and *tiraz*-style textiles discussed in this book, mainly from the central Islamic lands, constitute only a fraction of that textile world.[2] This introduction offers the reader some background by highlighting a number of the historical developments in textiles and fashion, looking at surviving garments and representations of garments, and tracing how they are described in historical literature.

BEFORE THE BIRTH OF ISLAM

The clothing culture of Byzantium and the late Roman Empire was class conscious in the types of garments worn and the fabrics used. This can be observed in the mosaic decorations of various buildings in Ravenna, notably the sixth-century basilicas of Sant'Apollinare Nuovo and San Vitale. The clerestory of the nave in Sant'Apollinare contains representations of apostles, prophets and evangelists dressed in the Hellenistic Roman tradition, in long white robes decorated with two *clavi* front and back, as well as two bands on the lower sleeve (fig. 1.1). A toga

1.1   Figure of an apostle or evangelist, 6th century. Mosaic. Sant'Apollinare Nuovo, Ravenna, consecrated 504 CE.

Detail, fig. 1.33 (p. 34)

1.2   The Three Magi, wearing trousers and Phrygian caps as a sign of their Oriental origin, 6th century. Mosaic. Sant'Apollinare Nuovo, Ravenna, consecrated 504 CE.

is draped over the left shoulder. A long frieze above the colonnade to the right of the altar features a procession of virgins holding laurel wreaths. They wear ornate and bejewelled dresses over long white ornamented undergarments, the back of the head and left shoulder covered by a white tasselled veil. The procession is led by the Three Magi, all dressed to underline their Eastern origin, in short tunics worn over variously patterned trousers, with capes of differing colours flung over their shoulders and fastened with clasps (fig. 1.2). What stands out here are the Phrygian caps. The colour range and ornamentation, as well as the decoration of the men's clothes, are dazzling. They portray an Iranian dress culture distinct from that of imperial Rome and Byzantium.

Similar short tunics decorated with ornamented borders and worn over trousers are seen on two male figures on a limestone sarcophagus relief from Palmyra in Syria dating from the late Roman period, now in the Musée du Louvre (fig. 1.3). At the edge of the eastern Roman Empire and close to its border with the Iranian world, Palmyra was a melting pot of cultures and traditions. The Parthian period in Iran

1.3   Standing figures, sarcophagus relief, Roman Empire, first half of the 3rd century CE. Limestone, 68.5 × 50 × 24 cm. Musée du Louvre, Paris, inv. no. AO 15556.

1.4   Arsacid prince (life-size), Shami, Khuzestan Province, Iran, *c.* 50 BCE–150 CE. Cast bronze, height 1.9 metres. Iran Bastan Museum, Tehran, Iran.

(*c.* 250 BCE–224 CE) was dominated by constant conflict with Rome, first the republic and then the empire. To the Romans, the Parthians were barbarians, inferior culturally. The famous imperial portrait of Augustus from Prima Porta in the Musei Vaticani in Rome, dated to *c.* 20 BCE, references the Parthians exactly in this way.[3] The portrait, a marble copy of a lost bronze original, shows Augustus as a military victor, dressed as a general with an elaborate breastplate covered in propagandistic imagery. The central scene comprises a Parthian warrior or ruler returning a Roman military standard to a

Roman soldier – a reference to a historical moment when Augustus managed to retrieve the Roman standard lost in battle in 53 BCE by his general Crassus. The Parthian figure is shown in clothing decidedly different from that used by Romans, a tunic worn over trousers.[4] It is this type of clothing from Parthian Iran that is referenced in the Ravenna mosaics, a type that had become ingrained in Roman ideology to denote oriental otherness. An imperial figure of a kneeling barbarian from the early first to early second century, found on the Palatine Hill in Rome and now in the Museo Archeologico Nazionale in Naples, portrays a kneeling Iranian dressed in Parthian clothing with a Phrygian cap.[5] The figure is a particularly clear and naturalistic representation of the pleated tunic and trousers, which are worn over what appear to be leather boots. A small ceramic figurine found in Syria and now in the British Museum shows a similarly dressed mounted archer, albeit far less naturalistic and with a wild beard.[6] An impressive life-size bronze statue of an Arsacid prince found in Shami in the southern Iranian province of Khuzestan represents the Iranian counterpart to Roman imperial portraits (fig. 1.4). The prince, with his staunch and uncompromising gaze fixed straight ahead, wears a short jacket, fastened by a belt, and a pair of baggy pleated trousers and boots. Given that this costume was ultimately derived from that of earlier nomadic invaders from central Asia, it is possible that the leggings serve as a protective layer when mounted on a horse.

The imperial garments seen in the two well-known apse mosaics in the basilica of San Vitale in Ravenna of Emperor Justinian I (r. 527–65) and his wife, Theodora, are as impressive as those of the Magi discussed above (figs 1.5, 1.6). Apart from their jewelled crowns, both Justinian and Theodora wear a long robe over which a flowing purple chlamys is draped, bejewelled and presumably woven with gold thread. They both stand out from their entourage because of the imperial purple colour of their cloaks. Theodora's attendants wear an array of multicoloured and patterned robes, some of which are also studded with pearls. This is in stark contrast to the figure of Abraham, who appears above the left colonnade before the entrance to the apse of the church. He is seen stepping out of his house in a simple, short, earth-coloured tunic, decorated with two *clavi* over his shoulders and small circular medallions on the sleeves and the lower edge of the tunic; the garment

1.5   Emperor Justinian and Bishop Maximian, accompanied by clergy and military guards, *c.* 547 CE. Mosaic. San Vitale, Ravenna.

1.6   Empress Theodora and her court, *c.* 547 CE. Mosaic. San Vitale, Ravenna.

leaves his legs bare. On the other side of the mosaic, representing the sacrifice of Isaac, Abraham is shown, by contrast, wearing a more ecclesiastical-looking outfit of a long white robe with a toga flung over his shoulder (fig. 1.7). A red woollen tunic in Cleveland, attributed to seventh- or eighth-century Egypt during the Umayyad caliphate, is of the same type as the one worn by Abraham in the mosaic discussed above, with its *clavi* and roundels (fig. 1.8). Despite its attribution, this tunic is a garment firmly rooted in the Roman tradition and was most likely produced by Christian weavers.

As already indicated, the dress culture of the lands beyond the eastern border of the Byzantine Empire was very different from that of the Hellenistic Mediterranean. That difference is perhaps best illustrated by a well-known rock-cut relief at Naqsh-i Rostam near Persepolis in southern Iran. The relief commemorates the victory of Shahpur I (r. 240–70) over the Roman army under Emperor Valerian at Edessa in southern Turkey in 260 CE (fig. 1.9). It shows Shahpur seated on a horse and wearing a large crown that has a *korymbos*, a spherical headdress

1.7   Abraham, *c.* 547 CE. Mosaic. San Vitale, Ravenna.

1.8   Woollen tunic with decorated bands and roundels, Egypt, 7th–8th century CE. Undyed linen, dyed wool (weft-faced plain weave, with slit- and dovetailed-tapestry weave, supplementary weft wrapping, embroidery), 205 × 170.2 cm. Cleveland Museum of Art, The A.W. Ellenberger, Sr, Endowment Fund, inv. no. 1972.46.

1.9   Rock-cut relief depicting the triumph of Shahpur I over the Roman emperor Valerian, reign of Shahpur I, Naqsh-i Rostam, Fars Province, Iran, after 260 CE.

1.10   Caftan (coat) with *senmurv*s (mythical creatures), Eastern Iranian world, 9th century CE, found at Moshchevaya Balka burial mound, Karachayevo-Cherkessk Republic. Silk and fur, l. 140 cm. State Hermitage Museum, St Petersburg, inv. no. K3-6584.

with diadems, suspended from it, and dressed in a loosely fitting shirt and trousers, both of which cling to his body and feature exaggerated pleats. The Roman emperor Valerian, on the other hand, is seen kneeling in front of Shahpur, evidently humiliated, with a standing attendant at his side. Both Romans wear short tunics fastened by belts and short capes over their shoulders, typical of Roman military dress. Shahpur's outfit is of the same kind as those seen on many Sasanian relief-silver hunting plates, such as one in the Metropolitan Museum, New York, which shows the emperor Yazdgard I (r. 399–420) wearing a knee-length tailored shirt over baggy trousers.[7] A caftan or coat now at the Hermitage Museum in St Petersburg, excavated at the Moshchevaya Balka burial mound in the north-western Caucasus, is a surviving example of

a type of garment similar to those worn by the royal figures mentioned above (fig. 1.10). It comprises a dark compound-woven silk base fabric, featuring a succession of connected medallions with pearl borders, each containing what is often seen as one of the defining representations of Sasanian art: the *senmurv*, or *simurgh*, a mythical creature attested in Middle Persian texts. The *senmurv* is usually represented as a hybrid creature with a long feathery tail (like that of a peacock), the clawed feet of a bird of prey and a dog's head. The coat itself is constructed of several parts with a tapering waist and short sleeves, and was probably worn over a lighter undergarment in combination with trousers. That these types of garments and cloth were used as far afield as central Asia is shown by a fresco from the palace at Afrasiab, near Samarkand, the ancient

1.11   Wall-painting depicting ambassadors from Chaganian and Chach paying homage to King Varkhuman of Samarkand, 648–51 CE, Afrasiab palace, near Samarkand. Fresco.

Sogdian capital.[8] The fresco contains three figures of ambassadors paying homage to King Varkhuman (r. 640–70 CE), all of whom are identified as Turkic (fig. 1.11). Two of them wear long coats with prominent repeats of medallions containing *senmurv*s and what appear to be boars' heads and geese or peacocks in a variety of colours, including reddish-browns and blues.[9] The *senmurv*s on the coat of the first figure in the sequence are very similar to those seen on the garment from Moshchevaya Balka, albeit contained in a lattice of pointed cartouches. The geese (ducks or peacocks) on the coat of the central figure correspond to those on a tailored child's coat at the Cleveland Museum of Art, made of a multicoloured silk fabric from central Asia and dated to the eighth century (fig. 1.12).[10] The garments in the painting relate to the coat, not only in their design but also in terms of colour palette: dark red, cream, dark blue, green and yellow. The child's coat is part of a full outfit comprising a pair of trousers, made from cream-coloured Chinese silk from the Tang dynasty, also at Cleveland, and a short-sleeved shirt in the Pritzker Collection in Chicago, and boots at the

1.12   Child's coat, probably Sogdia (now Uzbekistan), 8th century CE. Silk samite (weft-faced compound twill), 51.4 × 84.5 cm. Cleveland Museum of Art, Purchase from the J.H. Wade Fund, inv. no. 1996.2.1.

Hirayama Ikuo Silk Road Museum in Japan, made from the same Sogdian multicoloured silk.[11]

Dress in urban Arabia before Islam and during the time of the Prophet Muhammad was characterized, as is often still the case today, by several layers of clothing, for both men and women, with minimal or no tailoring, resulting in a relatively unstructured look that covered the whole body. The fundamental elements of a female or male outfit were the following: undergarments, such as the *'izar*, a cloth wrapped around the waist (perhaps similar to the modern-day *wuzar* worn in many parts of the Arabian peninsula); the *qamis* (from Latin *camisia*), a shirt-like long garment worn over the *'izar*; the *thawb*, a gown worn over the *qamis*; and then garments such as the *jubba* (a woollen tunic), *hulla* (a long, flowing coat), *qaba'* (a sleeved robe slit in front) and the *farruj* (similar to the *qaba'* but slit in the back), all of which were worn on top of everything else.[12] Both men and women covered their heads. For men the *'imama* (a turban-like garment that played a much greater role later under the caliphates) is already attested at that early date, as are various veil-like cloths for women, such as the *mandil* (a large square), as well as the *qina'* (which covered the face) and the *burqu'* (a cloth suspended in front of the lower face).[13] Several *hadith*s mention that the Prophet Muhammad presented his own clothes to chosen companions and members of his extended family. A symbolically important precedent for the informal presentation of robes is recorded in Ibn al-Athir's *Al-kamil fi al-tarikh* ('The complete history'), in which the Prophet is reported to have taken off his *burda*, a type of mantle, and handed it to the poet Ka'b ibn Zuhayr upon hearing one of his poems.[14] The bestowal of clothes (discussed in chapter 2) by caliphs of the Umayyad, Abbasid and Fatimid dynasties upon members of their courts, dignitaries or vassals became a prominent extension of the caliphal status quo and a symbol of authority.

When the Arabs conquered parts of the Mediterranean world and Iran they were confronted with very established and developed systems of clothing: on the one hand the dress of the late Roman Empire and Byzantium as seen by visual examples from Ravenna, Palmyra and Egypt with its cloaks, dalmatics and tunics, and on the other the world of Iranian and central Asian clothing as exemplified by the dress seen on the Sasanian reliefs at Taq-i Bustan, or murals at Afrasiab near Samarkand, with their silken overcoats and baggy trousers and boots. In time, aspects of these clothing traditions were adopted and adapted by Arab and non-Arab Muslims.

THE UMAYYADS

Some of the earliest representations of fashion and clothing under the caliphs of the Umayyad dynasty can be found in three architectural sites that all are connected to caliphal patrons: the palace of Qasr al-Hayr al-Gharbi near Palmyra in Syria; the palace of Khirbat al-Mafjar in the west bank of the Jordan Valley; and the bathhouse complex of Qusayr 'Amra near Amman in Jordan. Qasr al-Hayr al-Gharbi was built under the Umayyad caliph Hisham ibn 'Abd al-Malik (r. 724–43), as attested by a foundation inscription over the entrance, which dates the building to 109 AH / 727 CE. Two princely figures have survived: one from the façade is a standing male wearing a knee-length pleated short shirt over baggy trousers (fig. 1.13), similar to the costume worn by Sasanian royalty discussed above. A very close comparison with this example appears in the central roundel of the so-called 'Cup of Solomon' (fig. 1.15), also known as the 'Cup of Khusraw', a precious sixth-century bowl, made of carved rock crystal and garnet cameos mounted in a gold frame, from the treasury of the cathedral of St Denis, now in the Cabinet des Médailles in Paris; the vessel features an enthroned Sasanian ruler wearing a knee-length baggy pleated shirt over trousers, seated wide-legged, in an attitude similar to that of the figure at Qasr al-Hayr al-Gharbi. The other princely figure was once located on the second floor of the interior façade of the bath complex, overlooking a courtyard colonnade; what remains is a fragment of the lower half of a figure wearing a long garment, over which is flung a prominently pleated toga-like wrap. He is seated on what is perhaps a wood or ivory throne with both sandal-clad feet resting on a footstool (fig. 1.14). Traces of pigments have survived, notably in red, green and brown. While the first (see fig. 1.13) clearly adheres to an Eastern costume tradition, the second (see fig. 1.14) is firmly in the Hellenistic tradition of the Mediterranean. A painting that once covered the floor of the reception room in the palace's east wing is also of interest. It features a mounted archer hunting whose outfit is rooted in the Sasanian dress tradition, while above him two courtiers within a colonnade playing musical instruments wear outfits that may represent Arab dress, floor length shirts, worn over trousers, and shawls flung over their shoulders (fig. 1.16). A small fragment of a mural from the former second floor

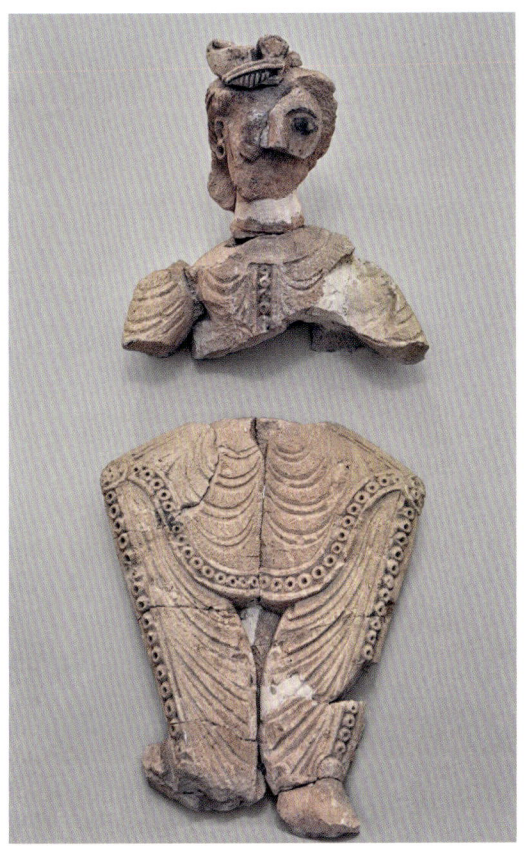

1.13 Fragmentary standing male figure, *c.* 727 CE, found at Qasr al-Hayr al-Gharbi, Syria. Stucco. National Museum, Damascus.

1.14 Fragmentary seated figure, *c.* 727 CE, found at Qasr al-Hayr al-Gharbi, Syria. Limestone, 1.06 × 0.9 metres. National Museum, Damascus, inv. no. 09.

1.15 Bowl, known as the 'Cup of Solomon' or 'Cup of Khusraw', Iran, 6th century CE. Rock crystal, with garnet cameos, in gold frame, diam. 28 cm. Cabinet des Médailles, Paris, inv. no. 56.95, Chab. 2538.

shows the face of a curly-haired and bejewelled female figure wearing a shawl wrapped around her head and covering her shoulders, with the ends neatly tucked away (fig. 1.17). It has been suggested that she is an Arab singer, many of whom were brought from the Hijaz to Syria to sing at the Umayyad court.[15]

Female figures are also present at Khirbat al-Mafjar, a site that has been connected with the nephew and successor of the caliph Hisham, al-Walid II ibn Yazid (r. 743–44), particularly during his time as heir apparent. Al-Walid's excesses are described in some detail in the historical sources, and the ostentatious architecture of the palace complex at Khirbat al-Mafjar is testimony to his many eccentric personality traits in seeking a variety of physical pleasures, and to his love for poetry.[16] A case in point is the well-known 'Tree of Life' mosaic in the small audience room of the bathhouse, which features a lion attacking a group of gazelles below a large tree bearing fruit, which has been interpreted as a poetic expression of earthly love.[17] Several surviving figures of scantily clad women sculpted in stucco from the large bathhouse wear loincloths perhaps equivalent to the *'izar* described above (fig. 1.18). The cloth seen here, rolled up around the waist and then tucked in to secure it from sliding down, seems to be made of a loosely falling fabric in a colour palette of dark reds and purples.

Red is also a prominent colour in another well-known figure from Khirbat al-Mafjar, the standing prince (fig. 1.19). This imposing figure was once located within an apsidal recess above the arched entrance to the music room of the bathhouse, which appears much like a triumphal arch. The prince stands on a plinth supported by two seated lions, confronting the viewer. His imposing facial features – large almond-shaped eyes, half-length hair and a well-groomed pointed beard – are complemented by his carefully curated outfit: a long red coat with a beaded border, belted at the waist, is worn over a pair of darker red baggy trousers and what might have been boots; in his left hand he holds onto a long sword. There is no way to say that the figure is that of al-Walid, as it lacks an

inscription to identify it conclusively, but similar figures (often referred to as the 'standing caliph type') can be seen on Umayyad coinage that is dated to before the language reform of al-Walid's grandfather 'Abd al-Malik ibn Marwan (r. 685–705) in the 690s.[18] The long coat worn over baggy trousers is clearly a reference to Sasanian dress customs, and corresponds to the princely figure from Qasr al-Hayr al-Gharbi, discussed above. If the figure is indeed that of al-Walid ibn Yazid, one might be tempted to see a highly confident individual with an acute sense of self-presentation, and knowledge of how dress can convey notions of power.

Qusayr 'Amra, a small bathhouse complex once part of a larger settlement in the Jordanian desert near Amman and within the vicinity of the oasis of al-Azraq, presents an extraordinary cycle of paintings, now badly damaged and restored several times, which has also been connected to al-Walid ibn Yazid. The complex was built at some time between 723 and 743. It consists of a multi-nave reception hall, to which is attached a bathhouse of Roman type. The building is decorated richly throughout with paintings that fall into the categories of princely representation, courtly pastimes, hunting and allegory. They are examples of the adaptation of late antique culture and iconography. Of great interest are the costumes seen in the paintings, many of which are examples of Hellenistic dress in the Mediterranean, but some of which also offer an insight into Arab dress codes at the time of the Umayyad caliphs. In the central aisle of the main reception hall is a painting of a prince, identified by an inscription above as 'al-amir'. He is seated on a throne below an arched, colonnaded canopy and wears a multicoloured robe similar to that of the princely figure at Qasr al-Hayr al-Gharbi, discussed above (see fig. 1.14).[19] On either side he is accompanied by a female standing figure who appears to draw a curtain. The figure on the prince's right wears a long flowing white shirt similar to a *qamis*, with a dark blue shawl draped over her shoulders, while the shirt of the other figure is darker. The walls along the aisle are flanked by courtly figures placed within a colonnade, most of whom are dressed in long robes reminiscent of Byzantine dress. All around the central aisle are representations of dancing figures and musicians. The bearded figure of a seated lute player stands out, as he is dressed in a patterned long robe with wide sleeves and has a long shawl draped over his shoulders (fig. 1.21).

1.16   Floor-painting of courtiers and a hunting scene, *c.* 727 CE, found at Qasr al-Hayr al-Gharbi, Syria. Plaster, painted in *secco*, 5 × 4.85 metres. National Museum, Damascus, inv. no. QHG.

1.17 Fragment of a wall-painting of a female figure (possibly an Arab singer), *c.* 727 CE, found at Qasr al-Hayr al-Gharbi. Fresco, 41 × 39 cm. National Museum, Damascus, inv. no. QHG.

1.18 Female figure, Khirbat al-Mafjar palace, near Jericho, 724–43 CE. Painted stucco. Rockefeller Archaeological Museum, East Jerusalem.

1.19 Figure of a prince, Khirbat al-Mafjar palace, near Jericho, 724–43 CE. Painted stucco. Rockefeller Archaeological Museum, East Jerusalem.

1.20   Wall-painting of a prince reclining on a daybed, Qusayr 'Amra bathhouse complex, near Amman, Jordan, 723–43 CE, main reception hall, west aisle. Fresco.

His face is more accentuated and naturalistic than that of the other figures, with finely chiselled features and a thin moustache; one might assume that he represents an Arab courtier, presumably in Arab costume.

A large painting in the western aisle features a barefoot prince, identified by an inscription above as Walid ibn Yazid, stretched out on a daybed, supported by bolsters (fig. 1.20). He wears a long light blue shirt with wide loose sleeves, made from what appears to be a light and partly sheer fabric, and a cream-coloured turban. His lap is covered by a lattice-patterned brown blanket. Two figures, perhaps female, are seated on the side of the daybed. Both wear pinkish shirts and tight-fitting cloths wrapped around their heads with the ends suspended on their left sides, and have blankets, one in an orange-yellow, the other dark blue, draped over their left shoulders. Behind the daybed a figure holding a pen and a large scroll-like sheet presumably represents a scribe. His costume consists of a long dark greyish-blue dotted robe, with a corresponding hemispherical hat. Over his

shoulders he wears an orange-yellowish shawl that is suspended all the way down his left side. An attendant on the end of the daybed, with bare chest and wearing a loincloth, operates a feathery fly-whisk.

While this painting and its significance within the overall programme of paintings at Qusayr 'Amra has received relatively little scholarly attention, another painting immediately adjacent on the flanking wall has been the subject of much debate. It features a group of six princely figures, some identified by inscriptions, paying homage to the figure stretched out on the daybed (fig. 1.22). The painting is badly damaged, but recent restoration has revealed some remarkable details, previously overlooked. Of the six, the Byzantine emperor, the Sasanian emperor Khosrow II Parviz, the Visigothic king Roderic and the Axumite Negus (emperor of Ethiopia), can be identified – as Oleg Grabar suggested, 'a Family of Kings'.[20] In the first row the figure of the Byzantine emperor is dressed in a long light blue mantle patterned with an overall design of rosettes. Under the mantle he wears a cream-coloured long shirt, with a brown border accentuated by small blue dots. Khosrow, whose head bears a Sasanian crown, wears a long blue robe with an indistinguishable pattern and a large pinkish cape draped over his shoulders. Roderic appears to be wearing a pair of brown trousers under a pinkish light robe, with a sky-blue cape held together with what seems to be a jewelled clasp. In the second row, the only figure that can be identified is the Axumite Negus, between Khosrow and Roderic, whose clothes are not easily identifiable. What seems certain is that he wears a brownish robe, of which a beaded border is visible between the figures in front of him. Directly adjacent to the group of the six kings is a large fresco showing a female figure standing in a water basin almost nude, clothed with a sheer loincloth. On her left, a group of wrestlers wearing loincloths are seen exercising.

In the eastern aisle of the reception hall, the barrel-vaulted ceiling is decorated with figures representing various trades (fig. 1.23). All are dressed in Roman-style short tunics. Below, two barefoot male figures are seen slaughtering what looks like an oryx antelope (fig. 1.24). Both wear long white shirts that are tucked in between their legs so as not to get in the way of the action. In the lunette above, two allegorical figures in Hellenistic clothing create a stark contrast to the butchery happening below (fig. 1.25).

Looking at these three Umayyad sites creates an insight into how the Umayyads used dress as a political marker. The images of princes enthroned or posing seem to be symbolic of status rather than representations of individuals. Their choice of Byzantine and Sasanian modes of dress is perhaps not necessarily a reflection of actual clothing styles, but tokens of what the Umayyads saw as imperial symbolism, accepted and universally understood idioms of royalty. It has been suggested that the Umayyads did not develop a royal iconography of their own, but in this context it is interesting how the image of the lounging prince at Qusayr ʿAmra differs from this standardized mode, particularly in respect of the contrast between his costume and the costumes of the 'Six Kings'.[21] He

1.21   Wall-painting of a lute player, Qusayr ʿAmra bathhouse complex, near Amman, Jordan, 723–43 CE, main reception hall, central aisle. Fresco.

1.22   Wall-painting of six kings paying homage to the reclining prince (see fig. 1.20), Qusayr ʿAmra bathhouse complex, near Amman, Jordan, 723–43 CE, main reception hall, west aisle, Fresco.

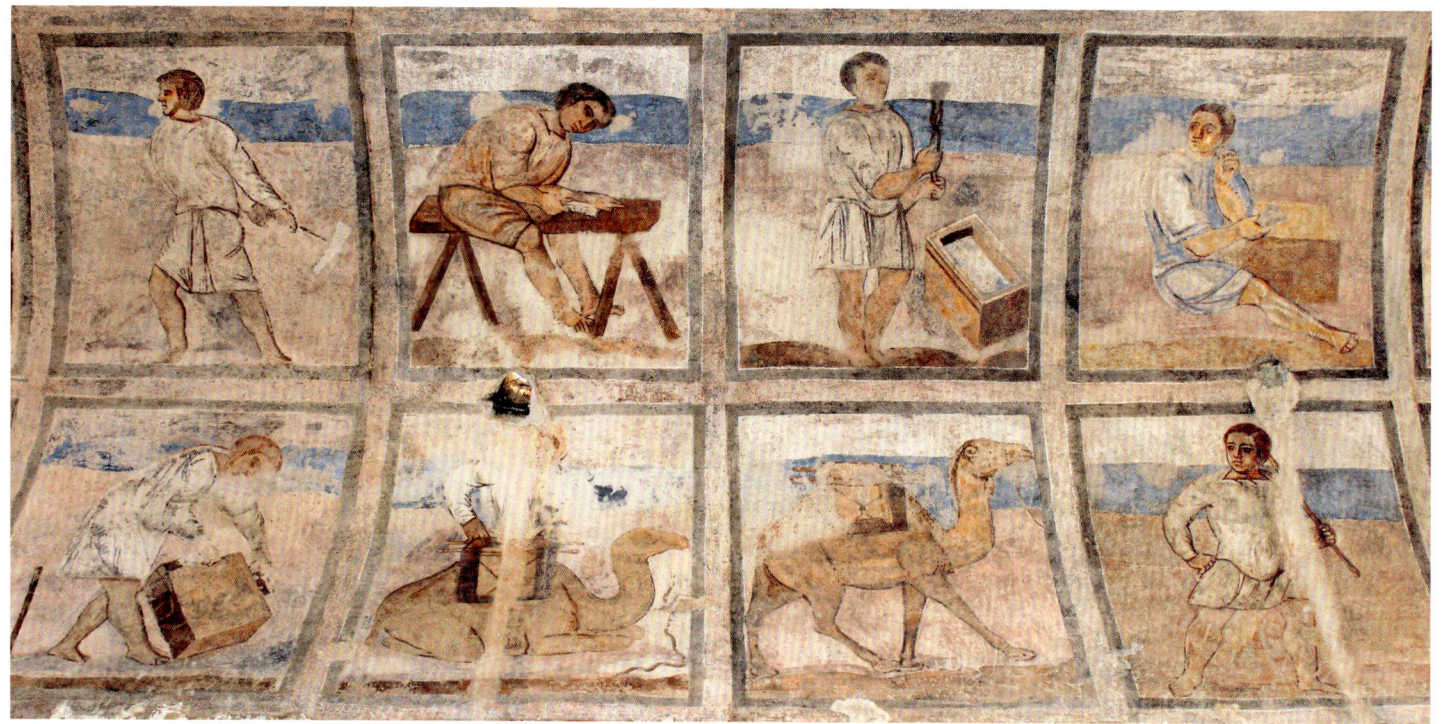

1.23   Painted ceiling depicting figures representing trades, Qusayr 'Amra bathhouse complex, near Amman, Jordan, 723–43 CE, main reception hall, east aisle. Fresco.

1.24   Wall-painting of two men slaughtering an antelope, Qusayr 'Amra bathhouse complex, near Amman, Jordan, 723–43 CE, main reception hall, east aisle. Fresco.

1.25   Two allegorical figures, Qusayr 'Amra bathhouse complex, near Amman, Jordan, 723–43 CE, main reception hall, lunette, east aisle. Fresco.

and his courtiers wear clothes that set them apart from the dress culture of the conquered. It seems that they represent perhaps the first step in creating an 'Islamic' notion of dress that amalgamated and adapted different cultural traditions, but distinguished the Muslim ruling elite from non-Muslims.[22] We know that the Umayyads began to esteem more luxurious modes of dress than the companions of the Prophet Muhammad. The caliph Sulayman ibn 'Abd al-Malik (r. 715–17), for example, is reported to have worn a green flowing robe with a matching turban, and to have liked long and wide sleeves, perhaps similar to what we see at Qusayr 'Amra.[23] He also wore trousers (a *sirwal*) as part of his outfits.[24] Al-Walid II was known to have worn special clothes for prayer called *thiyab al-khilafa* (caliphal garments).[25]

The earliest dated examples of a caliphal textile are six dispersed fragments that once belonged to a single piece, and were recovered in the late nineteenth century from a grave in Akhmin, the ancient Panopolis in Upper Egypt (fig. 2.4).[26] The fragments are rugged remnants of a once magnificent textile which would have been a sheer luxury for its owner. They comprise a compound-woven silk fabric with designs in mustard and muted blue on a dark red ground. It is very likely that the fragments once belonged to a large rectangular shawl, perhaps decorated with a repeat pattern of beaded roundels and multi-lobed flowers in between, bordered at both ends with beaded bands.[27] Importantly, two of the fragments are inscribed in an early form of Arabic script, embroidered in yellow silk between the border and the main field of roundels, the earliest surviving textile *tiraz* inscription, a type of institutionalized inscription discussed in the following chapters and in the Catalogue. The inscription follows a standard sequence: the name and titles of the caliph Marwan, a statement that the piece was commissioned or ordered, what appears to be the lost name or title of an administrator, and then the location of the *tiraz* workshop in Ifriqiya, a province spanning most of the north African Mediterranean coast. The date of the piece could fall into the reign of either of two Umayyad caliphs called Marwan – namely, Marwan ibn al-Hakam (r. 684–85) or Marwan II ibn Muhammad al-Himar (r. 744–50), the last ruler of the Umayyad dynasty. It is impossible to say which of the two was the textile's patron. The epigraphic style of the inscription conforms to script styles found in contemporary papyri, linking it to Umayyad scribal practice. That the inscription was

embroidered onto the compound-woven silk ground fabric opens up questions of manufacture. It would have been very complicated to weave such an inscription as part of the compound weave, so it was added later. It is, therefore, likely that the textile was not woven in Ifriqiya, but was produced elsewhere and was later personalized. From an aesthetic point of view, the beaded roundels might point to Sasanian influence.[28] Indeed, references to Sasanian motifs can be found in Umayyad art. (One might think of the winged motifs found in the mosaics of the Dome of the Rock in Jerusalem.) Dye analysis performed on the fragments has been inconclusive, some of the dyes pointing to a Mediterranean and others to an Eastern place of production.[29] Indeed, the Byzantine emperor within the group of the 'Six Kings' at Qusayr 'Amra, wears a robe decorated with an all-over pattern of rosettes. The embroidered inscription indicates that the notion of *tiraz* as a marker of administrative requisition extending to textiles was already established and clearly defined under the Umayyads, similar to the marking of state documents with a *protocollon* (preliminary sheet) to record administrative procedure (see chapter 2).

THE ABBASIDS

The Abbasid revolution of 750, which saw the Umayyad caliphate overthrown, resulted in a sea change in the caliphate's political and administrative culture. The move of the Abbasid capital to Madinat al-Salam (Baghdad) in 762 under al-Mansur (r. 754–75) brought the caliphate's centre of gravity closer to its eastern provinces in Iran, Khurasan and central Asia, and opened up new opportunities for trade and industry along the Silk Road and maritime routes to Asia. The Abbasids employed mostly Persian administrators, often non-Arab Muslims (*mawali*) and an army of Turkish slaves, a move that resulted eventually, some two centuries later, in the gradual disintegration of their power. Abbasid court culture borrowed much from that of the Sasanians. Not only was their first capital located near the Sasanian capital Ctesiphon, but Abbasid architecture also looked back in its monumentality, theatricality and visual impact to Sasanian buildings such as the Taq-i Kisra, still standing at the time of the Abbasid dynasty. The idea of Baghdad as a circular city, with its caliphal palace and congregational mosque at the centre, stressed the caliph's position as a singular leader of a world empire and religion. Dress and clothing played an important part in that new court culture.

Dress was a marker of social status, profession, sex and ethnic affiliation.[30] The philologist Abu al-Tayyib Muhammad al-Washsha (d. 936) describes in great detail the dress customs of fashionable society in the Abbasid capital city. In his *Kitab al-muwashsha*, a handbook of rules of good society for the aristocrats of Baghdad, he outlines how an outfit should be composed: a fine undershirt (*ghilala*) under a heavier lined *qamis*, both of fine linen (*dabiqi* produced in Egypt, or *jannabi* from Iran); a lined mantle (*durra'a*) from Alexandria, or a *jubba* from Nishapur in linen, silk or *mulham* (a mix of cotton and silk); and a Yemeni cloak cover from Aden called *rida'* or a *mitraf* from Sus in Iran with decorative borders (*muhashshat*); the head was clothed with a *taylasan* (a veil-like trapezoidal fabric) of Nishapuri *mulham*, often large enough to cover the turban.[31]

Al-Washsha's discussion of male dress codes is generally more encompassing than that of female dress. His descriptions provide some insight into fabrics and their colour – for example, discussing striped and banded linen (*shurub muzanmara*), and coloured *qasab* (a linen decorated with gold or silver) decorated with silk-embroidered roundels.[32] Caliphs would often present clothing to chosen courtiers as a sign of close companionship, but also to mark investiture to public office. This practice was called the *khil'a*, already in place under the Umayyads, but institutionalized by the Abbasids. Such an outfit often consisted of a *qamis*; trousers (*sirwal*); a *taylasan*; a long mantle, open in the front with long wide sleeves (*durra'a*) of Egyptian linen (*dabiqi*) or a sleeved robe (*qaba'*); a turban (*'imama*) made from a gilded fabric called *washy*; and a lined *ghilala*. All of these garments could form outfits of different values, from a mere 1,090 to 30,300 dinars.[33] The sources are full of anecdotes about the dress of caliphs and their viziers, according to their particular preferences. Ibn al-Furat (*fl.* 855–924), vizier three times under the caliph al-Muqtadir (r. 908–32), was fond of fine clothes, such as cloaks (*kisa'*), turbans and cloths worn over the turban, all made of *dabiqi*.[34] The caliph al-Muqtadir himself sometimes wore a caftan of Tustari cloth.[35] The warehouses of the Abbasid caliphs were stuffed with thousands of pieces of clothing of various kinds, as attested by the *Kitab al-hadaya wa al-tuhaf* ('Book of gifts and rarities'), probably written by the twelfth-century Egyptian author Qadi ibn al-Zubayr.[36] After the death of Harun al-Rashid (r. 786–809), his son al-Amin (r. 809–13) had an inventory of his father's wardrobe compiled by his vizier al-Fadl ibn al-Rabi', which contained tens of thousands of items, such as furnishings, suits of armour, and garments including turbans, various types of shirts and cloaks, trousers, fur-lined items, capes and hoods.[37] Al-Fadl was surprised when he made the inventory: 'I brought in the scribes and the treasury keepers and kept on counting for four months. I had never imagined that the treasuries of the caliphate could contain all the things I oversaw [there]!'[38] The account of the Umayyad caliph Hisham ibn 'Abd al-Malik's estate looked sparse in comparison, with quantities of garments and clothing counted only in the hundreds.[39]

Another vivid account of clothing is provided by an author called Abu al-Qasim, who probably lived in Baghdad in the ninth or tenth century, in a satirical account of the dress of the citizens of Isfahan and the interior decoration of their houses. It is worth quoting the passage on clothing here in full:

> By Allah, I do not see a single one of you wearing a garment of reddish Dabiqi (*shuqairi*), nor *Dabqawi* (from Dabqa in the Delta), nor of *Qirati Zuhairi* (perhaps he means a stuff with embroidered all-over patterns in the shape of the coins called *qirat*, a fraction of a dinar, and manufactured in the *Zuhairiyya* Quarter of Baghdad), nor reddish woven stuff (*baft qushairi*), nor Aden cloaks (*rida'*), nor *takhtandj*, nor *rakhtandj*, nor garments of *qasab*-linen of *samannud* and *Damsisi* (from Damsis in Egypt), and *Tinnisi*, and *Dimyati*, nor yet *Mudjalali* (?) stuff, nor figured (*washi*) material of brocade (*dibadj*) with the woven gold (*al-dhahab al-mansuj*) and the intermingled ambergris, with beautiful markings (*hasan al-tawshifi*) as if it were woven of the blossoms of the Spring (*Rabi'*), nor yet transparent *Shinzi* stuffs like thin air or the mirage, nor napkins (*shustaqat*) which are used for wiping the mouth in polite assemblies, of *qasab*-linen of unbleached material with a border (*mu'lam mukhawwam*), nor striped material (*muraiyash*), nor material ornamented (*muwashshah*) with Maghribi (north African) gold, nor *'attabi Dabiqi* with a border, and embroidered with gold (*mu'lam muthaqqal*).[40]

1.26   Dirham (presentation coin (?)) of al-Mutawakkil (r. 847–861 CE), Iraq?, dated 241 AH / 855–56 CE, obverse. Silver, diam. 30 mm, weight 4.35 g. Kunsthistorisches Museum, Vienna, inv. no. MK OR 7283.

What seems to be clear, even from the few references provided here, is that the Abbasid world was mad about clothing and fiercely international in the types of fabrics traded between Baghdad and the provinces, but also in the larger overseas networks that it deployed. This is indicated by the common use of geographic references in describing fabrics. We get a very good sense of the sheer variety by looking at the *tiraz* and *tiraz*-style textiles that have survived in Egyptian graves, which will be discussed further in the course of this book. Despite being grave goods and hence perhaps not reflecting the whole variety of clothing and textiles used during the early caliphates, they do show a huge multiversity of cloth types and qualities, including products that were made across the Islamic world and had reached Egypt through international trade routes, diplomatic exchanges and official government requisitions.

Visual representations of caliphal dress from the high point of the Abbasid caliphate in the ninth century are almost absent. A unique portrait of the caliph al-Mutawakkil (r. 847–61) can be seen on the obverse of a silver dirham minted in 241 AH / 855–56 CE by his son, the future caliph al-Muʿtazz (r. 866–69), now in the Kunsthistorisches Museum in Vienna (fig. 1.26). The dirham was probably a presentation coin – that is, minted to mark a specific anniversary – which was then dispersed to chosen individuals. The shoulder-length portrait comprises a frontal view of the caliph. Prominent

facial features are his large eyes, nose, moustache and double-pointed beard, as well as the ears, from which are suspended what appear to be earrings, and a *kaffiya* covering his head held by an *ʿagal* made from a twisted rope. He wears a robe with a pearl-band collar. The caliph's headgear is markedly Bedouin. Rather than pushing a public image based on foreign models, as seen under the Umayyads, perhaps al-Mutawakkil sought to assert Arabness in an environment where Arabs were a minority, outnumbered by a Persian administration and a Turkish slave army.[41] In this context, dress was used to carry a political message. What might have gone on behind palace walls, where only select courtiers were ever able to be in the presence of the caliph, is of course another matter. Here the dress code was surely more culturally diverse, as related in the literary sources. This is also the picture that emerges by looking at what has survived of the decoration of Abbasid palaces.

Hardly ever discussed in the literature is the evidence recovered during the excavations at Samarra in Iraq between 1911 and 1914 and recorded in sketchbooks by the archaeologist Ernst Herzfeld, now held at the Metropolitan Museum in New York. In 836 the caliph

1.27   Reconstruction of part of a wall-painting, 9th century CE, depicting two dancers, based on fragments found in the 'harem' at Dar al-Khilafa palace, Samarra. Watercolour on paper, 59.3 × 56.4 cm. Metropolitan Museum of Art, New York, Ernst Herzfeld Papers, Harris Brisbane Dick Fund, 1943, inv. no. eeh516.

al-Muʿtasim (r. 833–42) moved his court from Baghdad
to a newly founded capital at Samarra, where he built
extensive palace complexes along the River Tigris. The
city was further extended under al-Mutawakkil, with
a large congregational mosque and a palace for his son
al-Muʿtazz. The palaces were decorated with polychrome
wall stucco, but also cycles of wall-paintings featuring
floral, zoomorphic and anthropomorphic decoration.
The paintings comprising figures are mostly of scenes
connected to courtly pastimes and leisure. A well-known
painting found at the 'harem' at the Dar al-Khilafa, also
called the Jawsaq al-Khaqani, the main palace of the
Abbasid caliphs at Samarra, features two female dancers
holding large bottles pouring drink into cups (fig. 1.27).[42]
The women's costumes are composed of hip-length shirts

worn with long skirts of the same colours, red and blue,
that have patterned borders. Both women wear scarves
draped front to back over their upper arms. A painting
of two ceramic fragments found at the same site shows
a female figure wearing a tightly fitted short-sleeved
dress in red with accentuated borders around collar and
left sleeve, the base fabric decorated with yellow and
black 'leopard' dots (fig. 1.28). A tapestry-woven wool
fragment in the Textile Museum, Washington, DC, once
part of sumptuous furnishing fabric produced in Upper
Egypt during the Tulunid period (868–905), features a
figure wearing a dotted garment similar to that of the
painted figure at Samarra (fig. 1.29). The Tulunid dynasty
was founded by the Turkic governor Ahmad ibn Tulun
(r. 868–84), who had been sent to Egypt from Samarra

1.28   Watercolour painting of fragments of two painted ceramic
jars, 9th century CE, depicting the upper bodies of human figures,
found near the throne room at Dar al-Khilafa palace, Samarra. Ink
and watercolour on paper, 35 × 25 cm. Metropolitan Museum of Art
Libraries, New York, Ernst Herzfeld Papers, Harris Brisbane Dick
Fund, 1943, inv. no. eeh1220.

1.29   Textile fragment, Egypt, 9th–10th century CE, depicting
a seated courtly figure, acquired by George Hewitt Myers, 1938.
Linen and wool tapestry weave, 38.1 × 26.7 cm. Textile Museum,
Washington, DC, inv. no. 721.14.

under al-Mu'tazz and eventually established independent control over Egypt's military and economy. Louise Mackie suggested that the Tulunids adopted the courtly style favoured at Samarra, as is clear when one compares the dress of the figures in the painting and the fabric.[43] Photographs of a set of fragments of a wall-painting feature female figures dressed only in polychrome patterned 'izars, fastened around the waist (fig. 1.30); they are similar to the bathing figures found at Qusayr 'Amra, discussed above, and those seen on a number of Sasanian silver-gilt ewers and bottles.[44] While the focus in these is on the various patterns, such as scales and lattices, the 'izar seen on yet another painted fragment focuses on the way the pleats are suspended down the figure's legs to the patterned border at the hem (fig. 1.31). A very different set of images, on

painted jars, was found near the throne room of the Dar al-Khilafa. All of them feature male bearded figures with moustaches, seen in frontal view, wearing what look like striped kaffiyas. The one best preserved (fig. 1.32) wears a long brownish qamis, decorated with a lattice design accentuated with blue and black cross shapes, with a blue and white striped shawl flung over his shoulders, and holds a staff with both hands. The figure and its costume are reminiscent of the individual represented on the silver dirham of al-Mutawakkil discussed above, a decidedly 'Arab' approach to dress. The function of these jars within the court context remains a puzzle.

A stark contrast to the austerity of these figures is provided by a fragment of a wall-painting, also found near the throne room (fig. 1.33). It features a standing

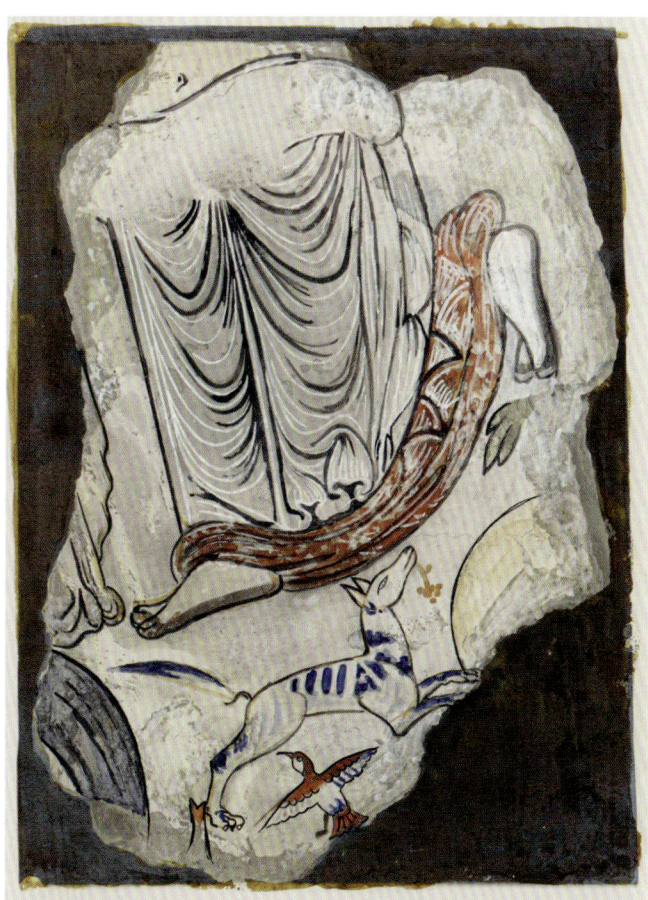

1.30 Reconstruction of photographs of a fragmentary wall-painting, 9th century CE, depicting dancers, found in the 'harem' at Dar al-Khilafa palace, Samarra. Hand-coloured photographs pasted to paper, with pencil outlines, 35 × 25 cm. Metropolitan Museum of Art Libraries, New York, Ernst Herzfeld Papers, Harris Brisbane Dick Fund, 1943, inv. eeh1220.

1.31 Photograph of a fragment of a wall-painting, 9th century CE, depicting the lower half of a dancer, found in the 'harem' at Dar al-Khilafa palace, Samarra. Hand-coloured photograph mounted on cardboard, 29.5 × 23.5 cm. Metropolitan Museum of Art Libraries, New York, Ernst Herzfeld Papers, Harris Brisbane Dick Fund, 1943, inv. no. eeh1019.

1.32   Drawing of a painted jar, 9th century CE, depicting
a robed male figure, found near the throne room at
Dar al-Khilafa palace, Samarra. Watercolour on paper,
29.4 × 23.5 cm. Metropolitan Museum of Art Libraries,
New York, Ernst Herzfeld Papers, Harris Brisbane Dick
Fund, 1943, inv. no. 1020.

1.33   Drawing of fragments of a painted ceramic jar, 9th century CE,
depicting a standing figure in a floral print robe, found near the throne
room at Dar al-Khilafa palace, Samarra. Watercolour on paper,
60 × 45 cm. Metropolitan Museum of Art Libraries, New York, Ernst
Herzfeld Papers, Harris Brisbane Dick Fund, 1943, inv. no. eeh588.

figure, possibly turbaned, in Persian or central Asian dress
– that is, a green tailored coat made from a fabric patterned
with red and yellow flowers, tied around the waist with a
belt, and worn over a pair of pinkish dotted baggy trousers.
Similar outfits can often be found in figures that decorate
lustre-painted ceramics from the tenth century, which have
been attributed to the workshops of Basra in southern Iraq.

No garments or outfits have survived from Abbasid
Iraq other than the inscribed textiles found in Egypt,
made from cotton with small embroidered inscriptions
(see Catalogue, Part I, cat. nos 95–106). These speak of a
vivid exchange of goods between the centre of the Abbasid
Empire and Egypt, its main economic powerhouse. Only
one Egyptian inscribed fragment was found during the
excavations of Samarra (see fig. 2.12). It must have been

a random survival, after the court had shifted back from
Samarra to Baghdad at the end of the ninth century.[45] The
textiles found in Egypt are obviously not representative
of Abbasid court costume alone and it is very likely that
we are missing the largest portion of what must have once
been a stunningly colourful and luxurious dress culture.

THE BUYIDS

In the tenth century, Abbasid power began to decline
with the rise of Shi'ism in the eastern provinces and the
establishment of an Iranian dynasty founded by 'Ali ibn
Buya, who in 934 conquered Fars and made Shiraz his
capital. In 945 his youngest brother, Ahmad ibn Buya,
conquered Iraq and established his capital at Baghdad
after taking control of the Abbasid administration as *amir*

al-umara', but retaining the caliph al-Mustakfi (r. 944–46) as vassal figurehead. Al-Mustakfi awarded honorific titles to several members of the Buyid family, including *Mu'izz al-Dawla* ('Glorifier of the State') for Ahmad. After several Buyid amirs ruled over Baghdad, in 988 Abu Nasr Firuz Kharshadh (r. 988–1012), a son of the amir 'Adud al-Dawla (r. 949–83), also known by his honorific title *Baha' al-Dawla* ('Splendour of the State'), took control of Baghdad. The Buyids were looking back to Iranian customs, and at the same time had to straddle Abbasid court protocol. This probably included dress codes. A gold medal issued at Baghdad in 365 AH / 975–76 CE by 'Izz al-Dawla portrays on the obverse a seated prince cross-legged, holding a cup and flanked on either side by an attendant.[46] The reverse of the medal shows a lute player seated cross-legged. The prince as well as the lute player wear tailored garments of the type found at Samarra (discussed above). A related gold medal, albeit uninscribed, in the Freer Gallery of Art shows a seated prince on the reverse, crowned and wearing a tailored open coat held at the waist with a belt, and trousers (fig. 1.34). The obverse of the medal depicts a crowned princely figure as a falconer mounted on horseback, again wearing a coat open in the front, fastened with a belt, over trousers. Depictions of dress can also be found in the illustrations of a well-known copy dated 400 AH / 1009–10 CE of the *Kitah suwar al-kawakib al-thabita* ('Book of fixed stars') by the astronomer 'Abd

1.35   Figure of Andromeda, manuscript illumination, 'Abd al-Rahman al-Sufi, *Kitab suwar al-kawakib al-thabitah* ('Book of fixed stars'), dated 1009–10 CE, p. 165. Ink and watercolour on paper, 27 × 18 cm (page). Bodleian Library, University of Oxford, MS Marsh 144.

1.34   Seated prince, reverse of a medallion, Iran, 11th–12th century CE. Gold, 5.2 × 4.3 cm, weight 29 g. Freer Gallery of Art, Washington, DC, inv. no. F1943.8.

al-Rahman al-Sufi (903–86), active under the Buyid amir 'Adud al-Dawla in Shiraz (fig. 1.35). The figures are clothed in what appear to be very light garments with exaggerated pleating, with open coats over shirt and trousers in the Persian style. While the figure of Andromeda wears a headband, the figure of Auriga, in contrast, wears a turban wound in several layers.[47] How much these garments constitute historical dress, or are merely symbolic of the Iranian tradition to which the Buyids saw themselves connected, may be debated.

Perhaps the only complete garment with a Buyid connection was a dark blue silk tunic in the Textile Museum, Washington, DC, now taken apart for the sake of readability of the inscriptions and their display in a museum context. Made from fabric that carried the names and titles of Baha' al-Dawla, it was excavated near Rayy

1.36   Tunic, Shiraz, Iran, or Madinat al-Salam, Iraq, *c.* 1000 CE, acquired by George Hewitt Myers, 1927. Silk samite (weft-faced compound twill), maximum width 130.8, width of sleeve 29.2 cm. Textile Museum, Washington, DC, inv. no. 3.116. Reproduced from A.U. Pope and Phyllis Ackerman, *A Survey of Persian Art from Prehistoric Times to the Present*, vol. VI, Oxford, 1938–39, p. 984.

in the 1920s and acquired by George Hewitt Myers in 1927 (fig. 1.36).[48] It featured a tapered body to which were attached two long straight sleeves, with a square tasselled piece at the back shoulder (fig. 1.37). The inscriptions, in a monumental Kufic, were on the sleeves and the shoulder piece; they are woven in golden-yellow silk as a complementary weft with twill interlacing as an integral element of the base fabric, which is a silk samite (a type of twill compound weave).[49] The inscription comprises part of the titles of the Buyid amir Baha' al-Dawla, but the fabric was cut in such a way as deliberately to omit his name. Below this part of the inscription is a dedication to a certain Abu Sa'd Zadanfarrukh ibn Azadmard the Treasurer (*al-khazin*), who is known from contemporary historical sources.[50] Recent scholarship has suggested convincingly that the tunic was made some 150 years after the time of Abu Sa'd Zadanfarrukh, during the reign of the Seljuqs in Iran, perhaps for a descendant of his, and that the textile to which the fragments once belonged was originally a banner that served as the insignia of his public office.[51]

Abbasid customs relating to robes of honour are discussed in the *Rusum dar al-khilafah* ('Customs at the abode of the caliph') by the tenth-century author Hilal

1.37   Fragment of a banner made of *tiraz* fabric, commissioned by Baha' al-Dawla for Abu Said Zadanfarrukh ibn Azadmard, Shiraz, Iran, or Madinat al-Salam, Iraq, *c.* 1000 CE, tailored into the shoulder on the back of the tunic shown in fig. 1.52. Silk samite (weft-faced compound twill). 54.61 × 43.82 cm. Textile Museum, Washington, DC, inv. no. 3.116C.

al-Sabi'.⁵² In one chapter, devoted to the investiture of 'Adud al-Dawla, Hilal distinguishes between robes of honour for the commander of the army (umara' al-juyush), those for the vizier (al-wazir) and those distributed on a regional level (al-wilayat). The passage provides information on two issues: the role of inscriptions on vestments and the varying grades of vestments according to office. Hilal's descriptions make it clear that vestments were graded by rank, distinguished not only by the decoration of the garments, but also by various types of supplementary insignia. Army generals (ashab al-juyush), for example, received the most elaborate vestments: a plain black turban, two black garments, one with a hoop and one without, a red gilded or embroidered susi cloth, and a loose, sleeveless dabiqi garment, with a frontal opening. In addition, a sword, two quivers, a standard and horses were presented.⁵³ Conquerors (ashab al-futuh) received a supplementary collar, armbands, sword and belt.⁵⁴ The standards given to army commanders, in white silk and inscribed in ink, seem to have been of particular importance. Because Hilal listed the contents of the standards' inscriptions in some detail, we can assume that they played a vital role as part of the vestment. While one side was inscribed with the shahada, a quotation from the Quran (surah 9:33) relating to the jihad, and a phrase referring to the amir al-mu'minin ('Commander of the Faithful') as the upholder of God's command, the other presented, among quotations from the Quran (surah 2:131, and surah 32:40–41), a caliphal protocol mentioning the name of the caliph: 'Bismillah al-rahman al-rahim li-'Abdallah ibn Ja'far al-imam al-Qa'im bi-Amr Allah amir al-mu'minin atala Allah 'umruhu'.⁵⁵

The investiture of 'Adud al-Dawla by the Abbasid caliph al-Ta'i' (r. 974–91) included also various presentation items, such as a seat of honour with cushions inscribed with the name of al-Muti'.⁵⁶ The difference in importance between the army officers (umara') and the viziers (wuzara'), mentioned in Hilal al-Sabi''s account, is described in detail in the Muqaddima, an introduction to history by Ibn Khaldun, who used the terms 'sword' (al-sayf) and 'pen' (al-qalam) for these two groups of caliphal officials. While the 'sword' was actively involved in establishing and retaining the caliph's power, the 'pen' merely consisted of administrators and agents, exercising authority on behalf of the ruler.⁵⁷ This would explain the more elaborate robes of honour given to military commanders as described by Hilal al-Sabi'.

Although Hilal's text does not mention inscribed garments as part of the khil'a, his extensive description and the content of the inscriptions on the banners presented to military commanders as part of their khil'a show that inscriptions were visually important, at least on these items. The choice of inscriptions on the standard, relating to the jihad and the position of the amir al-mu'minin, was certainly intentional and, perhaps, politically charged.

THE SELJUQS

The type of cut used in the tunic at the Textile Museum in Washington made from a Buyid banner was typical of garments from the Seljuq period: it was probably open in the front, buttoned and fastened with a belt, with long narrow sleeves.⁵⁸ Several similar complete garments of comparable construction have survived from Seljuq Iran or central Asia. One in the Sarikhani Collection is made of dark blue silk samite decorated with a pattern of golden roundels that comprise a border of floriated Kufic containing two confronted birds (fig. 1.38). Like the Buyid garment in the Textile Museum, Washington, DC, discussed above (see fig. 1.36), this also came from a burial, as is indicated by the decomposition of the robe on its back. A cushion and face cover of the same fabric were found with it.⁵⁹ The inscription contains benedictory phrases. A silk coat in The al-Sabah Collection, reportedly found in central Asia, and dated somewhat later, is made of fabric of similar design that has an overall pattern of paired birds.⁶⁰ Garments of this type are represented in the figures of attendant courtiers in the wall-paintings of the audience hall in the Ghaznavid palace at Lashkari Bazar in Helmand province, southern Afghanistan (fig. 1.39). The courtiers are dressed in long-sleeved coats that fasten on the left side, with a collar folded over to the right and a belt around the waist with a sash hanging down in front. One robe is decorated with a pattern of teardrops, the other with a pattern of large roundels comprising borders with floral scrolling and scrolls in the central panel. The figures also wear trousers and boots, and hold maces in their right hands. They coincide very closely with a description of an audience in 429 AH / 1038 CE of the Ghaznavid sultan Mas'ud I of Ghazna (r. 1030–40) by the contemporary historian of Mas'ud, the Ghaznavid civil servant Abu

1.38   Robe, Iran, 11th–12th century CE. Silk samite (weft-faced compound twill), length 124 cm. Sarikhani Collection, Oxfordshire, inv. no. I.TXT.1021.

al-Fadl Bayhaqi (d. 1077). In the passage he describes the courtiers and their dress in some detail:

> All around the hall, standing against the panels, were the household *ghulams* (*ghulaman-i khassagi*) with robes of Saqalatun, Baghdadi and Isfahani cloth, two pointed caps, gold-mounted waist sashes, pendants and golden maces in their hands. On the dais itself, to both left and right of the throne, were ten *ghulams*, with four-sectioned caps on their heads, heavy, bejewelled waist sashes, and bejewelled sword belts. In the middle of the hall were two lines of *ghulams*; one line was standing against the wall, wearing four-sectioned caps. In their hands they held arrows

and swords, and they had quivers and bow cases. There was another line, positioned down the centre of the hall, with two-pointed caps, heavy, silver-mounted waist sashes, pendants and silver maces in their hands. The *ghulams* of both these lines all wore cloaks of Shushtari brocade.[61]

Several polychrome stucco figures have survived from archaeological contexts that also broadly conform to the description of the costume provided in Abu al-Fadl Bayhaqi's description of the courtiers. These figures have been linked to the kind of courtly context provided by the paintings in the audience hall of Lashkari Bazar.[62] They have been attributed to western Iran under Seljuq rule between 1050 and 1150, perhaps under the rule of Sultan Sanjar (r. 1118–57).[63] The Seljuqs were, like the Ghaznavids, of Turkic origin and competed with them over areas in eastern Iran. Perhaps the most prominent of these sculptures are two at the Metropolitan Museum of

1.39   Wall-painting depicting courtiers, audience hall of Lashkari Bazar palace, Afghanistan, first half of 11th century CE. Fresco. Reproduced from Daniel Schlumberger, *Lashkari Bazar: une résidence royale ghaznévide et ghoride*, 2 vols, Mémoires de la Délégation Archéologique Française, 18, Paris, 1978, vol. I, pl. 123.

1.40   Standing figure with a crown, Iran or Afghanistan,
late 12th – early 13th century CE. Painted stucco,
143 × 51.5 × 25.4 cm. Metropolitan Museum of Art, New York,
Gift of Mr and Mrs Lester Wolfe, 1967, inv. no. 67.119.

1.41   Standing figure of a courtier from a palace frieze,
Iran, 1150–1250 CE. Painted stucco, h. 101.6 cm. Detroit
Institute of Art, Purchase, inv. no. 25.64.

Art in New York (fig. 1.40) and one at the Detroit Institute
of Art (fig. 1.41).[64] Another more fragmentary figure is in
The al-Sabah Collection.[65] All of them are characterized by
full-frontal posture, Sasanian-style crowns or headdresses,
patterned knee-length cloaks studded with jewel-like
ornaments, *tiraz* bands with legible but non-historical
Kufic inscriptions ('non-historical' means not inscribed
with a dated and localized caliphal protocol), jewelry
worn around the neck, belts with suspended sashes, and
decorated swords held diagonally in front.[66] Prominent
colours are light blue and red with traces of gilding.[67]

While the heads of the painted figures at Lashkari Bazar
are shown in three-quarter profile, the stucco figures look
straight at the viewer, which has led to the proposition
that they were intended to accompany the ruler's throne.[68]
The fact that all feature cloaks with prominent *tiraz*
bands on the upper sleeves, as well as crowns and jewelled
ornaments, points to a princely context. What a reception
with the ruler enthroned and attended by courtiers might
have looked like is suggested by a scene on a small silver
dish at the Hermitage Museum, which has been attributed
to early eleventh-century Iran or Afghanistan under the

1.42   Dish depicting a courtly scene, Iran or Afghanistan, early 11th century CE. Silver with gilding, cast and carved, diam. 10.3 cm. State Hermitage Museum, St Petersburg, acquired by the State Purchasing Commission from a private collector, 1953, inv. no. S-499.

Ghaznavids (fig. 1.42).[69] It features a seated prince wearing Sasanian-style dress and crown, attended by two courtiers in Turkic dress (not unlike the stucco figures discussed here, or the painted figures at Lashkari Bazar) wearing horned or double-pointed hats, similar to those described in the passage by Abu al-Fadl Bayhaqi quoted above.

THE ABBASID REVIVAL

Images of seated rulers persisted among the heirs of the Seljuqs long after the Seljuq Empire had disintegrated and through what has been referred to as the Abbasid Revival, from 1118 to 1258. A very important player in northern Iraq in the period before the mid-thirteenth-century Mongol invasions was the amir Badr al-Din Lu'lu' (r. 1234–59), originally an Armenian slave and later successor to the Zengid amirate of Mosul. Recognized by the Abbasid caliph al-Mustansir (r. 1226–42), he carried the title *al-malik al-rahim* ('the merciful king'). Apart from a series of metal objects inscribed with his name and titles, he is remembered in a series of patron's portraits executed for the frontispieces of copies of the *Kitab al-aghani* ('Book of songs') by the tenth-century poet Abu al-Faraj al-Isfahani (fig. 1.43).[70] One type represents the haloed Badr al-Din seated cross-legged on a high chair, attended by members of his court to either side; the other shows Badr al-Din as

a falconer mounted on a horse. In both he wears a lavishly patterned coat in blue and gold with inscribed golden *tiraz* bands on the upper sleeves that feature his name legibly in black Naskh. He also wears a pair of similarly patterned trousers and a pointed hat with a fur lining, emphasizing his Turkic affiliations.

A glimpse into the dress of the cultured urban bourgeoisie in late Abbasid Baghdad is provided by the illustrations of the *Maqamat* ('Assemblies') of Abu Muhammad al-Qasim ibn 'Ali ibn Muhammad ibn 'Uthman al-Hariri of Basra (1054–1122), poet, linguist and civil servant under the Seljuqs. Two manuscript copies of the work are particularly well known, one in the Bibliothèque Nationale de France (fig. 1.44), the other in the Oriental Institute, Academy of Sciences in St Petersburg.[71] The copy in the Bibliothèque Nationale was copied and illustrated in Baghdad by Yahya ibn Mahmud al-Wasiti around 1236–37. The stories are tales of adventures of the hero Abu Zayd from Saruj, and

1.43   Portrait of Badr al-Din Lu'lu' enthroned with attendants, manuscript illustration, frontispiece to Abu al-Faraj al-Isfahani, *Kitab al-aghani* ('Book of songs'), probably northern Iraq (Mosul), 1218–19 CE, fol. 1. Pigments and shell gold on paper, 30.6 × 22 cm (page). Feyzullah Library, Millet Kütüphanesi, Istanbul, inv. no. 1566.

1.44 Yahya ibn Mahmud al-Wasiti, 'Listening to a Theologian', manuscript illustration, Abu Muhammad al-Qasim ibn 'Ali ibn Muhammad ibn 'Uthman al-Hariri, *Maqamat* ('Assemblies'), 1237 CE, fol. 85v. Pigments on paper, 35 × 26 cm, Bibliothèque Nationale, Paris, MS Arabe 5847.

are told by a certain al-Harith, a merchant who travels between places, some of them exotic. The miniatures are lively illustrations of the text and exude a certain drama. Most striking is the sheer variety of dress codes, colour and pattern, for both female and male protagonists. Even though the copies date from a time just before the Abbasid caliphate came to an end in Baghdad, it seems that they reflect a varied and complex society that had retained many of its traits from earlier times, as described in ninth- and tenth-century texts such as those of Abu al-Tayyib Muhammad al-Washsha mentioned earlier. The exuberance of the various shirts, cloaks and shawls is especially noticeable; they are worn with a variety of headdresses, such as turbans with long sashes. Also, the differentiation of social and ethnic groups is expressed prominently by clothing. The costume of government officials or members of the religious elite stands out as being more layered and complex. Golden bands decorate borders and sleeves, perhaps a reference to inscribed *tiraz* bands. Certainly, these illustrations are a reference to the function of such bands as emblems of status. There is also a very clear notion of 'Arabness' among the urban middle class in these paintings, despite the fact that Baghdad had been effectively subdued by Iranian and Turkic governments for a good 150 years. The weight here is on types of dress that look back to earlier periods when the Abbasids were at their zenith, rather than the foreign fashions favoured by the Buyid or Seljuq elite.

THE FATIMIDS AND THEIR LEGACY

A certain 'Arab' notion of dress seems also to have been favoured among the elite of the Fatimid dynasty who ruled Egypt from 973 to 1171. One of the earliest representations of Fatimid courtly life is a marble relief at the Bardo Museum, Tunis, which shows a ruler seated cross-legged and holding a conical cup, attended by a female musician playing a flute (fig. 1.45). The ruler wears a tunic with long sleeves, decorated with epigraphic bands on its upper sleeves, an ornamented belt at the waist and a winged Sasanian-style crown. The female figure wears a long shirt-like dress also decorated with bands on the sleeves. In a way, the representation of rulership carries on the precedent set by the Abbasids, a hybrid of Arab and Iranian attitudes to dress. The marble relief dates most likely from before the Fatimids took Egypt and established the centre of their caliphate in Al-Qahira (Cairo). It probably was once located at a palatial complex in their capital al-Mahdiya, founded by the caliph al-Mahdi (r. 909–34) in 921. Once the Fatimids had made their capital in Al-Qahira, following the conquest of Egypt under al-Mu'izz (r. 953–75), it seems that a courtly style developed that was more refined, and more lavish and extravagant than that of earlier times. While the great Fatimid palaces in Al-Qahira have disappeared, there is quite a wealth of representations of courtly activity in luxury works of art of the eleventh and twelfth centuries. A carved ivory plaque that might once have belonged to a piece of furniture (now in the Museum für Islamische Kunst in Berlin), features a wealth

1.46   Detail of a panel depicting courtly activities, Egypt, 11th–12th century CE. Carved ivory, 30.3 × 5.8 × 1–1.5 cm. Museum für Islamische Kunst, Berlin, inv. no. I 6375.

1.45   Seated ruler with a musician playing a pipe, relief, 10th century CE, from the fortress city of Mahdia (now Tunisia). Marble, 53 × 35 cm. Bardo Museum, Tunis.

of figures feasting and hunting, accompanied by musicians and attendants (fig. 1.46). The lively activity and drama of the figures is underlined by a great attention to dress: patterned cloaks and tunics, turbans, baggy trousers, wide flowing sleeves – not unlike those shown in the illustrations of the *Maqamat*, discussed above.

Similar representations once decorated the palaces of the Fatimids, as is indicated by surviving wood beams, now in the Museum of Islamic Art in Cairo.[72] Fatimid lustre ceramics show similar courtly figures. A fine fragment of a lustre painted dish at the Benaki Museum in Athens depicts a seated musician wearing an ornamented robe with epigraphic *tiraz* bands on the sleeves (fig. 1.47). The figure is suggestive of the sheer splendour of the Fatimid court. That Fatimid court style trickled down into the middle classes may be indicated by a painting in a *muqarnas* (carved vault) fragment from Fustat, now in the Museum

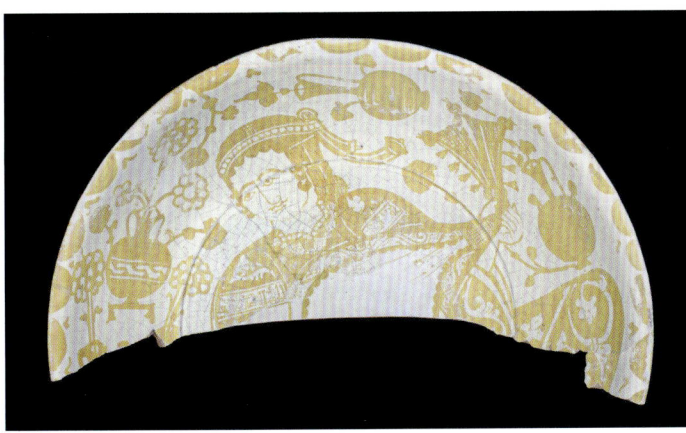

1.47 Fragment of a dish depicting a seated musician, Egypt, 11th century CE. Earthenware, lustre painted, diam. 38 cm. Benaki Museum, Athens, inv. no. 11121.

of Islamic Art in Cairo (fig. 1.48). It features a figure seated cross-legged and raising a beaker, who wears a tunic with a floral pattern over a pair of trousers. Prominent are the carefully wound turban, but also the shawl worn over the back with its ends flying out from underneath the arms, which is accentuated by decorative bands at either end.

In a ground-breaking article that considers surviving textiles from Egypt in various international collections, Lisa Golombek questioned the extent to which these textiles may be representative of all early Islamic textile production in Egypt.[73] She juxtaposed surviving examples of *tiraz* textiles with literary sources, and raised two main areas of concern: materials and types of garments. While the literary sources mention a large variety of materials, including silk, wool and *qasab* with gold filé, Golombek argued that the *tiraz* group contains largely fragments of linen or cotton clothes, with silk used only sparsely, for inscriptions or decorative bands. The range of *tiraz* garments is also limited to summer outfits, undergarments, turbans, shawls, sashes, napkins, presentation towels and possibly furnishings, such as curtains. Indeed, the Fatimid treasury accounts show how varied textiles at the Fatimid court were, in contrast to surviving *tiraz* textiles.[74]

The Fatimid treasury at the time of the caliph al-Amir (r. 1101–30) is described in detail by the civil servant Qadi Rashid ibn al-Zubayr in his *Kitab al-dhakha'ir wa al-tuhaf* ('Book of treasures and rarities'), a work used and quoted by al-Maqrizi in his topographical and historical description of Egypt, the *Kitab al-mawa'iz wa al-'itibar fi*

dhikr al-khitat wa al-athar.[75] The contents of the *khizanat al-kiswa* ('treasury of clothing') contained not only the wardrobe of the caliph and his family, but also items distributed to the various ranks of courtiers.[76] Although these accounts do not describe the appearance of garments in detail, they do provide some data about materials. The outfits described most carefully are those of the caliph, his brother Abu al-Fadl Ja'far and the senior princess.[77] These contain the largest number of individual items, ten or eleven for the caliph, five for his brother and sixteen for the princess. Linings and garments worn beneath other items, including tunic-like garments such as the *ghilala* and the *wasitani*, appear to have been mainly of linen, as were mantles ('*ardi*). In some cases the linen fabric contained silk, though whether this was tapestry-woven or embroidered is not known. The materials of what appear to be mostly outer garments are not stated in the lists concerning the caliph's outfit, but the outer garments in all four outfits all used large amounts of gold, the value of which was considerable. The caliph's first ceremonial costume contained two robes and a turban, which

1.48 Wall-painting depicting a seated figure, architectural fragment from the bathhouse of Abu Su'ud, Fustat, Egypt, 11th century CE. Fresco, 24.5 × 60 cm. Museum of Islamic Art Cairo, inv. no. 12880.

together were made with around 1,066.5 *mithqal* (*c.* 4.5 kg) of gold: the gold in the *thawb* amounted to 375.5 *mithqal* (1.589 kg), and in his turban to 325 *mithqal* (1.486 kg).[78] Whether the ground fabric of these items was silk is unknown. In the first princess's outfit, however, her second veil and her two cloaks were made of silk, but without gold. Although they are much less detailed, the lists outlining the outfits of relatives and palace officials also mention a large number of garments that were made of silk, either gilded or gold-embroidered.[79] Only the lowlier ranks of the court hierarchy, such as servants, captains and sailors of the caliphal barges, were given 'Alexandrian', 'Sus' and 'Damietta' cloth, which may well have been linen fabrics produced in these centres.[80] It is clear that gold-decorated textiles and silks, but also plain linens or linens woven with silk, were part of the palace wardrobe, depending on garment types and the rank of the wearer. Yet surviving *tiraz* textiles misrepresent this picture, giving almost no evidence for homogeneous silk and very little for the use of gold. Since gold was a precious commodity, it is unsurprising that textiles woven or embroidered with gold thread were much more expensive than textiles without. Looking back to the Fatimid period, the Mamluk author Ibn Duqmaq, for example, stated, while describing the products of the various textile centres in the Nile Delta, that in Tinnis and Damietta a cloth or garment embroidered in gold could be worth about a thousand dinars, whereas one without was worth only one or two hundred dinars.[81]

Egyptian textiles were internationally sought after in the tenth and eleventh centuries, as described in a well-known passage by the Persian traveller Nasir-e Khosrow in which he discusses the products of the workshops of Tinnis and Damietta. He describes a material called *qasab*, probably a fine linen that was often coloured, and which was used for men's turbans and headdresses (*wiqaya*), as well as women's clothing.[82] Nasir-e Khosrow refers to a particularly special variety in white, woven in what he refers to as the *kargah* ('sultan's' workshop). Khosrow praises the weavers of the royal outfits and the high value of their products, but also asserts how difficult it was for a foreign buyer to procure them: 'I have heard that the ruler of Fars (one of the Buwayhids) had sent 20,000 dinars to Tinnis to buy a complete set of royal robes (*yek-dast djama-ye-khass*). His agents stayed several years in the town without being able to manage this transaction.'[83]

One of the few references to *tiraz* bands is found in a statement by Ibn Abi Tayyi, who commented that:

I have heard a certain person say that he was present at the 'Investiture' at al-Kasr which used to take place in summer and winter, the value (of the stuffs given away) then being more than six hundred thousand dinars. The emirs used to be invested with garments of *dabiki*, and turbans with gold *tiraz* borders, these two items worth five hundred dinars. The greatest emirs were invested with necklaces (*tawq*), bracelets (*siwar*), and ornamented swords … In 516 AH. (1122 AD) the various articles upon which money was spent came to 14,305 pieces.[84]

But what about inscriptions, which feature so prominently in surviving *tiraz* textiles? These Fatimid treasury lists do not give any detailed information concerning inscriptions, though the value of the gold thread was specified in great detail. The different types of garments and outfits described in these passages reflect the ranks of the recipients. Their appearance was measured in terms of quality, richness, quantity and value, rather than the impact of inscriptions.[85]

In contrast, relatively few *tiraz* textiles have survived that were either woven or embroidered with gold; the majority that do come from the Fatimid period.[86] One of these is the so-called 'Veil of St Anne', which dates from 1096–97 and represents one of the best-preserved complete garments from the Fatimid period with a caliphal inscription (figs 1.49, 1.50).[87] Preserved in the church of St Anne at Apt, in southern France, the veil was probably brought to France during the early Crusades and served as a sacred relic of St Anne, whose cult had developed there during the twelfth century.[88] Raimbaud de Simiane and Guillaume de Sabran, lords of Apt, and Isoard, the town's bishop, are all known to have taken part in the First Crusade. The Veil of St Anne is a large rectangular linen cloth comprising a full-loom width and length. It bears a series of inscriptions that mention the names and titles of caliph al-Musta'li (r. 1094–1101) and his vizier al-Afdal, as well as the famous textile production centre Damietta in Lower Egypt as its place of production. The Veil is made from a very lightweight and sheer undyed linen-based fabric, perhaps like the *sharb* fabrics so celebrated in historical accounts. Both fringes of the

1.49   Veil of St Anne, Damietta, Egypt, 1096–97 CE. Linen, silk and gold thread (plain weave with in-woven polychrome silk tapestry), 150 × 310 cm. Cathedral of St Anne, Apt, France.

length are decorated with tripartite bands featuring the caliphal inscriptions. The central portion carries another band which serves as a linkage to two small roundels that contain a pair of harpies (human-headed birds) encircled by an inscription with the name of the vizier. The band terminates at the selvedge of one side in a larger roundel containing a pair of addorsed sphinxes, again encircled by text. This roundel extends into two volutes on either side, and could well have been the centre of the whole garment worn over the back and shoulder. But how exactly the Veil was worn is not entirely clear, as there are no signs of tailoring. Some scholars have proposed that it could have been folded to create a garment similar to the modern *bisht*, a light overcoat.[89] In that case the two bands would have been attached to the volutes to form the front of the garment and the selvedge of that side would have been closed up.

A fragment of a volute with a roundel containing two confronted gazelles, which was once part of a garment similar to the Veil of St Anne, is at the Metropolitan Museum in New York.[90] This one is made of a lightweight fabric dyed in dark blue that highlights the yellow silk used for the decorative tapestry work. In the Veil of St Anne it is the use of gold thread that marks the textile's exceptional status as a caliphal garment. Of similar size to the Veil, yet far less luxurious in its use of materials, is another complete loom width and length that survived as a relic in France after the Crusades: the so-called Shroud of Cadouin at the abbey of Cadouin in the Dordogne (fig. 1.51).[91] First mentioned in archival records in 1214, it was believed to have come into the possession of the

1.50   Detail of the Veil of St Anne (fig. 1.49) showing a roundel in the central band featuring a pair of addorsed sphinxes set within a Kufic inscription.

1.51   Shroud of Cadouin, Egypt, 1094–1101 CE. Linen, silk (linen plain weave with in-woven polychrome silk tapestry), 113 × 281 cm. Cadouin Abbey Museum, France.

Bishop of Puy, Adhémar de Monteil, after the capture of Antioch, during the First Crusade. As a holy relic it was associated with Jesus Christ himself, and was long considered to be the Holy Shroud, the cloth believed to have enshrouded the body of Jesus for his burial. Like the Veil of St Anne, the Shroud carries caliphal inscriptions mentioning the caliph al-Musta'li, but unlike the former it does not have a central band, nor use gold thread. The fabric seems also of lesser quality. The fact that these two textiles are the only examples of caliphal production to have survived intact as objects is remarkable, as they crossed over cultures and religious practice, were repurposed and assigned new symbolic meanings. In this they join the many hundreds of luxury objects that crusaders brought back from the Holy Land, which made medieval Europeans curious about the riches of the Middle East. Likewise, the thousands of archaeological textiles that survived in Egyptian graves because their caliphal associations made them special were also repurposed and assigned new symbolic functions as burial shrouds (see chapter 2).

Only a handful of complete garments have survived in Egyptian burials. The earliest is a small burial tunic at the Textile Museum, Washington, DC, with an embroidered *tiraz* in the name of the Abbasid caliph al-Muqtadir (r. 908–32) on one of its sleeves (fig. 1.52).[92] Another rare

complete child's tunic, this one dating from the Fatimid period, as is proven by its tapestry-woven sleeve bands, is in the Museum of Cairo University.[93] This tunic, too, was tailored; and it is decorated with non-epigraphic tapestry-woven bands reserved for the sleeves, which are purely decorative. Both tunics are made from linen-based fabric of an almost tight-weave structure, of comparable quality. Both consist of individually cut sections of cloth sewn together, with the main part of the tunic formed from an oblong piece of cloth with a slit cut into the mid-section to form the head opening; the sleeves are short and attached to the mid-section of the main cloth. In order to provide the tunic with enough volume to cover the body of its wearer, two trapezoidal pieces of cloth are inserted between the main body and sleeves.

Several garment fragments with epigraphic bands have survived which must have once belonged to adult tunics of similar construction. All are made from inscribed linen *tiraz* textiles, cut out of larger cloths and of funerary origin. One of them (fig. 1.53) is dated to the period of al-Muqtadir.[94] The inscription, which is similar in style to the tunic at Washington, is also upside down, but in this case below a pocket, suggesting that the fragmentary cloth may well have once been part of the left side of the front of a shirt or tunic, with the pockets above the heart;

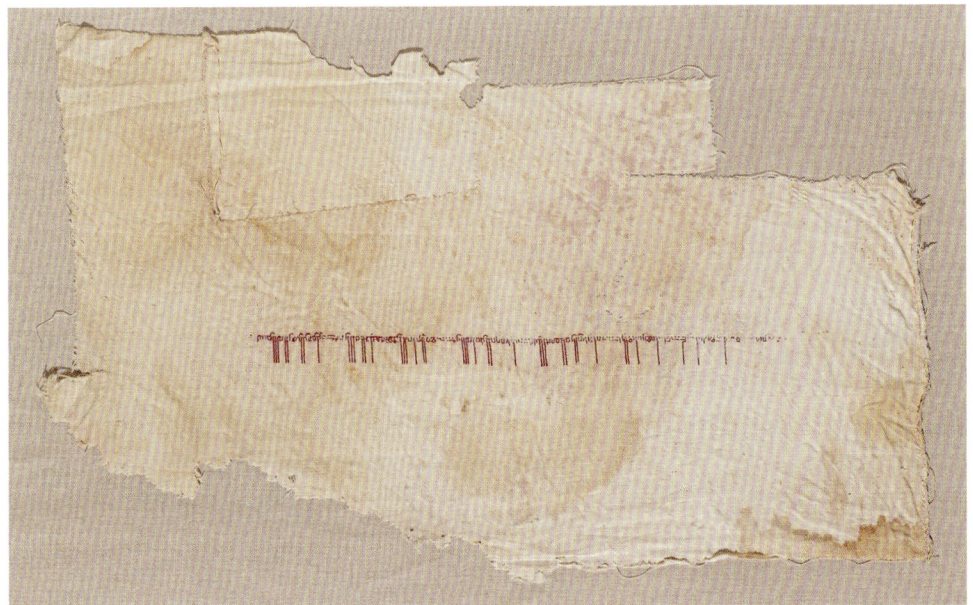

1.52 Tunic with *tiraz* inscriptions (running vertically on left-hand sleeve), dated 306 AH / 918–19 CE, acquired by George Hewitt Myers, 1936. Linen, with silk embroidery, 64.77 × 99.06 cm. Textile Museum, Washington, DC, inv. no. 73.444.

1.53 Fragment of a textile with a *tiraz* inscription (upside down below remnants of a pocket), tailored garment, Egypt, dated 921–22 CE. Linen, with silk embroidery, 54.6 × 30.5 cm. Abemayor Collection, Royal Ontario Museum, Toronto, inv. no. 978.76.70.

1.54   Fragment of a *tiraz* textile, formerly inset into a tailored garment, Egypt, 1048–58 CE. Linen, silk (linen plain weave with in-woven polychrome silk tapestry), 17.5 × 26.1 cm. Cleveland Museum of Art, John L. Severance Fund, inv. no. 1950.552.

1.55   Fragment of a *tiraz* textile, probably inset from a sleeve, Egypt, 1027–36 CE. Linen, silk (linen plain weave with in-woven polychrome silk tapestry), 42 × 62.6 cm. Cleveland Museum of Art, John L. Severance Fund, inv. no. 1950.554.

1.56   Fragment of a *tiraz* textile, probably inset from a sleeve, Egypt, 1045–58 CE. Linen, silk (linen plain weave with in-woven polychrome silk tapestry), 20.3 × 51.8 cm. Cleveland Museum of Art, Gift of Ruth Blumka in Memory of Leopold Blumka, inv. no. 1974.187.

here, as in the other case, an existing fabric was re-used or repurposed. A fragment of a larger *tiraz* inscription from the reign of the Fatimid caliph al-Mustansir (r. 1036–94), in the Cleveland Museum of Art, was once inset into a tailored garment made from the same fabric, with multiple stitching on both sides of the inscription band (fig. 1.54). Remnants of a pocket appear above the band, suggesting that this was perhaps not a sleeve band, as one might think at first sight, but again a piece placed on the front side of a garment. Two further Fatimid fragments in Cleveland might in fact represent sleeve bands (figs 1.55, 1.56). Both comprise finely tapestry-woven caliphal inscriptions with floriated Kufic: one bears the name of al-Zahir (r. 1021–36), the other that of al-Mustansir.

Two very rare complete adult linen tunics from Egypt, one in the Ashmolean Museum, Oxford (fig. 1.57), the other in The al-Sabah Collection (see cat. no. 54 and pp. 544–45), show that adult and children's tunics, like the ones discussed above, were similar in shape and construction.[95] Carbon dating suggested a mid-tenth-century date (930 +/–35 years) for the Ashmolean tunic, which on account of the similarities between the two pieces would seem to apply also to the tunic in Kuwait.[96] Tailored from pieces of cloth cut to the same basic shapes as the child's tunic just described, the two garments share the same basic construction and are of similar size: the Ashmolean piece is *c.* 170 cm long and 140 cm wide, while the Kuwait piece is slightly shorter, at 132 cm long. In both pieces the

1.57   Tunic with *tiraz*-style inscriptions, Egypt, 11th century CE. Linen, with silk embroidery, *c.* 170 × 140 cm. Ashmolean Museum, Oxford, purchased with the assistance of the Art Fund, the MLA/V&A Purchase Grant Fund, and the Friends of the Ashmolean, 1998, inv. no. EA1998.210.

1.58   Royal mantle of Roger II, Palermo, Sicily, dated 528 AH / 1133–34 CE. Silk, embroidered with gold thread, decorated with gold sheet, gems, pearls, 146 × 354 cm. Kaiserliche Schatzkammer, Hofburg, Vienna, inv. no. WE XIII 14.

1.59   Roger II of Sicily ('Rogerios Rex'), crowned by Jesus Christ ('IC'), 12th century CE. Mosaic. Santa Maria dell'Ammiraglio (church of the Martorana), Palermo, Sicily.

collar opening is fastened on the left side with a small cloth button. The collar of the Kuwait tunic is tighter and has a band collar. On the front and sleeves, both tunics are decorated with almost identical bands of large epigraphic decoration in a loosely embroidered silk, imitating a Kufic inscription with a continuous sequence of *alif*s or *lam*s linked by a knotted motif, differing only in colour: blue on the Ashmolean piece, yellowish-beige on the Kuwait piece. The character of both Kufic-style inscriptions, which consist of stumpy letters with hook-like stem terminals, points to the period in Egypt towards the end of Abbasid and the beginning of Fatimid rule. The disproportionally wide sleeves are striking on both pieces. These are what we see in some of the pictorial representations discussed above. It is likely that one would have worn another layer on top of such a tunic, perhaps a cloak or a shawl.

One last example to consider here is an iconic garment that offers a visual memento of the splendour of Fatimid court costume: the ceremonial robe of the first Norman king of Sicily, Roger II, made in the royal treasury (*khizana al-malakiyya*) in Palermo (Madinat al-Siqiliyya), probably by Muslim craftsmen, inscribed in Arabic and dated 528 AH / 1133–34 CE (fig. 1.58).[97] Its bright red silk base is embroidered on a large scale with gold thread and pearls, as well as encrusted with gold sheet and precious stones. As a garment, it links three clothing traditions – medieval European, Byzantine and Islamic. In doing so, it embodies the Norman programme of *convivencia* on an island that had been at the crossroads of diverse cultures for centuries. While firmly rooted in the culture of Christian Europe, the Normans in Sicily adapted to and adopted many aspects of Byzantine and Islamic culture that suited their identity and lifestyle as rulers within the political landscape of the Mediterranean at the time of the Crusades. Dressed in elaborately ornamented and jewel-encrusted robes as a Byzantine ruler, crowned by Jesus Christ himself in a famous mosaic at the Martorana church in Palermo (fig. 1.59), Roger II also enjoyed pastimes known from Abbasid Baghdad, Umayyad Córdoba and Fatimid Cairo (Al-Qahira).⁹⁸ A painting of a ruler seated cross-legged, dressed in a long Arab *qamis* with wide sleeves and armbands not unlike the shirt in The al-Sabah Collection discussed earlier, and holding a drinking cup while he is attended by courtiers, is only one of this type in the

1.60   Seated ruler attended by courtiers, detail of a ceiling panel depicting a banquet, Cappella Palatina, Palermo, Sicily, 12th century CE. Pigments on wood. Cappella Palatina, inv. no. CP0853.

muqarnas ceiling of the Cappella Palatina, Roger's chapel at the Royal Palace in Palermo (fig. 1.60). Built in 1132, with its hybrid programme of Byzantine mosaics and painted Islamic ceiling, the chapel is, like the robe, a symbol of Norman cultural adaptability and calculated display of opulence. The ceiling has been discussed as one of the best examples of Islamic painting, and has been linked to a tradition of painting from north Africa that was influenced by Abbasid style.⁹⁹ It seems that it was most likely created by Muslim craftsmen. The coronation robe, too, was probably made at least in part by Muslim craftsmen, who were trained in embroidering using gold thread and pearls. This is indicated by several Arabic inscriptions on the *alb,* a ceremonial shirt that is likely to have been part of the original outfit, but was altered later under Roger's grandson William II of Sicily (r. 1166–89). The handwritten inscriptions take the form of short notes on strips of textile inserted into the lining which record the work of embroidering with pearls by Arab and Latin craftsmen of the royal workshop under the supervision of their masters – a work of collaboration by people with different specializations.¹⁰⁰ As a garment, the mantle of Roger II represents a melting of different traditions in form, manufacture and iconography. Its shape is that of a ceremonial cape or chasuble, worn by medieval European clergy and royalty. While its base fabric is probably Byzantine, the embroidery in gold thread and pearls links it to traditions of the Islamic Mediterranean. Its iconography – comprising a pair of addorsed lions, each subduing a camel – has been much debated. It has been linked to an earlier Eastern tradition of combatant felines and seen as a symbol of Norman cultural domination over Islam, but perhaps a more tempting interpretation would be as an allegory of the victory of good over bad government. This notion is underlined by the content of the inscription, which invokes a sequence of benedictory rhymes concerned with a state of happiness, beauty, well-being and hope.¹⁰¹ Apart from the mantle's multiple layers of meaning, it is a reminder of the opulence of royal dress in the Islamic world in the use of gold thread and other precious materials, as, for example, in the caliphal outfits documented in the Fatimid treasury lists. While these are lost, we can still marvel at Roger's mantle, as did many who attended the coronations of the emperors of the Holy Roman Empire in the centuries to come.

CHAPTER 2

INSCRIPTIONS AS SYMBOLS
OF THE CALIPHATE

DEFINING *TIRAZ*

Adolf Grohmann, the well-known Austrian historian of Islamic papyrology, defined the term *tiraz* in his entry for the *Encyclopaedia of Islam* of 1934 as follows:

> The word is borrowed from the Persian and originally means 'embroidery'; it then comes to mean a robe adorned with elaborate embroidery, especially one ornamented with embroidered bands with writing upon them, worn by a ruler or person of high rank; finally, it means the workshop in which such materials or robes are made. A secondary development from the meaning 'embroidered strip of writing', border or braid in general, applied not only to inscriptions woven, embroidered, or sewn on materials, but also to any inscriptions on a band of any kind, whether hewn out of stone, done in mosaic, glass or faience, or carved in wood … The name *tiraz* then becomes the special name for the inscriptions officially stamped upon the rolls of papyrus in the factories themselves. The two last meanings are limited to a few occurrences …; when papyrus ceased to be made in the middle of the tenth century AD these two meanings of *tiraz* disappeared.[1]

Grohmann implied a chronological sequence regarding the textile context: originally the word meant embroidery in Persian, it then came to signify an embroidered inscription, and finally it denoted the type of workshop of manufacture. Scholars have since tended to follow this definition, while applying it almost entirely to textiles.[2] They were perhaps influenced by the *Muqaddima*

('Introduction' or 'Prolegomenon') of the fourteenth-century historian Ibn Khaldun (1332–1406), who defined *tiraz* as follows:

> It is part of royal and governmental pomp and dynastic custom to have the names of rulers or their peculiar marks embroidered on the silk, brocade, or pure silk garments that are prepared for their wearing. The writing is brought out by weaving gold thread or some other coloured thread of a colour different from that of the fabric itself into it.[3]

About twenty years before Grohmann, another Austrian papyrologist, Josef von Karabacek, had already suggested a much more balanced definition of *tiraz*. Comparing protocols used on papyri with those on coins and textiles, he demonstrated that the formulas used on all three followed largely the same patterns.[4] They commonly included Quranic phrases, the given name (*ism*), sometimes a teknonym (*kunya*), and title or honorific (*laqab*) of a ruling caliph, and administrative information relating to who had ordered the item and where and when it had been made.[5] Because papyri were used only as a medium for official documents up to the tenth century, Karabacek's discussion focused on the Umayyad and early Abbasid periods, which he also saw as the zenith of the Islamic usage of official *tiraz* inscriptions.

Karabacek strongly opposed the widely used translation of *tiraz* as simply 'embroidery', emphasizing its meanings as 'manufactory' and 'border', particularly 'inscription border'.[6] For him, the term *tiraz* was also synonymous with *dar al-tiraz*, a place of production believed to have been situated in the palace complexes of the Abbasid caliphs, where items were made for the use of the court. He stressed that presenting and wearing textiles or garments decorated with 'borders' and 'inscription borders' were sovereign rights of the ruler, that these borders were made using differing techniques, and that the inscriptions contained set caliphal protocols.

Detail, fig. 2.3 (p. 56)

It is likely that the term *tiraz* had different meanings at different times and therefore no single definition of the term is possible. However, since the overwhelming number of surviving textile inscriptions, as well as literary references, date from the Umayyad, Abbasid and Fatimid periods, it is necessary to determine what the term meant in those periods and how it was used.

A passage in the *Kitab al-mahasin wa al-masawi* ('Book of merits and faults') of the early medieval Islamic historian Ibrahim ibn Muhammad al-Bayhaqi, active under the caliph al-Muqtadir (r. 908–32), describes how the philologist and Quran reader al-Kisa'i (c. 737–805), a confidant and former teacher of the Abbasid caliph Harun al-Rashid (r. 786–809), asks him about the origin of formulas in coin inscriptions. These were essentially the reason for perhaps the most defining event of the Umayyad period, the language reform of the Umayyad caliph 'Abd al-Malik ibn Marwan (r. 685–705), which laid the foundation for the establishment of an Islamic polity independent from Byzantine supremacy and replaced Greek as the chancery language used by the early Islamic administration.[7]

One day Harun, holding a dirham in his hand, asked al-Kisa'i who had introduced the text on the coin. Al-Kisa'i told him that the Umayyad caliph 'Abd al-Malik had one day seen the Greek protocol (*tiraz*) on an Egyptian papyrus scroll from a state manufacture, and when its content was translated for him he was angry that the official inscription did not represent Islam properly. He also thought it problematic that such inscriptions were applied to all other products of state manufacture. 'Abd al-Malik therefore ordered his brother, the governor of Egypt, 'Abd-al-'Aziz ibn Marwan, to change the Byzantine *tiraz* on all objects inscribed in this way, such as textiles, papyri and curtains, to an Islamic one containing *surah al-tawhid* (surah 113) and parts of the *shahada* in surah 3:18, stressing the oneness of God.[8] 'Abd al-Malik further ordered the destruction of all remaining Byzantine papyrus scrolls and punishment for individuals who held on to them. As a consequence, the Byzantine emperor opposed 'Abd al-Malik's order and wrote to him, trying to convince him to change back to the old Greek protocol. After several unanswered attempts, the Byzantine emperor warned 'Abd al-Malik that he would issue coins in gold and silver inscribed with phrases that would ridicule the Prophet Muhammad. 'Abd al-Malik replied that in addition to the changes to papyri, the inscriptions on coins had been irrevocably changed and provincial governors had already been notified.

The term *sikka* denotes the caliphal prerogative to issue coins. It has been well documented that 'Abd al-Malik instigated a change to the early Muslim coinage, away from the figural Byzantine and Sasanian types to purely Islamic epigraphic types.[9] The coin evidence also suggests that the *sikka* as a concept developed only under the Umayyads, particularly under 'Abd al-Malik, as, in the first few decades after the Islamic conquest, the coinage that had been issued in Byzantine and Sasanian territories continued to circulate. This coinage was subsequently supplemented in Iran by Sasanian-type coins and in former Byzantine territories by modified Byzantine types. The Sasanian-style coins were minted by provincial governors and inscribed with their names rather than those of the caliph.[10] Following 'Abd al-Malik's victory over his rival 'Abdallah ibn al-Zubayr in 692, he instigated institutions that enabled him to build a centralized state; the reform of the coinage in 696–97 was part of this objective. 'Abd al-Malik's coinage moved away from previous Byzantine- and Sasanian-inspired models to purely Islamic ones, entailing the removal of all images and symbols from coins, substituting phrases from the Quran and mentioning the name of the Prophet Muhammad. This has been interpreted as an expression that the *sikka* was a right vested in the caliph by God and his Messenger (fig. 2.1).[11]

The text also provides evidence that 'Abd al-Malik ordered the introduction of Arabic as the official language for the *tiraz* inscriptions, not only on coins, but also on papyri (*tiraz al-qaratis*), vessels and clothes (*wa hiya tuhmal fi al-awani wa al-thiyab*). The act of inscribing (*yutarraz*) also embraced other media produced in Egypt, which the text does not specify ('*mimma yutarraz min saturi wa ghayriha min 'amal hadha al-balad*'). The term *tiraz* could also refer to non-Muslim formulas, such as the Greek inscriptions used by the Byzantines ('*ma fi 'amalihim min al-qaratis al-mutarraza bi-tiraz al-rum*').

Surviving papyri from Egypt provide us with evidence for the official changes in language as described above. The *protocollon*, a preliminary sheet preceding the first sheet of a papyrus scroll, bore texts often referred to as the 'papyrus protocol'.[12] In a similar way to coins and *tiraz* textile inscriptions, these contained religious formulas and institutional information: the name of the current caliph, the governor of Egypt or the name of the *'amil*, names of provincial officials, the name of the

2.1   Dinar of 'Abd al-Malik ibn Marwan, unknown mint, dated 77 AH / 696–97 CE. Gold, diam. 2 cm, weight 4.17 g. The al-Sabah Collection, Kuwait, inv. no. LNS 251 N.

papyrus mill where the scroll was made and often the name of its supervisor.[13] Until around 693–95 papyrus protocols were usually written in Greek, following the Byzantine tradition.[14] Extant papyri, however, indicate that al-Bayhaqi's account is imprecise with regard to the language reform. Rather than substituting Arabic for Greek, 'Abd al-Malik introduced bilingual protocols. Only from the time of Hisham ibn 'Abd al-Malik (r. 724–43) were protocols written in Arabic alone.[15] A well-known group of documents written for the Umayyad governor of Egypt Qurra ibn Sharik (in office 709–15) attests this. Qurra, a scribe (*katib*) by training, had been appointed by the Umayyad caliph al-Walid I (r. 705–15) to reorganize the economic affairs of the province. The Qurra papyri are perhaps the fullest account of any provincial governor in Egypt, given their state of survival and richness of content.[16] Two papyrus fragments in the Corpus Papyri Raineri at the Österreichische Nationalbibliothek in Vienna are significant for a discussion of how the term *tiraz* applies to papyri (fig. 2.2). One is inscribed 'mimma 'amara … bi-'amalihi fi tiraz' ('of what was ordered in the *tiraz*'), the other 'fi tiraz al-'ar (?) […]' ('in the *tiraz* of 'Ar (?) […]'.[17] Obviously *tiraz* refers here to a workshop in which the item was made or inscribed.

2.2   Papyrus fragment, inscribed in Arabic, al-Ashmunayn, Egypt, *c.* 864–73 CE. Papyrus and ink, 7.6 × 16.9 cm. Österreichische Nationalbibliothek, Vienna, Archduke Rainer Collection, inv. no. A.P. 04057.

2.3   Bottle with relief decoration, Jurjan, 8th century CE.
Unglazed ceramic, h 36 cm, diam. 22 cm. L.A. Mayer Memorial
Museum, Jerusalem, inv. no. C 40–69.

An unglazed ceramic bottle in the L.A. Mayer
Memorial Museum in Jerusalem is also of some
importance in this discussion (fig. 2.3).[18] The bottle
has a drum-shaped body on a tall circular foot, a long
tubular neck, straight spout and bow-shaped handle. It
is decorated with moulded designs, some of which have
been compared to jewelry. One of those, a necklace-like
moulded pendant suspended from the base of the spout,
has been compared particularly to similar necklaces
that decorate animal sculptures at Khirbat al-Mafjar.[19]
The most interesting feature of the object, however, is a
circular Kufic inscription on one side of the drum-shaped
body, which has a protocollary formula following the
benedictory part of the inscription: 'Blessing and goodness
to its owner … drink to his good health … of what
Muhammad made … in the *tiraz* of Jurjan' (see detail, p.
52).[20] The inscription states clearly that the item was made
in a *tiraz* workshop in Jurjan.[21] Without explanation, Eva

Baer dated the object to the eleventh to twelfth century.[22]
However, based on decorative and epigraphic comparisons
the bottle should rather be dated to the Umayyad or early
Abbasid period. First, the jewel-like device suspended
from the ribbon around the bottle's spout is reminiscent
of the ornaments worn by the stucco female figures that
decorate the waiting room of the bath complex of the
Umayyad palace at Khirbat al-Mafjar (see fig. 1.18).[23]
The overall arrangement of small-scale patterning also
compares to the overcrowded complexity of many of
the geometric and vegetal designs in the mosaic of the
music room there and its wall decorations.[24] Secondly, the
content of the inscription's protocollary formula and its
letterforms support an earlier date. The formula *mimma
'amala* (as well as its passive form *mimma 'umila*) in the
ewer's inscription was, furthermore, used on a variety
of early Islamic objects, including textiles, to about the
middle of the ninth century.[25] The style of the inscription,
however, allows a firmer attribution to the seventh or
eighth century, particularly the letterforms of the *'ayn*,
the *lam–alif*, the terminal *lam*, the *kaf* and the *sad*.[26]
Although comparative tables published by Grohmann and
based on a variety of media would suggest a date between
650 and 750, comparisons with the epigraphy of dated
papyrus inscriptions indicate the possibility of a date well
into the eighth century.[27] An Umayyad or early Abbasid
attribution of the bottle does not need to conflict with an
attribution to Jurjan in Iran. Jurjan had been an important
administrative centre of the Sasanians, and it became an
important Arab settlement, with its own governor, after
the Islamic conquest. Owing to its location close to the
Caspian Sea, it was a convenient trading post.[28] The city
had a prosperous silk industry, and was also a centre
of some industrial importance.[29] Furthermore, finds of
unglazed ceramics were made in Jurjan – albeit related
to those from Nishapur, which date from the ninth to
tenth centuries.[30]

The papyri and the bottle support the textual
evidence provided by al-Bayhaqi, discussed above,
that refers to *tiraz* inscriptions on papyri (*qaratis*) and
vessels (*awani*).[31] Not only did both types of object carry
protocollary *tiraz* inscriptions, but their inscriptions
sometimes also identified them as products of a *tiraz*
workshop, implying that the term had a dual meaning.

Surviving examples show that by the end of the
Umayyad period *tiraz* textiles were indeed inscribed in
Arabic. A very important piece in this context is a silk

2.4   Composite image of fragments of a *tiraz* textile naming Marwan ibn al-Hakam (r. 684–85) or Marwan ibn Muhammad (r. 744–50), eastern Mediterranean or central Asia, embroidered in Ifriqiya (modern Tunisia), 7th–8th century. Silk samite (weft-faced compound twill), with silk embroidery; piece (a) 30.3 × 50.7 cm; piece (b) 5.5 × 45 cm; piece (c) 15.21 × 21.5 cm; piece (d) 8.9 × 10.2 cm; piece (e) 39.5 × 49 cm; piece (f) 6.5 × 17 cm. Pieces (a) and (b) Victoria and Albert Museum, London, Purchased from the Reverend Greville John Chester in 1888, inv. nos 1314–1888, 1385–1888; piece (c) Victoria and Albert Museum, London, inv. no. T13-1960, given by the Whitworth Art Gallery, Manchester; piece (d) Brooklyn Museum, New York, Gift of Pratt Institute, inv. no. 41.1265; piece (e) Whitworth Art Gallery, University of Manchester, inv. no. T.8496; piece (f) Musée Royaux des Beaux-Arts, Brussels, inv. no. JS.Tx.0606.

textile embroidered with a *tiraz* inscription (fig. 2.4) in the name of Marwan ibn al-Hakam (Marwan I; r. 684–85) or Marwan ibn Muhammad al-Jaʿdi al-Himar (Marwan II; r. 744–50), the last ruler of the Umayyad dynasty.[32] It has survived as several dispersed fragments that once belonged to a complete loom width and length, which are now shared between four museums. They were recovered in the late nineteenth century from a grave in Akhmim, the ancient city of Panopolis in Upper Egypt. The fragments are rugged remnants of a once magnificent textile that comprised a compound-woven silk fabric with designs in mustard and muted blue on a dark red ground. A reconstruction has suggested that the textile was a large rectangular shawl, decorated with a repeat of beaded roundels and multi-lobed flowers, bordered at both ends with beaded bands.[33] Importantly, two of the fragments are inscribed in an early form of Arabic script, embroidered in yellow silk between the border and the main field of roundels. The inscription follows a protocollary sequence mentioning the name and titles of the caliph Marwan; what appears to be the lost name or title of an administrator who commissioned or ordered the piece; and the location of the *tiraz* workshop that made it in Ifriqiya, a province spanning most of the north African Mediterranean coast. The piece might date from the reign of either of the Umayyad caliphs called Marwan. The epigraphic style of the inscription conforms to script styles found in the Qurra papyri mentioned above, and links it to late Umayyad scribal practice.[34] It is significant that the inscription was embroidered onto the compound-woven silk ground fabric, as this opens up questions of manufacture. From a technical point of view, it would have been very complicated to weave such an inscription into the compound weave – hence the use of embroidery. This means, however, that the textile itself might not have been woven in Ifriqiya, but was produced elsewhere, perhaps in Byzantium or central Asia. It has been suggested, from an aesthetic point of view, that the beaded roundels might point to Sasanian influence.[35] The piece might have been a diplomatic gift which was then embroidered in Ifriqiya to personalize it, and it was from there that it reached Egypt.

The basic scholarly definitions of the term *tiraz* are a hundred years old and more, and their validity has been questioned in recent decades with regard to textiles. Nancy Micklewright described the phrase 'tiraz textile' as a term of convenience rather than one with a clearly defined meaning. She had doubts about its uncritical use in scholarly literature, where it often denotes textiles that are made of a variety of materials, with different types of applied decoration, and inscriptions of varying degrees of legibility that may or may not include protocollary formulas:

> When all of the textiles that are decorated with bands, with or without inscription, or produced in state-controlled factories, are grouped together, the result is a hodgepodge of silk, linen, and cotton fabrics and various colours and weaves, decorated with woven, embroidered, and painted bands that may contain inscriptions, pseudo inscriptions, or ornament of other kinds.[36]

The protocollary *tiraz* textiles known from the archaeological record were indeed made in a wide variety of materials and techniques – linen, cotton, wool, silk and reed or grass – and decorated in tapestry, loop pile, or with different embroidery stitches, or even inscribed in ink (see chapter 3). The variety shows further that *tiraz* textiles encompassed not only items of clothing, as most linen or cotton fabrics would suggest, but also furnishing fabrics such as reed mats (see figs 3.1–3.5 and cat. no. 115) and even carpets, further complicating any definition.[37]

Then, of course, there is the problem of how to reconcile the objects that have legible inscriptions with those that are inscribed with text that only appears to be legible. Textiles with protocollary inscriptions or benedictory text display almost the same range of materials and techniques as textiles with repetitious meaningful and non-meaningful inscriptions. Often the latter imitate the epigraphic styles of the former. Using a strict, protocollary definition, the latter should not be called *tiraz*. Yet their closeness in materials, techniques and epigraphic styles to true *tiraz* implies that they were made to emulate and imitate these. They might even have been made in the same workshops, given the excellent quality that some display. It is possible that already in the early Islamic period the distinction between proper *tiraz* and 'lookalikes' was blurred, given that low literacy rates prevented people from reading inscriptions of any kind. There also existed a general tendency to inscribe objects with forms that were so abbreviated that they were unintelligible, as is evident from contemporary ceramics and metalwork. Perhaps one should adopt a more inclusive

2.5 Dome of the Rock, Haram al-Sharif, Jerusalem, Quranic inscription in mosaic above the inner colonnade, completed in the reign of the Umayyad caliph 'Abd al-Malik, 72 AH / 691–92 CE.

approach to defining *tiraz* – one that is not dogmatic, but leaves open room for various ways to look at a body of material that reflects the diversity and multi-layered character of the early Islamic period.[38]

INSCRIBED TEXTILES AS POLITICAL STATEMENTS
THE UMAYYADS AND ABBASIDS

'Abd al-Malik's challenge to Byzantine rule and his quest to establish an Islamic visual identity through Arabic public text has also been observed in Umayyad monumental inscriptions. Although not mentioned in al-Bayhaqi's account, these too provide evidence for the political intentions of the Umayyads. 'Abd al-Malik and his son al-Walid I undertook an ambitious building programme of religious complexes in Damascus, Jerusalem, San'a', Mecca and Medina. The one with perhaps the highest impact both historically and in modern scholarship was the Dome of the Rock, situated in the Haram al-Sharif in Jerusalem, which contains a construction inscription dated 72 AH / 691–92 CE.[39] The main inscription, executed in gold mosaic on a blue background, 240 metres long and situated above the

arches of the inner octagonal arcade, contains carefully chosen quotations from the Quran (fig. 2.5). Two other inscriptions are on copper plaques on the eastern and northern gates.[40] An important link in the semiotics of inscriptions in different media is provided by the inscription on the north door of the Dome of the Rock, which proclaims the prophetic mission of Islam: 'He it is who has sent his Messenger with the guidance and the religion of truth, so that he may cause it to prevail over all religions, however much the idolaters may hate it.[41] Oleg Grabar pointed out that this passage became the standard on all Muslim coins and that its first architectural usage was in the Dome of the Rock.[42] This underlines again that inscriptions were chosen intentionally to make political statements.

Similarly to coins and papyrus protocols and foundation inscriptions on public buildings of the early Islamic period, the formulas used in *tiraz* inscriptions followed specific protocols reflecting the different stages of the commissioning procedure, and the hierarchies to which the individuals mentioned belonged. Many textiles in The al-Sabah Collection are inscribed with such protocols, the contents of which are discussed in detail in the Catalogue in this volume. An inscription usually begins with a religious invocation introduced by the phrase 'bism'illah al-rahman al-rahim' ('in the name of God, the Merciful, the Compassionate'), then benedictory phrases, such as 'baraka min Allah', or 'ni'ma min Allah' (both mean 'blessing from God'), introducing the section that refers to the caliph as the servant of God ("abd Allah'), continuing with his *ism*, his given name, followed by his religious status as imam preceding his regnal name, the *laqab*, which then is followed by his title *amir al-mu'minin* ('Commander of the Faithful'). Then an important part is concerned with administrative information: the act of ordering ('*amara*) and who ordered the manufacture – often a vizier; the workshop in which the piece was made (this is where the word *tiraz* appears) and sometimes the type of workshop (*khassa* or '*amma*, private or public), followed by the location; then a part that records the execution of the order, introduced by the phrase "ala yaday', and the name and often the title of the person who handled the order – in many cases, officials of the central administration; at the end a date, which is when the item was made. Not all these components are always present, but it is important to remember that the content of these inscriptions was planned carefully, as they reflected and proclaimed a court hierarchy that culminated in the person of the caliph, who had ultimate control of the administration and had designated certain individuals to exercise power on his behalf.[43] Any unauthorized changes to these protocols were an affront to caliphal authority.

Textual and artefactual evidence exists from the Abbasid period that illustrates the importance of placing the caliph's name in official inscriptions as a political prerogative. Political power struggles within the Abbasid family resulted on several occasions in a change of control over *tiraz* manufacture, events that are reflected in *tiraz* inscriptions. Two surviving historical accounts show that the exclusion of the ruler's name from a *tiraz* inscription was an act that asserted political independence. In the first account, related by al-Azraqi, the sons of the Abbasid caliph Harun al-Rashid (r. 786–809) competed over the succession to the throne. According to al-Azraqi, Harun al-Rashid divided his empire between his sons Amin, Ma'mun and Qasim al-Mu'tamin, based on a contract in which Amin accepted Ma'mun as governor of Khurasan with control of tax (*kharaj*), *tiraz* manufacture (*turuz*), the postal service (*barid*), the royal treasuries (*buyut al-*

amwal), and the land taxes ('*ushr wa 'ushur*; lit. 'the tenth and tenths').[44] In a letter to Harun al-Rashid, Ma'mun agreed to his share in Khurasan and that of his brothers, and affirmed that he would not break the contract.[45] The geographer and historian Abu Zayd Ahmad ibn Sahl al-Balkhi (850–934) relates the same story, albeit in more detail: Harun al-Rashid proclaimed his successors during the *hajj* in the year 802 by posting a letter on the Ka'ba in which he had laid down that Amin should be his first successor, Ma'mun his second and Qasim al-Mu'tamin his third.[46]

After Harun's death, however, Amin proclaimed his son Musa heir-apparent in defiance of Harun's stipulation, awarded him Iraq, and at the same time forbade the Friday prayer (*du'a*') in the name of Ma'mun, introducing Musa's name instead; and he declared coins minted in the name of Ma'mun invalid.[47] At the same time, the vizier al-Fadl ibn Rabi' and a certain Bakr ibn al-Mu'tamir attempted to influence Amin to depose Ma'mun completely. Amin sent one of his adherents, 'Ali ibn 'Isa ibn Mahan, to lead an army against Ma'mun. The intention was to have Ma'mun arrested and brought to Baghdad alive. In response to this insult, Ma'mun introduced three measures: he stopped sending the land tax revenues (*kharajja*), assumed the title *amir al-mu'minin* ('Commander of the Faithful'), and ceased to include Amin's name in *tiraz* and coin inscriptions.[48] The *Tarikh al-Bayhaqi* by the Ghaznavid historian Abu al-Fadl Muhammad ibn Husayn Bayhaqi (d. 1077) relates that Ma'mun made the Shi'ite imam Abu al-Hasan ibn Musa ibn Ja'far 'Ali al-Rida his own heir-apparent, and had his and al-Rida's names inscribed on coinage and *tiraz* textiles.[49] Ma'mun also dispatched his own army under Tahir ibn al-Husayn and Harthama ibn A'yan, who defeated Amin's troops at Rayy.[50]

The second account, related by Ibn al-Athir, concerns the struggles between al-Muwaffaq, the major force behind the throne of the Abbasid caliph al-Mu'tamid (r. 870–92) and his viceroy of the eastern provinces, and the governor of Egypt, Ahmad ibn Tulun. After al-Muwaffaq had hindered a plot by Ahmad ibn Tulun to free the caliph from al-Muwaffaq's control, Ahmad ibn Tulun took his revenge by putting a stop to the inclusion of al-Muwaffaq's name in the *khutba* and *tiraz* inscriptions, an action disapproved of by the caliph al-Mu'tamid.[51] The *khutba* was a 'sermon' given by the *khatib* to the community as part of the

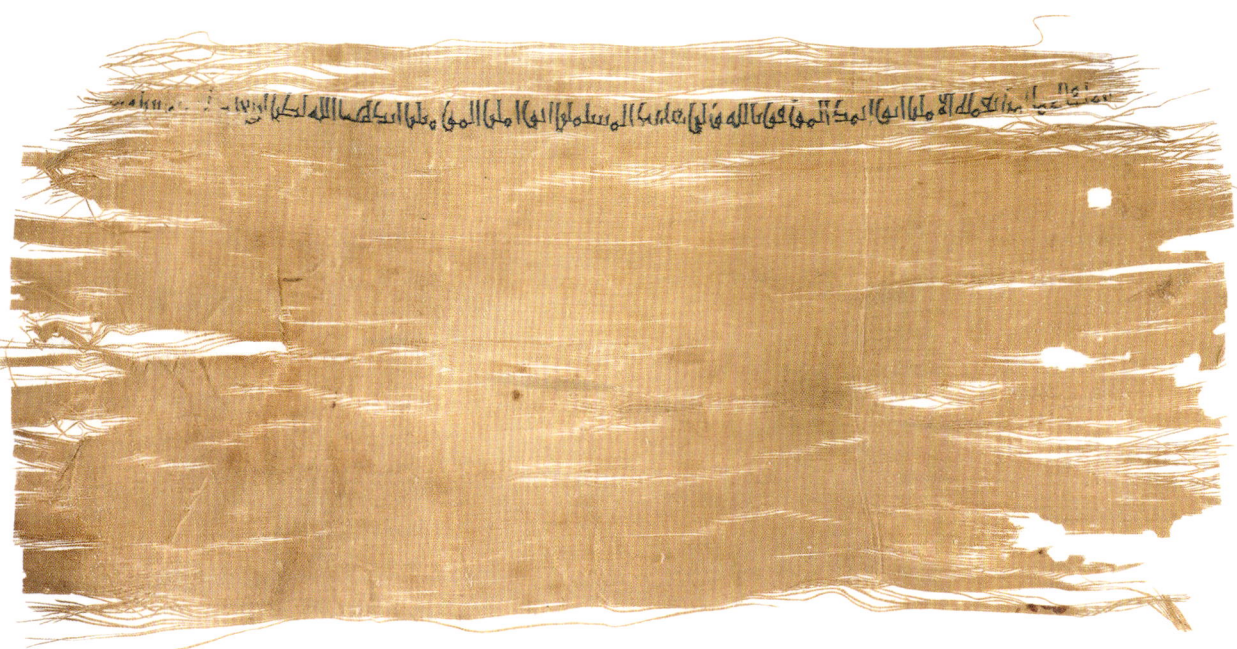

2.6   Fragment of a *tiraz* textile, Merw, Khurasan, dated 260 AH / 874–75 CE. *Mulham* (cotton and silk plain-weave fabric), with silk embroidery, 10 × 20.5 cm. Textile Museum, Washington, DC, inv. no. 73.4.

weekly Friday service.[52] The service consisted of various parts: the *hamdala* ('praise to God'), the *du'a' li al-mu'minin* ('prayer on behalf of the faithful'), the *salat* ('call to prayer') on the Prophet Muhammad, and two *khutba*s. In the *du'a' li al-mu'minin* it was a custom to mention the name of the ruling sovereign, in order to declare allegiance to him in his position as imam. Irene Bierman described this incident between al-Muwaffaq and Ahmad ibn Tulun as 'an overt tampering with the political formalities and indicators of power'.[53] The fact that al-Mu'tamid disapproved of Ahmad ibn Tulun's action underlines the significance of the control over *tiraz* inscriptions as a caliphal prerogative. Indeed, a textile published by Carl Johan Lamm and dated 258 AH / 872–73 CE (during the reign of the caliph al-Mu'tamid, who is mentioned in the inscription) states that it was ordered by one who appears to be the governor (*al-amir*), almost certainly Ahmad ibn Tulun himself.[54]

A number of surviving inscriptions record that they were ordered by Ahmad ibn Tulun's son Khumarawayh (r. 883–96).[55] Following the names of the Abbasid caliph al-Mu'tamid and, after 892, the caliph al-Mu'tadid, Khumarawayh is often referred to as 'mawla amir al-mu'minin', an honorific suggesting a close dependent relationship to the person of the caliph, but in reality merely a title that was conferred by the caliph on chosen subordinates in the administration, usually former slaves of non-Arab origin. Two of these inscriptions are interesting as they both date from 885–86 and also mention Khumarawayh: one is in the name of the caliph al-Mu'tamid, together with his son and heir-designate the 'amir Ja'far ibn amir al-mu'minin', while the other proclaims al-Mu'tamid's brother the 'amir Ja'far al-Muwaffaq bi-llah' as heir-apparent and de facto regent ('wali al-'ahd al-muslimin ibn amir al-mu'minin').[56]

In 884 al-Muwaffaq tried to regain control over Egypt from Khumarawayh, but eventually had to recognize the latter. A certain *amir* Ja'far is also mentioned in an inscription on a Yemeni textile in The al-Sabah Collection (cat. no. 109). This could be the same Ja'far al-Muwaffaq, son of al-Mu'tamid, who had been assigned to the western provinces while still a minor. It could also refer to al-Muwaffaq, regent over the eastern provinces, as he also styles himself 'ibn amir al-mu'minin'. An incident that supports the latter identification occurred during April 892, when the caliph al-Mu'tamid appointed his nephew Abu al-'Abbas Ahmad, son of al-Muwaffaq, later al-Mu'tadid (r. 892–902), his heir-apparent, and consequently his brother al-Muwaffaq's name was dropped from the *khutba*, on coinage and also *tiraz*.[57] Three surviving *tiraz* inscriptions provide evidence for these ongoing power struggles.[58] Abu Ahmad al-Muwaffaq is himself mentioned in two inscriptions as the individual who had ordered the textiles. Both items were made in Merw in the *tiraz al-khassa*, one in 873–74 (fig. 2.6), the other in 890–91.[59] Another textile from a year later (891–92) provides material evidence for the change in succession mentioned in the account above.[60] The inscription mentioned on this textile had been ordered in the *tiraz al-khassa* in Merw by al-Mu'tadid the newly appointed successor of al-Mu'tamid. Al-Mu'tadid is also acknowledged in three Tulunid *tiraz* inscriptions that mention Khumarawayh's successor, Harun, the fourth Tulunid governor of Egypt (r. 896–904).[61]

Viziers are by far the largest group of individuals credited in *tiraz* textile inscriptions for initiating orders of textiles.[62] As the heads of the caliphal administration they were in charge of economic and political affairs. Many of them came from prominent families of scribes and entered the administration at lower rank as scribes (*kuttab*), from which position they rose to power. The most famous such families were the Banu al-Furat and the Banu al-Jarrah, both active largely during the reign of the Abbasid caliph al-Muqtadir (r. 908–32). Members of these dynasties competed with one another over the most senior post. This resulted in rapid appointments and dismissals over a relatively short period of time. Al-Muqtadir appointed a new vizier no fewer than fifteen times. Completely isolated from the reality of the empire, the caliph relied in all his decisions on partial information coming from advisers, who were supposedly trusted but perhaps were not always trustworthy. 'Ali ibn Isa ibn al-Jarrah, for example, was head of government three times, in 913–17, 918–23 and 927–28. Three textiles in The al-Sabah Collection document his name (cat. nos 12, 14, 26). Another vizier was Abu 'Ali Muhammad ibn 'Ali ibn Muqla, whose training as a scribe led him to reform the Arabic script. He was in charge in 928–30, 932–33 and 934–36, and his name appears on one textile in The al-Sabah Collection (cat. no. 27). The office of the vizier was also important during the Fatimid caliphate in Egypt. Three textiles in The al-Sabah Collection mention in their inscriptions that they were ordered by a vizier (cat. nos 120, 141, 143).

Abbasid viziers were aided by administrators allied to these family groups and hence were advanced or demoted depending on who was in power. This is evident from the wording of *tiraz* inscriptions themselves. Many

Abbasid inscriptions contain a formula towards the end that alludes to the execution of an order, often given by a vizier: it consists of the phrase "ala yaday" (lit. 'upon the hands of'; that is, 'through / by the agency of') and the name and often the title of the person who handled the order. The formula appears mostly in inscriptions from Egypt and Khurasan. While earlier scholars thought that the individuals mentioned were local factory supervisors – the *sahib al-tiraz* – it can be shown that some were as elevated as viziers, but most were in fact administrators in the central Abbasid administration. A prominent name that appears over and over again in *tiraz* inscriptions is that of Shafi' *mawla amir al-mu'minin*, often with the *nisba* Muqtadiri, showing his allegiance and close relationship to the caliph al-Muqtadir. Shafi' was probably a member of al-Muqtadir's court at Baghdad, who had likely entered into the service of al-Muqtadir as a slave, and was later a member of an influential group of eunuchs.[63] Four textiles in The al-Sabah Collection attest his name, all dating from al-Muqtadir's reign and of Egyptian manufacture (cat. nos 7, 10, 12, 14). One textile in The al-Sabah Collection, also from al-Muqtadir's reign, mentions a certain Bishr, who in the textile record is sometimes styled *al-khadim* ('the eunuch'), confirming his position as a slave and dependant of the caliph within the central administration (cat. no. 8).

THE FATIMIDS

The Fatimids, just like the Abbasids before them, saw control over *tiraz* production and the content of their inscriptions as a prerogative of the ruler. A significant account in the *Sirat al-ustadh jawdhar* ('The life of the master Jawdhar') by Abu 'Ali al-Mansur al-'Azizi al-Jawdhari, a biography of a private secretary of the Fatimid caliph al-Mu'izz (r. 953–75), illustrates how the correct wording of protocols was a matter of great concern to the caliph himself. The *Sirat* describes an incident in which al-Mu'izz's father, al-Mansur (r. 946–53), commanded the formula 'mimma 'umila 'ala yaday Jawdhar mawla amir al-mu'minin bi al-Mahdiya al-murdiyya' ('of what was made under the direction of Jawdhar, client of the Commander of the Faithful in Mahdia') to be inscribed on prayer mats ordered by Jawdhar from Mahdia in the province of Ifriqiya, in modern-day Tunisia.[64]

Artefactual evidence clearly shows that, by introducing new caliphal protocols in inscriptions on *tiraz* textiles, coins and important monuments, the Fatimids conveyed important political messages.[65] The Fatimids

2.7 Dinar of al-Muʿizz li-Din Allah ibn al-Mansur, Filastin, Palestine, dated 359 AH / 969–70 CE. Gold, diam, 2.05 cm, weight 3.89 g. The al-Sabah Collection, Kuwait, inv. no. LNS 513 N.

asserted their claim to lead the whole Muslim community by stressing their ancestral right to rule whenever public mention of the Fatimid caliphs was made. As Ismaʿilis, claiming descent from Ismail, the son of imam Jaʿfar al-Sadiq (d. 765), the Fatimids traced their lineage back to Fatima, a daughter of the Prophet Muhammad and wife of his cousin ʿAli. They challenged Abbasid doctrine, which saw the *sunna*, the tradition of the Prophet, as the law where the rightful succession was laid down. The first *khutba* given in the name of al-Muʿizz at the mosque of ʿAmr ibn al-ʿAs at Misr al-Fustat (Old Cairo) on 20 Shaʿban 358 AH / 20 July 969 CE excluded the name of the Abbasid caliph al-Mutiʿ (r. 946–74) and reserved particular blessings for al-Muʿizz's ancestors:

> God, bless our servant and friend, the fruit of prophecy, the scion of the rightly guiding and rightly guided (*mahdiyya*) clan, the servant of God, the *imam* Abu Tamim al-Muʿizz li-Din Allah, the Commander of the Faithful, just as

you blessed his fathers, the pure ones, and his ancestors, the rightly guided *imams*.[66]

The foundation inscription of the first Fatimid mosque in Al-Qahira, al-Azhar, finished in 970–71 on the orders of al-Muʿizz's general and conqueror of Egypt, Jawhar al-Siqilli, is of particular importance here, since it was the first large congregational mosque to be finished since Ibn Tulun. It stresses the ancestral link of the Fatimid caliphs to the Prophet's family through their ancestors.[67]

The caliph's ancestral link was also stressed in coin and textile inscriptions. Before the conquest of Egypt, al-Muʿizz introduced a new type of coin that departed from the Aghlabid–Abbasid model, which had been issued under his predecessors, stressing his Ismaʿili mission and allegiance to ʿAli ibn Abi Talib's status as the rightful successor to the Prophet Muhammad (fig. 2.7). He had the phrase 'And ʿAli ibn Abi Talib is the Nominee of the Prophet, Most Excellent Representative, and Husband of the Radiant Chaste One' ('wa ʿAli ibn Abi Talib wasiyy rasul naʾib al-fudul wa zawj al-zahraʾ al-batul') included on the obverse of coins, and also the phrase 'Reviver of the Sunna of Muhammad, Lord of the Messengers and Heir to the Splendour of the Rightly Guided Imams' ("abd Allah Maʿad Abu Tamim, al-imam al-Muʿizz li-Din Allah, amir al-muʾminin, muhyi sunnat Muhammad, sayyid al-mursilin, wa-warith majd al-aʾimma al-mahdiyyin'). After his succession, al-ʿAziz (r. 975–96) introduced the phrase 'the Servant of God and his Companion' ("abd Allah wa-waliyyuhu').[68]

The earliest surviving Fatimid *tiraz* textile inscription is also in the name of al-Muʿizz and was made in 345 AH / 956–57 CE, thirteen years before the conquest of Egypt in 969 CE (fig. 2.8).[69] It reads:

2.8 Fragment of a *tiraz* textile, Mansuriyya, north Africa, dated 345 AH / 956–57 CE. Cotton, with silk embroidery, 20.5 × 82 cm, Museum of Islamic Art, Cairo, inv. no. 13165.

In the name of God, the Sovereign, the evident Truth, and may God honour (Muhammad) Seal of the Prophets and his pure family, blessings from God (and satisfaction) and … joy and peace and happiness and majesty and greatness and favour and goodwill to the servant of God and the friend of God Ma'add Abi Tamim (imam al-Mu'izz li-Din Allah), Commander of the Faithful, may God send blessings upon him and his pure ancestors and honourable descendants, and salute them with thorough salutation … the year three hundred and forty five.[70]

As public texts and carriers of political messages, common phrases shared between the *khutba* and inscriptions on key monuments, coins and textiles referred to the caliph's pure lineage. Inscriptions furthermore contained phrases of Shi'i importance, such as blessings upon the 'pure imams' ('al-a'imma al-zahirin'), and references to 'Ali and the ruling caliph as a 'Friend (or Companion and Ally) of God' ('wali Allah') and imminent victory. Often Fatimid *tiraz* textile inscriptions blessed the father of the ruling caliph.[71] These phrases were intended to underline and announce a Fatmid caliph's legitimate right to rule and exercise control. Consequently, their use was a prerogative of the ruler, who controlled the wording and adapted the message according to political need. Several examples of textiles with relevant inscriptions are in The al-Sabah Collection (see cat. nos 131, 132, 139, 142, 144, 150, 152).

THE DISPLAY OF *TIRAZ* INSCRIPTIONS

Two significant public displays of *tiraz* inscriptions existed during the Abbasid period: the *kiswa* (covering of the Ka'ba in Mecca) and the *khil'a*, the presentation of robes of honour to court dignitaries as a sign of office on appointment, and on an annual basis to court employees as part of their salaries.[72] Several *kiswa* inscriptions were recorded by al-Maqrizi in his *Khitat*.[73] The *kiswa* was made in Egypt during much of the early Islamic period, from where it was dispatched annually to Mecca. Since the Ka'ba was the most important Islamic religious monument, the patronage of the manufacture of the *kiswa* was a caliphal prerogative, or in later times a prerogative of those claiming caliphal status, such as the Mamluk and Ottoman sultans. It was an outward symbol of the custodianship over Mecca, first exercised by the Prophet Muhammad.

Abbasid customs relating to robes of honour as outlined in the *Rusum dar al-khilafah* by Hilal al-Sabi' were discussed in chapter 1.[74] The text elaborates on the investiture of the Buyid amir 'Adud al-Dawla by the Abbasid caliph al-Ta'i' (r. 974–91). In keeping with Abbasid customs, the robes conferred on the commander of the army (*umara' al-juyush*), the vizier (*al-wazir*) and regional officials (*al-wilayat*) reflected the appropriate rank of their recipients, being graded hierarchically and distinguished by decoration and insignias.

The dictionary of physicians by Ibn Abi Usaybi'ah, the *'Uyun al-anba' fi tabaqat al-atibba'* ('A literary history of medicine'), provides evidence for the *khil'a* as part of court salaries, and lists all those items that were presented every Muharram to the physician of Harun al-Rashid, Bakhtishu' ibn Jibra'il. Bakhtishu' received payments of two kinds. One was part of his public remuneration (*rasm al-'amma*), the other his private remuneration (*rasm al-khassa*), presumably paid by Harun al-Rashid himself. While the public fee was paid as large sums of money, the private fee was paid in cash but also in copious amounts of textiles of various kinds, many of which were described in Ibn Abi Usaybi'ah's text as *tirazi*. Among these items there were twenty pieces of *al-qasab al-khass al-tirazi*, twenty pieces of *al-mulham al-tirazi*, ten pieces of *al-khazz al-Mansuri*, ten pieces of *al-khazz al-mabsut*, three garments (*thiyab*) of *al-washi al-yamani*, three robes of *al-washi al-nasibi*, three *tayalisa* (headscarves) and various furs.[75] The items listed were certainly all types of garments that well-dressed members of the upper class in Baghdad used as part of their wardrobe, as mentioned in Abu al-Tayyib Muhammad al-Washsha's account (see chapter 1). Furthermore, this passage clearly establishes that luxury fabric types, such as *qasab* and *mulham* (see chapter 3), were used in the court context and also bore *tiraz* inscriptions. This ties in with surviving *mulham* fabrics in The al-Sabah Collection (cat. nos 105, 107).[76]

A passage in the *Kitab al-hadaya wa al-tuhaf* ('Book of gifts and rarities') describes the visit of the Byzantine embassy to the court of the Abbasid caliph al-Muqtadir (r. 908–32) in Baghdad in 917.[77] Although it does not concern the presentation of robes of honour, this passage describes very clearly the display of inscribed furnishing fabrics. Owing to the importance of the visit of the Byzantine envoy, al-Muqtadir's vizier, Abu al-Hasan ibn al-Furat, ordered that the caliph's palace, the *dar al-sultan*, should be filled with large numbers of armed men, while all other palaces should be hung with draperies, measures that were no doubt taken to impress the foreign envoy. According to the text, 38,000 draperies were used out of the *khizanat al-farsh* ('treasury of furnishings'), most of which were heavily embroidered in gold, with depictions of animals. Among 25,500 items of mainly Chinese, Armenian and *wasiti* origin (from Wasit), there were also a large number of embroidered *dabiqi* hangings. Very significantly, the text also states that 8,000 of these items were inscribed with the commissioner's order, names of past caliphs and other names.[78]

Another account of what the Byzantine ambassadors saw in the presence of the caliph is related by the historian al-Khatib in his *History of Baghdad*:

> Finally, they came again to the presence of the Caliph Muktadir, whom they found in the Palace of the Crown upon the bank of the Tigris. He was arrayed in clothes of Dabik-stuff embroidered in gold, being seated on an ebony throne overlaid with Dabik-stuff embroidered in gold likewise, and on his head was the tall bonnet called qalansuwah. Suspended on the right of the throne were nine necklaces, like prayer beads, and to the left were seven others, all of famous jewels, the largest of which was of such a size that its sheen eclipsed the daylight. Before the Caliph stood five of his sons, three to the right and two to the left. Then the ambassadors, with their interpreter, halted before Muktadir, and stood in the posture of humility, with their arms crossed.[79]

In a passage from the *Kitab al-aghani* ('Book of songs'), Harun al-Rashid's vizier, al-Fadl ibn al-Rabi', is described receiving a visitor during an audience: al-Fadl was seated on a *susandjird* carpet embroidered in gold, which was inscribed with a protocol mentioning the person who had ordered the piece, a certain Hammad 'Ajrad, a regional governor.[80] These instances illustrate very clearly the importance given to displaying inscribed textiles under the Abbasids.

Public displays of inscribed textiles were also central to the Fatimids' political propaganda. The sets of clothing handed out to high officials and their families were often inscribed with elaborate *tiraz* bands, which provided a means of establishing a hierarchical order in court.[81] However, texts describing such investitures were often not very precise in their descriptions of inscribed textiles. Al-Maqrizi referred to various texts describing annual investitures at the Fatimid court in which members of the caliphal family, as well as all ranks of officers and employees, received clothing.[82] The different types of garment described in these passages reflected the ranks of the recipients, and their appearance was measured in terms of quality, richness, quantity and value, rather than the impact of inscriptions.[83] While the amount and value of the gold thread was accounted for in great detail, these lists did not give any detailed information concerning inscriptions. The only reference to *tiraz* bands is found in a statement by Ibn Abi Tayyi, who discusses an investiture at the Fatimid palace (quoted in chapter 1).[84]

Surely it must have been an immense honour to receive a textile inscribed with the caliph's name, but it seems that inscriptions themselves did not necessarily act as emblems of rank. More likely the recipient's status was evident in whether garments were woven with silk and gold, were jewelled, coloured, of good quality and high monetary value, or whether the outfit included fur trimmings, turban jewels, gold swords and stirrups and elaborate belts. The relative uniformity, in style, arrangement and colour of surviving *tiraz* textiles, like those conserved in The al-Sabah Collection, would support this. Materials, on the other hand, such as silk and gold thread, and the linen-based fabrics into which they were woven, vary immensely in quality (see chapter 3).

Ibn Tuwayr's *Nuzhat al-muqlatayn fi akhbar al-dawlatayn al-fatimiyya wa al-salah'iya* ('A history of the Fatimid and Ayyubid dynasties'), probably composed by a secretary in the chancery of the late Fatimid or early Ayyubid dynasties, contains a very detailed and chronological account of the different stages of the Fatimid new year procession.[85] The description of the clothing and materials worn by the caliphal entourage is particularly interesting, as it contains references to inscribed text.[86] After prayer, the caliph proceeded to the *khizanat al-kiswa al-khassa*, his private store of clothing, in order to choose the clothing to be worn by him and his closest entourage during the procession. He chose for himself a turban with a *taj*, a crown-like ornament. Then the caliph was presented with the *yatima*, a large pearl, which was placed on the front of the caliph's horse, arranged with other precious stones in a crescent shape. The value of these items was considerable. Then the parasol was mounted, which matched the caliph's dress. This parasol consisted of a wood lance, with gold ribs rising to a semi-spherical shape. It was covered by gold-embroidered *dabiqi* cloth. After this, two caliphal standards of white silk embroidered with gold were brought, which were to be carried by two commanders of the caliphal entourage. Then twenty-one standards inscribed with the phrase 'nasr min Allah wa fath qarib' ('victory from God and a near conquest') were brought. The standards were also inscribed in three bands (*tirazat*). These were to be carried by mounted horsemen of the private *sibyan al-khass* ('the young guard' or 'the youth of the caliph's private personal guard'). The caliphal sabre, placed in a golden sheath encrusted with precious stones, was carried by an important amir, one of the most notable dignitaries and the grandest of the carriers of insignias. Another distinguished amir seems to have carried the caliph's lance, decorated with pearls, together with a large gold shield.

Visual records of the Fatimid period paint a vivid picture of the widespread presence of inscribed garments in the court context. These include works in stone, ceramic and wood. A stone relief found in the palace complex at Mahdia, dated to the early Fatimid period, and depicting a seated ruler holding a cup, shows that *tiraz* bands could function as armbands placed across the upper portion of a sleeve (see fig. 1.45).[87] Fatimid lustre-painted ceramic vessels from the tenth and eleventh centuries show, furthermore, that *tiraz* bands were also placed on the tails or in the folds of turbans (see fig. 1.47).[88]

The record of surviving *tiraz* textile inscriptions produced in Egypt shows a change in epigraphic aesthetic towards a highly decorative, often floriated, monumental script from the beginning of the caliphate of al-Muti' (r. 946–74), when Egypt was ruled by the Ikhshidid dynasty, shortly before the Fatimids conquered Egypt.[89] Examples in The al-Sabah Collection are cat. nos 37 and 38. Writing on the development of floriated Kufic, Adolf Grohmann suggested two stages. By the second half of the ninth century, Kufic letterforms had developed 'foliations', that is, split hastae or long letter stems, which often took the form of a leaf. In Egypt, Palestine and the Hijaz the gradual transformation from 'foliated' to 'floriated' Kufic (where letterforms terminated in full half-palmette leaves) took place by the mid-ninth century.[90] Grohmann argued that, under the Fatimids, Kufic inscriptions became fully invaded by vegetal decoration for the first time, as the inscriptions on the minarets of the mosque of al-Hakim in Cairo (1003) show.[91] Yasser Tabbaa revised Grohmann's observations by

distinguishing between private and public inscriptions, and rejected Grohmann's idea of gradual development. Although in private inscriptions, as on funerary steles, foliations occurred in the ninth century, public inscriptions, such as those on the Nilometer (dated 861 and 873), retained an austere style of unfoliated Kufic.[92] Fatimid public inscriptions at al-Azhar and the al-Hakim mosque, Tabbaa suggested, were so completely different from preceding inscriptions in terms of the number of vegetal motifs growing out of letters that this style must have been an original Fatimid creation in Egypt, from where it spread throughout the Middle East in the course of the eleventh century.[93]

Grohmann's and Tabbaa's observations can be confirmed when looking at *tiraz* textiles. As already mentioned, caliphal *tiraz* inscriptions had already undergone an aesthetic change before the Fatimids, under the Ikhshidids, with the appearance of floriated Kufic. Under al-Mu'izz and al-'Aziz (cat. no. 123), these letterforms continued, at least into the rule of al-Hakim, under whom large inscriptions of the Ikhshidid type continued to be produced.[94] At the same time, however, textile inscriptions developed further into types with more pronounced vegetal forms, which were smaller in size and more integrated with the decorative background, as is also illustrated by examples in The al-Sabah Collection from the reigns of al-Zahir (cat. nos 142, 143) and al-Mustansir (cat. nos 144, 145, 149, 150, 152).

GIFTING *TIRAZ* TEXTILES

Ceremonial rituals of bestowing robes were a means of extending the ruler's status to his subjects. A miniature from the *Jami' al-tawarikh* ('Compendium of chronicles') commissioned by the Ilkhanid vizier Rashid al-Din (in office 1277–1316) showing Mahmud ibn Sebuktekin, the first independent Ghaznavid ruler, surrounded by his nobles and wearing a robe that he had received from the caliph al-Qadir bi-llah (r. 947–1031), illustrates this point (fig. 2.9).[95] Coming from the hand of the ruler, such robes symbolized his beneficence but also the link between subject and master. The verb *khala'a* implies the removal of one's robes, and in a further sense means the bestowing of robes ('khala'a 'alayhi khil'a').[96] It appears that during the early Islamic period two customs of bestowal existed, one informal, the other formal. The informal bestowal of robes by the caliph consisted of the presentation of his own used clothing to chosen individuals of the caliphal circle. The formal bestowal of clothing was practised

2.9   Mahmud ibn Sebuktegin donning a richly decorated robe of honour sent by the Abbasid caliph al-Qadir (r. 947–1031) in 1000 CE, manuscript illustration, Rashid al-Din, *Jami' al-tawarikh* ('Compendium of chronicles'), *c.* 1306 or 1314–15 CE, fol. 121r. Pigments on paper. University of Edinburgh Library, Or. MS 20.

in official investitures of army or government officials upon their appointment, and to a wider extent in the annual distribution of clothing to the employees of the court. Owing to the survival of literary texts, particularly concerning the Fatimids, which ascribe to the bestowal of the caliph's own clothes the power to transmit blessing (*baraka*) to the recipient, interesting questions can be raised.

A precedent for an informal presentation of robes is recorded in Ibn al-Athir's collection of *hadith*s *Al-kamil fi al-tarikh* ('The complete history'; see chapter 1). The Prophet Muhammad took off his *burda* and handed it to the poet Ka'b ibn Zuhayr upon hearing one of his poems.[97] It is significant in this context that, according to tradition, the poet al-Busiri was composing a poem, later known as the *qasida al-burda*, when he was cured of a paralytic stroke when the Prophet Muhammad threw his mantle over the writer's shoulders.[98] The poem, titled *Al-kawakib al-durriyya fi madh khayr al-barriyya* ('Celestial lights in praise of the best of the creation'), was believed to transmit supernatural powers and is still today recited at burials, in order to extend *baraka* (blessing) to the deceased.[99]

The informal habit of presenting clothes that had been worn by the Prophet Muhammad or his family or companions was continued later in the Umayyad period, as attested by several instances of the Umayyad caliph al-Walid II (r. 743–44) taking off his clothes and presenting them to his favourite poets at his pleasure palace Khirbat al-Mafjar. On the occasion of a performance by the poet Hakam al-Wadi, al-Walid first presented the poet with money and had his clothes sent to him afterwards.[100] On other occasions al-Walid was usually drunk, as when the young poet Hammad al-Rawiyah was given the two garments al-Walid was wearing.[101] Another time, al-Walid was so enchanted by a song of the poet Ibn 'Aishah that he kissed him on his head, stripped naked and presented the poet with his clothes.[102] While it could be argued that al-Walid did not know in these last instances what he was doing, the first passage clearly shows al-Walid's intention to reward and honour a poet he liked. Such a gift provided a sign of appreciation, but also a physical link to the caliph himself and a mark of personal friendship or companionship bridging rank.

The *Kitab al-wuzara' wa al-kuttab* ('Book of viziers and scribes') of al-Jahshiyari (early tenth century) reports an incident in which the Abbasid caliph Harun al-Rashid (r. 786–809) invested his vizier Ja'far ibn Yahya ibn Khalid ibn Barmak (in office 793–803) with administrative posts and rewards, such as control of the post office (*barid*) and the *tiraz* of all the *kuras* (a type of administrative provincial unit), and afterwards embraced him with his own robe, possibly as a sign of affection.[103]

Under the Fatimids, texts report the giving of personal items of clothing as involving a certain degree of benediction. This is illustrated by an encounter between the Fatimid caliph al-Mu'izz (r. 953–75) and his private secretary Jawdhar, related in the *Sirat al-ustadh jawdhar*, which shows that during the Fatimid period the presenting of worn caliphal robes was still practised. Al-Mu'izz presented a pair of slippers worn by al-Mansur (r. 946–53), one of al-Mu'izz's ancestors (his father), to Jawdhar as a benediction:

> We know that you like wearing slippers, so we have sent to you two slippers of silk that were used by al-Mansur and then we too have used them whenever we needed them, so use them knowing that from God is the baraka and blessing.[104]

It is significant that al-Mu'izz explicitly stated that al-Mansur and he himself had worn those slippers before passing them on to Jawdhar. It is because they had been worn by two imams that they carried caliphal *baraka*. In presenting these slippers, al-Mu'izz passed caliphal *baraka* on to Jawdhar, and in doing so honoured him.

These anecdotes show that *khala'a* in the original sense of the word was often a personal rather than an institutional act: it was a matter between a ruler and a favourite subject, sometimes involving the donning of garments actually worn by the ruler himself, a predecessor or a religious leader. In this context the ruler extended benediction by presenting a worn garment. While the anecdotes quoted here relate to donations to living persons,

caliphs also presented their own used clothes as shrouds and burial outfits for the interment of chosen subjects. As will be discussed later, some evidence for the presentation of burial outfits by the Prophet or his companions also exists in *hadith* literature. These instances add a new dimension to the *khil'a* ritual, as a source of benediction not only for the living but also for the dead.

The most detailed account of a Fatimid caliph presenting his own clothes for the burial of an individual of his close circle is again in the *Sirat al-ustadh jawdhar*, where one story describes how Jawdhar sent al-Mu'izz a letter to ask for the gift of one of his garments so that he could use it as his own shroud:

> He [Jawdhar] sent a note to Our Master to ask him for one of his proper garments to serve him as a shroud when he should die, because of the blessing attached to it. After the caliph had read this note, he felt honoured and sent him numerous garments.[105]

In response to Jawdhar's request, al-Mu'izz sent outfits of the four caliphs under whom Jawdhar had served: a robe of so called Merwian (*marwi*) cloth and a tunic from al-Mansur; two garments from al-Qa'im, one with a plain lining (*libas mubattan musmat*); a tunic from al-Mahdi; and finally a lined garment of Merwian cloth with a tunic beneath it from al-Mu'izz himself.[106] With this gift, al-Mu'izz included a message for Jawdhar, in which he said:

> Receive all of this with the blessing which is contained therein. Conserve these garments until the time of which you spoke [i.e. his death], after which God will have prolonged your life so that you will join us in the pilgrimage to the sacred house of God [Mecca] and the visit to the grave of our ancestor Muhammad [at Medina], so that this will be a joy to your eyes by the grace of God to his friends, God willing.[107]

Al-Mu'izz alludes here to the time after Jawdhar's death, assuring him of life thereafter and the participation in caliphal piety.

Al-Mu'izz's gift can be compared to a number of *hadith*s and anecdotes relating to the time of the Prophet Muhammad, the caliphal and Fatimid periods.[108] Three *hadith*s concerning the life of the Prophet confirm the special status of garments worn by the Prophet Muhammad himself.

In an incident related in the *Kitab al-tabaqat al-kabira* ('The major book of classes'), a collection of *hadith*s collected by the ninth-century Iraqi historian Ibn Sa'd, the Prophet Muhammad was given a woollen mantle, which he then presented to a man who had made a request to wear this mantle. Public opinion criticized the man on the grounds that he had taken advantage of the Prophet, who needed the garment himself but would not refuse a beggar's request. The man justified his presumption by explaining that he wanted the mantle for his shroud (*kafan*).[109] The anecdote allows speculation that garments given away were not only an honour for the receiving person, but also an act of benevolence on the part of the bestower.

A tradition in the *Risalat al-itiqadat al-imamiyyah* ('Treatise of the creeds of the imamate') of the tenth-century Shi'ite historian Ibn Babawayh al-Saduq, active in Baghdad, contains an anecdote in which the Prophet Muhammad buried Fatimah bint Asad, mother of his son-in-law 'Ali (r. 656–61), in his own shirt and instructed her in her grave what to answer when questioned by the Angel of Death to avoid the 'torment of the grave'.[110]

Regarding the account of the enshrouding of the Prophet Muhammad himself, Ibn Sa'd mentions a tradition related by 'Abdallah ibn Numayr, according to which the Prophet was first wrapped in three white Yemeni cotton cloths, but then the shroud was subsequently changed.[111] One sheet was taken by his companion Abu Bakr (r. 632–34), who wanted to use it as his own shroud. But in the end he sold it and gave the proceeds to charity, because he reasoned that he himself did not deserve to use it.[112]

For the Rashidun caliphs who immediately followed the Prophet Muhammad and for those who claimed descent from him, the aspect of 'sacred' benevolence emanating from them may have partly served to underline their own religious and political status. Ibn Sa'd mentions an incident in which the caliph, and companion of the Prophet, 'Umar ibn al-Khattab (r. 634–44) sent five outfits (*athwab*) selected from his storehouses or treasury (*khaza'in*) to Zaynab bint Jahsh, a daughter of one of the Prophet Muhammad's cousins, so that she could choose one for her funeral.[113] This incident relates to the one mentioned above between the Fatimid caliph al-Mu'izz and his secretary Jawdhar, since, in both, the leader of the Muslim community dispatches burial outfits from the treasury to a chosen individual. It may be significant

that we do not possess information on the presentation of funerary outfits under the Umayyads and Abbasids. Yet two further accounts for this custom under the Fatimid caliphs al-'Aziz (r. 975–96), and al-Hakim (r. 996–1021) do exist. It may well be that garments of members of the Prophet's close family were believed to emanate *baraka* to a greater extent than those of more distant relatives.

How exaggerated and overwhelming caliphal benevolence could be is illustrated by a passage from al-Maqrizi in which the caliph al-'Aziz provided fifty funerary shrouds (*kafan*) and other funerary paraphernalia, including various embalming substances (*hanut*), for the burial of his vizier Ya'qub ibn Killis; thirty of the shrouds were woven with gold.[114] That al-'Aziz took a great interest in the funeral is furthermore documented by his commission to his chief *qadi*, Muhammad bin al-Nu'man, to wash the deceased vizier. Al-'Aziz also conducted the funeral procession and read the prayer of the dead. After the funeral, guardians reading from the Quran were instructed to remain by the grave for weeks, and administrative offices stayed closed for eighteen days.[115]

The instance described here was partly personal, partly political. Another example of a caliph providing a funerary outfit for a public personage is documented in the reign of al-Hakim, but this one lacks the personal aspect. The twelfth-century historian Jamal al-Din 'Ali ibn Zafir al-Azdi describes an incident of prime political and religious importance to the status of al-Hakim, whose alleged personal excesses are well known.[116] In Rajab 409 AH (13 November – 12 December 1018 CE), a certain Hasan bin Haydara al-Farghani al-Akhram declared that God had descended upon al-Hakim. Al-Hakim invested al-Akhram with precious garments, and eight days later allowed him to take part in the caliphal procession of 2 Ramadan. Public opinion must have disapproved severely of al-Akhram, as he was assassinated by a spectator during the procession. It is significant that the text mentions explicitly that al-Akhram was then wrapped in a shroud and placed in a coffin, both supplied by the palace, while the assassin, who had been executed, was instantly buried by a crowd. Obviously, the religious importance of al-Akhram for al-Hakim prompted his involvement in the investiture and later on in the funeral.

If the caliph's own used clothes could contain some of his *baraka*, it is possible that textiles inscribed with his name could also have carried caliphal *baraka*. That the caliphal name was particularly revered if pronounced or

2.10   The prophet Joshua ordering the property taken at Jericho to be destroyed, manuscript illustration, Rashid al-Din, *Jami' al-tawarikh*
('Compendium of chronicles'), *c.* 1306 or 1314–15 CE, fol. 10v. Pigments on paper. University of Edinburgh Library, Or. MS 20.

written is documented in anecdotes mentioned by al-Maqrizi.[117] For example, the Fatimid vizier al-Ma'mun ibn Bata'ihi kissed his letter of appointment from the caliph upon receiving it.[118] Likewise, al-Maqrizi reported that a *qadi* (judge) kissed a document sent by the caliph which announced that he should take part in the procession of the *'id al-fitr*.[119] Kissing documents signified great respect but could also have created a physical link between the receiver and the caliphal sender. In an illustration in the *Jami' al-tawarikh* ('Compendium of chronicles'), commissioned by the Ilkhanid vizier Rashid al-Din in the fourteenth century, a follower of the Prophet Joshua is shown rubbing the sash of Joshua's veil against his cheek as a sign of reverence, thereby creating a physical link to Joshua (fig. 2.10).

While there are sporadic accounts of conferring a caliph's own clothes under the Umayyads, it seems that the ritual of conferring *khila'* on dignitaries and court employees and their families became formalized only during the Abbasid period, after which the practice was carried on under the Fatimids and Mamluks.[120] Formalizing the *khila'* ritual must have brought with it the need to cater for a large number of subjects in the annual investitures. While the higher dignitaries and administrative officers may have received garments of spectacular richness, the lower ranks of the court hierarchy must have received cheaper garments. These must have been mass-produced, given the huge numbers of court employees. Perhaps it is this kind of material that is represented by surviving *tiraz* textiles. While some of them can surely be classified as extraordinarily fine and rich, the great majority are of a more basic nature and do not correspond to the grandiose garments mentioned in medieval texts. It is more likely that what survives was the 'standard wardrobe of the court and represent[s] the numerous undergarments, and perhaps some of the lighter summer mantles', as proposed by Lisa Golombek.[121]

The degree of standardization in the materials, techniques of manufacture and aesthetic (discussed in chapter 3) seems to underline the fact that these garments were mass-produced. What mattered to the people receiving them was the association with the caliph, symbolized by the inscriptions. Because they were inscribed with the names of caliphs and given out on their orders, they must have been thought to bear the benedictory qualities that the caliphs' own clothes were believed to carry. Eventually, the benedictory qualities carried by the inscriptions became the reason why *tiraz* textiles were used as shrouds in Egypt. While *tiraz* textiles must already have been in circulation under the Abbasids and early Fatimids, it is likely that the dispersal of the Fatimid treasury under al-Mustansir (r. 1036–94) made *tiraz* even more widely available to the public.

THE FUNERARY CONTEXT
TIRAZ TEXTILES AS RELICS

While the great majority of *tiraz* textiles survived as burial shrouds in Egyptian graves, a small number were preserved in Christian ecclesiastical contexts, some in western Europe after the First Crusade, and some in Sub-Saharan Africa. While some of these survivals were used as ceremonial garments, others assumed the status of relics in popular belief, and were carefully preserved.[122] The best-known pieces are the so-called 'Veil of St Anne' (dating from 1096–97), which is kept in the church of St Anne at Apt, a town in the southern French département of Vaucluse (see figs 1.49, 1.50),[123] the Shroud of Cadouin ('Suaire de Cadouin'), now in the abbey of Cadouin in the Dordogne (see fig. 1.51),[124] and the late Fatimid veil once used to wrap the relics from the reliquary of St Andrew (dated 1288) of the Sacro Convento of San Francesco at Assisi.[125] (The Veil of St Anne and the Shroud of Cadouin have been discussed in some detail in chapter 1.) In addition to these large and well-preserved pieces, some minor fragments of Egyptian textiles survived in other European churches, often as no more than minute scraps sewn into liturgical vestments,

perhaps because they were thought to have been in physical contact with the saintly figure who wore the garments from which they came.[126]

Some very important finds of *tiraz* textiles were made in the mid-twentieth century, during conservation work on a church in Däbrä Dammo in the province of Tigrai, just south of the Eritrean border in Ethiopia.[127] The church, called the 'Large Church' of Enda Abuna Aragawi, was part of a monastery complex, which dates back at least to the eighth century, if not earlier, as suggested by Kushan and Umayyad or Abbasid coins found in the convent area.[128] The recovery of a group of Abbasid and Fatimid *tiraz* textiles hidden in a closed recess within the church was of great significance. Of the published specimens, four are of documentary value. One is inscribed in the name of the Abbasid caliph al-Muʿtamid (r. 870–92), one in the name of al-Muktafi (r. 902–08) and two in the name of al-Muttaqi (r. 940–44).[129] They had perhaps been used to cover relics and sacred objects, and were therefore disposed of in a hidden space. Their state state of preservation is remarkable, with the glaze applied to the base fabric still largely intact. Two small Abbasid fragments of Iraqi origin with silk embroidered inscriptions on a cotton ground, similar to cat. no. 95, have survived in a psalter of 1050, which was part of the treasury of the church of St Michaelis in Lüneburg, where they once served as covers for pages containing painted illustrations (fig. 2.11).[130] How the textile from which the fragments were once cut reached northern Germany is unknown, but there were close diplomatic relations between the Ottonian emperors and Byzantium.[131] Hence, the textile could well have come from Constantinople, particularly given the diplomatic relations and exchange of gifts, including textiles, between the Abbasid caliphate in Baghdad and the Byzantine court in Constantinople under al-Muqtadir.[132]

One item relevant to this discussion did not survive as a relic, but as part of a papyrus cache now in the Erzherzog Rainer Collection at the Österreichische Nationalbibliothek in Vienna, and was therefore found neither in a settlement nor at a burial site. This is a strip of a silk-embroidered linen *tiraz* textile, inscribed in the name of the Abbasid caliph al-Muqtadir and his vizier Abu Ahmad al-ʿAbbas ibn al-Hasan, and is datable to 908–10. The piece was found wrapped in a papyrus letter, probably contemporary with it, concerning an order for textiles.[133]

The surviving *tiraz* corpus shows a predominance of undyed linen or cotton fabrics, which are inscribed in

2.11   Fragment of a *tiraz* textile, Iraq, 10th century CE. Cotton, with silk embroidery, 12.4 × 18.8 cm. Museum Lüneburg, inv. no. A 18b.

silk embroidery or tapestry. In contrast, among the textile finds from excavations of early Islamic settlement sites, such as Nahal Omer[134] and Nahal Shahaq now in Israel,[135] Ghirza in Libya[136] and Fustat,[137] textiles comparable to our *tiraz* corpus were either not present, or at best very rare. At Fustat only two caliphal *tiraz* textiles from the reign of al-Muqtadir (r. 908–32) were found among roughly 3,000 fragments of various types of materials of different qualities.[138]

At Samarra, the central seat of government and residence of the Abbasid caliphs from al-Muʿtasim (r. 833–42) to al-Muʿtamid (r. 870–92), excavations in the first quarter of the twentieth century by a German team of archaeologists, led by Friedrich Sarre and Ernst Herzfeld, brought to light finds that were exceptionally rich, comprising grand architecture, elaborate wall stucco, ceramics, glass, paintings and some coins, representative of a grand palatial environment.[139] (Examples of the wall-paintings, depicting figures in all sorts of fashionable outfits, are discussed in chapter 1.) From among this rich record

of finds, only one textile from the excavations by Sarre and Herzfeld has been published, a tiny inscribed Egyptian *tiraz* textile of silk-embroidered linen, made in Tinnis during the reign of the Abbasid caliph al-Muʿtamid (fig. 2.12). It was discovered in a subterranean passage between the harem and the Large Courtyard of the Jawsaq al-Khaqani palace.[140] This textile is the only token of a court once praised in medieval literature for its massive use of luxury textiles, many of which were imported from Egypt.

TIRAZ TEXTILES AS BURIAL SHROUDS

Although the provenances and exact find-spots of most extant *tiraz* textiles are unknown, there is evidence, both external and internal, to suggest that most such textiles were excavated on burial sites. This provenance is attested by eyewitness accounts of individuals present at excavations, by recent scientific excavations and by the internal evidence of decay.

There are several eyewitness accounts by scholars who attended excavations of burial sites that yielded *tiraz*

2.12   Fragment of a *tiraz* textile, Tinnis, reign of the Abbasid caliph al-Mu'tamid, 870–92 CE, found at the Jawsaq al-Khaqani palace, Samarra, 1911–13. Linen, with silk embroidery, 18 × 12 cm. Museum für Islamische Kunst, Berlin, inv. no. I 8275.

textiles. Ernst Kühnel wrote in 1952 that his colleague Husayn Rashid of the Arab Museum in Cairo took him in 1938 to the opening of graves in Fustat to show him the technique by which *tiraz* textiles were taken off the deceased.[141] Already in 1927, in a catalogue of the Islamic textiles in the Schlossmuseum, Berlin, Kühnel had mentioned that many of the textiles in European museums were excavated on Egyptian burial sites, particularly Akhmim (Panopolis), al-Mansha (Ptolemaïs), and Dayr al-Azam and Drunka, both near Assyut (Lycopolis).[142] In another account ʿAbd al-ʿAziz Marzuq records:

> During my work in the excavation of the Museum of Islamic Art in Cairo, in 1937–1939 at Ein as-Sira near Fustat, I observed that each dead body was wrapped in a series of linen shrouds. Sometimes there was a silk shroud over the linen ones, and this silk in many cases, fell into dust at the first touch. From the Kufic inscription tapestried, embroidered or painted on these shrouds we learn that they belong to the Abbasid and Fatimid periods.[143]

Leigh Ashton, though not writing as an eyewitness himself, confirmed the funerary origins of many *tiraz* textiles in his review of the exhibition of Islamic textiles in Paris in 1935: 'Within recent years a large number of shrouds with inscriptions containing the names of Abbasid and Fatimite Caliphs have been recovered from a cemetery at a place known as Basatin, about three miles south of Cairo.'[144]

Another eyewitness account was given by the late historian of Islamic art Layla ʿAli Ibrahim, who was present when her father Dr ʿAli Ibrahim monitored excavations of burial sites in Fustat some time between 1930 and 1932, during which many of the *tiraz* textiles now in the Museum of Islamic Art in Cairo were found.[145] A few visual records of these excavations exist. A photograph from an album that belonged to Layla ʿAli Ibrahim, possibly taken during an excavation at al-Khadra al-Sharifa, a funerary structure on the southern edge of Qarafa al-Kubra, the great Southern Cemetery of Fustat, shows the examination of an enshrouded body placed on a stretcher (fig. 2.13).[146] A guard stands at the side and an administrator sits at a table taking notes. Another photograph, published by the textile historian Suʿad Maher, which is clearly a detailed view of the previous scene, focuses on the cutting away

of a section of shroud over the corpse's head (fig. 2.14).[147] To date, these photographs comprise the only pictorial evidence of the exhumation and examination of the deceased in the Southern Cemetery during the 1930s.[148] But however important these photographic records are, they fail to provide precise data concerning find-spots. Only one *tiraz* textile excavated then is known to have a secure provenance, a fragment in the name of ʿAbd al-Rahim ibn Ilyas, heir-presumptive to the throne of the Fatimid caliph al-Hakim (r. 996–1021); according to Layla ʿAli Ibrahim, it was found in a grave within the mausoleum at al-Khadra al-Sharifa.[149]

Most surviving *tiraz* textiles may have been found in the Southern Cemetery or the nearby cemeteries at ʿAin al-Sira and Basatin, but provenances known for a few *tiraz* textiles in European and American museums indicate that, in addition to the Southern Cemetery, other burial sites were excavated as well: cemeteries in Erment, close to Luxor,[150] the Fayyum[151] and Akhmim.[152] Archival research into collecting Islamic artefacts from Egypt may still be in its infancy, but recent studies have focused on how a group of American collectors in Egypt during the time of the British occupation became interested in Islamic textiles. They often knew each other well and were connected by ties of education and society.[153] Likewise, one of the leading dealers in Cairo in the 1920s was Maurice Nahman, head cashier at the Crédit Foncier d'Égypte in Cairo, who sold many works to American museums, but also dealt with major collectors based in Egypt, such as the Greek philanthropist Antonis Benakis.[154] Two further names appear over and over again in museum registers, the *Répertoire chronologique d'épigraphie arabe* and the general literature on *tiraz* textiles: Phocion J. Tano and Michel E. Abemayor.[155] Theirs were the largest private collections at the time, and most of their pieces were sold directly to museums and collectors in North America.

The excavations of the first half of the twentieth century did not meet the standards of modern archaeological science, which records the stratigraphy and deposition of objects, and studies the physical environment in which objects are deposited. The main aim at that time was the mere recovery of objects, regardless of their archaeological context: a kind of treasure hunt. As a result, vital knowledge about geographical distribution, the numerical relationship between different types of *tiraz* textiles and dating of sites, and particularly how pieces were wrapped around the corpses on which they were

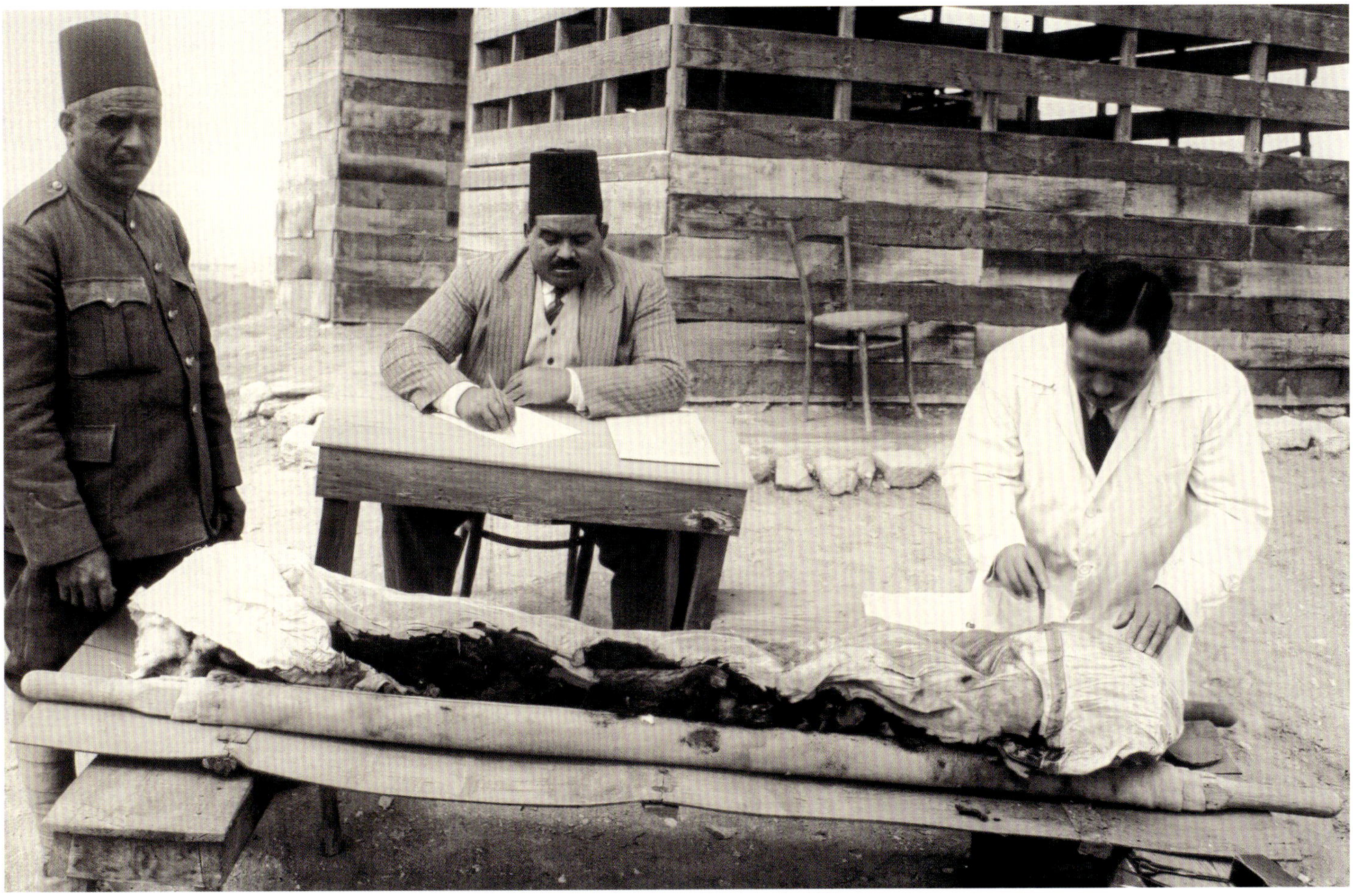

2.13   Members of staff from the Museum of Islamic Art, Cairo, examining an enshrouded corpse, during excavations at al-Khadra al-Sharifa, Southern Cemetery, Cairo, early 1930s. Photograph Jochen Sokoly, after an album of Layla 'Ali Ibrahim (d. 2002), Cairo.

found, or information on the pathology of the bodies, was lost forever. This kind of data could have provided a fuller picture of the social and historical context. But there was largely no interest in recording precise find-spots and archaeological contexts, as most excavations were conducted clandestinely. This was perhaps owing to the fact that, according to Islamic theology and practice, burials should not be disturbed, and had excavations been known about they would have incurred the disapproval of the local community; but secrecy also protected the find-spots of what were regarded as precious trade goods. The habit of cutting away sections of shrouds with *tiraz* bands and significant decoration destroyed any trace of what a complete garment would have looked like. Dealers then fragmented individual textiles even further, probably for commercial reasons, as indicated by two inscribed

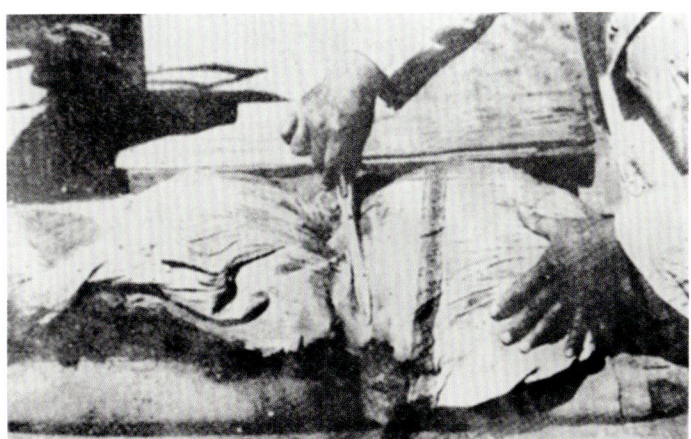

2.14   Member of staff from the Museum of Islamic Art, Cairo, cutting away a portion of the textile covering the head of an enshrouded corpse, during excavations at al-Khadra al-Sharifa, Southern Cemetery, Cairo, early 1930s. Reproduced from S. Maher, *Al-nasij al-islami*, Cairo, 1977, pl. 191.

2.15   Fragment of a *tiraz* textile, Madinat al-Salam, Iraq, 917–23 CE. Printed and embroidered *mulham* (cotton and silk plain-weave fabric), 28 × 34.3 cm. Abegg-Stiftung, Riggisberg (Bern), inv. no. 1520.

mulham fragments, one in the Abegg-Stiftung, Riggisberg, the other in the Museum for Islamic Art, Berlin, both of which form two parts of the same textile and comprise clean scissor cuts (fig. 2.15).[156]

Although data concerning archaeological context is almost non-existent, most surviving *tiraz* textiles provide internal evidence suggesting that they were burial finds. The way many fragments have decayed suggests contact with decomposed bodies. Large stained areas and areas where the textile structure has vanished suggest that the textiles were in contact with organic fluids resulting from human decomposition, which accelerated the textiles' own natural decay. The fabric is often 'eaten' into, leaving rough-edged holes; sometimes the organic fluids left encrustations on the textiles. Furthermore, the stains often form patterns, which must have been caused by folds in the textile over the body.[157] Where textiles were not in close contact with body fluids, they survived remarkably well.

While the overwhelming majority of *tiraz* textiles were found in the first half of the twentieth century, their recovery from burials has continued in recent decades, but now through scientifically controlled excavations. Several specimens were found in the burials of Qasr Ibrim, now flooded by the Aswan Dam, once located in Egyptian Nubia on the border to modern-day Sudan, and the site

of an early medieval metropolitan city of the Meroitic province of Lower Nubia and the site of an episcopal bishopric with a stone-built cathedral dedicated to the Virgin Mary. Excavations in 1964 and 1966 undertaken by the Egypt Exploration Society investigated a cemetery connected to the cathedral where several important ecclesiastical burials were found. The individuals were wrapped in a sequence of several shrouds, and some were still wearing their burial clothing. The shrouds comprised a range of *tiraz* textiles spanning from the Abbasid all the way to the Fatimid dynasty. The Abbasid inscriptions were embroidered and compare to the types discussed in the Catalogue. Several textiles also document the Fatimid caliphs al-Aziz (r. 975–96) and al-Hakim (r. 996–1021). Interestingly the excavations recovered a full tunic and trousers, the tunic comprising an embroidered *tiraz* on its sleeve. Several large sheets were recovered, some full lengths and loom widths, up to 4 m long and 80 cm wide, that had been folded with their sides sewn up to create a body bag to contain the deceased.[158]

However, excavations by the Institut Français d'Archéologie Orientale du Caire at Istabl 'Antar, an area in the southern part of the Southern Cemetery in Cairo, under the supervision of Roland-Pierre Gayraud in the late 1980s and early 1990s, yielded some of the most important evidence for interpreting the use of *tiraz* textiles in burials.[159] Various human burials were found, several of which contained bodies wrapped in shrouds; these were the first Muslim burials to be excavated and recorded scientifically.

Two funerary enclosures came to light at Istabl 'Antar, in which several tombs were found, some of which were mass graves containing up to six individuals; others were unoccupied.[160] A very important find of an enshrouded body was made in Tomb 12 of the second funerary enclosure (B6), reconstructed by the team as a partly subterranean structure with a flat roof and a staircase leading down into the burial chamber.[161] A comparable find of an enshrouded body was made adjacent to the complex, where the individual was buried in a pit, rather than in a built structure.[162] Both individuals were wrapped in a succession of large shrouds that consisted of plain undecorated linen. In both cases, raw cotton was used underneath the shrouds to wrap the head and feet of the corpse.

The burial found in Tomb 49, situated in a Fatimid mausoleum (B7) excavated in 1994, was markedly different. There a corpse was found lying in a collapsed coffin, wrapped in a sequence of inscribed *tiraz* shrouds, the inscription bands covering the face,

and the enshrouded body then covered with a reed mat (fig. 2.16).[163] Two of the shrouds (1 and 3) could be dated. The third (2) was decorated with a non-protocollary inscription datable to the tenth century on the basis of its script. The outermost shroud (1) carried the date of 320 AH / 932–33 CE, its inscription prominently visible on the deceased's face. It was made of *mulham*, embroidered in blue chain stitch, in a style and technique common in Iraq and eastern Iran and similar to those seen in cat. no. 95 in The al-Sabah Collection. This textile had been imported into Egypt from either Iraq or the Iranian world, where embroidered *mulham* was produced. It came as a surprise that the shroud beneath the other two (3) contained an inscription mentioning the *ism* ('given name') 'al-Ma'add', making it possible to date the piece to the reigns of the Fatimid caliphs al-Mu'izz (r. 953–75) or al-Mustansir (r. 1036–94), both of whom had used that *ism*. The archaeological context of the early Fatimid period would make a dating of the *tiraz* inscription to al-Mu'izz more likely.[164] Given that the Fatimids did not conquer Egypt until 969, the body could not have been deposited before the arrival of al-Mu'izz in Cairo shortly after. Therefore, we are provided here with a date *post quem*. The Abbasid shroud was already antique when it came to be used

2.16 Enshrouded corpse in a grave, Istabl 'Antar, Southern Cemetery, Cairo. Roland-Pierre Gayraud, IFAO, Cairo.

in this burial, as the dates of manufacture of the two garments must be a minimum of thirty-eight years apart, probably much more. Roland Pierre-Gayraud nicknamed the individual in Tomb 49 'Barbarossa', due to his henna dyed beard, and was able to ascertain that the Iraqi textile was brand new, with the primer or glaze used to prepare the cotton-silk mix for the embroidery still intact, and fold marks showing that it had been folded in a chest or cupboard where it had been stored until it was eventually used in this burial.[165] Gayraud, furthermore, suggested that the individual, who had died either shortly before or after the Fatimid court arrived in Cairo in 973, may have been buried by al-Mu'izz's wife and al-'Aziz's mother Darzan al-Sayyida al-Mu'izziyya, also called Taghrid, who had been charged with burying the deceased members of the Fatimid family and court who had been brought to Egypt in their coffins.[166]

The burial of Tomb 49 relates closely to what is seen on the photograph from Layla 'Ali Ibrahim's album, discussed earlier (see fig. 2.14). Both feature long pieces of cloth wrapping the whole of the deceased's body, the underside decomposed. At the head and foot of the bodies the cloths are folded over. The folded section of cloth wraps the head very tightly and comprises a *tiraz* band. According to Layla 'Ali Ibrahim, it was common that *tiraz* bands were found draped over the head of the deceased, a point to which we shall return.[167]

The documents found in the Geniza at Fustat provide some of the best insights into the composition of burial outfits used in medieval Egypt. Although they describe the burial garb of Jewish people, comparison with the few descriptions of outfits of high-ranking Muslims suggests that there was very little difference. The Geniza accounts confirm that tunics were an integral part of the deceased's clothing, but they also mention items such as cloaks, trousers, underwear, handkerchiefs, veils, skullcaps and wound-up turbans.[168]

Two surviving small burial tunics intended for children in Washington, DC, and Cairo are described in chapter 1 (see fig. 1.52). Both are heavily stained, but intact. The tunic in the Textile Museum, Washington, DC, is inscribed with an embroidered *tiraz* in the name of the Abbasid caliph al-Muqtadir (r. 908–32).[169] Running in perpendicular fashion on the back of the sleeve the inscription is positioned upside down, suggesting the garment was tailored out of a larger sheet already inscribed, and the inscribed area was reserved for the

sleeve intentionally, even though the tailor did not understand the nature of the piece he was sewing into the garment and inserted it the wrong way up. Another child's tunic, dating from the Fatimid period, is in the Museum of Cairo University.[170] It, too, was tailored with the tapestry-woven bands reserved for the sleeves, either re-cut from a larger garment or a length of cloth. A number of fragments which must have once belonged to adult tunics cut in a similar fashion with inscriptions on sleeve segments or below breast pockets have been discussed earlier (see figs 1.53–1.56). In one, the inscription is located below a pocket, upside down, in the same way as the tunic in Washington, suggesting that the fragmentary cloth was once part of a larger textile that was cut and tailored into a garment, a case of re-use of a larger fabric, perhaps even specifically for burial. An example of just such a large, almost intact sheet is in the Benaki Museum, Athens, comprising a full-loom width and length with a darned decorative band and embroidered inscription in red.[171] The two very rare complete adult linen tunics, in the Ashmolean Museum, Oxford (see fig. 1.57), and in The al-Sabah Collection (cat. no. 54), discussed in chapter 1, relate to the children's tunics above and are also rare survivals of complete tailored garments.[172] That both have a funerary origin is clear from the large amount of decomposition and staining with bodily fluids affecting both pieces; yet they have survived remarkably well.

In the 1990s a Polish team of archaeologists excavated a Christian monastery at Naqlun, in the Fayyum oasis south of Cairo.[173] The burials there, of male and female individuals, included one of a mother and child. Many of the bodies were laid to rest in coffins, most wrapped in large linen sheets, decorated with tapestry-woven and embroidered bands, some of which were epigraphic, some zoomorphic. Even the coffins were sometimes wrapped in large sheets, or mats made of reed or rushes. The earliest firmly datable textile found at Naqlun was one inscribed with the names and titles of the Fatimid caliph al-Hakim (r. 996–1021). Another featured an inscription that places the piece in the reign either of al-Zahir (r. 1021–36) or of al-Mustansir (r. 1036–94).[174] Most of the other decorated textiles featured *tiraz*-style bands, however, that would fit into the second half of the eleventh or first half of the twelfth century, particularly the reigns of the Fatimid caliphs al-Mustansir, al-Musta'li (r. 1094–1101) and al-Amir (r. 1101–30). One textile, a compound-woven silk, with monumental kufic letters mirroring each other, was clearly imported from Spain.[175] Grave goods, including crosses, identified the individuals buried at Naqlun as Christian. Interestingly, a necklace made of Abbasid silver dirhams was also found.[176] Together with the textual accounts in the Geniza documents describing the burial outfits of Egyptian Jews, the Christian burials at Naqlun and Qasr Ibrim, described above, suggest that there was a certain amount of overlap between the burial practices of Jews, Christians and Muslims in respect of clothing and the wrapping of the dead, and that customs were not always as clear cut as we might like to see them. Both Jews and Christians had adapted to the presence of Islam in Egypt by the eleventh century, and perhaps they had begun to emulate certain practices.[177] Of course, this complicates the attribution of many of the textiles in museums, as we really do not know whether the burials from which they came were Jewish, Christian or Islamic, a problem only scientific archaeological methods could have resolved.

OTHER BURIAL TEXTILES

Apart from funerary clothing, the archaeological evidence from Istabl 'Antar also suggests that reed mats were used in burials to wrap enshrouded bodies loosely or to cover the ground on which they were laid. In Tomb 49 the body was found *in situ*, wrapped in an undecorated, and rather crude, reed mat similar to one found at Naqlun (see fig. 2.16). In Tombs 15 and 10, reed mats were found covering the ground. Apart from being used to wrap and support the deceased, mats were also used to cover wood planks arranged over the deceased, as can be seen from photographs of the Fustat excavations published by Su'ad Maher.[178] In such circumstances the decomposition of the corpse would not have affected the mats at all. These finds may shed some light on the origins of three complete examples, in the Metropolitan Museum, New York,[179] and the Benaki Museum, Athens[180] (see figs 3.1, 3.3, 3.4). The excellent state of preservation of these mats, however, almost certainly results from the sheltered archaeological conditions of burials. In contrast, a mat in The al-Sabah Collection (cat. no. 115) is only a fragment of a much larger piece, and looks as if it was cut out.

The large mat in the Benaki Museum is inscribed in Kufic characters in a style common during the tenth century. The inscription comprises invocations to God and benedictory phrases dedicated to the owner. Most importantly, the inscription states that this mat was made in a *tiraz al-khassa* in Tabariyya (Tiberias). The mats in the Metropolitan Museum and the smaller one in the Benaki Museum are inscribed in a style of Kufic comparable with that of the large Benaki mat but comprise only benedictory phrases. Historical texts provide evidence that reed mats were inscribed with caliphal protocollary inscriptions and were used for prayer. An account in the *Sirat al-ustadh jawdhar*, quoted above, tells us that the Fatimid caliph al-Mu'izz once asked his private secretary Jawdhar to order reed prayer mats from Mahdia inscribed with the caliphal protocol, which would have been similar to the extant pieces described here.[181]

The *Kitab dhikr al-mawt wa-ma ba'dahu* ('Book of the remembrance of death and the afterlife') of the imam Abu Hamid Muhammad ibn Muhammad al-Ghazali (d. 1111), the famous Shi'ite theologian active under the Seljuq vizier Nizam al-Mulk as a teacher at the Nizamiyya madrasa, describes in one chapter the death of the Prophet Muhammad and his interment. In this account the Prophet, who had been washed by his own family and clothed in his designated burial clothes, was laid during interment on a mat covered with some of his own garments.[182]

The burials at Istabl 'Antar provide diverging evidence for the use of coffins. In several of the burials found in the Abbasid funerary enclosure, such as those from Tombs 10 and 12, the deceased had been deposited without a coffin. In the Fatimid funerary enclosure, however, coffins were found in the burials of Tombs 47, 49 and 55. In a burial within a mausoleum (*qubba*), one coffin was found that contained a number of skeletons. In the 1930s at al-Khadra al-Sharifa, another Fatimid structure, a burial was found containing a corpse wrapped in a *tiraz* in the name of the caliph al-Hakim and his heir-designate, 'Abd al-Rahim ibn Ilyas, which had been placed in a coffin.[183] A foundation stone found *in situ* in the 1930s, inscribed in the name of al-'Aziz's mother, Darzan al-Sayyida al-Mu'izziyya, also called Taghrid, suggested that al-Khadra al-Sharifa was commissioned by a prominent member of the Fatimid family and therefore was likely to have contained burials of family members. Gayraud suggested that the use of coffins was limited to those two Fatimid structures, the one excavated by his team and al-Khadra al-Sharifa, and that this use of coffins was a particular Fatimid custom: the ancestors of al-Mu'izz were brought to Cairo in coffins after the Fatimid conquest and deposited in the Fatimid palace, while other members of the family were buried at Istabl 'Antar, where they remained until they were plundered during the reign of al-Mustansir (r. 1036–94).[184] Many of the burials at these two sites may well have been of members of the intimate circle of the Fatimid dynasty.

Although scant archaeological evidence of Egyptian Muslim burials is available, there seems to be one important common factor: the deceased were wrapped in large linen or cotton shrouds and the head was given particular attention. While in the Abbasid burials found at Istabl 'Antar the heads were cushioned with raw cotton, in the Fatimid burials there and at al-Khadra al-Sharifa inscribed textiles were used for this purpose, with the *tiraz* bands placed over the eyes of the deceased. That we have evidence for this in Tomb 49 (see fig. 2.16) and from Layla 'Ali Ibrahim's and Su'ad Maher's photographs (see figs 2.13, 2.14) means that this was no mere coincidence, but had deeper significance and was perhaps a common practice among followers of the Fatimids.[185] The dressing and wrapping of the body was a matter of great importance and the preparation of the body for burial was always given great care. Al-Bukhari recorded a *hadith* that illustrates the importance of covering the deceased correctly. During the Battle of Uhud in the early years of Islam, the body of one of the fallen soldiers, Mus'ab ibn 'Umayr, could not be properly covered by his mantle (*burda*) since it was too short. It left either his head or his feet exposed. The Prophet Muhammad advised that his head should be covered by the mantle and his bare feet should be covered with rushes.[186] This *hadith* suggests that covering a person's head properly was more important than covering the feet. From the extant burials discussed above it is clear that generally great care was taken to wrap the deceased, regardless of whether or not a coffin was used.

Another important issue which the finds from Tomb 49 in Istabl 'Antar raise is the concurrent use of textiles with Abbasid and Fatimid caliphal inscriptions on the same body.[187] This raises questions relating to the age of the shrouds at the time of burial and the religious context in which the burial took place. The fact that the Abbasid shroud was at least thirty-eight years old when it was buried and had probably never been used suggests that it had not been specifically made for this burial. It is possible that it was chosen for burial by the deceased or his family. It is also possible that this textile only came into circulation after the conquest of Egypt under al-Mu'izz (r. 953–75) or perhaps al-'Aziz (r. 975–96), or even

as late as the dispersal of the Fatimid treasury between 1067 and 1072 under the caliph al-Mustansir. However, if one accepts Roland-Pierre Gayraud's suggestion that the burial of Tomb 49 at Istabl 'Antar and others in its vicinity were of members of the Fatimid family and court, then it is also entirely possible that al-Mu'izz's wife Taghrid chose textiles from the treasuries found in Cairo after the conquest. When the Fatimids took over Cairo in the tenth century they obviously confiscated the treasuries and storehouses that had been built up by the Tulunids and Ikhshidids who had controlled Egypt before them. Given these dynasties' connection to the Abbasid caliphate, the treasuries contained numerous artefacts from Iraq and the eastern provinces of the Abbasid empire that had reached Cairo as diplomatic gifts. The textiles found at Qasr Ibrim, which are for the most part much earlier than those found at Naqlun and of Egyptian production, could well have been diplomatic gifts as well, many perhaps from the Abbasid governors in Cairo, as well as the Fatimids, as has been suggested recently.[188] Yet, the time of the dispersal of the Fatimid treasury in the eleventh century would in fact fit with the dating of textiles found at Naqlun. It may also explain how such textiles might have reached the Christian part of the population at that time.

It has been suggested that in the very early Islamic period the deceased were predominantly buried in clothes that they had worn during their lifetime.[189] Literary evidence supports this suggestion. In a deathbed declaration preserved among the Geniza documents, an individual expressly mentions that besides a washed turban and other robes, new trousers and a new waistband should be included in his funerary outfit, suggesting that the other items had already been used by him.[190] An anecdote concerning a conversation between the Rashidun caliph Abu Bakr and his daughter 'Aisha describes how Abu Bakr chose a used garment as his shroud, despite the protestations of his daughter, asserting that: 'The living have more of a right to new clothes.'[191]

But why did people wear used clothes as burial outfits? The two main reasons could have been cost and religious beliefs. Garments in the medieval Islamic world tended to be very expensive. It has therefore been argued that when the value of a burial outfit was expressly stated in wills or lists of the estates of the deceased, outfits were likely to have been new.[192] The price was thus a way to distinguish new from old in these documents.

Some of the burial accounts found among the Geniza documents refer to the cost of tailors, indicating that the garments mentioned had to be made before the burial.[193] Theological opposition may have also contributed to the use of previously worn garments in burials. 'Puritan' tendencies in early Islam, opposing any kind of luxury and believing that the living needed new things more than the dead, were probably the underlying cause.[194] It was often recommended to use garments that the deceased had worn during prayer.[195]

Tiraz textiles such as those discussed here survived in burials because they were selected for their special nature, be it a caliphal inscription, a prominent epigraphic band or the nature of the materials. Many were already antique when they were employed in burials. Different religious groups used inscribed and decorated textiles for varying reasons. For a Christian, the rationale for using a *tiraz* inscribed with formulas from the Quran might have been not religious but social – to fit in with the Muslim community, for example, or because the inscribed textile represented a treasured luxury item. For Sunni Muslims the names of caliphs would have signified a spiritual link to the caliphate, perhaps also not predominantly from a religious point of view but in keeping with traditions regarding the Prophet's shroud and the giving of shrouds by the early caliphs that were circulating at that time.[196] For a follower of Ismaili doctrine, the name of the Fatimid caliph itself would have been sacred, however. It emanated blessing, and represented a physical link to the person of the caliph, who was believed to exercise intercessory powers on the day of judgment.[197] In a conversation between the Fatimid caliph al-Mu'izz and the Fatimid theologian Qadi al-Nu'man (d. 974), the caliph alludes to these powers:

> O Nu'man, we [i.e. the Ismaili imams] are the portals of God and the conduit [vehicle, channel] to God. He who gets closer to God through us and uses us as mediator will be accepted. And whoever seeks intercession (*tawassul*) through us will be answered. He who asks for forgiveness through us will be forgiven. But those who have sinned are not equal to those who have not. That is why there are ranks in heaven. And that is the easiest form of God's punishment.[198]

Wrapping the face with the inscription may have provided the deceased with a means of testifying to their Fatimid allegiance and identity after resurrection and during the judgment.

CHAPTER 3

MAKING *TIRAZ* TEXTILES:
MATERIALS AND MANUFACTURE

The mention of a place of manufacture is an important part of many *tiraz* inscriptions, as much as it is important for most types of protocollary inscriptions in the early Islamic world. The place of manufacture identified the item's origins and often was connected with the presence of a caliphal workshop or sometimes a coin mint. *Tiraz* inscriptions thus provide a valuable historical dimension that allows studying the making of textiles and the way they were inscribed and decorated in a structured manner.

Significantly, *tiraz* inscriptions represent evidence for geographically diverse places of production, both inside and outside Egypt. The fact that these too were found in Egypt tells us that Egypt had a wide-ranging network of political, diplomatic and trade connections both in the Mediterranean and in the regions of the Near and Middle East, central Asia, and the Indian Ocean.

The knowledge that a group of items was made in a particular location allows us to establish common features regarding material, spinning, weave, and types of tapestry or embroidery, which facilitate the attribution of textiles to specific locations or clusters of locations in cases where a place of production is lost or not mentioned in an inscription. Clusters of material and technology can also help to understand craft practice, and in consequence the movement of materials and techniques. Furthermore, they can shed light on issues of socio-economic importance, such as the nature and movements of craftspeople and their technological memory.

MATERIALS
LINEN
Flax (Lat. *Linum usitatissimum* / Arab. *katan*: 'flax', but also 'linen') belongs to the family of bast fibre plants, the stems of which contain a fibrous layer beneath their bark consisting of bundles or strands of cellulose fibre. These

strands help to hold the plant upright and are constructed of long, thick-walled cells that overlap one another, filled with non-cellulosic material in order to hold them together. Like this, the strands can run the whole length of the stem.[1] The cellulitic fibres can be extracted from the stem by a sequence of operations that begins with the decomposition of the plant stem. When extracted, processed and dried, the natural spin direction of the flax fibres is an 'S'. The necessary steps are explained below in more detail.

Twenty-six different varieties of flax have been distinguished in the documents from the Geniza in Fustat (Old Cairo).[2] The varieties were probably not botanical types but local and qualitative variations of the same flax plant.[3] The colour and texture of the flax material were the primary factors in the grading of different qualities, which depended directly on some of the production processes undertaken at village level. However, chemical and microscopic analysis has so far not been carried out to distinguish different flax varieties among surviving Islamic textile samples made of linen. It appears that many of the raw linen types took their names from the places where they were produced. Thus it appears that the main flax-producing regions were Upper Egypt, the Fayyum and the Nile Delta in Lower Egypt (see map, pp. 12–13). Linen textiles in The al-Sabah Collection originate particularly from the urban centres of Lower Egypt (cat. nos 1–54, 120–187). From there, the raw material was traded by intermediary merchants either to the main Egyptian weaving centres or ports on the Mediterranean for shipment overseas. The majority of the well-known weaving centres, as recorded in *tiraz* inscriptions, were located within flax-growing regions, and thus the raw materials did not have to be transported far. Merchants would often visit villages in person to attend the processing of the raw flax material into a tradable product of suitable quality.[4] Already at this early stage, the quality and the price of certain types of flax were influenced by the care with which the plants were processed, thus affecting the quality of all products later made from them. Therefore,

Detail, Cat. 75 (LNS 1 T)

it is important to consider the sequence of processes undertaken to extract linen fibres from raw flax plants.

After being gathered from the field, flax plants were retted – soaked in water – so that the fibres could be separated from their woody cores. While soaking, the plants fermented. Two methods of retting existed: dew-retting and water-retting. In the first, the plants were spread on the ground and left in the open for several weeks, subjected to rain and dew; in the second the plants were tied up into bundles and immersed in water pools for about ten to fourteen days. After retting, the soaked plants were turned regularly while they dried. The Geniza documents state that this first stage of raw flax production was conducted by the farmers themselves, as indicated by its trade name *muzari'in* ('flax of the farmers').[5] Retting had a darkening effect on the raw flax. Dew-retted flax tended to be grey, whereas water-retted flax was more yellowish to buff. Over-retted flax tended to lose strength, and its ability to hold tension was weakened.[6]

Once retting was completed, the flax fibres had to be separated from their woody core. This was done by passing the plant stems through fluted rollers or by beating them. Workers had to be careful not to damage the fibrous strands, in order to keep them long enough for further treatment. Then the broken bark had to be separated from the fibres of the broken flax stems by scrutching – that is, by beating the material with a blade of wood or metal against a vertical wood board with a slot cut in the middle or the side.[7] The bundles of fibre strands were then combed or 'hackled' by pulling them through a succession of pins and combs. Finally, they were arranged parallel to one another, and long and short fibres were separated. The material was then ready for spinning.[8]

That the last two stages were carried out by workers other than the farmers is suggested by the trade name *sunna'* for the raw combed material, the 'flax of the workers'.[9] Because the quality of the raw flax material depended largely on how diligently the combing and cleaning were carried out, it was in the interest of merchants to exert some influence on these procedures. Before the raw flax material reached the textile workshops it must have passed through the hands of many different merchants, depending on where it was traded to.

Once the raw fibre material had reached a textile production centre, further work had to be done on the fibres in order to prepare them for spinning. The material had to be bleached and blanched, processes for which various chemicals were used. If the raw flax was intended to remain colourless, it could then be spun. The material had to be treated further if it was to be dyed.[10]

COTTON

Unlike linen, which is made from fibres that occur in the plant stem, cotton (Arab. *qutn*) is made from the seed boll of the cotton plant (Lat. *Gossypium herbaceum*, or *G. arboreum*) – the flossy, hairy material attached to the seeds. When the plant ripens and the boll opens, the floss comes out and can then be harvested by hand. Each cotton seed can produce up to 20,000 fibres and a single boll contains *c.* 150,000 fibres.[11]

Cotton fibres are single cells growing off the skin of the seed. They consist of an outer membrane of cellulose filled with liquid. This very fact conditions their physical properties. Cotton has short filaments up to 2.5 cm long that, in a raw state, are tangled together. This is one of the main drawbacks for spinning cotton. First the filaments have to be disentangled and then they have to be spun tight enough to make the yarn sufficiently thick to withstand further tension during weaving. When spun, the filaments pull out of the yarn quite easily, so yarns and fabrics thin over time. Flax filaments, by contrast, are relatively long and make finer, stronger and longer-lasting yarn. As regards tensile properties, cotton is at a clear disadvantage compared with linen because it holds less weight. Cotton naturally twists in the 'Z' direction and is spun accordingly. Owing to its homogeneous surface, cotton yarn is much softer and smoother than that made from flax, and the material made from it wears more quickly than linen, a fact that might explain why in medieval Egypt cotton played a subordinate role.[12]

The origins of cotton cultivation are not absolutely certain. Some research has maintained that *G. arboreum* and *G. herbaceum* both descended from cotton varieties growing wild in areas as diverse as Upper Guinea, the Upper Nile Valley, India, Pakistan and Baluchistan, Arabia, Sudan and parts of the Sahara, and south-west Africa and Angola.[13] Archaeological data from the Indian subcontinent, however, suggests that the origins of cotton lie there.

Detail, Cat. 119 (LNS 18 T)

The Islamic period saw the establishment of cotton industries in the eastern Islamic world, such as in Iran, Khuzestan and Iraq, but also in Mediterranean countries, such as Syria, north Africa, the Maghrib, Spain and Sicily.[14] There is, however, some uncertainty about the production of cotton in Egypt, a subject of debate for most of the twentieth century. Rudolf Pfister and Carl Johan Lamm were the first scholars to address this problem seriously, having based their views on the examination of extant textiles. Both scholars agreed in general terms that cotton was not produced in Egypt before the end of the Fatimid period, and that the available evidence suggests those cotton fragments found in Egypt were all imported – though neither denied the possibility that cotton was woven in Egypt in the early Islamic period.[15] On the basis of the Geniza documents, S.D. Goitein suggested that during the early medieval period cotton does not seem to have been grown in Egypt, but was imported – for example, from Sicily and Tunisia.[16] Lisa Golombek and Veronika Gervers, too, followed the opinion that until the twelfth century only linen was produced in Egypt, whereas by that time developed cotton industries already existed in India, Persia, Iraq and Yemen.[17] Maurice Lombard suggested – on the basis of a passage by al-Muqaddasi, who mentioned cotton threads as part of a list of Egyptian products – that cotton was imported into Egypt as a raw material and then spun there.[18]

Almost all Abbasid cotton *tiraz* textiles fall into three geographic areas well known in the medieval literary sources as production centres: the capital region of the Abbasids with Madinat al-Salam (Baghdad) at its centre (cat. nos 95–106); Khurasan, with its capital Merw and the city of Nishapur (cat. nos 107–108); and the Yemenite capital San'a' (cat. nos 109–113; see map, pp. 12–13). It is possible that these cotton textiles reached Egypt as trade items, but it is also conceivable that they were brought as part of official exchanges, since they are inscribed with caliphal protocols.

One rare cotton textile found in Egypt has a Fatimid origin and was almost certainly brought to Egypt from outside (fig. 2.8). It bears an inscription in the name of the Fatimid caliph al-Mu'izz and is dated 345 AH / 956–57 CE. Pre-dating the Fatimid conquest of Egypt by thirteen years, it is likely to have been produced outside Egypt, possibly at al-Mansuriya, the Fatimid capital of the province of Ifriqiya.[19] It is very likely that the piece was brought to Egypt from Ifriqiya by a follower of the Fatimids and was deposited there in a burial at a later date.

In addition to *tiraz* textiles, a large number of Gujarati resist-dyed cotton textiles, which had clearly been imported from India, were found at Fustat.[20] Examples of these are in The al-Sabah Collection (cat. nos 116–118). While it has been thought that most of this Indian material arrived in Egypt during the Ayyubid and Mamluk periods, carbon dating carried out on samples stamped with Kufic inscriptions suggests dates as early as the Fatimid period.[21] Much of this material is decorated with designs that can be compared with contemporary Indian designs, further reinforcing the assumption that the textiles concerned were imports.

WOOL

Wool has been largely excluded from studies on *tiraz* textiles, though it had been important in Egypt during the pre-Islamic period and continued to be so in early Islamic times. One of the reasons may be that wool was the major decorative and ground material in Coptic textiles, many of which are undated and are usually attributed on stylistic grounds to the pre-Islamic or very early Islamic period.[22] Much of the Coptic material comprises designs belonging to the classical repertoire, such as Dionysiac and animal motifs and palmette scrolls. This has led scholars to assume that, therefore, they cannot be 'Islamic'. Lisa Golombek and Veronika Gervers, however, have questioned this, and proposed a reconsideration of the issue of 'Coptic' versus 'Islamic' textiles. In their view much of the decorative repertoire of these textiles compares with Abbasid or Fatimid material: for example, repeating medallions filled with geometric motifs, stylized birds and animals, and conventionalized human figures. Furthermore, they regarded these attributions given by scholars as preconceived on the basis of the material: wool was 'Coptic' and silk was 'Islamic'.[23]

Golombek's and Gervers's view is not unfounded. A study undertaken by Rudolf Pfister, who examined the colourants of a number of decorative wool bands from linen tunics commonly labelled as 'Coptic', found that some of these had been dyed with lac dye, which was an insect-based red colourant imported from India.[24] Pfister argued that lac dye gradually replaced the locally produced *kermes* or cochineal in Egypt, and suggested that these textiles were produced after the Muslim conquest of Egypt. The attribution of the Coptic weavings to the Islamic period was also strengthened by the fact that Egyptian wool and silk textiles with Arabic inscriptions

Detail, Cat. 55 (LNS 68 T)

were predominantly dyed with lac dye.[25] Pfister's findings suggest that though, after the Muslim conquest, textiles in Egypt continued to be produced by Copts according to materials, designs and weaving techniques used before, there were subtle but very decisive changes owing to the increase in international trade within the Indian Ocean region. With the Muslim conquest, Egypt was linked to an already existing network of Arab sea trade.

On the basis of textual sources, Maurice Lombard suggested that wool textiles in Egypt were predominantly produced in the Saʿid (Upper Egypt) (cat. nos 50–55) and the Fayyum (cat. nos 74–93), two areas traditionally associated with the production of Coptic textiles (see map, pp. 12–13).[26] Surviving wool textiles from Bahnasa,[27] Akhmim[28] and Qays[29] confirm this. Most of these examples are tapestry-woven in wool on linen warps. From the Fayyum, wool textiles made in Sanhur and Tuttun have survived.[30] Exceptions are the textiles from Tuttun, which comprise wool base fabric with the inscription and decoration woven in wool and linen.[31] Another wool-on-wool tapestry woven with a fragmentary inscription contains the name of the last Umayyad caliph, Marwan ibn Muhammad (r. 744–50).[32]

While the majority of surviving fragments in this group can be attributed to distinct geographical areas and a relatively limited period from between the beginning of Islamic rule in Egypt up to the Tulunid period, there is evidence that *tiraz* textiles continued to be produced with inscriptions in wool well into the later Fatimid period. A fragment in the Rietberg Museum in Zürich datable to the reign of al-Zahir (r. 1021–36) is decorated in fine multicoloured wool thread on a linen base.[33] Frequent references to wool production and trade in the Geniza documents suggest that wool retained its importance well into the Fatimid period.[34] Further references can be found in the *Hudud al-ʿalam* ('The regions of the world'), which mentions, for example, that Tinnis and Damietta produced wool and linen stuffs at very high price.[35] Wool items were also present among the textile finds at Fustat, mostly as floor coverings, but some also as clothing fabrics.[36] There is, consequently, enough extant and literary evidence to suggest that wool had a far greater importance, both geographically and chronologically, as a material for the production of *tiraz* textiles than has been hitherto portrayed in the scholarly literature.

SILK

A dichotomy existed in early Islamic Egypt between silk and wool, comparable with the relationship between linen and cotton. Like linen, wool was an indigenous Egyptian product, while silk was, like cotton, an imported material. Although silk was present in pre-Islamic Egypt, largely as imported compound-weave fabrics from Syria, its use in early Islamic times as a medium for inscribing linen textiles was a novelty. Following the Coptic tradition, the earliest Egyptian *tiraz* textiles were inscribed in wool on a linen ground, sometimes even in wool on a wool ground, as discussed earlier. It appears that this changed with the arrival of the Abbasids, who brought about a significant eastward shift in the arts of Islam. The Abbasids brought with them, it seems, the habit of inscribing cotton textiles in silk, which was adapted in Egypt to inscribing in silk on linen-ground fabric: silk-inscribed linen textiles predominate from the early ninth century onwards.

The character of silk as an imported material can further be illustrated on the basis of the unique compound silk textile discussed in chapter 2, which survives in six fragments embroidered with an inscription containing a caliphal protocol in the name of Marwan and mentioning its manufacture in a *tiraz* workshop in Ifriqiya (see fig. 2.4).[37] It is not clear where the textile might have been woven, perhaps in Byzantium or central Asia, since the inscription was embroidered later onto the finished cloth. Whether or not the piece could have been produced in Egypt is uncertain, too. Louise Mackie has suggested that the drawloom, a comlex mechanical loom operated by two weavers which can raise warp threads individually or in groups to insert wefts as required by the pattern, was introduced there only in the thirteenth century.[38] Given the similarities between the decoration of the silk fragments and that of contemporary monuments in the Bilad al-Sham (Greater Syria and Palestine), there is also a possibility that it was manufactured in Syria, particularly Damascus, which according to historical sources had an old and well-established silk industry.[39]

REED AND GRASS

Reed has also been excluded from most studies on *tiraz*. Although it is not an orthodox textile material, it can be woven on a loom in much the same way as textile yarns. The material was used in the medieval Islamic world to produce floor mats. The few surviving items illustrate that reed was woven to a high standard of craftsmanship.

The inscriptions on these items are comparable in epigraphic aesthetic to a number of *tiraz* textile inscriptions. Furthermore, the *tiraz* workshops in which these mats were manufactured were probably part of the same institutional set-up as those producing linen and silk *tiraz* textiles.

The most important surviving item providing evidence for the manufacture of reed mats in *tiraz* workshops is a mat made in a *tiraz al-khassa* in Tabariyya ('Tiberias'), now in the Benaki Museum, Athens (fig. 3.1).[40] Its inscription does not provide a caliphal name and contains only invocations and blessings 'to its owner' ('li-sahibihi'). Étienne Combe suggested that the piece should be dated to the mid-tenth century on the basis of its epigraphy. By comparing the inscription to those on linen *tiraz* textiles of the period, Combe's dating can be confirmed.[41] The surviving part of an inscription on a mat fragment in the Museum für Islamische Kunst, Berlin, features (in a script comparable with that used in the Athens example) the word *tiraz* as well as the beginning of the word *al-khassa* (fig. 3.2), suggesting that this fragment has a similar date and origin.[42] Other complete examples of similar composition and workmanship, with benedictory inscriptions though without a place of manufacture, are in the Metropolitan Museum, New York (fig. 3.3), and the Benaki Museum, Athens (fig. 3.4).[43] A fragment of a reed mat of similar quality and with a stylistically comparable inscription is in The al-Sabah Collection (cat. no. 115).

Tabariyya as a centre for the manufacture of mats is well documented in medieval literary sources. The historian al-Muqaddasi, writing before 985–86, states that the merchants of Tabariyya exported long pieces of mats.[44] Much later, in 1047, the traveller Nasir-e Khosrow stated that mats were made in Tabariyya, which served as prayer mats.[45] In the twelfth century, the geographer al-Idrisi stated that Tabariyya produced mats called *al-samaniyya* which were highly praised and were not produced anywhere else than in Palestine.[46] A passage in the biography of the Fatimid court secretary Jawdhar describes how Jawdhar was asked by his master al-Mui'zz to order inscribed reed prayer mats from Mahdia, the inscriptions of which al-Mu'izz had thought out very carefully.[47] The use of reed prayer mats under the Fatimids is further documented by al-Maqrizi's account of the contents of the *khaza'in al-farsh* ('treasury of furnishings'), which was part of the Fatimid

3.1   Inscribed floor mat, Tabariyya, mid-10th century CE. Plain weave with flax or hemp warp and reed or esparto grass weft, with brocaded decoration, 223 × 115 cm. Benaki Museum, Athens, inv. no. 14735.

3.2   Fragment of an inscribed floor mat, attributed to Tabariyya, mid-10th century CE. Plain weave with flax or hemp warp and reed or esparto grass weft, 44.5 × 20 cm. Museum für Islamische Kunst, Berlin, inv. no I. 68/63.

3.3   Inscribed floor mat, attributed
to Tabariyya, first half of the 10th
century CE. Plain weave with flax or hemp
warp and reed or esparto grass weft,
with brocaded decoration, 161 × 86 cm.
Metropolitan Museum of Art, New York,
Purchase, Joseph Pulitzer Bequest, 1939,
inv. no. 39.113.

3.4   Inscribed floor mat, Tabariyya, 10th century CE, with repetition of *baraka* ('blessing'). Plain weave with flax or hemp warp and reed or esparto grass weft, with brocaded decoration, 57 × 45 cm. Benaki Museum, Athens, inv. no. 14743.

3.5   Detail of a fragment of a floor mat, showing the weave structure, probably Tabariyya, 10th century CE. Hemp warp and flattened esparto grass weft, cat. no. 115.

treasury: reed mats (*husur*) were listed among the tents and their contents.[48]

The reed mats at the Benaki Museum, the Museum für Islamische Kunst and the Metropolitan Museum are of high quality and share details of manufacture upon close inspection. Their ground fabric consists of hemp warps into which a double weft of fine flattened reed strands has been woven. The mat fragment in The al-Sabah Collection (cat. no. 115) was woven in a very similar manner (fig. 3.5). The use of textile rather than reed material for the warp suggests that the mats were woven on a conventional textile loom. Not only are the materials used very fine, the layout must also have involved careful planning. Both fringes are carefully knotted, a couple of weft bands are placed in exact order at each end, and an intricately woven lattice-shaped band frames the main field, which itself contains the carefully spaced inscriptions on either end. Aesthetically, and perhaps technically, these pieces are comparable with the large turban-cloths woven in Egypt during the same period.[49]

GOLD THREAD

In medieval society, textiles woven with gold thread were very highly esteemed, perhaps not only for their material value, but also their glittering aesthetic. In medieval texts, the use of gold thread is usually indicated by the term *mudhahhab*, derived from *dhahab* ('gold').[50] Gold thread was used at the Abbasid court, as the *Kitab al-aghani* ('Book of songs') mentions in an account of an audience with al-Fadl ibn al-Rabi', vizier of Harun al-Rashid, in which a *susanjird* carpet is described as embroidered in gold.[51] However, the most sumptuous descriptions of garments woven or embroidered with gold thread are perhaps in the accounts concerning the contents of the Fatimid treasury.[52] Several of the descriptions provide information on the sheer weight of the gold used in the decoration of the garments: in the first ceremonial costume of the Fatimid caliph the weight of the gold used in his *thawb* amounted to 375.5 *mithqal* (1.589 kg), while the gold in his turban weighed 325 *mithqal* (1.486 kg).[53] Looking back to the Fatimid dynasty, the Mamluk author Ibn Duqmaq, attested that a gold-embroidered cloth or garment made in Tinnis and Damietta was far more valuable than one without (see chapter 1, pp. 43–44).[54]

Only 32 of 1,821 recorded historical *tiraz* textiles are decorated with gold thread.[55] Only three from the Abbasid period are known; the rest are Fatimid.[56] The earliest Fatimid specimen dates from 964–65 during the time of al-Mu'izz; the latest is the 'Veil of St Anne', which dates from 1096–97 during the reign of al-Musta'li (discussed in chapter 1).[57] A passage about the city of Dabiq in al-Maqrizi's topographical and historical description of

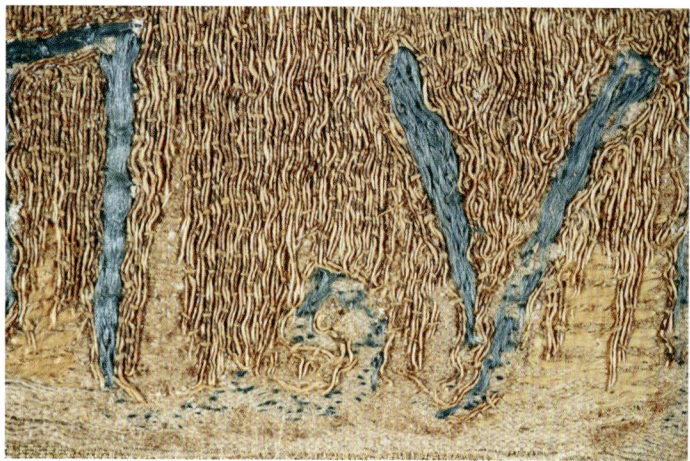 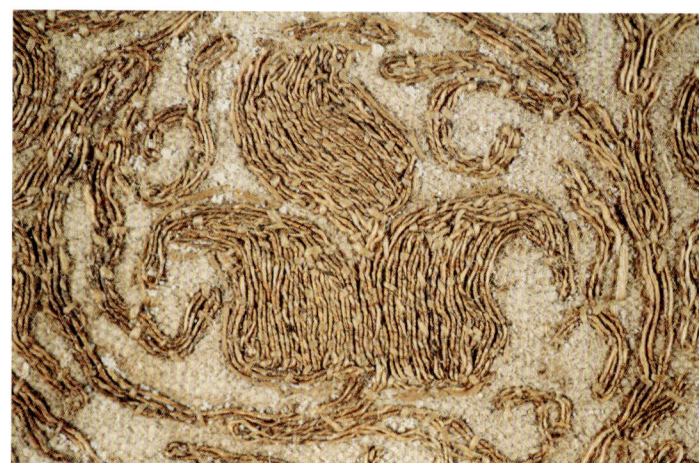

3.6a, b   Details of the gold-thread embroidery on a *tiraz* textile fragment, Khurasan, 12th century CE. *Mulham* (silk and cotton plain weave) with embroidery in silk and gold thread (silk wrapped in gilded animal substrate), cat. no. 108.

Egypt, the *Kitab al-mawa'iz wa al-'itibar fi dhikr al-khitat wa al-athar* describes the textile products made there; it mentions at some length the fact that various textile and garment types comprised woven decoration in heavy gold thread, which was highly prized. Al-Maqrizi further mentions that these gold-woven products were introduced under the Fatimid caliph al-'Aziz in 975–76 and continued to be used until his death in 996.[58]

Very few samples of gold thread from *tiraz* textile fragments have been examined scientifically in order to determine the technique used. One is a Fatimid textile inscribed with the name of al-Hakim, now in the Musée des Tissus, Lyon.[59] The examination was made on a small section of a strip of gold, which is wound around a core of yellow silk. Chemical analysis showed that the metal used is an alloy of around 75 per cent gold, 25 per cent silver and traces of copper. Examination under an electron microscope was able to establish the method by which the strip of gold was obtained. The uneven structure of the surface and the fringe suggested that the strip had been beaten flat from gold wire after cooling. The gold wire, in turn, had been made by stretching a gold ingot during the cooling process. Once the continuous thread was beaten flat, it was rolled by hand around a silk core. Microscopic examination of other Fatimid specimens in the Royal Ontario Museum, Toronto, undertaken in 1995, shows that an alternative method of producing gold thread was to gild a base of animal substrate, usually very fine skin obtained from the gut; it seems that the gilded skin was then cut into fine strips, which were wound around a

silk core, employing a technique similar to that used later under the Ilkhanids in Iran and central Asia (fig. 3.6a, b).[60] In the process of decomposition, the gold has sometimes peeled off, leaving the skin exposed, a feature clearly detectable under the microscope.

THE SPINNING OF YARN

Spinning is a process in which raw fibres are twisted into yarn. In traditional societies a hand-held spindle was used for this purpose. The spindle is rotated at high speed while the textile fibres are pulled out from the raw bulk, twisted by rotating the material between the thumb and index finger. Then the newly twisted portion of the thread

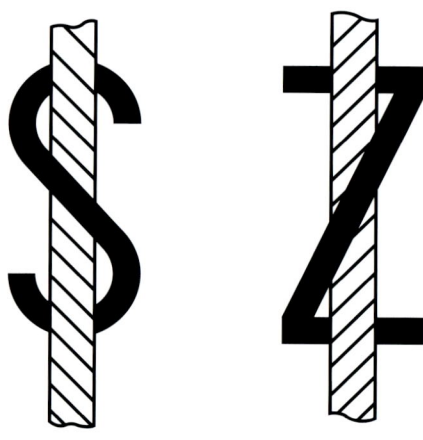

3.7   The two possible twist directions for the spinning of yarn: anti-clockwise ('S' twist) and clockwise ('Z' twist).

is wrapped around the spindle. During this process the three constituting factors of a thread are decided: its twist direction, thread thickness (diameter) and the degree to which (that is, how tightly or loosely) the fibres are twisted.

Threads can be twisted only clockwise or anti-clockwise. An anti-clockwise twist is called 'S', while a clockwise twist is called 'Z' (fig. 3.7). The one chosen depends on the spinner's hand movement, though this in turn is influenced by the fibre of which the thread is made. The choice of spin direction is bound by traditional knowledge passed down from generation to generation, which rests on two main factors: natural raw materials spin in one or the other direction (linen is naturally inclined to spin in the S-direction, while cotton is Z-inclined); and natural raw materials were native to certain geographical areas in the ancient period. As a result, the geographical predominance of certain textile materials influenced which spin direction was used in the production of yarn in a given area. For example, as linen was the predominant crop of Egypt, yarns produced there were spun in the S-direction. Since in Syria, Iraq, eastern Iran and India it was cotton that was grown predominantly, in the yarns from those countries Z-spinning was used. In turn, the occurrence of a 'foreign' twist direction in the products of a given region could be interpreted as the effect of the arrival of foreign workers, particularly since the choice tended to be conservative and was unlikely to change accidentally.

Other diagnostic features of yarn are its thickness and the degree by which individual fibres are twisted. These two factors are dependent on each other and also affect the yarn's quality. The thickness of yarn depends on the amount of raw material pulled out from the fibre bundle and also how tightly the material is twisted. The thickness of linen yarn used in Egypt during the early Islamic period tended to be between 0.1 and 0.4 mm. Some exceptionally fine threads (0.05 mm), as well as exceptionally thick ones (0.5–0.6 mm) have also survived.[61] The degree by which the threads are twisted depends on the tension applied to the raw material. Three broad groups can be differentiated on the basis of the samples examined here: threads with little tension are twisted between 10 and 20 degrees, medium tension between 20 and 30, and high tension between 30 and 45 degrees.

Thickness and twist degree are interrelated: the finer the thread, the higher the degree of the twist. This should come as no surprise, because in order to achieve very thinly spun yarn the amount of material used has to be limited. A small amount of material has to be twisted to a higher degree to give the thread more internal stability, preventing fibres from pulling out easily and the yarn from disintegrating. Likewise, if a thicker thread is required, the larger number of fibres pulled out from the bundle of raw material limits the application of tension. A good-quality thread is twisted evenly from constantly equal amounts of fibre. Louisa Bellinger suggested that the production of such fine Z-spun linen threads relied on the expertise of craftsmen from Iraq working in Egypt.[62]

THE WEAVING OF CLOTH
WEAVE TYPES

Weaving a fabric entails passing weft threads at right-angles under and over warp threads to create a close network. The configuration of warp and weft threads is primarily conditioned by the mechanical basics of the weaving process. However, this in itself can depend on the physical properties of the materials to be woven. The action of weaving requires a framework to fix the warp threads, normally two parallel beams between which the warps are attached – in short, a loom. It ensures that the warps are kept under tension to form one dimension of the fabric, and provide the foundation for the interlacing of the looser weft threads. In antiquity this basic principle was achieved in various manners. A movable loom could be attached to a steady medium, in which case the weaver had to work to keep the warps under tension, insert the weft and beat it down. Since this set-up was movable the weaver could carry his work with him, hence it is often found in nomadic societies. In settled societies, a frame to which the set-up could be attached was developed to provide more stability. Loom development often depended primarily on the weaving materials, but to a large extent it also related to the development of clothing and fashion.[63] Yet the socio-economic implications of weaving technology should be borne in mind too, since weaving involves the physical abilities of the weaver. The development of looms seems to have been influenced by a drive to rationalize the workforce in order to increase production.

A type of weave is defined by the position of warps and wefts crossing each other. Of the various traditional types of weave, 'plain weave' is the simplest and the commonest. Its characteristic is the alternate under-

3.8a, b   Details of fragments of linen plain-weave fabric, showing density and weave consistency: (a) *dabiqi*, cat. no. 156, (b) *sharb*, cat. no. 141, both Egypt, 11th century CE.

and over-crossing of a single warp thread by the weft threads (fig. 3.9). To judge from surviving *tiraz* samples, plain weave appears to be the only technique used for weaving linen *tiraz* fabrics during the medieval period in Egypt. Imported cotton *tiraz* textiles found in Egypt were likewise woven in plain weave.

WEAVE CONSISTENCY

Weave consistency – that is, the closeness or looseness of a weave – is determined by the number and thickness of threads. The thickness of threads in turn depends on how tightly they are twisted. These features can be measured numerically, which is necessary for the assessment of

fabric types. For example, fabrics with the same thread counts can be of completely different consistency. While one may be made of very fine threads and its fabric may be translucent and light in weight, the other may be made of coarser, thicker and heavier threads and be very tightly woven (as exemplified by the samples in fig. 3.8a, b). Both pieces may have the same thread count, yet be of different consistency and consequently of a different fabric type. If a thread count is given on its own, as is usually the case in most *tiraz* literature, it does not provide complete information on a fabric.[64]

The number of warp and weft threads per centimetre are dependent on each other; in most cases the number of warps exceeds that of the wefts slightly ('predominant-warp'). Very few textiles exist in which warps and wefts are exactly equal ('balanced plain weave') or in which the number of wefts exceeds that of warps ('predominant-weft' or 'weft-faced'). Likewise, very few textiles have excessively more warps than wefts ('warp-faced'). Most textiles contain between fifteen and thirty warps per centimetre and the weft is roughly proportional. The reason for the predominance of warps as opposed to wefts is that the warps were arranged first on the loom, before the weaving process began. This allowed the weaver to predetermine the density of the fabric by placing the warps either close together (for a dense fabric) or far apart (for a loosely woven fabric). Then the wefts did not have to be beaten in too much, making the weaving process itself easier for the weaver. The fairly narrow parameters for numbers of warps and wefts suggest standardization within workshops. Textiles with the same thread counts could be of different consistency – tight, close or gauzy – depending also on how thick and tightly twisted the yarns were.[65]

BASE FABRICS

The most common fabric types produced in early Islamic Egypt should be considered here briefly. The literary sources provide us to some extent with definitions, establishing characteristics of fibres and fabrics. In the following sections it is shown that many extant fabrics fit these definitions, thus confirming the literary sources to a degree. That medieval authors often referred to the best textile varieties known to them when they made qualitative statements about textiles should not be problematic. If one is aware of this bias, it can still help to define the characteristics of a type, regardless of qualitative questions. The names of fabric types

were frequently derived from trade names or places
of production, sometimes referring to the same types
produced in different localities.

Dabiqi

A linen fabric frequently mentioned in medieval literary
sources was *dabiqi* (fig. 3.9a, b). It is likely to owe its
name to the ancient city of Dabiq, which was probably
located on the Nile Delta, but during the Islamic period
must have lost its importance in textile production.
The trade name *dabiqi* was given to textiles of a certain
type, which were produced in a great variety of textile
centres in Egypt and abroad. Goitein notes that among
the Geniza material he did not find a single document
referring to the city of Dabiq.[66] However, there are
two Fatimid textile fragments that bear the name of
Dabqu.[67] Dabqu, sometimes Dabquwa or al-Dabiqiyya,
is mentioned by medieval authors, such as Ibn Hawqal,
al-Bakri, al-Idrisi and Yaqut. However, it is by no means
certain that these names refer to the ancient Dabiq.[68]
Anna Contadini has drawn attention to a crucial
distinction between *dabiqi* and *dabqawi* material,
attested in the *Hikayat abu al-qasim al-baghdadi* ('The
portrait of Abu al-Qasim al-Baghdadi') by Muhammad
bin Ahmad Abi al-Mutahhar al-Azdi, which suggests that
Dabiq and Dabqu were not one and the same.[69] Whereas
dabqawi described a material woven in Dabqu and was
thus a geographically derived term, *dabiqi* described a
general textile type that was produced in many different
centres and appears frequently in the literary sources.[70]
For example, al-Bakri mentions that both Tinnis and
Damietta produced *dabiqi*.[71] Al-Ya'qubi also attests Tinnis
as a major centre for the production of this cloth.[72] In
describing the products of the Delta region, Ibn Hawqal
stated that Tinnis and Damietta produced *dabiqi* among
other types of cloth, and that their products surpassed
those of other Delta locations in quality and luxury.[73]
Al-Idrisi also mentions the quality of *dabiqi* produced
in Tinnis and Damietta, probably copying from Ibn
Hawqal's account, as Serjeant suggested.[74] Both Yaqut and
al-Qazwini mention the town of Asyut in Upper Egypt
for its production of *dabiqi* stuffs.[75]

A passage in al-Tanukhi's *Nishwar al-muhadara
wa-akhbar al-mudhakara* ('Cream of conversation and
recollections'), about a man who dealt with the mother
of al-Muqtadir (r. 908–32), describes *dabiqi* as a close-
woven stuff, sometimes used for the inner lining of the

3.9a, b   Details of fragments of linen *dabiqi* plain-weave fabric, showing
density and weave consistency: (a) cat. no. 150, Egypt, 1036–94 CE; (b) cat.
no. 120, Egypt, 975–96 CE.

soles in sandals.[76] Al-Ya'qubi also notes that the *dabiqi*
fabrics of Tinnis were of close texture, fine and with a
'velvety' surface (*mukhmal*).[77] Al-Azdi described *dabiqi*
as having a velvet-like pile and being softer than silk.[78] To
judge from these comments, the qualitative standards for
the yarn must have been high. To achieve softness, the
fibres had to be clean and free from irregularities such
as knots or thickenings. Important, also, was the early
harvest of the raw flax, as flax from late harvests tended
to be much harder.[79]

Dabiqi was such a well-known and esteemed
material throughout the early Islamic world that the
Arabic sources frequently compared even the textile

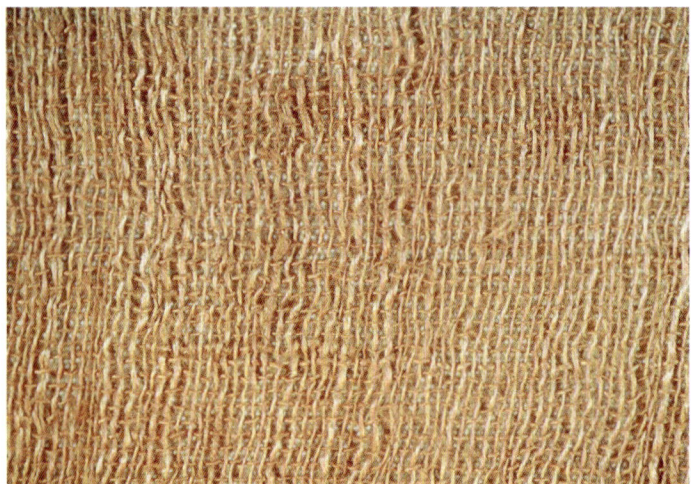

3.10a, b   Details of fragments of linen *sharb* predominant-warp plain-weave fabric, showing density and weave consistency: (a) cat. no. 129, Egypt, 996–1021 CE; (b) cat. no. 33, Egypt, early 10th century CE.

of Khuzestan and Fars, *dabiqi* was to some extent copied: in his *Nishwar al-muhadara*, al-Tanukhi, for example, relates a story about the Abbasid vizier 'Ali ibn 'Isa, who envied the beautiful robe made of Shustari *dabiqi* ('qamis dabiqi shustari') of one of his visitors, a certain Qadi Abu 'Umar.[82]

Dabiqi* was a versatile fabric, used for both clothing and furnishings. The Fatimid treasury lists give a good idea of the various types of garments made from *dabiqi*. They list the *wasitani*, possibly a belted robe,[83] the *ghilala*, possibly an undergarment in the shape of a tunic,[84] the *'ardi*, a mantle,[85] and the *mula'a*, a wrap.[86] The *qamis*, a shirt, is mentioned in an anecdote from the *Kitab al-aghani* involving the Abbasid caliph al-Mu'tasim (r. 833–42).[87] In another anecdote about the plentiful clothing of a man from Baghdad, al-Tanukhi mentions among his garments the *durra'a al-dabiqiyya*, a type of shirt.[88] Goitein's survey of Geniza documents has likewise shown that *dabiqi* was used for a wide variety of clothing: undergarments (*ghilala*), outer-wear (*thawb* or *mula'a*) and accessories (*mandil*).[89] Evidence of *dabiqi* used for furnishing is known from as early as the Abbasid period: the topography of Baghdad by al-Khatib al-Baghdadi tells of boats lined with *dabiqi*.[90] The same author also mentions a throne upholstered in gold-embroidered *dabiqi*.[91] The Fatimid treasury lists speak primarily of curtains in the caliph's *majlis* ('throne room') and of tents made of *dabiqi*.[92]

Sharb

Sharb is another type of textile mentioned frequently in the sources (fig. 3.10a, b). In contrast to *dabiqi*, *sharb* was a very loosely woven fabric. The very best quality was extremely light in weight, as al-Maqrizi states, and it seems to have been very thin, as it was often used as turban-cloth, according to the Geniza documents.[93] Ibn Hawqal mentions in a description of the products of Tinnis and Damietta that the *sharb* and *dabiqi* stuffs produced there were of a quality 'which nothing on earth can approach for price and beauty, softness and luxury, thinness and fineness'.[94] The combination of these diagnostic factors meant that the yarns for such a fabric had to be both very thin and strong: since there is much more internal tension in a loosely woven fabric than in a tightly woven one, its yarns are pulled much more. Flax from late harvests, naturally more woody, has both qualities.[95] The fibres can be twisted to a high degree to make the yarn thin and sturdy enough not to pull out too easily.

products from non-Egyptian locations to it. Al-Mas'udi, for example, describes the textiles of the Caucasus in his *Muruj al-dhahab* ('The meadows of gold') as follows: 'In their country there are various kinds of cloth made of linen of a kind called *tala*, finer than *dabiqi* and more lasting in wear.'[80] Speaking about the central Asian city of Urgench, in his *Lata'if al-ma'arif* ('The book of curious and entertaining information'), al-Tha'alibi mentions that: 'The muslins (*karabis*) called *arandj* are among its specialities. They say that the *aimiri* kind of them does not fall short of the *haffi* of Nishapur, the *munaiyar* of Rayy, the poppy-coloured kind (*kashkashi*) of Jurdjan, and the *dabiqi* of Egypt.'[81] In the famous textile production centres

Several surviving textiles, all Fatimid, with sheer or gauzy weave were woven of dyed yarn, predominantly in blue.[96] Various sources indicate that *sharb* was sometimes woven with gold but rarely indicate whether the gold thread was woven as part of the ground fabric, or simply as a decorative band.[97] Of the latter type a number of examples exist among the *tiraz* corpus.[98] The combination of a ground fabric dyed blue and decoration executed with gold thread must have made an impressively luxurious effect and may have evoked royal connotations.[99] Two such specimens, both Fatimid, have survived.[100]

According to most literary sources, *sharb* seems to have been produced predominantly in the Nile Delta, notably at Tinnis, Damietta and Shata – their products being the best quality.[101] Extant *tiraz* textiles support this picture and account for production in Tinnis,[102] Damietta,[103] Tuna,[104] Shata[105] and Bura.[106] While the sources stress Delta production, Misr (that is, Misr al-Fustat, the first Arab settlement after the conquest of Egypt between 639 and 646) is hardly mentioned by them; nevertheless it is documented by extant material.[107] However, two sources mention places of production unattested by extant *tiraz* textiles: Yaqut, quoting Ibn Zawlaq (before 997), mentions that *sharb* was produced in Abwan[108] and Biyawrnabara,[109] both in the vicinity of Damietta; al-Idrisi, copying Ibn Hawqal or his source, mentions Mahallat al-Dakhil, Samnud and Dumayra as further locations, also both near Damietta (see map, pp. 12–13).[110]

Sharb seems to have been the preferred material for turbans, as attested by several literary sources.[111] Other uses included underwear[112] and cloaks.[113] A number of surviving *tiraz* textiles seem once to have been the ends of large lengths, possibly turban-cloths.[114] Some of them are loom widths and still have a fringe. The only complete surviving *sharb* textile, a large rectangular sheet, is the so-called 'Veil of St Anne' (see fig. 1.49);[115] its use as a garment is discussed in chapter 1. An examination of the piece has revealed that there are neither sewing marks nor arm-slits, suggesting that the piece was either used as a veil, loosely thrown over another garment, or possibly as a turban-cloth.[116]

'Asb

'Asb corresponds with what is known in south-east Asia as *ikat*, a textile technique in which the yarn is tie-dyed, so that it is multicoloured (fig. 3.11a, b). On the loom

3.11a, b   Details of fragments of cotton *ikat* warp-faced and predominant-warp plain-weave fabrics, showing density and weave consistency: (a) cat. no. 111, (b) cat. no. 113, both Yemen, 10th century CE.

such yarns are then used as warps and arranged in such a way that the intervals of coloured segments produce a pattern.[117] The term *'asb* originates from the root *'asaba* ('to tie, bind or wrap'), and is derived from the technical process. Lane, Lamm and Serjeant have cited most of the available literary sources on *'asb*.[118] Judging from a review of these sources, Alfred Bühler came to three conclusions in his monumental work on the history of *ikat* textiles: (1) *'asb*, and not *washi*, is the proper term to define textiles made using the *ikat* technique; (2) out of a variety of possible locations for the production of *ikat*s, Yemen was the only location in the Islamic world for which the *ikat* technique is attested without question; and (3) cotton is the only material that the sources mention as a base material for *ikat*s.[119]

With regard to the blue dye used in most Yemeni *ikat*s, Pfister found that this was obtained by using indigo, a material for which Yemen and Oman were particularly famous and which was traded from there to Egypt.[120] Three cotton *ikat tiraz* textiles have been recorded, whose inscriptions state that they were made in Sana'a'.[121] Three other cotton *ikat*s, attributable to Yemen, carry inscriptions mentioning Zaydi imams but lacking a place of production.[122] All these clearly provide material evidence for what the literary sources tell us about *ikat*s. A number of very similar cotton *ikat*s have survived, some with painted non-historical inscriptions and others without.[123] By comparison with the extant historical *tiraz* items, these too can be attributed to Yemen.

While Yemeni pieces, such as the examples mentioned above and discussed in the Catalogue (cat. nos 110, 111, 113), are made of cotton, a number of *ikat* pieces exist that are made of linen, sometimes linen woven with silk.[124]

3.12   *Ikat* fragment with a *tiraz* band, Egypt, 11th–12th century CE. Linen, silk (plain weave with tapestry weave), resist-dyed (*ikat*), 25.4 × 22.5 cm. Detroit Institute of Art, Gift of Dorothea Russell, inv. no. 31.18.

A very prominent item, a fragment in Detroit, stands out because it includes tapestry-woven decoration belonging to the Egyptian decorative repertoire of the late Fatimid period (fig. 3.12).[125] Bühler, however, questioned an Egyptian origin for this small group and suggested that the Z-twist common in the yarns of which they are made would rather point to a non-Egyptian origin; he followed Bellinger's suggestion that, under the Fatimids, Z-spun linen was no longer as frequent as under the Abbasids.[126] However, dated *tiraz* textiles suggest that Z-spun linen was not infrequently used under the Fatimids, particularly in the eleventh century, the period to which the fragment in Detroit can be attributed on stylistic grounds.[127] Bühler also agreed with Adele Weibel, who had seen the piece and suggested that the ground fabric was non-Egyptian and that the wefts of a previous decorative band had been removed in Egypt and replaced by a tapestry-woven band.

Be that as it may, two *ikat* fragments in the Metropolitan Museum have similar tapestry-woven bands datable to the eleventh century, which seem to have been woven in the process of weaving the ground fabric. In one, the tapestry weave is limited to the actual design elements set in reserve against the background of the *ikat* ground fabric (fig. 3.13).[128] The other has a band of tapestry-woven heart shapes, the base of which is undulating rather than straight horizontal, as should have been the case had the weft threads of a previous band been pulled out and replaced (fig. 3.14).[129] Given that in the early Islamic period linen was predominantly produced and woven in Egypt, and Z-spinning was still practised under the Fatimids, it is not unreasonable to regard the Detroit *ikat* fragment and others of a similar kind as products of Egyptian workshops.[130] Given the international character of the Egyptian marketplace, with products and people coming from the Indian Ocean region via the Red Sea, it is possible that imported *ikat*s were copied in Egypt, perhaps by immigrant craftsmen, as the few surviving examples discussed here suggest.

Mulham

In contrast to *dabiqi*, *sharb* and possibly also *'asb* (or *ikat*), *mulham* fabrics were not indigenous Egyptian products (fig. 3.15). The word *mulham* is derived from the Arabic word *luhma* ('weft'). Dozy suggested that *mulham* referred to a fabric in which the weft was not silk.[131] Lamm reasoned that since a fabric made of silk warp and wool weft was called *khazz*, *mulham* must have denoted a fabric

3.13   *Ikat* fragment, mid-11th century CE, found at Fustat, Egypt. Linen, silk (plain weave with tapestry weave), resist-dyed (*ikat*), 24.1 × 43.2 cm. Metropolitan Museum of Art, New York, Rogers Fund, 1927, inv. no. 27.170.28.

3.14   *Ikat* fragment, Eygpt (probably found at Fustat), 11th–12th century CE. Linen, silk (plain weave with tapestry weave), resist-dyed (*ikat*), 10.8 × 15.2 cm. Metropolitan Museum of Art, New York, Rogers Fund, 1927, inv. no. 27.170.4.

with silk warp and either cotton or linen weft.[132] Because
of its properties – the silk element in the ground fabric
produced a very soft and smooth ivory-coloured surface
– this material was very highly esteemed. The literary
passages about *mulham* collected by Lamm and Serjeant
suggest that Abbasid Merw was the most renowned centre
of production of this material. From there, the making of
mulham seems to have spread to other parts of the Abbasid
empire, particularly Iran and Iraq.[133]

For example, Ibn al-Faqih's tenth-century version
of the *Kitab al-buldan* ('Book of the countries') states
that the *mulham* cloths of Merw were the finest of their
kind.[134] Tha'alibi's *Lata'if al-ma'arif* also notes that *mulham*
was a particular speciality of Merw.[135] According to the
literary sources, other centres producing *mulham*s were
Nishapur,[136] Isfahan[137] and Khawarizm.[138] That *mulham*
stuffs were highly esteemed is suggested by Ibn Rusta
(active in the tenth century); quoting a certain Harun
ibn Yahya, he described a procession of the Byzantine
emperor in the Hagia Sophia in Constantinople, in
which 5,000 eunuchs were dressed in white *mulham*
stuffs from Khurasan.[139]

The importance of Merw as a centre for the
production of *mulham* is reflected by the number of
surviving specimens.[140] Of twenty historical *mulham*s,
four were produced in Merw, according to their
inscriptions (see Catalogue, §I.5, figs A–B).[141] Lamm
further suggested that the word *mulham*, derived, as we
have seen, from the root *luhma* ('weft'), denotes a fabric
in which the weft is predominant over the warp.[142] Indeed,
most of the fragments now generally regarded as *mulham*
are very tightly woven, warp-faced fabrics in which the
silk warps dominate over the cotton wefts in such a way
that the latter are hardly seen.[143] Because of the thinness of
the silk threads it was easier to arrange the silk warp first,
and then shoot in the coarser cotton wefts. The reverse
would have been a much more laborious process since
the shuttle would have had to go across the loom many
more times to weave wefts in the fine silk. In many extant
mulham fabrics, the number of silk warps exceeds that of
the cotton wefts by three times (see fig. 3.15).

Because of the slippery consistency of the fabric and
its polished finishing, *mulham* was very well suited to
silk embroidery, particularly chain stitch (see fig. 3.15).
All the recorded *tiraz* textiles in *mulham* are embellished
with chain-stitch embroidered inscriptions. An example
from the reign of the caliph al-Mu'tadid (r. 892–902), with

3.15   Detail of a fragment of *mulham* (silk and cotton warp-faced plain
weave), with an inscription in silk embroidery in chain stitch, Iraq,
10th century CE, showing density and weave consistency, cat. no. 105.

3.16   *Tiraz* fragment, from the reign of the Abbasid caliph al-Mu'tadid
(r. 892–902 CE), attributed to eastern Iran or Khurasan. *Mulham* (silk and
cotton plain weave), with embroidery, 37.5 × 35.6 cm. Metropolitan Museum
of Art, New York, Gift of George D. Pratt, 1931, inv. no. 31.19.2.

3.17 Textile fragment, probably Mesopotamia or eastern Iran, 12th century CE. *Mulham* (silk and cotton warp-faced plain weave), embroidered in metallic thread, gilded overall, 23.37 × 75.05 cm. Textile Museum, Washington, DC, Acquired by George Hewitt Myers, 1931, inv. no. 73.276.

an elaborately designed and chain-stitch-embroidered inscription in a style reminiscent of the so-called New Style in Quranic calligraphy, with pronounced angular letter forms and extremely elongated upper letter stems, is in the Metropolitan Museum, New York (fig. 3.16). In order to appreciate fully the artistic environment out of which these embroidered *tiraz* textiles came, it is useful to consider a few specimens attributed to the eastern Abbasid caliphate, which are noteworthy for their elaborately embroidered figural decoration. One is a *mulham* fragment in the Textile Museum in Washington, DC, attributed by Lamm to twelfth-century Iraq, and embroidered in coloured silk floss and gold thread with pairs of confronted winged horses, bordered above and below by bands of pseudo-Kufic repeat inscriptions (fig. 3.17).[144] Gaston Wiet published three other textiles in private collections, all of which comprise large embroidered overall designs on what appears to be a *mulham* ground fabric.[145] Two other fragments are in the Boston Museum of Fine Arts: one with a variety of embroidered roundels containing lions or griffins and peacocks is said to have been found near Baghdad; the other is embroidered with lion figures (figs 3.18, 3.19).[146] Given that *mulham* was so closely linked with Khurasan, as attested by several surviving *tiraz* inscriptions on *mulham* naming Merw and Nishapur (see Catalogue, §I.5, figs A–D), it is entirely possible that the figural embroideries mentioned here were produced there too, and that an Iraqi attribution is perhaps too limiting. Figural

3.18 Embroidered textile fragment, Mesopotamia or eastern Iran, 10th–11th century CE, found in Egypt. *Mulham* (silk and cotton plain weave), embroidered in silk and metal-wrapped thread, 11 × 9 cm. Boston Museum of Fine Arts, Helen and Alice Colburn Fund, inv. no. 31.445.

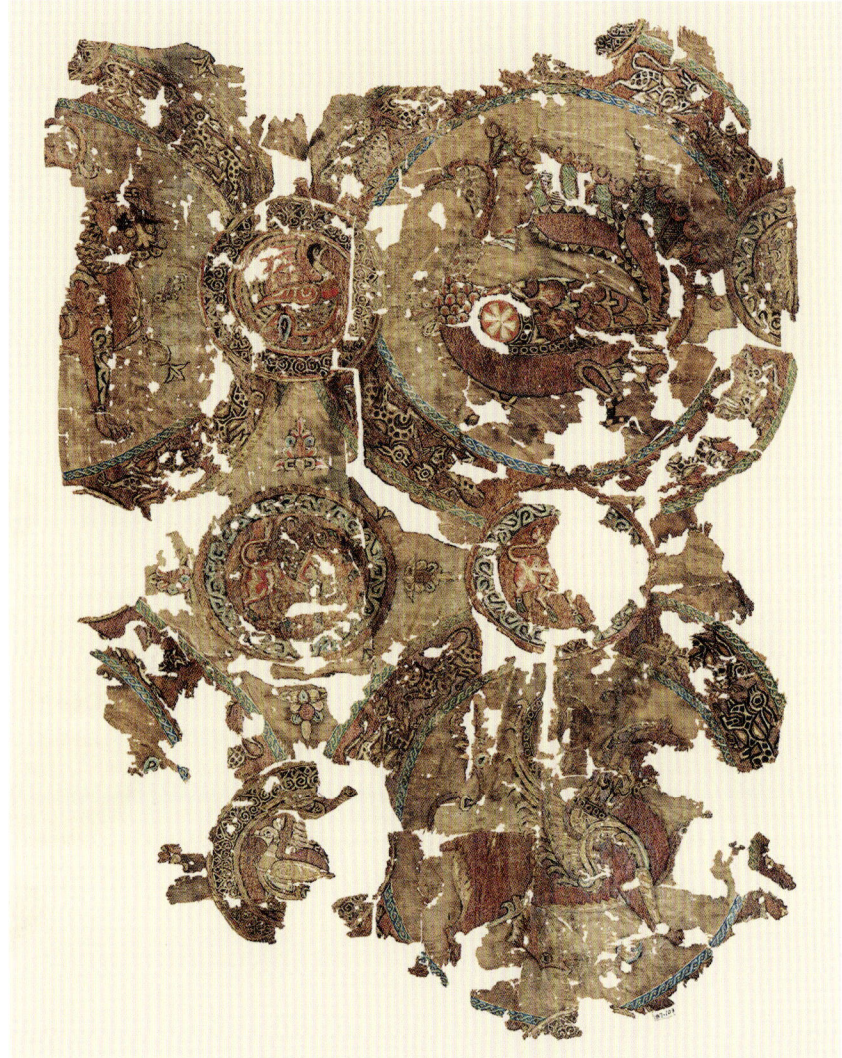

3.19 Textile fragment with mythological animals in roundels, Mesopotamia (Madinat al-Salam(?)), 10th–11th century CE. *Mulham* (silk and cotton plain weave), embroidered in silk and metal-wrapped thread, 68.5 × 50.5 cm. Boston Museum of Fine Art, Archibald Cary Coolidge Fund, inv. no. 37.103.

embroidery is rarely found on Egyptian pieces, and when it is it tends to be cruder than that from Iraq or Iran. The combination of *mulham* and embroidery in these examples underlines the likelihood that we are dealing here with an Eastern non-Egyptian tradition.

WEAVE QUALITY

The idea of weave quality has rarely been addressed so far in studies on *tiraz* textiles.[147] Yet the quality of a fabric is a diagnostic factor in its description and classification. The different types of fabric described in the previous section can be sorted according to quality. A *dabiqi* textile is not superior to a *sharb* textile because it is more closely woven. Neither is a *sharb* qualitatively superior to a *dabiqi* because

its threads tend to be finer and twisted more tightly. Therefore, it is necessary to evaluate quality for each textile type individually.

Abi al-Mutahhar al-Azdi's *Hikayat abu al-qasim al-baghdadi* ('The portrait of Abu al-Qasim al-Baghdadi') describes in very visual terms the exquisite aesthetic of a type of *dabiqi* from Egypt called *mutawakkili*, presumably named after the Abbasid caliph al-Mutawakkil (r. 847–61). It was:

> embroidered with a *tiraz* border, with a velvet-like pile (*mukhmal*), made in Egypt, with two badges (*'alam*), and two bands (*zunnar*) and their patterns of fine thread, of perfect length,

exquisite width, with a short pile, bordered with a fringed (?) border (*hashiya mashqaqa*), softer than *qazz*-silk and finer than floss-silk (*khazz*).[148]

In a description of al-Mutawakkil's clothing, al-Mas'udi stated in his *Muruj al-dhahab* ('The meadows of gold') that the caliph wore *mulham* cloth, which in al-Mas'udi's time (the tenth century) was still manufactured under the name of *mutawakkili*, a cloth 'of a very beautiful weave, and of an excellent colour'.[149] A passage that stresses the lightness and delicacy of the fabric can be found in a description of the linen products of the city of Tawwaj, in Fars near Kazerun province in southern Iran, by Yaqut in his geographical dictionary *Mu'jam al-buldan* ('Dictionary of countries'):

It is a fine cloth of light delicate weave (*raqiqa muhalhala al-nasaj*), as if it were very fine sieve-cloth (*munkhal*), but its colours are lovely and it has golden tiraz borders (*tiraz mudhahhaba*), a piece being sold for a sum of money … Sometimes there is made an excellent close-woven kind which sells well.[150]

While the previous passages are more concerned with the overall effects of material and decoration, a passage from the *Al-isharah ila mahasin al-tijara* ('The indicator to the virtues of commerce') written by the twelfth-century author Abu al-Fadl Ja'far ibn 'Ali al-Dimashqi, describes the diagnostic factors of fabric quality more precisely, allowing us to define the notion of textile quality in medieval Islamic society:[151]

People's tastes vary in regard to the *tiraz* borders and the ornamented embroideries (*rukum* / inscriptions), but they are agreed in the preference of that which is of the finest thread, and closest of weave, of the purest white, of the best workmanship, red, and golden; and, where *dabiqi* is concerned, whatever is beautiful even if raw (*kham*); but when it is compressed (*maqsur*) it is not esteemed.[152]

This passage defines three areas of qualitative distinction very clearly: the density of weave, the fineness and purity of spun threads, and the colour of the material. Of these three, the density of the weave is a diagnostic factor not

only of quality but also of fabric types, as has been shown in the last section. It therefore must be seen in combination with other factors and can be expressed numerically by a thread count combined with measurements of the diameters of warp and weft threads. For fabric colour, finish and degree of workmanship, one can only rely on description. Ultimately, in an evaluation of the overall quality of a textile which uses the combination of both numerical and descriptive factors, there always remains a subjective element.

The absence of impurities, such as discolouring or woody fragments, raises certain materials above others, particularly if the material has a clean, white appearance with a smooth touch. The yarns have to be spun finely and evenly, and the weave should not be too loose, even in a loosely woven fabric. Workmanship also plays its part, but the above text does not define whether this applies to the decoration or the fabric. One may speculate that it applies to both. A well-woven or embroidered inscription must have raised the esteem and value of a piece of cloth just as much as a base fabric that was free from irregularities. The author also added a specification for *dabiqi*, namely that it is better *kham* ('raw' or 'unprocessed') than *maqsur* ('restricted', 'shortened' or possibly 'compressed'). While *maqsur* may mean a polished or burnished fabric that had been treated with starch, *kham* may mean a fabric that had not been treated at all.

It has been shown earlier that, for both *dabiqi* and *sharb*, the thread quality was decisive for the finished fabric. The best-quality yarn had to be very fine and thin in diameter, which was achieved by using little fibre material spun very tightly.[153] As opposed to loosely spun yarn, the fibres held together better, consequently lasted longer and resulted in an overall smoother surface of the finished fabric.

The technical analysis of each textile provided in the Catalogue attempts a grading of the quality of *tiraz* textiles for the first time. See the 'Note on the Catalogue Entries' (p. 126) for a full explanation of the grading system.

DYEING

When it came to textiles, the medieval Islamic world was extremely colour-conscious, as vivid descriptions of colours in the Geniza documents show. Goitein, for instance, mentions a document in which textiles of 'gazelle-blood' colour, 'pure violet', 'musk colour', 'silvery' and 'intense yellow' were ordered.[154] Colours were known by the names of many different shades, perhaps sometimes named after the dyeing material. Two Geniza trousseau lists contain items in colours such as 'cloud blue', 'pomegranate red', 'pearl-coloured', 'ash grey', 'sky blue', 'emerald' and 'sand-coloured'.[155] It is possible that such a variety of colours was the result of specialization among dyers in one particular colour and dyeing material. This is suggested by different epithets recorded for dyers in the Geniza, such as *qirmizini* (or *qirmizi*), *za'afarani*, *summaq*, *arjawani* and *munnayyir*, all derived from materials used as colourants.[156]

The relation between dyed and undyed *tiraz* textiles contrasts starkly with the proliferation of colours as portrayed in the Geniza documents. The ground fabrics of the vast majority of extant dated *tiraz* textiles are undyed.[157] Relatively few dyed ones have survived, and those that have are in a limited range of colours: a number of Yemeni cotton *ikat*s in blue,[158] and textiles with wool or linen and wool ground from Egypt in a reddish tone and blue.[159] Of surviving Egyptian linen fabrics several are blue,[160] green,[161] black,[162] or multicoloured in blue, green and beige.[163]

Egyptian *dabiqi* or *sharb* linens and most imported cotton from the Abbasid period are likely to have been undyed, except Yemeni cotton *ikat*s. The only dyed Egyptian fabrics from the Abbasid period are in wool or wool and linen mix. Under the Fatimids, the dyed linen textiles recorded are entirely of Egyptian manufacture, and the majority (i.e. all items excluding *ikat*s) are loosely woven *sharb* fabrics.[164] For both the Abbasid and Fatimid periods, Egyptian *dabiqi* fabrics tended to be undyed, it seems. A Geniza letter written in or around 1085–86 describes a piece of ambergris (*'anbar*) as 'whiter than *dabiqi* garments (*thiyab*)'.[165] The Cairo Geniza documents, which speak about 'cloud'-, 'manna'-, 'lead'-, 'silver'-, 'borax'-, 'starch'-, 'snow'- and 'pearl'-coloured *dabiqi* textiles, suggest that the notion of uncoloured fabrics was defined very subtly in medieval society and appreciated in its own right.[166]

A count of the occurrences of coloured and uncoloured garments in the Geniza documents by Goitein has yielded results similar to those presented above regarding the predominance of white and the relatively limited range of colours.[167] Part of the explanation could be that the choice of colours for clothing was dictated and limited by religious terms. It seems that the choice of white for burial clothes prevailed over that of coloured garments:

Lamm mentions – without identifying his source – that, according to Islamic tradition, in Paradise white garments are worn.[168] The Prophet Muhammad is said to have recommended white garments for both the living and the dead, a colour in which he himself was enshrouded.[169] Fatimid *hadith* literature, for example, recommends white garments and condemns the use of red garments.[170]

Perhaps a more fruitful way to explain the problem is by considering the overall aesthetic of clothing items – that is, the juxtaposition of decorated and undecorated areas. The surviving *tiraz* fragments are characterized by large undecorated areas – only occasionally dyed – against which are set bands of coloured inscriptions or decorative bands. This aesthetic is characteristic of at least Abbasid and Fatimid textiles, a fact suggested not only by the surviving *tiraz* fragments but also by contemporary literature.

With regard to Islamic garments, it would be very tempting to search for a religious explanation for this aesthetic as, at least in the Fatimid period, there existed religious recommendations regarding the use of silk in men's costume, where it had to be limited to borders.[171] However, perhaps a technical explanation is more appropriate. Taking into account that linen is an extremely colour-resistant material and animal fibres are easier to dye, the only areas where colour could be used more extensively were the silk or wool borders of textiles. An eleventh-century account from the Geniza documents confirms that dyeing was an expensive process.[172] The document states that the cost of materials for dying 66 pounds of unbleached silk was 300 dinars. Crimson was valued at 85 dinars and was the single most expensive item. The other dyes mentioned were antimony, black and green. Their value in the account came to 24 dinars. Expenses incurred, such as customs dues, were 25 dinars. Finally, the dyers' wages were rated at 20 dinars. Since some of the silk had been lost in the process of handling, another 20 dinars were added. The total bill came to 474 dinars, of which 129 dinars were spent on dyeing alone. This was almost 50 per cent of the cost of the raw silk. Obviously, the proportion between the cost of dye-stuff and raw material depended largely on the quality of the material to be dyed. What exactly the cost to dye linen would have been is not clear, but given the resistance of linen to dye-stuffs, it is likely that it would have been even higher.

Given these technical problems, coupled with the immense cost in Egypt of the silk material alone, it is not surprising to find that silk was used so sparingly and that coloured silk was reserved for the *tiraz* bands. But even here the proliferation of colours was limited, as far as the inscriptions were concerned, and colours were more varied in the accompanying decorative bands. Single, undecorated inscriptions were usually subject to standard colour choices. The more integrated an inscription was with the surrounding decoration, the more it became part of the overall interplay of colours, and the less effective its independent visual message was. This is particularly the case with later Fatimid inscriptions, while the majority of Abbasid and early Fatimid inscriptions were undecorated. The colours documented in *tiraz* inscriptions are red, blue, black, yellow, green, brown, golden and undyed against a coloured background.[173]

It is very likely that colour choices were limited by the availability of colourants, many of which were imported, just like raw silk. Very few studies have explored the chemical nature of colourants in medieval textiles but, as the dyer's account above shows, they were rare and expensive commodities. Studying the nature of colourants, Pfister discovered that the red dye used in Egyptian *tiraz* textiles with wool inscriptions was sometimes lac dye, derived from the insect *Cartheria lacca*, which was traded exclusively from India. This eventually replaced other red insect-based dyes, such as *kermes* or cochineal, and

plant dyes used in Egypt, such as *Rubia tinctorum*. The Arab invasion of Egypt and the increased influence of international trade with the Indian Ocean facilitated the importation of such foreign dyes.[174] Pfister examined a large number of fragments with decoration reminiscent of Coptic designs, many of which he dated to the period after the Muslim conquest of Egypt owing to his finds of lac dye – a surprising finding, since common consensus would have attributed them to pre-Islamic Egypt.[175] More significantly, he examined a selection of fabrics that can be firmly attributed to the Islamic period because of the presence of *tiraz* inscriptions or pseudo-inscriptions. Most of these samples were Fayyumi wool textiles, mostly of the type with animated friezes in the Coptic tradition, bordered by contorted Kufic pseudo-inscriptions (similar to those discussed in the Catalogue – see cat. nos 74–92). Another group consisted of items that were datable to the Abbasid or even Fatimid periods because of the style of their inscriptions or decoration.[176] Of these, two dated *tiraz* inscriptions stood out. One was dated 88 AH / 707–08 CE and inscribed with the name of a certain Samu'il ibn Murqus; the other was inscribed with the name of Abu al-Fath al-Fadl ibn Ja'far, vizier of al-Radi, and Misr (Misr al-Fustat) as the place where it was made.[177] The materials of both inscriptions, wool in the first and silk in the

Detail, Cat. 77 (LNS 66 T a–c)

second, were dyed with lac dye. They thus illustrate that lac dye was used for both wool and silk and over a long period of time.[178] Without the examination of more dated specimens, it can only be speculated that lac dye was used also under the Fatimids.

Indigo (*nil*) was another very important colourant, which had its origins in India and was introduced from there to the Islamic world via the Arabian Sea and the land route through Afghanistan.[179] Indigo was a natural source of blue colour. Its etymology reflects its Indian origin: the Arabic term *nil* is derived from the Sanskrit word for blue, *nila*.[180] Indigo was obtained from the leaves of two varieties of the same bush, *Indigofera tinctoria* and *Indigofera argentea*. While the first was native to the southern Deccan, the second was native to the northern Deccan and Gujarat. It was probably from Gujarat that most of the indigo that reached the Islamic world was traded.[181] Since the process of obtaining the colourant from the plant material was long and laborious, indigo was expensive – a fact reflected in literary accounts describing attempts to cheat in the use of indigo.[182] The cultivation of indigo in the Islamic world progressed gradually from east to west. Important plantations were in Afghanistan, Iran (Kirman and Khuzestan), Syria, Sudan, Sicily and Egypt.[183] In Egypt the cultivation took place in the Fayyum and the Nile Delta, where the Gujarati *Indigofera argentea* was planted. It was from there that indigo spread further west.

Indigo was also produced in Yemen, as is not only suggested by surviving *ikat* textiles made in Sana'a' but also attested by a number of medieval historians.[184] That the indigo from Yemen was considered of high quality and very desirable is suggested by al-Muqaddasi, who travelled in the Tihama during the tenth century, and who compared the indigo produced there to lapis lazuli.[185]

As both indigo and lac dye were very expensive imported colourants, it is not surprising to find that they were used only sparingly. Their predominance among surviving *tiraz* textiles might be explained by the fact that they were seen as fit for inscribing a caliphal protocol on an otherwise undecorated textile, precisely because they were such expensive commodities. We can only speculate that red and blue might in fact have been visually identifiable as royal colours, as was the use of gold. It is perhaps, then, no coincidence that one of the most sumptuous Qurans ever produced was written in gold on blue vellum, and others have survived that were written in ink on red, orange or pink vellum.[186] A passage from the

Kitab al-bayan al-mughrib fi akhbar muluk al-andalus wa al-maghrib ('Book of the amazing story of the history of the kings of al-Andalus and Maghreb') by the eleventh-century Andalusian author Ibn Idhari, noted by Josef von Karabacek, is significant in this context. It describes a letter sent through an envoy in 338 AH / 949–50 CE by the Byzantine emperor Constantine VII Porphyrogenitus to the Spanish–Umayyad caliph 'Abd al-Rahman. The letter was written in gold on vellum coloured hyacinth purple and was sealed by a golden seal weighing four *mithqal*s – a most ostentatious missive.[187] Karabacek further states, without identifying his source, that the use of red papers ('al-waraq al-ahmar') was the prerogative of chanceries and of those important personages who corresponded with the ruler, and was a sign of great status.[188] Furthermore, a manuscript of the *'Umdat al-kuttab* ('Staff of the scribes', or 'Pillar for penmen'), a work by the tenth-century author Ahmad ibn Muhammad ibn Isma'il ibn al-Nahhas, on the scribe's tools, mentions in a chapter on papermaking that paper was dyed with indigo and lac dye, two colourants also found in early Islamic textiles.[189] We may also think of the famous Blue Quran, a folio of which is in The al-Sabah Collection (the majority of dispersed surviving folios are preserved in the museums in Raqqada and Qayrawan in Tunisia).[190] Its deep blue vellum underlies text written in bold gold lettering, applied as gold leaf on a substrate of resin; its colouring is similar to what is found in some *tiraz* textiles from Yemen.[191]

INSCRIBING *TIRAZ*

Tiraz textile inscriptions can be divided into three groups according to the method of their production. In the two main groups, inscriptions are woven or embroidered. In the third group they are printed, painted or written. This formal division extends to the content of the inscriptions. The majority of caliphal protocollary inscriptions are either embroidered or woven. Very few exist that were executed in a non-textile medium: three Yemeni *ikat*s with painted inscriptions are such examples.[192] Because of the rarity of these painted inscriptions, the technicalities of weaving and embroidering inscriptions have been given precedence in most studies on *tiraz*.

Embroidery is a means of applying decoration by stitching individual threads onto a base fabric in order to make up an intended pattern. Tapestry is a process of weaving decoration into the base fabric by inserting discontinuous weft threads of a different colour; the consistency and material may differ from the base fabric, and the number of weft threads per centimetre greatly exceeds that of the warps. Both embroidery and tapestry have to be executed by trained and skilled craftsmen. Tapestry seems to have been a technique largely used in Egypt, where its history goes back to Pharaonic times.[193] Embroidery, on the other hand, seems to have been a specialism of the eastern Islamic lands, from where it came to Egypt. Whenever craftsmen moved from one area to another, they took with them their particular craft knowledge, which in time infiltrated local techniques.

EMBROIDERY

The theory that textile techniques were geographically specific and that their transmission depended on the movement of craftsmen prompted the textile historian Louisa Bellinger to suggest that silk embroidery was first introduced in Egypt by a foreign workforce sent by the Abbasids, a theory still widely accepted. Another factor indicating foreign influence was the occurrence of Z-spun linen in Egypt, an area that Pfister and Lamm had already studied. The combination of silk embroidery and Z-spinning, they argued, showed the influence of craftsmen used to working with cotton, a material common in the eastern Islamic world, but not in Egypt. Although the origins of Islamic embroidery (*raqm*) had already been attributed to Iran and Iraq by Karabacek in his work on the *susanjird* technique, it was really Bellinger who looked at the technicalities for the first time.[194] Based on her observations on specimens in the Textile Museum in Washington, DC, Bellinger argued that when embroidered *tiraz* inscriptions were introduced into Egypt, the stitches that had developed out of inscribing cotton or *mulham* ground fabrics with silk were adapted to the special requirements of linen.[195]

Bellinger showed that Egyptian embroidery stitches were more varied in type than eastern ones, a fact she attributed to the novelty status of embroidery in Egypt. Unlike eastern stitches, Egyptian stitches were counted: the thread was inserted between the yarns of the ground fabric at regular intervals. With the exception of one stitch type, they also exerted some strain on the ground fabric. Stem stitch and back stitch pulled together the threads on which they were worked (fig. 3.20).[196] Flat stitch exerted a diagonal pull on the face and a straight pull on the back of the fabric (fig. 3.21).[197] Satin stitch comprised a series of flat stitches that cover a section of the ground fabric

3.20 Detail of a fragment of linen *dabiqi* plain-weave fabric, with an inscription in silk embroidery in flat and back stitch, Egypt, 911–12 CE, cat. no. 8.

3.21 Detail of a fragment of linen *dabiqi* plain-weave fabric, with an inscription in silk embroidery in flat and back stitch, Egypt, early 10th century CE, cat. no. 16.

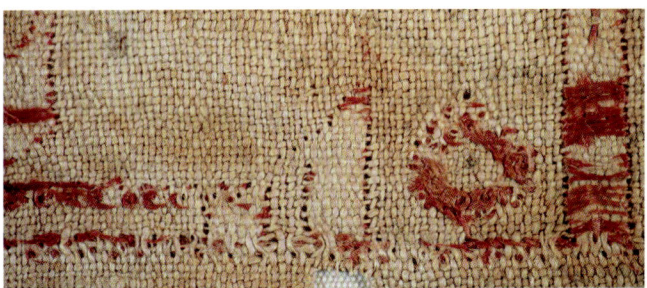

3.22 Detail of a fragment of linen *dabiqi* plain-weave fabric, with an inscription in silk embroidery in satin and chain stitch, Egypt, 8th–9th century CE, cat. no. 1.

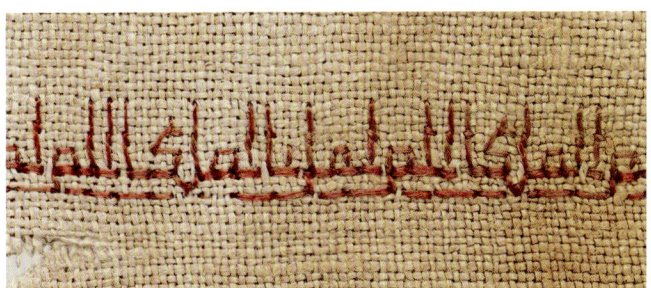

3.23 Detail of a fragment of linen *dabiqi* plain-weave fabric, with an inscription in silk embroidery in stem and couching stitch, Egypt, late 9th century CE, cat. no. 6.

(fig. 3.22). Braiding exerted a pull on the face of the fabric.[198] Couching, in contrast, had no obvious pull on the material (fig. 3.23).[199] Bellinger suggested that these counted stitches were used partly because of the sturdy properties of linen, but also because linen fabric is not suited to be prepared with a wheel or to be written on in ink to create outlines for the embroidered text.[200] A Khurasani glazed *mulham* textile in the Textile Museum, Washington, DC, dated to 283 AH / 896–97 CE shows traces of wheel marks, indicating that the chain-stitch embroidered inscription was first deliniated before it was embroidered (fig. I.5.B).[201] This is contrary to embroidery techniques in Egypt, where the threads of the base material were counted in order to decide the frequency of stitches as a more practicable method for inscribing linen.[202] This can be clearly seen in the examples in The al-Sabah Collection presented here. It was also a technique that weavers in Egypt had already been used to in tapestry weaving, where the designs were woven into carefully counted warps. In many *tiraz* inscriptions, the baselines of inscriptions were pronounced, probably owing to the fact that Egyptian embroiderers almost always pulled out a weft thread to mark the base of the inscription.[203] This was a remnant of an old tapestry-weaving tradition. From this baseline the stems of letters were then developed on counted threads.

Bellinger was able to distinguish diagnostic features of the embroideries of three Egyptian centres from which a good number of examples have survived: Alexandria, Tinnis and Misr al-Fustat.[204] She noted that Alexandrian inscriptions were small and delicate, with a downward ending to the tails. Their baseline was laid first, the stitches of the small letters and stems started just below the baseline, and the reverse was much like the face (fig. 3.23). Embroidery from Tinnis was characterized by little crosses near the heads of the stems, and the reverse side showed a marked diagonal slant to the stitches. In inscriptions from Misr al-Fustat the baseline of the reverse was heavier than that of the face, and one or more lines of back stitching often ran above the low letters, thereby reinforcing the stems (fig. 3.24a–c); they couched down the stems, which on the face showed as small dots between the stems.

While the embroidery from Misr al-Fustat was characterized by confident stitches that provided body to the inscriptions, the inscriptions embroidered in Alexandria were much less confident, their upper lines often rather thin and their baseline very accentuated

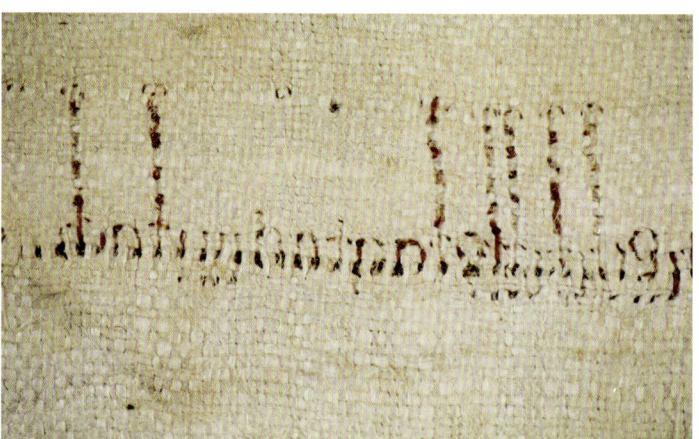

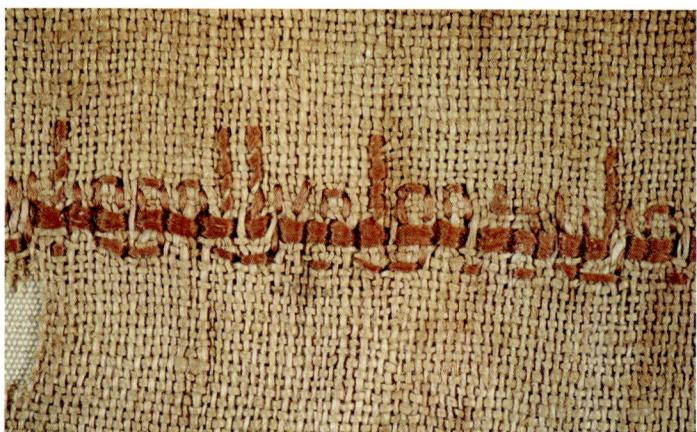

3.24a–c   Details of fragments of linen *dabiqi* plain-weave fabric, showing inscriptions embroidered in silk, Misr al-Fustat, Egypt, 10th century CE: (a) cat. no. 12, embroidery in back and flat stitch; (b) cat. no. 14, embroidery in chain stitch; (c) cat. no. 26, embroidery in back, flat and couching stitch.

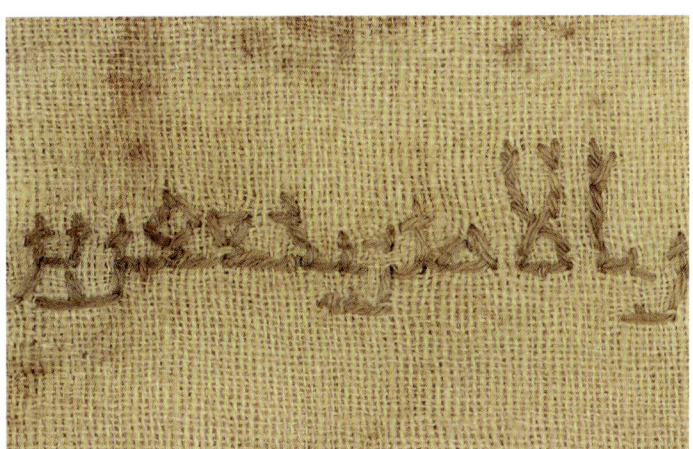

3.25a, b Details of fragments of linen *dabiqi* plain-weave fabric, showing inscriptions embroidered in silk: (a) cat. no. 5, Alexandria(?), Egypt, late 9th century CE, embroidery in couching and stem stitch; (b) cat. no. 3, Alexandria, Egypt, 9th century CE, embroidery in flat and chain stitch.

3.26a–c Details of fragments of cotton plain-weave fabrics, showing inscriptions embroidered in cotton: (a) cat. no. 111, *ikat*, Yemen, 10th century CE, embroidery in couching stitch; (b) cat. no. 109, Yemen, second half of the 9th century CE, embroidery in back stitch; (c) cat. no. 110, Yemen, 900 CE, embroidery in couching stitch.

(fig. 3.25a, b). Embroidery was also practised in Yemen, with inscriptions composed of thin lines of yarns that are couched onto the base fabric (fig. 3.26a–c). Chain stitch was used predominantly in Iraq and Khurasan (fig. 3.27a–c). It featured a series of looped stitches that connected to each other in a chain-like pattern. This type of stitch was particularly well suited to more slippery materials, such as glazed cotton or *mulham*, since it did not have to rely on the counting of threads of the ground fabric to insert the needle, as was the case with the stitches used on Egyptian linen. As a consequence, this type of stitch also allowed more freedom in shaping the letters, resulting in types of script with rounded letter shapes, bow-shaped lower letter terminals and swan-neck upper hastae often terminating

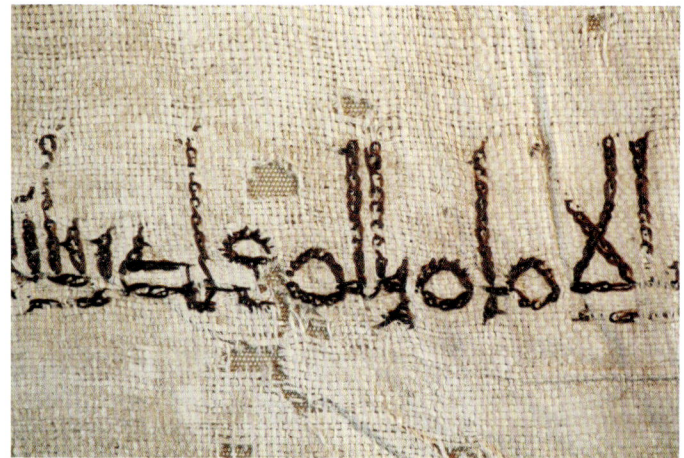

3.27a–c   Details of fragments of cotton *dabiqi* plain-weave fabric, showing inscriptions embroidered in silk in chain stitch: (a) cat. no. 96, Baghdad, Iraq, 920–21 CE; (b) cat. no. 97, Iraq, 932–33 CE; (c) cat. no. 95, Iraq, 912–13 CE.

3.28   Detail of a fragment of cotton *dabiqi* plain-weave fabric, with an inscription written in ink, Iraq or Egypt, 10th century CE, cat. no. 106.

in foliations or even floriations. Generally, these types of inscription were reminiscent of the swelling and thinning letter shapes of text copied in manuscripts, shapes that are also found in textile inscriptions written in ink on cotton (fig. 3.28).

Because of the predominance of tapestry-woven *tiraz* inscriptions under the Fatimids – only one embroidered specimen is in the Textile Museum collection in Washington, DC – Bellinger assumed that tapestry weaving replaced embroidery under the Fatimids, an event she linked to the decline of Abbasid power in the second quarter of the tenth century (fig. 3.29).[205] This assumption needs reconsideration in the light of evidence that has emerged since she was writing. At least thirteen Fatimid textiles made in Egypt with embroidered inscriptions can be documented.[206] One example datable to the reign of al-ʿAziz is in The al-Sabah Collection (fig. 3.30). Although it is very tempting to assume that embroidery disappeared under the Fatimids, a theory that sees embroidery as a foreign craft that ceases when the foreign caliphate loses power, it is not borne out by the textile evidence. Furthermore, the literary sources seem to support the view that embroidery persisted under Fatimid rule. In the Fatimid treasury lists, recorded by al-Maqrizi in his *Khitat*, embroidered costumes are listed on several occasions, indicating that they were not a rare commodity and had far more prominence than the extant textile evidence leads us to believe.[207] It is possible that the *tiraz* evidence is not entirely representative on this point, but

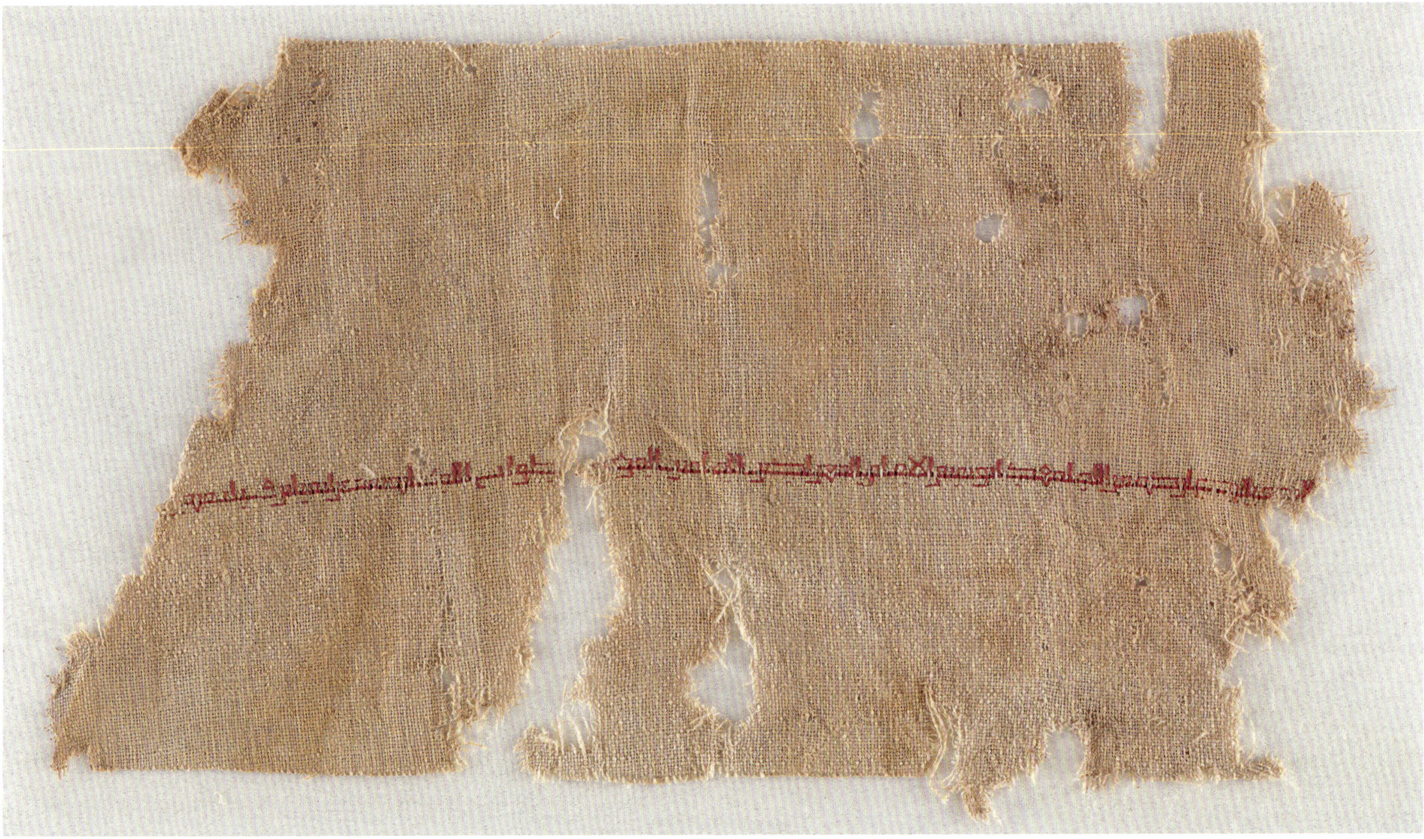

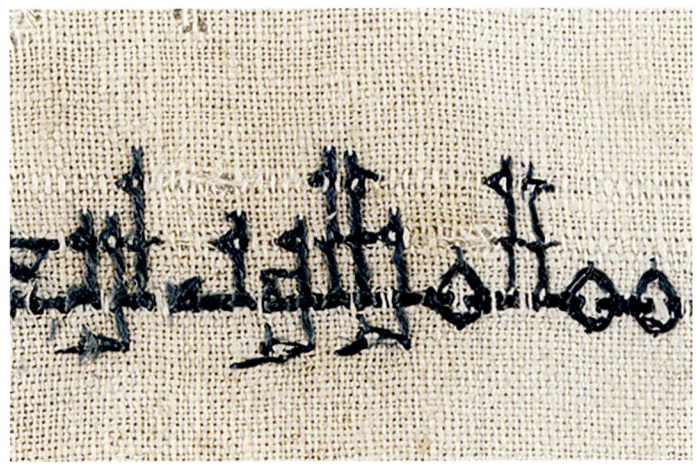

3.29   *Tiraz* fragment from the reign of the Fatimid caliph al-Muʿizz (d. 975), dated 360 AH / 971 CE, Misr al-Fustat, Egypt. Linen (plain weave), embroidered in silk in back stitch, width 14 cm. Textile Museum, Washington, DC, Acquired by George Hewitt Myers, 1931, inv. no. 73.30.

3.30   Detail of a fragment of linen *dabiqi* plain-weave fabric, with an inscription embroidered in silk in couching and chain stitch, Egypt, late 10th century CE, cat. no. 120.

nevertheless the overwhelming presence of tapestry-woven inscriptions under the Fatimids begs for an explanation.

TAPESTRY

While Bellinger stressed the foreign contribution of imported workmen in Egypt, she barely considered what happened to the traditional Egyptian technique of tapestry weaving, which had been employed by local Copts for centuries before Islam. The question that requires an answer is: given the impact of foreign craftsmen, what happened to the Coptic traditions in the early Islamic period? The question is significant, as several early Islamic sources indicate that the main workforce in the Delta region were Copts. In his geographical dictionary, Yaqut, relying on an earlier source, mentions, for example: 'One of the curious things about Damietta and Tinnis is that the weavers in them who make these fine garments are Copts of the lowest, humblest, and meanest of people as regards food and drink.'[208]

Egyptian tapestry weaving was a craft that developed out of using wool. Wool is not well suited for embroidery on linen, since its fibres are not homogeneous and catch easily on the woody surface of linen fibres. By working wool yarn into the ground fabric as a weft, some of these problems could be overcome. Nevertheless, two fundamental challenges existed for weavers working with wool tapestry: how to accommodate the bulkiness of the wool yarns and how to lock the tapestry-woven areas into the ground fabric so that these would not loosen up, resulting in possible loss of fabric or the shifting of decorated sections. Bellinger showed that wool tapestry was woven on paired warps, thus reducing the number of times the wool weft had to pass between the warps.[209] This made it easier for the weaver, and also eased internal tension between the tapestry-woven area and the ground fabric. Wool tapestry on paired warps can be found on at least two *tiraz* textiles, both dating from late Umayyad or early Abbasid times.[210] The second challenge of locking the tapestried area into the ground fabric could be addressed in two ways. The ground fabric weft could be compressed and beaten together so closely that the tapestry could not move out of place. Or the tapestry could be woven on paired warps that had been crossed in order to lock into place the inserted wool wefts. This way the tapestried area had more support and the demarcation between tapestry and base fabric

3.31a, b   Details of fragments of tapestry weave, with the weft threads of the linen ground fabric compressed and beaten together closely, in combination with crossed and paired warps, to fix the position of the tapestry in place; (a) cat. no. 60, Bahnasa(?), Egypt, 9th–10th century CE; (b) cat. no. 187, Egypt, 11th–12th century CE.

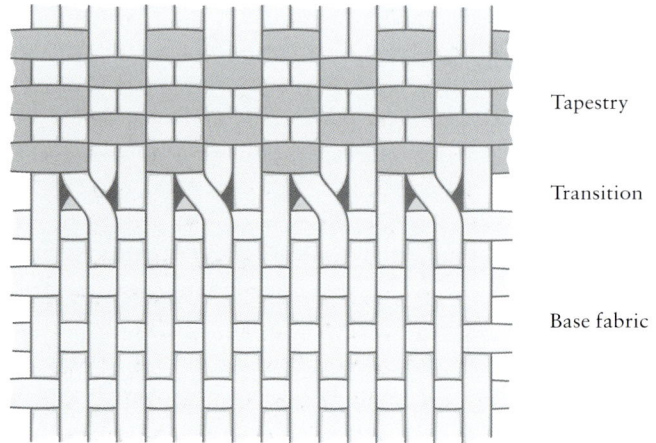

Tapestry

Transition

Base fabric

3.32a, b   Details of fragments of tapestry weave with slit and toothed coloured areas: (a) cat. no. 75, Fayyum, Egypt, late 9th to 11th century CE; (b) cat. no. 59, Qays(?), Egypt, 8th–9th century CE.

3.33a, b   Details of tapestry inscriptions with letter stems woven on only two warps and wrapped in silk yarn: (a) cat. no. 155, Egypt, 11th century CE; (b) cat. no. 150, Egypt, 1036–94 CE.

was strengthened and less flexible. This was particulary important in the case of a sheer base fabcric. While the first solution was more suited to uneven decoration, such as an inscription, the second was more suited to areas of decoration with a border running parallel to the wefts of the ground fabric. In some textiles both techniques are found simultaneously (fig. 3.31a, b). The first major study dedicated to this technique was undertaken by Daniël de Jonghe and Marcel Tavernier, who showed that the pairing and crossing of warps was a technique found in a large number of pre-Islamic Coptic tapestries. A second shed rod was inserted into the loom so that it was possible to change the sequence of the warp threads.[211] Another way of locking different colour areas into place

in tapestry weave was to build them up in a stepped or diagonal manner that resulted in demarcations between differently coloured areas that appear slit and toothed, the slits referring to gaps left between two adjacent blocks of colour. (fig. 3.32a, b).

Considering the pre-Islamic Coptic origins of the technique of pairing and crossing warps, its presence in the earliest Islamic textiles from Egypt is significant. It indicates that the weavers must have been Copts. This is easily understandable, given the continuity in the medium in which they were working – wool tapestry – before and after the birth of Islam. But what happened to Coptic techniques when silk, a foreign material, was introduced to Egypt?

3.34   Detail of a fragment of tapestry-woven inscription, stabilized by additional wefts of the same material as the base fabric (linen) woven in to support the letters, cat. 124, Egypt, 975–96 CE.

3.35a, b   Details of tapestry-woven inscriptions, having the letter stems tied to the background of the tapestry band: (a) cat. no. 160, Egypt, 11th century CE; (b) cat. no. 136, Egypt, late 10th to 11th century CE.

Bellinger suggests that there was a certain degree of continuity. While there seems to be little occurrence of crossed warps, the use of paired warps continued in some workshops. Bellinger mentioned that Misr al-Fustat, Damietta and Tuna still used paired warps occasionally, whereas Bura, Shata and Tinnis produced tapestry only on single warps.[212] Although the use of paired warps in silk tapestry can be understood as a sign of the continuity of Coptic craftsmanship, the de facto disappearance from silk tapestry of the technique of crossing warps might mean that traditional techniques were adapted to new materials, resulting in the change of craft.

Many inscriptions woven in silk were executed on counted warps. Unlike a horizontal band, which had a straight border between tapestry and ground fabric, an inscription contained a large number of letter stems protruding upwards from the horizontal baseline right into the ground fabric, causing potential weakness and the challenge of linking tapestry and ground fabric together. In small inscriptions this was less of a problem. These were often woven on only two warps, so that the silk yarn was wrapped around the thin letter stems, resulting in a small slit between the stem and the surrounding ground fabric (fig. 3.33a, b). In order to stabilize the area around the inscription, wefts of the same material as the base fabric were often woven in more densely (fig. 3.34). Another technique used for small inscriptions to link the tapestry-woven letter stems to the base fabric for greater stability was to tie the yarns used for the tapestry weave to the base fabric. This can be illustrated particularly well by Fatimid *tiraz* textiles in the name of al-Zahir.[213] Examples in The al-Sabah Collection show a similar technique (fig. 3.35a, b). Here, little knots made in the weaving process secure the stems to the background of the band; each little knot is made when part of the stem is finished and then carries over to the next letter stem. In larger inscriptions the slits between stems and ground fabric were problematic, since in some inscriptions the stems, and consequently the slits, could be several centimetres high. The stability of the inscription and the ground fabric would have been weakened considerably by the pull exerted by the letter stems.

While crossed and paired warps were suitable for even and horizontal bands, they were not really very practical for inscriptions that had more vertical than horizontal edges. The problem of supporting the stems of a large inscription was solved by pulling out a certain

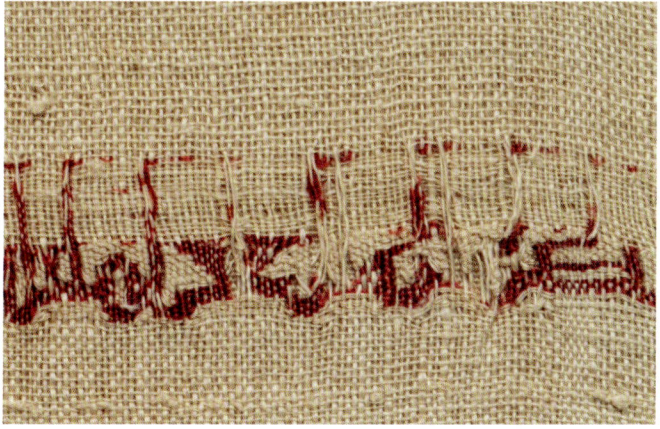

3.36a, b   Details of tapestry-woven inscriptions, having the upper letter stems 'floating' on the base fabric: (a) cat. no. 39, Egypt, 10th century CE; (b) cat. no. 130, Egypt, late 10th to 11th century CE.

number of warps for all letters above the baseline of the inscription and weaving the tapestry on those isolated warps. Behind these isolated warps, the weaving of wefts into the ground fabric continued, whereas spaces between the low letter stems were often filled out with supplementary wefts. The letter stems above the baseline of the inscription then had a backing of floating wefts (fig. 3.36a, b).[214] The textile conservator Mary Ballard observed that among twelve textiles in the Detroit Institute of Arts that had tapestry-woven inscriptions in this technique, there were items where the slit was closed with a finishing back stitch, predominantly on very tall letter stems.[215] The weaving of floating wefts behind the tapestry-woven area also had its roots in Coptic traditions. The same technique can be found in the woven decoration of a number of Coptic textiles, including at least two tunics dating from the third to seventh

centuries (for a similar example see fig. 3.37).[216] From a technological point of view, this suggests that Copts continued to be heavily involved in the textile industry and that they adapted to new materials and subjects, as the examples clearly show.

Although not much research has been conducted on the nature of the looms used to weave *tiraz* textiles, the fact that the textiles exhibit a certain continuity of Coptic weaving techniques would suggest that the looms on which they were woven had been used since pre-Islamic times. Since tapestry weaving cannot be executed on a drawloom, the most likely type used by Coptic weavers were cloth-looms. Cloth-looms fall into two broad categories distinguished by the operation of the heddle, a device attached to every other warp thread, allowing the weaver to lift up the warps alternately in order to insert the weft. This motion can be conducted either by hand or mechanically. If it is conducted mechanically, the single hand-operated heddle is replaced by a pair of frame-heddles, one controlling the even-numbered, the other the odd-numbered warps, which are attached to a pair of foot-operated treadles.

In the absence of extant looms or their depictions, it is necessary to turn to surviving Coptic garments in order to reconstruct the way they were woven and what types of loom were used. A study of a selection of complete tunics found that they were all woven in one, so that they required minimal tailoring.[217] The tunics fell into two groups, according to how they were stitched together and the sleeves were attached. In one group, the garments were partitioned along the sleeves with a slit for the neck and the sides were stitched together; this shows that they were made on a wide warp set-up, allowing the full length of the tunic to be woven, including the front and back part of the garment with sleeves and collar. An example in an excellent state of preservation is in the Khalili Collection (fig. 3.38).[218] In the other group, the tunics were woven on a much smaller set-up of warps, about half the size of those used for the first group; here, the front and back of the garment were woven one above the other and needed partitioning on one side. The shoulder area and one side only had to be stitched together. Furthermore, the sleeves were woven separately and attached to the finished tunic. Owing to the use of a smaller warp set-up, this kind of tunic produced less wasted thread material. Whether or not these two groups correspond to a chronological development is not known.[219] It has been

3.37   Tunic with Dionysian ornament, probably Akhmim (formerly Panopolis), Egypt,
probably 5th century CE. Undyed linen, tapestry-woven wool decorations, 174.6 × 135 cm.
Metropolitan Museum of Art, New York, Gift of Edward S. Harkness, 1926, inv. no. 26.9.9.

suggested that they were woven on different looms: the
first group on vertical looms and the second on horizontal
foot-powered treadle-looms.[220]

    Although both types of loom function according to
the same basic principle, there are factors that distinguish
them markedly. Looms with a hand-operated heddle tend
to be positioned upright, so that the warp is positioned
vertically. The cloth can then be beaten downwards,

taking advantage of gravity. Since it is very likely that
Coptic looms developed out of those used in Pharaonic
Egypt, some very early representations of looms in
Pharaonic contexts can illustrate the techniques involved.
Wall-paintings in the Eighteenth Dynasty tombs of
Thot-nefer, Nefer-hotep and Nefer-rotep at Thebes
show that vertical looms consisted of rectangular frames
made of thick beams and were operated by craftsmen

3.38 Wool tunic, Upper Egypt, 8th–9th century CE.
Dark blue wool with ornament in wool tapestry
weave, 223 × 108 cm. Nasser D. Khalili Collection,
inv. no. TXT 1.

seated on backless stools (fig. 3.39).[221] A representation of a loom in a pre-Dynastic and Middle Kingdom model of a weaver's workshop from the tomb of Nehen Kwetre at Thebes illustrates the problems involved in weaving horizontally, albeit in this case without a foot-operated treadle (fig. 3.40).[222] The model comprises a loom placed horizontally on the ground and operated by two weavers: one inserts the weft, the other beats the weft into the

3.41   Detail of a fragment of wool fabric with a weftless band between the fringe and tapestry-woven decorative band, Egypt, 10th–13th century CE, cat. no. 90.

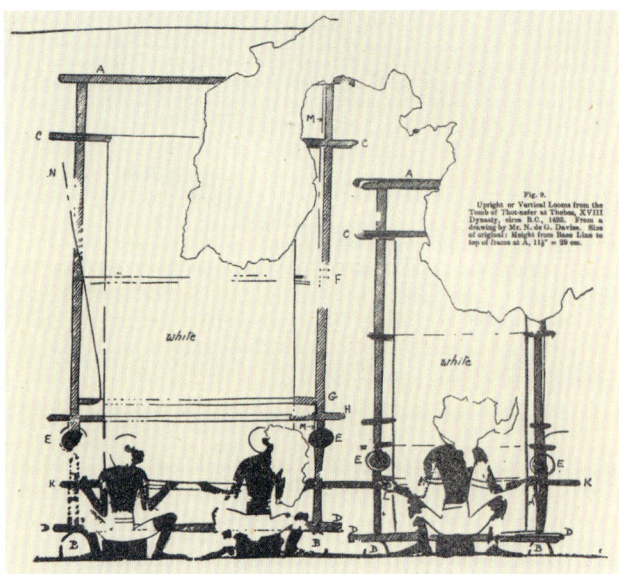

3.39   Wall-painting of a weavers' workshop, tomb of Thot-nefer, Thebes, XVIII Dynasty. c. 1425 BCE. Reproduced from Roth H. Ling, *Ancient Egyptian and Greek Looms*, Halifax, 1913, p. 10, fig. 9.

3.40   Model of a weavers' workshop, tomb of Meketre, tomb TT280, Thebes, Middle Kingdom, XII Dynasty, c. 1981–1975 BCE. Wood, plaster, pigments, c. 56 × 36 cm. Egyptian Museum, Cairo.

warp. To beat in the weft required some force because of the physically difficult motion of the horizontal heddle.[223] Vertical looms could be operated by one weaver alone. It has been suggested that with vertical looms, cloth widths of two metres or more could be achieved, and lengthwise rotatable cloth-beams provided the facility to weave great lengths, as indicated by a number of exceptionally long specimens of Pharaonic linen cloth.[224]

We can only speculate what types of cloth-looms Coptic weavers used in the early Islamic period to weave *tiraz* textiles. It is perfectly possible that both vertical and horizontal looms were common. But some of the technicalities of weaving an inscription, as described above, would perhaps point more towards the vertical loom than the horizontal, in the context of *tiraz* textiles. The counting of warps for the inscriptions may be easier on a vertical set-up, as well as the segregation of warps for the shafts of large inscriptions. Several full widths of *tiraz* textile cloths have survived, including a very small number of complete lengths.[225] Although the widths of these textiles can vary immensely, there are some that are close to the dimensions of tunics that were woven on a vertical loom.[226] Many of these textiles are characterized by the presence of a 'weftless' band between the fringe and the tapestry-woven decorative bands, probably caused when the ends of the warps were wound around the two rotatable upper and lower beams of the loom.[227] These beams held the warps in place and allowed the weaver to roll up the finished portions of the fabric. In

3.42a–c   Details of a fragment of tapestry-woven band with an inscription having at least one line woven upside down, the letter stems woven first, Damietta, Egypt, 1012–13 CE, cat. no. 128.

some cloths, supplementary silk wefts were inserted into these bands after the fabric was woven, in order to fill the void (fig. 3.41). In most textile fragments the baselines of inscriptions face away from these bands, suggesting that in a piece with inscriptions at either end of the cloth at least one inscription was woven upside down, implying that the letter shafts were woven first. The same applies to textiles with confronted inscriptions at either end (fig. 3.42a–c).

A very striking fragment of a textile made in the name of the Fatimid caliph al-Hakim (r. 996–1021) at the

Benaki Museum in Athens gives a unique insight into the habit of weaving upside down (fig. 3.43).[228] It comprises a relatively small inscription band, in which the weaver suddenly changed the style, layout and direction of the inscription. At the beginning of the tapestry-woven band the inscription is upside down in relationship to the decorative band with bird cartouches above, comprising thin letters. It then changes abruptly to one flipped facing the right way up with very bold letters and a different decorative band above. Because the change in the style of

3.43   *Tiraz* fragment, Egypt, 996–1021 CE. Silk tapestry on linen. Benaki Museum, Athens, inv. no. 15190.

the band left a vertical break, the inscription must have been woven sideways, from right to left.

Another variation in weaving an inscription is documented by the inscriptions contained in the borders of the figural roundels of the 'Veil of St Anne' (see fig. 1.49). Its warps represent the long side of the rectangle, while the wefts constitute the short side. The radiating inscriptions contained in the borders of the roundels of the central decorative band show very clearly that an inscription did not need to be upright to be woven and could even be woven with the letter stems at an angle. The same applies to the figural decoration contained in the roundels: this too was woven on its side. These details indicate that weavers were not aware of the content of the inscriptions they wove and that in fact they had to remember only the sequence of shapes within an inscription or a decorative pattern, a matter facilitated by working on counted warps.

THE CHRONOLOGY AND GEOGRAPHY OF TECHNIQUES

Extant *tiraz* fragments show that tapestry weaving was exercised throughout the Umayyad, Abbasid and Fatimid periods, a finding hardly surprising if one considers that tapestry was an indigenous Egyptian technique. There seems, however, to be a marked difference in the occurrence of wool and silk tapestry in *tiraz* textiles, wool tapestry being far less common.[229] Silk tapestry, on the other hand, is documented as early as the reign of the Abbasid caliphs Harun al-Rashid (r. 786–809) and his

son al-Amin (r. 809–13).[230] A fragment in The al-Sabah Collection from Harun's reign comprises an inscription in silk satin stitch accompanied by a decorative band tapestry-woven in silk (cat. no. 1). Although evidence is patchy until the early tenth century, from the reign of al-Muqtadir (r. 908–32) onwards an almost continuous sequence of tapestry-woven specimens exists until the end of the Fatimid period (an example dated to 912–13 during the reign of al-Muqtadir is cat. no. 10).

The chronology of silk embroidery in Egypt provides a significant contrast to the tapestry-woven examples.[231] The earliest extant silk-embroidered *tiraz* textile from Egypt is dated 831–32.[232] From the decade between 854 and 864 an almost continuous sequence can be documented until the end of Abbasid rule in Egypt, when it seems to come to a virtual halt.[233] The abundance of Abbasid embroidered *tiraz* textiles from then on contrasts starkly with the scarcity of Fatimid examples: only twelve extant specimens have been documented.[234] Nevertheless, they cover the reigns of the first three Fatimid caliphs to reign over Egypt, al-Muʿizz (r. 953–75), al-ʿAziz (r. 975–96) and al-Hakim (r. 996–1021).

Given the impact that silk embroidery was supposed to have made on the Egyptian textile industry by introducing a new material by means of a new technique, it is surprising to find that the earliest silk-embroidered textile dates only from 831–32, a good twenty or thirty years after the earliest silk tapestry was made in Egypt. The chronological problem can be resolved by turning to *tiraz* textiles from the eastern provinces of the Abbasid empire, which were, after all, believed to have been the inspiration for the introduction of embroidery into Egypt. The earliest example, a Yemeni *ikat*, is dated 815–16, which conforms roughly with the period from which the earliest silk tapestries date.[235] Although this item is embroidered in cotton on a cotton ground fabric, rather than in silk, it marks the early arrival of eastern *tiraz* textiles in Egypt. Imports must undoubtedly also have included silk embroidery. This would suggest that silk embroidery was introduced into Egypt perhaps in the second half of the eighth century. It must have had a very prompt impact on tapestry weaving, to judge from the fragments from Harun al-Rashid's and al-Amin's reigns. The existence of these items would suggest that tapestry weaving with silk did not develop gradually; rather, the craftsmen in Egypt took on the challenge of the new silk medium almost instantly.

There is enough evidence to suggest that until the end of the Abbasid period, silk tapestry and embroidery were used concurrently. Although caliphal embroidered *tiraz* textiles from the Fatimid period may tempt one to conclude that tapestry eventually replaced embroidery, given that many more tapestry-woven examples have survived than embroidered ones, non-historical *tiraz* textiles provide evidence that embroidery continued to be practised widely into the later Fatimid period.[236]

The demographic and economic environment in the Delta region has been sketched by Maurice Lombard. Using medieval texts, he delineates the Delta as highly populated, specialized solely in textile manufacture, and dependent on outside supplies of nourishment; its economic success was upheld by its geographic location, close to the supplies of raw flax from the fields, easy access to the Mediterranean and canal links to the capital Cairo and its markets.[237] The population consisted almost exclusively of Copts, as is indicated by one of the earliest historical sources available, an account by the patriarch Dionysus of Tell-Mahrè who accompanied the caliph al-Ma'mun (r. 813–33) in the early ninth century in order to bring under control a Coptic revolt against high taxes: he estimated the population of Tinnis at 30,000 Copts.[238] Under these circumstances the Abbasids must have had to rely on Coptic expertise: even if they moved Iraqi craftsmen to Egypt, the physical presence of these workers must have been minimal. At the same time the Abbasids had a very tight financial grip on the local population. This was ensured by the direct appointment of governors and other high officers from Baghdad, who were directly responsible to the caliphal administration.[239] Against this background, it is likely that the Abbasid central administration also exercised a high level of control over the textiles produced for the court in Egypt and sought ways to utilize the expertise of the local workforce to suit their own tastes.

The establishment of the Tulunids in Egypt began a process of independence for Egypt's economy from central Abbasid hegemony, a development that came to fruition under the Fatimids. Egypt became an important centre for international trade, linking the Mediterranean with the Indian Ocean region. The textile industry played a key part in this process, particularly in the Delta region, with its access to established sea routes and inland waterways. The technological changes brought by the Abbasids from the east of their empire left a long-lasting legacy well into the Fatimid period and beyond. It is clear that Copts made a significant contribution to the Egyptian textile industry. Without the ability of Coptic weavers to react to new challenges, the expansion of the industry from the early Islamic period onwards would not have been possible.

CATALOGUE

NOTE ON THE HISTORY
OF THE COLLECTION

Some of the textiles presented here were acquired sporadically by The al-Sabah Collection early on in its formation, perhaps in the late 1970s or early 1980s – a time when this material was no longer as sought after as it had been in the first half of the twentieth century. However, the bulk of the collection was added as a body from the antiquarian book dealer H.P. Kraus in New York.

Hans Peter Kraus (12 October 1907 – 1 November 1988), known professionally as H.P. Kraus, was born in Vienna, where he trained as a librarian and, after having worked with the publishers R. Lechner in Berlin and Ernst Wasmuth in Berlin, took up residence. He started his own antiquarian business in 1932. In 1939 he and his mother fled from the Nazi occupation of Austria and emigrated to the United States. In New York, Kraus founded a rare-book dealership that specialised in the acquisition and resale of entire collections, but he also dealt in important medieval manuscripts and early modern incunables.[1] His professional focus was firmly on the arts of the western European book, and the Islamic world was marginal to his illustrious career. Kraus published regular catalogues of his stock, which became reference works in their own right.[2] In 1972 the German art historian Ernst J. Grube published in New York a catalogue of Persian paintings that Kraus had acquired in the sale of Hagop Kevorkian's collection at Sotheby's in 1967.[3] Prompted to explain why he had taken on Persian arts, Kraus explained that he delighted in variety.[4] Perhaps this is what brought him to consider what would have seemed to him the rather obscure group of inscribed and decorated archaeological *tiraz* textiles that form the basis of this book.

Kraus's company prepared a typescript catalogue of his collection containing readings of the historical inscriptions, rudimentary technical data and short discussions providing context (see opposite). This catalogue was far less opulent than his usual publications and consisted of photocopied pages with images inserted into the text manually, with the occasional image photocopied in colour and later pasted in. The binding consisted of a hard board with green waxed linen. How many of these catalogues were produced is unknown.[5] Who undertook the task of reading and contextualizing the textiles is not clear. Given the nature of the material only a few individuals active at that time would have had the training and expertise to undertake this task. Richard Ettinghausen had worked on a catalogue of the *tiraz* textiles at Dumbarton Oaks that was never published. Before emigrating to the United States in the early 1930s, he had worked in Berlin with Ernst Kühnel, himself the undisputed authority on *tiraz* textiles. However, as Ettinghausen died in 1979, it is unlikely that he was involved in the work. Yet he must have known Kraus well, given their shared background of emigration. Ernst Grube, another of Kühnel's students, might also have worked on the material, given his earlier involvement with Kraus's company and his experience in reading inscriptions. Perhaps the most likely cataloguer, however, was Oleg Grabar, who had worked on inscriptions with historical data in his catalogue of Tulunid coinage from Egypt.[6] While Kraus's catalogue was generally well compiled, some of the inscriptions were not read correctly and references were rather generic, showing only a superficial knowledge of the subject. This would seem to indicate that whoever worked on the catalogue was not a specialist in the field of *tiraz* textiles, and familiar only with the general literature. But then the primary purpose of the catalogue was to serve as a sale catalogue and not as an academic reference book.

The collection sold by Kraus was one of the last to become available on the open market. In 1978, a much larger collection – about a thousand inscribed or decorated *tiraz* textiles from the collection of the American–Egyptian antiquities dealer Michel Abemayor – had been sold to the Royal Ontario Museum, Toronto. Abemayor had moved his stock to New York after the Egyptian revolution of 1952, led by Gamal Abdel Nasser. By that time, interest in *tiraz* textiles and decorated early Islamic textiles in general had waned and they were no

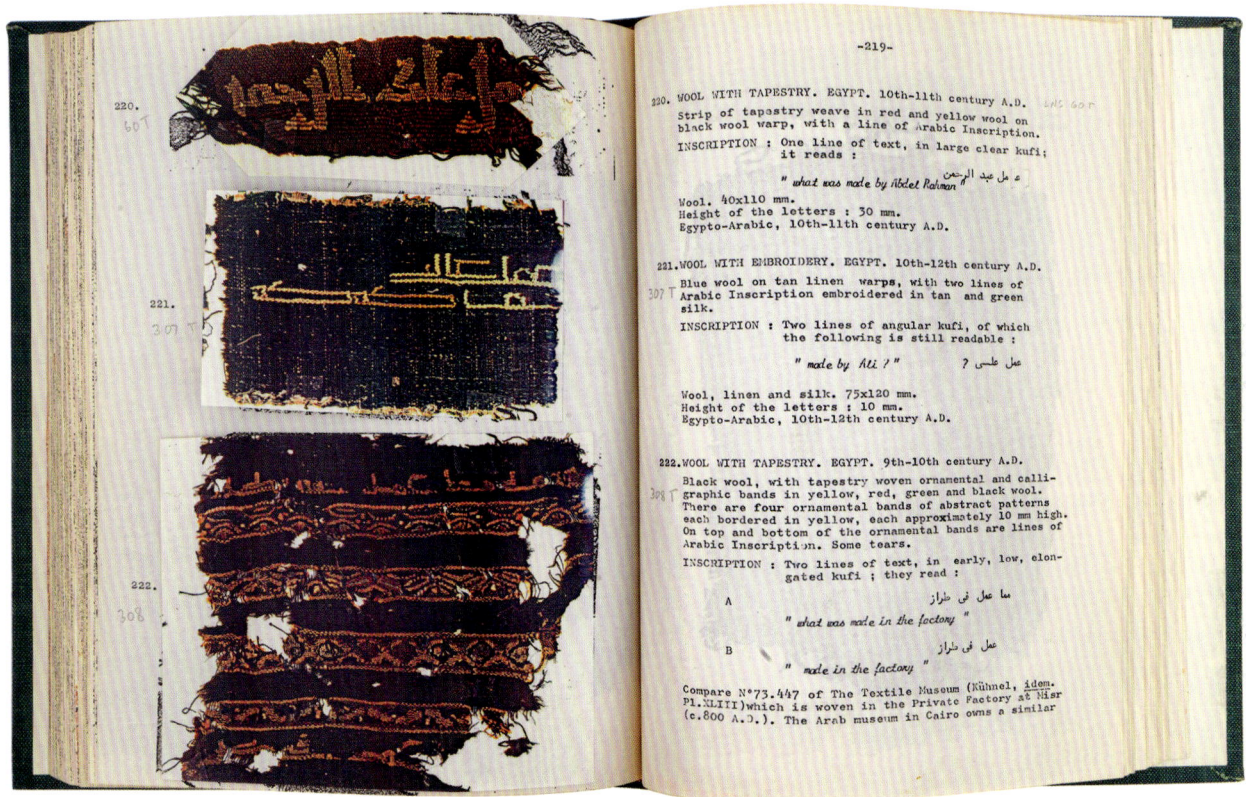

The typescript sale catalogue *Islamic Textiles*, prepared by H.P. Kraus, New York, n.d.

longer as popular with collectors and benefactors in the USA as they had been in the first half of the century.[7] That might explain why these two large collections were still available in the late 1970s. The Abemayor Collection was acquired through a gift to the Royal Ontario Museum owing to the foresight of the textile curator Veronica Gervers, who, together with Lisa Golombek, published some of the most important pieces.[8] Until today much of this collection still remains unpublished.[9] It is, therefore, fortunate that the Kraus collection was acquired by The al-Sabah Collection in its entirety, allowing for thorough study and its publication in the current volume.

NOTE ON THE CATALOGUE ENTRIES

ORGANIZATION

The 189 entries in the catalogue cover the *tiraz* textiles in The al-Sabah Collection in Kuwait. (For the definition of *tiraz* adopted here, see chapter 2, pp. 53–59.) While the overwhelming majority of surviving *tiraz* textiles were made and found in Egypt (the urban centres of Lower Egypt and the Nile Delta, the urban centres of the Nile Valley and Upper Egypt, the Fayyum) and date from the Umayyad, Abbasid and Fatimid dynasties (661–1171 CE), a much smaller group represents non-Egyptian material. Other regions or textile cultures represented or discussed here are those of Iraq, Khurasan, Yemen, Palestine and the Indian Subcontinent. It is for this reason that the secondary division within the catalogue is geographical.

The catalogue is organized in two main parts: Part I covers textiles produced under or during the Abbasid caliphate and Part II those produced in Egypt under the Fatimid caliphs. Part I is further subdivided into eight sections, according to the regions and cultures in which the textiles originated. Within each section the texts are ordered chronologically and grouped by dynasty.

Each entry has an illustration of the textile, and top matter giving a description of its appearance, details of the materials and techniques used in the making of the piece, and a transcription and translation of the inscription (if there is one); provenance, and inventory number in The al-Sabah Collection are also given. Many entries have a list of 'related works' (see below) and most have a commentary discussing points of interest about the subject of the entry and its connection with the related works.

TOP MATTER

HEADWORD

The headword consists of a brief definition of the item and its origins – the name and regnal dates of the caliph under which it was manufactured if they can be established, or a more general reference to the caliphate if nothing more exact is possible. There follows a statement of the place of origin and the date of manufacture (sometimes a year,

sometimes no more than a century or a span of centuries). Precise dates derive from the inscription and are given in the form 240 AH / 854–55 CE; in the headword (as elsewhere in the book), century dates are given according to the reckoning in the Common Era only.

DESCRIPTION

A prose description of the piece details its appearance, the materials, colours and techniques used to create it, the style of the inscription and the arrangement of the decorative elements.

MATERIALS

All the materials used in the textile (that is, both the ground fabric and the decoration) are listed in this section. It also names the type of weave and the technique(s) used in the decorative parts of the textile.

DIMENSIONS

The dimensions given are maxima (many of the items are of irregular shape); where the textile is in multiple pieces, these are identified, and the dimensions of each piece are given. The maximum height of the letters in the inscription follows; multiple dimensions are given where the piece has more than one register of inscription and the letter heights differ in each one.

GROUND FABRIC

The ground fabric is described in three sections. The first lists the material(s), the weave and the texture. For definitions of different types of fabric referred to in relation to texture (for example, *dabiqi* or *sharb*), see chapter 3, pp. 93–101. Three grades, expressed by numbers, have been devised to describe the quality: very good (1), good (2) and medium (3). For greater flexibility, nuances of quality within a main grade have been expressed by phrases such as 'good-very good' or 'medium-good'. These grades reflect a combination of qualitative factors, numerical and subjective, and are independent of the constraints of textile types. Because the different qualitative factors were not always equally balanced, the grades of quality represent a compromise.

The thread count represents the number of threads per cm for the warp and the weft of the ground fabric; the direction of twist is given for each. For an explanation of the direction of twist, see chapter 3, pp. 92–93, and fig. 3.7. Occasionally the number of threads is given per 0.5 cm, in which case that unit is named explicitly (for example, 'weft 8 per 0.5 cm S-spun' [cat. no. 181]).

The thread thickness in mm is given for the warp and weft of the ground fabric, and the tightness of the twist (see the description of the thread count above) is defined as 'tight', 'medium', or 'loose'.

DECORATION

The decoration of the textile may generally be executed in either tapestry or embroidery (there are instances where a textile comprises both tapestry-woven and embroidered decoration); each of these techniques has its own heading.

The materials and techniques and the colours of the threads used for the production of the tapestry-woven parts of the textile are listed. Where relevant the following details are given: the number of picks per cm (the number of threads that are inserted into the warp to create a design) and the direction of twist (see the description of the thread count above), the thickness of the thread and the tightness of the twist (see the description of the thread thickness above). For further description of the technicalities of tapestry weaving see chapter 3, pp. 112–20, and figs 3.31–3.36)

The materials and techniques and the colours of the threads used for embroidery are listed, including (where relevant) the stitches and what elements they are used for.

PROVENANCE

Most of the textiles were formerly in the H.P. Kraus collection, which is explicitly named, together with the number given to the piece in the typescript sale catalogue (Kraus n.d.; see page 124 for further information about the collection).

INVENTORY NUMBER

The inventory number in The al-Sabah Collection ends the top matter. Where the item is in multiple pieces, the number may have a suffix in lower-case letters: in such cases, 'a' in the inventory number corresponds to 'piece (a)' in the catalogue entry.

RELATED WORKS

Related works are textiles that can be compared to a textile in The al-Sabah Collection historically or formally and attempt to provide context. They can provide supplementary examples from the same reign of a caliph identified in an inscription, or an administrator mentioned, or a location or workshop. They can also serve to support an attribution where a reading is inconclusive or an inscription is non-historical based on comparison with the known corpus of Egyptian and non-Egyptian *tiraz* textiles. Related works can also provide context for form and style with regard to inscriptions and decoration.

The lists of related works can be found at the end of the catalogue, while each catalogue entry gives the exact location of the related works for that entry at the end of the top matter. For each related work, the location and inventory number are given, followed by its publication history. Where the administrative data – date and place of manufacture and the name and title(s) of the authorizing officer – are known from an inscription on the textile, they are listed in parentheses; the maximum letter height of the inscriptions is supplied where it is known and relevant to provide context for the attribution. Where relevant, the absence of such data is explicitly mentioned. A 'non-historical' inscription is one that does not employ a dated and localized caliphal protocol.

INSCRIPTION

Transcription

Reading and transcribing *tiraz* textile inscriptions is not easy. Various factors come into play: condition; epigraphic style of script and its general legibility; mistakes and omissions. Often an inscription represents a combination of these factors and hence the reader has to navigate content based on experience and prior knowledge of content found in related examples. While every attempt has been made here to read and transcribe the Arabic text as represented on the textile, there are cases where the wording of inscriptions could not be deciphered. Such cases are indicated explicitly. Most of the inscriptions are incomplete, because they have lost parts of the text due to the fact that the fabrics into which they were embroidered or woven were removed from the larger pieces of cloth to which they once belonged. Furthermore, all the textiles discussed here were part of funerary outfits and almost all comprise signs of decomposition caused in burial.

Where text could be read a system of symbols is used to indicate where part of an inscription is missing or where it could not be read. While *tiraz* inscriptions were planned, both in terms of content and form, they often contain mistakes, usually due to human error on the part of the craftspeople executing them. Spelling mistakes are generally common, but sometimes names or titles are entirely missing or only represented in part, sometimes the order is confused. The same applies to benedictory and Quranic phrases, as well as administrative content. The reading of the inscriptions reflects loss, emissions or mistakes and uses the following symbols within the transcriptions and translations:

[...] = there is a lacuna in the text / inscription text is lost; sometimes a word or phrase is included within a square bracket to complete a reading where it is clear what should follow

(...) = there is text but it is indecipherable; sometimes a word or phrase is included within a bracket to suggest a likely reading

Sic or ! (or a combination) = indicates a mistake, an unusual word or a single letter that deviates from the norm, where the text can be clearly read (that is, there is no question of possible misreading of unclear text)

? = indicates an unkown, sometimes within brackets '(...)' or after a word or phrase; this can be a whole part of an inscription, or sometimes only a word where '?' indicates a tentative suggested reading

Translation
The transcribed Arabic text is translated into English. While the Arabic texts run continuously, in the translation different parts of an inscription (the Basmalla, the *du'a*, the caliphal names and titles *ism*, *kunya* and *laqab*) and administrative information are separated by colons and within by commas. Capitalization occurs for the name and attributes of God, the caliphs' or administrators' names and titles, and a capitalised word introduces each segment separated by a colon. The translations follow a simplified system to indicate likely or tentative suggested readings with '[...]' or '(...)' used when whole parts of text are missing or undecipherable. They have mostly been omitted to cut into complete words to make the reading of the translation easier for the non-specialist and non-Arabic speaker.

Commentary
In the commentary, the epigraphic style of Arabic inscriptions here is in most cases referred to as 'Kufic', commonly understood and used to denote a variety of angular types of script, primarily found in Quranic or monumental inscriptions from the beginning of the Islamic era in the seventh up to the eleventh century, or 'Naskh', commonly understood as a cursive script which began replacing 'Kufic' from the eleventh century onwards. 'Pseudo-epigraphic' refers to inscriptions which are meaningless in terms of content, illegible and mimic readable inscriptions in style or aesthetic. References to inscriptions may include the term 'confronted', which means that an entire line, words or a word in the inscription are arranged facing each other horizontally.

PART I
THE ABBASID CALIPHATE

1

URBAN CENTRES OF
LOWER EGYPT AND THE NILE DELTA

Textile workshops in the Delta were located in two urban agglomerations consisting of a main centre and a number of satellite locations: Tinnis and Tuna in one, and Damietta, Shata, Bura and Dabiq in the other.[1] Both were located in and around the Buhayrat al-Manzala, a large lagoon on the eastern side of the Nile Delta. While Tinnis and Tuna were located on two islands within the lagoon, Damietta and its conurbation were situated on its western shore, possibly on small islands or peninsulas. Alexandria, though it was on the easternmost border of the Delta, was, strictly speaking, not a Delta location, since it differed considerably in socio-economic terms from the isolated industrial and trade centres Tinnis and Damietta (see map, pp. 12–13), which were entirely dependent on the outside world for survival, and existed only for the sake of textile production. In contrast, Alexandria was an ancient city with a long history, and had an urban structure comparable with that of Misr al-Fustat, a centre with a port to which goods were brought from far afield to be traded all over the Mediterranean.

Although we have a good idea of Alexandria's importance from historical accounts, only fourteen textiles that were made there are known today.[2] The Egyptian textile historian M.A.A. Marzouk has shown that Alexandria was an active textile production centre from pre-Islamic times up to the Mamluk period.[3] Misr al-Fustat's position on the southernmost tip of the Delta made it the perfect location for trade with the Delta on the one hand, and the Fayyum and Upper Egypt on the other, perhaps also the ports on the Red Sea. It was connected to the agglomerations of Tinnis and Damietta by the branches of the Nile and canals, which facilitated the transportation of goods in both directions, and it was reachable from Upper Egypt on the Nile.[4] South of Misr al-Fustat several important trade and production centres flourished along the Nile – the Fayyum oasis, and in Upper Egypt Bahnasa, Qays and Ashmunayn – all of which are well documented in the historical literature and surviving examples of inscribed textiles. However, textiles from Misr al-Fustat and the Delta provide a more chronologically balanced picture, documenting continuous production from Umayyad and early Abbasid times up to at least the later Fatimid periods.[5]

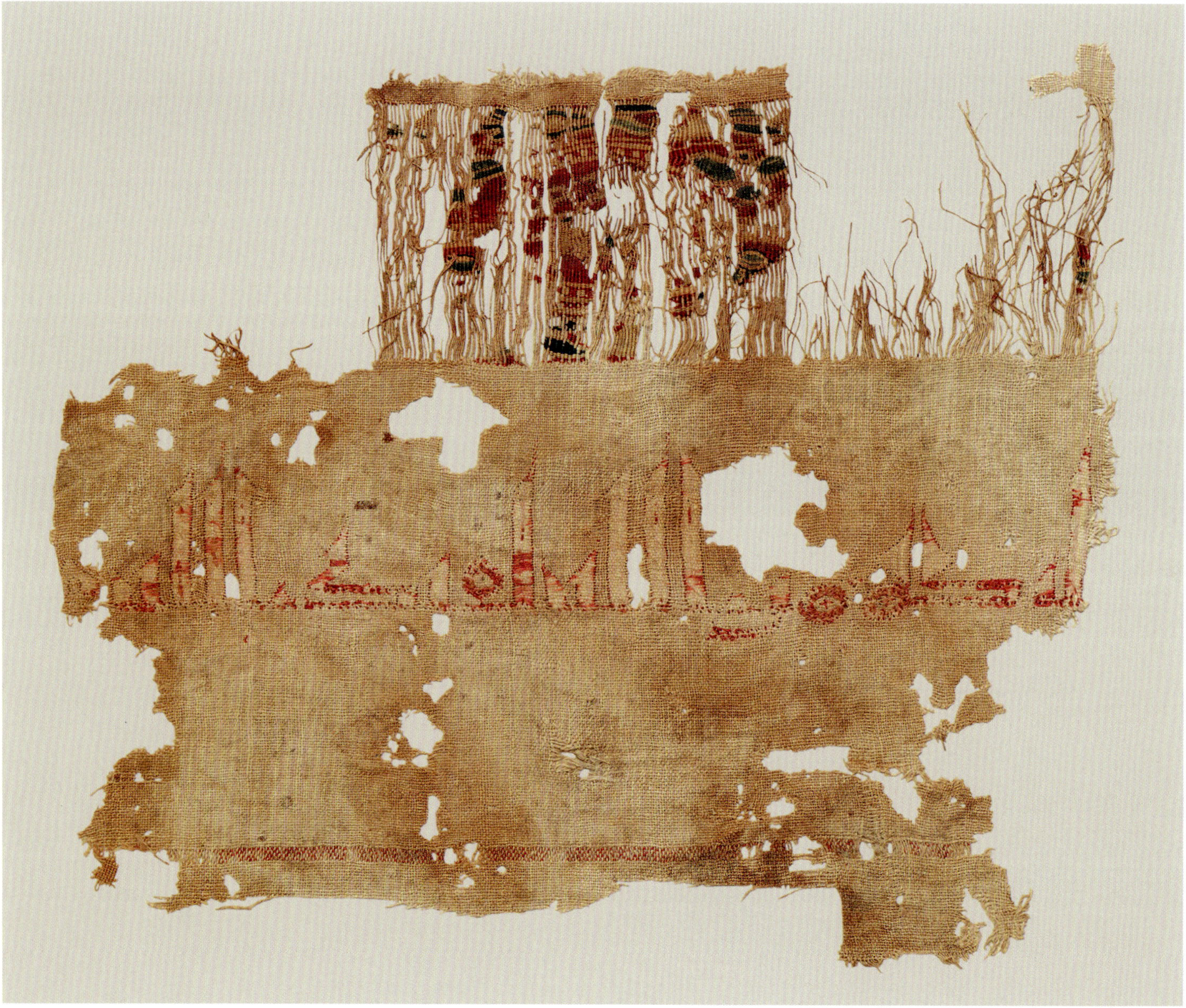

TEXTILES WITH CALIPHAL INSCRIPTIONS

Cat. 1 *TIRAZ* FRAGMENT FROM THE REIGN OF THE ABBASID CALIPH HARUN AL-RASHID (r. 786–809)

Egypt, 8th to 9th century CE

Description: Fragment of undyed linen with a Kufic inscription embroidered in satin and chain stitch in red silk, accompanied by a decorative band tapestry-woven in red, green, blue, ochre and yellow silk (4.5 cm), which once comprised a sequence of medallions with a beaded border containing a zoomorphic figure, probably a quadruped.

Materials: linen and silk: plain weave and embroidery

Dimensions: h. 14.5 cm, w. 18.2 cm; max. letter height 3.7 cm

Ground fabric: linen warp and weft, undyed, balanced plain weave, tight texture (*dabiqi*); good quality (2)

Thread count: warp 25 Z-spun, weft 21 S-spun

Thread thickness: warp 0.3 mm tight twist, weft 0.3 mm tight twist

Tapestry: silk, dyed (red, green, blue, ochre, yellow); woven on paired and crossed warps

Embroidery: silk (red), satin stitch (hastae), chain stitch (baseline, terminals and rounded letters)

Provenance: Ex H.P. Kraus collection, no. 13

Inv. no. LNS 141 T

Related works: See page 500

Inscription: [...] [ب]ـركة من الله لعبد الله هـ[ـرون] [...]

[...] Blessing from God to the servant of God Harun [...]

This is a rare fragment of a textile that combines an embroidered caliphal inscription with a tapestry-woven decorative band. Both inscription and decorative band are in silk and the ground fabric is a linen plain weave, which indicates Egyptian manufacture. The inscription refers to the *ism* (given name) of the caliph introduced by the term *'abd Allah* ('servant of God'). The following letter could be *ha*. Therefore, the only possible *ism* would be, it seems, that of Harun al-Rashid, who is referred to as "abd Allah Harun amir al-mu'minin' in two *kiswa* inscriptions recorded by al-Maqrizi;[6] an extant example with a tapestry-woven inscription documenting both the caliph's *ism* and *laqab* is in the Museum für Islamische Kunst in Berlin (Related works 1).

The style of epigraphy seen here supports a late eighth-century date, as does the decorative band with its pearl-band border, which can be found in Egyptian wool textiles from that period. Significantly, a textile at the Textile Museum in Washington, DC, comprising an early, possibly ninth-century form of Kufic inscription, accompanied by two tapestry-woven bands similar to the one seen here, was made in a *tiraz al-khassa* workshop in Misr (Related works 2). A rare piece in an epigraphic style similar to the present one, also executed in satin stitch, comprising the beginning of the *basmallah*, is in the Keir Collection (Related works 3).

Examples of the combination of an embroidered inscription with a tapestry-woven decorative band can be found in several extant textiles. However, none of them compares with the present piece either in terms of material or content of inscription. The first is a linen ground fabric with the inscription and decorative band in wool, stating its manufacture in the *tiraz al-khassa* in Misr (Related works 4). On the basis of its epigraphic style it can be dated to the eighth century. The second is a *mulham* fabric in Cairo with an embroidered inscription stating its manufacture in Merw in 278 AH / 891–92 CE (Related works 5). The third is a cotton ground fabric with an embroidered inscription stating its manufacture in San'a' in 289 AH / 901–02 CE (Related works 6).

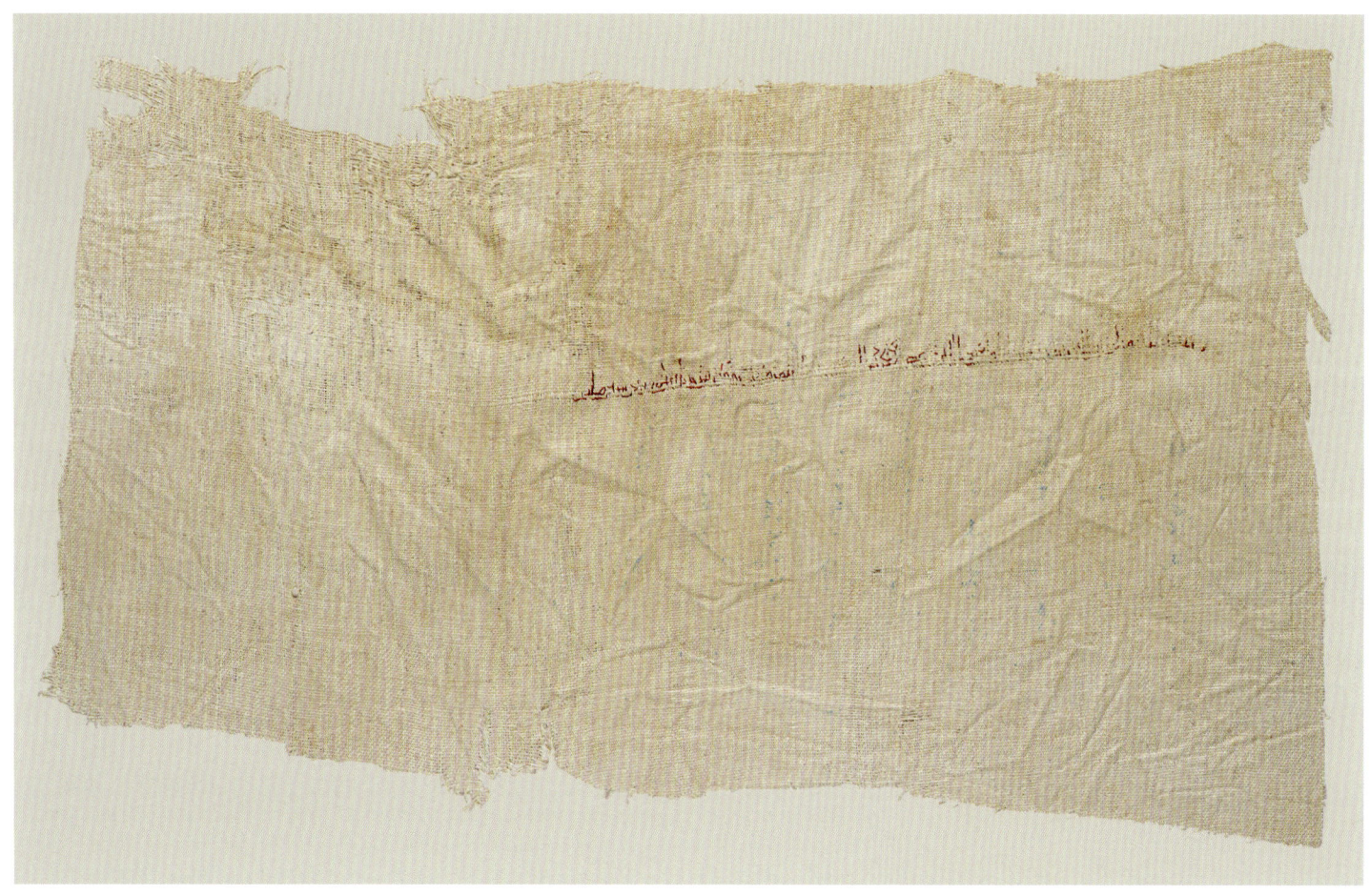

Cat. 2   *TIRAZ* FRAGMENT FROM
THE REIGN OF THE ABBASID
CALIPH AL-MUTAWAKKIL
(r. 847–61)
Egypt, 240 AH / 854–55 CE

Description: Fragment of undyed linen, roughly
rectangular, with one line of Kufic
inscription embroidered in red silk;
the inscription is small, rather thin
and coarse, and the letters have
horizontal tails.

Materials: linen and silk: plain weave
and embroidery

Dimensions: h. 21.5, w. 33.1 cm;
max. letter height 0.8 cm

Ground fabric: linen warp and weft, undyed,
predominant-warp plain weave,
tight texture (*dabiqi*); good–
medium quality (2–3)

Thread count: warp 22 S-spun, weft 15 S-spun

Thread thickness: warp 0.5 mm slight–medium twist;
weft 0.15–0.3 mm medium–tight
twist

Embroidery: silk, dyed (red), couching stitch

Provenance: Ex H.P. Kraus collection, no. 36

Inv. no. LNS 160 T

Related works: See page 500

Inscription: بسم الله الرحمن (الرحيم) (...) الله لعبد الله (...) بلله (...)مما عمل بسنة اربعين مئتان

In the name of God, the Merciful, [the Compassionate] (...) God to the servant of God (...) bi-llah (...) of what was made in the year two hundred and forty

Although the name of the caliph is no longer clearly readable, the date 240 AH / 854–55 CE places this item in the reign of the Abbasid caliph al-Mutawakkil (r. 847–61). Of the ten known *tiraz* fragments that have survived from his reign (for a number of these see the listing in cat. no. 3), one in the Textile Museum, Washington, DC (Related works 1), is very closely related to the present piece in terms of epigraphy and execution. Both inscriptions are executed in the same feeble stitch and are roughly comparable in proportions, the letters of the inscription in the Washington example being slightly larger (1.4 cm, compared with 0.8 cm). The Washington piece states its manufacture in Misr in the year 245 AH / 859–60 CE. Given that the two inscriptions are so similar, it is tempting to believe that this piece, too, was made there.

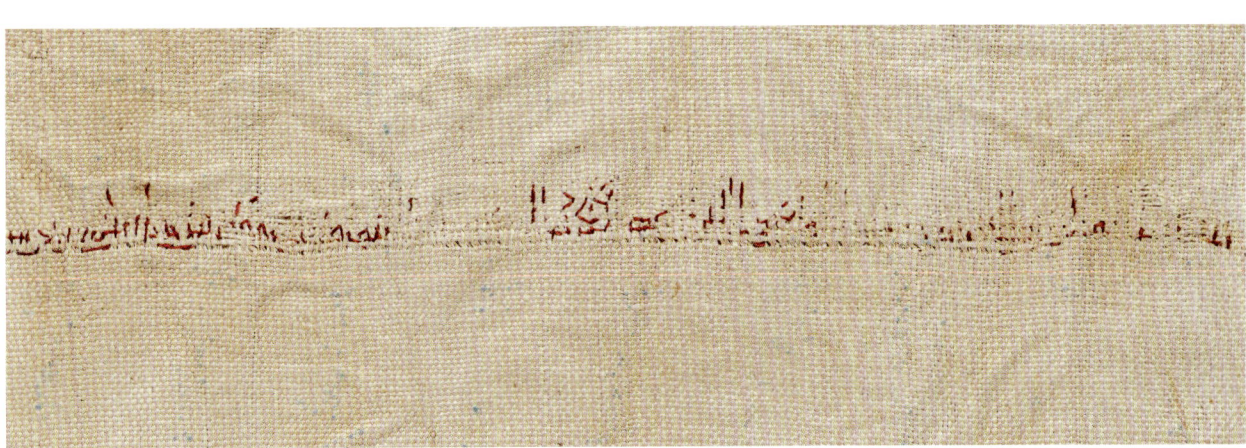

Cat. 3 *TIRAZ* FRAGMENT
ATTRIBUTED TO THE
REIGN OF THE ABBASID
CALIPH AL-MUTAWAKKIL
(r. 847–61)
Egypt, 9th century CE

Description: Fragment of undyed linen, roughly
rectangular, with one line of
Kufic inscription embroidered in
greenish-blue silk, with two plain
bands woven in brownish silk
below.

Materials: linen and silk: plain weave
and embroidery

Dimensions: h. 8.8, w. 13.6 cm;
max. letter height 1.3 cm

Ground fabric: linen, undyed, predominant-warp
plain weave, close weave (*dabiqi*);
good–medium quality (2–3)

Thread count: warp 23 S-spun, weft 15 S-spun

Thread thickness: warp 0.2–0.3 mm slight–medium
twist; weft 0.3 mm slight–medium
twist

Embroidery: silk (greenish-blue), flat stitch
(hastae), chain stitch (lower
terminals); two silk supplementary
weft float bands

Provenance: Ex H.P. Kraus collection, no. 35

Inv. no. LNS 159 T

Related works: See page 500

Inscription:

[...] [اصـ]ـير المؤمنين ايده الله مما عمل بالا سـ(كندرية) بط[راز] [...]

[...] [Comm]ander of the Faithful. May God strengthen him. Of what has been
ordered in Ale(xandria) at the ti[raz] [...]

The style of epigraphy seen here is reminiscent of that found in several *tiraz*
inscriptions from the reign of al-Mutawakkil (r. 847–61). Two very closely
related examples are in the Textile Museum, Washington, DC (Related works 1
and 2). They share with the present piece relatively short hastae, rounded lower
terminals and a fully developed *lam–alif*. Furthermore, they share identical
technical details. While the letters above the baseline are executed in flat stitch,
the lower terminals are executed in chain stitch. The inscription on the second
Washington piece states its place of production as Misr and its date as 240 AH
/ 854–55 CE; its ordering formula – 'mimma 'umila' ('of what was made') –
compares with that used in the present piece.

Although, generally, very few such early examples of *tiraz* inscriptions exist,
there are a number of other *tiraz* textiles extant from al-Mutawakkil's reign.
Not all of them have been published in photographic form, but those that have
show a variety of epigraphic styles that differ from this one. Related works 3
and 4 show a type that comprises a rather feeble line of inscription, executed in
couching stitch. Other published *tiraz* textiles from al-Mutawakkil's reign are
in the Museum of Islamic Art, Cairo (Related works 5–7), and Tano Collection
(Related works 8; whereabouts unknown).

The only place of production recorded by extant *tiraz* inscriptions from the
reign of al-Mutawakkil is Misr.[7] Other Delta locations are recorded on items
from the reign of Abbasid caliphs immediately before and after al-Mutawakkil.
From al-Wathiq's reign (r. 842–47), two *tiraz* textiles made in Tuna have
survived, one in the Museum of Islamic Art, Cairo (Related works 9), the other
in the Cleveland Museum of Art (Related works 10). From al-Musta'in's reign
(r. 862–66) a textile made in Tinnis and dating from 248 AH / 862–63 CE has
survived, now in the Textile Museum, Washington, DC (Related works 11). The
wording of the inscription after 'mimma 'umila', where the place of production
is mentioned, is controversial. While previously this part has been read as
'bi-al-Ashmunayn', the present author cannot confirm this reading.[8] There is a
discernible *lam–alif*, followed by a *sin or shin*, but the secure identification of
the letters following is not possible.

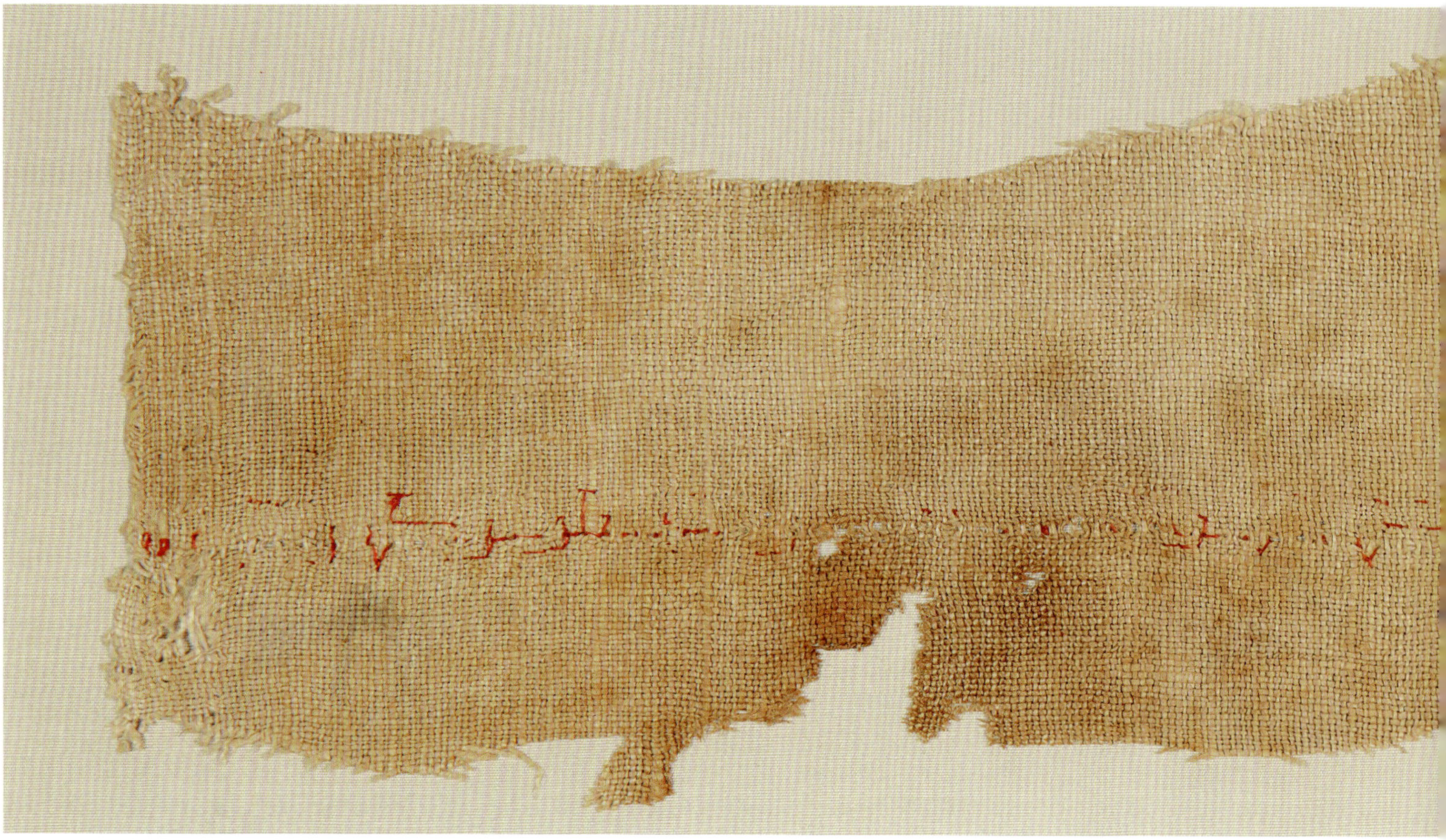

Cat. 4 *TIRAZ* FRAGMENT
ATTRIBUTED TO THE
REIGN OF ONE OF TWO
ABBASID CALIPHS,
AL-MUTAWAKKIL (r. 847–61)
OR AL-MU'TAMID (r. 870–92)
Egypt, 9th century CE

Description: Fragment of undyed linen
embroidered in red silk, with one
line of thin Kufic inscription.

Materials: linen and silk: plain weave
and embroidery

Dimensions: height 8.1, w. 31.9 cm;
max. letter height 0.9 cm

Ground fabric: linen, warp and weft, undyed,
balanced plain weave, tight texture
(*dabiqi*); medium quality (3);
selvedge on left side of inscription;
remains of a seam on the right side
of the inscription

Thread count: warp 13 S-spun, weft 16 S-spun

Thread thickness: warp 0.5–1.0 mm medium twist,
weft 0.5–0.6 mm medium twist

Embroidery: silk, dyed (red) couching stitch

Provenance: Ex H.P. Kraus collection, no. 38

Inv. no. LNS 162 T

Related works: See page 500

Inscription:

بسم الله الرحمن الرحيم ا (!) بركة [...] [مؤ]منين بركة (من) [...]

In the name of God the Most Merciful, the Most Compassionate. *Alif* (!) blessing [...] [fai]thful. Blessing (from) [...]

The inscription must once have contained a caliphal protocol, which is now illegible. However, the epigraphic style of the inscription with its feeble stitches and squared letterforms is comparable with that of a *tiraz* textile inscription in the Textile Museum, Washington, DC, which dates from the reign of the Abbasid caliph al-Mutawakkil (r. 847–61 CE) and was produced in Misr (Related works 1). Both share, particularly, the prominent horizontal bars above the hastae. Another *tiraz* textile with an inscription in a comparable epigraphic style is in the name of the Abbasid caliph al-Mu'tamid (r. 870–92). It is dated 273 AH / 886–87 CE and was also made in Misr. Like the present inscription, this one is characterized by feeble and rather squared letterforms (Related works 2).

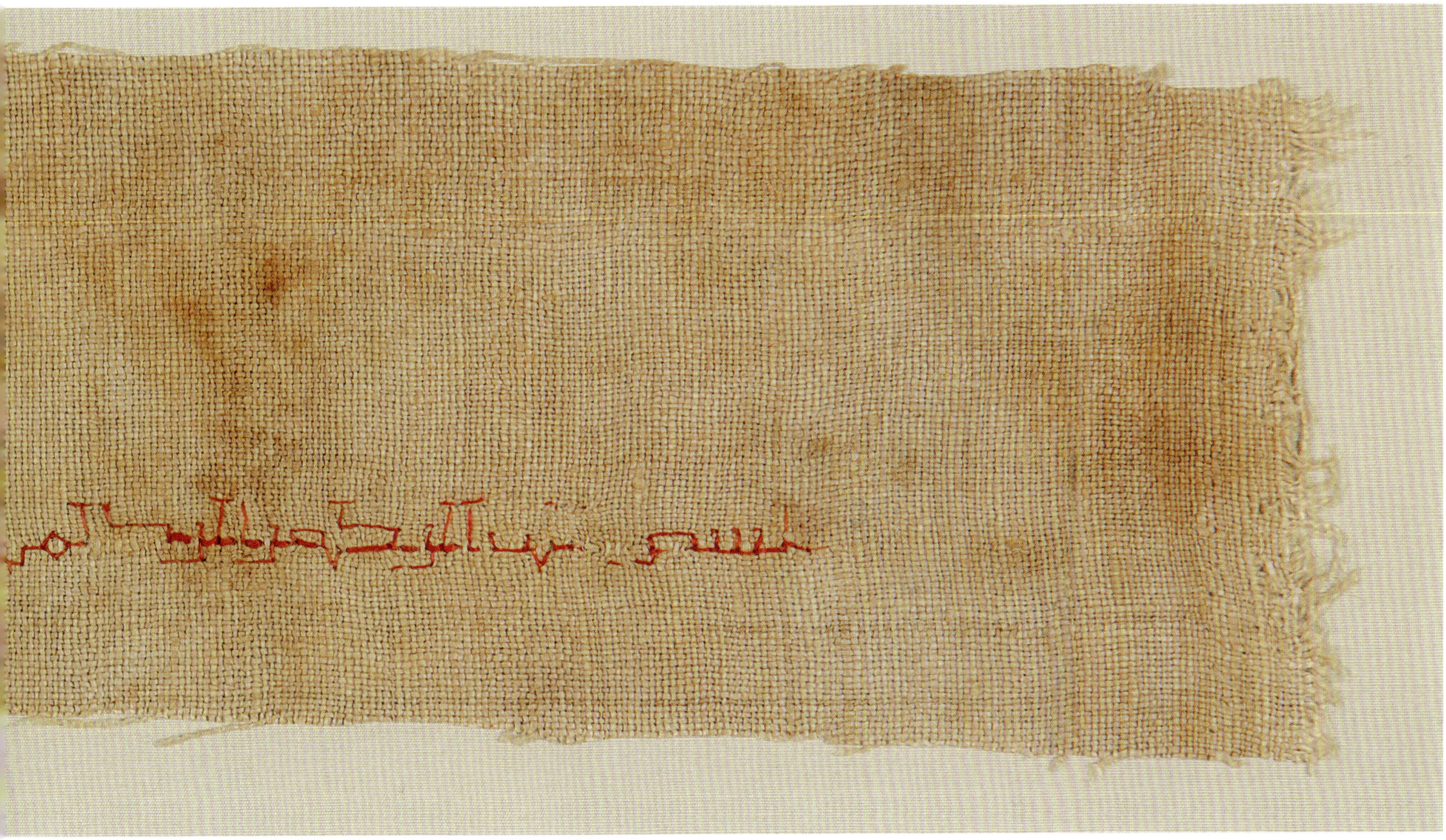

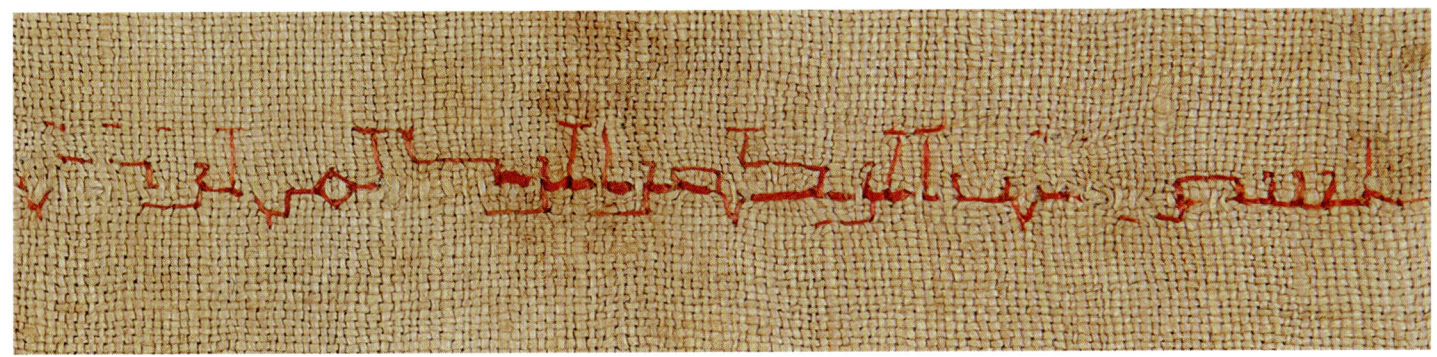

Cat. 5 *TIRAZ* FRAGMENTS FROM THE REIGN OF THE ABBASID CALIPH AL-MU'TADID (r. 892–902)
Egypt, 282 AH / 895–96 CE

Description: Fragment of undyed linen with woven decoration in beige and brownish linen and blue (faded) silk; it has one line of Kufic inscription in thin, small-sized Kufic with horizontal tails embroidered in red silk, accompanied by two brocaded bands (which were probably part of a tripartite band): one comprising a sequence of squares containing X-shapes set apart above and below by two thin indigo bands; the other (below) comprising a sequence of rectangular compartments containing a lattice design, each lozenge enclosing a diamond or cross shape, and, between these lattice compartments, vertical separation bars containing small diamond shapes.

Materials: linen and silk: plain weave, brocaded and embroidery

Dimensions: h. 10.0 cm, w. 29.0 cm; max. letter height 1.5 cm

Ground fabric: linen warp and weft, undyed, balanced plain weave (*dabiqi*), close texture, some irregularities; medium quality (3)

Thread count: warp 16 S-spun, weft 11 S-spun

Thread thickness: warp 0.3 mm slight–medium twist, weft 0.4–0.5 mm slight–medium twist

Embroidery: silk, dyed (red), couching and stem stitch; decorative band: silk, undyed and dyed (blue), supplementary weft

Provenance: Ex H.P. Kraus collection, no. 40

Inv. no. LNS 164 T

Related works: See page 500

Inscription:

بسم الله الرحمن الرحيم بركة من الله لعبد الله الامام المعتضد بالله امير المؤمنين عزه الله ما عمل (ب)ـالسكندرية (؟) سنة (اثنين ثمانين مئتان)

In the name of God, the Most Merciful, the Most Compassionate. Blessing from God to the servant of God al-Imam al-Mu'tadid bi-llah the Commander of the Faithful, may God bless him. Of what has been made (in) Alexandria(?) in the year (two hundred and eighty-two)

The inscription mentions the Abbasid caliph al-Mu'tadid (r. 892–902), albeit omitting his *ism*, but the reading of the place name and the date is not clear. It has been suggested that the place of production should be identified as Iskandariya (Alexandria).[9] In this inscription *kaf* (as in 'baraka') and *dal* (as in "abd Allah') are of the same shape, like two small semi-circles placed on top of each other. The same shape appears in what appears to be the place name, preceded by a *sin*, where it could represent a *kaf*, yet there seems to be no *dal* before the *ra*. In a logical sequence the place name should then be followed by the date preceded by the word 'sanat' ('year').

The epigraphic style of the inscription is characterized by a relatively feeble line of script with a pronounced line below the baseline of the inscription, to which are connected the lower terminals. The same epigraphic style can be found among a small number of *tiraz* textiles that date from the reigns of the caliphs al-Mu'tamid (r. 870–92) and al-Mu'tadid (r. 892–902) (Related works 1–7). Of these, no. 1 was made in Alexandria. Like these, the inscription in the present piece is also accompanied by a geometric band comprising a lattice design made up of sequences of lozenges, albeit in much simpler form and less finely brocaded.

Cat. 6   *TIRAZ* FRAGMENT FROM
THE ABBASID DYNASTY
Egypt, late 9th century CE

Description: Fragment of undyed linen, roughly
rectangular, with one line of
inscription embroidered in red silk.

Materials: linen and silk: embroidery

Dimensions: h. 14.0 cm, w. 20.0 cm;
max. letter height 1.0 cm

Ground fabric: linen warp and weft, undyed,
balanced plain weave, dense
texture (*dabiqi*), regular; good
quality (2)

Thread count: warp 20 S-spun, weft 17 S-spun

Thread thickness: warp 0.3–0.4 mm slight–medium
twist, weft 0.3–0.4 mm slight–
medium twist

Embroidery: silk, dyed (red), couching and
stem stitches

Provenance: Ex H.P. Kraus collection, no. 157

Inv. no. LNS 263 T

Related works: See page 500

Inscription: [...]الر[...] (حمد؟) لله (كله؟) الملك لله له الملك لله له الملك لله له (...؟...)

[...] [Pr](aise?) be to God (a complete one). Sovereignty belongs to God, to Him, Sovereignty belongs to God, to Him, Sovereignty belongs to God, to Him (...?...)

In terms of embroidery stitches and epigraphy, the inscription here compares with two dated inscriptions from Alexandria and Misr, 272–73 AH / 885–87 CE, during the reign of al-Mu'tamid (r. 870–92) (Related works 1 and 2). The stitches are counted and rather thin. The lower letter terminals extend horizontally below the baseline, a feature also prominent in both comparative pieces.

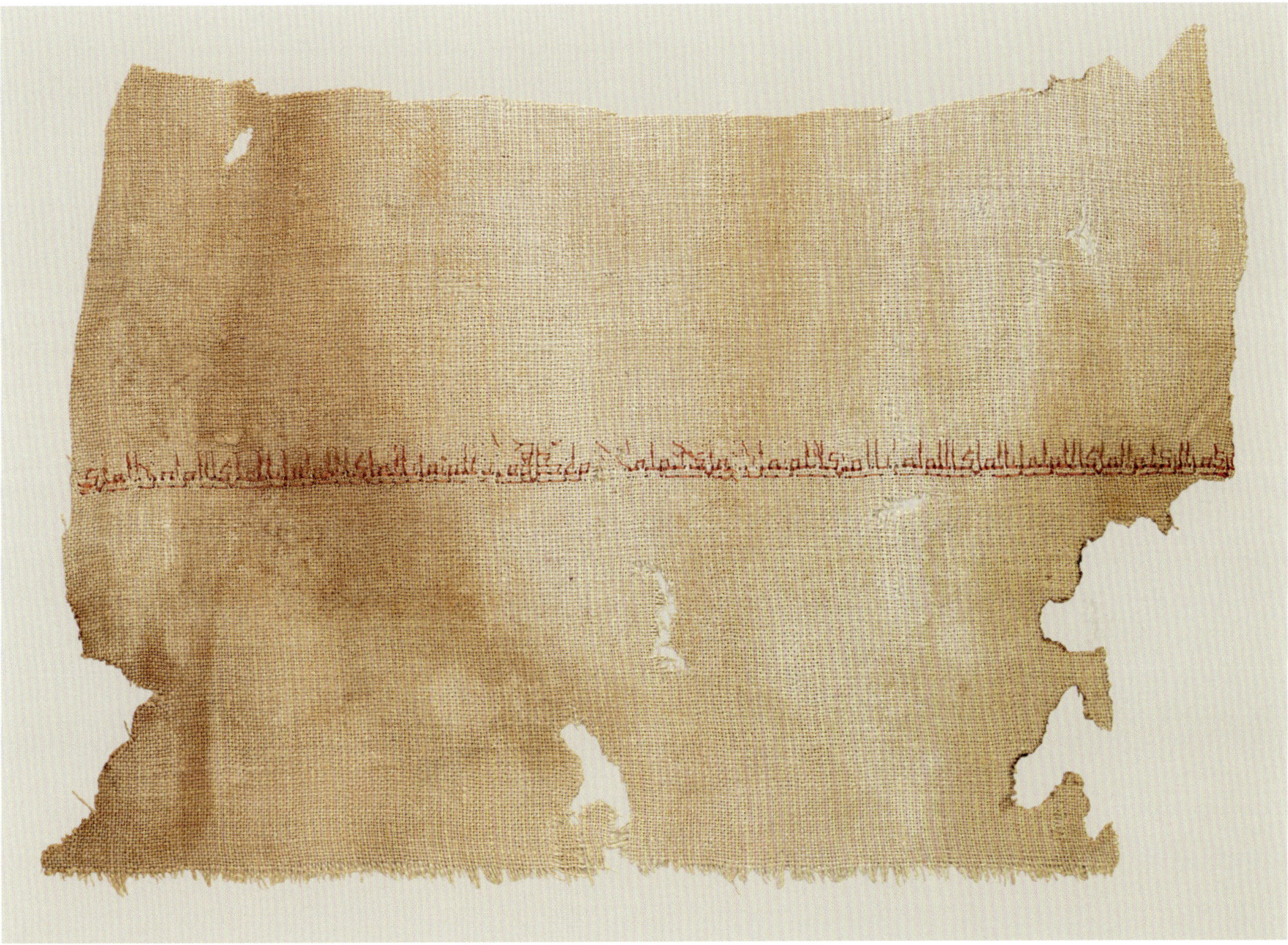

Cat. 7 *TIRAZ* FRAGMENT FROM
THE REIGN OF THE ABBASID
CALIPH AL-MUQTADIR
(r. 908–32)
Egypt, 295 AH / 907–08 CE

Description: Fragment of undyed linen, roughly
rectangular, with one line of text
embroidered in red silk in small
angular letters, with elongated
hastae.
Materials: linen and silk: plain weave
and embroidery
Dimensions: h. 15.0 cm, w. 16.5 cm;
max. letter height 1.3 cm
Ground fabric: linen warp and weft, undyed,
balanced plain weave, tight texture
(*dabiqi*); medium quality (3)
Thread count: warp 14 Z-spun, weft 15 S-spun
Thread thickness: warp 0.3–0.6 mm medium twist,
weft 0.3–0.5 mm medium twist
Embroidery: silk, dyed (red), couching stitch,
back stitch
Provenance: Ex H.P. Kraus collection, no. 8

Inv. no. LNS 136 T

Related works: See page 500

Inscription:

[...] شفيع م (!) امير المؤمنين سنة خمس وتسعين و مئتان - علي

[…] Shafi' *mim*(!) the Commander of the Faithful. In the year two hundred and
ninety-five – 'Ali

The reading of the name Shafi' (for a commentary on his biography, see cat. no.
12) conforms with that of other inscriptions where the *ya* appears with a long
hasta (Related works 1–3). A final *'ayn* is clearly visible. The word 'mawla' has
been amalgamated with the word 'amir'. A similar mistake is found in a *tiraz*
inscription in the Cleveland Museum of Art, (Related works 4), and one in the
Keir Collection (Related works 5), where after Shafi''s name the first word of his
title *mawla amir al-mu'minin* is abbreviated as 'maw'. Two inscriptions have
survived that are dated or datable to 295 AH / 907–08 CE and mention the name
of Shafi' *mawla amir al-mu'minin*: the first, explicitly dated 295 AH / 907–08 CE,
was ordered by the vizier in Tinnis at the *tiraz al-khassa* (Related works 6); the
second, datable to 295–96 AH / 907–09 CE, was ordered by the vizier al-'Abbas
ibn al-Hasan at the *tiraz al-'amma* in Misr (Related works 7). One can compare
the style of epigraphy, which is characterized by a rather feeble line of script with
a pronounced baseline and medium-height hastae, to the items from the reign
of al-Muqtadir later in this catalogue (cat. nos 8, 12, 15–18) and a number of
comparable inscriptions from his reign (Related works 8 to 20).

Cat. 8 *TIRAZ* FRAGMENT FROM THE REIGN OF THE ABBASID CALIPH AL-MUQTADIR (r. 908–32)

Egypt, 299 AH / 911–12 CE

Description: Fragment of undyed linen base fabric embroidered in red silk, with one line of Kufic inscription.

Materials: linen and silk: plain weave and embroidery

Dimensions: h. 10.5 cm, w. 22.0 cm; max letter height 1.4 cm

Ground fabric: linen warp and weft, undyed, balanced plain weave, dense texture (*dabiqi*); good quality (2)

Thread count: warp 24 SZ-spun, weft 19 S-spun

Thread thickness: warp 0.2–0.4 mm loose–medium twist, weft 0.3 mm loose–medium twist

Embroidery: silk, dyed (red), back and flat stitch

Provenance: Ex H.P. Kraus collection, no. 1

Inv. no. LNS 129 T

Related works: See pages 500–01

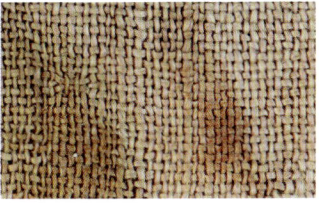

Inscription:

[...] من الله نعمة من الله من جعفر الامام المقتدر بالله اميرالمؤمنين اطال الله بقاه مما امر الوزير على بن محمد اعزه اللة بعمله فى طراز مصر على يدى بشر مولى سنة تسع تسعين مئت[ـان] [...]

[...] from God, prosperity from God to Ja'far al-imam al-Muqtadir bi-Allah the Commander of the Faithful, may God prolong his existence. Of what the vizier 'Ali the son of Muhammad, may God bless him, ordered to be made in the *tiraz* of Misr, under the direction of Bishr the client, in the year two hund[red] and ninety-nine [...]

This textile contains a protocol in the name of the Abbasid caliph al-Muqtadir, normally introduced in caliphal protocols with the phrase 'baraka min Allah li-'abd Allah Ja'far', but here instead with 'ni'ma min Allah min Ja'far', obviously a mistake. It was ordered from a *tiraz* workshop in Misr in the year 299 AH / 911–12 CE by the vizier 'Ali bin Muhammad, and the order was processed by the intermediation ("ala yaday') of Bishr, who is referred to simply as *mawla*, rather than more formally as *mawla amir al-mu'minin*.

The combination of administrative data contained in the present inscription adds to the known corpus of *tiraz* inscriptions significantly. For the year 299 AH / 911–12 CE, the textile evidence has so far been limited to six textiles (two of which only possibly date from 299 AH / 911–12 CE and were ordered by Muhammad ibn 'Ubaydallah), to which the present one can now be added. No other textile is known to have survived from the year 299 AH / 911–12 CE that was manufactured in the *tiraz al-'amma* in Misr, by order of 'Ali ibn Muhammad through the intermediation of Bishr. The same combination of data can be found, however, in a textile inscription from 296 AH / 908–09 CE (Related works 7), and on two dated 298 AH / 910–11 CE (Related works 15 and 16).

The vizier 'Ali ibn Muhammad, short for Abu al-Hasan 'Ali ibn Muhammad ibn Muqla, is attested in inscriptions as early as 296 AH / 908–09 CE and as late as 306 AH / 918–19 CE and again in 310–12 AH / 922–24 CE (Related works 7–13). This evidence confirms his dates of office known from literary sources – namely, 296–99 AH / 908–12 CE, 304–06 AH / 917–19 CE and 311–12 AH / 923–24 CE, under the caliphs al-Muqtadir and al-Qahir.[10] Ibn Muqla was born in Baghdad in 272 AH / 885–86 CE. His career began as a collector of land taxes in Fars, after which he was given an important post as secretary, in charge of the opening and the dispatch of official letters, in the central administration under the vizier Ibn al-Furat around 296 AH / 908 CE.[11] While he continued to be allied to Ibn al-Furat when he was vizier a second time from 304–06 AH / 917–19 CE, he began working against the interests of his master. Hence he was appointed by the vizier 'Ali ibn 'Isa during the latter's second vizierate (305–16 AH / 917–28 CE) to direct the *diwan* of public estates.[12] Ibn Muqla himself served as vizier in 316–18 AH / 928–31 CE.

In 320–21 AH / 932–33 CE al-Qahir appointed him again for six months, but the relationship between the caliph and vizier was difficult and Ibn Muqla tried (unsuccessfully) to get al-Qahir deposed. Ibn Muqla fled Baghdad, but upon returning in 322 AH / 934 CE managed to get the caliph imprisoned and deposed; under the new caliph, al-Radi, he held the vizierate again until 324 AH / 936 CE.[13] Economic and financial crises, as well as challenges from regional governors, marked the end of the independent caliphate. With the appointment of Ibn Ra'iq, the governor of Wasit in Iraq, as the *amir al-umara'*, Ibn Muqla's property and that of his family was confiscated and he was subsequently disgraced. Imprisoned and mutilated, Ibn Muqla died on 10 Shawwal 328 AH / 20 July 940 CE.[14] As an individual trained in the art of writing and copying letters, one of Ibn Muqla's most significant and lasting contributions was the reform of the Arabic script. He devised a system of proportionate script in which letters were sized and constructed according to the size of the nib of

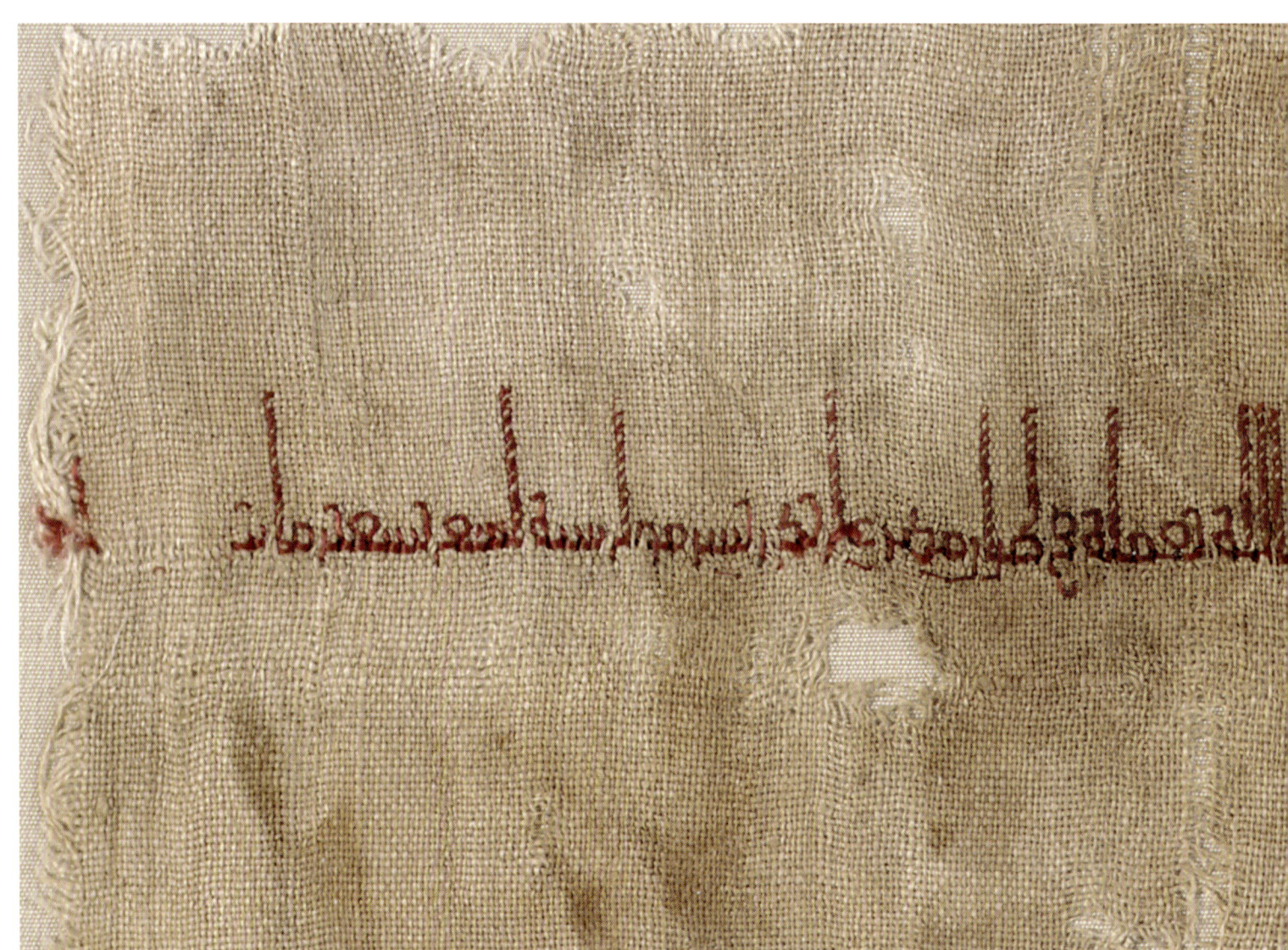

the reed pen. This system transformed the copying of the Quran from the late tenth century onwards.

The name of Bishr appears on six textiles dated 296–301 AH / 908–14 CE (Related works 7, 10, 14–17). Bishr, who in the present inscription bears the title *mawla amir al-mu'minin*, is known from other *tiraz* inscriptions, dated 296 AH / 908–09 CE, one from Damietta, where he is referred to as Bishr *al-khadim* (servant or slave) (Related works 14). The literary sources mention various characters named Bishr. In al-Tabari's history of the Abbasid caliphate, for example, a certain Bishr al-Afshini is mentioned, a *mawla* of Muhammad ibn Abi Saj, a high member of the military and governor under al-Muwaffaq.[15] Muhammad ibn Abi Saj was nicknamed al-Afshin. Bishr was probably a eunuch and a member of the caliphal administration. Eunuchs were frequently referred to as *khadam* in the literature. Bishr was probably involved at a high level in the negotiations with the Qarmatians who were besieging the city of Kufa in 293 AH / 906–07 CE, for the same year Tabari's text describes how the caliph Al-Muktafi bestowed robes of honour (*khil'a*) on Bishr al-Afshini and the vizier al-'Abbas ibn al-Hasan in Baghdad as recognition of their victory. In 302 AH / 914–15 CE Bishr was governor of Tarsus on behalf of the central authorities, and with military support arranged by the vizier 'Ali ibn 'Isa. Given the prominent military career of the historical Bishr, particularly in the Bilad al-Sham (Greater Syria), it is likely that he is identical with Bishr al-Khadim, who was appointed governor of Damascus and Aleppo by the caliph al-Qahir in 321 AH / 933 CE and killed there the same year by the Ikhshidid Muhammad ibn Tughj. The precise naming of Bishr al-Khadim in Tabari's text makes it quite certain that he is not one of various other characters called Bishr, mentioned by Ibn Miskawayh, who were known with other additional names.[16]

The textile inscriptions mentioned above that include Bishr's name may date from the time after his campaign in Kufa and perhaps before he was made governor of Tarsus, a period that perhaps he spent at the court in Baghdad. From the literary, as well as the textile evidence, it is clear that he was a contemporary of Shafi' al-Muqtadiri, a fellow eunuch who is known from as many as eighty *tiraz* inscriptions (see cat. nos 7, 10, 12, 14). As mentioned above, Bishr is known from a textile dated 296 AH / 908–09 CE and made in Damietta, by order of the vizier Abu al-Hasan 'Ali ibn Muhammad (Related works 14). In the same year he is mentioned on a textile manufactured in the *tiraz al-'amma* in Misr (Related works 7). This suggests that the assignment of the administrative execution of an order for particular locations was by no means static – that is, the same person could handle assignments for a variety of locations. That the vizier in office relied on a variety of executives in the same year is suggested by the evidence of a textile in the Royal Ontario Museum, Toronto, dated 299 AH / 911–12 CE, ordered by the vizier Abu al-Hasan 'Ali ibn Muhammad in Tinnis by intermediation of Shafi' *mawla amir al-mu'minin* (Related works 5).

In terms of epigraphic style, the present piece relates to a number of textile inscriptions from Misr during al-Muqtadir's reign. Examples in the Kelsey Museum of Archeology in Ann Arbor and the Bouvier Collection are particularly closely related (Related works 7, 16), though there the hastae are more vertically pronounced; however, the terminals below the baseline are rather angular, a feature not found in the present piece. It is likely that all three of these pieces were produced by different hands, perhaps even different workshops.

Cat. 9   *TIRAZ* FRAGMENT FROM
THE REIGN OF THE ABBASID
CALIPH AL-MUQTADIR
(r. 908–32)
Egypt, 300 AH / 912–13 CE

Description: Fragment of undyed linen ground
fabric, with one complete line
of Kufic inscription (l. 32.3 cm)
embroidered in couching and
chain stitch in red silk.

Materials: linen and silk: plain weave
and embroidery

Dimensions: h. 16.5 cm, w. 36.7 cm;
max. letter height 2.1 cm

Ground fabric: linen warp and weft, undyed,
balanced plain weave, close
texture (*dabiqi*), regular structure;
very good quality (1)

Thread count: warp 22 S-spun, weft 22 S-spun

Thread thickness: warp 0.3–0.4 mm slight–medium
twist, weft 0.3–0.5 mm slight–
medium twist

Embroidery: silk, dyed (red), couching on three
warps, warp thread drawn to mark
the baseline of the inscription

Provenance: Ex H.P. Kraus collection,
New York

Inv. no. LNS 52 T

Related works: See page 501

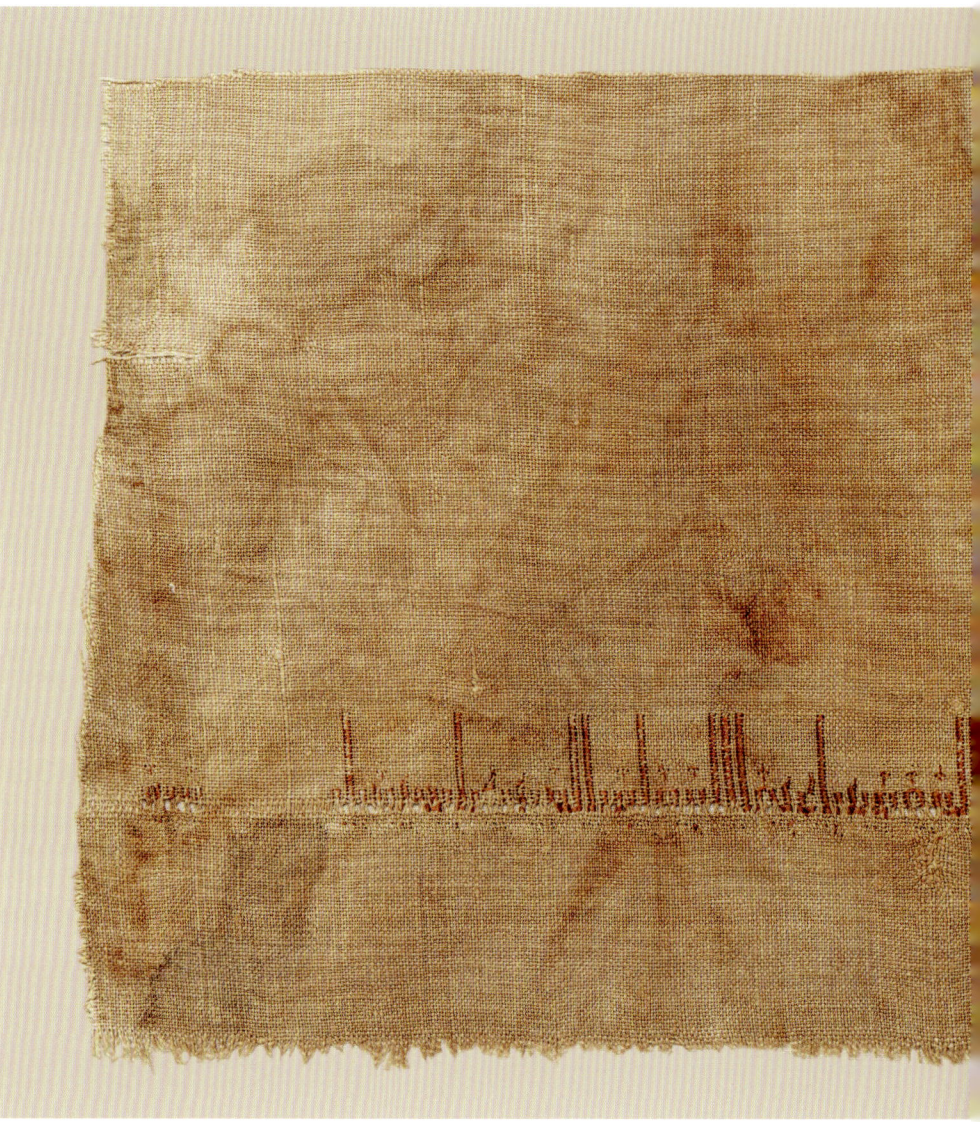

Inscription:

بسم الله الرحمن الرحيم عز من الله [...] المقتدر بالله امير المؤمنين (١) عزه الله ما امر [الوزير] بط[ا]ز سنة ثلث مائة

In the name of God, the Most Merciful, the Most Compassionate. Glory from God [...] al-Muqtadir bi-llah, the Commander of the Faithful, (M)ay God bless him. What has been ordered by [the vizier] in the *ti[ra]z*, in the year three hundred

This *tiraz* inscription is a complete length, mentions the name of the Abbasid caliph al-Muqtadir and provides a date of 300 AH / 912–13 CE. The place of production is not mentioned, but the piece was produced in an unspecified *tiraz* workshop. The style of script seen here is composed of relatively broad letters with a pronounced vertical (as opposed to a thin line, as seen in many

other inscriptions), a characteristic achieved by embroidering each letter on quadruplets (or other equal sets) of counted warp threads. The letters on the baseline such as *mim*, *ha* and *qaf* are square-shaped rather than rounded, as only one thread is carried over straight to form the upper side of the letter. The prime and central *ba*, *ta*, *nun* and *sin* are angular, and the upward stems of *alif* and *lam* ascend in a straight and broad line. Some of the upper terminals of the low letters are embellished by small arrowhead-like pointed finials. Rounded letter terminals below the baseline, in the case of terminal *mim*, *ra* and *waw*, are bordered by a non-functional festoon. The festoon is chain stitched in order to achieve the rounded shape of the crescents, which would not have been possible on counted threads with couching. A related example dated 295 AH / 907–08 CE featuring this particular style of epigraphy is in the Royal Ontario Museum, Toronto (Related works 1).

Cat. 10   *TIRAZ* FRAGMENT FROM
THE REIGN OF THE ABBASID
CALIPH AL-MUQTADIR
(r. 908–32)
Egypt, 300 AH / 912–13 CE

Description: Fragment of undyed linen, roughly
rectangular, showing some
discolouration and tears, having a
tapestry-woven band with one line
of large bold Kufic text woven in
dark blue silk.

Materials: linen and silk: plain weave
and tapestry

Dimensions: h. 22.5 cm, w. 38.0 cm;
max. letter height 2.5 cm

Ground fabric: linen warp and weft, undyed,
warp-faced plain weave, gauzy
texture (*sharb*); very good–good
quality (1–2)

Thread count: warp 28 S-spun, weft 14 S-spun

Thread thickness: warp 0.1–0.15 mm tight twist,
warp 0.2 mm tight twist

Tapestry: silk, dyed (dark blue); slit; hastae
woven on warps lifted up from the
base fabric; selvedge on the left side
of the inscription

Provenance: Ex H.P. Kraus collection, no. 28

Inv. no. LNS 152 T

Related works: See pages 501–02

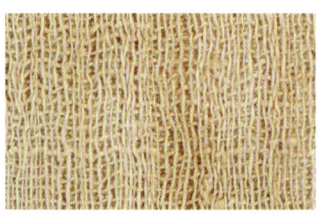

Inscription: [...] [ال]ـخاصة بمصر على يدي شفيع مولى امير المؤمنين سنة ثلث مائة (بركة)

[…] [al-]khassa in Misr under the direction of Shafi' the client of the Commander
of the Faithful in the year three hundred (blessing)

The beginning of this inscription has lost most of its silk tapestry, but it is still
possible from the voids in the ground fabric to distinguish the missing letters. The
word before ''ala' ends with a *sad* and a *ra*. Connected before that was a round
letter on the baseline, which must be a *mim*. The word can thus be read as Misr.
In the normal sequence of a *tiraz* inscription the place of manufacture should be
preceded by the type of workshop and in this case there is a long letter stem with
what appears to be a *ha* or *kha* and a round final letter, which could be a terminal
ta marbuta. A possible reading could thus be '(a)l-khassa', as in *tiraz al-khassa*.

At least forty-six textiles with tapestry woven inscriptions from the
period of al-Muqtadir have been documented (Related works 1–46). This
tiraz inscription adds to the existing corpus significantly. Of the five known
inscriptions mentioning the name of Shafi' *mawla amir al-mu'minin* executed
in tapestry, none were produced in the *tiraz al-khassa* in Misr. Only one item,
dated 316 AH / 928–29 CE, was produced in Misr, albeit in an unspecified *tiraz*
workshop (Related works 46). Of the other textiles, two were made in Tinnis
and one in Damietta (Related works 8, 12, 18). In one the place of production is
lost (Related works 20). Among this group the present piece is the one with the
earliest date of production.

The epigraphic style seen here is typical of tapestry-woven inscriptions of the
period of al-Muqtadir, with their rather angular letters of even thickness on and
above the baseline, and pronounced bow-shaped lower terminals. In comparison
with embroidered inscriptions, relatively few such tapestry-woven examples
have survived from al-Muqtadir's reign. The reverse is true of the reigns of his
immediate successors al-Qahir and al-Radi. Perhaps the example most closely
related to the present piece from al-Muqtadir's reign, comprising almost exactly
the same size of script, is in the Royal Ontario Museum, Toronto, the end of a
caliphal inscription dating from 300 AH / 912–13 CE (Related works 6). Another
example with a comparable type of script, but in a much larger size, is in the
Kelsey Museum of Archeology, Ann Arbor (Related works 14), and another
with an confronted inscription is in the Royal Ontario Museum, Toronto
(Related works 9).

Cat. 11   *TIRAZ* FRAGMENT FROM
THE REIGN OF THE ABBASID
CALIPH AL-MUQTADIR
(r. 908–32)
Egypt, early 10th century CE

Description: Fragment of undyed linen, with
one line tapestry-woven Kufic
inscription in dark blue silk.

Materials: linen and silk: plain weave
and tapestry

Dimensions: h. 15.5 cm, w. 59.1 cm;
max. letter height 1.6 cm

Ground fabric: linen warp and weft, undyed,
balanced plain weave, close texture
(*sharb*); very good–good quality
(1–2)

Thread count: warp 28 S-spun, weft 20 S-spun

Thread thickness: warp 0.15–0.25 mm tight twist,
weft 0.15 mm tight twist

Tapestry: silk, dyed (dark blue); slit; hastae
woven on warps lifted up from
the base fabric

Provenance: Ex H.P. Kraus collection, no. 30

Inv. no. LNS 154 T

Related works: See page 502

Inscription: بسم الله الرحمن الرحيم بركة من الله لعبد الله جعفر الامام المقتدر بالله [...]

In the name of God, the Most Merciful, the Most Compassionate. Blessing from
God to the servant of God Ja'far al-Imam al-Muqtadir bi-llah [...]

The epigraphic style of the inscription here, with its barely distinguishable flat letters on the baseline and lower terminals integrated into the baseline, is rare, but seems to be a phenomenon limited chronologically to al-Muqtadir's reign (r. 908–32) and shortly after. A complete inscription from al-Muqtadir's reign, almost identical in style and content, is in the Royal Ontario Museum, Toronto (Related works 1). Its content finishes after the name and title of the caliph, suggesting that the present inscription, also, was not intended to contain any administrative data. The letter height of both inscriptions is roughly comparable, the letters in the Toronto example being 1.9 cm as against 1.6 cm here. Other inscriptions exist from the reign of al-Muqtadir and al-Qahir (r. 932–34), which are related in epigraphic style, but are not identical with the present one. Although, in most of these, the letters on the baseline are quite flat, they are far more distinguishable from one another. In one in the Royal Ontario Museum, Toronto (Related works 2), dated 320 AH / 932–33 CE, the lower letter terminals are integrated into the baseline, as in the present piece. In another item from al-Muqtadir's reign, in the Royal Ontario Museum (Related works 3), dated 300 AH / 912–13 CE, the letters are flat on the baseline, but have pronounced bow-shaped lower terminals.

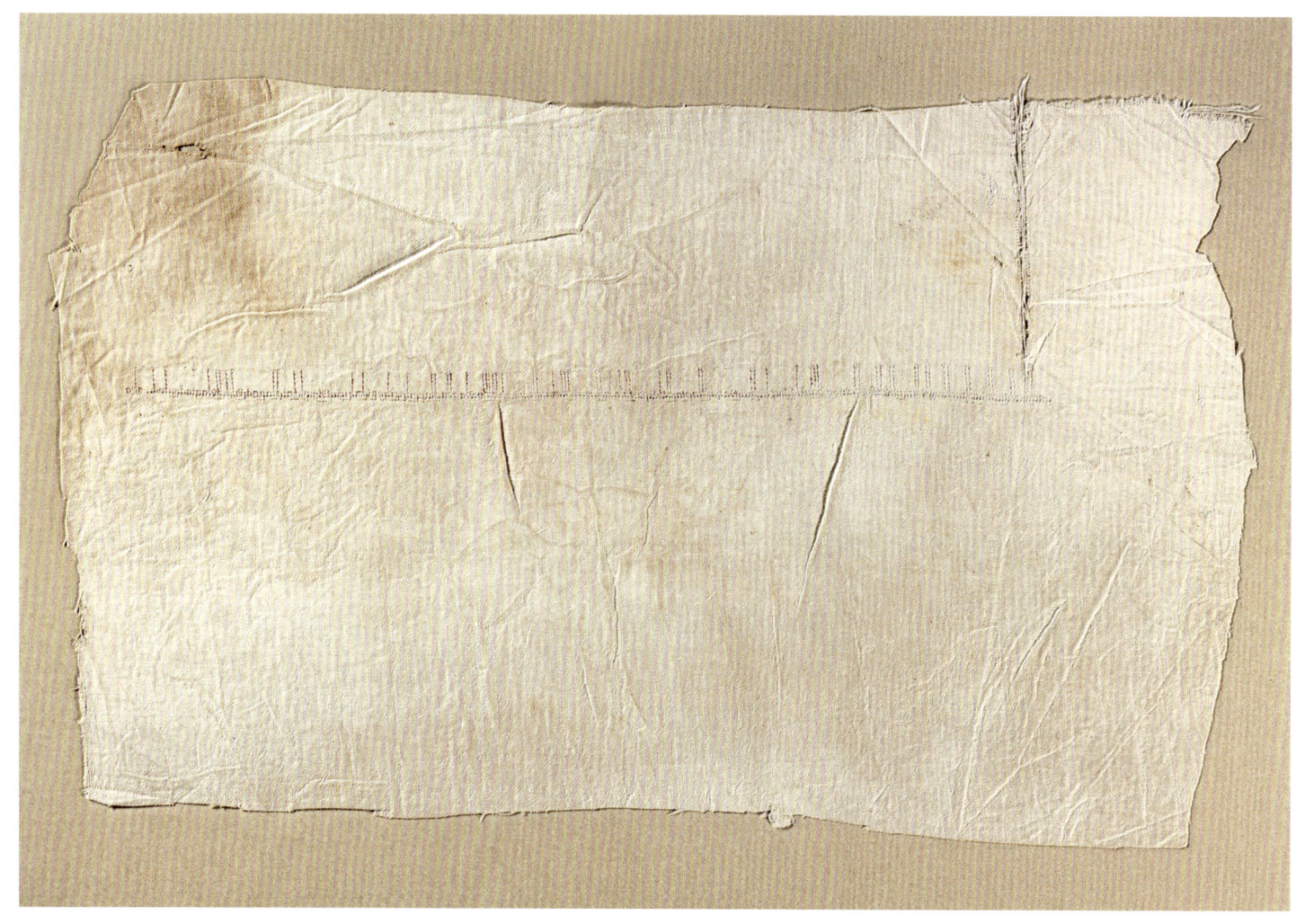

Cat. 12   *TIRAZ* FRAGMENT FROM
THE REIGN OF THE ABBASID
CALIPH AL-MUQTADIR
(r. 908–32)

Egypt, 300 AH / 912–13 CE

Description: Fragment of undyed linen, with
one line of Kufic inscription
embroidered in red silk in
couching, flat and back stitch.

Materials: linen and silk: plain weave
and embroidery

Dimensions: h. 24.0 cm, w. 38.5 cm;
max. letter height 0.8 cm

Ground fabric: linen warp and weft, undyed,
balanced plain weave, dense
texture (*dabiqi*), regular structure,
glazed and polished; good quality
(2)

Thread count: warp 16 SZ-spun, weft 17
SZ-spun

Thread thickness: warp 0.15–0.6 mm slight–medium
twist, weft 0.3–0.6 mm slight–
medium twist

Embroidery: silk, dyed (red), couching, back
and flat stitch

Provenance: Ex H.P. Kraus collection, no. 2

Inv. no. LNS 130 T

Related works: See page 502

Inscription:

بسم الله الرحمن الرحيم الحمد لله رب العلمين نعمة من الله و يمن للخليفة جعفر الامام المقتدربالله امير المؤمنين اطال الله بقاه ما
امر الوزير علي بن عيسى [...][...] على يدي شفيع مولى امير المؤمنين بطراز العامة بمصر سنة ثلث مائة

In the name of God, the Most Merciful, the Most Compassionate. Praise be
to God, the Lord of the worlds. Prosperity from God and fortune to the caliph
Ja'far al-Imam al-Muqtadir bi-llah the Commander of the Faithful, may God
prolong his existence. Of what the vizier 'Ali the son of 'Isa has ordered [...]
under the direction of Shafi' the client of the Commander of the Faithful, in the
tiraz al-'amma in Misr, in the year three hundred

The inscription mentions its date of production in the year 300 AH / 912–13 CE.
It was ordered by the vizier 'Ali ibn 'Isa by intermediation of Shafi' *mawla amir
al-mu'minin* and produced in the *tiraz al-'amma* in Misr. The epigraphic style is
typical of the period, and is characterized by a broad baseline with pronounced
hastae of *lam* and *alif*. The letters ascending from the baseline are embroidered
in back and flat stitch with one thread. Hence their appearance is rather feeble.
The letters are undecorated. This epigraphic style is not exclusive to the reign of
al-Muqtadir, as there is evidence from previous and successive periods. It seems
that this style was used in Misr and Tinnis.

Of the 401 textiles known from the reign of al-Muqtadir, this piece is
important as it relates to a textile in Washington dating from the year 300 AH,
also ordered by the vizier 'Ali ibn 'Isa, who so far has been thought to have begun
his tenure in Muharram 301 AH / August 913 CE (Related works 1).[17] On the
evidence of the Washington piece, Kühnel suggests that 'Ali ibn 'Isa may have
been installed before that date. The evidence of the present piece, now the second
known item, suggests that the historical constellation provided by the inscription
is not coincidental. Furthermore, the two pieces share the same aesthetic and
almost identical wording of the inscription, with only very minor differences: the
present inscription reads 'na'ama min Allah wa yumn li al-khalifa', rather than
'baraka min Allah li al-khalifa'; 'atala Allah' rather than 'ayyaduhu Allah'; and
'ma amara al-wazir' ('what the vizir ordered') rather than 'mimma amara al-
wazir' ('of what the vizir ordered'). The present inscription also omits the word
'bi-'amalihi' ('to be made').

Important here is the mention of the vizier together with his executive, as
these two individuals were acting on behalf of the ruling caliph and represented
an administrative hierarchy. The order 'mimma amara bi-'amalihi' or 'ma
amara bi-'amalihi' was usually given by the vizier to be executed ("ala yaday';
lit. 'upon the hands of') by a second person. Ernst Kühnel believed that this
second individual was the superintendent of the caliphal *tiraz* workshops, who
oversaw the production locally in Egypt.[18] However, both the textile evidence
and the biographies of some of these individuals suggest that they were, rather,
administrators within the central caliphal diwans who were overseeing the
financial transactions.[19] This is evident from the example of Shafi', the individual
mentioned here.

Shafi' al-Muqtadiri is the character who is by far the most often mentioned
as the executor of orders, 'ala yaday in *tiraz* inscriptions.[20] He is also one of the
few whose biography can be established fairly precisely from literary sources.
He was active under the caliphs al-Muqtadir (r. 908–32), al-Qahir (r. 932–34)

and al-Radi (r. 934–40). The earliest surviving textile mentioning his name was made in 295 AH / 907–08 CE and the last one in 326 AH / 937–38 CE. For twenty-eight years Shafi' seems to have been predominant, but not exclusively so. Other contemporary individuals are mentioned as executors, *'ala yaday* in *tiraz* inscriptions during that time. Despite Shafi''s frequent appearances, his biography has not been written yet. We know the date of neither his birth nor his death. His *nisba* (denotation of belonging), 'al-Muqtadiri', coupled with the title *mawla amir al-mu'minin*, both accompanied his name frequently and indicate that he was of extremely high status – so high, indeed, that he was allowed to include his name in the inscriptions that documented the administrative process on behalf of the caliph. It is very likely that Shafi' was a non-Arab member of the Abbasid caliphal administration, and he probably came into the service of al-Muqtadir as a slave; hence the *nisba* 'al-Muqtadiri' which denotes belonging to the caliph.

From the historical literature we can ascertain that Shafi' was a member of al-Muqtadir's court at Baghdad and head of an influential group of eunuchs.[21] He was a member of the caliph's counsel, together with Muqtadir's mother, his uncle, Mu'nis *al-khazin* ('treasurer'), Mu'nis *al-khadim* ('eunuch' or 'slave') a police prefect, and Sawsan, *hajib* ('chamberlain'). He was involved in a number of conspiracies and plots at court. Together with the caliph's chamberlain Nasr, Shafi' conspired against the vizier Ibn al-Furat, and had him arrested on 28 Jumada I 306 AH / 10 November 918 CE. Under the vizierate of Ahmad al-Khasibi (11 Ramadan 313 AH / 4 December 925 to 11 Dhu al-qa'da 314 AH / 27 January 927 CE), Shafi' replaced the director of the postal service (*diwan al-barid*), the eunuch Shafi' al-Lu'lu'i, after the latter had died. The postal service, which included the secret service, was one of the offices assigned to the most favoured of the caliph's private circle. Shafi' is mentioned in Hilal al-Sabi''s *Kitab al-wuzara* ('The book of viziers') in a list of directors of *diwan*s, reconfirming his high administrative position.[22]

Two related *tiraz* inscriptions, one in the Textile Museum, Washington, DC, the other in the Museum of Islamic Art in Cairo, are noteworthy here, as they

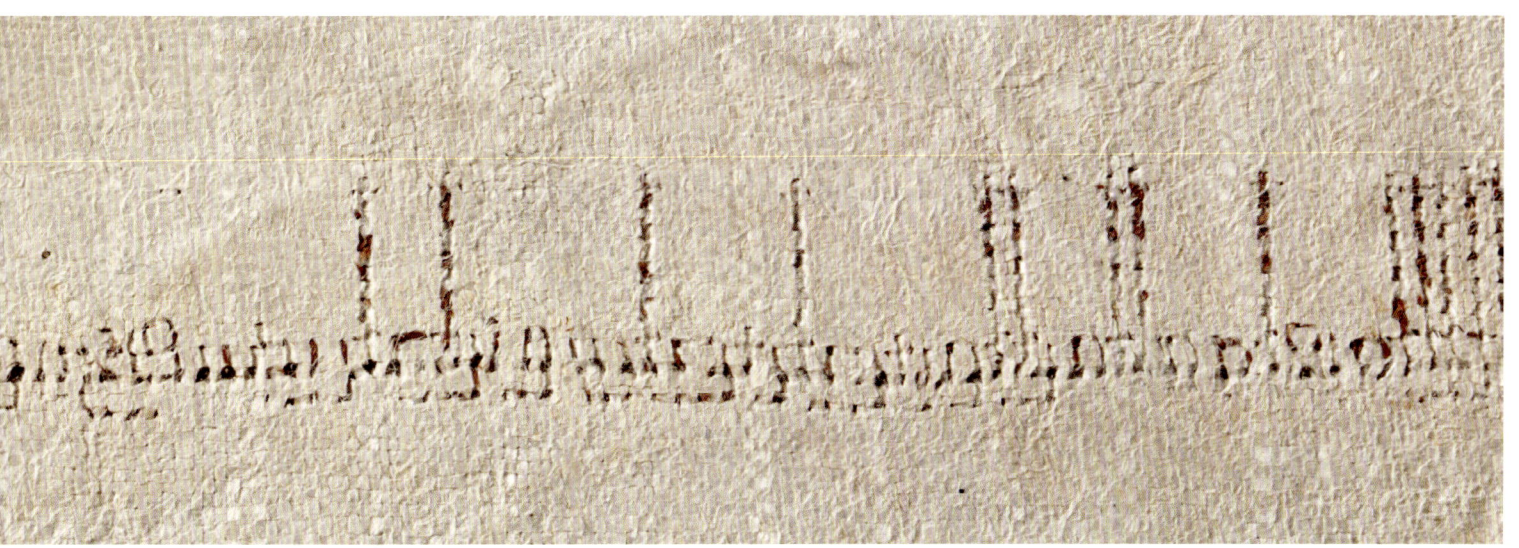

too were ordered under the execution of Shafi' at the *tiraz al-'amma* in Misr in 300 AH / 912–13 CE. That in the Textile Museum was ordered by an unnamed vizier (Related works 2). It shares with our piece the style of epigraphy and its embroidery stitches, but uses a slightly different protocol in referring to the Prophet Muhammad as the Seal of the Prophets ('khatim al-nabiyin') and features a different benedictory phrase alluding to the caliph – 'baraka min Allah wa ghibta'. Furthermore, the word 'baraka' appears at the end of the inscription after the date. The inscription on the textile in Cairo has lost its ordering formula and the name of the ordering vizier (Related works 3).

According to the Mamluk historian al-Dhahabi (1274–1348), 'Ali ibn 'Isa ibn Da'ud ibn al-Jarrah, who is mentioned in the inscription here as vizier, was born between 857 and 863, probably in Baghdad, as he was known as al-Baghdadi.[23] He was made vizier in 913 and held his office three times 913–17, 918–23, and 927–28. 'Ali ibn 'Isa died at the end of the year 946, at the age of ninety. Al-Dhahabi mentions primarily his piety and status as a man of religious learning, as he refers to two of 'Ali ibn 'Isa's works, the *Fi al-du'a* ('About prayer'), and the *Ma'ani al-Qur'an* ('The meanings of the Quran'). A collection of his letters exists. Al-Dhahabi describes 'Ali ibn 'Isa generally as a knowledgeable, honest and generous man. However, he relates nothing regarding 'Ali's office as vizier and administrator of al-Muqtadir. 'Ali ibn 'Isa's name appears in forty-five extant *tiraz* inscriptions, the great majority from the reign of al-Muqtadir in 301–18 AH / 913–31 CE, two from al-Qahir's (r. 932–34) and one from al-Radi's reign (r. 934–40).[24]

Both the present textile and its counterpart in the Textile Museum, Washington, DC, are part of a group of at least twenty-six extant textiles dating from the year 300 AH / 912–13 CE. Of these several were made in a variety of locations in- and outside Egypt, five in Misr (Related works 2–5, and 7–10), one possibly in Tinnis (Related works 11) and two in Madinat al-Salam (Baghdad) (Related works 12–13). Others lack a known place of manufacture (Related works 14–25). These textiles represent the multiplicity of epigraphic styles used within one year.

Cat. 13   *TIRAZ* FRAGMENT FROM
THE REIGN OF THE ABBASID
CALIPH AL-MUQTADIR
(r. 908–32)

Description: Fragment of undyed linen, with
one line of Kufic inscription
embroidered in dark-brown silk
chain stitch.

Materials: linen and silk: plain weave
and embroidery

Dimensions: h. 12 cm, w. 25 cm;
max. letter height 2.5 cm

Ground fabric: linen warp and weft, undyed,
predominant-warp plain weave,
closely woven (*dabiqi*), regular;
good quality (2)

Thread count: warp 26 S-spun, weft 11 S-spun

Thread thickness: warp 0.3–0.5mm medium twist,
weft 0.3mm loose–medium
twist

Embroidery: silk, dyed (brown), chain stitch

Provenance: Ex H.P. Kraus collection, no. 10

Inv. no. LNS 138 T

Related works: See page 502

Inscription: [...] [عب]ـد الله جعفر الإمام المقتدر بالله أمير المومـ[ـنين] [...]

[...] [se]rvant of God Ja'far al-Imam al-Muqtadir bi-llah the Commander of the
Fai[thful] [...]

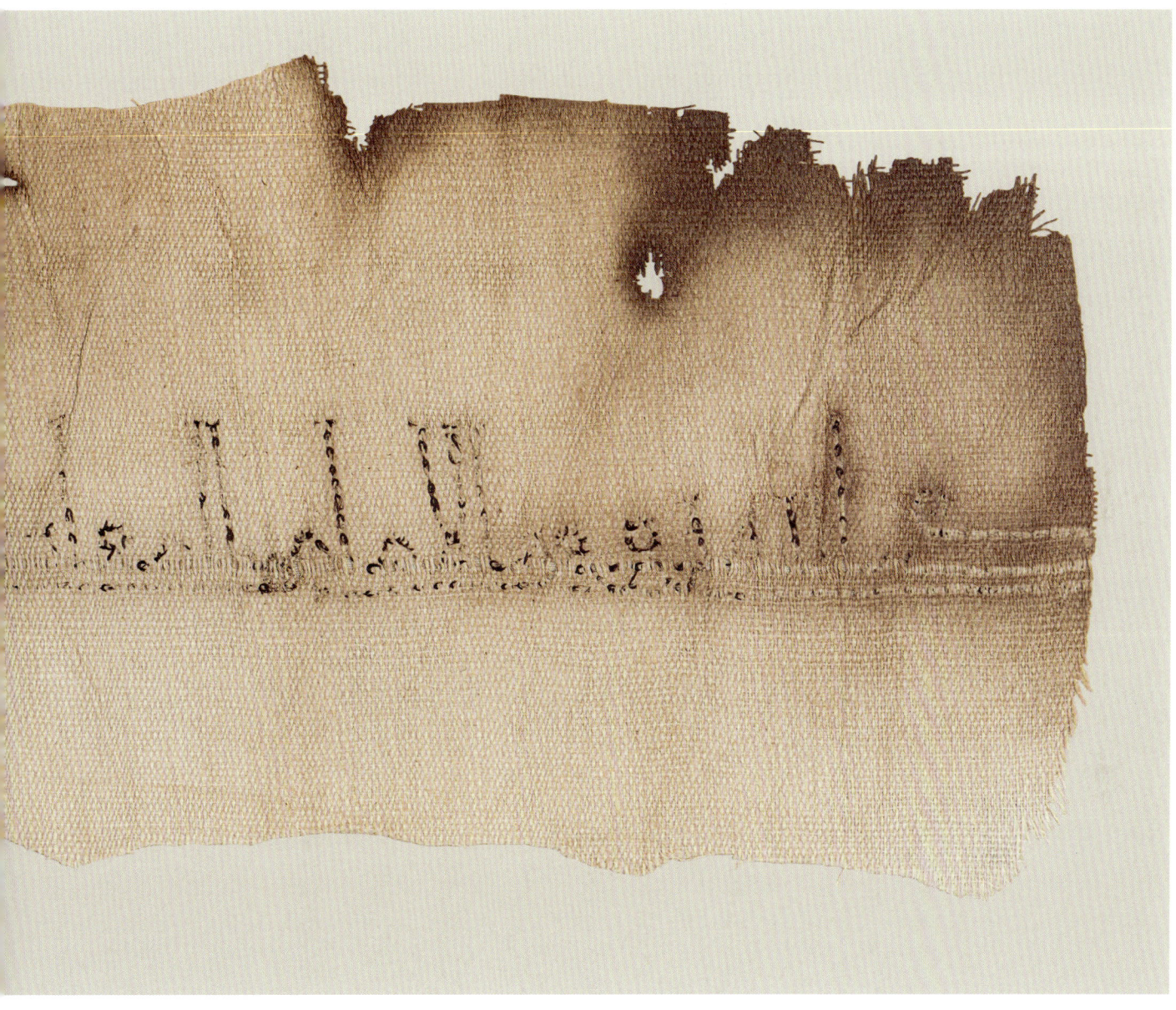

This piece belongs to a group of textiles all characterized by their chain-stitched inscriptions in an epigraphic style that has its origins in the eastern Islamic world – that is, Iraq or Khurasan (Related works 1–6). They are, however, Egyptian in origin, as is indicated by several inscriptions documenting Tinnis (Related works 1–4) and Misr (Related works 5). All of these comprise linen ground fabrics and the execution of the embroidery is not as refined as that of Iraqi or Iranian examples, suggesting that they are Egyptian adaptations of an imported style. Textiles with inscriptions in a similar epigraphic style were produced in Baghdad, such as the examples from the reign of al-Muqtadir discussed in the catalogue section on Iraq (cat. no. 96). The Egyptian adaptations, too, all date from al-Muqtadir's reign.

Cat. 14 *TIRAZ* **FRAGMENT FROM THE REIGN OF THE ABBASID CALIPH AL-MUQTADIR**
(r. 908–32)
Egypt, 302(?) AH / 915–16(?) CE

Description: Fragment of undyed linen, roughly rectangular, with one line of Kufic inscription in red silk.

Materials: linen and silk: plain weave and embroidery

Dimensions: h. 13.0 cm, w. 13.5 cm; max. letter height 1.3 cm

Ground fabric: linen warp and weft, undyed, balanced plain weave, close texture (*dabiqi*), regular structure; good quality (2)

Thread count: warp 16 S-spun, weft 21 S-spun

Thread thickness: warp 0.25–0.3 mm slight–medium twist, weft 0.25–0.3 mm slight–medium twist

Embroidery: silk, dyed (red), couching, back and flat stitch, warp thread drawn to mark the baseline of the inscription

Provenance: Ex H.P. Kraus collection, no. 3

Inv. no. LNS 131 T

Related works: See pages 502–03

Inscription:

[...] [الـمـ]ـقتدر بالله امير المؤمنين ايده الله ما امر الوزير على بن عيسى بعمله بمصر علي يدي شفيع سنة اثنين ثلث مائة – بركة

[...] [al-M]uqtadir bi-llah the Commander of the Faithful, may God strengthen him. Of what the vizier 'Ali the son of 'Isa has ordered to be made in Misr under the direction of Shafi', in the year three hundred two – blessing

The inscription mentions the *laqab* (regnal title) al-Muqtadir, the name of his vizier 'Ali ibn 'Isa, his executive Shafi', Misr as place of manufacture and a date of possibly 302 AH / 915–16 CE. The date is not clearly legible as most of the silk embroidery has vanished. There is clearly a digit after the remnants of the word 'sanat' (year) and before 'mi'a' (100), which ends in the letter *nun* and is preceded by a number of letter shafts, the second of which is higher than the rest. A possible reading may be 'ithnan' (two). However, the dates of 'Ali ibn 'Isa's tenure are known from the historical literary record: 913–17, 918–23, and 927–28.[25] Hence a reading of 302 AH / 915–16 CE as a date would be justified.

Only one other textile dating from 302 AH / 915–16 CE has been recorded. This is a fragment with an embroidered inscription in the Benaki Museum, Athens (Related works 1). It mentions the name of the caliph al-Muqtadir and was ordered by the vizier 'Ali ibn 'Isa, while omitting the name of its place of manufacture and the executive. Since the present inscription comprises more administrative data, it contributes new information to the known corpus of *tiraz* textiles.

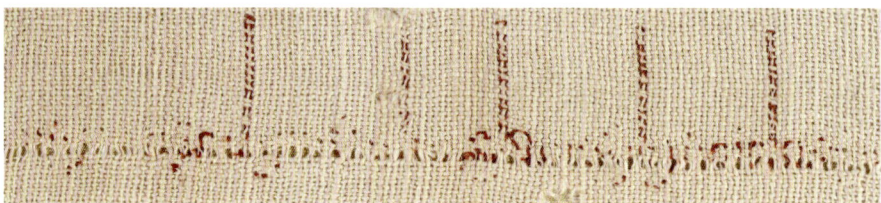

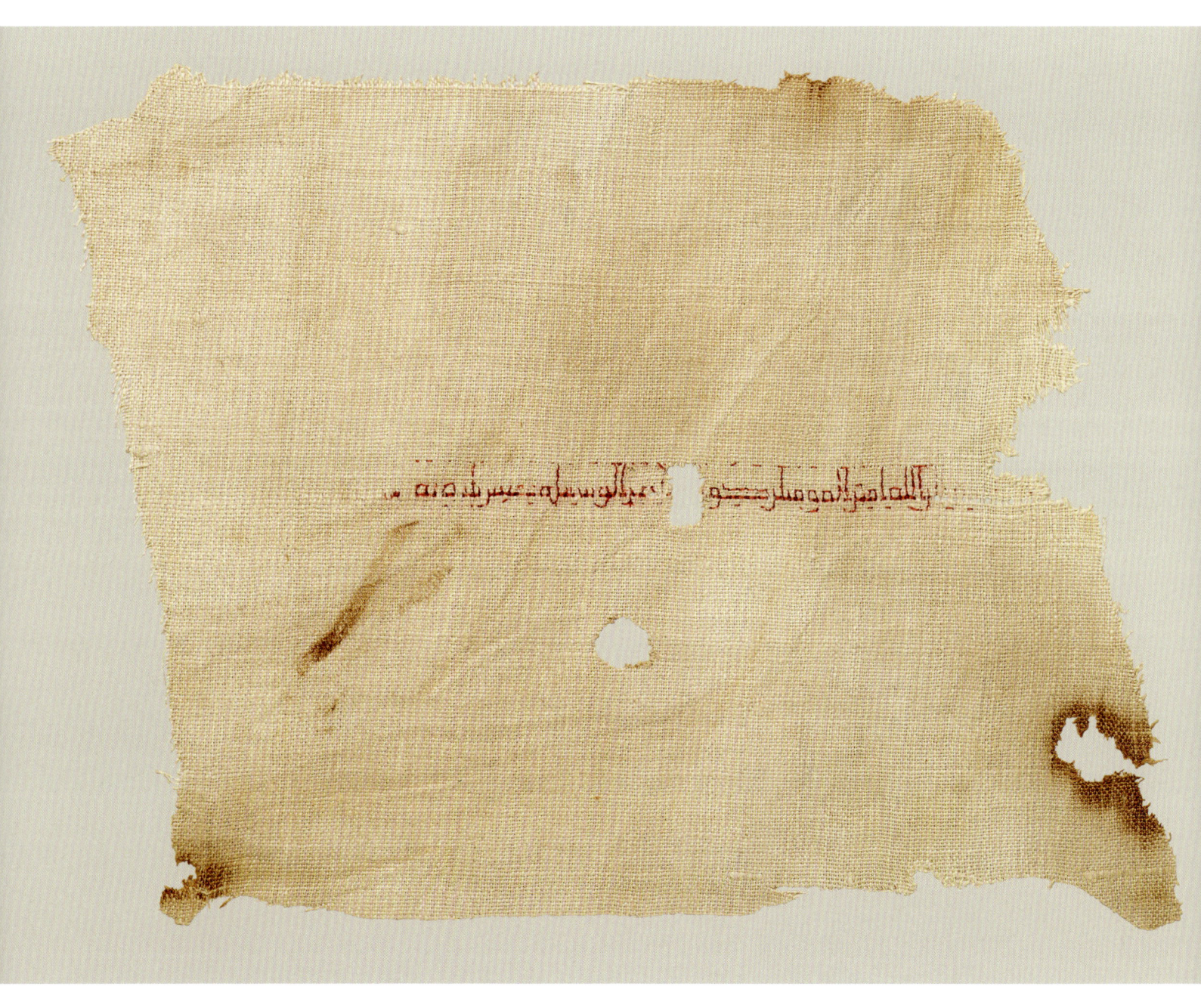

Cat. 15 *TIRAZ* FRAGMENT FROM
THE REIGN OF THE ABBASID
CALIPH AL-MUQTADIR
(r. 908–32)
Egypt, 310 AH / 922–23 CE

Description: Fragment of undyed linen
embroidered in red silk with one
line of Kufic inscription.

Materials: linen and silk: plain weave
and embroidery

Dimensions: h. 18.5 cm, w. 21.7 cm;
max. letter height 1.0 cm

Ground fabric: linen, undyed, predominant-warp
plain weave, dense texture (*dabiqi*);
good quality (2)

Thread count: warp 22 S-spun, weft 14 S-spun

Thread thickness: warp 0.3–0.5 mm loose–medium
twist, weft 0.3 mm loose–medium
twist

Embroidery: silk (red), back and flat stitch

Provenance: Ex H.P. Kraus collection, no. 9

Inv. no. LNS 137 T

Related works: See page 503

Inscription:

[...][المقت]در بالله امير المؤمنين ص(ـلـ)ـو(ات الله) (ما) امر الوزير سنة عشر ثلث مائة

[...] [al-Muqta]dir bi-llah the Commander of the Faithful. B(e)n[edictions of God]. (What) the vizier ordered in the year ten three hundred

Only one item dated 310 AH / 922–23 CE compares with the present piece in terms of epigraphic style, size and colour of the inscription (Related works 1). It was made in Misr, by order of the vizier Hamid ibn al-'Abbas by intermediation of Shafi' *mawla amir al-mu'minin*. Its inscription carries more complete administrative data, as the present piece refers only to the order by the vizier, who remains unnamed, and does not mention the intermediary, nor the workshop and its location. A large number of *tiraz* pieces made in Misr during other years of al-Muqtadir's reign compare with this one in terms of epigraphic style and its execution in red silk embroidery (Related works 2–14). It is plausible that this item, too, was made in Misr.

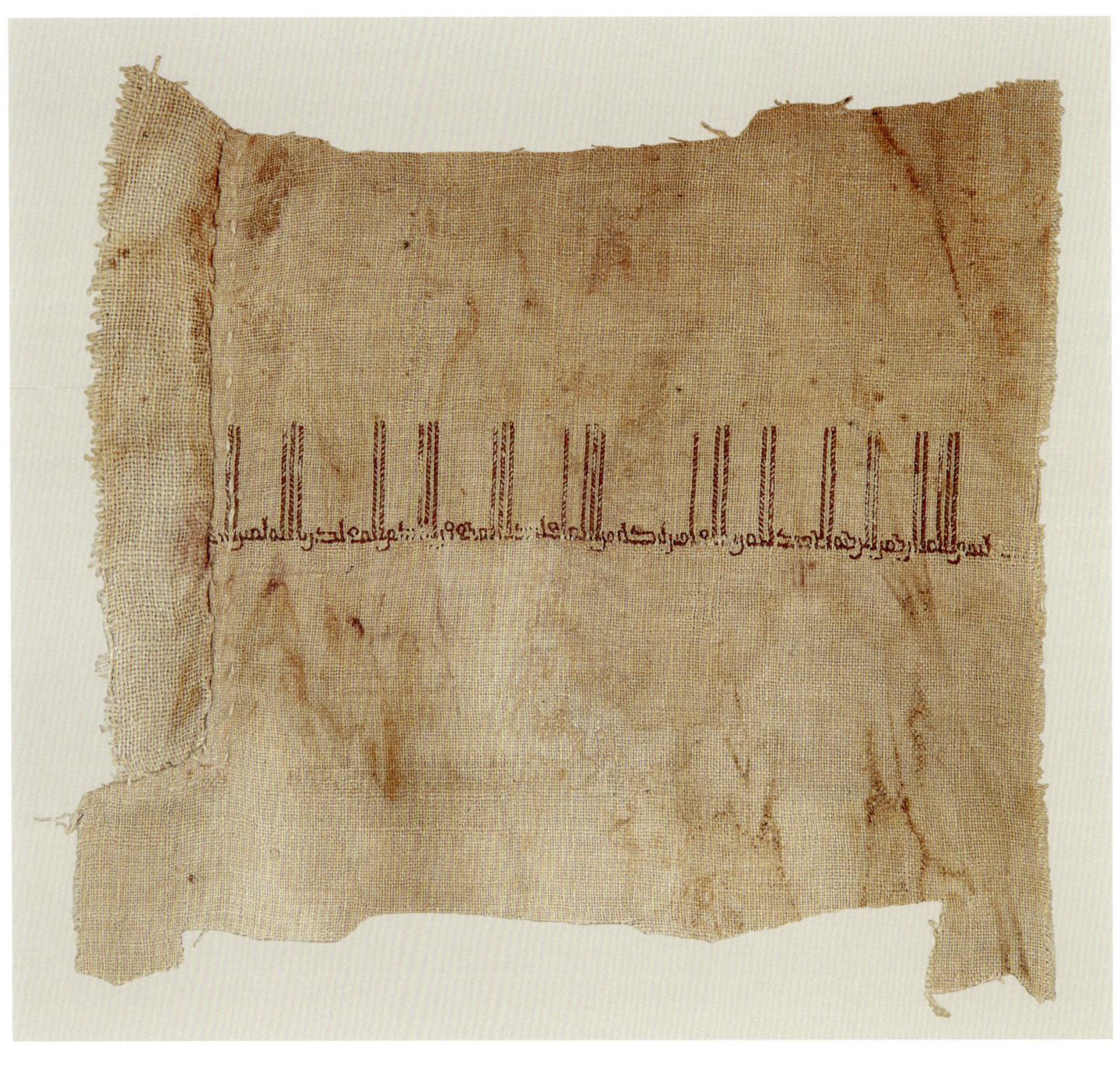

Cat. 16 *TIRAZ* FRAGMENT FROM
THE REIGN OF THE ABBASID
CALIPH AL-MUQTADIR
(r. 908–32)
Egypt, early 10th century CE

Description: Fragment of undyed linen
embroidered in red silk, with
one line of Kufic inscription.

Materials: linen and silk: plain weave
and embroidery

Dimensions: h. 13.7 cm, w. 14.3 cm;
max. letter height 2.1 cm

Ground fabric: linen, undyed, balanced plain
weave, tight texture (*dabiqi*);
very good quality (1); seam on
the left side

Thread count: warp 26 S-spun, weft 23 S-spun

Thread thickness: warp 0.25 mm loose–medium
twist, weft 0.15–0.25 mm loose–
medium twist

Embroidery: silk, dyed (red), back and flat stitch

Provenance: Ex H.P. Kraus collection, no. 4

Inv. no. LNS 132 T

Related works: See page 503

Inscription:

بسم الله الرحمن الرحيم الحمد لله رب العلمين بركة من الله لعبد الله جعفر الامام المقتدر بالله امير الـمـ[ؤمنين] [...]

In the name of God, the Most Merciful, the Most Compassionate. Praise be to
God the Lord of the worlds. Blessing from God to the servant of God Ja'far al-
Imam al-Muqtadir bi-llah the Commander of the Fai[thful] [...]

The inscription is almost identical with one in the Bouvier Collection, to such a
degree that one could well attribute them to the same hand (Related works 1).
Not only are the shapes of the individual letters comparable, but the height of
the inscription is exactly the same, and the rhythmic appearance of the upper
hastae is identical. The two pieces are executed in the same stitches, with the
direction of the stitches (particularly on the upper hastae) following the same
pattern. Since both pieces are fragmentary, having lost the administrative
data once contained in the inscription, a secure attribution to a particular
year, workshop and location is not possible. However, it is likely that both are
products of the workshops at Misr and date from around 300 AH / 912–13 CE,
as is suggested by the closeness to a number of related inscriptions (Related
works 2–10).

It is noteworthy that the present fragment was once part of a tailored
garment as it has a seam on the left side. Where exactly the present fragment
would have been located within that garment is not clearly identifiable;
the angular shape of the seam suggests possibly an attached pocket. As the
inscription does not continue beyond the seam it was probably cut intentionally.
A number of full garment fragments made from *tiraz* textiles have survived
(see chapter 1).

Cat. 17 *TIRAZ* **FRAGMENT FROM THE REIGN OF THE ABBASID CALIPH AL-MUQTADIR**
(r. 908–32)
Egypt, early 10th century CE

Description: Fragment of undyed linen ground fabric, with one line of Kufic inscription embroidered in red silk.

Materials: linen and silk: plain weave and embroidery

Dimensions: h. 11.9 cm, w. 31.8 cm; max. letter height 0.6 cm

Ground fabric: linen, undyed, balanced plain weave, tight texture (*dabiqi*); good quality (2)

Thread count: warp 22 S-spun, weft 20 S-spun

Thread thickness: warp 0.3–0.4 mm medium twist, weft 0.3–0.4 mm medium twist

Embroidery: silk, dyed (red), back and flat stitch

Provenance: Ex H.P. Kraus collection, no. 6

Inv. no. LNS 134 T

Related works: See page 503

Inscription:

بسم الله الرحمن الرحيم الحمد(لله رب) العلمين بركة من الله بركه من الله لعبد الله جعفر الامام المقتدر بالله امير المؤمنين ايده الله
ما امر الوزير بطر(از) العا[مة] [...]

In the name of God, the Most Merciful, the Most Compassionate. Praise be
to (God the Lord) of the worlds. Blessing from God. Blessing from God to
the servant of God Ja'far al-Imam al-Muqtadir bi-llah the Commander of the
Faithful, may God strengthen him. Of what has been ordered by the vizier in
the tir(az) al-'a[mma] [...]

The reading of the inscription towards the left is conjectural after the phrase
'ayyaduhu Allah', as much of the silk has disappeared and only the stitches
remain. The comparison with other similar inscriptions suggests a reading of
'ma amara al-wazir bi-tiraz al-'amma'. Of what remains one can identify that
there is a *waw* followed by *ya* and *ra*, *ta*, *ra* and *alif*, and another set of *alif*, *'ayn*
and *alif*. The epigraphic type seen here is characterized by the small size of the
letters (max. letter height 0.6 cm), particularly the upper stems of *alif* and *lam*,
which are much taller in other contemporary inscriptions. In the case of these
letters, only one warp thread is couched, which means that the letters do not
appear very broad. The baseline is embroidered on two or three warps. *Mim*,
'ayn and *fa* are near circular. The letters are plain – that is, there are no foliations
above the baseline or meaningless lower terminals or festoons below.

Several *tiraz* textiles from the reign of al-Muqtadir exist that can be compared
with this piece in terms of epigraphic type, particularly the tiny letter size (Related
works 1–8). While most inscriptions during al-Muqtadir's reign, and indeed most
of the early Abbasid period, are characterized by an emphasis on the vertical, by
rather thin elongated *alif* and *lam* with a standard letter height of around 1.0 cm,
the inscriptions in this and the related works listed here, comprise a standard
letter height between 0.5 and 0.8 cm. Chronologically these inscriptions span
much of al-Muqtadir's reign, so it is difficult to date the present piece accurately
to a particular cluster. The place of production of all (except one textile, whose
inscription does not specify a location) is Misr. It is therefore very likely that
this piece, too, was made in Misr. The workshop type *tiraz al-'amma* is found in
three cases conforming with our piece. The ordering of the textile is in almost all
cases credited to the vizier, who is always named, though his name seems to be
omitted in this case. Most of the comparative inscriptions feature the full caliphal
and administrative protocol and mention, in addition to the vizier and the place
of production, the name and title of the person in charge of the administrative
execution of the order: in four cases this is Shafi' al-Muqtadiri, who carried the title
mawla amir al-mu'minin and was an important member of al-Muqtadir's court
(see above, pp. 157–59). Given the fragmentary state of the al-Sabah inscription,
it is perfectly possible that it may also at one time have contained his name.

Cat. 18 *TIRAZ* FRAGMENT FROM THE REIGN OF THE ABBASID CALIPH AL-MUQTADIR (r. 908–32)

Egypt, early 10th century CE

Description: Fragment of undyed linen, with one line of Kufic inscription embroidered in red silk.

Materials: linen and silk: plain weave and embroidery

Dimensions: h. 25.9 cm, w. 41.1 cm; max. letter height 1.1 cm

Ground fabric: linen warp and weft, undyed, balanced plain weave, close texture (*dabiqi*), glazed and polished; good quality (2)

Thread count: warp 19 S-spun, weft 18 S-spun

Thread thickness: warp 0.3–0.5 mm medium twist, weft 0.3–0.5 mm medium twist

Embroidery: silk, dyed (red), back and flat stitch

Provenance: Ex H.P. Kraus collection, no. 7

Inv. no. LNS 135 T

Related works: See pages 503–04

Inscription:

(بسم الله الرحمن الرحيم الحمد لله رب) العلمين [صلى] الله (على محمد خاتم النبيين عز لعبد الله جعفر) الامام المقتدر بالله امير المؤمنين اطال الله بقاه[...]

(In the name of God, the Most Merciful, the Most Compassionate. Praise be to God, the Lord) of the worlds [benedictions from] God (upon Muhammad the Seal of the Prophets. Glory to the servant of God Ja'far) al-Imam al-Muqtadir bi-llah the Commander of the Faithful. May God prolong his existence [...]

The epigraphic style of this piece is characterized by short upper hastae. At the same time, the embroidery has been executed very carefully and regularly. The textile relates to a number of items that have inscriptions in a comparable epigraphic style from the period of al-Muqtadir (r. 908–32) (Related works 1–9). The evidence given here suggests that these textiles were products of the workshops in Misr and their occurrence is chronologically spread from the beginning of al-Muqtadir's reign to its end. In fact, it seems that the style continued into the reign of the Abbasid caliph al-Radi (r. 934–40), as is suggested by two textiles from Misr in the Textile Museum, Washington, DC (Related works 10–11). Both were ordered from Misr, one by the vizier 'Ali ibn Muhammad by intermediation of Shafi' *mawla amir al-mu'minin*, the other from the *tiraz al-khasssa* by the vizier Muhammad ibn 'Ali by intermediation of 'Ubayyid *mawla amir al-mu'minin*.

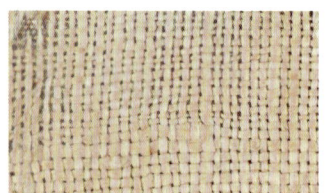

Cat. 19 *TIRAZ* **FRAGMENT FROM THE REIGN OF THE ABBASID CALIPH AL-MUQTADIR** (r. 908–32)

Egypt, early 10th century CE

Description: Fragment of undyed linen embroidered in brown silk, with one line of Kufic inscription.

Materials: linen and silk: plain weave and embroidery

Dimensions: h. 24 cm, w. 40.3 cm; max. letter height 2.2 cm

Ground fabric: linen warp and weft, undyed, balanced plain weave, dense texture (*dabiqi*), glazed and polished; good quality (2)

Thread count: warp 22 S-spun, weft 20 S-spun

Thread thickness: warp 0.3–0.6 mm medium–tight, weft 0.25–0.6 mm medium–tight

Embroidery: silk, dyed (dark brown), couching over four warps (stems) and chain stitch (lower letter terminals)

Provenance: Ex H.P. Kraus collection, no. 12

Inv. no. LNS 140 T

Related works: See page 504

Inscription: بسم الله الرحمن الرحيم [عز] من الله للخليفة جعفر الامام المقتدر بالله امير المـؤ[منين] [...]

In the name of God, the Most Merciful, the Most Compassionate. [Glory] from God to the caliph Ja'far al-Imam al-Muqtadir bi-llah the Commander of the Fai[thful] [...]

The script here is composed of broad letters with a pronounced vertical (as opposed to a thin line, as seen in many other inscriptions), a characteristic achieved by embroidering each letter on quadruplets (or other equal sets) of counted warp threads. The low letters such as *mim*, *ha* and *qaf* are square-shaped rather than round, as only one thread is carried over straight to form the upper side of the letter, the prime and central *ba*, *ta*, *nun* and *sin* are angular, and the stems of *alif* and *lam* ascend in a straight and broad line. Some of the upper terminals of the low letters are embellished by small arrowhead-like pointed finials. Rounded letter terminals below the baseline, in the case of terminal *mim*, *ra* and *waw*, are bordered by a non-functional festoon. The festoon is chain stitched in order to achieve the rounded shape of the crescents, which would not have been possible on counted threads with couching. A number of examples with comparable inscriptions from the reign of al-Muqtadir have survived (Related works 1–19). The chronology of this epigraphic style continues into the reigns of the caliphs al-Qahir (r. 932–34) (Related works 20) and al-Radi (r. 934–40) (Related works 21–26),[26] and there is evidence for its use in Tinnis and Misr. The inscriptions share a similar height of letters (*c*. 2.0 cm), the stems of *alif* and *lam* do not terminate in pointed spearheads, and the balance between vertical height and horizontal spacing is almost equal. The use of a multi-plaited *lam–alif* here is a striking

feature, albeit rare among this group. It can also be found in a *tiraz* at the Royal Ontario Museum, Toronto (Related works 7). This fragment is dated 306 AH / 918–19 CE and was made in an unspecified *tiraz* workshop in Tinnis. It would be tempting to attribute the present inscription to the same place of production. The appearance of the caliphal *laqab* (regnal title) al-Muqtadir is also similar among the inscriptions in this group and may suggest manufacture in the same set of workshops.

Cat. 20 **TIRAZ FRAGMENT ATTRIBUTED TO THE REIGN OF THE ABBASID CALIPH AL-MUQTADIR** (r. 908–32)
Egypt, early 10th century CE

Description: Fragment of undyed linen, with one line of Kufic inscription embroidered in red silk.

Materials: linen and silk: plain weave and embroidery

Dimensions: h. 6 cm, w. 17 cm; max letter height 1.9 cm

Ground fabric: linen warp and weft, undyed, predominant-warp plain weave, close texture (*dabiqi*), regular; good quality (2)

Thread count: warp 26 S-spun, weft 19 S-spun

Thread thickness: warp 0.15–0.4 mm loose–medium twist, weft 0.3 mm loose–medium twist

Embroidery: silk, dyed (red), couching and chain stitch over three warps.

Provenance: Ex H.P. Kraus collection, no. 11

Inv. no. LNS 139 T

Related works: See page 504

Inscription:

[...] [بر]اكة من الله لعبد الله امير المؤمنين ايده [ال]له مما امر بع[ـمله] [...]

[...] [ble]ssing from God to the servant of God the Commander of the Faithful may [Go]d strengthen him. What has been ordered to be ma[de] [...]

It is noteworthy that the inscription omits both the *ism* (given name) and *laqab* (regnal title) of the ruling caliph, who is referred to here as "abd Allah amir al-mu'minin' with a lacuna between the two. After the term *'abd Allah* (servant of God) would normally appear the *ism*, followed by the religious designation *al-imam* (leader of the religious community) and then the caliph's *laqab*, followed by the honorific *amir al-mu'minin* ('Commander of the Faithful').

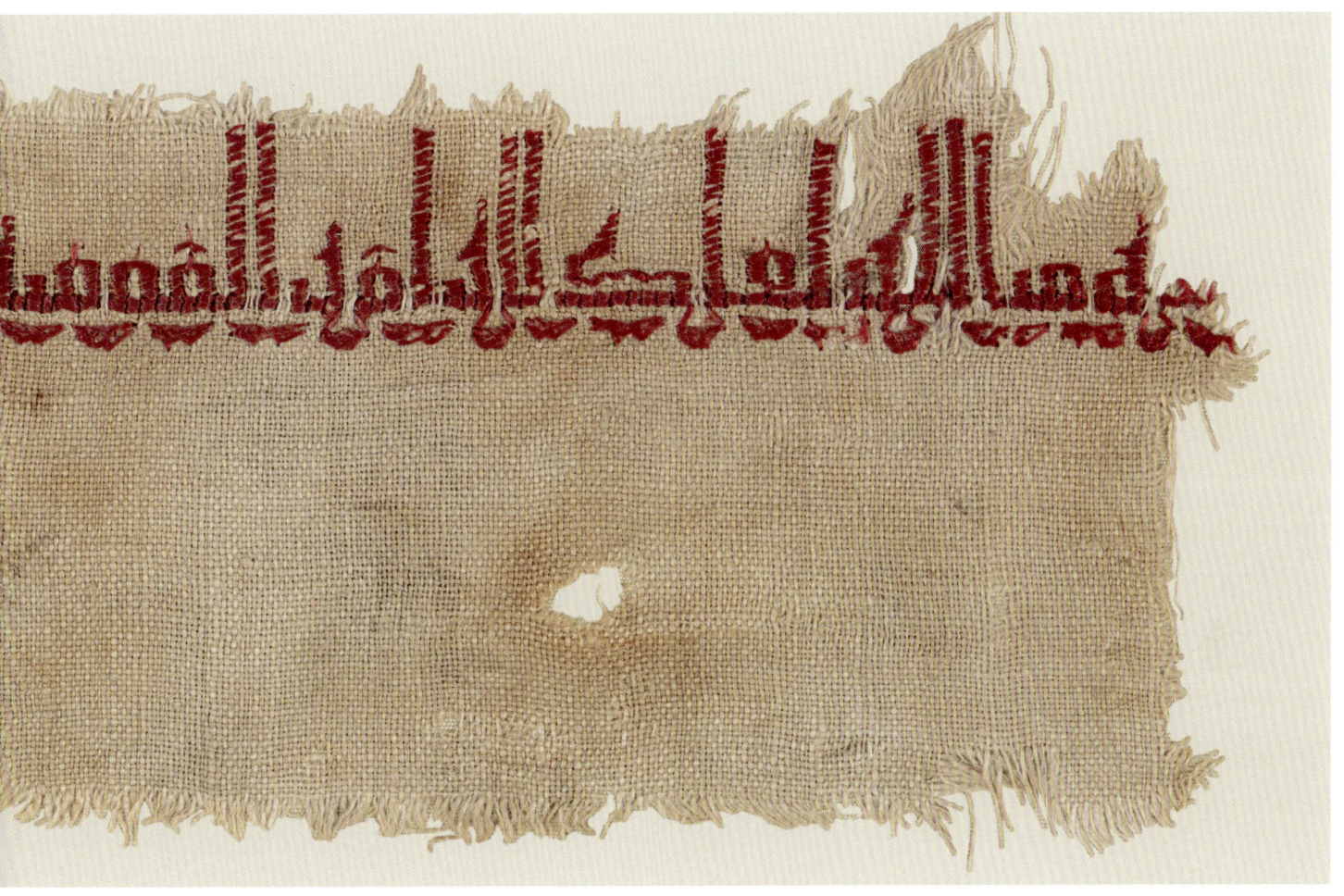

In technique and style, this inscription relates to cat. nos 19 and 22, which date from the reign of al-Muqtadir, possibly from around the first decade of the tenth century. Although the style continued under al-Muqtadir's successors al-Qahir and al-Radi, an attribution of the present piece to al-Muqtadir's reign is more likely on the basis of the close similarities with dated inscriptions from his reign: for example, a textile in the Metropolitan Museum of Art, New York, dated 310 AH / 922–23 CE, and another in the Royal Ontario Museum, Toronto, dated 305 AH / 917–18 CE (Related works 1, 2).

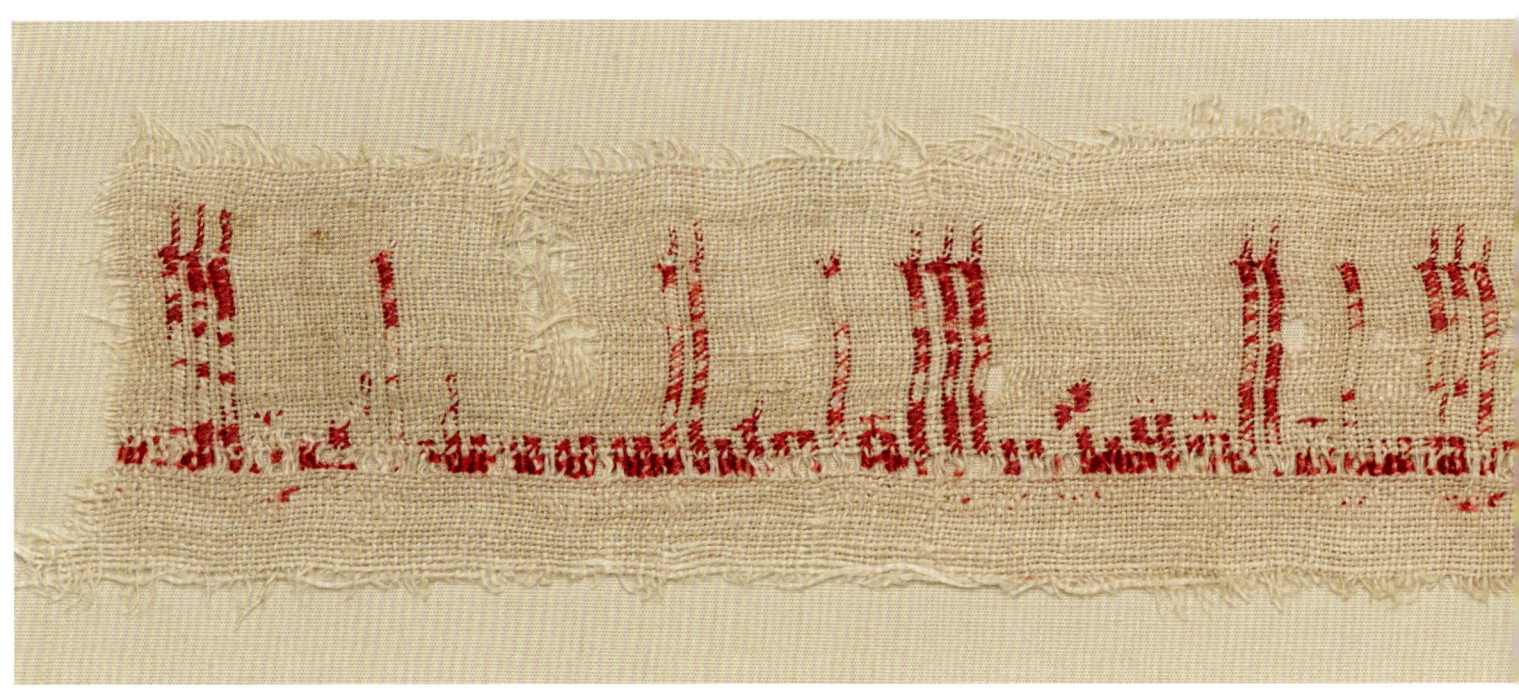

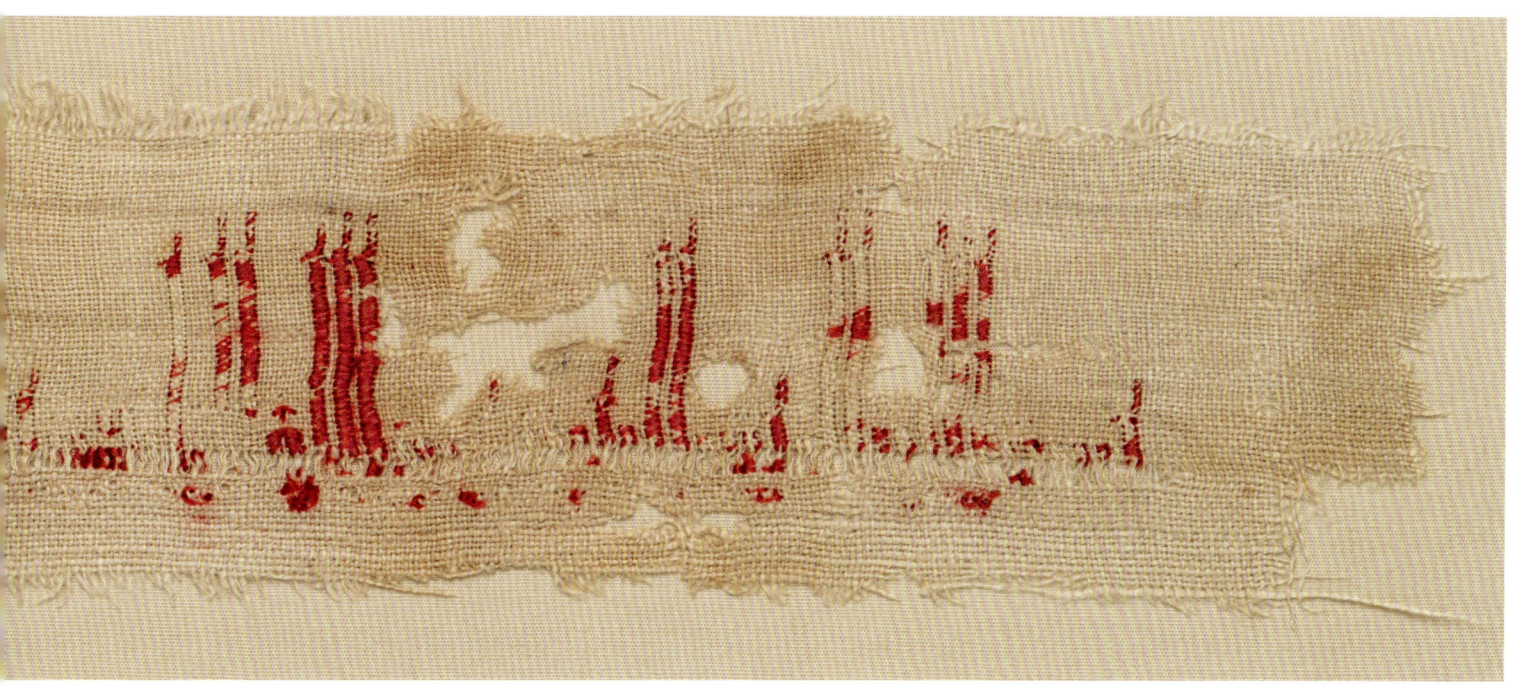

Cat. 21   *TIRAZ* FRAGMENT FROM
THE REIGN OF THE ABBASID
CALIPH AL-MUQTADIR
(r. 908–32)
Egypt, early 10th century CE

Description: Fragment of undyed linen, with
one line of Kufic inscription
embroidered in red silk.

Materials: linen and silk: plain weave
and embroidery

Dimensions: h. 6.1 cm, w. 29.2 cm;
max. letter height 2.9 cm

Ground fabric: linen warp and weft, undyed,
predominant-warp plain weave,
tight texture (*dabiqi*); good
quality (2)

Thread count: warp 19 Z-spun, weft 20 S-spun

Thread thickness: warp 0.3–0.5 mm medium twist,
weft 0.2 mm medium–tight twist

Embroidery: silk, dyed (red), back, flat, satin
and chain stitch

Provenance: formerly H.P. Kraus collection,
no. 14

Inv. no. LNS 142 T

Related works: See page 504

Inscription: بسم الله الرحمن الرحيم بركة من الله للخليفة جعفر الامام المقتدر بالله امير المؤمنين ايده الله [...]

In the name of God, the Merciful, the Compassionate. Blessing from God to the caliph Jaʿfar, the Imam Al-Muqtadir bi-llah, Commander of the Faithful, may God strengthen him […]

The epigraphic style of the inscription is characterized by its bold and angular letter shapes with a pronounced baseline, rounded chain-stitched lower terminals and spear-headed hastae. Inscriptions of this type have survived in some quantity from al-Muqtadir's reign (Related works 1–16). For comparison, see cat. nos 19 and 20, which have inscriptions executed in a similar technique.

Cat. 22   *TIRAZ* FRAGMENT
ATTRIBUTED TO THE
REIGN OF THE ABBASID
CALIPH AL-MUQTADIR
(r. 908–32)
Egypt, early 10th century CE

Description:	Fragment of undyed linen, with one line of Kufic inscription embroidered in red silk.
Materials:	linen and silk: plain weave and embroidery
Dimensions:	h. 23.5 cm, w. 35 cm; max. letter height 2.0 cm
Ground fabric:	linen warp and weft, undyed, balanced plain weave, dense texture (*dabiqi*), regular structure; good quality (2)
Thread count:	warp 21 S-spun, weft 20 S-spun
Thread thickness:	warp 0.4 mm slight–medium twist, weft 0.3–0.4 mm slight–medium twist
Embroidery:	silk, dyed (red), couching, flat and back stitch, very regular, weft thread drawn for the baseline of the inscription, stitches on sets of four warps
Provenance:	Ex H.P. Kraus collection, no. 5

Inv. no. LNS 133 T

Inscription: undecipherable

The inscription here belongs to the same group as cat. nos 19, 20 and 21. Although its content, which once must have contained a caliphal protocol, is no longer decipherable, enough silk has remained to judge the nature and quality of the embroidery, and consequently its possible attribution to a workshop. The hastae show careful and regular stitching on counted threads. The stems as well as the baseline were stitched on sets of four warps and one weft thread was pulled out from the fabric to mark the baseline. The baseline must have once been composed of several horizontal layers of stitches, and hence must have been quite pronounced. The stitches above the lower letters, ascending from the baseline in some cases, form small hood-like pointed terminals. Below the baseline there is a continuous series of stitches forming small crescents, more numerous than any possible letter terminals. Comparable inscriptions are attested for the workshops of Misr and Tinnis (see commentary for cat. no. 19).

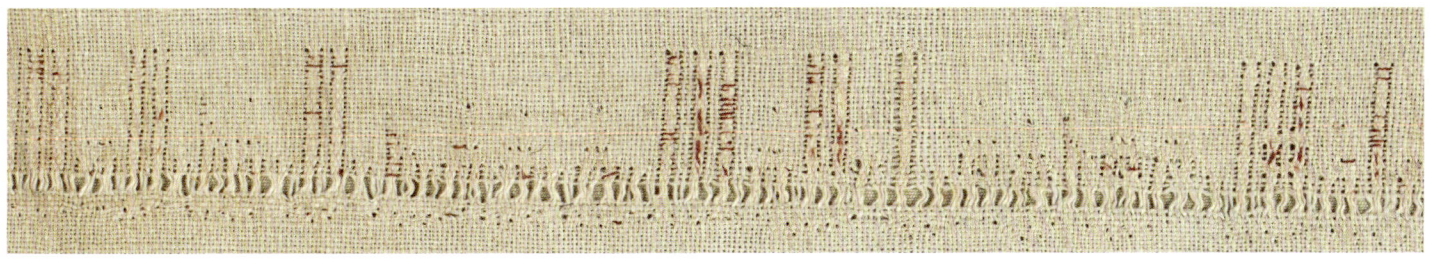

Cat. 23 *TIRAZ* FRAGMENT FROM
THE REIGN OF THE ABBASID
CALIPH AL-QAHIR
(r. 932–34)
Egypt, 10th century CE

Description: Fragment of undyed linen, with
one line of Kufic inscription
embroidered in red silk.

Materials: linen and silk: plain weave
and embroidery

Dimensions: h. 15.8 cm, w. 13.1 cm;
max. letter height 1.6 cm

Ground fabric: linen warp and weft, undyed,
balanced plain weave, tight texture
(*dabiqi*), some irregularities;
medium quality (3)

Thread count: warp 14 SZ-spun, weft 17 S-spun

Thread thickness: 0.3–0.4 mm slight–medium twist,
weft 0.3–0.4 mm slight–medium
twist

Embroidery: silk, dyed (red), flat stitch (hastae)
and chain stitch (lower terminals)

Provenance: Ex H.P. Kraus collection, no. 42

Inv. no. LNS 165 T

Related works: See pages 504–05

Inscription: [...] ابو منصور الامام القاهر بالله امير المؤمنين ايد[ه] [...]

[...] Abu Mansur al-Imam al-Qahir bi-llah the Commander of the Faithful,
may [God] strengthen [him] [...]

The embroidery stitches and the linen material of the ground fabric suggest
that this piece is of Egyptian manufacture, probably from a workshop in
Misr. A number of Egyptian *tiraz* textiles that have survived from the reign of
al-Qahir (r. 932–34) can be related to the present piece (Related works 1–26).
Particularly prominent for the style of script seen here are the festoon-like
lower letter terminals.

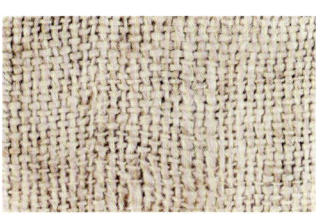

Cat. 24 *TIRAZ* **FRAGMENT FROM THE REIGN OF THE ABBASID CALIPH AL-QAHIR**
(r. 932–34)
Egypt, 10th century CE

Description: Fragment of undyed linen, with one line of Kufic inscription embroidered in red silk.

Materials: linen and silk: plain weave and embroidery

Dimensions: h. 19.7 cm, w. 27.9 cm; max. letter height 3.0 cm

Ground fabric: linen warp and weft, undyed, balanced plain weave, dense texture (*dabiqi*), glazed and polished; good quality (2)

Thread count: warp 15 S-spun, weft 13 S-spun

Thread thickness: warp 0.5–0.6 mm medium twist, weft 0.5–0.6 mm medium twist

Embroidery: silk, dyed (red), flat stitch and braiding (baseline and hastae), chain stitch (lower terminals)

Provenance: Ex H.P. Kraus collection, no. 37

Inv. no. LNS 166 T

Related works: See page 505

Inscription: بسم الله الرحمن الرحيم (عز؟) للخليفة محمد الامام القا[هر بالله] [...]

In the name of God, the Most Merciful, the Most Compassionate. (Glory?) to the caliph Muhammad al-Imam al-Qa[hir bi-llah] [...]

The epigraphic style of this inscription is characterized by fairly broad hastae with pointed tips, multiple twisted *lam–alif*s, upward triangular and pointed extensions of letters such as *dal*, *mim* and *ha*, and a festoon-like sequence of terminals below the baseline. Among published *tiraz* textiles from the reign of al-Qahir, this seems to be the only one in this particular epigraphic style. A related example from al-Qahir's reign, though not exactly identical, is in the Metropolitan Museum of Art, New York (Related works 1); it shares with this piece the pointed tips of the upper letter terminals.

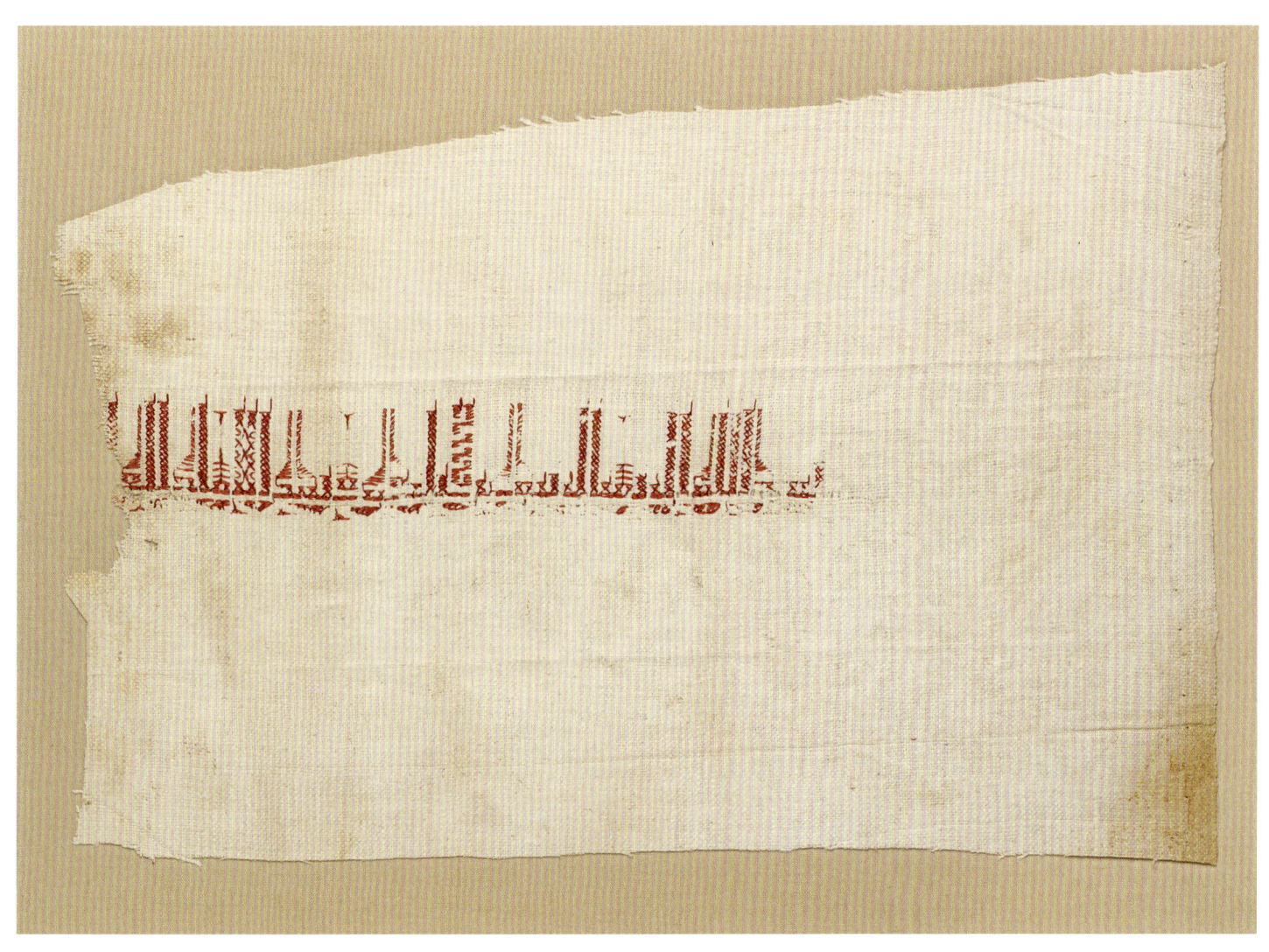

Cat. 25 *TIRAZ* **FRAGMENT FROM THE REIGN OF THE ABBASID CALIPH AL-RADI (r. 934–40)**
Egypt, 10th century CE

Description: Fragment of undyed linen with one line of dark blue silk tapestry-woven Kufic inscription.

Materials: linen and silk: plain weave and tapestry

Dimensions: h. 18.8 cm, w. 44 cm; max. letter height 1.6 cm

Ground fabric: linen warp and weft, undyed, balanced plain weave, gauzy texture (*sharb*); good quality (2)

Thread count: warp 24 S-spun, weft 25 S-spun

Thread thickness: warp 0.15–0.3 mm slight–medium twist, weft 0.1–0.2 tight twist

Tapestry: silk, dyed (dark blue); slit; hastae woven on warps lifted up from the base fabric; supplementary linen weft filling between the lower letters

Provenance: Ex H.P. Kraus collection, no. 31

Inv. no. LNS 155 T

Related works: See page 505

Inscription: [...] الله ونصر من الله وعز من الله لعبد الله ابي العباس (احمد) الراضي بـ[الله] [...]

[...] God and help from God, and glory from God to the servant of God Abi al-'Abbas (Ahmad) al-Radi bi-[llah] [...]

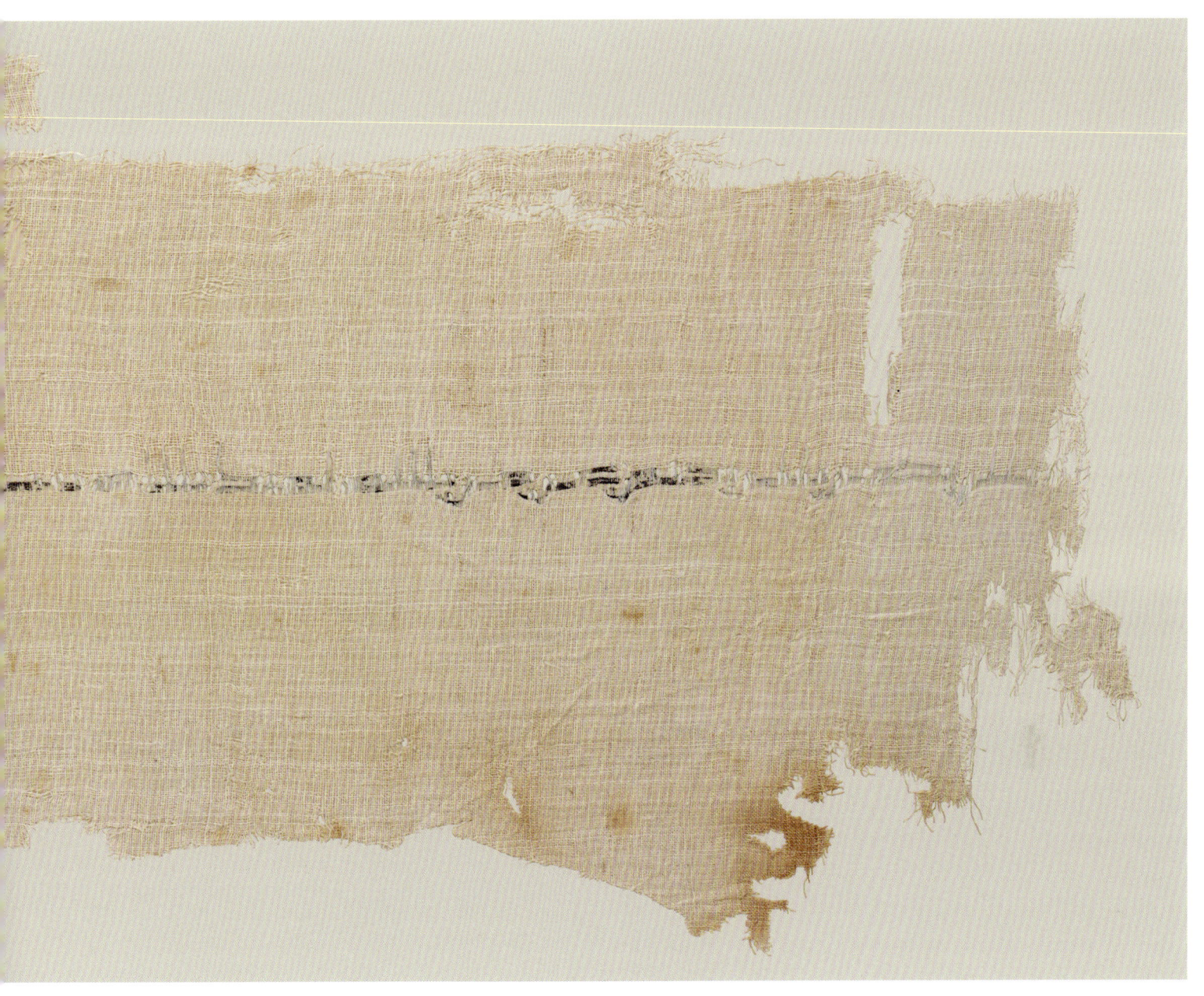

The epigraphic style of the inscription is very close to that of a dated *tiraz* textile inscription in the Textile Museum, Washington, DC, which was woven during al-Radi's reign (r. 934–40) at Shata in Egypt in 325 AH / 936–37 CE (Related works 1). Another closely related example from al-Radi's reign is in the Royal Ontario Museum, Toronto (Related works 2).

Cat. 26 *TIRAZ* FRAGMENT FROM
THE REIGN OF THE ABBASID
CALIPH AL-RADI (r. 934–40)
Egypt, 10th century CE

Description: Fragment of undyed linen, with
one line of Kufic inscription
embroidered in red silk.

Materials: linen and silk: plain weave
and embroidery

Dimensions: h. 12.6 cm, w. 29.7 cm;
max. letter height 0.7 cm

Ground fabric: linen warp and weft, undyed,
balanced plain weave, close texture
(*dabiqi*); good quality (2)]

Thread count: warp 21 S-spun, weft 17 S-spun

Thread thickness: warp 0.2–0.3 mm slight–medium
twist, weft 0.3 mm medium twist

Embroidery: silk, dyed (red), couching, back
and flat stitches

Provenance: Ex H.P. Kraus collection, no. 45

Inv. no. LNS 168 T

Related works: See page 505

Inscription:

[...] (لعبد الله محمد) الامام الراضي بالله امير المؤمنين ايده الله ما امر الوزير علي بن عيسي بعمله بمصر على يدي عبايد مو(لى) امير
المؤمنين سنة عشر(!sic) وثلث مائة [...]

[...] (to the servant of God Muhammad) al-imam al-Radi bi-llah the Commander of the Faithful, may God strengthen him. Of what has been ordered to be made by the vizier ʿAli ibn ʿIsa in Misr under the direction of ʿUbayyid the cli(ent) of the Commander of the Faithful. In the year three hundred and ten [*sic*] [...]

The reading of the inscription proposed differs from that in the Kraus sale catalogue.[27] The name of the vizier is clearly mentioned as ʿAli ibn ʿIsa and the place of production as Misr. The date is incorrectly written. The vizier mentioned here, ʿAli ibn ʿIsa ibn Daʾud ibn Jarrah, was actually not in office under al-Radi, but under al-Muqtadir in 301–04 AH / 913–17 CE and 314–16 AH / 926–29 CE.[28] It is curious that his name should be mentioned in a *tiraz* inscription of al-Radi. However, this is not unique. Of *c.* 126 known *tiraz* textile inscriptions known from al-Radi's reign, one in the Islamic Museum in Cairo also records the order by the vizier ʿAli ibn ʿIsa (Related works 1). Like the present piece, this was made in Misr and mentions the title *mawla amir al-muʾminin* of the executive (*ʿala yaday*), but not his name; the date, too, is unclear.

It is not entirely clear why these two inscriptions record the order of a vizier no longer in office. An explanation may be offered by the biography of ʿAli ibn ʿIsa and his circumstances at the caliphal court.[29] Born into a Persian family of bureaucrats, ʿAli's first appointment as vizier was in 300 AH / 912–13 CE under al-Muqtadir to replace the vizier Abu ʿAli Muhammad ibn ʿUbaydallah ibn Yahya al-Khaqani. His tenure lasted for four years, during which he tried to achieve financial stability for the state, despite the high costs of military spending in conflicts against the Fatimids and other rebellious movements that were challenging Abbasid power. ʿAli was dismissed and replaced in 304 AH / 916–17 CE with the vizier Ibn al-Furat. Yet ʿAli was already being consulted by the caliph a year later to decide whom to appoint to replace Ibn al-Furat. In 306 AH / 918–19 CE Hamid ibn al-ʿAbbas was appointed vizier, but owing to his incompetence ʿAli ibn ʿIsa was appointed as his deputy shortly afterwards and began to control

most of the affairs of the vizier. Because of his tight control of government spending and his relations with the Karamitian sect, 'Ali was once again thrown out of office, imprisoned and exiled to Mecca and San'a'. After the execution of Ibn al-Furat, 'Ali was appointed overseer of Egypt and Syria. Three years later in 314 AH / 926–27 CE he was again given the post of vizier.

Because of the increasing financial crisis of the Abbasid government, the empire was threatened by the Byzantines and the Karamitian sect, who began to advance on Baghdad. 'Ali ibn 'Isa had to ask the caliph and his mother for financial help to defend the city and to increase the salaries of soldiers, who by that time were mutinous. Although al-Muqtadir first refused 'Ali's resignation in the wake of these events, he was dismissed later and again imprisoned. After Al-Muqtadir had been deposed, 'Ali was released. When the caliph was restored, 'Ali was again employed in the administration. From 318 AH / 930–31 CE he was head of the *diwan*s and general adviser to his cousin, the vizier Sulayman ibn al-Hasan ibn Makhlad and then Abu al-Qasim 'Ubaydallah ibn Muhammad al-Kalwadani. 'Ali was exiled again under his second cousin and enemy Husayn ibn al-Qasim. He held minor administrative posts under the caliph al-Qahir (r. 932–34), and under al-Radi (r. 934–40) was brought back in 323 AH / 934–35 CE, after another period of exile, by the vizier Ibn Muqla in order to negotiate a peace agreement with the Hamdanids, with whom 'Ali had been accused of conspiring. In 325 AH / 936–37 CE 'Ali was general adviser to his brother, the vizier 'Abd al-Rahman ibn 'Isa ibn Da'ud ibn al-Jarrah for a period of three months. After the accession of the caliph al-Mutaqqi (r. 940–44), 'Ali was again assistant to his brother 'Abd al-Rahman, a post he held for about one week and which was his last appointment. 'Ali ibn 'Isa died in 334 AH / 945–46 CE at the age of 89.

The present inscription sheds important light on administrative procedure. From 'Ali ibn 'Isa's turbulent biography it is clear that he was involved intermittently in the Abbasid administration and exerted considerable influence, even when he was not himself vizier. It is thus understandable that his name should appear in a *tiraz* inscription at a time when he was no longer in office as vizier. The fact that two such inscriptions are now known excludes the possibility of a mistake in the choice of name. 'Ali must have been delegated by either the caliph or his vizier to commission textile orders. As *tiraz* inscriptions were subject to the same protocol as all official documents, 'Ali would have been referred to by his old title as vizier, an act of reverence and honour.[30] As 'Ali ibn 'Isa was adviser to his brother in 325 AH / 936–37 CE, it is tempting to date the piece to that year. However, because of his constant involvement in the caliphal administration at high level, he may have been delegated at any time after he was re-employed in the administration in 323 AH / 934–35 CE. Hence an exact chronological attribution is not possible.

In addition to the details mentioned above, the present inscription adds to a series of four textiles from al-Radi's reign, which record the same executive (*'ala yaday*) as in the present inscription, a certain 'Ubayyid, who in three cases is referred to as *mawla amir al-mu'minin* (Related works 2–5). The fact that three of these inscriptions were ordered from Misr fits with the present inscription. Of those four inscriptions, only one is in an epigraphic style comparable with the present piece (Related works 3).[31] This means that the choice of epigraphic style and the administrative procedure recorded in the inscriptions were separate issues. The same workshops were commissioned to produce diverse styles in diverse techniques.[32]

Cat. 27 *TIRAZ* FRAGMENT FROM THE REIGN OF THE ABBASID CALIPH AL-RADI (r. 934–40)
Egypt, 934–36 or 937–39

Description:	Fragment of undyed linen, with one line of Kufic inscription embroidered in red silk.
Materials:	linen and silk: plain weave and embroidery
Dimensions:	h. 32 cm, w. 32.5 cm; max. letter height 1.2 cm
Ground fabric:	linen warp and weft, undyed, balanced plain weave, dense texture, glazed and polished; good quality (2)
Thread count:	warp 16 S-spun, weft 14 S-spun
Thread thickness:	warp 0.5–1.0 mm medium twist, weft 0.3–0.6 mm medium twist
Embroidery:	silk, dyed (red), couching and back stitches
Provenance:	Ex H.P. Kraus collection, no. 44
	Inv. no. LNS 167 T
Related works:	See page 505

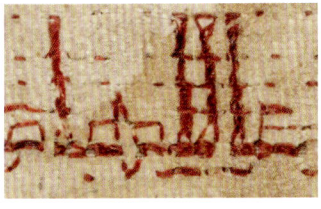

Inscription:

بسم الله الرحمن الرحيم صلى الله على محمد النبي عز لعبد الله محمد الامام الراضي بالله امير المؤمنين اطال الله ما امر الوزير محمد بن علي سنة (اثنان؟) ثلث مائة

In the name of God the Most Merciful, the Most Compassionate. God's blessings be upon Muhammad the Prophet. Glory to the servant of God Muhammad al-imam al-Radi bi-llah the Commander of the Faithful. May God prolong his (life). Of what has been ordered by the vizier Muhammad ibn 'Ali, in the year three hundred (and two?)

The epigraphic style of the inscription can be found in a number of *tiraz* textiles from the reign of al-Radi. Florence Day summarized the style as follows:

> the tall letters (here *lam* and *alif* only) are composed of two vertical threads laid on the surface of the cloth and held in place by stitches making four bars; these are continued horizontally the whole length of the inscription in a darning stitch; below the inscription darning stitches with the tails horizontal make another straight line. The tall letters have

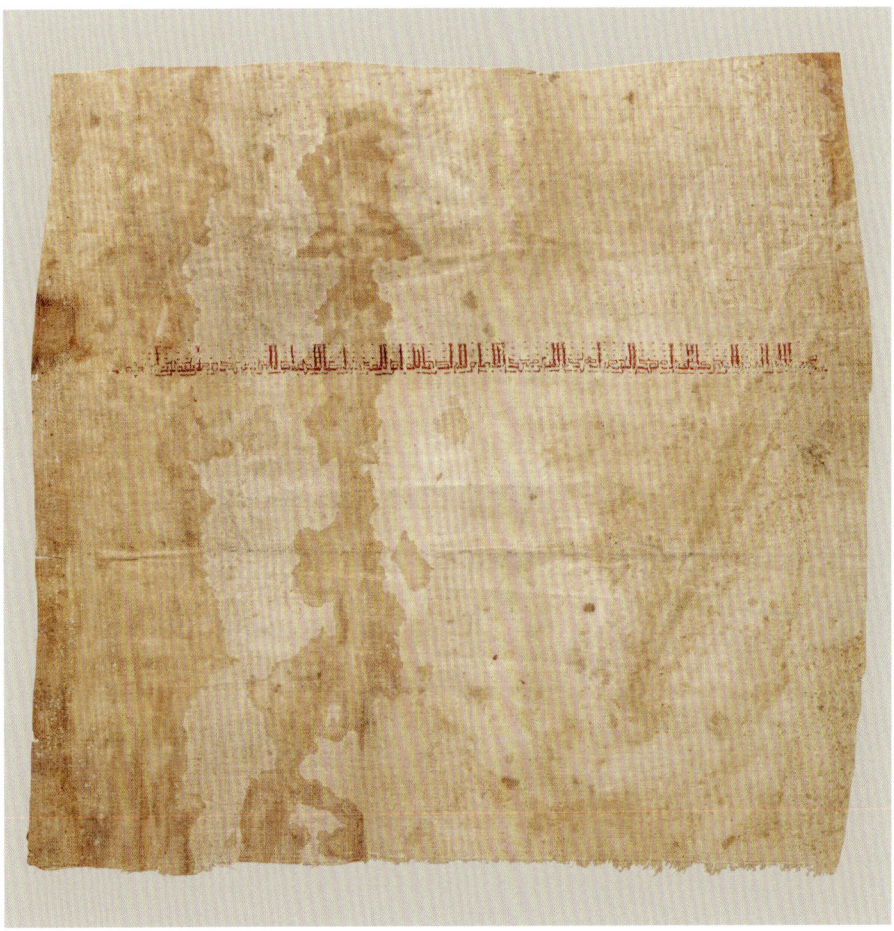

V-shaped finials, the low ones have finials in the shape of right angles. The style is involved, decoration being put before clarity; *dal* and *ha* have the same form, *mim*, *ta*, *ha* and *waw* have two tails, in some words the letters are out of order.³³

Prominent features are the angular approach to the shape of the letters and lower terminals, and the use of gridlines to form the background of the inscription. Noticeable also is the shape of the letter *'ayn*, which is composed of a trefoil. These inscriptions are generally difficult to read, as the letter shapes are often contorted. Their sizes are comparable to the present piece, ranging from 0.9 cm to 1.5 cm.

Many of these inscriptions record the order by one of al-Radi's viziers, Muhammad ibn 'Ali, who was in office in 322–24 AH / 933–36 CE and 326–27 AH / 937–39 CE (Related works 1–6). He is also known as Ibn Muqla, a *katib* who reformed the Arabic script (for his biography, see cat. no. 8). Two of the works related to the present piece have inscriptions that almost exactly match its wording, particularly after the *basmallah* where the phrase 'salla Allahu 'ala Muhammad al-nabi 'izz li-'abd Allah' is quite unusual. Those inscriptions that have survived complete do not mention a place of production, and usually the correct reading of the date is difficult or ambiguous. Kühnel attributed the group to the *khassa* workshops of Misr on the basis of a piece in the Textile Museum, Washington, DC, which shows a similar epigraphic style, but is different in terms of execution and size (Related works 5). However, a piece in the Royal Ontario Museum, Toronto, which mentions the *tiraz al-khassa* in Misr as its place of manufacture, is much closer in epigraphic style to the present piece (Related works 6).

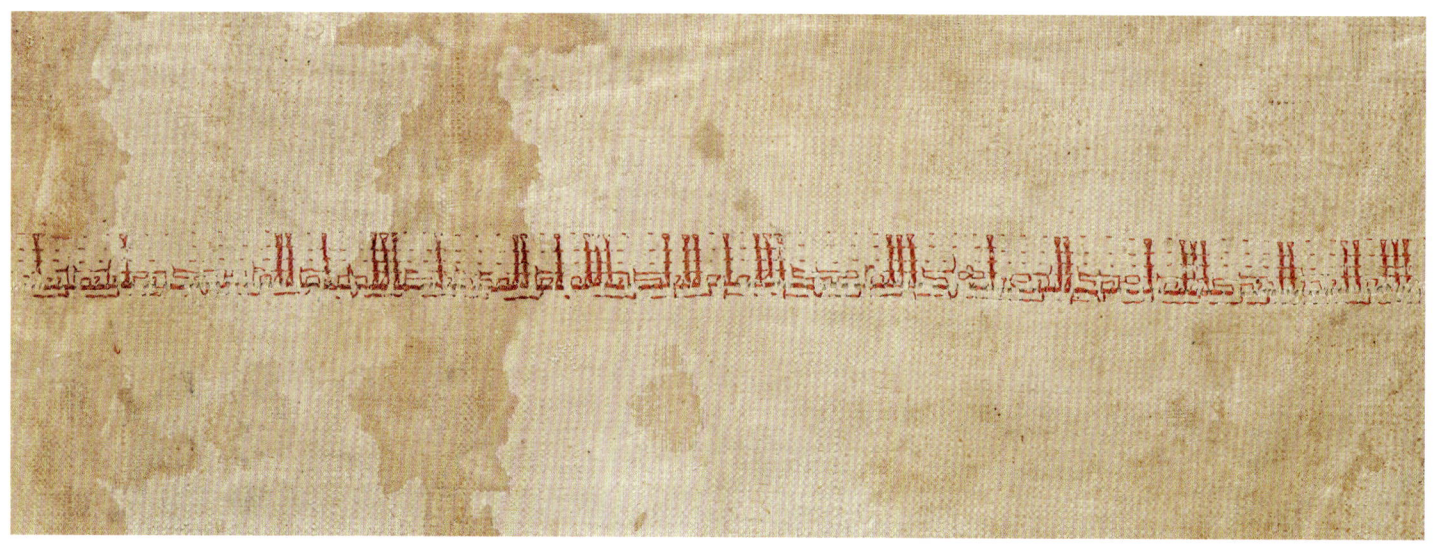

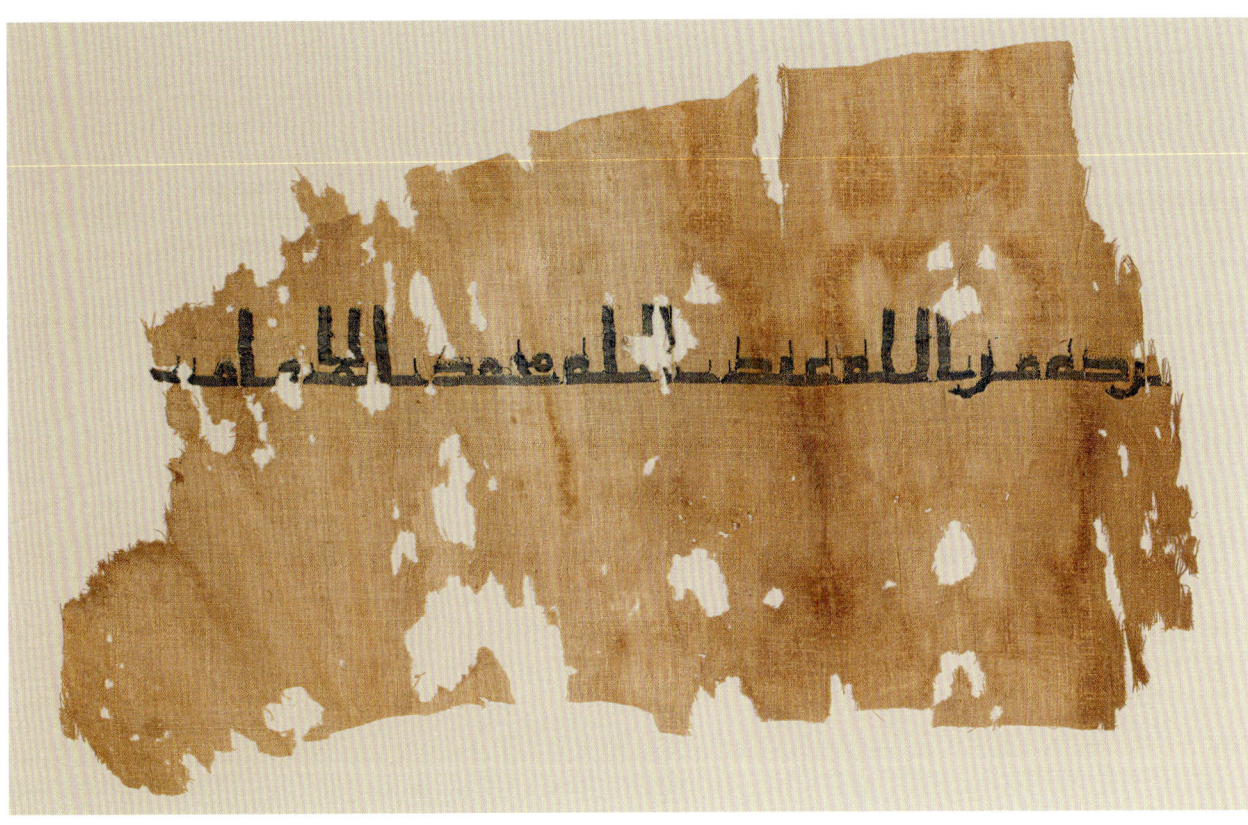

Cat. 28 *TIRAZ* FRAGMENT FROM
THE REIGN OF THE ABBASID
CALIPH AL-RADI (r. 934–40)
Egypt, 10th century CE

Description: Fragment of undyed linen, with one
line of Kufic inscription tapestry-
woven in greenish-blue silk.

Materials: linen and silk: plain weave
and tapestry

Dimensions: h. 18.3 cm, w. 29.7 cm;
max. letter height 2.2 cm

Ground fabric: linen warp and weft, undyed,
predominant-warp plain weave,
close texture (*dabiqi*); very good
quality (1)

Thread count: warp 35 S-spun, weft 22 S-spun

Thread thickness: warp 0.1–0.25 mm tight twist,
weft 0.1–0.15 mm tight twist

Tapestry: silk, dyed (greenish-blue); hastae
woven on warps lifted up from
the base fabric

Provenance: Ex H.P. Kraus collection, no. 46

Inv. no. LNS 64 T

Related works: See page 505

Inscription:

[…] [ب]ـركة من الله عبد الله محمد الامام […]

[…] [ble]ssing from God to the servant of God Muhammad the imam […]

The epigraphic style seen here, with its rather angular letterforms and use of
blue silk, is typical for tapestry-woven inscriptions during the period of al-Radi
(r. 934–40). Noticeable is the curved terminal *nun*. Curved terminals below the
baseline of the inscription, rather than angular ones, are found in a number of
Kufic tapestry-woven inscriptions from al-Radi's reign. One, a textile in the
Textile Museum, Washington, DC, was made in Shata and is dated 325 AH /
936–37 CE (Related works 1). Others are in the Royal Ontario Museum, Toronto,
and the Cleveland Museum of Art (Related works 2–5). The text of the present
inscription contains a very noticeable mistake in the syntax of the sentence: it
omits 'li-' before "abd Allah' ('[…] baraka min Allah [li-]'abd Allah Muhammad
al-imam a[l-Radi] […]'), a mistake also found in Related works 3.

Cat. 29 *TIRAZ* **FRAGMENT FROM THE REIGN OF THE ABBASID CALIPH AL-RADI (r. 934–40)**
Egypt, 10th century CE

Description: Fragment of undyed linen, with two lines of an addorsed Kufic inscription tapestry-woven in dark blue silk.

Materials: linen and silk: plain weave and tapestry

Dimensions: h. 14.4 cm, w. 12.7 cm; max. letter height 3.0 cm

Ground fabric: linen warp and weft, undyed, predominant-warp plain weave, gauzy texture (*sharb*); good quality (2)

Thread count: warp 32 S-spun, weft 23 S-spun

Thread thickness: warp 0.1 mm very tight twist, weft 0.1 mm very tight twist

Tapestry: silk, dyed (dark blue); letters above the baseline woven on warps lifted up from the base fabric

Provenance: Ex H.P. Kraus collection, no. 49

Inv. no. LNS 169 T

Related works: See pages 505–06

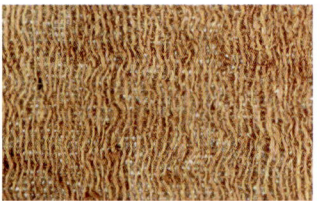

Inscription:

Line 1:

[...] [العبد الـلـله ابي العباس محمد الامام [الراضي بالله] [...]

[...] [to the servant of G]od Abi al-'Abbas Muhammad al-Imam [Al-Radi bi-llah] [...]

Line 2:

[...] [ا]مير المؤمنين اطا[ل الله] [...]

[...] [the C]ommander of the Faithful, may [God pro]long [...]

Of some forty-seven *tiraz* textiles with inscriptions in tapestry weave that have survived from the time of al-Radi, eight have confronted inscriptions (Related works 1–8). Of these, four were made in the *tiraz al-khassa* in Misr. Five are dated or datable to 323–26 AH / 934–38 CE. This is striking, as another three single-line inscriptions from al-Radi's reign mention Misr as a place of manufacture, of which two were made in the *tiraz al-khassa* (Related works 9, 10). It may also be significant that besides a *tiraz* inscription in Washington that mentions Shata as its place of production (Related works 11), three more have survived, which were made in the *tiraz al-khassa* in Damietta (Related works 12–14).

Cat. 30   *TIRAZ* FRAGMENT
ATTRIBUTED TO THE
REIGN OF THE ABBASID
CALIPH AL-RADI (r. 934–40)
Egypt, 10th century CE

Description: Fragment of undyed linen, with
one line of Kufic inscription
tapestry-woven in dark blue silk,
accompanied by a tapestry-woven
decorative band comprising a
palmette scroll (h. 2.0 cm) with
ochre leaves issuing from a blue
stem.

Materials: linen and silk: plain weave
and tapestry

Dimensions: h. 14.9 cm, w. 18.6 cm;
max. letter height 3.0 cm

Ground fabric: linen, undyed, warp-faced plain
weave, gauzy texture (*sharb*);
good quality (2)

Thread count: warp 30 S-spun, weft 12 S-spun

Thread thickness: warp 0.1–0.15 mm tight twist,
weft 0.1–0.15 mm tight twist

Tapestry: silk, dyed (dark blue); slit and
toothed; hastae woven on warps
lifted up from the base fabric

Provenance: Ex H.P. Kraus collection, no. 29

Inv. no. LNS 153 T

Related works: See page 506

Inscription:

[…] صلى الله علي […]

[…] God's blessings be upon [Muhammad Seal of the Prophets] […]

The epigraphic style of the inscription, with its uniformly thick letters on and
above the baseline and the bow-shaped lower terminals, is very close to a dated
tiraz textile inscription in the Textile Museum, Washington, DC, which was
woven during al-Radi's reign (r. 934–40) at Shata in Egypt in 325 AH / 936–37 CE
(Related works 1). Another closely related example from al-Radi's reign is in the
Royal Ontario Museum, Toronto (Related works 2).

Cat. 31 *TIRAZ* FRAGMENT ATTRIBUTED TO THE REIGN OF THE ABBASID CALIPH AL-RADI (r. 934–40)

Egypt, 10th century CE

Description: Fragment of undyed linen, with one line of Kufic inscription tapestry-woven in dark blue silk, with a red band woven in red silk (h. 0.5 cm) along an untwisted fringe.

Materials: linen and silk: plain weave and tapestry

Dimensions: h. 32.7 cm, w. 56.7 cm; max. letter height 3.5 cm

Ground fabric: linen warp and weft, undyed, warp-faced plain weave, gauzy texture (*sharb*); good quality (2); untwisted fringe

Thread count: warp 21 S-spun, weft 15 S-spun

Thread thickness: warp 0.15–0.2 mm tight twist, weft 0.15–0.2 mm tight twist

Tapestry: silk, dyed (dark blue); letters above the baseline woven on warps lifted up from the base fabric; discontinuous supplementary linen weft filling

Provenance: Ex H.P. Kraus collection, no. 60

Inv. no. LNS 179 T

Inscription:

[...] [صلي ال]له على ا (!) محمد خاتم النبيين (...؟...) على اله الطيبين الاخيار (الاتقياء الانقياء الابرياء) (و) سلم تسليما [...]

[...] blessings of Go]d upon *alif*(!) Muhammad the Seal of the Prophets (...?...) upon his family the good, the excellent (the pious, the immaculate, the honest) (and) salute them with worthy greetings of peace [...]

It is noteworthy here that the silk threads with which the inscription was woven are carried from one hasta to the next, and that the inscription was executed in layers as indicated by the three horizontal lines connected to letters of different sizes. The hastae are lifted up from the ground fabric and the silk warp is carried over from behind and then woven on these segregated warps. This is a common technique, which is found throughout the later Abbasid period, when large inscriptions became part of the *tiraz* repertoire. The style of the epigraphy suggests a date in the 10th century, perhaps during the reign of the caliph al-Radi (r. 934–40).

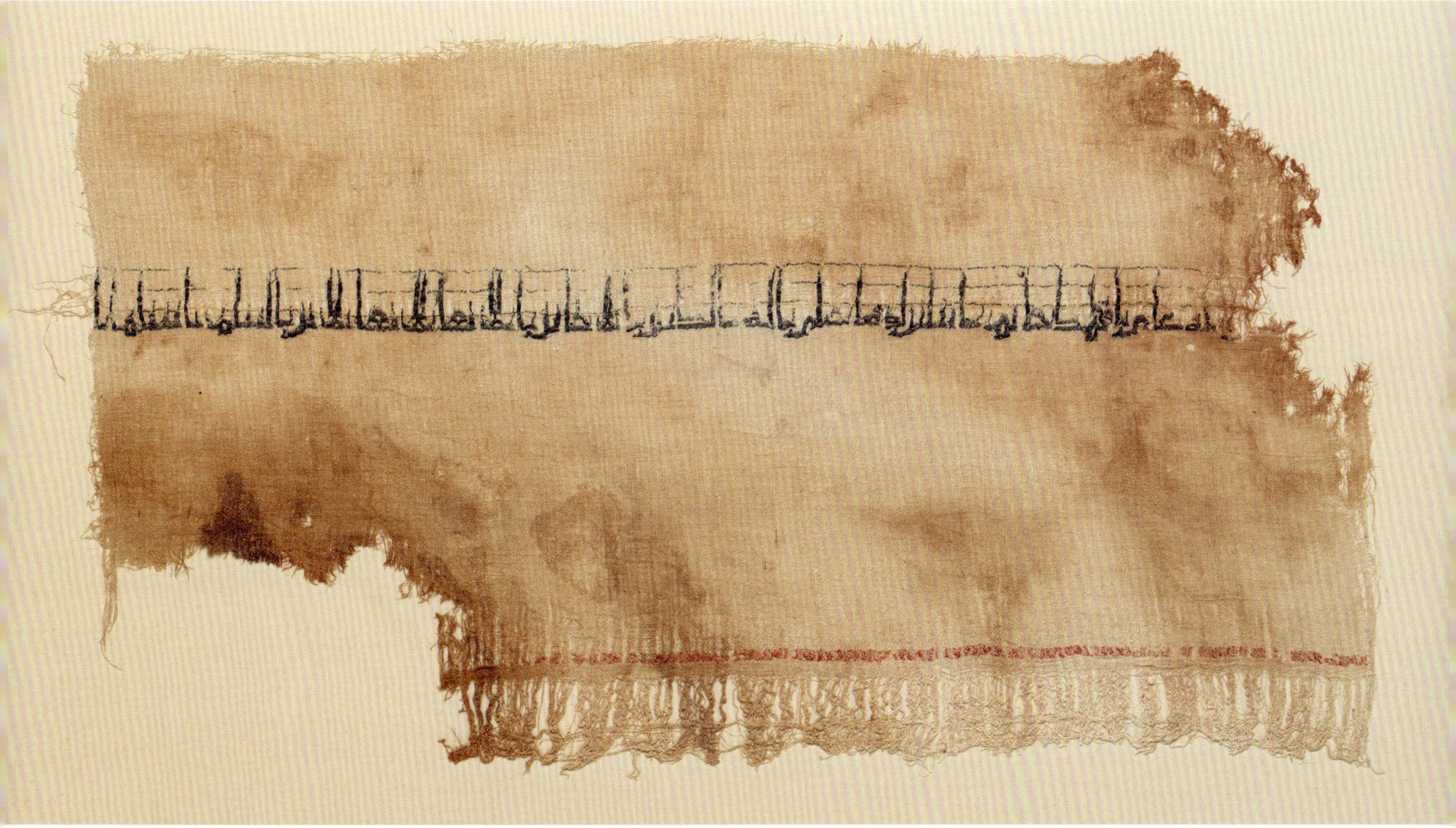

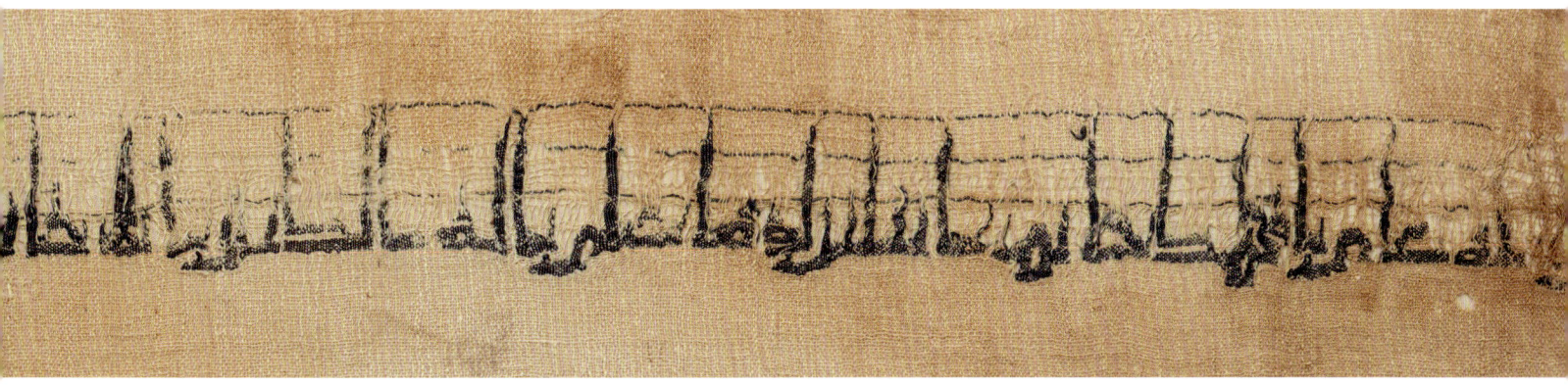

Cat. 32 *TIRAZ* FRAGMENT FROM
THE REIGN OF THE ABBASID
CALIPH AL-RADI (r. 934–40)
Egypt, 10th century CE

Description: Fragment of undyed linen, with
two lines of an addorsed Kufic
inscription tapestry-woven in dark
blue silk (letter height varying
between 2.4 and 2.8 cm, with space
of 1.2 cm between), accompanied
by a silk tapestry-woven decorative
band (h. 1.3 cm) in red, greenish-
blue and ochre with the remains of
what appears to have been a floral
scroll; parallel to the decorative
band is a weftless band along the
remains of the untwisted fringe.

Materials: linen and silk: plain weave and
tapestry

Dimensions: h. 22.5 cm, w. 29.5 cm;
max. letter height 2.5 cm

Ground fabric: linen warp and weft, undyed,
predominant-warp plain weave,
gauzy texture (*sharb*); good quality
(2); untwisted fringe

Thread count: warp 25 S-spun, weft 20 S-spun

Thread thickness: warp 0.1–0.25 mm tight twist,
weft 0.1 mm tight twist

Tapestry: silk, dyed (red, greenish-blue,
ochre); hastae woven on warps
lifted up from the base fabric,
with supplementary weft behind
for support; decorative band
woven on paired warps

Provenance: Ex H.P. Kraus collection, no. 48

Inv. no. LNS 63 T

Related works: See page 506

Inscription:

Line 1:

[...] [العبا]س الامام الراضي بالله امـ[ـير] [...]

[...] [al-'Abba]s al-Imam Al-Radi bi-llah Comm[ander] [...]

Line 2:

[...] [امیـ]ـر المؤمنین ایده الله [ما] امر الوزیر ا[...]

[...] [Comman]der of the Faithful, may God strengthen him. [What] has been ordered by the vizier *alif* [...]

This piece belongs to a group of tapestry-woven textiles from al-Radi's reign (r. 934–40) that almost all have dark blue silk tapestry-woven inscriptions in a rather angular simple Kufic, some of which are also addorsed, like the present example (see also cat. no. 29). Most of these do not have supplementary bands of tapestry-woven decoration, but one in the Textile Museum, Washington, DC, does, though its band is more defined than that on the present piece, comprising a sequence of multicoloured lozenges (Related works 1). Four known pieces from al-Radi's reign have two addorsed lines of Kufic tapestry-woven inscription, which mention that they were ordered by a vizier. One of these, a piece in the Benaki Museum, Athens, was ordered by the vizier Muhammad ibn 'Ali in 326 AH / 937–38 CE (Related works 2). The others mention the name of Abu al-Fath al-Fadl ibn Ja'far and are datable to 324–26 AH / 935–38 (Related works 3–5). The name of the vizier mentioned on the present textile begins with an *alif*, and therefore it is possible that it is Abu al-Fath al-Fadl Ja'far who is referred to here. A piece in the Royal Ontario Museum, Toronto, made in Damietta mentions the name of the vizier Ahmad ibn Muhammad (dated 329 AH / 940–41 CE), albeit in a single line of inscription (Related works 6).

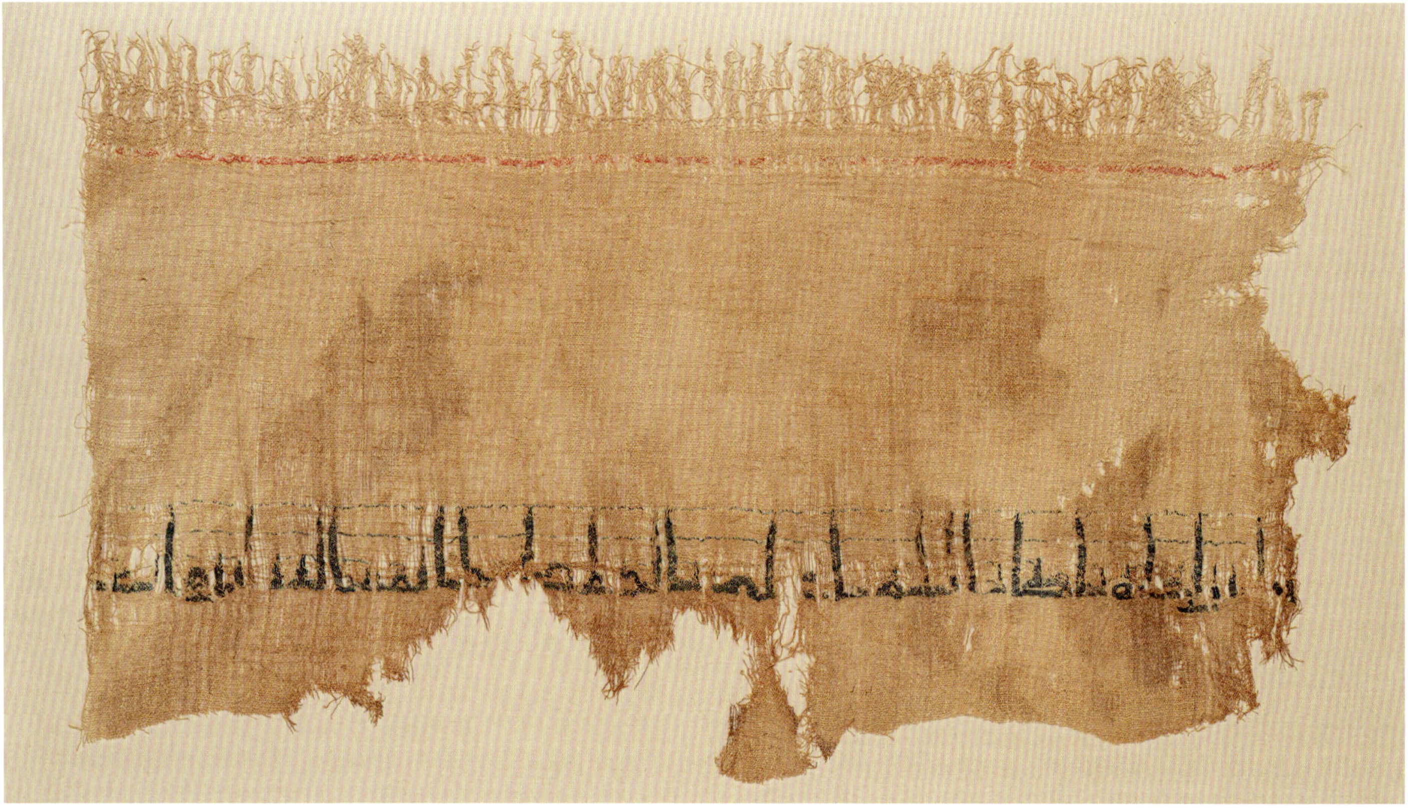

[Image of the tiraz fragment]

Cat. 33 ***TIRAZ* FRAGMENT FROM THE ABBASID DYNASTY**
Egypt, 10th century CE

Description: Fragment of undyed linen, fringed, with one line of Kufic inscription tapestry-woven in dark blue silk, and a band in red silk (h. 0.5 cm) below the fringe.

Materials: linen and silk: plain weave and tapestry

Dimensions: h. 24.8 cm, w. 41.5 cm; max. letter height 3.5 cm

Ground fabric: linen warp and weft, undyed, predominant-warp plain weave, gauzy texture (*sharb*): good–medium quality (2–3); untwisted fringe

Thread count: warp 19 S-spun, weft 13 S-spun

Thread thickness: warp 0.1–0.15 mm tight twist, weft 0.1–0.15 tight twist

Tapestry: silk, dyed (dark blue); letters above the baseline woven on warps lifted up from the base fabric, with silk yarns carried over from hasta to hasta

Provenance: Ex H.P. Kraus collection, no. 52

Inv. no. LNS 171 T

Inscription: [...] بقأه النبيين (!) خاتم محمد(!الـ) علي (!)ا (اطالله؟) بركة (!)[...]ا[...] [...]

[…] […] *alif* (!) blessing (may God prolong?) (!) upon the (!) Muhammad the Seal (!) of the Prophets, permanence […]

The inscriptions here (and in cat. no. 34) are not entirely readable. However, individual phrases and words that are used in caliphal *tiraz* inscriptions can be read.[34] This suggests that the present inscription is a corrupted version of a caliphal protocol. The style of the epigraphy, in conjunction with the use of phrases such as 'al-hamdu li-llah rab al-'alamin', even when they are abbreviated – as in the case of 'salla allahu 'ala (Muhammad al-nabi)' – suggests a date in the first half of the 10th century, perhaps during the reign of the caliph al-Radi (r. 934–40). A standard formula used in inscriptions of his reign is 'bismillah al-rahman al-rahim al-hamdu li-llah rab al-'alamin salla Allahu 'ala Muhammad al-nabi baraka min Allah'.

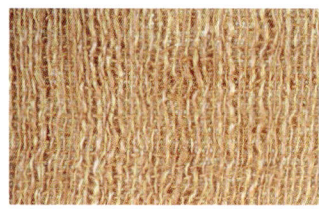
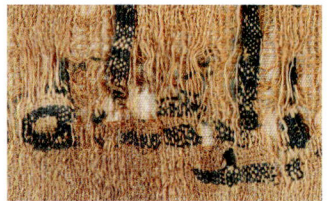

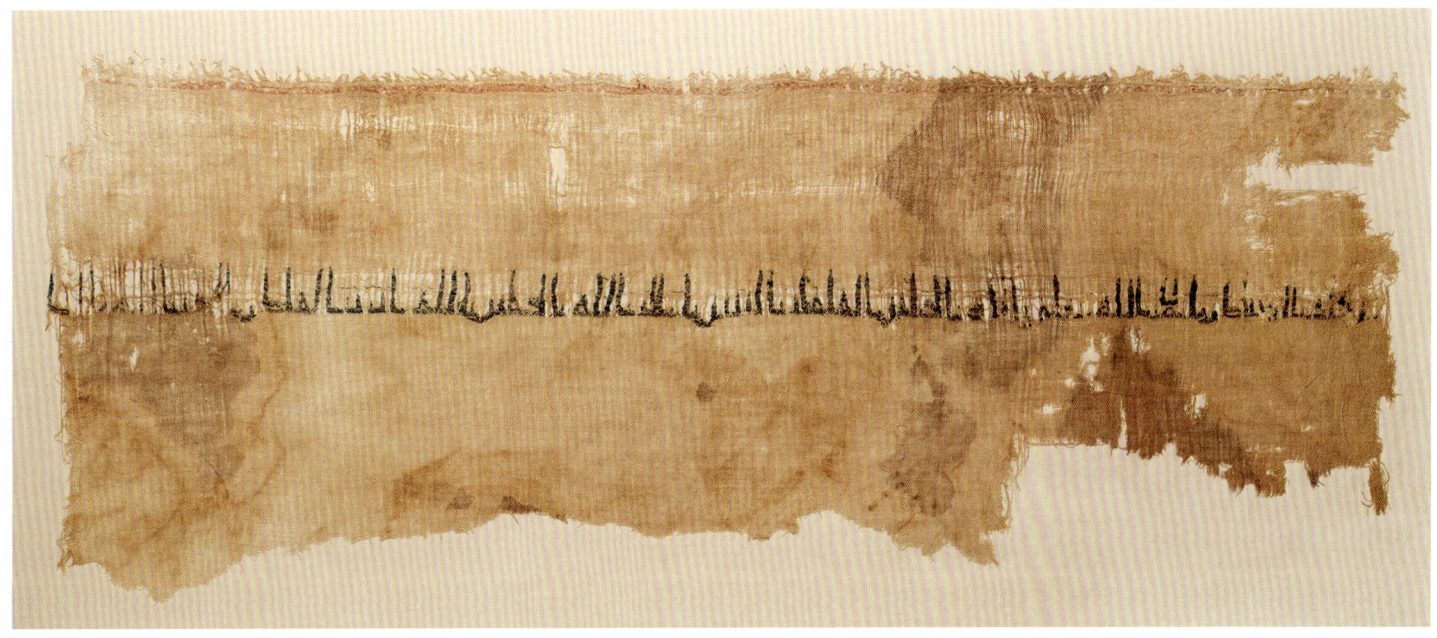

Cat. 34   *TIRAZ* **FRAGMENT FROM THE ABBASID DYNASTY**
Egypt, early 10th century CE

Description: Fragment of undyed linen, with one line of Kufic inscription tapestry-woven in dark blue silk, and a band in red silk (h. 0.5 cm) below the untwisted fringe.

Materials: linen and silk: plain weave and tapestry

Dimensions: h. 33.8 cm, w. 82.3 cm; max. letter height 3.7 cm

Ground fabric: linen warp and weft, undyed, predominant-warp plain weave, gauzy texture (*sharb*); good–medium quality (2–3); untwisted fringe

Thread count: warp 18 S-spun, weft 13 S-spun

Thread thickness: warp 0.15 mm tight twist, weft 0.15 mm tight twist

Tapestry: silk, dyed (dark blue); letters above the baseline woven on warps lifted up from the base fabric; supplementary silk weft band in red below the fringe

Provenance: Ex H.P. Kraus collection, no. 53

Inv. no. LNS 172 T

Inscription:[35]   (...) الملك (...) الله (...) لااله ا ؟) علي (الله المبين الخاتم النبيين ا النبيين) الا الله (الله نصر) (ا)الرحيم [...]

[...] [t]he Most Compassionate, (God help) except God, upon (God the Manifest, the Seal of the Prophets *alif*?) there is no God (...) God (...) the King (...)

A stylistically similar inscription is discussed in the commentary of cat. no 33.

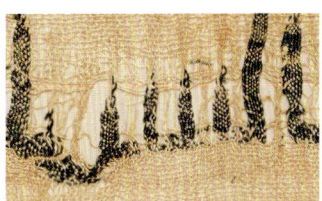

Cat. 35 *TIRAZ* FRAGMENT FROM
THE ABBASID PERIOD
Egypt, early 10th century CE

Description: Fragment of undyed linen, with
one line of Kufic inscription
tapestry-woven in dark blue silk.

Materials: linen and silk: plain weave and
tapestry

Dimensions: h. 16.0 cm, w. 39.0 cm;
max. letter height 2.6 cm

Ground fabric: linen warp and weft, undyed,
predominant-warp plain weave,
loose texture (*sharb*); good quality
(2); selvedge on the right side of
the inscription

Thread count: warp 19 Z-spun, weft 12 S-spun

Thread thickness: warp 0.15–0.25 medium twist,
weft 0.15 tight twist

Tapestry: silk, dyed (dark blue); letters above
the baseline woven on warps lifted
up from the base fabric

Provenance: Ex H.P. Kraus collection, no. 51

Inv. no. LNS 170 T

Inscription: بسم الله الرحمن الرحيم الملك الحق المبين الحمد الله [رب] (الـعـالـمـين) [...]

In the name of God, the Most Merciful, the Most Compassionate. The King, the
Manifest Truth, praise be to God [the Lord] (of the world) […]

The reading of the inscription after the *basmallah* is not quite clear. Neither is
the reading of the word 'al-mulk'. Inscriptions of the same type have survived
from the reigns of the caliphs al-Muqtadir, al-Qahir and al-Radi.

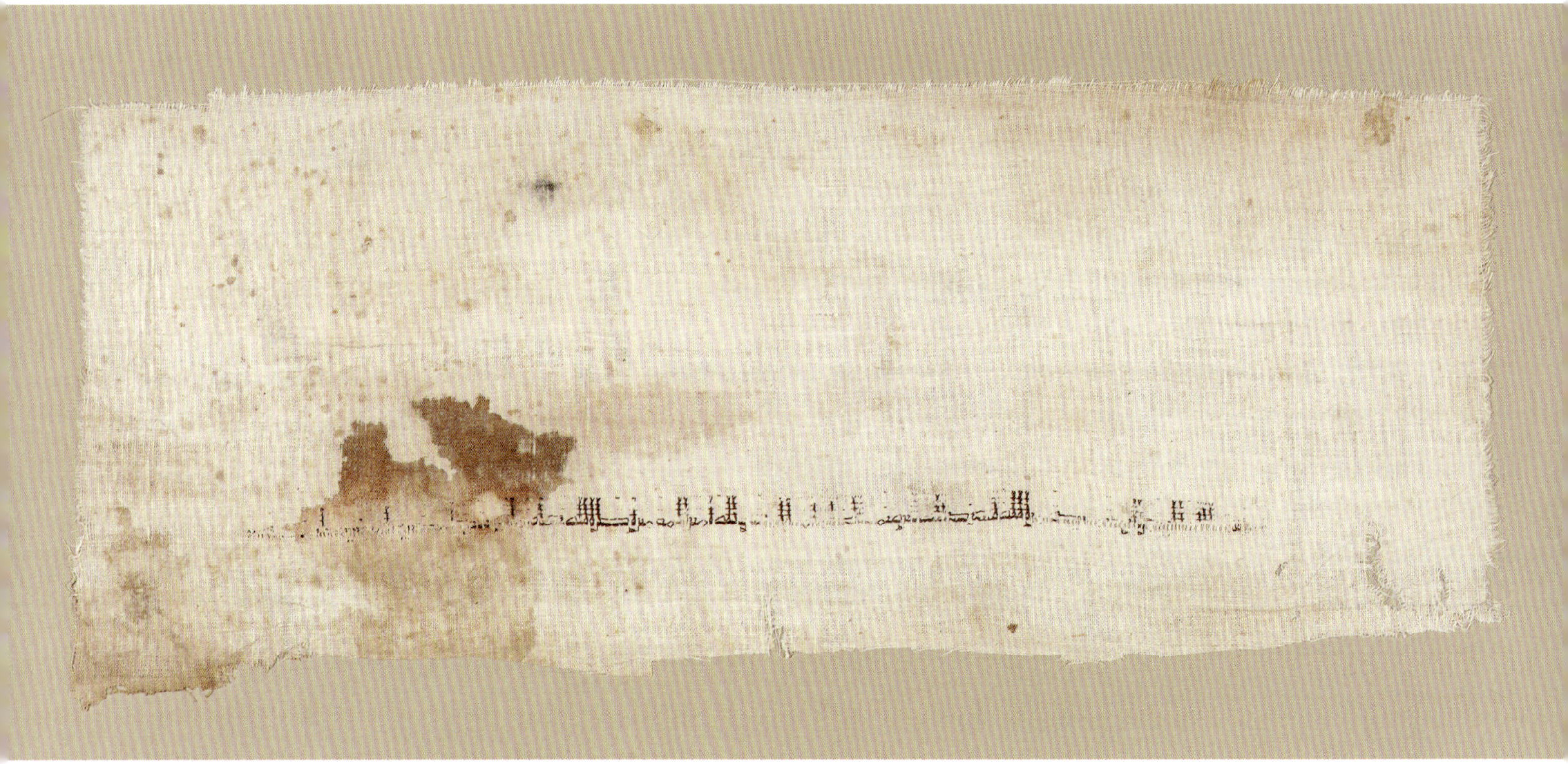

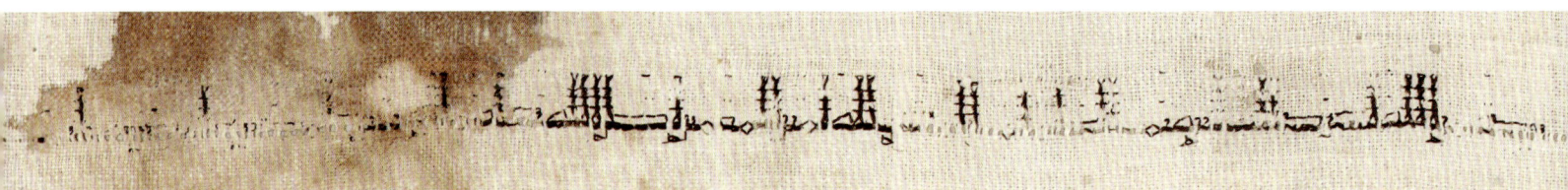

Cat. 36   *TIRAZ* FRAGMENT FROM
THE REIGN OF THE ABBASID
CALIPH AL-MUTTAQI
(r. 940–44)
Egypt, mid-10th century CE

Description: Fragment of undyed linen. with
one line of Kufic inscription
embroidered in dark brown silk.

Materials: linen and silk: plain weave
and embroidery

Dimensions: h. 20.6 cm, w. 48.5 cm;
max. letter height 1.2 cm

Ground fabric: linen warp and weft, undyed,
balanced plain weave, close texture
(*dabiqi*), glazed and polished;
good quality (2)

Thread count: warp 14 S-spun, weft 17 S-spun

Thread thickness: warp 0.4–0.6 mm medium twist,
weft 0.3–0.5 mm medium twist

Embroidery: silk, dyed (dark brown), couching,
back and flat stitch

Provenance: Ex H.P. Kraus collection, no. 54

Inv. no. LNS 173 T

Related works: See page 506

Inscription: بسم الله الرحمن الرحيم بركة من الله لعبد الله ابرهيم الامام [المتقي] لله امير المؤمنين اطال الله بقاه [...]

In the name of God, the Most Merciful, the Most compassionate. Blessing from God to the servant of God Ibrahim al-Imam [al-Muttaqi] li-allah the Commander of the Faithful. May God prolong his existence [...]

The epigraphy of the present piece is characterized by a stout appearance, with letters such as *ta*, *kaf* and *dal* prominently elongated in relation to the height of the hastae. Furthermore, the hastae are crossed by short horizontal bars which are probably caused by the yarn being carried over to the next hastae. This suggests that the inscription was embroidered in horizontal layers, rather than being built up from right to left.[36] To date, five specimens with a comparable style of epigraphy are known. (Related works 1–5). Most of these examples were made in Misr, as stated in the inscriptions. This might suggest that the present piece, too, was made there. The section of the inscription that should contain the place of production is damaged to the extent that a reconstruction of the inscription would be close to conjecture. However, several letters in this section may have been a *ta* or *sad*, components of the words *tiraz* and Misr. Yet, the inscription is too short to have contained the place of production together with the ordering vizier.

The characteristics described above can also be found in two further types of embroidered inscription of different epigraphic styles, but executed on the same basic principle. These also seem to be products of the workshops in Misr. The first group of these is characterized by letters on the baseline to which wedge-shaped terminals are attached, while the lower terminals are comparable to the ones seen here. Kühnel attributed this type to Misr.[37] A piece of this group in the Royal Ontario Museum, Toronto, is datable to 322–24 AH / 933–36 CE or 326–27 AH / 937–39 CE during the reign of al-Radi, and refers in its inscription to its manufacture in the *tiraz al-khassa* in Misr (Related works 6). In the second group a horizontal line links only the tips of the hastae and the letters are undecorated. An example that was also made in a Misr workshop, but dates from a much earlier period during the reign of al-Muqtadir, is in the Textile Museum, Washington, DC (Related works 7).

Cat. 37   *TIRAZ* FRAGMENT FROM
THE REIGN OF THE ABBASID
CALIPH AL-MUTIʿ (r. 946–74)
Egypt, 10th century CE

Description: Fragment of undyed linen, with
an addorsed Kufic inscription
tapestry-woven in dark blue silk.

Materials: linen and silk: plain weave and
tapestry

Dimensions: h. 22.5 cm, w. 29.0 cm;
max. letter height 5.3 cm

Ground fabric: linen warp and weft, undyed,
predominant-warp plain weave,
gauzy texture (*sharb*); good quality
(2); selvedge on the right side of
the *basmallah*

Thread count: warp 20 S-spun, weft 16 S-spun

Thread thickness: warp 0.15–0.2 mm tight twist,
weft 0.15–0.2 mm tight twist

Tapestry: silk, dyed (dark blue); letters above
and below the baseline woven
on warps lifted up from the base
fabric; discontinuous weft filling

Provenance: Ex H.P. Kraus collection, no. 55

Inv. no. LNS 174 T

Related works: See page 506

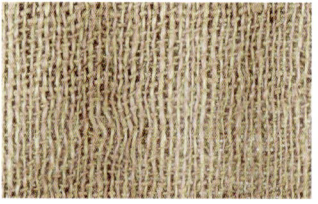

Inscription:

Line 1:   بسـم الله الرحمن الرحيم لعبد [الله] [...]

In the name of God the Most Merciful, the Most Compassionate. To the servant
of [God] [...]

Line 2:   [...] الامام المـ(ـو !) طيع لـلله امير المـ(ـؤ مـنيـ)ـن

[...] al-Imam al-M(u!)tiʿ li-llah the Commander of the Fai(thfu)l

This fragment can be attributed to the reign of al-Mutiʿ (334–63 AH / 946–74 CE),
rather than al-Mustakfi (333–34 AH / 944–46 CE).[38] Although the spelling of al-
Mutiʿ li-llah in one line of the inscription is faulty – an additional *sinna* is located
between *mim* and *ta* and what should be 'li-llah' reads 'bi-llah' – there can be
little doubt that it is al-Mutiʿ who is referred to here. His *ism*, al-Fadl, often
follows immediately after the *basmallah* in *tiraz* inscriptions from his reign,
particularly those with relatively short protocols (Related works 1–2).

The inscription contains several further spelling mistakes. In some cases,
letters were added and sometimes left out, so that the meaning of some of the
words can be ascertained only from the context. This is particularly the case after
the *laqab* (regnal title) of the caliph, where normally his title *amir al-muʾminin*
should follow. Here, it appears that *amir* has been dropped and *al-muʾminin* was
first abbreviated and then conflated with another unidentifiable word. It seems in
general that the inscription is very compressed. Both of the lines probably carried
the same text. In reconstruction, the text, and with it the width of the textile,
should be about double the size that has survived. The relatively small width of
the textile explains the compression of the two lines of inscription and perhaps
also the garbled end of one of them, as the weaver ran out of space.

The style of the epigraphy, with its undecorated and quite angular letters,
woven in dark blue, goes back to the period of al-Muqtadir, and is frequently
used under his successors. It is only under al-Mutiʿ that floriated tapestry-woven
inscriptions appear. It seems that this earlier style existed side by side with the
newer floriated style for a period. A number of examples showing a comparable
epigraphic style have survived, most of which do not provide any information
as to where they were manufactured (Related works 3–15). Two of these
mention Shata as a place of production (Related works 3 and 7). There is some
circumstantial evidence from *tiraz* textiles from al-Mutiʿ's predecessors that this
group may have been produced in the Delta. A piece from al-Mustakfi's reign
with an addorsed tapestry-woven inscription in blue, in the Textile Museum,
Washington, DC, was made in Damietta (Related works 17). There is also,
however, some evidence for the production of these textiles in Misr already
during the reign of al-Radi (r. 934–40).[39] Hence, a firm attribution to one
particular centre is not possible for the al-Sabah textile on that basis.

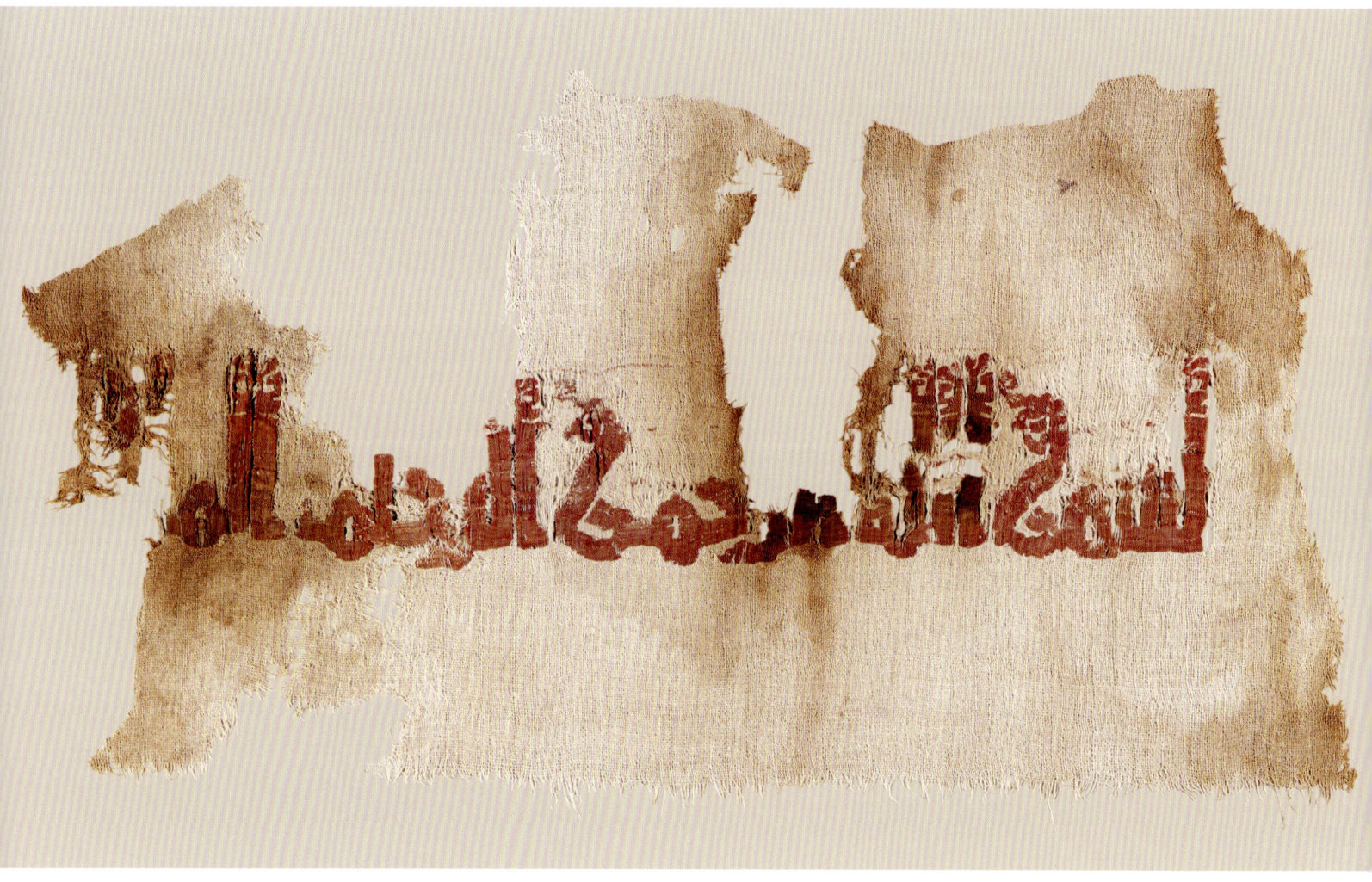

Cat. 38 *TIRAZ* FRAGMENT
ATTRIBUTED TO THE
REIGN OF THE ABBASID
CALIPH AL-MUTI' (r. 946–74)
Egypt, 10th century CE

Description: Fragment of undyed linen, with
one line of monumental foliated
Kufic inscription executed in red
silk tapestry weave.

Materials: linen and silk: plain weave
and tapestry

Dimensions: h. 24 cm, w. 43 cm;
max. letter height 6.6 cm

Ground fabric: linen warp and weft, undyed,
predominant-warp plain weave,
regular structure, loose texture
(*sharb*); good–medium quality
(2–3)

Thread count: warp 19 S-spun, weft 13 S-spun

Thread thickness: warp 0.15–0.25 mm medium twist,
weft 0.15 mm tight twist

Tapestry: silk, dyed (red); the hastae of *alif*
and *lam* woven on warps lifted
up from the base fabric, the linen
wefts continuing behind, with
occasional linen supplementary
weft filling worked into the
tapestry of each hasta and carried
over to the next (both methods
make sure that the hasta stays
in its place)

Provenance: Ex H.P. Kraus collection, no. 64

Inv. no. LNS 69 T

Related works: See pages 506–07

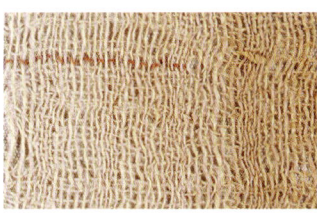

Inscription:

بسم الله الرحمن الرحيم المـ[...]

In the name of God, the Most Merciful, the Most Compassionate, al-M[...]

The style of epigraphy seen here is characterized by its monumental size, its colour (red), and its very finely foliated letter stems above the baseline, such as *alif*, *lam* and terminal *nun*. This fragment can be attributed to the reign of the Abbasid caliph al-Muti' (r. 946–74) on grounds of the epigraphy and a comparison of the content of this inscription with other known specimens.

The height of the present inscription is *c.* 6.6 cm, which is well within the range of inscriptions quoted in Related works 1–20. To judge from these, this size represents the mid-range of monumental inscriptions during al-Muti''s reign. There is evidence for both tiny and massive textile inscriptions. Sizes above 10.0 cm are not uncommon during al-Muti''s reign, as Related works 9, 14–16 and 20 show. Epigraphically, these inscriptions show certain developments of script that are departures from the early Kufic types. Very prominent is the terminal *nun*, which bends upwards above the baseline in reverse S-shape motion, rather than below the baseline where it would look more like a *ra*. The long letter stems above the baseline are foliated: the *alif* and *lam* with half-split palmettes within the bounds of the hasta, in terminal *nun* with half-split palmettes that fan out. Very prominent in these inscriptions is the way the phrase 'bismillah' is written: 'bism' and 'Allah' are separated. In comparable inscriptions from the reign of the Fatimid caliph al-Mu'izz (r. 953–75), whose monumental *tiraz* inscriptions otherwise continued the same aesthetic as those of al-Muti', the two words are joined.[40]

Another peculiarity of monumental inscriptions from al-Muti''s reign is the mentioning of the caliph's *laqab* (regnal title) after the opening *basmallah* without the introductory protocol that would normally be found in *tiraz* inscriptions. This may be a result of the large sizes of these inscriptions. There are small-size inscriptions from al-Muti''s reign comprising the full caliphal protocol. The present inscription has, after the *basmallah*, the beginning of al-Muti''s name ('al-M') and, following this, the remnants of the fanned half-split palmette of what can be interpreted as the hasta of a *ta* bending backwards. It seems that these kinds of monumental-style inscriptions were introduced during the Ikhshidid period, particularly the reign of al-Muti'. Dated examples fall mainly into the 960s, shortly before the arrival of the Fatimids in Egypt. The style was subsequently taken on by the Fatimids under al-Mu'izz, then al-'Aziz (r. 975–96) and continued to be used well into the reign of al-Hakim (r. 996–1021).

Regarding the type of ground fabric found among the *tiraz* textiles mentioned here, they almost all comprise loosely woven linen ground fabric, rather than closely woven fabric. The Arabic term for this type of fabric is *sharb*, which was used for turban-cloths and shawls.

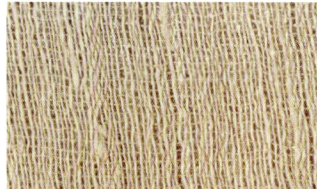

Cat. 39   *TIRAZ* **FRAGMENT FROM**
THE ABBASID DYNASTY
Egypt, 10th century CE

Description: Fragment of undyed linen, with
one line of Kufic inscription
tapestry-woven in dark blue silk.

Materials: linen and silk; plain weave
and tapestry

Dimensions: piece (a) (right): h. 13.7 cm,
w. 37.1 cm; max. letter height 3.6 cm
piece (b) (left): h. 19 cm, w. 49.5 cm;
max. letter height 3.6 cm

Ground fabric: linen warp and weft, undyed,
predominant-warp plain weave,
gauzy texture (*sharb*); good quality
(2); selvedge on the left side of the
inscription

Thread count: warp 26 S-spun, weft 16 S-spun

Thread thickness: warp 0.1–0.15 mm tight twist,
weft 0.1–0.15 mm tight twist

Tapestry: silk, dyed (dark blue); slit and
toothed; hastae woven on warps
lifted up from the base fabric

Provenance: Ex H.P. Kraus collection,
nos 26 (part a) and 27 (part b)

Inv. no. LNS 151 T

Related works: See page 507

Inscription:

Part a (right):   [...] خا[تم] على محمد الله صلى و العلمين رب لله والحمد (كفاً؟) و [الله]...]

[...] God and (sufficient?) and praise be to God the Lord of the worlds and God's
blessings be upon Muhammad the Se[al] [...]

Part b (left):   [...] [الله]لعبد وسعادة (؟) ونعمة الله من بركة الطيبين اله علي و النبيين تم[...]

[...] (seal) of the Prophets and upon his family the good. Blessing from God and
prosperity(?) and happiness to the servant [of God] [...]

The inscription on this piece is interesting, as it omits the caliphal protocol, stopping in the middle of the phrase 'li-'abd (Allah)' after which the *ism* (given name) and *laqab* (regnal title) of the ruling caliph should follow. As this is very rare in *tiraz* textile inscription, the omission was probably not accidental. Rather than being a mistake on the part of the weaver, one may speculate that the size of the letters and consequently the length of the inscription were at odds with the choice of width for the cloth and hence the length had to be cut down. The particular style of tapestry-woven inscription seen here with letters of even thickness on and above the baseline, and curved and pointed terminals below the baseline, in blue silk, spans the reigns of the caliphs al-Muqtadir (r. 908–32) (Related works 1, 2), al-Radi (r. 934–40) (Related works 3–8), al-Mutaqqi (r. 940–44) (Related works 9), al-Mustakfi (r. 944–46) (Related works 10) and al-Muti' (r. 946–74) (Related works 11–15). There is evidence for its survival into the early Fatimid period under the caliph al-Mu'izz (r. 953–75) (Related works 16).

Cat. 40 *TIRAZ* FRAGMENT FROM
THE ABBASID DYNASTY
**Egypt, first half of the
10th century CE**

Description: Fragment of undyed linen with
a cursive inscription of Quranic
content, handwritten in brownish
ink, remnants of a tapestry-woven
inscription, and remnants of an
untwisted fringe.

Materials: linen and ink: plain weave and
tapestry with handwriting

Dimensions: h. 21.3 cm, w. 67.7 cm;
max. letter height 4.5 cm

Ground fabric: linen warp and weft, undyed,
predominant-warp plain weave,
close texture (*dabiqi*); very good
quality (1); untwisted fringe

Thread count: warp 25 S-spun, weft 22 S-spun

Thread thickness: warp 0.15–0.3 mm slight–medium
twist, weft 0.1–0.15 mm medium–
tight twist

Provenance: Ex H.P. Kraus collection,
New York or Vienna, no. 284

Inv. no. LNS 354 T

Related works: See page 507

Inscription:
Line 1 (tapestry): undecipherable

Line 2 (ink):
شَهِدَ اللَّهُ أَنَّهُ لا إِلَهَ إِلَّا هُوَ وَالْمَلائِكَةُ وَ أُوْلُوا الْعِلْمِ قَائِم[ا بِالْقِسْطِ]

Allah bears witness that there is no god but He – as do the angels, and those
endowed with knowledge – upholding justice. (Quran 3:18)

This piece and cat. no. 41 together once formed part of the larger end of the same
shawl or sheet, as indicated by the surviving fringe on the present piece and the
continuous content of the handwritten inscription. Cat. no. 41 is unusual as it
shows the beginning of what must have been a caliphal *tiraz* inscription, now

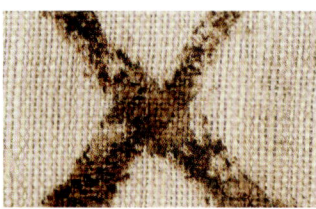

fragmented. Its epigraphic style, size and colour choice is typical for the period of al-Radi (r. 934–40). A very closely related piece is in the Textile Museum, Washington, DC (Related works 1); this too was woven in blue, and the terminals of the low letters are curved, while the letters on the baseline are joined in an angular fashion. The inscription in ink on both pieces was applied at a later stage and quotes Quran 3:18–19 (Surah al-'Imran), representing the *shahada*.[41] It is difficult to date. Features such as the triangular base of the *lam–alif* or the angular *kaf* in 'hakim', however, indicate that the inscription is medieval, perhaps as early as the tenth century.

Considering that most extant *tiraz* textiles have been recovered from Islamic burials, it is significant to find a Quranic surah written by hand on a textile that would have been used as a shroud. However, in this context it was meant to supersede the already present, presumably caliphal, inscription. Surah al-'Imran ('The family of 'Imran') is the third chapter of the Quran, part of the Medinan surahs, and references the events of the battles of Badr and Uhud. Verse 18 is concerned with the character and reward of the faithful, while verse 19 is concerned with Islam as the true religion. These verses, and particularly the *shahada*, may have had significance in the context of death. While it would be important for a Muslim to be reminded of the virtues of adhering to Islam and to confess them, a dying person is supposed to recite the *shahada* in order to prepare for death, and should be reminded, even after death, by those near to him to remember the *shahada*. Hence it was common to recite the Quran by the grave after burial. Writing the *shahada*, or Quranic verses in general, on a shroud seems to be a common practice until the present day; one can find it, for example, among contemporary Shi'a communities.[42] However, it is not clear if this practice might also have been prevalent among Sunni communities in the tenth century. The present piece seems to be the only surviving textile with such a formula written on it in such a crude and unrefined calligraphic style.

Most extant *tiraz* textiles do not have additional handwritten inscriptions, to judge from the published and known corpus of examples. However, given the often very fragmented nature of these textiles, it is perfectly possible that sometimes such handwritten additions were discarded by dealers in favour of the caliphal inscriptions. The handwriting on these textile fragments surely represents a secondary stage in their use, a conscious adaptation for burial according to specific beliefs. It is therefore also likely that they were used for burial after they had been used or stored for some time, in the way suggested by finds in the burials of Istabl 'Antar (see chapter 2), where shrouds from different periods and locations of production were found on the same body.

Cat. 41 *TIRAZ* FRAGMENT FROM
THE ABBASID DYNASTY
**Egypt, first half of the
10th century CE**

Description: Fragment of undyed linen, with
one line of Kufic inscription
tapestry-woven in blue silk,
comprising the beginning of a
caliphal *tiraz* inscription, above
a cursive inscription of Quranic
content, handwritten in ink, and
remnants of an untwisted fringe.

Materials: linen, silk, and ink: plain weave
and tapestry with handwriting

Dimensions: h. 25.6 cm, w. 84.0 cm;
max. letter height 1.5 cm

Ground fabric: linen warp and weft, undyed,
predominant-warp plain weave,
close texture (*dabiqi*); very good
quality (1); untwisted fringe

Thread count: warp 27 S-spun, weft 22 S-spun

Thread thickness: warp 0.1–0.3 mm slight–medium
twist, weft 0.2 mm medium twist

Tapestry: silk, dyed (dark blue); letters above
the baseline woven on warps
lifted up from the base fabric;
supplementary inscription
applied by hand in black ink

Provenance: Ex H.P. Kraus collection,
New York or Vienna, no. 285

Inv. no. LNS 91 T

Related works: See page 507

Inscription:

Line 1 (tapestry): بسم الله الرحمن الرحيم بركة من الله ونعمة من الله وسعادة من (الله) [...]

In the name of God, the merciful the Almighty, blessing from God and
benefaction from God and happiness from (God) [...]

Line 2 (inscription in ink): [...] لا اله الا هو العزيز الحكيم. ان الدين عند الله الإسلام [...]

[...] There is no God but God, He is the Exalted in Power, the Wise. The religion
before God is Islam. [...] (Quran 3:18–19)

A commentary on the handwritten and tapestry-woven inscriptions found here is
included in the note to cat. no. 40.

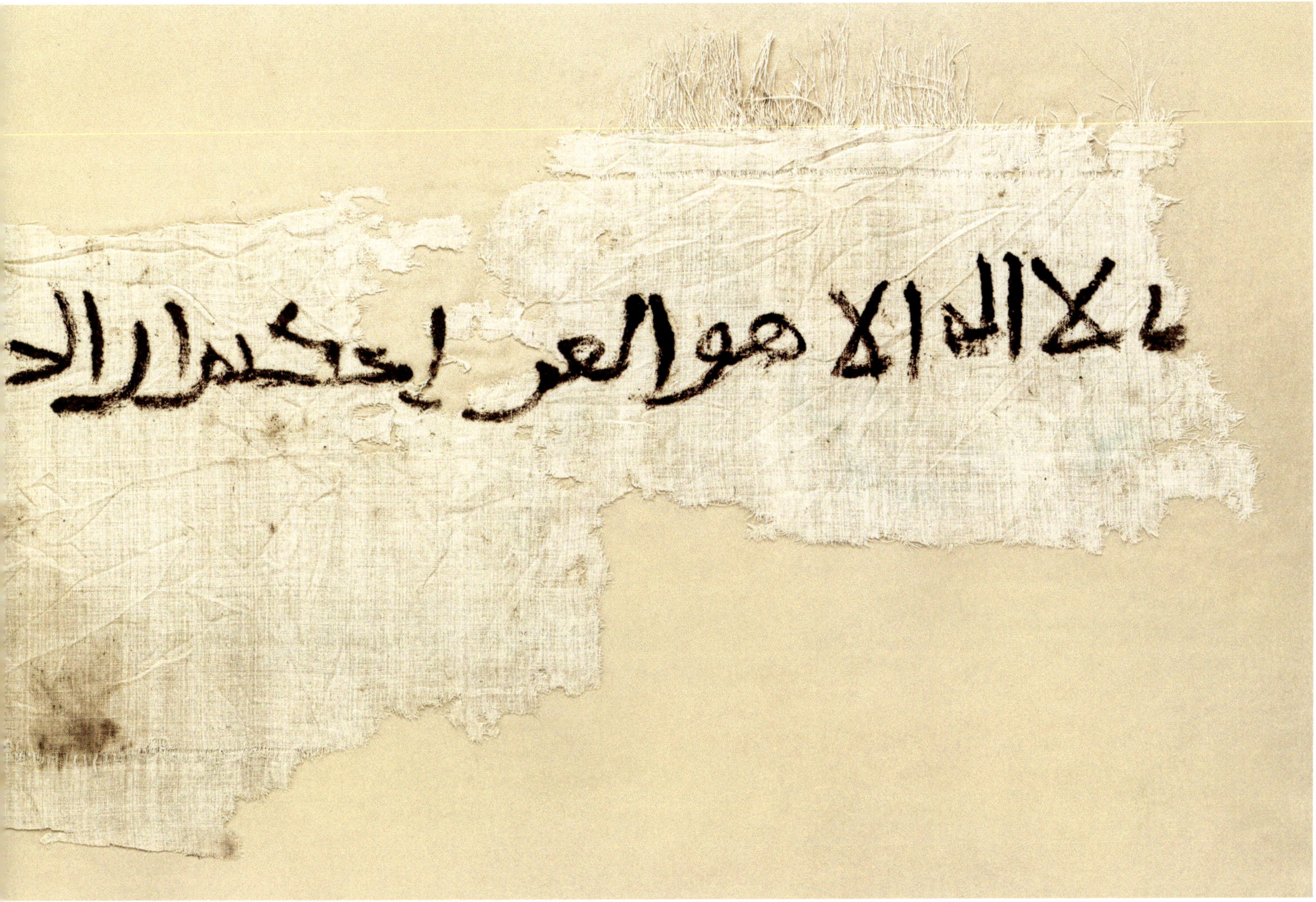

TEXTILES WITH A MAKER'S MARK

Cat. 42 *TIRAZ* **FRAGMENT FROM THE ABBASID DYNASTY**
Egypt, 9th to 10th century CE

Description: Fragment of undyed cotton, fringed at one end, with two lines of Kufic inscription embroidered in black silk.

Materials: cotton and silk: embroidery

Dimensions: h. 16.0 cm, w. 25.5 cm; max. letter height 1.5 cm

Ground fabric: cotton warp and weft, undyed, predominant-warp plain weave, loose texture (*sharb*); medium–poor quality (3–4)

Thread count: warp 15 Z-spun, weft 11 Z-spun

Thread thickness: warp 0.3–0.5 mm tight twist, weft 0.3–0.5 mm tight twist

Embroidery: silk, dyed (dark brown), couching stitch; supplementary red cotton weft; untwisted fringe

Provenance: Ex H.P. Kraus collection, no. 244

Inv. no. LNS 326 T

Related works: See page 507

Inscription:

Muhammad the son of Sulayman

محمد بن سليمان

This maker's mark is interesting as it mentions a name, a certain Muhammad the son of Sulayman. The piece was obviously once part of a larger textile, which perhaps was inscribed with a caliphal protocol, placed strategically close to the fringe so as not to disturb the overall aesthetic. The epigraphic style of the inscription can be compared with that of a *tiraz* from the reign of al-Muʿtamid (r. 870–92) produced in Misr in 273 AH / 886–87 CE (Related works 1), so an attribution to the later ninth century or perhaps the beginning of the tenth century might be justified.

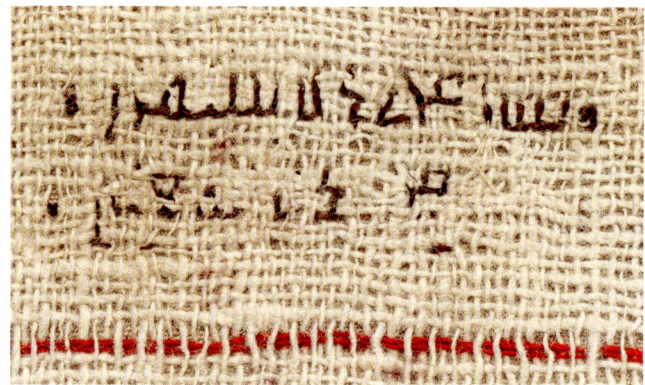

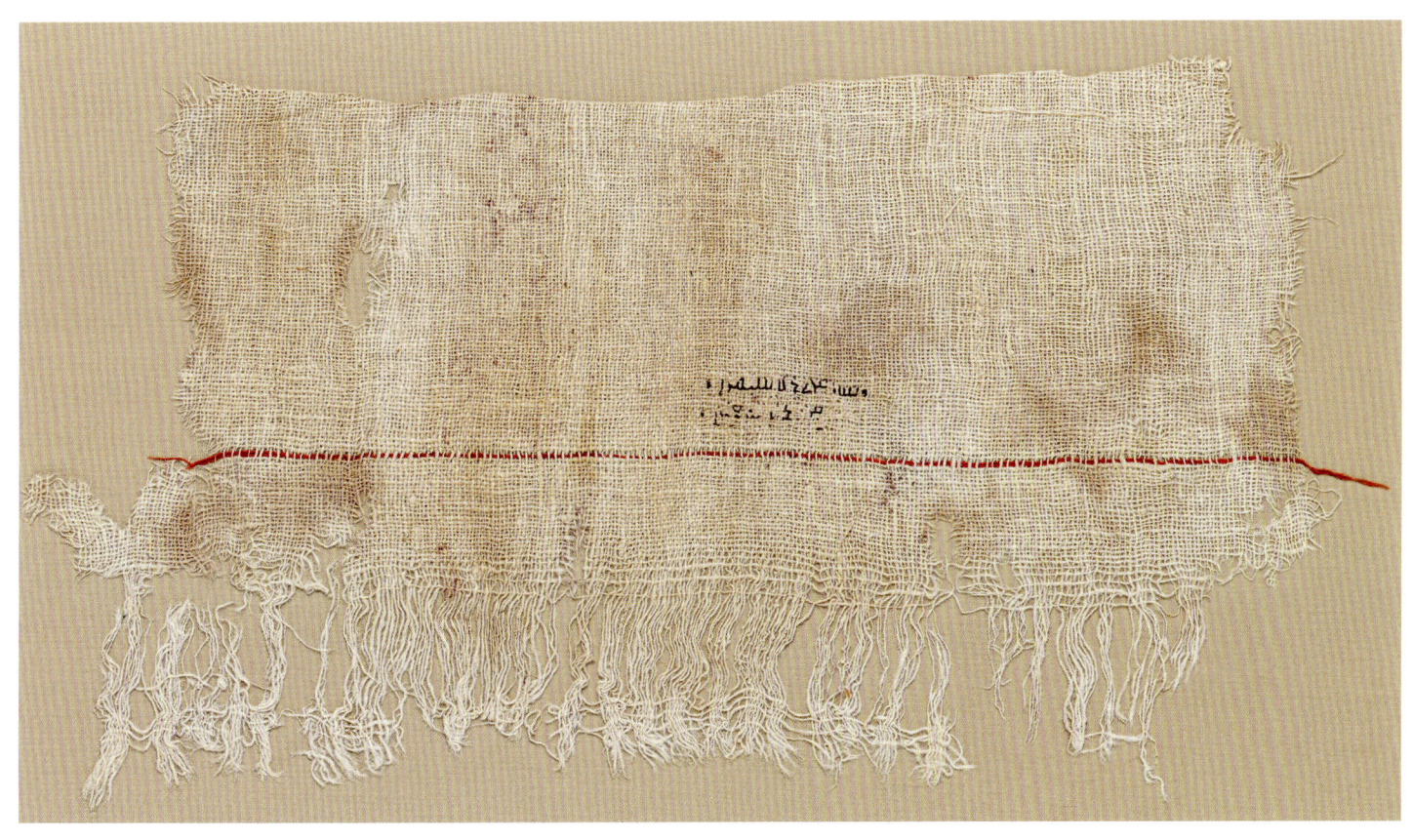

Cat. 43 *TIRAZ* **FRAGMENT FROM THE ABBASID DYNASTY**
Egypt, 9th to 10th century CE

Description: Fragment of undyed cotton, with three horizontal lines and one vertical line of Kufic inscription embroidered in black silk in small characters with high stems.

Materials: cotton and silk: embroidery

Dimensions: h. 15.5 cm, w. 10.5 cm: max. letter height 1.4 cm

Ground fabric: cotton warp and weft, undyed, balanced plain weave, dense texture (*dabiqi*), glazed and polished; very good–good quality (1–2)

Thread count: warp 27 Z-spun, weft 28 Z-spun

Thread thickness: warp 0.2–0.4 mm slight–medium twist, weft 0.2–0.4 mm slight–medium twist

Embroidery: silk, dyed (dark blue), couching and blanket stitch

Provenance: Ex H.P. Kraus collection, no. 242

Inv. no. LNS 324 T

Related works: See page 507

Inscription:

بركة و سلامة و الخير معين لصحابه

Blessing and safety and the good, aid to its owner

Factory marks such as this one and those in cat. nos 42 and 44 have not received much attention. Unlike caliphal inscriptions, which are usually placed very prominently along the central portion of one or both ends of a large sheet or shawl, factory marks are often placed at a corner of a large sheet or along a shawl's fringe or selvedge, and are very hard to decipher. Therefore, they seem not to have been as interesting to scholars as *tiraz* inscriptions with caliphal protocols. There are many fragments with similar marks in various museum collections. Ernst Kühnel mentions at least six at the Textile Museum, Washington, DC.[43] They would have been cut off by dealers and removed from the larger textiles to which they must surely once have belonged, consequently detaching them from their context. On their own, these marks can tell only a very limited story. In terms of date, the style of script might indicate the late ninth or early tenth century. The fact that in this case, like Related works 1 and 2, the inscription is embroidered on cotton might indicate an Iraqi origin, but then the type of embroidery and style of script seem to point to Egypt. Cat. no. 44 is noteworthy as the inscription mentions a certain 'Amr the son of Muhammad , and cat. no. 42 mentions a certain Muhammad the son of Sulayman.

Cat. 44 *TIRAZ* FRAGMENT FROM
THE ABBASID DYNASTY
Egypt, 9th to 10th century CE

Description: Fragment of undyed cotton,
roughly rectangular, with one
horizontal and one vertical line
(the former partly legible, the
latter not) of Kufic inscription
embroidered in blue silk in small
characters with high stems.

Materials: cotton and silk: tapestry weave

Dimensions: h. 9.0 cm, w. 11 cm;
max. letter height 1.0 cm

Ground fabric: cotton warp and weft, undyed,
balanced plain weave, dense
texture (*dabiqi*), polished;
good–medium quality (2–3)

Thread count: warp 14 Z-spun, weft 16 Z-spun

Thread thickness: warp 0.5–0.6 mm medium twist,
weft 0.5–0.6 mm medium twist

Embroidery: silk, dyed (blue), couching and
back stitch

Provenance: Ex H.P. Kraus collection, no. 243

Inv. no. LNS 325 T

Related works: See page 507

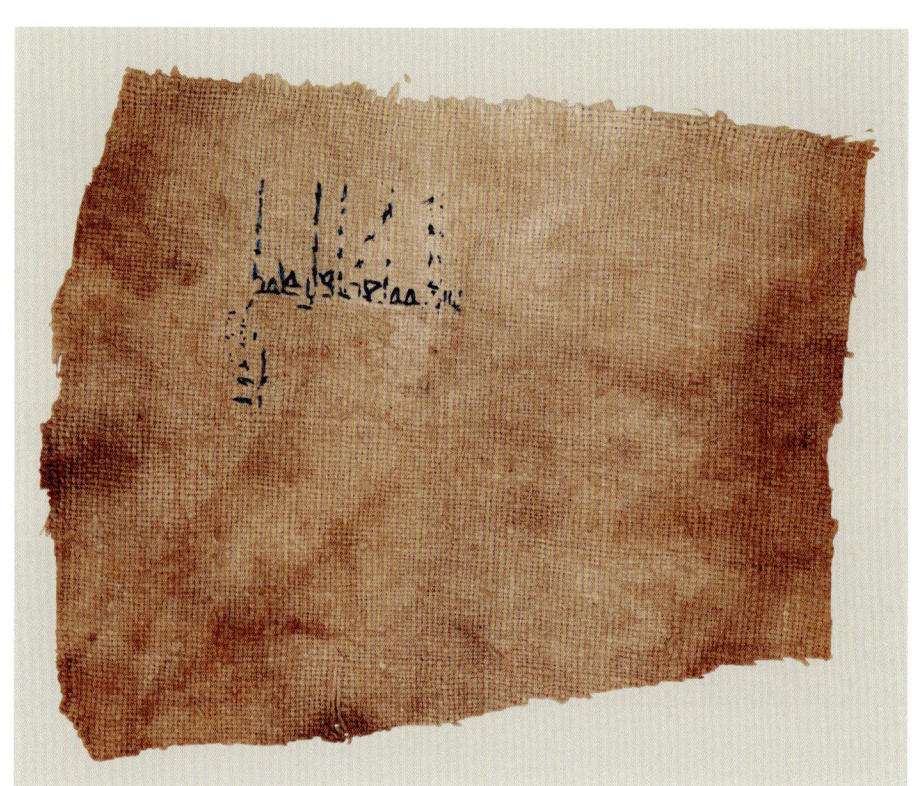

Inscription: سلامة لعمرو ابن محمد

Safety to 'Amr the son of Muhammad

Similar inscriptions are discussed in the commentary of cat. no. 43.

TEXTILES WITH REPETITIOUS, NON-MEANINGFUL
OR ABBREVIATED INSCRIPTIONS

Cat. 45   ***TIRAZ* FRAGMENT FROM THE ABBASID DYNASTY**
Egypt, 10th century CE

Description: Fragment of undyed linen, roughly rectangular, with one line of repetitious inscription embroidered in green silk.

Materials: linen and silk: embroidery

Dimensions: h. 7.5 cm, w. 16.0 cm; max. letter height 0.6 cm

Ground fabric: linen warp and weft, undyed, balanced plain weave, dense structure (*dabiqi*); medium quality (3)

Thread count: warp 15 SZ-spun, weft 13 Z-twist

Thread thickness: warp 0.4–0.6 mm slight–medium twist, weft 0.25–0.3 mm medium–tight twist

Embroidery: silk, dyed (light blue, light green), couching stitch

Provenance: Ex H.P. Kraus collection, no. 144

Inv. no. LNS 252 T

Inscription: repetition of

Sovereignty belongs to God

الملك لله

Cat. 46   *TIRAZ* FRAGMENT FROM
THE ABBASID DYNASTY
Egypt, 10th century CE

Description: Fragment of undyed linen, roughly
rectangular, with one line of
repetitious non-meaningful
text with elongated letter stems
embroidered in dark blue silk.

Materials: linen and silk: embroidery

Dimensions: h. 12.5 cm, w. 44.0 cm;
max. letter height 0.8 cm

Ground fabric: linen warp and weft, undyed,
predominant-warp plain weave,
dense texture (*dabiqi*); good
quality (2); seam above the
inscription attaching a piece of
tailored fabric (probably a pocket)

Thread count: warp 24 S-spun, weft 14 S-spun

Thread thickness: warp 0.3–0.5 mm slight twist,
weft 0.4–0.5 mm slight twist

Embroidery: wool, dyed (dark blue), couching
and back stitch

Provenance: Ex H.P. Kraus collection, no. 194

Inv. no. LNS 292 T

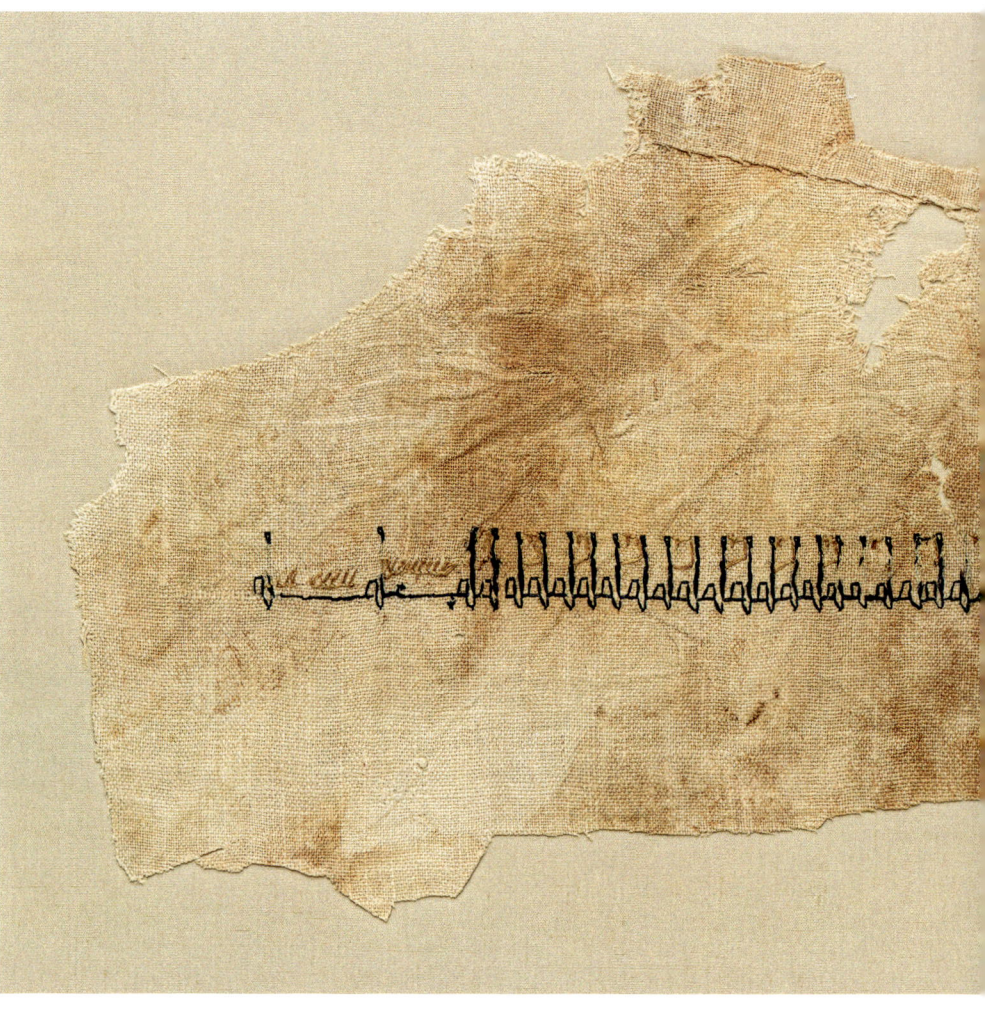

Inscription: epigraphic repetition of   له له له له

Cat. nos 46–52 are examples of inscriptions that are in a style related to caliphal inscriptions, but are mere repetitions of letters, to emulate the look of proper inscriptions. The examples here date mostly from the first half of the tenth century, probably from the reign of al-Muqtadir or al-Radi. In epigraphic style they mostly emulate inscriptions from Iraq, both in technique and appearance, but are of Egyptian production. Iraqi inscriptions were executed in chain stitch, often in blue silk, on cotton; the textiles here have linen base fabrics. The inscriptions are characterized by pronounced upper letter stems, such as the *alif*, and swelling lower terminals of the letters *ra* and *waw*, which would often form a festoon-like sequence below the baseline. These are characteristics that can also be observed here, but their execution is far less skilled than in the Iraqi examples. It is likely that the inscriptions here were copied from Iraqi originals without a knowledge of inscriptional content, merely to emulate a distinctive style.

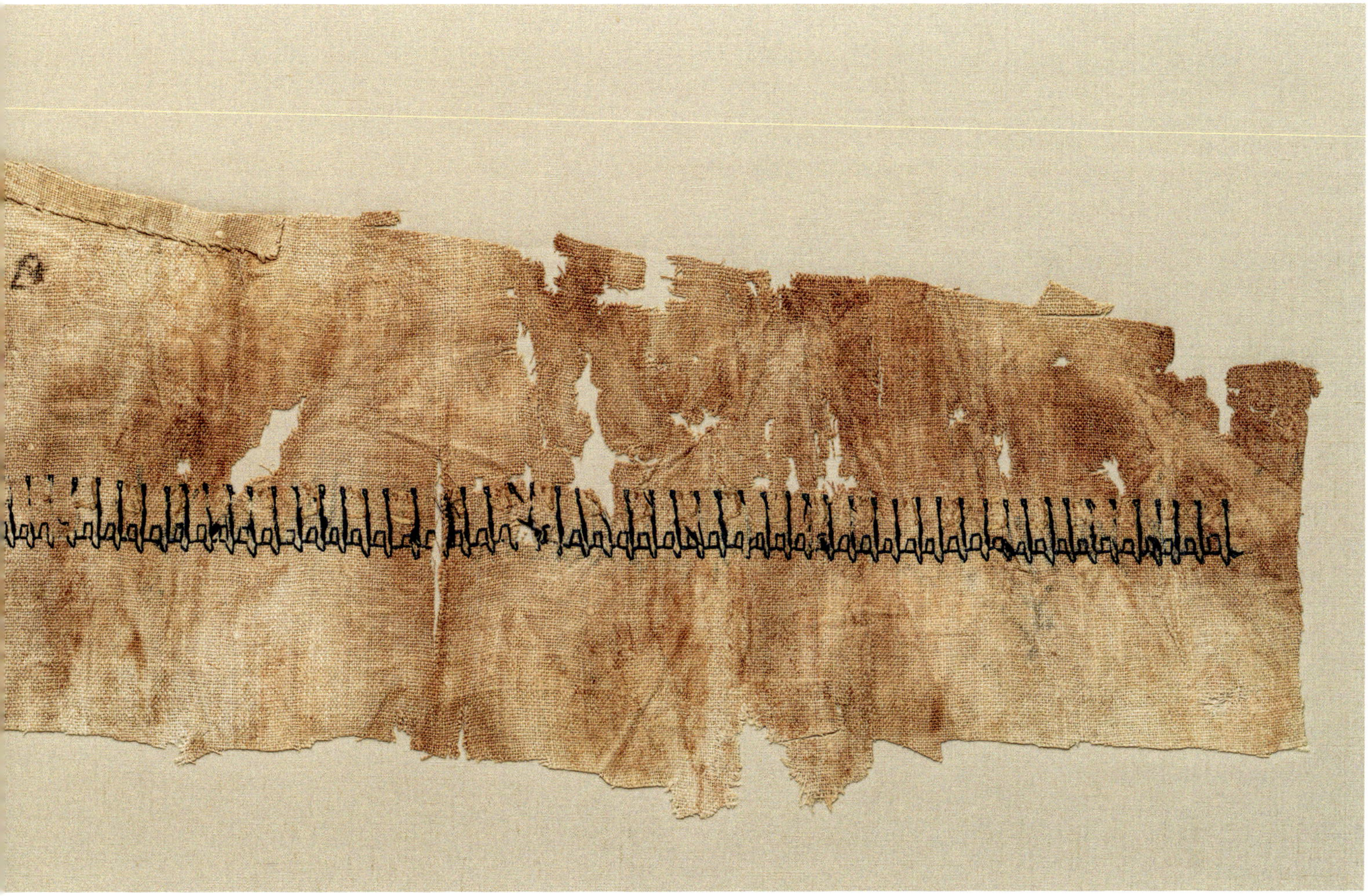

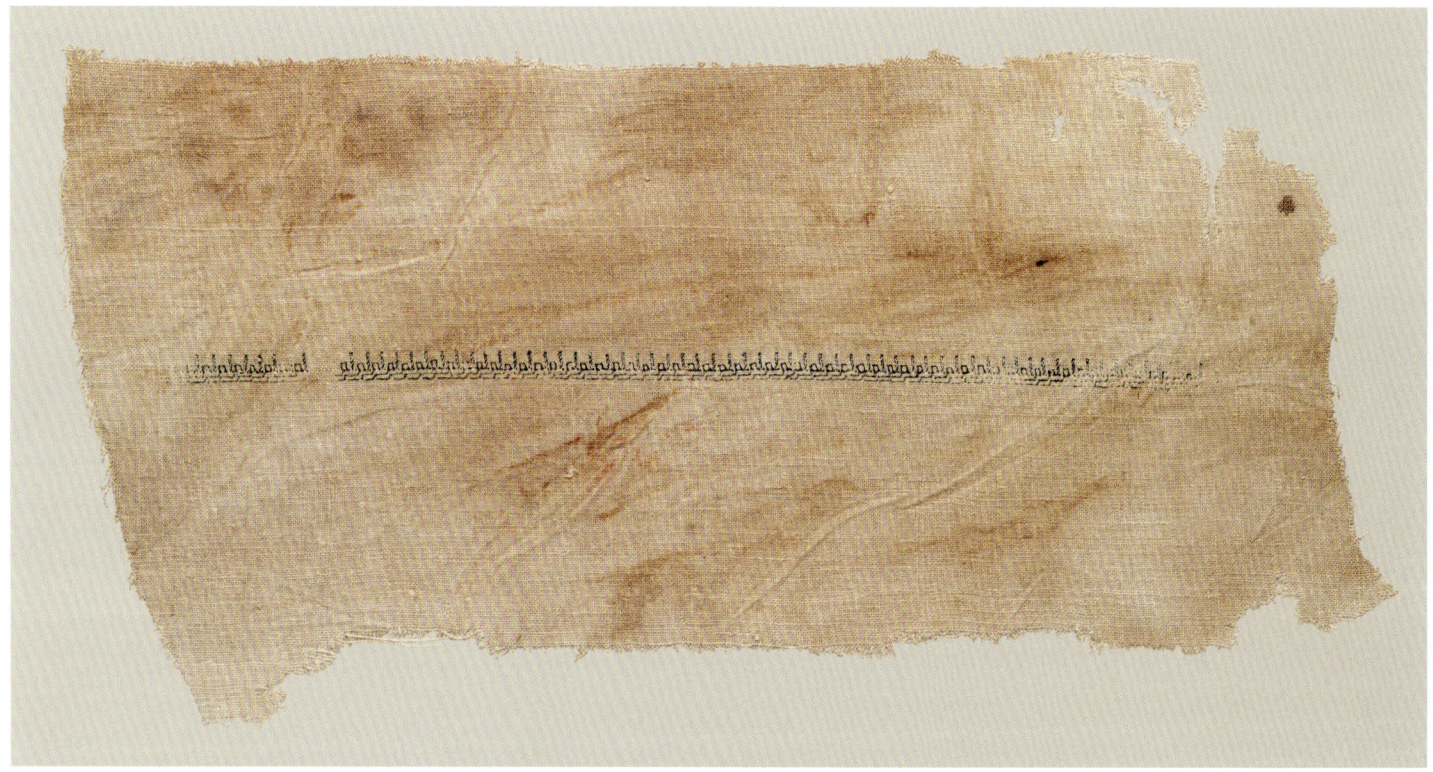

Cat. 47   *TIRAZ* **FRAGMENT FROM THE ABBASID DYNASTY**
Egypt, 10th century CE

Description: Fragment of undyed linen, with one line of repetitious non-meaningful text embroidered in green silk.

Materials: linen and silk: embroidery

Dimensions: h. 19.3 cm, w. 36.7 cm; max. letter height 0.7 cm

Ground fabric: linen warp and weft, undyed, balanced plain weave, dense texture (*dabiqi*); good quality (2)

Thread count: warp 20 S-spun, weft 17 S-spun

Thread thickness: warp 0.4–0.5 mm slight–medium twist, weft 0.4–0.5 mm slight–medium twist

Embroidery: silk, dyed (dark blue), couching, back and flat stitch

Provenance: Ex H.P. Kraus collection, no. 193

Inv. no. LNS 291 T

Inscription: epigraphic repetition of

ڡ ڡ ڡ

Cat. 48 *TIRAZ* FRAGMENT FROM
THE ABBASID DYNASTY
Egypt, 10th century CE

Description: Fragment of undyed linen, large
and roughly rectangular, with
one line of repetitious text with
elongated stems embroidered in
brown silk.

Materials: linen and silk: embroidery

Dimensions: h. 20.9 cm, w. 36 cm;
max. letter height 1.0 cm

Ground fabric: linen warp and weft, undyed,
balanced plain weave, close texture
(*dabiqi*), glazed and polished;
very good–good quality (1–2)

Thread count: warp 19 Z-spun, weft 22 Z-spun

Thread thickness: warp 0.25–0.5 mm medium twist,
weft 0.4–0.5 mm medium twist

Embroidery: silk, dyed (dark red), couching
and chain stitches

Provenance: Ex H.P. Kraus collection, no. 187

Inv. no. LNS 286 T

Inscription: epigraphic repetition of

For God or Sovereignty

لله or ملك

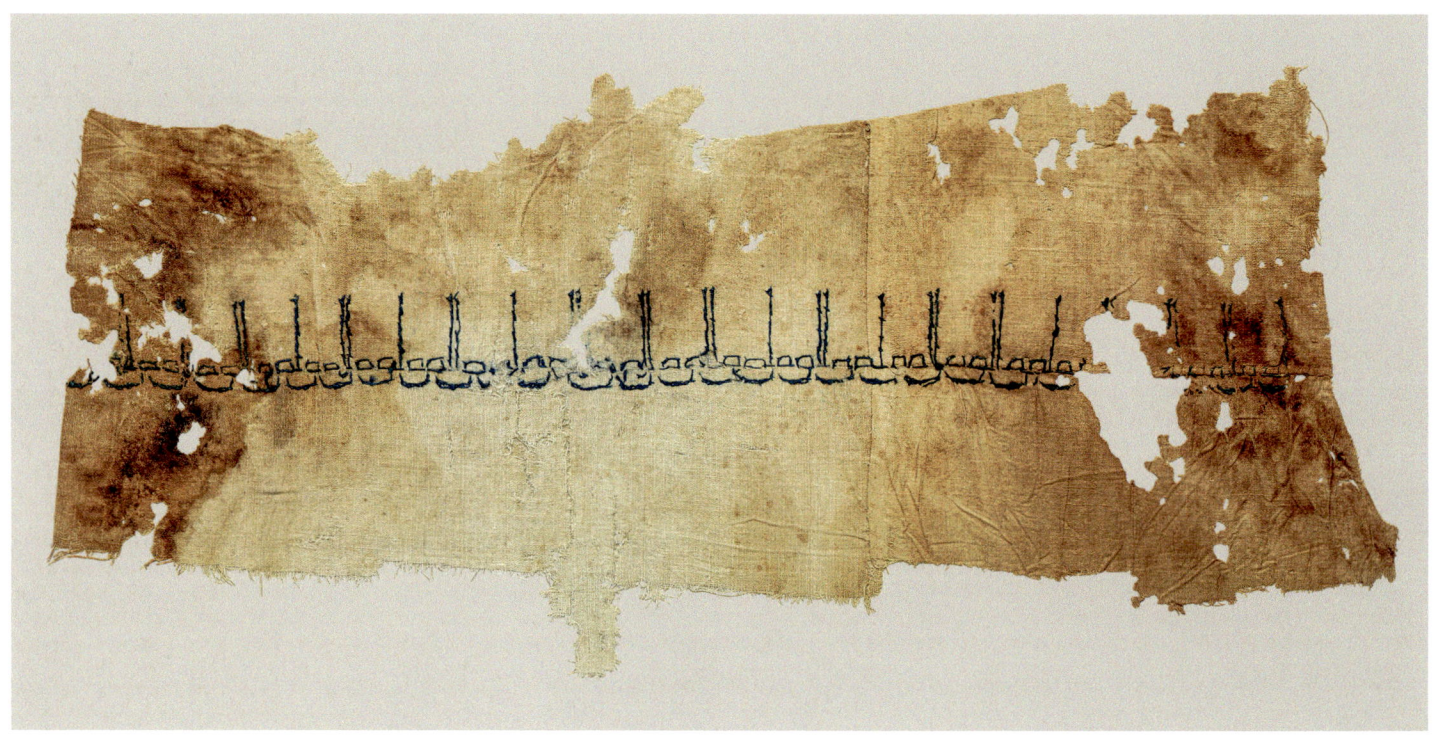

Cat. 49 *TIRAZ* FRAGMENT FROM
THE ABBASID DYNASTY
Egypt, 10th century CE

Description: Fragment of undyed linen, roughly
rectangular, with one line of
repetitious text with elongated
stems embroidered in dark blue
linen; the fragment has a seam.

Materials: linen and silk: embroidery

Dimensions: h. 19.8 cm, w. 43.6 cm;
max. letter height 3.2 cm

Ground fabric: linen warp and weft, undyed,
predominant-weft plain weave,
dense texture (*dabiqi*); good
quality (2); seam in the right
third of the inscription, with the
embroidery executed over it

Thread count: warp 22 S-spun, weft 31 Z-spun

Thread thickness: warp 0.15–0.4 mm slight twist,
weft 0.1–0.3 mm medium twist

Embroidery: linen, dyed (dark blue), S-spun,
couching and chain stitch

Provenance: Ex H.P. Kraus collection, no. 196

Inv. no. LNS 294 T

Inscription: epigraphic repetition of

God or For God

آاله or لله

The repeated inscription may be read as the word 'Allah' or 'li-llah' ('God'
or ' For God'). The textile conserves a seam towards the right-hand end of
the inscription; the inscription is embroidered on top of the seam.

Cat. 50   *TIRAZ* FRAGMENT FROM
           THE ABBASID DYNASTY
           Egypt, 10th century CE

Description: Fragment of undyed linen, with
                one line of repetitious inscription
                with elongated stems embroidered
                in blue silk.

Materials: linen and silk: embroidery

Dimensions: h. 15.0 cm, w. 16.5 cm;
                max. letter height 3.0 cm

Ground fabric: linen warp and weft, undyed,
                balanced plain weave, dense texture
                (*dabiqi*); medium quality (3)

Thread count: warp 20 S-spun, weft 18 S-spun

Thread thickness: warp 0.2–0.5 mm medium–tight
                twist, weft 0.2–0.5 mm medium–
                tight twist

Embroidery: silk, dyed (dark blue), chain stitch

Provenance: Ex H.P. Kraus collection, no. 199

Inv. no. LNS 297 T

Inscription: repetition of

Blessing from God

بركة من الله

Cat. 51 *TIRAZ* **FRAGMENT FROM THE ABBASID OR EARLY FATIMID DYNASTY**
Egypt, 10th century CE

Description: Fragment of undyed linen, roughly rectangular, with two lines of inscription consisting of a decorative repetition of 'Allah' embroidered in red silk, and one line, damaged, embroidered in light blue silk.

Materials: linen and silk: embroidery

Dimensions: h. 12.5 cm, w. 21.4 cm; max. letter height 7.7 cm

Ground fabric: linen warp and weft, undyed, balanced plain weave, dense texture (*dabiqi*); medium quality (3)

Thread count: warp 12 S-spun, weft 11 S-spun

Thread thickness: warp 0.4–1.0 mm slight twist, weft 0.4–1.0 mm slight twist

Embroidery: silk, dyed (light blue, red), chain stitch

Provenance: Ex H.P. Kraus collection, no. 198

Inv. no. LNS 296 T

Related works: See page 507

Inscription:

Lines 1 and 2: repetition of God

الله

Line 3:

In the Name of God […]

بسم الله [...]

Cat. 52   *TIRAZ* **FRAGMENT FROM THE ABBASID OR EARLY FATIMID DYNASTY**
Egypt, 10th century CE

Description: Fragment of undyed linen, roughly rectangular, in two pieces, with one line of text and (above) a band of decoration imitating calligraphic shapes, all embroidered in dark blue silk.

Materials: linen and silk: embroidery

Dimensions: h. 10.0 cm, w. 12.0 cm; max. letter height 6.6 cm

Ground fabric: linen warp and weft, undyed, predominant-warp plain weave, close texture (*dabiqi*); medium quality (3)

Thread count: warp 11 S-spun, weft 8 S-spun

Thread thickness: warp 0.5–1.0 mm medium twist, weft 0.5–1.0 mm medium twist

Embroidery: silk, dyed (dark blue), chain stitch

Provenance: Ex H.P. Kraus collection, no. 197

Inv. no. LNS 295 T

Related works: See page 507

Inscription: undecipherable

Cat. 53   *TIRAZ* **FRAGMENT FROM THE ABBASID DYNASTY**
Egypt, 9th century CE

Description: Fragment of undyed linen, with one line of repetitious Kufic inscription embroidered in reserve against an embroidered red background, and (below) a band of beaded decoration embroidered in blue.

Materials: linen and silk: embroidery and supplementary weft

Dimensions: h. 7.5 cm, w. 10.6 cm

Ground fabric: linen warp and weft, undyed, balanced plain weave, close texture (*dabiqi*), regular; very good quality (1)

Thread count: warp 22 S-spun, weft 20 S-spun

Thread thickness: warp 0.15–0.3 mm slight–medium twist, weft 0.3 mm slight–medium twist

Embroidery: silk, dyed (red, blue), back stitch, supplementary weft open-work

Provenance: art market, 1970s–1980s

Inv. no. LNS 51 T

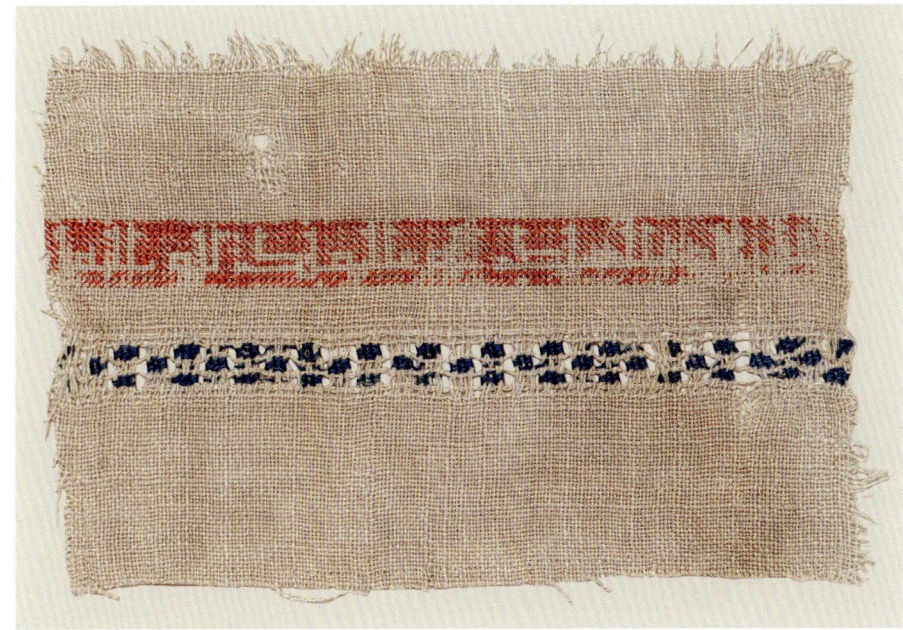

Inscription: repetition of

The kingdom is God's

الملك لله

Cat. 54 **SHIRT (*THAWB*) FROM THE ABBASID OR EARLY FATIMID DYNASTY**
Egypt, mid-10th century CE

Description: Shirt (*thawb*) of undyed linen, wide, with wide sleeves and a round vertical collar, embroidered with a broad *tiraz* band around each sleeve near the end, and with two bands down the front, extending from shoulder to hem; the embroidered bands bear what appear to be repetitious Kufic inscriptions of the word 'li-llah', interrupted by angular palmette-like motifs.

Materials: linen and silk: embroidery

Dimensions: h. 132 cm, w. 192 cm

Ground fabric: linen warp and weft, undyed, warp-faced(?) plain weave, dense texture (*dabiqi*); good quality (2)

Thread count: warp 28 S-spun, weft 11 S-spun

Thread thickness: warp 0.4 mm medium twist, weft 0.3 mm tight twist

Embroidery: silk, undyed (ivory), S-spun three-plied, 1–1.5 mm slight twist, satin stitch

Tailoring: original seams in running stitch, repairs in back stitch, with linen fabric of different colour and texture on back, front and sleeves

Provenance: art market, 1970s–1980s, reportedly from Egypt

Published: Jenkins, Keene and Bates 1983, pp. 104–05; Curatola et al. 2010, p. 88, no. 60

Inv. no. LNS 57 T

Related works: See page 507

Inscription: repetition of   لله

To God

This garment is constructed of several cut pieces of linen: a single long rectangular piece for back and front, with an opening for the head but otewise uncut on the shoulder, to which are attached sleeves each comprising a rectangular piece of cloth from shoulder to chest of the body of the garment; two pieces are set into either side below the sleeves, one trapezoid covering the length between sleeve and lower hem, another lozenge-shaped set between the sleeve and the trapezoidal side piece. The collar is constructed out of the same fabric and sewn onto the shoulder, back and front, and the opening for it is covered by a flap that reaches the peak of the shoulder with a knob-like textile button at the end of the open collar, fitting into a looped rope attached to the neck part of the collar; the closure of the collar cannot be seen by one confronting the wearer of the garment. At some point, a large piece of linen was set into the frontal part of the tunic, perhaps to repair it, carefully respecting the existing embroidered inscription.

Only the frontal areas of the garment carry the epigraphic decoration. This consists of a repetition of the word 'la'a' or 'li-llah', with three different renderings of the letter shape between the *lam* and *alif*: a tripartite knotted stem, a short stem with a star-shaped knot, and a six-partite knotted stem. On the sleeves, the embroidery covers the seams, suggesting that it was applied after the two pieces of fabric forming the sleeve had been sewn together. On the front, the inscription friezes run along the seams from the shoulders down. In the tradition of adornment in the Islamic world, it is possible that the embroidery there was applied after the fabric had been cut, but before it was sewn to construct the shirt. However, on the lower part of both sleeves the embroidery can be seen runing over the seams, which suggests that the embroidery was applied after the garment had been constructed and sewn together.

Only very few complete early Islamic garments from Egypt have survived. A similar tunic in the Ashmolean Museum, Oxford (Related works 1; fig. 1.57), relates remarkably closely to the present piece: they share the basic construction, as well as the formal features of the epigraphic bands. In contrast to the al-Sabah garment, however, the Ashmolean tunic features two bands in dark blue silk running down the front of the garment. It was acquired by a Greek collector in Alexandria in the first half of the twentieth century, and its condition suggests that, like many *tiraz* textiles, it had been used as a shroud. Carbon dating on the Oxford piece has provided a tentative date of 930 CE +/– 35 years. On this basis, the tunic here can be dated accordingly. An earlier child's tunic is in the Textile Museum, Washington, DC (Related works 2; fig. 1.52). This piece is inscribed in red embroidered silk on a linen ground fabric, carries the name of the Abbasid caliph al-Muqtadir and states that it was made in Misr in the year 306 AH / 918–19 CE. The inscription is located on the back of one sleeve and positioned upside down.[44]

Related are also a number of non-inscribed, but decorated linen child's tunics. One, in the collection of Cairo University, can be dated to the Fatimid period on the basis of the tapestry-woven bands located on both sleeves (see chapter 1).[45] Twelve unpublished tunics are in the textile collection of the Royal Ontario Museum, Toronto.[46] These tunics are decorated mainly along the collar in brown silk or wool embroidery, comprising small standardized geometric designs. Their date is not certain.

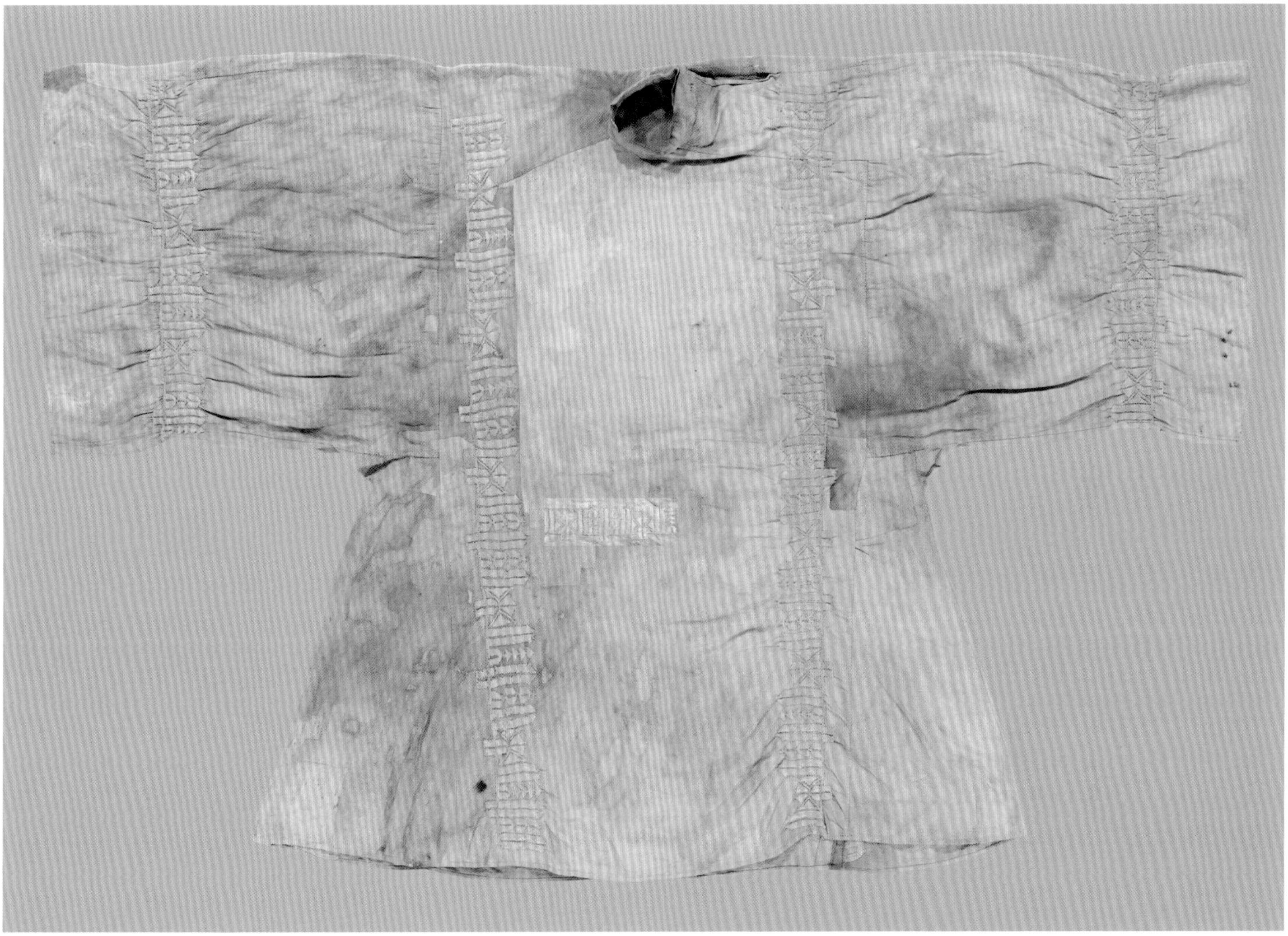

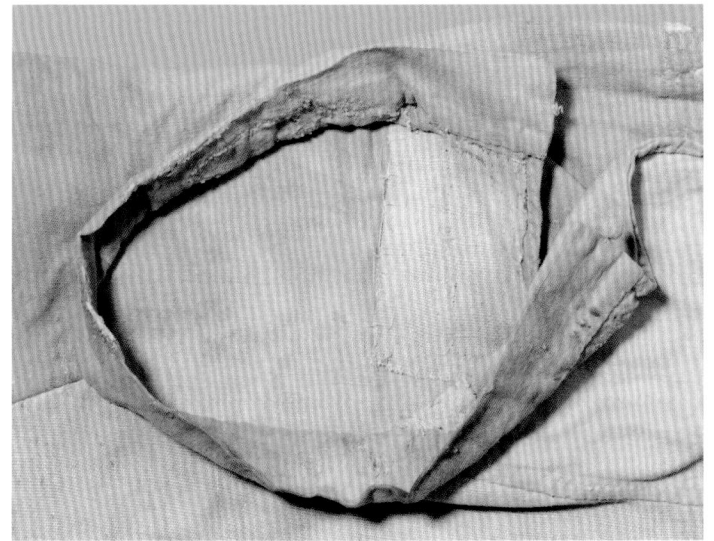

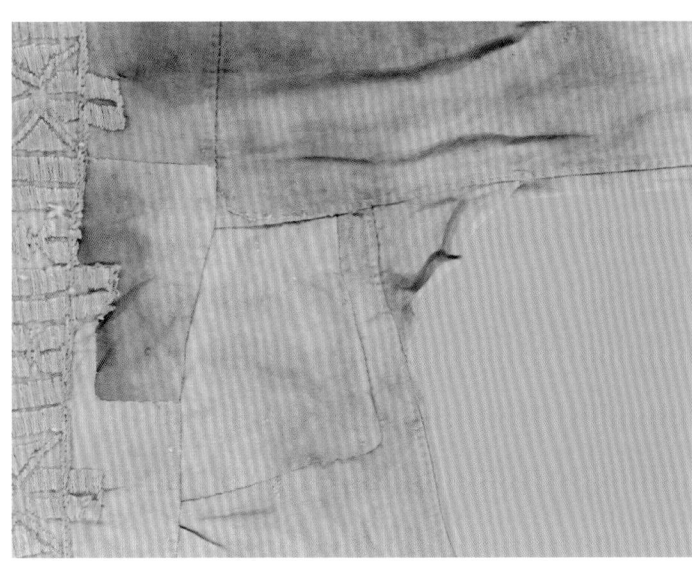

2

THE URBAN CENTRES OF
THE NILE VALLEY AND UPPER EGYPT

While the Nile Delta was famous for its linen textiles, the economic historian Maurice Lombard has suggested that wool textiles were predominantly produced along the Nile, all the way to Upper Egypt (Sa'id), but also in the al-Fayyum oasis, which was traditionally associated with the production of textiles for Coptic consumption.[1] The Fayyum is treated separately in this catalogue, as the textiles produced there were quite distinct in terms of materials and aesthetics and form their own group.

Literary sources list a number of textile centres along the Nile. In his *Kitab al-tanbih wa al-ishraf* ('Book of admonition and revision') the tenth-century geographer al-Mas'udi mentions the *tiraz* workshops of Bahnasa, Asyut and Akhmim.[2] Ibn Hawqal and al-Idrisi both mention the town of Taha as a place of *tiraz* production.[3] The *tiraz* workshops of Ashmunayn, the ancient Oxyrhynchus, were mentioned in the twelfth-century geography of al-Idrisi, who says that 'in its *tiraz* factories, they make curtains and carpets of wool which are called after the city'.[4] Ibn Hawqal noted that 'linen is brought from it and many garments are dispatched to Cairo (Misr) and elsewhere'.[5] The production of so-called 'cut' carpets ('al-farsh al-qutu') is further mentioned by al-Ya'qubi.[6] These references are interesting, as carpet fragments from Ashmunayn have indeed survived. The city of Qays is mentioned by Ya'qubi as part of the Fayyum, but it was actually located just south of Bahnasa. He says: 'The town of Qais is there, where the Qaisi garments and the excellent robes are made, also the town of Bahnasa (Oxyrhynchus) where the Bahnasa curtains (*sutur*) are made, and the town of Ahnas where the robes are made.'[7]

Perhaps the most elaborate description of a town in Upper Egypt can be found also in al-Idrisi, who writes about Bahnasa:

It is at Bahnasa that there were and still are *tiraz* factories where they weave for royal use (*khassa*), the precious curtains which are known as Bahnasi, the sultan's cloth (*makati'*), the large tents, and the *mutakhaiyar* (chosen?) cloth. In it

are many *tiraz* factories belonging to the public ('*amma*), where merchants evaluate the precious curtains, the length of one of which is thirty *dhira'*, more or less. No curtains, robes, or other cloths made of wool and cotton are made there without the names of the *tiraz* factories being placed upon them, whether it is the royal (*khass*) *tiraz*, or the public *tiraz* factories, a prescribed custom which the preceding age established, and those workers who came after them followed, up to this present time of ours. These curtains, carpets (*fursh*) and robes are renowned throughout the earth.[8]

The presence of a prominent Coptic population is documented by Yaqut and Qazwini, who discuss the churches of Asyut.[9] It is perhaps no surprise, then, that Asyut is mentioned as a place where a so-called Armenian type of manufacture was practised, based on the local production of wool.[10] Nasir-e Khosraw describes this in some detail:

In this Asyut, they weave cloth (*dastar*) of sheep wool, which has no equal in the world, and fine wools which are taken to Persia and which they call Misri (Egyptian). All this is from Upper Egypt, for in Cairo itself they weave no wool. I myself have seen in Asyut a cloth (*futa*) manufactured of sheep's wool, the like of which I have not seen in Lahawar (Lahore), nor Multan, so that I thought it silk (*harir*) from the look of it.[11]

Surviving woollen *tiraz* textiles confirm what Arab geographers tell us. The names of the most important centres are documented in several surviving *tiraz* inscriptions: Bahnasa, Akhmim, Ashmunayn[12] and Qays. Generally these are rare among the huge corpus of early Islamic *tiraz* inscriptions, but the fact that they did survive is significant, as they challenge the overbearing presence of textiles made in the Nile Delta and allow the textile historian to study material that is probably more connected to pre-Islamic and indigenous Egyptian craft traditions. Perhaps the reason for their rare survival is that the woollen textiles of Upper Egypt were often furnishing fabrics, rather than clothing, as is also suggested by literary sources mentioned here.

The town of Bahnasa is perhaps documented by the largest group of fragments surviving from Upper Egypt. All of these are in the Museum of Islamic Art in Cairo and are discussed in more detail below in individual catalogue entries.[13] Most of them feature prominent inscriptions that are usually dedicated to unnamed patrons, as is the case with cat. no. 60. Two of the textiles in Cairo are particularly important as they document the *tiraz al-khassa* in Bahnasa, confirming literary evidence.[14] The Bahnasa textiles appear, on account of their epigraphy, to date from the Tulunid period in the ninth century.[15]

The *tiraz* workshop in Akhmim is documented by an inscription on a pile-knotted rug fragment in the Textile Museum, Washington, DC, thus confirming literary evidence about the town as a centre for the production of pile-knotted rugs mentioned above.[16] A textile from Ashmunayn has survived, albeit from the reign of the Fatimid caliph al-Zahir (r. 1021–36), but nevertheless documenting the existence of a *tiraz al-khassa* in the city.[17]

One example woven in Qays, now in the Museum of Islamic Art in Cairo, is dated, 168 AH / 784–85 CE, which falls within the reign of the Abbasid caliph al-Mahdi (r. 775–85).[18] It is a fragment of a much larger piece and characterized by several bands of decoration with intricately tapestry-woven animal and floral designs, one of which contains an inscription in an early form of Arabic script from the end of a protocol, giving the year of production. Two textiles that are of similar manufacture and aesthetic and have been attributed to Qays can be dated to the reign of Harun al-Rashid (r. 786–809) on account of their inscriptions. The inscription on one in the Bouvier Collection records the order of a certain amir Isma'il.[19] Two Egyptian governors with the *ism* Isma'il were active in 181–82 AH / 797–99 CE under Harun al-Rashid, which suggests a late eighth-century date for that piece.[20] The other textile, in the Museum für Islamische Kunst in Berlin, is inscribed with a protocol that mentions Harun al-Rashid's name and titles.[21] The textiles described in this section can be related to the latter pieces in the use of an epigraphic style characterized by low letters of even thickness that seem to 'crawl', a style attributed by Grohmann to the time between the late Umayyad period and a short transition period under the early Abbasids, before a more pronounced Abbasid style was developed in the ninth century.[22]

Cat. 55 *TIRAZ* FRAGMENT FROM
THE UMAYYAD OR ABBASID
DYNASTY
**Egypt, probably Qays or
Misr, 8th to 9th century CE**

Description: Fragment of tapestry-woven
coloured wool, comprising three
registers: the two outermost
contain a Kufic inscription in
yellow on a red ground, separated
from the central band by beaded
borders; the central band (5.3 cm)
features a lattice design with
lozenges alternating in red and
yellow, each full lozenge containing
a multi-petalled flower and each
half-lozenge at the edge containing
a multi-beaded half medallion, the
yellow lattice grid beaded in blue
and accentuated by blue and red.

Materials: wool: tapestry weave
Dimensions: h. 13.5 cm, w. 17.9 cm;
max. letter height 1.3 cm
Ground fabric: wool warp, dyed (dark blue),
weft lost
Thread count: warp 13 S-spun
Thread thickness: warp 0.4–0.5 mm tight twist
Tapestry: wool, dyed (red, mustard yellow,
dark blue, light red, light green);
c. 32 picks per cm; 0.15 mm
medium–tight twist
Provenance: Ex H.P. Kraus collection, no. 223

Inv. no. LNS 68 T

Related works: See page 507

Inscription:

Line 1:

[...و]حمد[م] بن عمّار زيـ(ـع) [...]

[...] ʿAziz ʿAmmar the son of Muhammad and [...]

Line 2:

[...ـن]بـ عمّار عزيز حبه(صا) [...]

[...] its owner ʿAziz ʿAmmar the son [...]

This piece and the following textiles (cat. nos 56–59) belong to a distinct group that share certain technical characteristics and aesthetic. They are all tapestry-woven in multicoloured wool in a limited range of colours (red, mustard yellow, dark blue) on blue wool warps. All comprise bands of decoration, and inscriptions with separating bands between. The decoration usually appears crowded and comprises predominantly lattice designs, lozenges and beaded borders. The base colour tends to be red, the designs being in yellow and red and the inscriptions in yellow only. The style of the inscriptions is angular and the letter terminals wedge-shaped.

Probably the most important example of this group is a piece in the Museum of Islamic Art in Cairo (Related works 1), comprising a broad register containing the inscription band and bands of geometric and floral designs, accompanying a main field with confronted fish and floral arrangements. It is dated 168 AH / 784–85 CE during the reign of the Abbasid caliph al-Mahdi (r. 775–85) and the inscription mentions that it was made in Qays, a well-known textile centre in Upper Egypt. Further related fragments are in the Bouvier Collection (Related works 2–6). One of these mentions that it was ordered by a certain ʿamir Ismaʿil' (Related works 2). As most of the surviving examples preserve only fragments of the inscription and decorative bands, one may speculate that these too once accompanied larger arrangements comprising zoomorphic or floral representations. This is the case with the piece in Cairo, mentioned above.

The present inscription refers to the individual mentioned here as its owner (*(sa)hibihi*), indicating that the piece was made for a private patron. The same can be found in another piece in the Bouvier Collection (Related works 4). There the inscription continues with the term *mimma*, which normally introduces a phrase recording the order of the textile, the place of production and often a date. In another fragment, the term *mimma* can still be read (Related works 5). A fifth fragment in the Bouvier Collection features two bands of diamond shapes not unlike those in the present piece, accompanying two bands of inscription in a style of script similar to the one seen here (Related works 6). The fragmentary inscription has been read as a protocol mentioning the *tiraz al-khassa* in Misr. A complete linen sheet in the Textile Museum, Washington, DC, features text tapestry-woven in wool in a style of script that

would indicate an eighth-century date, but with a reference to the *tiraz al-khassa* in Misr.[23] Like the present piece, it also features bands of diamond shapes. Kühnel refers to the textiles of Upper Egypt, particularly Qays and Bahnasa, as a comparison, and alludes to Coptic traditions.[24] However, the Washington piece is fundamentally different from the textiles discussed here, as there the wool tapestry is limited to distinctive bands within a linen base fabric.

Cat. 56   *TIRAZ* FRAGMENT FROM
THE ABBASID DYNASTY
Egypt, 9th century CE

Description: Fragment of wool dyed black,
roughly rectangular, with four
decorative bands tapestry-woven
in yellow, red, green and dark blue
wool; these bands are bordered by
two calligraphic bands, tapestry-
woven in yellow and red.

Materials: wool: plain weave and tapestry

Dimensions: h. 13.6 cm, w. 19.2 cm;
max. letter height 0.8 cm

Ground fabric: wool warp and weft, dyed (black),
predominant-weft plain weave,
dense texture; good quality (2);
selvedge: wool warp, dyed (red),
and wool braiding (dark blue,
dark green)

Thread count: warp 30 S-spun, weft 10 S-spun

Thread thickness: warp 0.5 mm slight twist,
weft 0.5 mm tight twist

Tapestry: wool, dyed (yellow, red, green
and dark blue)

Provenance: Ex H.P. Kraus collection, no. 222

Inv. no. LNS 308 T

Related works: See page 507

Inscription:

Line 1:

[...] مما عمل في طر[از] [...]

[...] of what has been made in the *tiraz* [...]

Line 2:

[...] عمل في طر[از] [...]

[...] (of what) has been made in the *tiraz* [...]

The inscription on this piece is significant as it mentions the textile's manufacture in a *tiraz* workshop. The only textiles woven from wool or from linen and wool that mention a *tiraz* workshop in an inscription are those from Misr, Bahnasa and the Fayyum. An attribution to the Fayyum seems unlikely, as the textiles produced there are fundamentally different in manufacture and aesthetic (see the discussion of textiles from the Fayyum below, pp. 263–300). In both of the surviving textiles from Misr and Bahnasa the woollen inscriptions are embedded in a base fabric of linen. Neither is the case here. To judge from the wool-on-wool tapestry, the colour range and the similarity to inscriptions associated with Upper Egypt, particularly Qays, an attribution to the latter seems more likely, particularly on account of the surviving caliphal textile from the period of al-Mahdi, listed above (Related works 1).

Cat. 57   *TIRAZ* **FRAGMENT FROM**
THE ABBASID DYNASTY
Egypt, 8th to 9th century CE

Description: Fragment of tapestry-woven wool
dyed dark blue, roughly square,
with a large decorative band
formed of three sections, tapestry-
woven in red, ochre and yellow.
The central and largest section of
the band is has an alternation of
eight-pointed stars in yellow, the
centre formed by an ochre circle,
and confronted triangles also in
yellow, themselves composed of
three ochre triangles; this central
section is framed by two bands of
red, yellow and blue lozenges. It
is framed by two smaller bands of
text, tapestry-woven in ochre and
undyed wool.

Materials: wool: plain weave and tapestry

Dimensions: h. 15.3 cm, w. 18.9 cm;
max. letter height 0.9 cm

Ground fabric: wool warp and weft, dyed (dark
blue), weft-faced plain weave,
dense texture; medium quality (3)

Thread count: warp 9 S-spun, weft 14 S-spun

Thread thickness: warp 0.5 mm tight twist,
weft 0.5 mm slight twist

Tapestry: wool, dyed (red, ochre, dark blue,
green); 36 picks per cm; slit and
toothed

Provenance: Ex H.P. Kraus collection, no. 219

Inv. no. LNS 306 T

Related works: See page 507

Inscription:

[…] to its owner […]

[...] لصاحبه [...]

This fragment relates particularly closely to a piece in the Bouvier Collection
(Related works 1), which is inscribed in a similar style of script in yellow on a
blue ground, with accents of red, particularly highlighting the joints between
letters. It is interesting that here, conforming with other examples in this group,
the inscription refers to an unnamed owner (*li-sahibihi*).

Cat. 58 *TIRAZ* FRAGMENT FROM
THE ABBASID DYNASTY
Egypt, 9th to 10th century CE

Description: Fragment of wool dyed black, with
three tapestry-woven decorative
bands with abstract motifs,
framed by two bands of text.

Materials: wool: plain weave and tapestry

Dimensions: h. 11.0 cm, w. 22.0 cm; max. letter
heights 2.0 cm and 1.0 cm

Ground fabric: wool warp and weft, dyed (black),
weft-faced plain weave, dense
texture; good–medium quality
(2–3)

Thread count: warp 11 S-spun, weft 20 S-spun

Thread thickness: warp 0.5 mm medium–tight twist,
weft 0.5 mm loose–medium twist

Tapestry: wool, dyed (red, ochre, green,
black); S-spun; slit and toothed

Provenance: Ex H.P. Kraus collection, no. 117

Inv. no. LNS 228 T

Inscription: repetition of

Prosperity and blessing and glory

نعمة و بركة وعز

Cat. 59 *TIRAZ* FRAGMENT FROM
THE ABBASID DYNASTY
Egypt, Qays(?), 8th to
9th century CE

Description: Fragment of coloured wool on blue
wool warp, with one line of Kufic
inscription in mustard on a red
background woven along the side
(that is, vertically in the direction
of weaving), with a selvedge above
(that is, beside) the inscription.

Materials: wool: plain weave and tapestry

Dimensions: h. 3.8 cm, w. 18.0 cm;
max. letter height 2.9 cm

Ground fabric: wool warp, dyed (dark blue), and
weft, dyed (red, ochre), weft-faced
plain weave, regular structure,
dense texture; good quality (2);
selvedge above the inscription

Thread count: warp 7 S-spun paired, weft 12
S-spun two-plied Z-spun

Thread thickness: warp 0.5 mm tight twist,
weft 0.25–0.3 mm tight twist

Tapestry: wool, dyed (ochre); S-spun; slit
and toothed; inscription woven
vertically

Provenance: Ex H.P. Kraus collection, no. 220

Inv. no. LNS 60 T

Related works: See page 507

Inscription:

[the w]ork of ʿAbd al-Rahman […]

[...] عبد الرحمن مل[ع]

This piece gives an interesting insight into the weaving habits of the medieval
craftsmen. The inscription here was not woven with its baseline running
parallel to the weft – that is, perpendicular to the warp. Instead, its baseline
runs parallel to the warp, which means that the weaver wove the inscription
on its side. As a weaver in the medieval period was unlikely to have been
literate, there was no need for him to be able to understand the inscription that
he was weaving. It was probably remembered as a sequence of shapes, rather
than individual letters. Furthermore, as the inscription is on its side and has
a selvedge on its right, it appears that the fragment was once part of a larger
border along the selvedge. In that case there would have been more decoration

in the centre of the garment, and the inscription would not have been its main focus. Perhaps this is why here the name of the maker, a certain 'Abd al-Rahman, is found – a feature rarely seen in early textiles from Egypt.

The epigraphic style and technical details, such as the colour and material of the warp, and those of the weft, relate to two textiles, one in the Museum of Islamic Art in Cairo, the other in the Bouvier Collection, both from the reign of the Abbasid caliph al-Mahdi (r. 775–85) (Related works 1–2). The calligraphy and the material and colour arrangement of warps and wefts in the present piece can also be compared to a second piece in the Bouvier Collection (Related works 3). It can therefore be suggested that the present fragment, too, comes from an Upper Egyptian workshop, perhaps Qays, and dates from around the late eighth to the early ninth century.

Cat. 60   *TIRAZ* FRAGMENT FROM
THE ABBASID DYNASTY
Egypt, Bahnasa(?), 9th
to 10th century CE

Description: Fragment of undyed linen, with
one line of bold Kufic inscription
tapestry-woven in ochre wool,
with a brocaded geometric band
above comprising a lattice within
a border enclosing small lozenges.

Materials: linen and wool: plain weave
and tapestry

Dimensions: h. 21.0 cm, w. 56.0 cm;
max. letter height 10.2 cm

Ground fabric: linen warp and weft, undyed,
balanced plain weave, dense
texture (*dabiqi*), irregularities;
medium quality (3)

Thread count: warp 15 S-spun, weft 15 S-spun

Thread thickness: warp 0.4–0.5 mm loose twist,
weft 0.4–0.6 mm loose twist

Tapestry: wool, dyed (ochre); 34 picks
per cm; S-spun; woven on crossed
and paired warps; brocading:
linen, S-spun

Provenance: Ex H.P. Kraus collection, no. 207

Inv. no. LNS 110 T

Related works: See pages 507–08

Inscription:

[...] [م]ـن الله لصاحبه ممـا[...]

[...] [fro]m God to its owner. Of what was [...]

Like cat. nos 61–63 below, the present piece belongs to a group of textiles that can be shown to have been produced in Bahnasa.[25] All of these share the same epigraphic characteristics, details of manufacture and aesthetic. A piece in the Bouvier Collection is almost identical with the present piece in the style of the script, featuring wedge-shaped hastae and terminals, and the choice of ochre wool (Related works 1). It comprises the *basmallah*, the beginning of a *tiraz* inscription, while the piece here features the dedication to the owner and the beginning of a phrase concerning the texile's manufacture.

The basis for attributing these items to Bahnasa is a group of seven pieces in the Museum of Islamic Art, Cairo, all of which mention this textile centre in their inscriptions (Related works 2–8). The inscriptions and decoration are all woven in wool on a paired linen warp, while the ground fabric consists of a linen warp and weft. The colour schemes of these items are mostly restricted to earthy tones, such as ochre, brown, murky blue, black or maroon. The inscriptions are sometimes woven in coloured wool set against an undyed linen background, and sometimes woven in undyed linen set against a background of dyed wool. The epigraphic style used is typical of the early Abbasid period, particularly Tulunid Egypt, and comprises a bold angular script with wedge-shaped terminals. While most of the comparable examples are fragmentary, three textiles with important historical information have survived. Two are wool on linen warp tapestry-woven, like ours, and comprise an inscription in a related style of script documenting their manufacture in the *tiraz al-khassa* at Madinat Bahnasa (Related works 2, 3). The other item, also in wool tapestry on linen, was also made in Bahnasa and carries a date that can be tentatively read as 230 AH / 844–45 CE (Related works 8). Another group of fragments in Cairo have inscriptions comprising only the name 'Bahnasa' in black wool on an undyed linen ground (Related works 5–7). The epigraphy on the latter pieces, with a prominent *ya* curving backwards below the baseline, relates to the former ones (Related works 2, 3, 8).

In none of the known inscriptions from this group does the blessing, usually 'baraka min Allah', allude to a specifically named person, but always to an unnamed owner or patron (*li-sahibihi*), as is the case in the al-Sabah example, usually followed by the phrase 'mimma 'umila' ('of what was made'). At the beginning of the fragmented inscription here is what could be read as a *nun* belonging to the word *min*, which is followed by 'Allah'. The brocaded band above the inscription seems to be unique to the present fragment, and if the same feature was once present in other fragments it has not survived in any of them. Similar brocaded bands can be found accompanying embroidered

inscriptions of the Abbasid period. A band with almost exactly the same design, executed in a similar loose stitch, can be found on a linen textile in Washington, made in Alexandria in 272 AH / 885–86 CE, with an inscription in the name of the Abbasid caliph al-Mu'tamid (r. 870–92 CE).[26] A similar, albeit more complicated, brocaded band can be found also on a *tiraz* textile from the period of al-Muqtadir (r. 908–32), also in the Textile Museum, Washington, DC.[27] Another example, in the Abegg-Stiftung, Riggisberg, perhaps also dating from the period of al-Muqtadir, is related to the latter, albeit without an inscription (Related works 9).[28]

The epigraphic style seen here is typical of the ninth century and can be found at that time throughout the Abbasid empire in inscriptions of public importance, such as those on mosques founded by local governors or rulers loyal to the Abbasid caliphs. By using an Abbasid style of script, they declared their loyalty to the Abbasid caliphate. These inscriptions are in a style of Kufic that is devoid of the foliated and floriated decoration that develops in the early tenth century, particularly under the Ikhshidids, and continues later under the Fatimids in Egypt. Several dated inscriptions from the early Abbasid period relate to this style of script: the Mosque of Bu Fatata in Sus, dated 223–26 AH / 838–41 CE,[29] the inscription around the courtyard of the Great Mosque in Sus, dated 236 AH / 850–51 CE,[30] the inscriptions around the pit of the Nilometer on Rhoda Island in Cairo, dated 247 AH / 861 CE,[31] the inscription around the dome and the mihrab of the Great Mosque of Qairawan, dated 248 AH / 862–63 CE,[32] inscriptions from the Great Mosque in Tunis, dated 250 AH / 864–65 CE,[33] and the inscriptions on the Mosque of Ibn Tulun in Cairo, dated 263–65 AH / 876–79 CE.[34] Wood inscription panels from the Nilometer and the Mosque of Ibn Tulun can be found in the David Collection (see cat. no. 66).

Cat. 61 *TIRAZ* **FRAGMENT FROM THE ABBASID DYNASTY**
Egypt, Bahnasa(?), 9th century CE

Description: Fragment of undyed linen, with one line of bold Kufic inscription tapestry-woven in undyed linen on ochre wool, and an interrupted double border of blue above and below.

Materials: linen and wool: plain weave and tapestry

Dimensions: h. 16.0 cm, w. 25.7 cm; max. letter height 6.7 cm

Ground fabric: linen warp and weft (remnants), undyed, plain weave, tight texture (*dabiqi*); medium quality (3)

Thread count: warp 13 S-spun, weft 14 S-spun

Thread thickness: warp 0.5 mm loose twist, weft 0.5 mm loose twist

Tapestry: wool, dyed (ochre, blue) and linen (undyed); 30 picks per cm; S-spun; 0.4 mm tight twist; woven on crossed and paired warps; slit and toothed

Provenance: Ex H.P. Kraus collection, no. 208

Inv. no. LNS 113 T

Related works: See page 508

Inscription:

In the name of Go(d) [...]

بسم الل(ـه) [...]

This fragment may also be a product of a Bahnasa workshop, as it relates in manufacture and epigraphic style to surviving examples discussed above (see cat. no. 60). Two *tiraz* inscriptions in the Bouvier Collection are particularly close to the present piece in terms of the arrangement of the inscription within a bordered band, and the epigraphic style featuring prominent wedge-shaped letter terminals. One includes a reference to a *khassa* workshop and the first three letters of what could either be the word *bi-madinat* ('in the city') or 'Misr', as suggested by Georgette Cornu (Related works 1).[35] Surely it is a reference to the location of the workshop mentioned before. At least two textiles have survived that document the *tiraz al-khassa* in Madinat al-Bahnasa (Related works 3–4). The second fragment in the Bouvier Collection (Related works 2) relates epigraphically and includes an inscription referring to manufacture for an unnamed patron, a feature commonly found in this group. The epigraphic style seen here compares to a number of historical inscriptions discussed above, as well as to carved wood panels in the Museum of Islamic Art, Cairo, which have been attributed to the rule of the Tulunids in the ninth century.[36]

Cat. 62   *TIRAZ* FRAGMENT FROM
THE ABBASID DYNASTY
Egypt, probably Bahnasa,
9th century CE

Description: Fragment of undyed wool, with one
line of Kufic inscription tapestry-
woven in blue wool, comprising the
beginning of the *basmallah*.

Materials: wool: plain weave and tapestry

Dimensions: h. 14.5 cm, w. 28 cm;
max. letter height 10.0 cm

Ground fabric: wool warp and weft, undyed,
weft-faced plain weave, tight
texture, regular; good quality (2)

Thread count: warp 7 two-plied Z-spun, weft 30
S-spun

Thread thickness: warp 0.5 mm tight twist,
weft 0.3 mm medium twist

Tapestry: wool, dyed (blue); 30 picks per cm;
S-spun; slit and toothed

Provenance: Ex H.P. Kraus collection, no. 209

Inv. no. LNS 58 T

Related works: See page 508

Inscription:

بسم ا[لله الرحمن الـ[ـرحيم]

[In the name of G]od, the Most Merciful, the [Most Compassionate]

The style of inscription of cat. nos 62 and 63 is almost identical with that found
on two fragments in the Museum of Islamic Art in Cairo, which were made
in Bahnasa (Related works 1, 2). The epigraphic details of these inscriptions,
particularly the final *ya* curving backwards and the pronounced hook-like letter
terminals, are indicative of a date up to the late ninth century. Indeed, one of
the pieces is tentatively datable to 230 AH / 844–45 CE (Related works 1). Both
of these fragments comprise linen warps with the inscription worked either in
wool or in undyed linen against a coloured wool background. One has, indeed,
remnants of the linen ground fabric (Related works 2).

Cat. 63 *TIRAZ* **FRAGMENT FROM THE ABBASID DYNASTY**
Egypt, 9th century CE

Description:
Fragment of undyed linen, with one line of Kufic inscription tapestry-woven in red wool on an undyed background.

Materials:
linen and wool: plain weave and tapestry

Dimensions:
h. 9.0 cm, w. 29.3 cm; max. letter height 5.5 cm

Ground fabric:
linen warp and weft, undyed, balanced plain weave, close texture (*dabiqi*); medium quality (3)

Thread count:
warp 13 S-spun, weft 13 S-spun

Thread thickness:
warp 0.5–1.0 mm slight twist, weft 0.4–0.6 mm slight twist

Tapestry:
wool, dyed (red); 34 picks per cm; S-spun; woven on crossed and paired warps; slit and toothed; discontinuous linen weft filling between letters

Provenance:
Ex H.P. Kraus collection, no. 200

Inv. no. LNS 302 T

Related works:
See page 508

Inscription:

[…] (بر)كة و يمن و غبطة [...]

[…] [bless]ing and fortune and beatitude […]

For a discussion of an inscription executed in a similar style see cat. no. 62.

 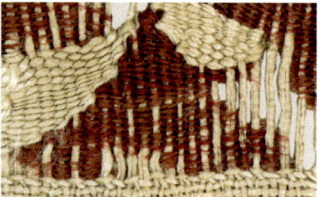

Cat. 64   *TIRAZ* FRAGMENT FROM
THE ABBASID DYNASTY
Egypt, 9th century CE

Description: Fragment of tapestry-woven wool,
with a Kufic inscription in undyed
wool on a dark brown background,
set within borders of undyed wool.

Materials: wool: plain weave and tapestry

Dimensions: h. 32.6 cm, w. 27.5 cm;
max. letter height 9.0 cm

Thread count: warp 6 S-spun two-plied Z-spun,
weft 20 Z-spun paired

Thread thickness: warp 0.5 mm tight twist,
weft 0.5 mm tight twist

Tapestry: wool warp, dyed (ochre), and weft,
undyed and dyed (dark brown),
weft-faced plain weave, dense
texture, coarse quality

Provenance: Ex H.P. Kraus collection, no. 212

Inv. no. LNS 304 T

Inscription:

[…] mad[ina?] […]

[…] مد […]

This fragment features the remnant of an inscription, which could be read as the two letters *mim* and *dal*, perhaps once referring to the textile centre Madinat al-Bahnasa, discussed earlier (cat. nos 60–63).

Cat. 65 *TIRAZ* FRAGMENT FROM
THE ABBASID DYNASTY
Egypt, 9th century CE

Description: Fragment of undyed wool and
linen, roughly square, with a Kufic
inscription tapestry-woven in red
wool and two decorative bands.

Materials: linen and wool: plain weave
and tapestry

Dimensions: h. 23.4 cm, w. 19.7 cm;
max. letter height 5.0 cm

Ground fabric: wool warp, undyed, linen weft,
undyed, weft-faced plain weave,
dense texture; good quality (2)

Thread count: warp 6 S-spun, weft 30 S-spun

Thread thickness: warp 0.5 mm tight twist,
weft 0.5–0.6 mm tight twist

Tapestry: wool, dyed (red, brown); 28 picks
per cm; S-spun; slit and toothed;
discontinuous linen weft filling
between letters

Provenance: Ex H.P. Kraus collection, no. 211

Inv. no. LNS 303 T

Inscription:

[…] Blessing from God […]

[…] بركة مـ(ـن الله) (…]

Cat. 66 *TIRAZ* FRAGMENT FROM THE ABBASID DYNASTY
Egypt, 8th to 9th century CE

Description: Fragment of wool, near rectangular, tapestry-woven in coloured wool on an undyed wool warp, with one line of Kufic inscription in mustard yellow on the red ground fabric. Beneath the inscription is a main decorative band (7.7 cm), bordered above and below by an undulating split-palmette scroll in mustard yellow on a dark blue ground; the band is made up of a sequence of cartouches with what appears to be stylized zoomorphic content in red and yellow, outlined in yellow, alternating with small lozenges containing four dots arranged cross-wise, out of which grow, above and below, two wing-like leaves accentuated at the tip and root in red and yellow; a plain-coloured band in greenish-blue runs along the lower edge.

Materials: wool: plain weave and tapestry

Dimensions: h. 20.0 cm, w. 24.9 cm; max. letter height 1.8 cm

Ground fabric and tapestry: wool, dyed (light green, red, yellow, dark blue) and undyed, weft-faced plain weave; tapestry slit and toothed

Thread count: warp 14 S-spun, weft c. 90 S-spun

Thread thickness: warp 0.4 mm tight twist, weft 0.05–0.1 mm loose twist

Provenance: Ex H.P. Kraus collection, no. 227

Inv. no. LNS 56 T

Related works: See page 508

Inscription:

(…?…) God

الله (…؟…)

This piece relates to a group of textiles that share certain technical and aesthetic characteristics, but are nevertheless different regarding manufacture. Bellinger identified that they are woven in wool weft on a two-plied wool warp, that the tapestry is toothed rather than slit, and that the yarns are spun in the Z-direction.[37] Aesthetically these textiles comprise decoration on a red ground, and often have palmette borders, pearl bands and sequences of leaves fanning out, all sharply executed in a subdued choice of the same colours. On the basis of the technical characteristics, Kühnel and Bellinger suggested an Eastern, rather than Egyptian, place of production for this group, possibly Iraq or Iran, particularly since they identified similarities with the textiles found at Dura Europos. Furthermore, some of the pieces comprise representations of birds set within flowering roundels, which belong to the Sasanian repertoire. The palmette scroll seen on the present piece is similar to one on a fragment in the Bouvier Collection attributed to Iran or Iraq (Related works 1).

The dating of the group has been based upon the evidence of a textile inscribed with the name of the Umayyad caliph Marwan II (r. 744–50) in the Textile Museum, Washington, DC (Related works 2). It comprises decoration of birds within roundels and its inscription is in a style current in the early eighth century. Epigraphic pieces, including the present one, comprise an angular style of Kufic with wedge-shaped terminal letters, for which a slightly later date in the early decades of the Abbasid caliphate would be justified.

Perhaps the most prominent piece of this group is a cushion cover in the Cleveland Museum of Art (Related works 3). Its inscription mentions its manufacture ('mimma 'umila') for an unnamed patron ('baraka min Allah li-sahibihi') in a *tiraz* workshop, the location of which is lost. The textile panel consists of a central field in two colours, green and dark red, decorated with two rows of pearl-band roundels containing figures of fluttering birds. The inscription runs along the edge of the central panel. The central panel is bordered by a tripartite band, composed of a continuous beaded design, a sequence of half-rosettes set against vine scrolls and a plain green band with floral sprays. The Cleveland textile allows us to judge the complexity of wool panels that were probably made in one piece as furnishing items, given that almost all other examples of this type of textile have survived as fragments. The inscription is the most complete example of any in this group – not a caliphal protocol, but a text invoking good wishes and blessings on the owner. Nevertheless, it mentions that the panel was made in a *tiraz* workshop. Stylistically the inscription fits a mid-ninth-century date during Tulunid rule, which also applies to the present piece. The rather angular style of script with its prominent circular *mim*, the *ya* bending backwards and the hook-like terminals of letters can be found in the inscriptions of the Nilometer in Cairo, built in 861 by order of the Abbasid caliph al-Mutawakkil (r. 847–61) and the Ibn Tulun mosque in Cairo (founded in 879).[38] Another related textile is in the Bouvier Collection, also mentioning its manufacture for an unnamed patron in a *tiraz* workshop using the formula 'baraka min Allah li-sahibihi' (Related works 4). Shepherd suggested a late eighth- to ninth-century date for the Cleveland textile, while Cornu proposed a ninth-century date for the

Bouvier piece, but both attributed them to Egypt, on the evidence of the linen (rather than wool) warps on which the wool tapestry was executed.[39]

A fifth textile in the Metropolitan Museum of Art, New York, represents a larger portion of a design that features floral rosettes containing striding horses with a band of script below, which includes remnants of the phrase 'mimma amara' ('of what was made'), and has a border not unlike that of the present piece (Related works 5). Dospěl Williams mentions that the New York piece was radiocarbon dated with 95 per cent confidence to 663–868 CE, which would confirm the circumstantial evidence of epigraphic style on which Shepherd's and Cornu's attributions were based, but would also allow for a larger window of possible dates, perhaps into the late 9th century.[40] Unlike Related works 3 and 4, its wool tapestry was worked on wool warps, suggesting perhaps an Eastern, origin. For an in-depth discussion of this piece see cat. no. 67. Even though our piece was woven in wool on warps, the fact that they are S-spun, rather than Z-spun, would perhaps suggest an Egyptian, rather than Eastern origin.

Cat. 67   **TEXTILE FRAGMENT FROM THE LATE UMAYYAD OR EARLY ABBASID DYNASTY**
Egypt or eastern Islamic world, mid-8th century CE

Description: Fragment of wool tapestry on wool warp, with decoration of alternating six-lobed flowers and remnants of what appear to be rosettes with a border of lotus flowers, in brown, mustard, green and light red on a crimson background.

Materials: wool: plain weave and tapestry

Dimensions: h. 30.0 cm, w. 10.0 cm

Ground fabric and tapestry: wool warp, undyed, and weft, dyed (red, black, dark blue, greenish-blue), weft-faced plain weave, dense texture; very good quality (1)

Thread count: warp 14 two-plied S-spun, weft 52 Z-spun

Thread thickness: warp 0.4 mm tight twist, weft 0.25 mm medium twist

Provenance: art market, 1970s–1980s

Inv. no. LNS 44 T

Related works: See page 508

This textile belongs to a group of fragments that share a number of characteristics: they are woven in Z-spun wool weft on two-plied SZ-spun wool warps, and, where areas of different colour meet, the tapestry is toothed rather than slit. Both characteristics can be found in this example.

A textile important for dating this group is in the Textile Museum, Washington, DC (Related works 1). Its fragmentary inscription in simple Kufic contains the remnants of the words 'mu'minin', then a *mim*, then a void, and 'amara bihi' at the end. Kühnel interpreted this as a fragmentary protocol of the last Umayyad caliph Marwan II (r. 744–50) and dated the fragment to his short reign. Apart from the technical details, the present fragment shares with that piece the particular multi-lobed rosettes (or flowers), a remnant of which can be seen on the left side of the Marwan textile, and the flowered friezes around the large medallions (or cartouches) that contain figures of birds. Kühnel and Bellinger attributed the Marwan textile to an Iraqi or Iranian workshop, mainly on the basis of the technical details, but also its aesthetic.[41] They argued that the Z-twist found there is an Eastern phenomenon, and that the toothed tapestry on two-plied warps was common in the wool textiles from Dura Europos, including the particular subdued colours, and differs from Coptic textiles, which usually feature wool tapestry worked on single warps, and slit rather than toothed. Furthermore, they stressed the Sasanian aesthetic found in the zoomorphic motifs of the Marwan piece. As the Umayyads were particularly active in Greater Syria, and the technical connection with Dura Europos has been suggested, a Syrian origin for these wool textiles may be feasible. Alternatively it is possible that these textiles originated in Abbasid Iraq, as they feature design elements, such as the arrangements of the rosettes, that can be found in Sasanian art, and eventually became part of a wider vocabulary of imperial design.[42]

An important complete textile belonging to this group is in the Cleveland Museum of Art, probably once a cushion cover (Related works 2). It is inscribed with a *tiraz* inscription stating its manufacture in a *tiraz* workshop. Dorothy Shepherd followed Kühnel's Iraqi or Iranian attribution of similar textiles, based on the large, Sasanian-style roundels containing bird figures. Recent scholarship, however, has attributed the piece to Egypt, in particular Bahnasa, based on the use of S-spun wool on linen warps.[43]

Several pieces in the Bouvier Collection are also closely related to textiles of this group.[44] Related works 3 and 4 are examples, with rosettes made up of an interlace of flowering buds, similar to the present piece. They have also been attributed to Iran or Iraq, like the Marwan textile.

Two very closely related textiles in terms of materials, colour and aesthetic are at the Metropolitan Museum of Art, New York (Related works 5, 6). Related works 5 features cartouches on a red ground, like the Marwan textile in Washington, and is inscribed in a similar style of script with the remnants of a protocol documenting the textile's requisition and manufacture ('mimma 'amara'). Carbon dating has suggested a late Umayyad or early Abbasid attribution.[45] The other textile is perhaps more closely related to the present piece aesthetically (Related works 6). Both may have been made in non-Egyptian workshops, perhaps in Iraq, given the shift of power from Greater Syria to Iraq under the Abbasids and the establishment of Baghdad as the centre of their empire. Related works 6 features a wide border with elaborated multi-petalled flowers similar to the ones seen here, composed of small elements, buds and intertwined stems on a red ground. It was probably once part of a larger textile with a central field in green.

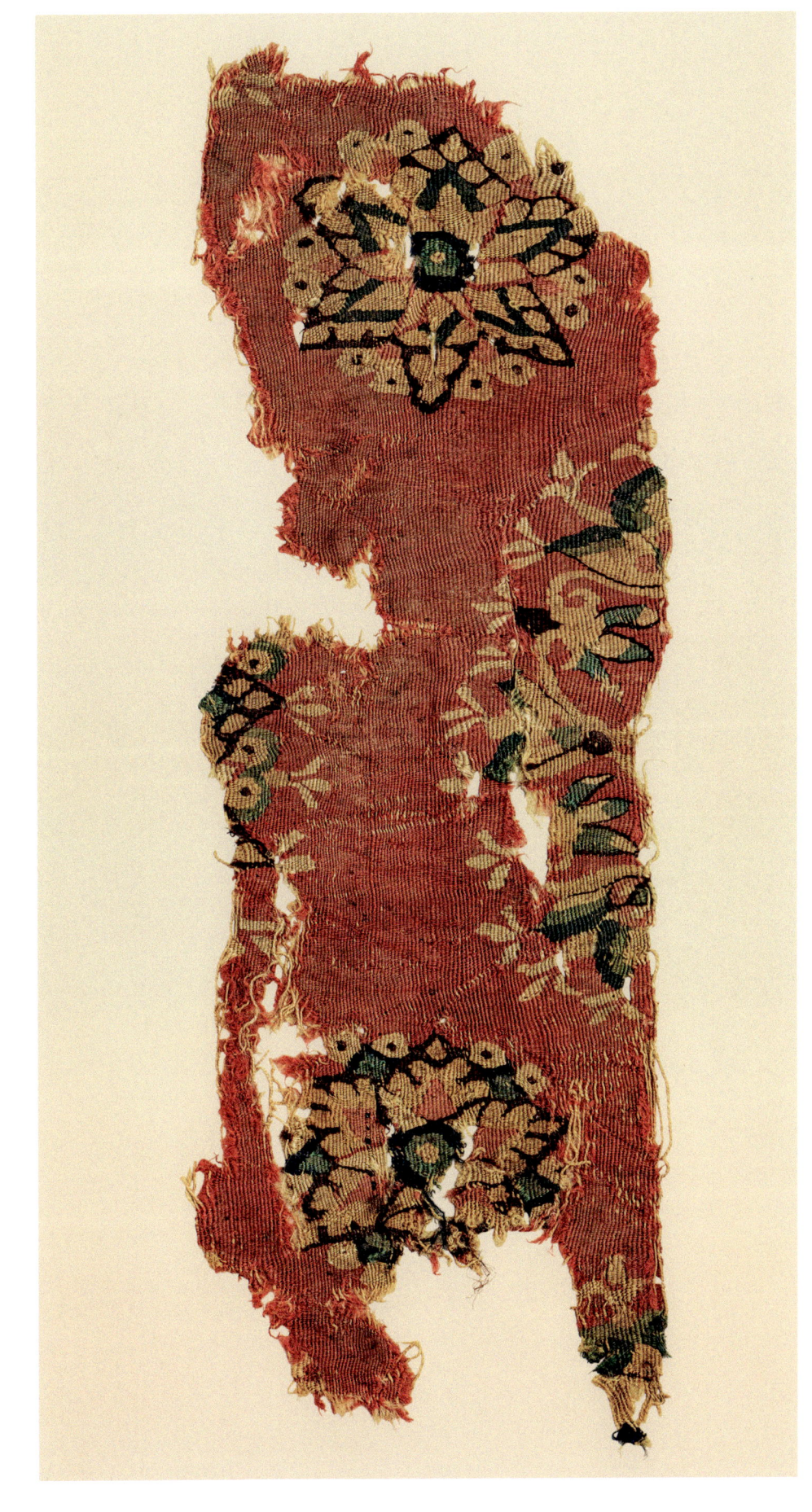

Cat. 68 *TIRAZ* **FRAGMENT FROM THE ABBASID DYNASTY**
Upper Egypt, 9th century CE

Description: Fragment (five pieces) of sand-coloured wool (a remnant of the ground fabric is visible on the upper edge of piece (a)) decorated in wool tapestry, comprising four registers: the uppermost is composed of a plain band in crimson (height 2.3 cm); the band beneath (height 6.0 cm) comprises a lattice design in blue, red and green; the band above the inscription (height 3.0 cm) comprises a sequence of acanthus(?) leaves in pink and blue on a green ground, placed to form triangular compartments enclosing triplets of small dotted circles in yellow and red and yellow and blue; the plaited Kufic inscription in crimson beneath (height 4.0 cm), constituting the lowermost register, has a lattice similar to the second register.

Materials: wool and linen: plain weave and tapestry

Dimensions: piece (a): h. 28.7 cm, w. 25.7 cm
piece (b): h. 5.0 cm, w. 5.0 cm
piece (c): h. 6.0 cm, w. 4.7 cm
piece (d): h. 4.5 cm, w. 2.2 cm
piece (e): h. 4.8 cm, w. 3.4 cm

Ground fabric: wool warp and weft, undyed, weft-faced plain weave, close, fairly regular; good–medium quality (2–3)

Thread count: warp 11 Z-spun two-plied S-spun, weft 11 per 0.5 cm Z-spun

Thread thickness: warp 0.5 mm slight twist, weft 0.3–0.5 mm medium twist

Tapestry: wool, dyed (crimson, pinkish, green, dark blue, light blue, dark brown, mustard) and undyed; 56 picks per cm; Z-spun medium twist; slit and toothed

Provenance: art market, 1970s–1980s

Inv. no. LNS 31 T a–e

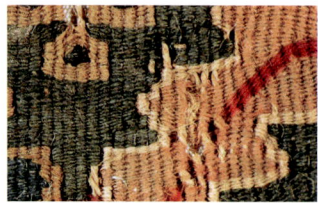

Inscription: [...] ه[...] حا(لمما) الله (عز؟) [بقا] م [...]

[...] *ha* [...] ha(limama) God (glory?) [permanence] *mim* [...]

Cat. 69   **TEXTILE FRAGMENT FROM
THE UMAYYAD OR EARLY
ABBASID DYNASTY**
**Upper Egypt, 8th to early
10th century CE**

Description: Fragment of undyed linen (a
remnant of the ground fabric is
visible in the upper right corner),
decorated in tapestry weave with
an arrangement of several bands
culminating in a large circular
ornament, all in multicoloured
threads on a mustard yellow
ground; the ornament comprises a
frame of rope pattern in mustard
on black or dark blue ground,
the circle filled with small dark
blue lantern-shaped motifs. The
outermost band (remnant in the
upper right corner) comprises rope
pattern in mustard on a dark blue
ground; working inwards, the
next two bands are composed of
an alternating sequence of pairs of
cream-coloured and single dark
blue lozenges; the central band is
composed of an overall pattern of
small layered and multicoloured
circular motifs running diagonally.

Materials: linen and wool: plain weave and
tapestry

Dimensions: h. 22.2 cm, w. 29.0 cm

Ground fabric: linen warp and weft, undyed,
balanced plain weave, close texture
(*dabiqi*), regular structure; good–
medium quality (2–3)

Thread count: warp 20 S-spun, weft *c.* 18 S-spun

Thread thickness: warp 0.3–0.5 mm slight–medium
twist, weft 0.3–0.5 mm slight–
medium twist

Tapestry: wool, dyed (blackish-blue, black,
ochre, green), and linen, undyed;
25 weft picks per cm; S-spun;
0.5 mm slight–medium twist;
woven on eight crossed and paired
warps; slit and toothed

Provenance: art market, 1970s–1980s

Inv. no. LNS 22 T

Related works: See page 508

The present piece belongs to a group of Egyptian tapestry-woven textiles that are defined by wool warps on linen weft. The famous cushion cover in the Cleveland Museum of Art (Related works 1), an iconic example, is discussed above in cat. no. 66. That piece features two prominent borders comprising a pearl-band pattern, perhaps more refined than those of the present piece. Two fragments in the Bouvier Collection are perhaps more closely related to our piece in terms of quality (Related works 2, 3). These two feature pearl-band borders that are integrated with a background of lozenges, creating something like a fluid wave pattern full of motion.

Cat. 70 *TIRAZ* FRAGMENT FROM
THE ABBASID DYNASTY
Upper Egypt, mid-8th to
mid-10th century CE

Description: Fragment (two pieces) of dyed wool
tapestry on two-plied wool warp,
comprising a succession of six-
pointed stars outlined in dark blue
on a mustard-coloured ground,
with smaller eight-pointed stars
between, and a broad blue border
below with a sequence of beige
calligraphic designs.

Materials: wool: plain weave and tapestry

Dimensions: piece (a) (right): h. 29.0 cm,
w. 57.5 cm
piece (b) (left): h. 12.7 cm,
w. 18.7 cm

Ground fabric wool warp, undyed, and weft,
and tapestry: undyed and dyed (blue, ochre);
weft-faced plain weave, slit; warps
two-plied S-spun, regular weave,
dense texture; good quality (2);
slit and toothed

Thread count: warp 9 S-spun two-plied Z-spun,
weft 32 S-spun

Thread thickness: warp 0.5 mm tight twist,
weft 0.5 mm slight twist

Provenance: art market, 1970s–1980s

Inv. no. LNS 24 T a, b

Related works: See page 508

Inscription: repetition of

Permanence

بقا

This fragment is of a heavy quality and hence may have once formed part of a
larger wall hanging or floor covering, perhaps similar to a *kilim*. We know from
literary evidence that the workshops of Bahnasa, in particular, produced high-
quality furnishing fabrics. A number of fragments of furnishing fabrics with
stylized geometric and figural motifs can be compared with the present piece
(Related works 1–4). These have been dated to the ninth century, but may well
date from a later period. A number of textiles from Egypt comprise brocaded
overall geometric patterns of eight-pointed stars, hexagons and octagons similar
to the ones seen here (Related works 5).

Cat. 71   TEXTILE FRAGMENT FROM THE ABBASID DYNASTY
Upper Egypt, mid-8th to mid-10th century CE

Description: Fragment of dyed wool tapestry on undyed wool warp, comprising three bands, the two outer ones composed of a sequence of cream-coloured rectangular motifs filled with brown pseudo-epigraphic ornaments; the central band has a sequence of brown hexagons containing mustard-coloured eight-pointed stars filled with smaller blue hexagons, each with a small, horizontally elongated cross-shaped motif in red at the centre.

Materials: wool: plain weave and tapestry
Dimensions: h. 10.3 cm, w. 24 cm
Ground fabric and tapestry: wool warp, undyed, and weft, undyed and dyed (red, brown, ochre, blue), weft-faced tapestry, plain weave, regular structure; good quality (2); slit and toothed
Thread count: warp 7 S-spun two-plied Z-spun, weft 40 S-spun
Thread thickness: warp 0.5 mm tight twist, weft 0.5 mm loose–medium twist
Provenance: art market, 1970s–1980s

Inv. no. LNS 23 T

Cat. 72   TEXTILE FRAGMENT FROM THE ABBASID OR EARLY FATIMID DYNASTY
Upper Egypt, 9th to 10th century CE

Description: Fragment of a wool tapestry-woven decorative band, comprising a central green-grounded cartouche containing a stylized figure of a peacock with elongated tail and holding a branch in its beak, woven in undyed linen and yellowish wool on a reddish ground bordered by green, reddish and yellowish bands, interspersed with small hexagons in undyed linen.

Materials: linen and wool: tapestry
Dimensions: h. 12.5 cm, w. 14.4 cm
Ground fabric and tapestry: warp undyed linen, weft dyed wool (red, ochre, blue) and linen, undyed; slit and toothed
Thread count: warp 16 S-spun paired (8 pairs), weft 28 S-spun
Thread thickness: warp 0.5 mm medium–tight twist, weft 0.4–0.5 mm tight twist
Provenance: art market, 1970s–1980s

Inv. no. LNS 92 T

Related works: See page 508

The execution, and choice of colour and subject matter are typical of the wool textiles produced in Upper Egypt in the ninth to tenth century. The colours of the wool used tended to be earthy tones and contrasted with areas woven in undyed linen. The tapestry is usually executed on paired warps, as is the case here. For comparison with birds and other zoomorphic figures and products of comparable workmanship, see a number of textiles in the Bouvier Collection (Related works 1, 2).

Cat. 73 **TEXTILE FRAGMENT FROM THE ABBASID DYNASTY**
Egypt, 9th to 10th century CE

Description: Fragment of undyed linen, with a medallion tapestry-woven in dark blue and red wool containing a single animal, perhaps a hare, probably once part of a larger composition.
Materials: linen and wool: tapestry weave
Dimensions: h. 20 cm, w. 25.6 cm
Ground fabric: linen warp, undyed, weft (lost)
Thread count: warp 8 Z-spun two-plied Z-spun
Thread thickness: warp 1.0 mm medium–tight twist
Tapestry: wool, dyed (dark blue, red); S-spun; 0.5 mm slight–medium twist; slit and toothed
Provenance: art market, 1970s–1980s

Inv. no. LNS 404 T

Related works: See page 508

A fragment featuring a leaping hare that looks very similar to the animal represented here is in the Brooklyn Museum, New York (Related works 1). Like the present piece it is woven in wool tapestry on linen warps, suggesting manufacture in Egypt. It has been attributed to the ninth century, when Egypt was under Tulunid rule and Coptic traditions enjoyed a revival. Another comparable example, in the Bouvier Collection, features a frieze of hares within small roundels, albeit more stylized (Related works 2). A fragment of a lion figure in the Bouvier Collection relates to the present piece very closely in terms of the use of linen and wool in the weaving of the tapestry (Related works 3). While the hare in the present piece was outlined in undyed linen set against a dark blue wool background, the reverse is the case for the piece in the Bouvier Collection: here the animal is outlined in dark blue wool and set against a background of undyed linen. In both, the tapestry comprises dovetailing and slits. A small fragment of a Coptic or late antique textile, dated to the fourth to seventh century, featuring a hare rendered in a naturalistic manner, is at the Harvard Art Museums; it provides a link to the much older local repertoire of Egyptian weavers.[46]

3

THE FAYYUM

The Fayyum (*al-Fayyum*) (from Coptic *Phiom*: 'the Sea') is an oasis, 7.5 km from north to south, and about 75 km from east to west, around a large lake located about 100 km south of Cairo in Middle Egypt, east of the Nile Valley (see map, pp. 12–13).[1] The cliffs that separate it from the river valley open up at one point, allowing a stream that branches off from the Nile near Asyut to enter the Fayyum basin; in medieval times the stream was known as Khalij al-Manha. The lake that was formed by these waters coming from the Nile was used for irrigation and hence the region was very fertile; rice and flax were the main crops. The Geniza documents speak of special Fayyumi varieties of flax, which merchants bought there to supply the markets of Cairo and Alexandria.[2]

The Fayyum formed an administrative province, called a *kura*, in the early Islamic period and also later, with its largest centre at Madinat al-Fayyum ('city of Fayyum'). The Fayyum oasis had been settled well before Pharaonic times and since then has played an important role in the economy of Egypt. Under the Ptolemaic dynasty, the city of Fayyum was known as Ptolemais Euergetis, then Krokodilopolis, then Arsinoë in Arcadia under Roman rule. In later Roman times Arsinoë became the seat of a bishop, a suffragan of Oxyrhynchus, the capital of the province and the metropolitan see. It plays a role in the Judaeo–Islamic legend of Joseph, who is said to have constructed the canal of al-Manha, and the association of the Fayyum with the Joseph legend is perhaps due to the presence there of an ancient Jewish settlement. Arabs invaded the Fayyum without difficulty during the time of the early Islamic conquests in the mid-7th century. Despite the Arab presence, Coptic Christianity continued to play the predominant role in the Fayyum for several centuries; a large number of prominent monasteries were established there, several of which have been excavated and studied. The finds of Islamic textiles from the eleventh and twelfth centuries, made by a Polish team of archaeologists at Deir al-Naqlun, the monastery of the Archangel Gabriel, about 16 km south of Madinat al-Fayyum are discussed in chapter 2.[3] These finds are significant as they show that not only Muslims were buried with *tiraz* shrouds, but that Christians also adopted the fashion for *tiraz* textiles as they began to integrate with aspects of Islamic culture.[4]

The Fayyum oasis was famous for its textiles before the Muslim invasion in the mid-seventh century. The *Futuh al-Bahnasa* ('Conquest of Bahnasa') describes the fine clothes, made from silk with gold embroideries, that the Coptic leaders wore when they met the Arab invaders.[5] The text also describes fine furnishing fabrics. Notable are the descriptions of a tent made from a material called *tardwahsh*, which was upholstered inside with polychrome silk in blue, red, green and black, embroidered with gold and silver thread, as well as pearls, and ornamented with figures of birds and wild animals. Carpets of polychrome silk were laid out, and furnished with cushions, couches and mats. The tent cords were also made of polychrome silk.[6]

A surviving archive of papyrus letters dating from 864 to 878 documents a partnership between two textile merchants from the Fayyum and one from Misr al-Fustat. These provide a very detailed glimpse into the economic foundations of the textile trade in the Fayyum and its trade networks beyond.[7] One of the merchants concerned was a certain Abu Hurayra Ja'far bin Ahmad bin 'Abd al-Mu'min, whose family not only sold textiles but also financed their production. A number of contracts concern the delivery of specified types of cloth to Ibn 'Abd al-Mu'min from various suppliers, probably weavers. The weavers were often paid in advance and then had to work according to specific requirements and timed schedules, depending on demand. The letters also provide an insight into the economic relationship between the capital Misr al-Fustat and other urban centres, where the finances came from, and the farmers and weavers of the Fayyum who benefited and were dependent on the inward flow of cash coming from the cities. It is likely that in the ninth century the farmers and weavers were still Christians, while the population of the large urban centres comprised more and more Muslims.

One of the earliest surviving *tiraz* textiles is the so-called 'turban of Samu'il bin Musa', which documents in its inscription its manufacture in the city of Sanhur in the Fayyum for an individual identified as Samu'il ibn Murqus.[8] It is a full-loom width and length of a linen ground fabric inscribed in Arabic with a text in a simple, unadorned early type of script executed in wool tapestry, accompanied by a colourful band comprising small birds within diamond-shaped cartouches. The inscription states the function of the textile – it was a wrap-around turban-cloth (*'imama*). Some controversy exists on the reading of the name of the dedicatee, as well as the date. Previously read as 'Samu'il bin Musa', recent scholarship has revised 'Musa' to 'Murqus' (Samuel son of Mark), thereby suggesting that the turban-cloth was made for a Christian patron.[9] The inscription places the manufacture of the cloth in the month of Rajab in the year 88 AH / 6 June–5 July 707 CE, which would date it to the Umayyad period. It has been suggested, however, that the maker must have omitted the digit for the hundred – a common feature of early Islamic inscriptions – and even failed to finish the word for eighty (*thamanin*). This would place the piece either in the year 188 AH / 804–05 CE or 288 AH / 901–02 CE, when Egypt was under Abbasid rule.[10] The diamond-shaped lozenges filled with small birds are indeed more reminiscent of Abbasid-period ornament than Umayyad, reminding us of the architectural decorations of Samarra, or Abbasid lustre ceramics.[11]

An important textile in the Musée du Louvre in Paris, woven in wool tapestry on wool warps, features a bilingual inscription. Its Arabic text states that it was made for an unnamed owner in a private workshop (*tiraz al-khassa*) in the city of Tebtynis (now Tuttun) within the governorate of the Fayyum (*kurat al-Fayyum*). It is accompanied by a Coptic inscription comprising a religious invocation to Christ to help a certain Raphael son of Ganarkhou.[12] The mention of the *tiraz al-khassa* confirms what Ibn Hawqal relates about the *tiraz* workshops of the Fayyum – namely, that 'In Faiyum there are large fine towns and well-known *tiraz* factories as well

as great estates, belonging to the sultan and to the public (*'amma*).'[13] Another related piece, albeit without a Coptic inscription, but with the same line in Arabic dedicated to an unnamed patron, belongs to the Museum of Islamic Art in Cairo.[14] The fragmented inscription on a third textile, in the Biblioteca Apostolica Vaticana, documents its manufacture in the *tiraz al-'amma* of a location now lost, albeit without mentioning a patron.[15] The style of its inscription and details of its making link it to the latter two textiles.

It is interesting that in the Louvre piece the Coptic and Arabic inscriptions are clearly demarcated in content: the Coptic (written in the Greek alphabet) is a personalized prayer, while the Arabic relates to the textile's production.[16] Another bilingual text can be found on the two ends of a shawl fragment in the Metropolitan Museum, New York, with a benedictory text in Coptic accompanied by a text in Arabic that is so highly stylized as to render it undecipherable.[17] Given that these textiles were excavated as funerary shrouds, it would seem plausible to attach to the Coptic prayers apotropaic symbolism relating to a deceased person, but the Arabic inscriptions are clearly rooted in the temporal world. It has been suggested that such textiles were inscribed and personalized to record a gift from father to son or daughter during his lifetime – a phenomenon documented in the Geniza documents – or gifts to members of the clergy such as priests or monks.[18] These textiles suggest that the *tiraz* practice was adopted and adapted by Christians in Egypt after the Islamic conquests (a topic discussed in connection with burial and funerary habits in chapter 2).

The dating of this group of textiles is a matter of debate. The date found on the turban of Samu'il ibn Murqus provides an anchor. Despite the uncertainty about whether the piece dates from the seventh, eighth or ninth century, it still gives us some understanding of what kinds of textiles were made in the Fayyum in the first centuries after the Islamic conquest. However, with its inscription and decorative band in wool woven into a larger base fabric of linen, the piece stands apart from the kinds of textiles represented by the bulk of the group. Most of these are tapestry-woven on wool, often in shades of black or very dark midnight-blue wool, a colour like that of the shawl in the Louvre mentioned above. A similar piece in the Katoen Natie Collection in Antwerp is a full-loom width of about a metre and is about 2.2 metres long, with twisted fringes at both ends and Coptic inscriptions citing Psalm 17:33–34 (Septuagint), as well as bands of stylized pseudo-Kufic script; it was subjected to radiocarbon dating,[19] which gave a date between 1029 and 1219 with a 95.4 per cent confidence level.[20] This would place the piece firmly in the Fatimid or early Ayyubid periods. Georgette Cornu attributed several pieces in the Bouvier Collection and the Biblioteca Apostolica Vaticana to the twelfth to thirteenth centuries on art-historical grounds, based on the absence of figural motifs, the focus on geometric designs, and the use of brocaded wefts for the designs, a technique found in Ayyubid and Mamluk textiles; but until these pieces can be carbon dated their attributions are debatable.[21]

The Bardo Museum in Tunis holds an early tunic important for the fact that it was tailored from a large Fayyumi cloth or shawl and is decorated with zoomorphic bands which relate to many of the fragments associated with Coptic weaving traditions.[22] Its size suggests that it was perhaps once the garment of a child or adolescent.[23] In terms of cut, the piece relates to other known garments, including one discussed earlier in the Catalogue (cat. no. 54). The bands, obviously cut out from larger bands like the ones running along the fringe of an uncut fabric, were inserted on both upper sleeves. The bands are different on the two sleeves: that on the right sleeve has a continuous sequence of hexagonal cartouches containing either stylized flowers or birds; the other shows a procession of striding felines. Both bands are accompanied by text in addorsed Kufic that can be read as 'al-mulk li-llah' ('the kingdom is God's').[24] In terms of epigraphy, the inscription relates to those on fragments traditionally dated earlier, including several in this section of the Catalogue (see cat. nos 78–86). The inscription on an important rug fragment in the Textile Museum, Washington, DC, which documents its manufacture in the *tiraz* of Akhmim in the year 203 AH / 818–19 CE, features letters with terminals similar to those found on the Bardo tunic and on those pieces presented here and in other collections.[25] They are characterized by small stepped pyramidal elements, which may be the consequence of the weaving process and the use of the slit and toothed technique.

In terms of cloth quality the fragments in this group are quite different from other wool textiles, such as the ones associated with Upper Egypt (see the Catalogue, §I.2). Unlike those, the wool in Fayyumi fragments seems to be quite coarse. It twists more heavily and therefore creates more internal tension in the fabrics. This observation may confirm that of al-Ya'qubi, who reported that: 'In Faiyum (town) coarse cloth (*khaish*) is made.'[26]

a   d   b

Cat. 74 *TIRAZ* **FRAGMENT FROM THE LATE UMAYYAD OR EARLY ABBASID DYNASTY**
Egypt, Fayyum, 8th to 9th century CE

Description: Fragment (five pieces) of black or very dark blue wool, comprising a broad band of polychrome decoration on a red ground within surrounding palmette-scroll borders. A central medallion in this band contains a mounted horseman within a pearl band in green with red and yellow dotted circles; on either side of the medallion are scenes of various subject matter presented in a sequential order, contained within the spandrels of a large scrolling plant; most of the designs are in mustard yellow with black outlines on a dark red ground, accentuated in green, ivory and blue (described as going out from the medallion). To the right of the medallion in order: void; two figures that appear to be sphinxes pictured above each other (they differ in their facial features from the lions depicted in the same disposition elsewhere on the textile); a human figure fighting two lions with a sword and stabbing one in the mouth; trees disposed sideways; a pair of sphinxes above each other (as before). To the left of the medallion in order: a pair of lions depicted above each other; a human figure fighting two lions with a sword and stabbing one in the mouth; void; lion eating what appears to be a human figure lying on the ground; void; trees disposed sideways; a pair of lions above each other. Above the main decorative band is a Coptic inscription in Greek characters in mustard yellow characters on a dark red ground; below the main band is an inscription in stylized Kufic inhabited by smaller stylized floral motifs in mustard yellow accentuated in red set against the dark blue base fabric.

Materials: wool: plain weave and tapestry

Dimensions: piece (a) (left of d): h. 20.2 cm, w. 37.5 cm; max. letter height 0.8 cm
piece (b) (left of c): h. 19.5 cm, w. 20 cm
piece (c) (left of e): h. 23.7 cm, w. 21.8 cm
piece (d) (left of b): h. 20.8 cm, w. 9.9 cm
piece (e) (right side): h. 20.3 cm, w. 19.6 cm

Ground fabric: wool (blackish-blue), weft-faced plain weave, dense texture; good quality (2)

Thread count: warp 10 S-spun, weft 44 S-spun

Thread thickness: warp 0.4 mm tight twist, weft 0.2–0.3 mm tight twist

Tapestry: wool, undyed and dyed (red, ochre, green, light blue); S-spun; tight twist; slit and toothed; thin long stems of floral decoration executed almost as floating wefts with binding in large intervals

Provenance: Ex H.P. Kraus collection, nos 296 (piece (a)), 297 (piece (b)), 298 (piece (c)), 299 (piece (d)), 300 (piece (e))

Inv. no. LNS 65 T a–e

Related works: See page 508

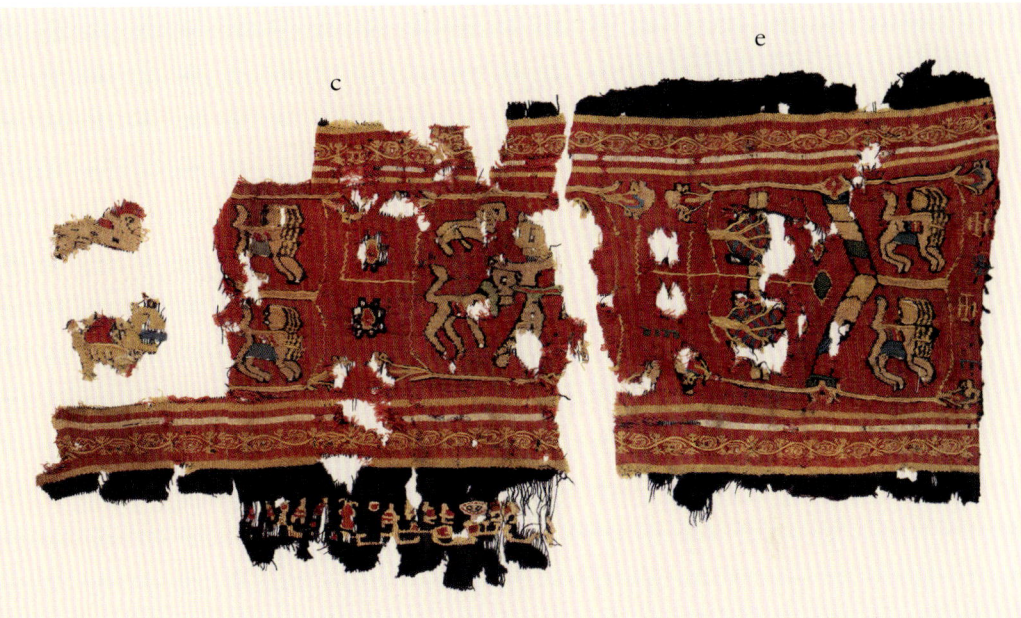

Inscription:
Arabic:

[...] المؤمنين [...]

[...] the believers [...]

Coptic: undecipherable

This is a good example of how pre-Islamic traditions permeated the Islamic period in Egypt. The subject matter seen here reflects the Christian heritage of the Egyptian Copts. It is very likely that the scenes depicted are not just decorative, but depict parts of a narrative. The fighting scenes between a human figure and pairs of lions are reminiscent of the account of Daniel in the lion's den in the Old Testament. Several Coptic textiles have survived that depict biblical and hagiographical accounts. Among the most prominent are those representing the story of Joseph,[27] the Adoration of the Magi,[28] and St George fighting the dragon;[29] a scene with figures taming lions, very close in its abstracted aesthetic to the present piece, was published by Volbach and Kühnel.[30] Most of these Coptic textiles have been dated to the sixth or seventh century. In all of them the figures are highly stylized, unlike earlier weavings, which are influenced by the Hellenistic aesthetic.

To find Coptic and Arabic inscriptions accompanying a decorative band indicates an early Islamic date. An example is a fragment in the Boston Museum of Fine Arts (Related works 1). An important piece in the Musée du Louvre, Paris, mentioning in an Arabic inscription its manufacture in a private (*khassa*) workshop in Tuttun in al-Fayyum, also carries an inscription in Coptic comprising an invocation asking Jesus Christ to help Raphael son of Ganarkhou (Related works 2).

The epigraphic style of the Arabic inscription seen here is typical of the products of al-Fayyum, with wedge-shaped letter terminals and irregular spacing between letters. Often Fayyumi inscriptions are also inhabited by zoomorphic motifs. Furthermore, the choice of colour and material, usually limited to a dark blue wool base fabric and decorative bands in red and yellow wool, with the inscriptions often in ivory, is common in the Fayyum and can be observed on the Louvre piece. Another related example in terms of inscription and aesthetic is in the Brooklyn Museum of Art (Related works 3).

While most of the examples with Christian scenes mentioned above have been attributed to the pre-Islamic period, there can be little doubt that the present piece dates from a period after the Islamic conquest, given the presence of an Arabic inscription. Although there seems to be some debate about the dating of Fayyumi textiles – Thompson dates the Brooklyn piece to the tenth or eleventh century, while Britton dates the Boston pieces to the eighth to tenth century – an early date for the present piece seems preferable, considering the naturalistic approach to the subject matter depicted.

Cat. 75 *TIRAZ* FRAGMENT FROM
THE ABBASID OR FATIMID
DYNASTY
**Egypt, Fayyum, late 9th
to 11th century CE**

Description: Fragment of dark blue wool, with
two decorative in-woven bands.
The lower band (h. 2.9 cm) is
plain and of a rusty red colour;
the other (h. 3.5 cm) is composed
of three registers, the central
one comprising a sequence
of confronted quadrupeds in
cream, mustard and blue on a
rusty red ground with stylized
trees in cream, mustard and blue
in between, and the two outer
registers comprising repetitive
stylized Kufic script in cream on
a rusty red ground.

Materials: wool and linen: plain weave
and tapestry

Dimensions: h. 28.7 cm, w. 59.1 cm;
max. letter height 1.3 cm

Ground fabric: wool warp and weft, dyed
(blueish-black), weft-faced plain
weave, close texture, regular
structure; good quality (2);
selvedge intact on the right side of
the smaller piece; ancient repairs

Thread count: warp 12 S-spun, weft 22 S-spun

Thread thickness: warp 0.3 mm tight twist, weft 0.3–
0.4 mm slight–medium twist

Tapestry: wool, dyed (red, ochre, black,
dark blue), and linen, undyed;
c. 44 picks per cm; S-spun;
0.4 mm tight twist S-spun,
0.3–0.4 mm tight twist; slit and
toothed

Provenance: art market, 1970s–1980s

Inv. no. LNS 1 T

Related works: See page 508

Inscription: repetition of
Sufficiency(?)

الكفا

The repeated inscription found on the present piece also appears on one in
the Bouvier Collection (Related works 4). It reads 'al-kifa', which may be an
abbreviation of 'al-kifa'iya' ('Sufficiency').

Cat. 76 ***TIRAZ* FRAGMENT FROM THE ABBASID OR FATIMID DYNASTY**
Egypt, late 9th to 11th century CE

Description: Fragment of wool dyed black, with three bands of decoration tapestry-woven in red, ochre and dark brown. The largest band consists of a central frieze with ducks and hares alternating in medallions, bordered by two friezes of Arabic inscription in tan wool on a red ground. Below it is a smaller band, also with a red ground, and a decorative scroll motif in dark and tan wool. The last band consists of a plain line of red wool with an inscription above it.

Materials: wool: plain weave and tapestry

Dimensions: h. 20.8 cm, w. 52.5 cm; max. letter height 1.0 cm

Ground fabric: wool warp and weft, dyed (blackish), balanced plain weave, gauzy texture; good–medium quality (2–3)

Thread count: warp 13 S-spun, weft 14 S-spun

Thread thickness: warp 0.3 mm tight twist, weft 0.3 mm tight twist

Tapestry: wool, dyed (red, ochre, dark brown); S-spun; tight twist; slit and toothed; wool supplementary weft

Provenance: Ex H.P. Kraus collection, no. 224

Inv. no. LNS 309 T

Related works: See page 508

Inscription: repetition of
Sovereignty belongs to God

الملك لله

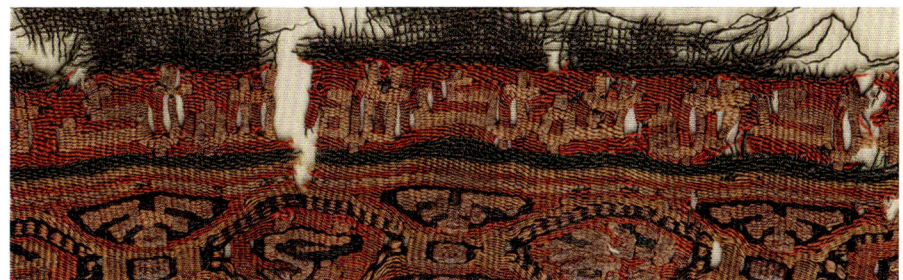

Cat. 77 *TIRAZ* FRAGMENT FROM
THE LATE ABBASID
OR EARLY FATIMID
DYNASTY
**Egypt, Fayyum, late 9th
to 11th century CE**

Description: Fragment (three pieces) of
wool dyed dark blue, with
a decorative band tapestry-
woven in multicoloured wool,
comprising three registers. A
central band has a sequence
of confronted quadrupeds in
mustard-coloured wool on a
red ground, accompanied by
stylized zoomorphic and floral
motifs, set between borders
of pairs of addorsed volutes;
on either side of this central
band runs a repetition of non-
meaningful text in pseudo-Kufic
script in mustard set against a
dark blue ground. Remnants of
the dark blue ground fabric are
visible between the inscription
and the central band.

Materials: wool and linen: plain weave,
tapestry and embroidery

Dimensions: piece (a) (left): h. 11.6 cm,
w. 22.3 cm; max. letter height
3 cm
piece (b) (right): h. 11.8 cm,
w. 12.6 cm
piece (c) (top right): h. 2.9 cm,
w. 14.1 cm

Ground fabric: wool warp and weft, dyed
(dark blue), balanced plain
weave, loose weave

Thread count: warp 13 S-spun, weft 7 per
0.5 cm S-spun

Thread thickness: warp 0.3 mm tight twist,
weft 0.15–0.2 mm tight twist

Tapestry: wool, dyed (red, black, ochre,
green), and linen, undyed;
c. 62 picks per cm; S-spun;
slit and toothed

Embroidery: linen, undyed; S-spun;
running stitch

Provenance: Ex H.P. Kraus collection,
no. 115

Inv. no. LNS 66 T a–c

Related works: See page 508

Inscription: epigraphic repetition of   لعا

The aesthetic of both script and zoomorphic decoration, plus the choice of materials, suggest a Fayyumi origin for this piece. The sequence of pairs of animals seen here is set within a field bordered horizontally and vertically, a feature seen also on a textile in the Biblioteca Apostolica Vaticana (Related works 1). The inscription on this piece mentions its workshop of production as a *tiraz al-khassa*, and alludes to an unnamed owner or patron (*li-sahibihi*).

Cat. 78 *TIRAZ* FRAGMENT FROM
THE LATE ABBASID OR
EARLY FATIMID DYNASTY
**Egypt, Fayyum, late 9th
to 11th century CE**

Description: Fragment of wool dyed dark blue,
with a band of repeated non-
meaningful text in pseudo-Kufic
script tapestry-woven in undyed
linen and red wool

Materials: wool and linen: plain weave
and tapestry

Dimensions: h. 8.2 cm, w. 26.2 cm;
max. letter height 1.8 cm.

Ground fabric: wool warp and weft, dyed (dark
blue), weft-faced plain weave,
dense texture; good quality (2)

Thread count: warp 13 S-spun, weft 22 S-spun

Thread thickness: warp 0.4–0.5 mm medium–tight
twist, weft 0.5–0.6 mm slight twist

Tapestry: linen, undyed (inscription), and
wool, dyed (red); slit and toothed;
discontinuous wool weft filling
between letters

Provenance: Ex H.P. Kraus collection, no. 110

Inv. no. LNS 223 T

Inscription: epigraphic repetition of ما

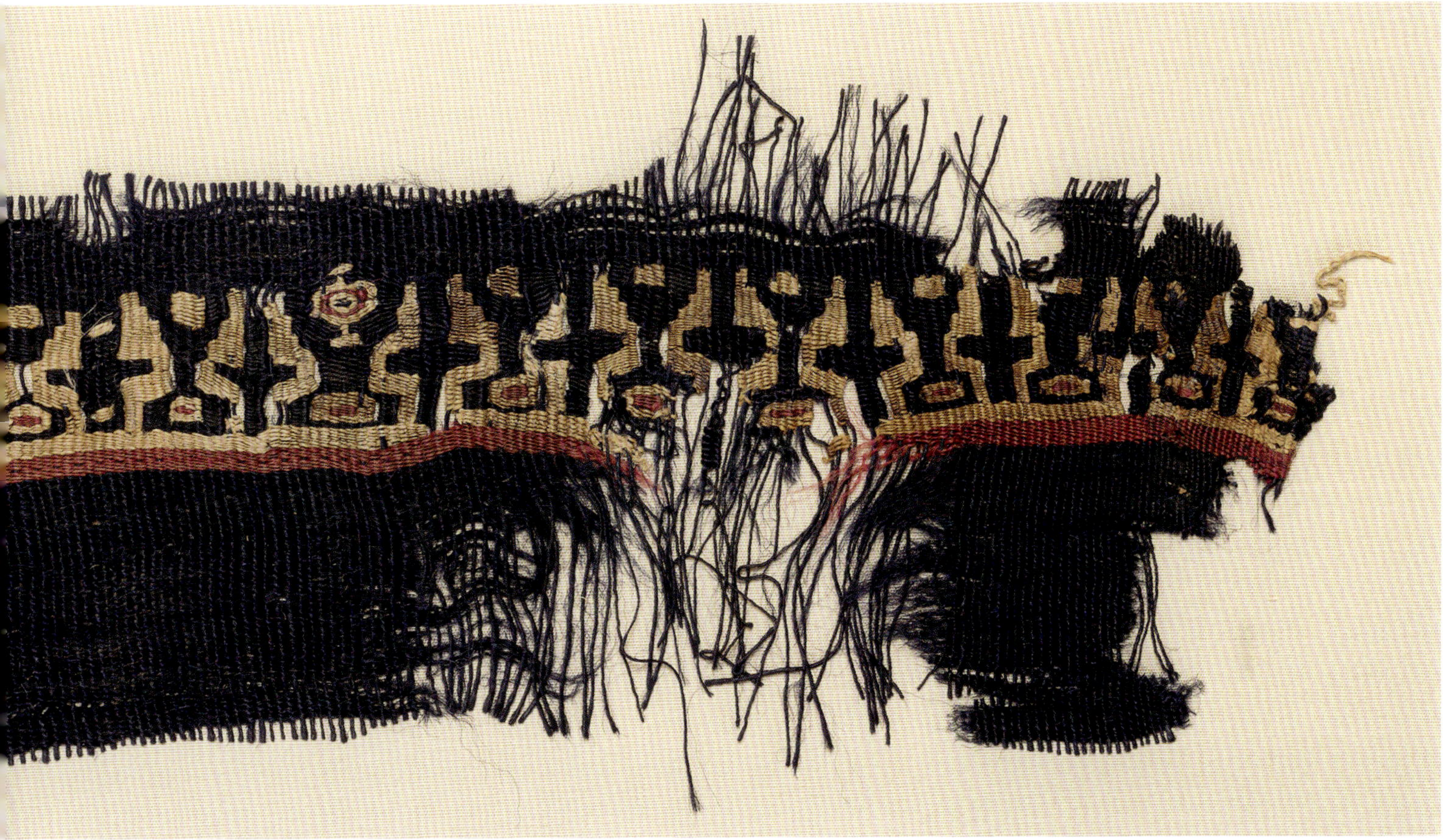

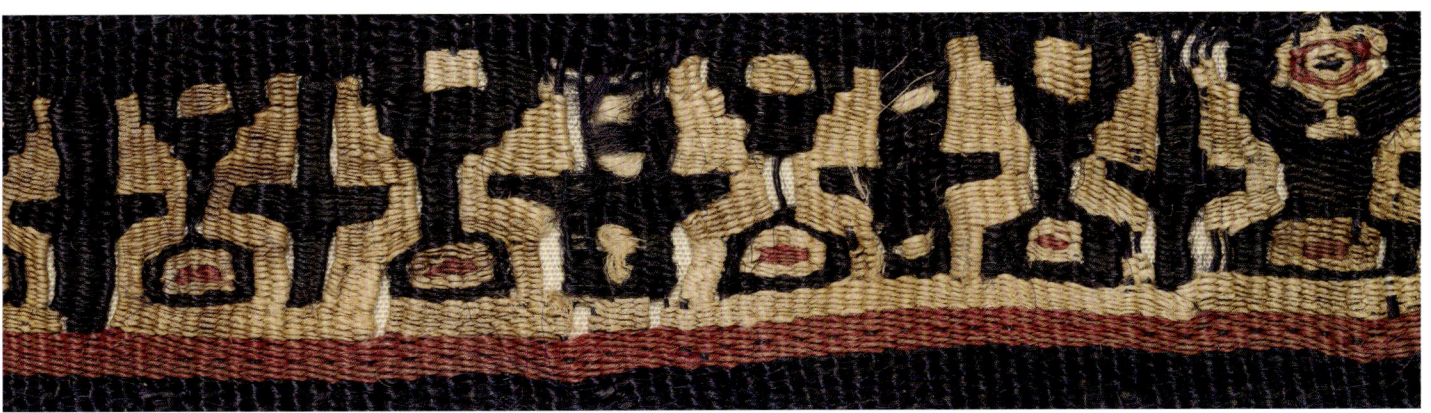

Cat. 79 *TIRAZ* FRAGMENT FROM
THE LATE ABBASID OR
EARLY FATIMID DYNASTY
**Egypt, Fayyum, late 9th
to 11th century CE**

Description: Fragment of wool dyed dark blue,
roughly rectangular, with two lines
of Kufic inscription tapestry-woven
in undyed linen; the space between
the letters is decorated with birds,
animals and floral motifs.

Materials: wool and linen: plain weave
and tapestry

Dimensions: h. 12.0 cm, w. 18.5 cm;
max. letter height 3 cm

Ground fabric: wool warp and weft, dyed (dark
blue), weft-faced plain weave, tight
texture; good quality (2); selvedge
on the left side of the inscriptions

Thread count: warp 11 S-spun, weft 26 S-spun

Thread thickness: warp 0.4 mm tight twist,
weft 0.6 mm slight twist

Tapestry: linen, undyed; slit and toothed;
discontinuous wool weft filling
between letters

Provenance: Ex H.P. Kraus collection, no. 109

Inv. no. LNS 222 T

Related works: See page 508

Inscription:

Line 1:

[...] الحمد لله بركة من ا[لله] [...]

[...] Praise be to God. Blessings from G[od] [...]

Line 2:

الله (لا؟) اله (الا؟)

God (there is no?) God (but?)

This fragment features a prominently stitched seam with some kind of piping on its left side, suggesting that it might once have been part of a sleeve.

Cat. 80 *TIRAZ* FRAGMENT FROM
THE LATE ABBASID OR
EARLY FATIMID DYNASTY
Egypt, Fayyum, late 9th
to 11th century CE

Description: Fragment of wool dyed black, with
three decorative bands tapestry-
woven in red and yellow wool. One
band contains a Kufic inscription
with decorative patterns of ducks
and floral motifs between the
letters. Above it, a narrower band
consists of a stylized floral pattern
framed by two horizontal lines;
the uppermost decorative band,
in yellow wool, is directly beneath
the fringed edge of the textile.

Materials: wool: plain weave and tapestry

Dimensions: h. 24.6 cm, w. 46 cm;
max. letter height 2.3 cm

Ground fabric: wool warp and weft, dyed
(blackish-brown), predominant-
weft plain weave, gauze texture;
good quality (2); twisted fringe

Thread count: warp 18 S-spun, weft 10 S-spun

Thread thickness: warp 0.3 mm tight twist,
weft 0.3 mm tight twist

Tapestry: wool, undyed and dyed (red,
pinkish); discontinuous wool weft
filling between letters

Provenance: Ex H.P. Kraus collection, no. 108

Inv. no. LNS 221 T

Related works: See page 508

Inscription:

الحمد لله (...؟...) الحمد لله (...؟...) ملك لله ملك لله (...؟...) [...]

[...] Praise be to God (...?...) Praise be to God (...?...) the kingdom is God's the
kingdom is God's (...?...) [...]

Cat. 81 *TIRAZ* FRAGMENT FROM
THE LATE ABBASID OR
EARLY FATIMID DYNASTY
Egypt, Fayyum, late 9th
to 11th century CE

Description: Fragment of wool dyed dark blue,
with a central band of decoration
framed by two bands of Kufic
inscription tapestry-woven in
undyed wool. The tapestry-woven
central band has an ochre filling
and a middle band of black wool
that forms several medallions
decorated with bird motifs in
ochre, blue and red.

Materials: wool and linen: plain weave
and tapestry

Dimensions: h. 11.0 cm, w. 10.0 cm;
max. letter height 2.5 cm

Ground fabric: wool warp and weft, dyed (dark
blue), weft-faced plain weave,
dense texture; good quality (2);
seam on the right side of the
inscription

Thread count: warp 12 S-spun, weft 40 S-spun

Thread thickness: warp 0.25 mm tight twist,
weft 0.4 mm slight–medium twist

Tapestry: linen, undyed (inscription), and
wool (decoration), dyed (red,
ochre, black, greenish-blue);
discontinuous wool weft filling
between the letters

Provenance: Ex H.P. Kraus collection, no. 111

Inv. no. LNS 224 T

Related works: See page 508

Inscription: repetition of
Sufficiency(?)

الكفا

This is probably a fragment from a sleeve, as the stitched seam on the right side
of the band and inscription indicates. Every element of this fragment is of good
quality: the deeply saturated tone of the dark blue wool base fabric, and the
carefully executed decorative band in a reddish tone with small lozenges
containing birds accentuated in a lighter blue tone. The complete garment
would have once been magnificent and belonged to a wealthy individual, as
both the materials and the quality of workmanship would have commanded a
hefty price. From a technical point of view, the fragment shows that the craft of
wool weaving continued from Greco-Roman times right into the Islamic period.
A complete tunic with a similar type of band comprising animals in small
cartouches is in the Bardo Museum in Tunis, originally bought in the Egyptian
art market (Related works 1).

Cat. 82   *TIRAZ* FRAGMENT FROM
THE LATE ABBASID OR
EARLY FATIMID DYNASTY
**Egypt, Fayyum, 10th to
11th century CE**

Description: Fragment of wool dyed dark blue,
with a large central decorative
tapestry-woven band framed by
two bands of Kufic inscription
tapestry-woven in undyed
linen; the central band has a
red background and a series of
medallions with floral and animal
motifs in ochre, blue and undyed
wool

Materials: wool and linen: plain weave
and tapestry

Dimensions: h. 11.5 cm, w. 10 cm;
max. letter height 1.3 cm

Ground fabric: wool warp and weft, dyed (dark
blue), weft-faced plain weave,
dense texture; good quality (2)

Thread count: warp 11 S-spun, weft 28 S-spun

Thread thickness: warp 0.3 mm tight twist, weft 0.4–
0.5 mm slight–medium twist

Tapestry: linen, undyed (inscription), and
wool, dyed (red, ochre, black,
greenish-blue); discontinuous wool
weft filling between the letters

Provenance: Ex H.P. Kraus collection, no. 112

Inv. no. LNS 225 T

Related works: See page 508

Inscription: repetition of

Sufficiency(?)

الكفا

Cat. 83 *TIRAZ* **FRAGMENT FROM THE LATE ABBASID OR FATIMID DYNASTY**
Egypt, 10th to 11th century CE

Description: Fragment of wool dyed dark blue with a central band of decoration bordered by two bands of Kufic inscription tapestry-woven in undyed linen and red wool, with bird figures decorating the spaces between letters; only the upper of the two lines of text is legible. The tapestry-woven central band (5.7 cm) has a red filling and medallions with birds and floral patterns in tan, green, ochre and black.

Materials: wool and linen: plain weave and tapestry

Dimensions: h. 11.5 cm, w. 17.5 cm; max. letter height of 2.6 cm

Ground fabric: wool warp and weft, dyed (dark blue), weft-faced plain weave, dense texture; good quality (2); selvedge on the left side of the inscription

Thread count: warp 9 S-spun, weft 26 S-spun

Thread thickness: warp 0.5 mm tight twist, weft 0.5 mm slight twist

Tapestry: linen, undyed (inscription), and wool, dyed (red, ochre, black, greenish-blue); discontinuous wool weft filling between the letters

Provenance: Ex H.P. Kraus collection, no. 118

Inv. no. LNS 229 T

Related works: See page 508

Inscription: repetition of: الملك له

Sovereignty belongs to him

The inscription here is possibly a corrupted version of 'al-mulk li-llah' ('Sovereignty is God's').

Cat. 84   **TEXTILE FRAGMENT FROM
THE LATE ABBASID OR
EARLY FATIMID DYNASTY**
**Egypt, Fayyum, 10th to
11th century CE**

Description: Fragment (two pieces) of wool,
with a tapestry-woven band in
wool and undyed linen, comprising
a frieze of zoomorphic and
pseudo-epigraphic decoration in
red, mustard, cream and blue on a
black ground, comprising pairs of
confronted birds against a stylized
tree of life, with small six-pointed
stars above the main field; the pairs
of birds are separated by a motif
resembling a letter stem with two
hook-like terminals.

Materials: wool and linen: tapestry
Dimensions: piece (a) (right): h. 4.2 cm,
w. 11.0 cm
piece (b) (left): h. 4.3 cm, w. 6.4 cm
Ground fabric: wool warp, dyed (black), weft lost
Thread count: warp 21 S-spun
Thread thickness: warp 0.25 mm tight twist
Tapestry: wool weft, dyed (red, ochre, black,
dark green), and linen, undyed; 36
picks per cm; S-spun; 0.3–0.5 mm
tight twist; slit and toothed
Provenance: art market, 1970s–1980s

Inv. no. LNS 50 T a, b

Related works: See page 508

A piece with a comparable frieze of zoomorphic and pseudo-epigraphic
decoration is in the Bouvier Collection (Related works 1).

Cat. 85 *TIRAZ* FRAGMENT FROM
THE LATE ABBASID OR
EARLY FATIMID DYNASTY
Egypt, Fayyum, 10th to
11th century CE

Inscription: repetition of

Victory with help from God (?) [or] Victory with God's help

نصر من الله

Description:	Fragment (three pieces) of wool dyed bluish-black, with a band of Kufic inscription with floral patterns filling the spaces between letters, tapestry-woven in red and yellow wool and undyed linen; some of the letters have disappeared.
Materials:	wool and linen: plain weave and tapestry
Dimensions:	piece (a) (right): h. 7.5 cm, w. 25.5 cm piece (b) (centre): h. 8.4 cm, w. 28.2 cm piece (c) (left): h. 4.3 cm, w. 3.2 cm max. letter height 2.0 cm
Ground fabric:	wool warp and weft, dyed (bluish-black), weft-faced plain weave, dense texture; good quality (2)
Thread count:	warp 11 S-spun, weft 18 S-spun
Thread thickness:	warp 0.3 mm tight twist, weft 0.4–0.5 mm slight–medium twist
Tapestry:	wool, dyed (red, yellow), and linen, undyed; slit and toothed; discontinuous wool weft filling between the letters
Provenance:	Ex H.P. Kraus collection, no. 110 (piece (a)), no. 114 (piece (b))

Inv. no. LNS 226 T a–c

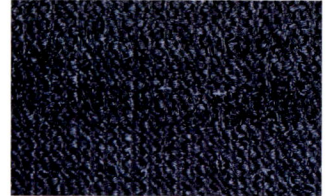

Cat. 86   *TIRAZ* FRAGMENTS FROM
THE LATE ABBASID OR
EARLY FATIMID DYNASTY
**Egypt, Fayyum, 10th to
11th century CE**

Description: Fragment of wool dyed black, with
two bands of inscription in undyed
linen: the upper, larger band carries
an inscription in Kufic tapestry-
woven in undyed linen; the lower
one carries a Coptic inscription
(in Greek characters) woven with
a supplementary undyed linen weft.

Materials: wool and linen: plain weave
and tapestry

Dimensions: h. 10.0 cm, w. 26.2 cm; max. letter
height (Arabic) 1.7 cm, max. letter
height (Greek) 0.7 cm

Ground fabric: wool warp and weft, dyed (black),
balanced plain weave, close
texture; good quality (2); selvedge
on the right side of the inscriptions

Thread count: warp 19 S-spun, weft 25 S-spun

Thread thickness: warp 0.3 mm tight twist,
weft 0.3 mm tight twist

Tapestry: linen, undyed (Arabic inscription);
slit and toothed; discontinuous
wool weft filling between the
letters; supplementary undyed
linen weft (Coptic inscription)

Provenance: Ex H.P. Kraus collection, no. 116

Inv. no. LNS 227 T

Related works: See page 508

Inscription:

Arabic: (؟) (...) بركة (؟) كاملة لصاحبه مما عمل (...) (؟)

(...) complete blessing (?) to its owner. Of what has been made (...) (?)

Coptic: undecipherable

Cat. 87 *TIRAZ* FRAGMENT FROM THE LATE ABBASID OR EARLY FATIMID DYNASTY
Egypt, Fayyum,
10th to 13th century CE

Description: Fragment of wool dyed dark blue, with two bands of repetitious epigraphic and geometric decoration. The broader band (3.6 cm) comprises two addorsed lines of Kufic inscription consisting of repetitions of the non-meaningful phrase *la'a* embroidered in undyed wool; between them is a band of small embroidered lozenges filled with stylized flowers in greenish-blue and reddish-brown, bordered by three thin woven bands in ivory, reddish-brown and mustard yellow, finished vertically towards the selvedge (left) with an arrangement of four embroidered stripes enclosing a lattice. A thinner band (1.8 cm), running along above the fringe, comprises a Kufic inscription again repeating the phrase *la'a* embroidered in undyed wool on a monochrome woven band in reddish-brown.

Materials: wool and linen: plain weave, tapestry and embroidery

Dimensions: h. 26.1 cm, w. 35.1 cm; max. letter height 0.6 cm

Ground fabric: wool warp and weft, dyed (dark blue), balanced plain weave, gauzy texture; good quality (2); braided fringe consisting of four warps; selvedge on the left side of the fragment

Thread count: warp 13 S-spun, weft 15 S-spun

Thread thickness: warp 0.3 mm tight twist, weft 0.3 mm tight twist

Tapestry: wool, dyed (reddish-brown, greenish-blue); supplementary weft

Embroidery: linen, undyed, and wool, dyed (reddish-brown, mustard yellow and ivory); S-spun; back and running stitch

Provenance: Ex H.P. Kraus collection, no. 228

Inv. no. LNS 67 T

Related works: See page 508

Inscription: epigraphic repetition of لاء

A very closely related textile to this and cat. nos 88–93 is in the Katoen Natie Collection (Related works 1), discussed in the introduction to this section (p. 263), which features a stylized epigraphic inscription similar to the one seen here. That textile survives as a complete loom length and width, with twisted fringes. The present piece would once have formed part of such a textile, perhaps intended as a shawl. While here the decorative band consists of two addorsed lines of epigraphic designs with a geometric band between, the Katoen Natie textile comprises a single line of epigraphic designs on either end, both accompanied by a Coptic inscription quoting from the Bible. The radiocarbon dating of the Katoen Natie textile to the eleventh to thirteenth century, coupled with the similarities in the Arabic pseudo-script, provide an anchor for the attribution of the present piece.

A fragment almost identical with the present one is in the Bouvier Collection (Related works 2). It shares not only the technique of manufacture, but also the representation of the inscription, the decorative bands, the choice of colours and the finish against the selvedge. Another fragment in the Bouvier Collection comprises a similar arrangement of both inscription and decoration, but features a band of differently organized lozenges (Related works 3). In both those textiles the epigraphic and decorative bands are brocaded, resembling what is found here. Georgette Cornu attributed the two Bouvier pieces to the thirteenth century during the Mamluk dynasty, arguing that the geometric approach and the execution of the decoration in brocading can be found in Mamluk textiles.[31]

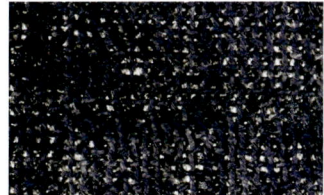 

Cat. 88 *TIRAZ* FRAGMENT FROM
THE LATE ABBASID OR
FATIMID DYNASTY
Egypt, 10th to 13th century CE

Description: Fragment of wool dyed black,
roughly rectangular, with
embroidered decoration in ochre,
green and red linen and wool in
several decorative bands. The first
consists of two confronted lines
of pseudo-epigraphic inscription
woven in ochre and red wool
with a line of stylized floral motifs
in ochre linen below. Next, a
larger central strip of decoration
has star motifs in undyed linen,
enclosing red and green lozenges,
separated by tree-like dividers; this
is framed by two smaller bands of
pseudo-epigraphic inscription that
repeat the letters in the first band.
Below is a narrow band formed
by stylized triangles, and, last, a
horizontal band woven in red wool,
running along the fringed edge.

Materials: wool and linen: plain weave
and embroidery

Dimensions: h. 31.4 cm, w. 31.5 cm;
max. letter height 0.5 cm

Ground fabric: wool warp and weft, dyed (black),
balanced plain weave, gauzy
texture; good quality (2); braided
fringe; selvedge

Thread count: warp 13 S-spun, weft 13 S-spun

Thread thickness: warp 0.25–0.3 mm tight twist,
weft 0.25–0.3 mm tight twist

Embroidery: linen, dyed (ochre), and wool,
dyed (red, green, orange);
S-spun; supplementary weft

Provenance: Ex H.P. Kraus collection, no. 229

Inv. no. LNS 312 T

Related works: See page 508

Inscription: epigraphic repetition of   لط

For a fragment with similar decoration and a discussion of related works see cat.
no. 87.

Cat. 89   *TIRAZ* FRAGMENT FROM
THE LATE ABBASID OR
FATIMID DYNASTY
Egypt, 10th to 13th century CE

Description: Fragment (two pieces) of wool
dyed black, with a band (1.3 cm)
consisting of two addorsed lines
of Kufic script repeating a single
word, executed as embroidery on
supplementary weft in undyed
linen.

Materials: wool and linen: plain weave with
embroidery, tapestry
and supplementary weft

Dimensions: piece (a) (right): h. 10.0 cm,
w. 21.2 cm; max. letter height
0.4 cm
piece (b) (left): h. 12.2 cm,
w. 21.4 cm; max. letter height
0.4 cm

Ground fabric: wool warp and weft, dyed (black),
balanced plain weave, gauzy
texture; good quality (2); untwisted
fringe with supplementary weft

Thread count: warp 18 S-spun, weft 18 S-spun

Thread thickness: warp 0.25 mm tight twist,
weft 0.25 mm tight twist

Embroidery: linen, undyed; S-spun;
supplementary weft with back
and running stitch

Provenance: Ex H.P. Kraus collection, no. 225

Inv. no. LNS 310 T a, b

Related works: See page 508

Inscription: repetition of

Happiness

اليمن

For a fragment with similar decoration and a discussion of related works see
cat. no. 87.

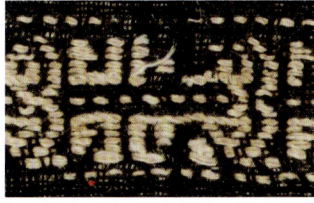

Cat. 90   ***TIRAZ* FRAGMENT FROM THE LATE ABBASID OR FATIMID DYNASTY**
Egypt, 10th to 13th century CE

Description: Fragment of wool dyed bluish-black, with three bands of tapestry-woven and embroidered decoration. The first band (4.0 cm) consists of a confronted geometrical pattern formed by the repetition of pseudo-epigraphic motifs embroidered in undyed and reddish-brown dyed wool. The second band (2.5 cm) consists of a geometrical pattern again of pseudo-calligraphic motifs embroidered in undyed linen and ochre and reddish-brown wool and framed between two bands tapestry-woven in reddish-brown wool. The last band is tapestry-woven in plain reddish-brown and runs along the fringed edge of the piece.

Materials: wool and linen: plain weave with embroidery and tapestry

Dimensions: h. 28.9 cm, w. 24.6 cm; max. 'letter' height 0.5 cm

Ground fabric: wool warp and weft, dyed (bluish-black), balanced plain weave, gauzy texture; good–medium quality (2–3); braided fringe; selvedge

Thread count: warp 13 S-spun, weft 11 S-spun

Thread thickness: warp 0.25–0.3 mm tight twist, weft 0.25–0.3 mm tight twist

Tapestry: wool, dyed (reddish-brown)

Embroidery: linen, undyed, and wool, dyed (ochre and reddish-brown); S-spun; supplementary weft

Provenance: Ex H.P. Kraus collection, no. 230

Inv. no. LNS 313 T

Related works: See page 508

Inscription: abstract epigraphic repetitions

For a fragment with similar decoration and a discussion of related works see cat. no. 87.

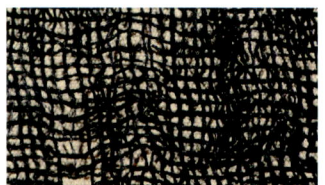

Cat. 91   *TIRAZ* FRAGMENT FROM
THE ABBASID OR FATIMID
DYNASTY
Egypt, 10th to 13th century CE

Description: Fragment of wool dyed black, with
four embroidered and tapestry-
woven decorative bands in undyed
linen and ochre, brownish-red and
green wool. The first band (1.0 cm)
has a repeated motif of birds in
undyed wool. The second band
(2.0 cm) consists of a geometrical
pattern formed by green, tan,
yellow and black lozenges. The
band below (1.0 cm) again has
repeated bird motifs. Lastly, a band
along the fringe (0.7 cm) is formed
by a Kufic inscription, with a
repetition of letters in a decorative
fashion.

Materials: wool and linen: plain weave
with embroidery, tapestry
and supplementary weft

Dimensions: h. 30.3 cm, w. 56.1 cm;
max. letter height 1.3 cm

Ground fabric: wool warp and weft, dyed (black),
balanced plain weave, gauzy
texture; good–medium quality
(2–3); twisted fringe; selvedge
on the right side

Thread count: warp 11 S-spun, weft 12 S-spun

Thread thickness: warp 0.2 mm tight twist,
weft 0.25 mm tight twist

Tapestry: supplementary paired weft, linen,
undyed; S-spun; supplementary
weft, wool, dyed (ochre,
brownish-red, green); S-spun

Embroidery: linen, undyed; S-spun; running
stitch

Provenance: Ex H.P. Kraus collection, no. 231

Inv. no. LNS 314 T

Related works: See page 508

Inscription: repetition of

For God

الله

For a fragment with similar decoration and a discussion of related works see cat.
no. 87.

Cat. 92 *TIRAZ* **FRAGMENT FROM THE LATE ABBASID OR FATIMID DYNASTY**

Egypt, 10th to 13th century CE

Description: Fragment of wool dyed bluish-black, with three tapestry-woven and embroidered decorative bands. The first band (3.3 cm) consists of an embroidered geometric pattern in red, blue and undyed wool, framed by two tapestry-woven plain friezes in ochre and tan wool, and two embroidered lines of repeated non-meaningful text in pseudo-Kufic script in undyed linen. The two lower bands (1.3 cm) also consist of repeated non-meaningful text in pseudo-Kufic script embroidered in undyed linen.

Materials: wool and linen: plain weave with embroidery, tapestry and supplementary weft

Dimensions: h. 15.0 cm, w. 43.4 cm; max. letter height 0.7 cm

Ground fabric: wool warp and weft, dyed (bluish-black), balanced plain weave, gauzy texture; good–medium quality (2–3); selvedge on the left side

Thread count: warp 14 S-spun, weft 14 S-spun

Thread thickness: warp 0.3 mm tight twist, weft 0.25–0.3 mm tight twist

Tapestry: wool, dyed (ochre, red, greenish-blue, orange); S-spun; supplementary weft

Embroidery: linen, undyed; S-spun; running stitch

Provenance: Ex H.P. Kraus collection, no. 240

Inv. no. LNS 322 T

Related works: See page 508

Inscription: epigraphic repetition of

لا

For a fragment with similar decoration and a discussion of related works see cat. no. 87.

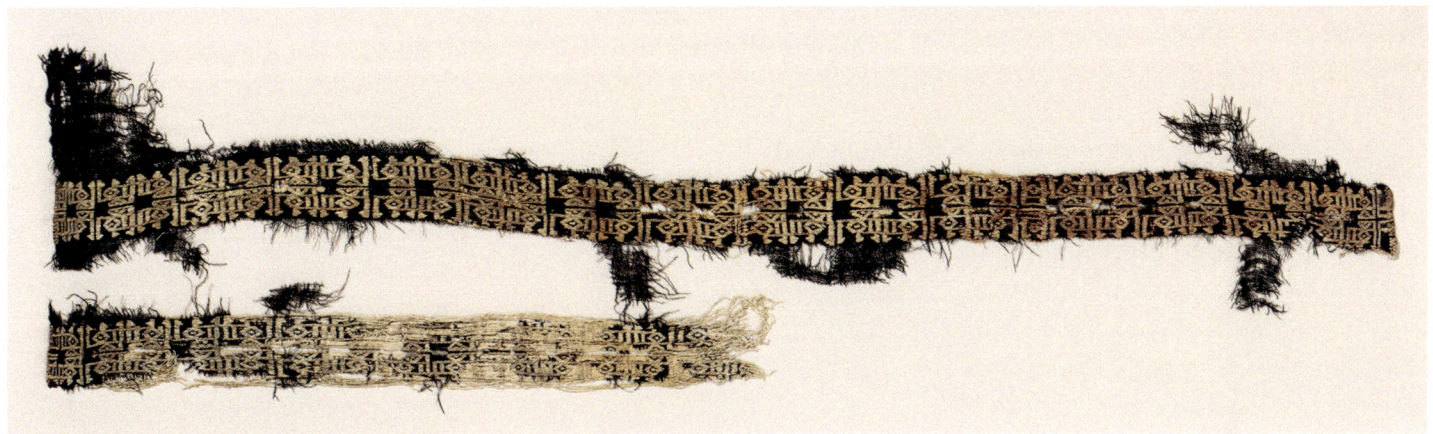

Cat. 93 *TIRAZ* FRAGMENT FROM THE LATE ABBASID OR FATIMID DYNASTY
Egypt, 10th to 13th century CE

Description: Fragment of wool dyed bluish-black, with a decorative band, embroidered in undyed linen consisting of confronted repetitions of a pseudo-Kufic inscription.

Materials: wool and linen: plain weave with embroidery

Dimensions: h. 16.2 cm, w. 61.5 cm; max. letter height 1.5 cm

Ground fabric: wool warp and weft, dyed (black), balanced plain weave, gauzy texture; good–medium quality (2–3); loom width with selvedges on both sides

Thread count: warp 11 S-spun, weft 11 S-spun

Thread thickness: warp 0.2 mm tight twist, weft 0.2–0.3 mm tight twist

Embroidery: linen, undyed; S-spun; supplementary weft

Provenance: Ex H.P. Kraus collection, no. 241

Inv. no. LNS 323 T

Related works: See page 508

Inscription: repetition of

God (...)

الله (...)

For a fragment with similar decoration and a discussion of related works see cat. no. 87.

Cat. 94 *TIRAZ* FRAGMENT FROM
THE ABBASID OR FATIMID
DYNASTY

Inscription: repetition (undecipherable)

Egypt, 10th to 11th century CE

Description: Fragment of wool dyed dark blue,
with a decorative band woven in
red and black carrying a pseudo-
epigraphic inscription embroidered
in undyed linen.

Materials: wool and linen: plain weave
with embroidery and tapestry

Dimensions: h. 7.8 cm, w. 28.8 cm;
max. letter height 1.0 cm

Ground fabric: wool warp, dyed (dark blue) and
weft, dyed (dark blue, red), weft-
faced plain weave, dense texture;
good quality (2); braided selvedge

Thread count: warp 10 S-spun, weft 22 S-spun

Thread thickness: warp 0.4 mm medium twist,
weft 0.5 mm slight twist

Embroidery: linen, undyed; S-spun, two-plied;
running stitch

Provenance: Ex H.P. Kraus collection, no. 253

Inv. no. LNS 331 T

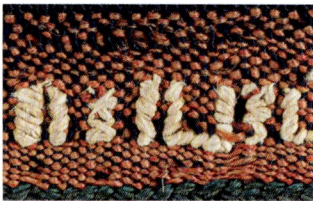

4

IRAQ

As the epicentre of the Abbasid empire, Iraq held a key position in the early Islamic world. By founding Baghdad (Madinat al-Salam: 'City of Peace') in 762 on a site north of the Sasanian capital Ctesiphon on the banks of the river Tigris, the Abbasid caliph al-Mansur (r. 754–75) was attempting to exert more control over the eastern parts of his empire, particularly Khurasan. The shift away from the Umayyad capital of Damascus brought with it new arrangements for administration of the empire, but also increased linkage between the various provinces of the empire through international trade. Baghdad, founded as a round city, embodied in its urban form the idea of an Abbasid hegemony that brought together divergent regions: it had four gates alluding to key cities or regions – Basra, Kufa, Damascus and Khurasan.

The Abbasid administration was dominated by dynastic families of bureaucrats of Iranian origin. Members of these families often headed the various government departments and rose to high positions within the closest circles around the caliph, some as viziers and personal advisers. They exerted huge power, and sometimes easily fell from grace. Many of the textile inscriptions discussed in this book document their names. The establishment of an administration on such a large scale brought with it a culture that placed particular emphasis on the written word. It is hence no surprise that Baghdad became a centre of learning that attracted the brightest literary scholars, scientists and translators. Likewise, members of the administrative class, the *kuttab*, became innovators of new epigraphic styles. One of the greatest was Ibn Muqla, who revised the Arabic script to embrace a more proportionate style of writing, perhaps similar to the inscriptions discussed in this section. Later on, scribes such as Ibn al-Bawwab and Yaqut al-Musta'simi introduced fully cursive hands. Surely the content of *tiraz* textile inscriptions and the way they looked was planned by members of the *kuttab* and, at least during the Abbasid caliphate, tightly controlled from Baghdad. Inscriptions from Egypt documenting members of the Abbasid administration in Baghdad, such as viziers and their secretaries, provide evidence for that (see cat. nos 7, 8, 10, 12, 14, 26, 27).

Baghdad as a place of production is documented in at least twenty-three *tiraz* inscriptions, including one in The al-Sabah Collection (cat. no. 98).[1] When a workshop type is mentioned in these Baghdadi inscriptions, it is always a *tiraz al-khassa*, unlike Egypt, where both *'amma* and *khassa* workshops are documented.[2] Examples are cat. nos 96 and 98. As the definitions of *khassa* and *'amma* in the textile context are still not entirely clear, it is perhaps justified to say that the exclusive usage of the term for textiles made in Baghdad might imply a difference in administrative structure or control to those in Egypt, where the large size of the industry and involvement of many different locations probably necessitated different structures of procurement and control. That Egyptian textiles were popular and numerous in Baghdad is discussed in chapter 1. One example was even found at Samarra, as mentioned in chapter 2.

The earliest inscription from Baghdad, in the Royal Ontario Museum, Toronto, dates from 260 AH / 874–75 CE during the reign of the caliph al-Mu'tamid (r. 870–92).[3] The latest are from the reign of the caliph al-Qadir (r. 991–1031), who had been appointed as caliph by the Buyid ruler Baha' al-Dawla.[4] While there are many references to Baghdad as a textile centre for production and trade in literary sources, with various parts of the city specialized in one or the other type of cloth, it is difficult to determine where textiles with caliphal protocols were produced.[5]

Apart from Baghdad, several centres in Iraq and Khuzestan produced textiles, such as Basra, Tustar (Shushtar), Wasit and Kufa.[6] Basra was a trade emporium connecting Iraq with the trade of the Indian Ocean basin, as far as China. None of these centres is documented in a *tiraz* textile inscription.

Iraqi *tiraz* textiles were widely dispersed through diplomatic channels, as examples found in Egypt prove. That they were also gifted to the Byzantine court is known from literary sources that discuss various embassies that visited Baghdad (see chapter 1).[7] This might explain the presence of an Iraqi textile at the Ottonian court, close in epigraphic style to the examples discussed here (see fig. 2.11).

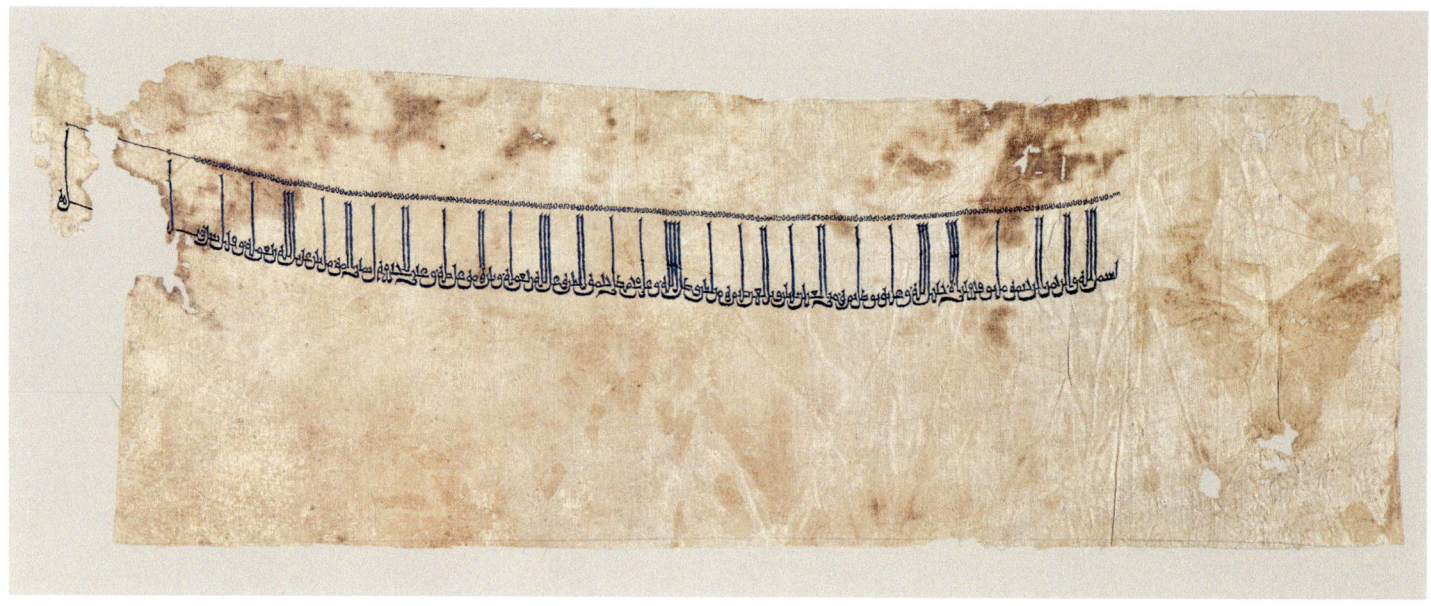

Cat. 95   *TIRAZ* FRAGMENT FROM
THE REIGN OF THE ABBASID
CALIPH AL-MUQTADIR
(r. 908–32)
Iraq, 300 AH / 912–13 CE

Description: Fragment of undyed glazed cotton,
with an inscription band (length
51.7 cm) comprising Quranic
content in Kufic script, a caliphal
dedication and date embroidered
in dark blue silk floss; a second,
smaller inscription with Quranic
content runs above the main
inscription.

Materials: cotton and silk: plain weave
and embroidery

Dimensions: h. 24.2 cm, w. 66.2 cm;
max. letter heights 4.2 cm (line 1),
0.4 cm (line 2)

Ground fabric: cotton warp and weft, undyed,
balanced plain weave, glazed and
polished, close texture (*dabiqi*),
regular structure; very good–good
quality (2); loom width
with selvedges right and left

Thread count: warp 22 Z-spun, weft 19 Z-spun

Thread thickness: warp 0.15–0.4 mm slight twist,
weft 0.25–0.4 mm slight twist

Embroidery: silk, dyed (dark blue), *c.* 0.5 mm,
chain stitch

Provenance: art market, 1970s–1980s

Published: Jenkins 1983, p. 42; Qaddumi 1996,
pp. 240–41, fig. 10a

Inv. no. LNS 19 T

Related works: See pages 508–09

Inscription:

Line 1:

بسم الله و [sic] الرحمن الرحيم و [sic] ما توفيقي الا (…؟…) الله و عليه توكلت و هو العرش (…؟…) العظيم مؤمن يتكل الله
علي محمد ا [sic] خاتم و [sic] النبيين و علي آله ر [sic] بعمله (…؟…) {بر}كة و عز لالخليفة امير المؤمنين عز الله نعمة و (…؟…)
سنة ثلث مائة

In the name of God and [*sic*] the Most Merciful, the Most Compassionate and
[*sic*] my success comes only (… ? …) (through?) God, upon him I have relied and
He the Great (… ? …) Throne. A Believer relies upon God, upon Muhammad
[*sic*] the seal [*sic*] of the prophets and upon his family *ra'* [*sic*] its fabrication (… ?
…) (ble)ssing and glory to the caliph the Commander of the Faithful. The glory
of God, prosperity and (… ? …). In the year three hundred

Line 2: largely undecipherable
Parts of Quran 11:88 (Surah Hud)

Until now, this fragment has been dated to 302 AH / 914–15 CE based on the
reading of the last two words of the inscription as 'ithnayn thulth mi'a'.[8] Here,
however, a reading of the last two words as 'sanat thulth mi'a' (300 AH / 912–
13 CE) is proposed. Either reading allows us to date the textile to the beginning
of the reign of the Abbasid caliph al-Muqtadir (r. 907–32). Two examples in the
Royal Ontario Museum, Toronto, are also dated to the year 300 AH / 912–13 CE
(Related works 1 and 2). Two further historical *tiraz* inscriptions from al-
Muqtadir's reign relate closely to the present one in terms of epigraphy and are
embroidered in blue silk chain stitch on cotton ground fabric (Related works 3
and 4). This type of script was not exclusive to the reign of al-Muqtadir and was
used over a period of perhaps up to thirty years, as indicated by a piece in the
Museum of Fine Arts, Boston, which is inscribed in the same style of calligraphy
and mentions the name of the Abbasid caliph al-Radi (r. 934–40).[9] An inscription

in a style that might be regarded as a further development of that in the present piece, dated to 390 AH / 999–1000 CE and with the name of the Buyid ruler Baha' al-Dawla, is in the Metropolitan Museum, New York, suggesting that this style of script was used over a long period and was linked to the workshops of Baghdad.[10]

The present inscription, which contains parts of Quran 11:88 (Surah Hud) (see also cat. nos 97, 100, 101, 102), is characterized by an epigraphic style with a low baseline, tall letter stems and pronounced cursive letter terminals below the baseline. This style must have been developed by calligraphers, as it embodies all the qualities of the pen: the balance between thick and thin script line and the well-proportioned curvature of low terminals. A number of textile fragments have survived in which this style was actually used for inscriptions applied to the fabric by pen using black ink (see cat. no. 106). Two such examples are in the Textile Museum, Washington, DC.[11] In one of these, the main inscription is also accompanied by a second, smaller inscription above.[12]

That these kinds of inscription are connected to Iraq, and perhaps Baghdad in particular, is supported by two textiles with comparable inscriptions, embroidered in blue silk on a cotton base fabric in Madinat al-Salam (Baghdad) during the reign of al-Muqtadir (Related works 1, and cat. no. 98). That these textiles had afterlives beyond burial is documented by the two cotton fragments embroidered in a similar style of script that were once inserted into an Ottonian psalter from the treasury of the Goldene Tafel ('golden panel'), once held at the Benedictine abbey of Sankt Michaelis in Lüneburg[13] (see chapter 2, p. 72, fig. 2.11). It is interesting to note that several examples in this style of script have survived that were embroidered on *mulham* (see cat. no. 105), which was a key product of Khurasan. The style of inscriptions from Khurasan, notably Merw, was, however, quite distinct from those represented by the present piece and those discussed below – less flowing and more angular. Is it possible that fabrics produced in Khurasan were later embroidered in the Abbasid capital Baghdad?

Cat. 96 *TIRAZ* FRAGMENT FROM
THE REIGN OF THE ABBASID
CALIPH AL-MUQTADIR
**Baghdad, Iraq, 308 AH
/ 920–21 CE**

Description: Fragment (two pieces) of undyed
glazed cotton, with one line of
Kufic inscription embroidered in
dark brown silk chain stitch.

Materials: cotton and silk: plain weave
and embroidery

Dimensions: piece (a) (right): h. 14.6 cm,
w. 11.2 cm; max. letter height 1.4 cm
piece (b) (left): h. 18 cm, w. 28.1 cm;
max. letter height 1.4 cm

Ground fabric: cotton (undyed), balanced plain
weave, glazed and polished, close
texture (*dabiqi*); medium quality
(3)

Thread count: warp 20 Z-spun, weft 20 Z-spun

Thread thickness: warp 0.15–0.5 mm slight twist,
weft 0.15–0.5 mm slight twist

Embroidery: silk, dyed (dark brown), chain
stitch

Provenance: Ex H.P. Kraus collection, nos 22
(piece (a)), 23 (piece (b))

Inv. no. LNS 149 T a, b

Related works: See page 509

Inscription:

Piece (a) (right):

[...] جعفر الإمام المقتدر بالله امـ [يراالمؤمنين] [...]

[...] Ja'far al-Imam al-Muqtadir bi-Allah the Com[mander of the Faithful] [...]

Piece (b) (left):

[...] [طرا]ز الخـ[اصة في] مدينة [السلا]م علي يـ[دي] [...] مولي أمير المؤمنين عزه الله سنة ثمان ثلث مائة

[...] [tira]z al-kh[assa in] Madinat al-Salam under the dire[ction] [...] of the client of the Commander of the Faithful, may God bless him. In the year three hundred and eight

This piece can be compared with two textiles that were produced in the *tiraz al-khassa* in Baghdad (Related works 1, 2). They are part of a larger group characterized by a specific style of Kufic embroidered in chain stitch, mostly in dark brown but also in red and blue (Related works 3–5). This style is related to the so-called 'New Style' of Abbasid scripts which was developed from the styles used in Abbasid administration and was then adopted in copying the Quran from the end of the ninth century onwards.[14] The new style is characterized by a more cursive approach to the line of script and the juxtaposition of rounded and angular letterforms, often of varying height and with pointed terminals. The latter characteristic is particularly visible in the *tiraz* textiles of the present group, where such letters as the rounded *mim* and terminal triangular *ha* appear. Another important feature is the stepped appearance of *alif* and *lam* as in 'Allah', with the joint between the second *lam* and the terminal *ha* extending below the baseline. That these inscriptions were copied in Egypt is evident from two examples in the same epigraphic style, albeit of lesser craftsmanship, which were made in Tinnis at the beginning of the tenth century (Related works 6, 7).

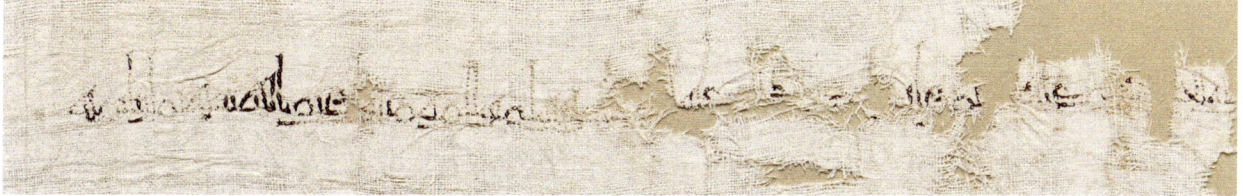

Cat. 97 *TIRAZ* FRAGMENT FROM
THE REIGN OF THE ABBASID
CALIPH AL-MUQTADIR
(r. 908–32)
Iraq, 320 AH / 932–33 CE

Description: Fragment (two pieces) of undyed
glazed cotton, with one line of
Kufic inscription (length *c*. 38.5 cm)
embroidered in red silk chain
stitch.

Materials: cotton and silk: plain weave
and embroidery

Dimensions: piece (a) (right): h. 19.4 cm,
w. 27.4 cm; max. letter height
2.9 cm
piece (b) (left): h. 10.5 cm,
w. 17.2 cm; max. letter height 2.9 cm

Ground fabric: cotton warp and weft, balanced
plain weave, dense texture (*dabiqi*),
regular structure; very good–good
quality (1–2)

Thread count: warp 26 Z-spun, weft 31 Z-spun

Thread thickness: warp 0.3–0.5 mm slight–medium
twist, weft 0.2–0.3 mm slight–
medium twist

Embroidery: silk, dyed (red), chain stitch

Provenance: art market, 1970s–1980s

Inv. no. LNS 30 T a, b

Related works: See page 509

Inscription:

بسم الله الرحمن الرحيم وما توفيقي الا بالله و عليه توكلت و هو رب العرش العظيم (...) يتوكل (...) جعفر بن المكتفي بالله سنة عشرين و ثلث مائة

In the name of God, the Most Merciful, the Most Compassionate. My success comes only through God. In him I put my trust. And he is the Lord of the mighty throne (...) trust (...) Ja'far the son of al-Muktafi bi-llah. In the year three hundred and twenty

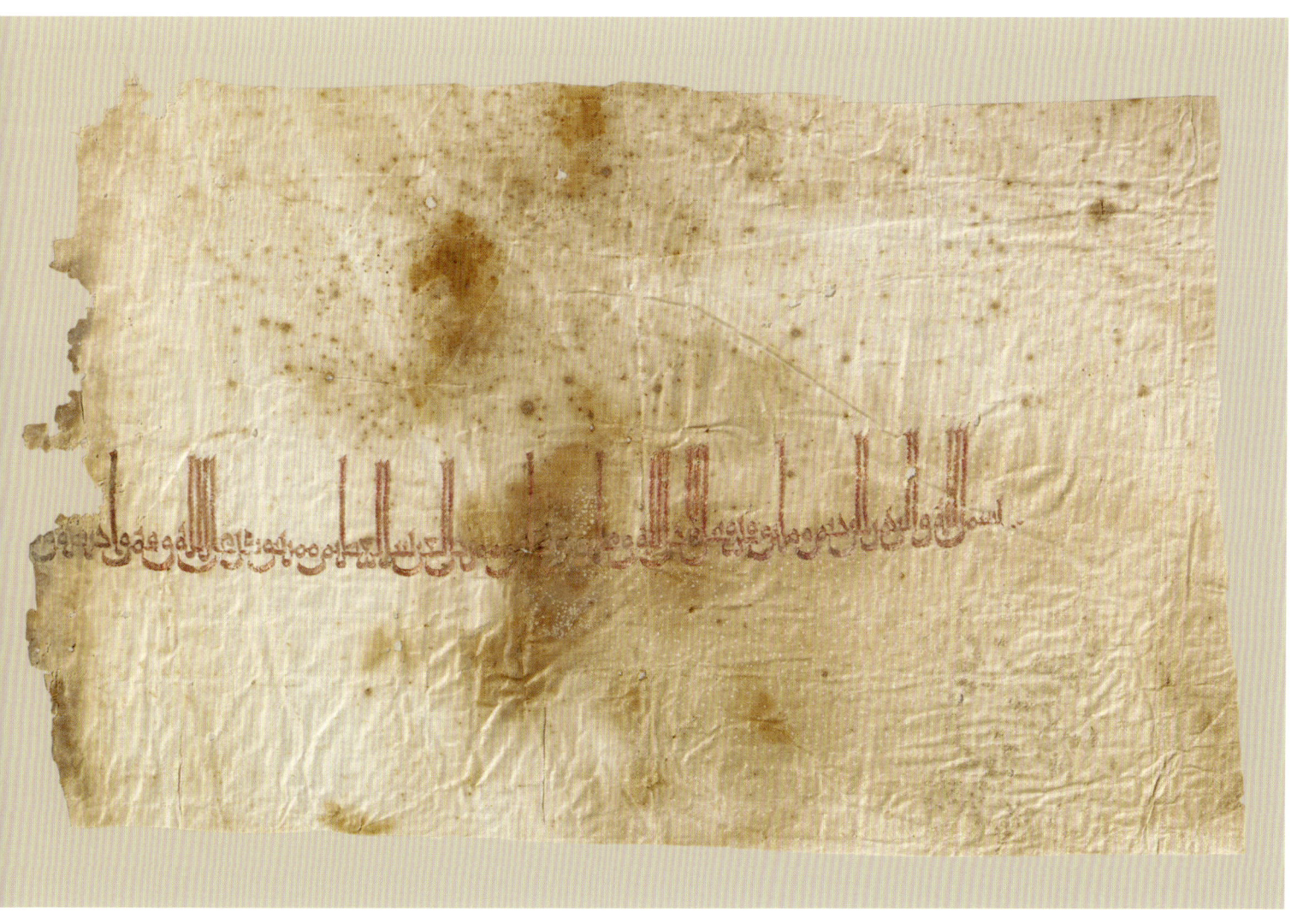

The inscription, which contains parts of Quran 9:129 (Surah at-Tawbah), and 11:88 (Surah Hud) (see also cat. nos 95, 100, 101, 102), states the year of manufacture as 320 AH / 932–33 CE, which was the last year of the reign of the Abbasid caliph al-Muqtadir (295–320 AH / 908–32 CE). It appears to mention al-Muqtadir's *ism* (given name), Ja'far, and a family relationship to the caliph al-Muktafi (r. 902–08) as 'ibn al-Muktafi bi-llah' ('Ja'far son of al-Muktafi bi-llah'). This is quite curious, as the caliph al-Muktafi preceded al-Muqtadir but was his half-brother, not his father. Al-Muqtadir's father was, in fact, Abu al-Abbas Ahmad ibn Talha al-Muwaffaq, known as al-Mu'tadid (r. 892–902), who was also the father of al-Muktafi. The fact that the name appears at the end of the inscription, where normally administrative information relating to the textile's manufacture would be found, is also curious. Several cotton textiles documenting the year 320 AH / 932–33 CE are known (Related works 1–4), two (Related works 3, 4) embroidered in Baghdad. Related works 1 and 4 are inscribed in the same style of script as the present piece.[15]

Cat. 98   *TIRAZ* FRAGMENT FROM
THE REIGN OF THE ABBASID
CALIPH AL-MUQTADIR
(r. 908–32)
Baghdad, Iraq, 908–32

Description: Fragment of undyed glazed cotton,
with one line of Kufic inscription
embroidered in dark blue silk chain
stitch.

Materials: cotton and silk: plain weave
and embroidery

Dimensions: h. 32.4 cm, w. 60.8 cm;
max. letter height 1.1 cm

Ground fabric: cotton warp and weft, undyed,
balanced plain weave, glazed and
polished, tight texture (*dabiqi*);
good quality (2)

Thread count: warp 20 Z-spun, weft 23 Z-spun

Thread thickness: warp 0.15–0.5 mm slight–medium
twist, weft 0.2–0.5 mm slight–
medium twist

Embroidery: silk, dyed (dark blue), chain stitch;
selvedge on the left side of the
inscription

Provenance: Ex H.P. Kraus collection, no. 21

Inv. no. LNS 148 T

Related works: See page 509

Inscription:

بسم الله الرحمن الرحيم الحمد لله رب العلمين والعاقبة للمتقين وصلالله على محمد النبي خاتم النبيين و علي آله اجمعين الطيبين الاخيار بركة من الله (... و علي ...) لالخليفة جعفر الامام المقتدر بالله امير المؤمنين صلي لله و (...) بعمله في طر(از) الخاصة بمدينة السلام سنة (...) و ثلث مائة

In the name of God, the Most Merciful, the Most Compassionate. Praise be to God the Lord of the worlds, and the ultimate outcome belongs to the righteous. And God's blessings be upon Muhammad the Seal of the Prophets and upon his family, the good, the excellent. Blessing from God (… and upon …) the caliph Ja'far al-Imam al-Muqtadir bi-llah the Commander of the Faithful. God's blessings upon and (…) its making in *tir(az) al-khassa* in Madinat al-Salam in the year (…) and three hundred

This textile is important as it mentions the *tiraz al-khassa* in the Abbasid capital Baghdad (Madinat al-Salam). It can be related to a textile at the Royal Ontario Museum, Toronto, which was also produced in Baghdad, in the year 300 AH / 912–13 CE (Related works 1), and another in the Boston Museum of Fine Arts (Related works 2). While a large number of surviving examples comprise a larger letter type than is seen here, often between 2.0 and 3.0 cm, the small size of script is also found in other extant pieces, where the inscriptions are between 0.4 and 1.4 cm in height. One in the Biblioteca Apostolica Vaticana (Related works 3), from the reign of al-Qadir (r. 991–1031), was made in the *tiraz al-khassa* in Madinat al-Salam, like the present piece. It is also striking that both inscriptions use almost the same religious formulas. It is interesting to note the difference in calligraphic style between the present piece and cat. no. 96 given that both were produced at the *tiraz al-khassa* in Baghdad at roughly the same time.

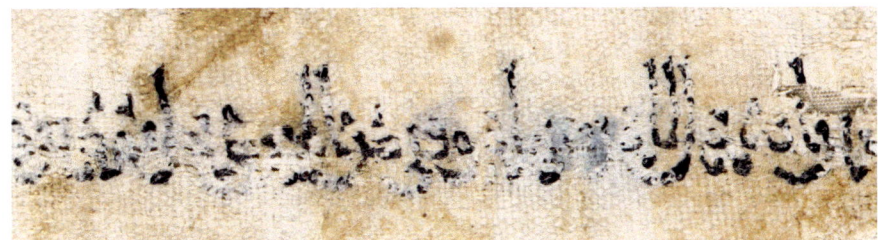

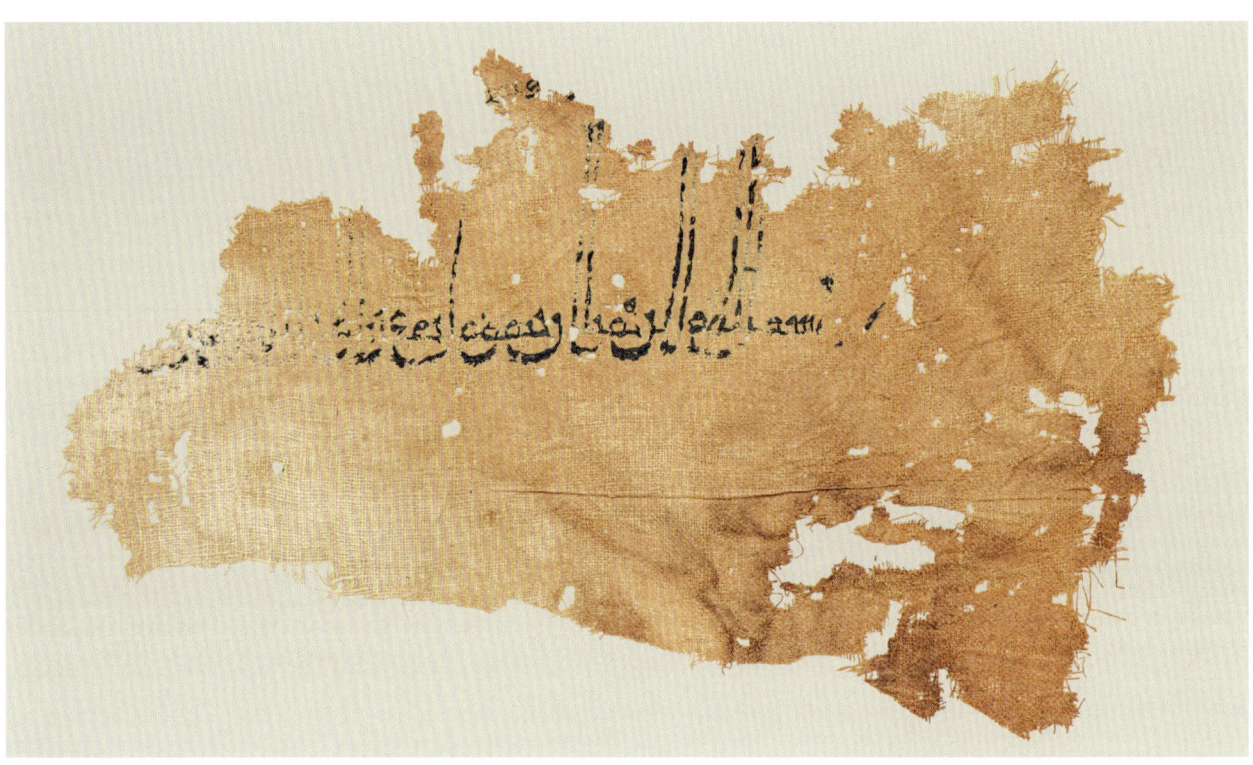

Cat. 99 *TIRAZ* FRAGMENT FROM
THE ABBASID DYNASTY
**Iraq, first half of the
10th century CE**

Description: Fragment of undyed glazed cotton,
with one main line of Kufic
inscription embroidered in blue
silk chain stitch, and a second
accompanying line above the
latter's hastae (*c.* 0.4 cm).

Materials: cotton and silk: plain weave
and embroidery

Dimensions: h. 8.0 cm, w. 16.3 cm;
max. letter height 4.3 cm

Ground fabric: cotton (undyed), predominant-weft
plain weave, glazed, tight texture;
good–medium quality (2–3)

Thread count: warp 20 Z-spun, weft 21 Z-spun

Thread thickness: warp 0.3–0.5 mm medium twist,
weft 0.3–0.5 mm medium twist

Embroidery: silk, dyed (dark blue), chain stitch

Provenance: Ex H.P. Kraus collection, no. 20

Inv. no. LNS 147 T

Inscription:

بسم الله الرحمن الرحيم و ما توفيقي الا بالله [...]

In the name of God, the Most Merciful, the Most Compassionate. And my
success comes only through God [...]

Cat. 100 *TIRAZ* FRAGMENT FROM
THE ABBASID DYNASTY
**Iraq, first half of the
10th century CE**

Description: Fragment of undyed glazed cotton,
with one line of Kufic inscription
embroidered in blue silk.

Materials: cotton and silk: plain weave
and embroidery

Dimensions: h. 29.3 cm, w. 24.8 cm;
max. letter height 2.8 cm

Ground fabric: cotton (undyed), predominant-weft
plain weave, glazed, close texture
(*dabiqi*); good quality (2)

Thread count: warp 22 Z-spun, weft 35 Z-spun

Thread thickness: warp 0.1–0.5 mm loose twist,
weft 0.1–0.4 mm loose twist

Embroidery: silk, dyed (dark blue), chain stitch

Provenance: Ex H.P. Kraus collection, no. 19

Inv. no. LNS 146 T

Inscription: [...] بسم الله و [sic] الرحمن الرحيم و ما توفيقي الا بالله و عليه توكلت و هو رب العرش العظيم

In the name of God and [*sic*] the Most Merciful, the Most Compassionate. My
success comes only through God and upon him I have relied and he is the Lord
of the Mighty Throne [...]

The text used here is Quranic, rather than historical. It is composed of
quotations from Quran 11:88 (Surah Hud), and 9:129 (Surah al-Tawbah).
Quotations from these Quranic verses can be found on a number of fragments
of the same type (see also cat. nos 95, 97, 101, 102).

Cat. 101 *TIRAZ* FRAGMENT FROM THE ABBASID DYNASTY
Iraq, first half of the 10th century CE

Description: Fragment (two pieces) of undyed glazed cotton, with one line of Kufic inscription embroidered in dark blue silk.

Materials: cotton and silk: plain weave and embroidery

Dimensions: piece (a): h. 17.8 cm, w. 17.7 cm; max. letter height 3.3 cm
piece (b): h. 16.2 cm, w. 24.3 cm; max. letter height 3.8 cm

Ground fabric: both pieces: cotton (undyed), balanced plain weave, glazed and polished, close texture; good–medium quality (2–3)

Thread count: piece (a): warp 23 Z-spun, weft 21 Z-spun
piece (b): warp 24 Z-spun, weft 24 Z-spun

Thread thickness: piece (a): warp 0.15–0.4 mm loose–medium twist, weft 0.2–0.5 mm loose–medium twist
piece (b): warp 0.15–0.4 mm loose–medium twist, weft 0.3 mm loose–medium twist

Embroidery: both pieces: silk (traces), dyed (dark blue), chain stitch

Provenance: Ex H.P. Kraus collection, nos 17 (piece (a)), 18 (piece (b))

Inv. no. LNS 145 T a, b

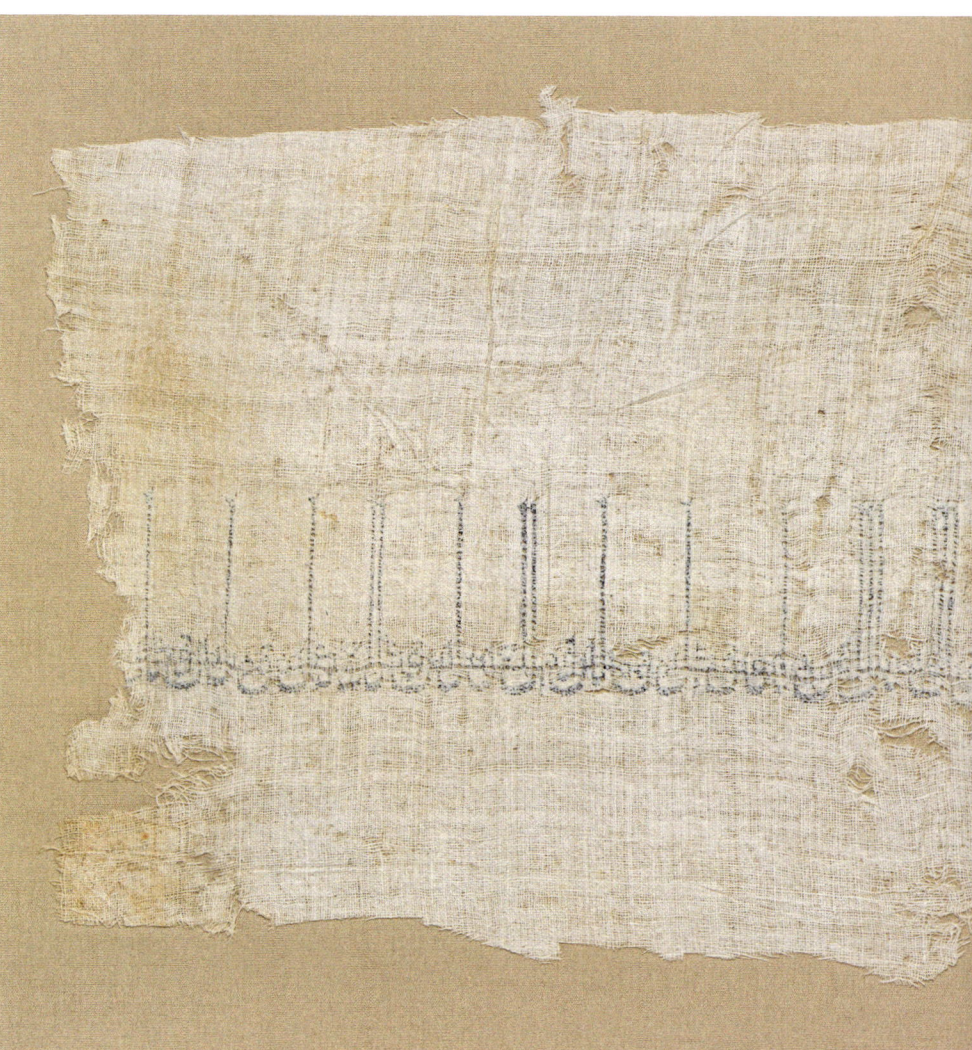

Inscription:

Piece (a) (left):

[بسم الـ[ـله (و!) الرحمن الرحيم و ما توفيقي الا بالله وعليه توكلت وهو رب العرش العظيم ومن توكل [...]

[In the name of G]od (and!) the Most Merciful, the Most Compassionate. My success comes only through God and upon him I have relied and He is the Lord of the Mighty Throne, and whoever relies upon [...]

Piece (b) (right):   بسم الله (و!) الرحمن الرحيم و ما توفيقي الا بالله وعليه توكلت [...]

In the name of God (and!) the Most Merciful, the Most Compassionate. My success comes only through God and upon him I have relied [...]

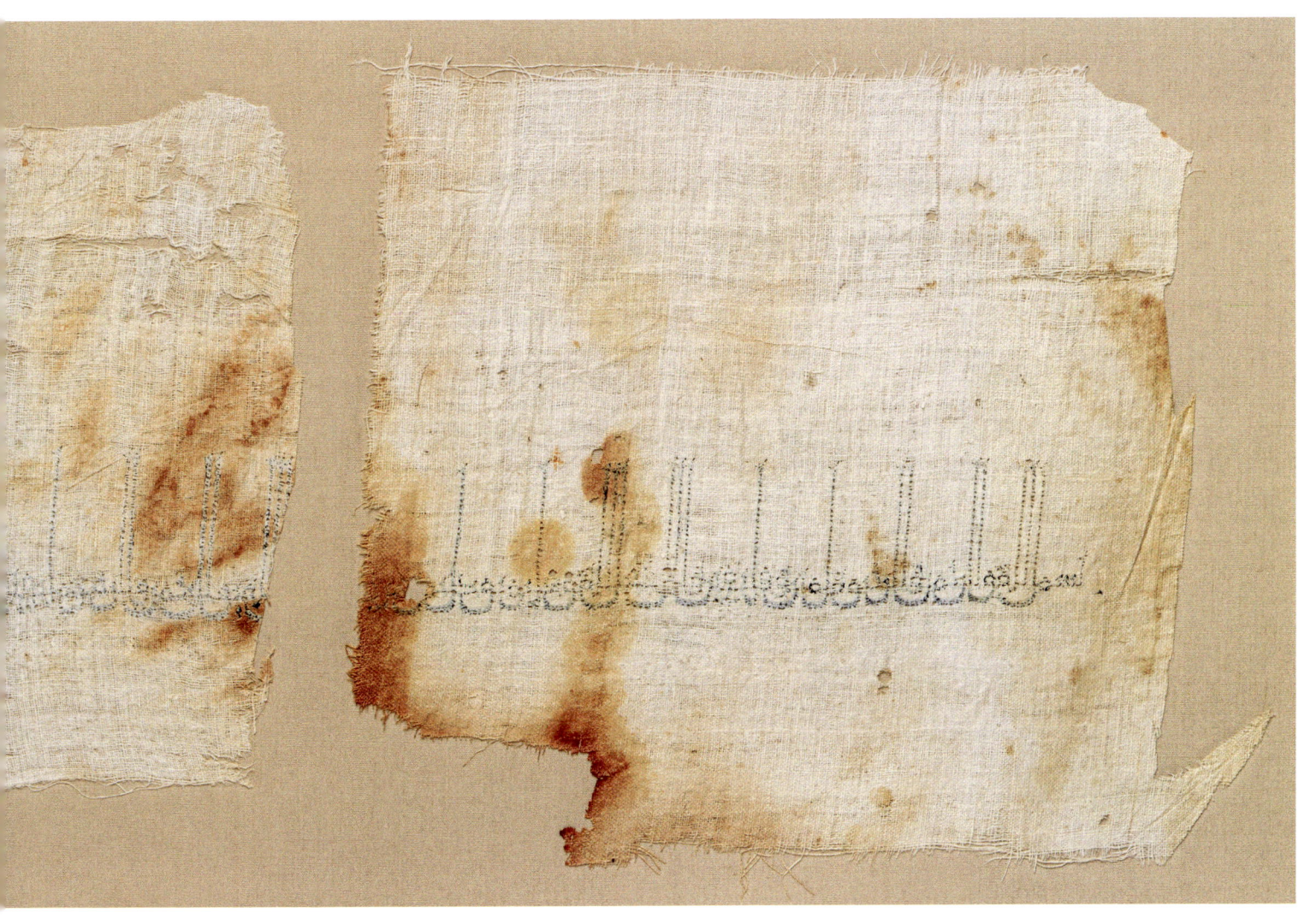

The inscriptions here contain parts of Quran 9:129 (Surah at-Tawbah) and 11:88 (Surah Hud) (see also cat. nos 95, 97, 100, 102). Although both fragments are extremely closely related in terms of material texture, epigraphic style and execution of the inscription, they must be from different textiles, as they differ slightly in the density of stitches and most obviously in the size of the inscription. The fabric of piece (a) is also marginally finer than that of piece (b).

Cat. 102   *TIRAZ* FRAGMENT FROM
THE ABBASID DYNASTY
**Iraq, first half of the
10th century CE**

Description: Fragment of undyed glazed cotton
ground fabric with a single line of
Kufic inscription embroidered in
dark blue silk, and with a selvedge
on the right side of the inscription.

Materials: cotton and silk: plain weave
and embroidery

Dimensions: h. 52 cm, w. 27.6 cm;
max. letter height 3.4 cm

Ground fabric: cotton, undyed, predominant-warp
plain weave, glazed, dense texture;
good quality (2); selvedge on the
right side of the inscription

Thread count: warp 24 Z-spun, weft 22 Z-spun

Thread thickness: warp 0.15–0.5 mm slight twist,
weft 0.1–0.4 mm slight twist

Embroidery: silk, dyed (dark blue), chain stitch

Provenance: Ex H.P. Kraus collection, no. 16

Inv. no. LNS 144 T

Inscription:

بسم الله الرحمن الرحيم و ما توفيقي الا بالله وعليه توكلت و هو رب العرش العظيم و من توكل على الله [...]

In the name of God, the Most Merciful, the Most Compassionate. My success
comes only through God, upon Him I have relied and He is the Lord of the
Mighty Throne. And whoever relies upon God [...]

The inscriptions here contain parts of Quran 9:129 (Surah at-Tawbah) and 11:88
(Surah Hud) (see also cat. nos 95, 97, 100, 101).

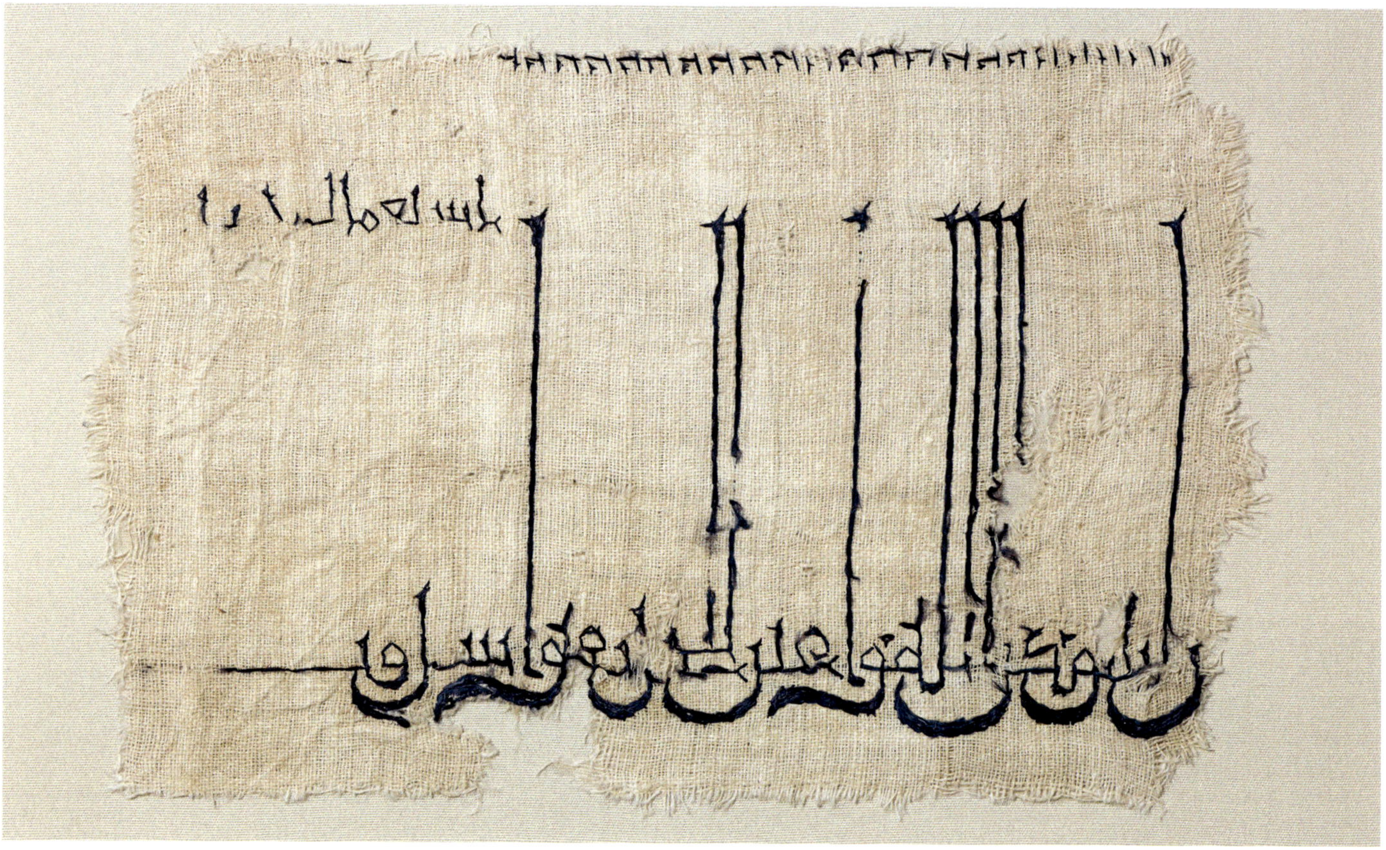

Cat. 103 **_TIRAZ_ FRAGMENT FROM THE ABBASID DYNASTY**
Iraq, 10th century CE

Description: Fragment of undyed cotton, roughly rectangular, with two lines of Kufic inscription embroidered in dark blue silk: the larger text has elongated upper letter stems and festoon-like lower terminals; the smaller text begins on the upper line formed by the letter terminals, to the left. An embroidered line on the upper edge may have been part of another text.

Materials: cotton and silk: plain weave and embroidery

Dimensions: h. 12.8 cm, w. 19.5 cm; max. letter height 8.6 cm

Ground fabric: cotton warp and weft, undyed, balanced plain weave, dense texture (_dabiqi_); good–medium quality (2–3)

Thread count: warp 18 Z-spun, weft 22 Z-spun

Thread thickness: warp 0.2–0.5 mm slight–medium twist, weft 0.15–0.4 mm medium twist

Embroidery: silk, dyed (dark blue), chain stitch

Provenance: Ex H.P. Kraus collection, no. 106

Inv. no. LNS 219 T

Inscription:

Line 1:

(... ? ...) (victory?) God (... ? ...) ... ?

(... ؟ ...) (نصر؟) الله (... ؟ ...)

Line 2:

That of which use is made

استعمال منه

Cat. 104 *TIRAZ* FRAGMENT FROM
THE ABBASID DYNASTY
Iraq, 10th to 11th century CE

Description: Fragment of undyed glazed
cotton with a single line of Kufic
inscription embroidered in dark
blue silk, with elongated upper
letter stems and festoon-like
lower terminals.

Materials: cotton and silk: plain weave
and embroidery

Dimensions: h. 13.5 cm, w. 18.5 cm;
max. letter height 3.1 cm

Ground fabric: cotton warp and weft, undyed,
balanced plain weave, glazed and
polished, close texture (*dabiqi*);
medium quality (3)

Thread count: warp 19 Z-spun, weft 15 Z-spun

Thread thickness: warp 0.25–0.5 mm slight–medium
twist, weft 0.3–0.4 mm slight–
medium twist

Embroidery: silk, dyed (dark blue), chain stitch

Provenance: Ex H.P. Kraus collection, no. 107

Inv. no. LNS 220 T

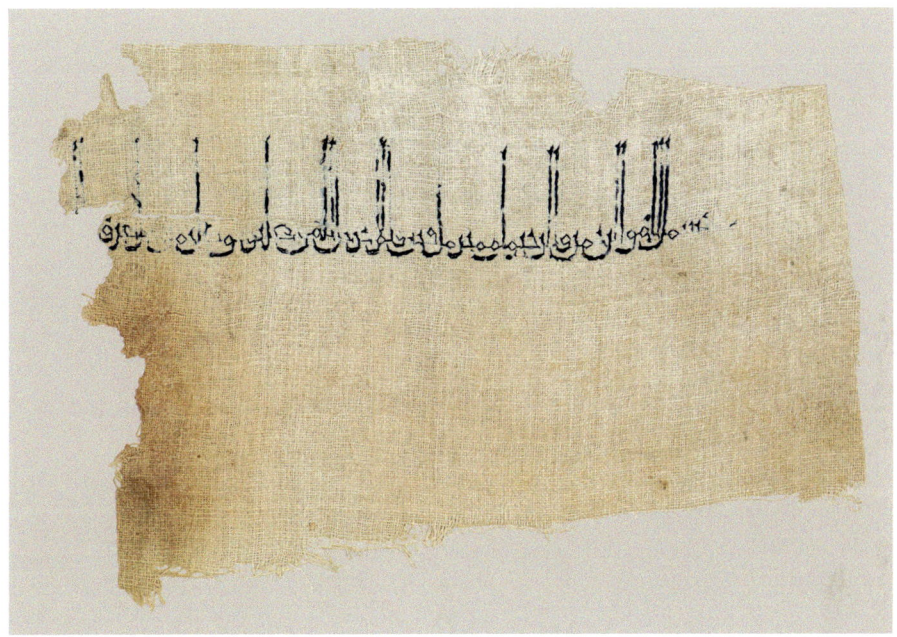

Inscription:

بسم الله الرحمن الرحيم (... ؟ ...)

In the name of God, the Most Merciful, the Most Compassionate (… ? …)

Cat. 105   *TIRAZ* **FRAGMENT FROM THE ABBASID DYNASTY**
Iraq, 10th century CE

Description: Fragment of undyed *mulham*, with one line of Kufic inscription embroidered in blue silk chain stitch.

Materials: cotton and silk: plain weave and embroidery

Dimensions: h. 2.9 cm, w. 14.7 cm; max. letter height 1.7 cm

Ground fabric: *mulham* (silk warp, cotton weft), undyed, warp-faced plain weave, tight texture; very good quality (1)

Thread count: warp 66 Z-spun, weft 30 Z-spun

Thread thickness: warp 0.05 mm loose–medium twist, weft 0.3 mm loose–medium twist

Embroidery: silk, dyed (blue), chain stitch

Provenance: Ex H.P. Kraus collection, no. 15

Inv. no. LNS 143 T

Related works: See page 509

Inscription:

[بسم ال]ـله الرحـمن الرحيم الحـمد لله رب العلمين والعـاقبة للمتقين و صلى الله ا (!) على محمد (؟) الله و خـا[تـ]ام النبي(ـين)ن
وا (!) عـ[ـلي] [...]

[In the name of Go]d the Most Merciful, the Most Compassionate. Praise be to God the Lord of the worlds, and the ultimate outcome belongs to the righteous, and God's blessings *alif* [*sic*] upon Muhammad(?) God, and the S[ea]l of the Proph[et]s and ⟨*alif*⟩ [*sic*] u[pon] [...]

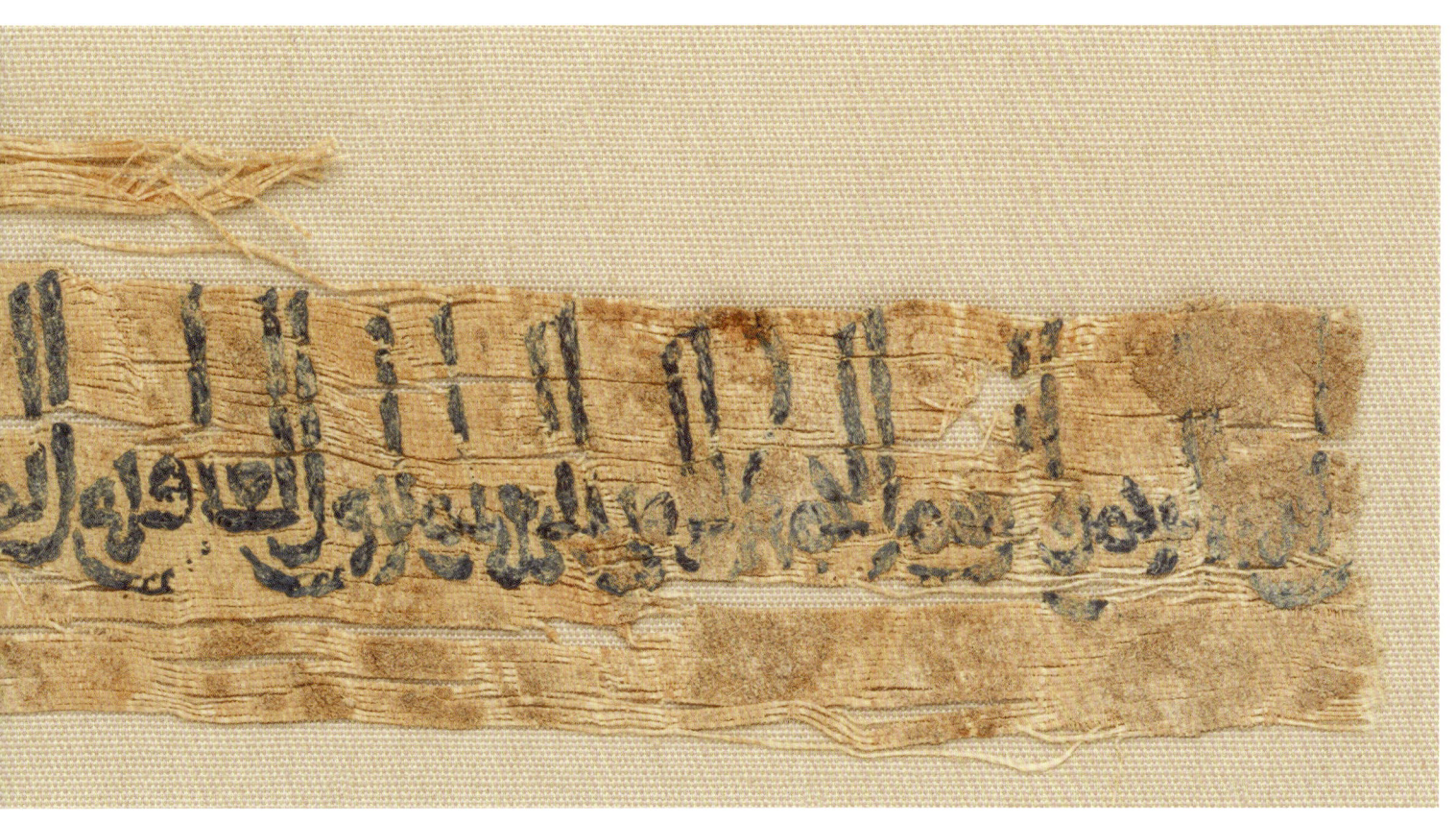

This fragment belongs to a small group of *tiraz* textiles which were all executed in blue silk chain stitch embroidery on *mulham* and which share the same style of epigraphy with the inscriptions on cotton base fabrics discussed above (see cat. nos 95–104). The inscriptions are characterized by an emphasis on calligraphic qualities, the varying thickness of hastae and elegantly curved lower terminals, the rhythm of hastae and balanced proportions of individual letters. The chronological range of these textiles spans the latter part of the reign of the Abbasid caliph al-Muqtadir (r. 908–32) (Related works 1–2), the reign of al-Radi (r. 934–40) (Related works 3), and up to the first half of al-Qadir's reign (r. 991–1031) (Related works 4–5.) The shroud dated 320 AH / 932–33 CE found in a burial at Istabl 'Antar (see chapter 2, pp. 77–78) also relates to the present piece in terms of epigraphic style and the *mulham* base fabric (see fig. 2.16). It is not entirely clear where the *mulham* fabrics mentioned here were produced. Of about twenty *mulham* textiles with historical *tiraz* inscriptions, four are known to have been produced in Merw,[16] one in Nishapur.[17] It is also known from literary sources that Merw was an important centre for the production of *mulham* (see chapter 3). On the other hand, it seems that the epigraphic style of inscriptions produced in Merw differed from that used in Baghdad – it was bolder, more angular and less fluid. Given the close political and economic links between the capital Baghdad and the province of Khurasan, it is possible that *mulham*s were produced also in Baghdad, or at least imported from Khurasan and then inscribed in Baghdad.

Cat. 106 *TIRAZ* FRAGMENT FROM
THE ABBASID DYNASTY
Iraq or Egypt, 10th century CE

Description: Fragment of undyed cotton, with
a Kufic inscription in black ink
(applied with a pen) consisting
of a benedictory phrase.

Materials: cotton: plain weave; ink
(inscription)

Dimensions: h. 10.2 cm, 18.3 w. cm;
max. letter height 4.9 cm

Ground fabric: cotton warp and weft, undyed,
balanced plain weave, dense
texture (*dabiqi*); medium quality
(3)

Thread count: warp 15 S-spun, weft 12 Z-spun

Thread thickness: warp 0.2–0.6 mm medium twist,
weft 0.15–0.6 mm medium twist

Provenance: Ex H.P. Kraus collection, no. 24

Published: Curatola et al. 2010, no. 151.

Inv. no. LNS 61 T

Related works: See page 509

Inscription:

بركة من الله وغبطة و نصر من الله و غبطة [...] [...]

[…] blessing from God and beatitude and help from God and beatitude […]

The epigraphic style seen here, characterized by its rhythmic arrangement of
letter stems with small wedge-shaped terminals, and the festoon-like sequence
of letter terminals below the baseline, is indicative of a date in the tenth to
eleventh century, when it can be found in silk-embroidered *tiraz* textiles from
Iraq, as two examples in the Biblioteca Apostolica Vaticana (Related works 1,
2) and the embroidered textiles discussed in this section show. Two textiles
with ink inscriptions that equal the present piece in their elegance and aesthetic
precision are in the Bouvier Collection (Related works 3, 4). Two ink-inscribed
pieces in the Textile Museum, Washington, DC, one cotton, the other linen,
comprise a style of inscription with similar festoon-like lower letter terminals,
but bending swan-neck upper letter terminals, a feature the present piece does
not exhibit (Related works 5, 6); yet one is on a cotton base fabric (Related
works 5), and the other a linen one (Related works 6). Kühnel suggested
an Egyptian origin for the latter piece.[18] Closely related are also three linen
fragments with ink inscriptions in the Metropolitan Museum of Art, New York,
which are closer in style to the present piece than the previously discussed items,
in that they lack the bending of upper letter stems (Related works 7–9). Given
their linen base fabric, it is likely that they are of Egyptian production.

The fact that the group largely shares the epigraphic style of the inscriptions,
but not the material on which they are executed, complicates an attribution of
pieces to a particular location. The present piece is executed on cotton, and its
inscription relates to styles used in Iraq, particularly Baghdad. As already seen
with the cotton and *mulham* textiles discussed above (see cat. nos 95, 97, 98
and 105), there seems to have been a certain overlap caused by the sharing of
materials or copying of epigraphic styles beyond geographic regions.

It is usually believed that inscriptions written in pen and ink copy
embroidered inscriptions. It is, however, worth considering that the aesthetic of
these inscriptions originates in the art of calligraphy, rather than textile craft,
and that they would have been executed with a reed pen by a calligrapher,
given the extraordinary quality of some of the surviving pieces. Embroidered
inscriptions in turn must have been the product of a multi-stage process: they
would have been designed by a calligrapher, then executed by an embroiderer,
who was a craftsman but made no creative input. He must have received texts
written out by a calligrapher, presumably on paper.

In order for textiles to be inscribed, the fabric would have to be treated in
advance to produce a surface slippery enough for a reed pen to produce crisp
text in ink that stayed on the surface for drying, rather than being absorbed by
the fibres and running into the fabric. The approach would have been similar to

that of writing on paper, as that, too, is made from plant fibre. In comparison with linen, cotton is far easier to prepare owing to the physical nature of its fibres, which are short, soft and absorbent. The very best papers were also made from cotton fibres. It was often treated with substances or glazes that allowed the fabric to be pressed, or burnished like paper, in order to produce a slippery and sometimes shiny surface, ready for the chain stitch embroidery used in Iraq and Khurasan. The same approach would have worked for inscriptions written with a reed pen in ink.

5

KHURASAN

In pre-Islamic and early Islamic times, the province of Khurasan covered a much larger geographical area than it does today in eastern Iran. It incorporated areas of central Asia and also Afghanistan, including Badakhshan and Tokharistan on the upper Oxus river and Bamiyan in the Hindu Kush (see map, pp. 12–13).[1] Khurasan was the region through which Alexander the Great entered the northern Indian subcontinent. It continued to serve as a gateway for the conquests of Mahmud of Ghazna, the Ghurid sultans, Timur and later the Mughals. Already during Sasanian times, Khurasan was an administrative unit, a satrapy, governed from its capital at Merw. In 653 Merw was conquered by Arab armies led by companions of the Prophet during the early wave of Islamic conquests. Unrest in Khurasan between the Arab minority and non-Arabs continued throughout the Umayyad period and culminated in Khurasani support to bring the Abbasid caliphate to power in 750. Under Abbasid control, Khurasan was central to the caliphate's economy, but also as a supplier of soldiers and administrators for matters of state. For example, members of the Khurasani family of the Barmakids, who had been in public office in Balkh as high priests and administrators during Sasanian times, moved to Basra in the late eighth century, where they converted to Islam, and from where they rose in the ranks of the Abbasid administration through their close association with caliphs such as al-Saffah (r. 749–54), al-Mansur (r. 754–75), al-Mahdi (r. 775–85) and Harun al-Rashid (r. 786–809).[2] The involvement of members of the caliphal court in Khurasan and the presence of the *tiraz* system early in the Abbasid caliphate is documented in the *Kitab al-aghani* ('Book of songs') of Abu al-Faraj al-Isfahani, who records that a certain Mu'alla ibn Tarif, a slave given by al-Mansur to al-Mahdi, who freed him, administered the *tiraz* and the *barid* (postal service) of Khurasan, before he became governor of Ahwaz.[3]

How closely the Abbasid caliphate was entwined with the *tiraz* system in Khurasan is documented by several *tiraz* textile inscriptions. The political and administrative influence in Khurasan of the de facto regent of the Abbasid caliphate, Abu Ahmad Talha ibn Ja'far al-Muwaffaq, who managed affairs of state for most of the reign of his brother al-Mu'tamid (r. 870–92), is documented by two inscriptions dating from 260 AH / 874–75 CE[4] (see fig. 2.6) and 277 AH / 890–91 CE,[5] both produced in Merw, the former in its *tiraz al-khassa*. In both, the text records that al-Muwaffaq issued the order himself. A textile inscription from 278 AH / 891–92 CE records an order in the *tiraz al-khassa* at Merw by al-Muwaffaq's son and successor as viceroy of Khurasan, al-Mu'tadid who in 279 AH / 892–93 CE became Abbasid caliph.[6] That Merw was a centre for the production of *tiraz* textiles is reflected by several other inscriptions: two from al-Mu'tadid's reign (r. 892–902), one in the Benaki Museum in Athens (dated 286 AH / 899–900 CE),[7] the other at the Museum für Islamische Kunst in Berlin (dated 287 AH / 900–01 CE);[8] three from al-Muktafi's reign (r. 902–08), one in the Museum of Islamic Art, Cairo (dated 293 AH / 906–07 CE),[9] one at Cairo University[10] and one at the Textile Museum, Washington, DC;[11] and one from al-Muqtadir's reign (r. 908–32) in the Museum für Islamische Kunst.[12] Some of these textiles comprise cotton base fabrics, some a mix of cotton and silk, called *mulham* in the historical primary sources.

That Merw was closely connected with the production of *mulham* is stated by al-Tha'alibi (961–1038):

The Arabs used to call every close woven garment brought from Khurasan 'Marawi' and every fine garment exported from it 'Shahidjani', because Merv in their eyes was the chief city of Khurasan and was called Marv Shahidjani. The name Shahidjani has persisted for the fine robes to this day. The particular article for which Merv is noted is the *mulham* cloth. One day Abu al-Fath al-Busti al-Katib said to me: 'Do you know a town, the first letter of which is a *mim*, whence four things are brought by way of gifts, the name of each beginning with a *mim*?' I replied, 'If you ask me to say offhand, I do not know, but I could think it over, and perhaps I might discover it.'

He answered: 'It is Merv, whence come *mulham*, pastry (*mulabban*), cake (*murri*) and brooms (*makanis*).[13]

Ibn al-Faqih's *Kitab al-buldan* ('Book of the countries', tenth century) states that the *mulham* cloths of Merw were the finest of their kind.[14] *Mulham* stuffs were also highly esteemed beyond the Islamic world, as attested by Ibn Rusta (active in the tenth century), who describes a procession of the Byzantine emperor in the Hagia Sophia in Constantinople in which 5,000 eunuchs were dressed in white *mulham* stuffs from Khurasan.[15] The luxuriousness and outstanding quality of *mulham* cloth is shown by two fragments in the Textile Museum in Washington, DC (figs I.5.A, I.5.B), which have elegant inscriptions in blue and red silk, the first of which possbily states its

manufacture in Merw. It has been suggested that, from Merw, the making of *mulham* spread to other parts of the Abbasid empire, particularly Iran and Iraq.[16] A *mulham* fabric from Iraq is discussed in the Iraq section of this catalogue (cat. no. 105, pp. 318–19). *Mulham*s were also produced in another important textile centre in Khurasan, namely Nishapur.[17]

Al-Muqaddasi seems to be the first author to mention Nishapur as a *tiraz* production centre. He proclaims: 'There is no equal to the brocade (*diwadj*), tiraz, clay (tin), Shahidjani (stuff), needles, knives, and white currants (*ribas*) of Nishapur.'[18] He also records that:

There are brought from Nishapur white *haffi* garments, and the *baibaf*, the *haffi* Shahidjani turbans ('*imama*), *rakhtandj* and *takhtandj*,

I.5.A   Fragment of a *tiraz* textile from the reign of al-Muktafi (r. 902–08), Merw(?), Khurasan. Cotton, with silk embroidery, 7 × 37 cm. Textile Museum, Washington, DC, acquired from Detroit Institute of Art, 1951, inv. no. 73.657.

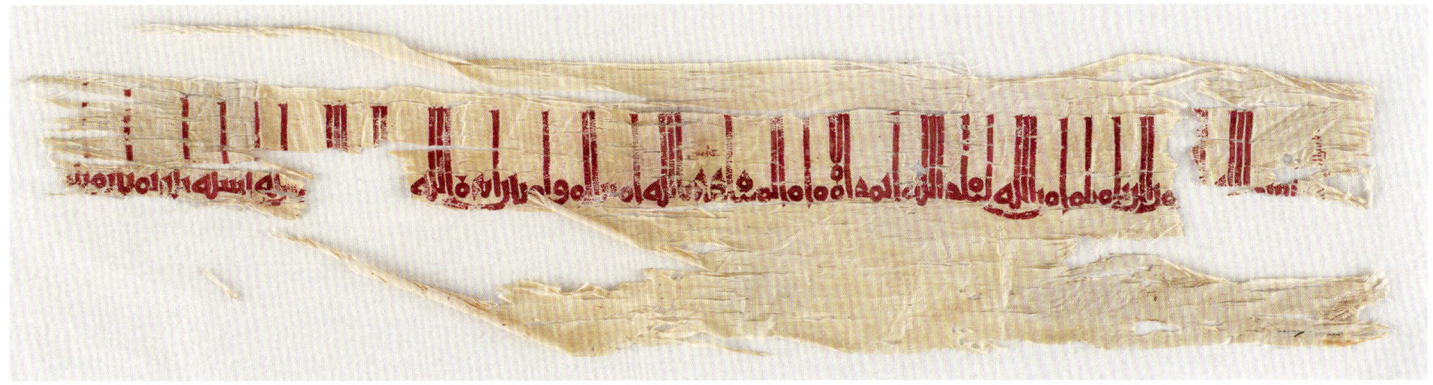

I.5.B   Fragment of a *tiraz* textile from the reign of the Abbasid caliph al-Mu'tadid (r. 892–902), Khurasan, dated 283 AH / 896–97 CE. Cotton, with silk embroidery, 14.8 × 66 cm. Textile Museum, Washington, DC, acquired by George Hewitt Myers, 1934, inv. no. 73.366.

I.5.C   Fragment of a *tiraz* textile from the reign of the Abbasid caliph al-Muʿtamid (r. 870–92), Nishapur, dated 266 AH / 880–81 CE. Silk (plain weave), with silk embroidery, 15.9 × 30.5 cm. Metropolitan Museum of Art, New York, Gift of George D. Pratt, 1931, inv. no. 31.106.27.

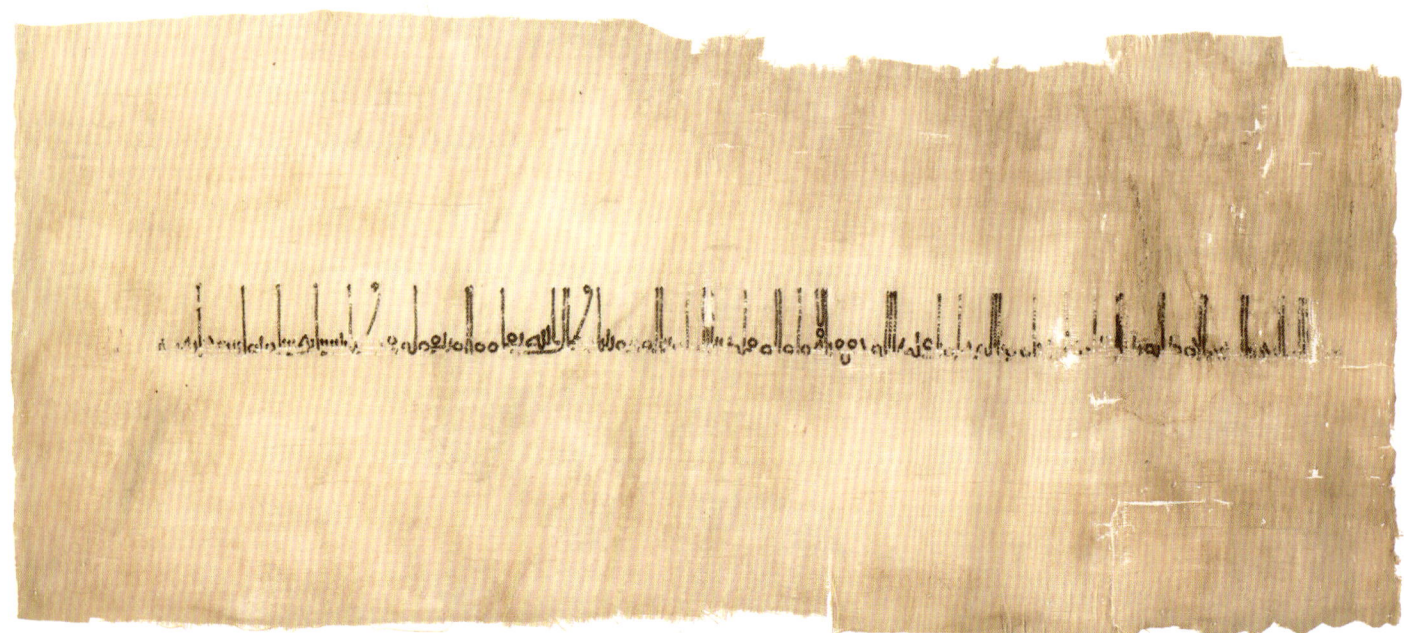

I.5.D   Fragment of a *tiraz* textile from the reign of the Abbasid caliph al-Muqtadir (r. 908–32), Nishapur(?), dated 298 AH / 910–11 CE. Cotton, with silk embroidery, 20 × 43.3 cm. Textile Museum, Washington, DC, Acquired by George Hewitt Myers, 1951, inv. no. 73.674.

veils called 'between garments' and the *mulham* stuff (with a double warp) with *kazz* silk, the cloth of one color (*musmat*), 'Attabi, Sa'idi, *zara'ifi*, *mushti*, striped cloaks (*hulla*), and garments of goat hair (*thiyab al-sha'r*) as well as expensive thread (*ghazl*) … From the districts of Nishapur come many coarse cloths.[19]

Another account, by al-Istakhri, mentions that: 'In Khurasan are the best stuffs of cotton and *ibrism* silk, which come from Nishapur and Merv, and the finest cloth (*bazz*) from Merv.'[20] In fact, a *tiraz* fragment at the Metropolitan Museum of Art, New York, attributed to Nishapur and dating from 266 AH / 880–81 CE during the reign of the caliph al-Mu'tamid (r. 870–92), comprises an inscription embroidered in red silk on a striped silk base fabric that records an order of his brother al-Muwaffaq (fig. I.5.C).[21] The fact that this fragment is striped correlates with the evidence about Nishapur given by al-Muqaddasi quoted above. The location mentioned in the inscription had traditionally been read as 'Bishapur' but, given the involvement of al-Muwaffaq in Khurasan, a reading of 'Nishapur' makes much more sense. Interestingly, another fragment that has been attributed to Bishapur based on a reading of the location by Kühnel may well also have been produced in Nishapur rather than

Bishapur (fig. I.5.D); its inscription, which is embroidered in dark brown silk on a cotton base fabric, relates very closely to those associated with Merw discussed earlier.[22]

Textiles from Khurasan, particularly Merw, were also much favoured at the Fatimid court, as an account in the *Sirat al-ustadh jawdhar* ('The life of the master Jawdhar') tells us.[23] One day Jawdhar, caliph al-Mu'izz's secretary, sent his master a letter asking him for a garment to use as his shroud. Honouring Jawdhar's request, al-Mu'izz sent outfits of the four caliphs under whom Jawdhar had been in service, including a robe of so-called Merwian (*marwi*) cloth from al-Mansur, and a lined garment of Merwian cloth with a tunic beneath it from al-Mu'izz himself. The Fatimid appreciation of Eastern textiles may also explain the use of an embroidered textile in the Museum of Islamic Art, Cairo, which may well be attributed to Khurasan on account of its inscription embroidered on *mulham* or silk in a style comparable with those of the Merwian textiles discussed above.[24] The textile (*c.* 85.0 × 62.0 cm) comprises a marriage contract in thirteen lines from the time of the Fatimid caliph al-Mustansir (r. 1036–94) written in blue ink in a cursive hand below the embroidered inscription.[25]

An important document for the history of textiles in Khurasan is the so-called 'Suaire de St Josse' in the Musée du Louvre in Paris (fig. I.5.E).[26] Woven in samite with seven colours of weft, the textile, probably a saddle

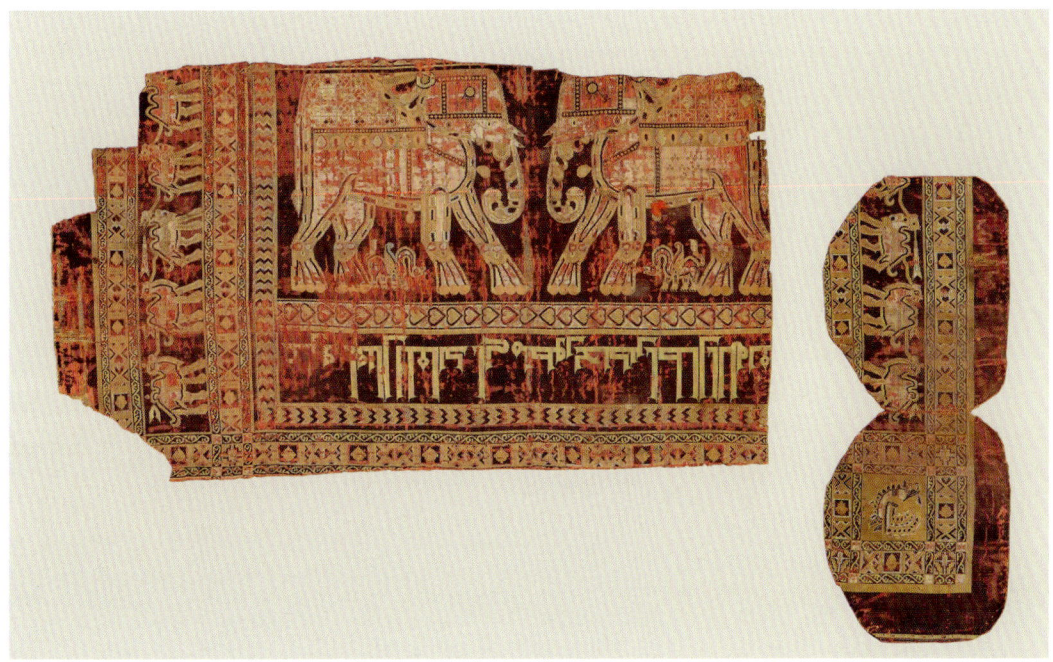

I.5.E   Suaire de St Josse, Khurasan or eastern Iran, before 961 CE, found as two pieces in the reliquary of St Josse, Saint-Josse-sur-Mer, France. Silk samite (weft-faced compound twill), 94 × 52 cm, 24.5 × 62 cm. Musée du Louvre, Paris, inv. no. OA7502.

cloth, which survives as two fragments, would once have been extraordinary to look at. It is not entirely clear what the exact layout of the different design elements was, but what has survived are two massive confronted elephants in a central field, above a band of inscription in monumental Kufic mentioning the name and title of a Turkish military general (*qa'id*) by the name of Abi Mansur Bugtekin.[27] The central field is contained by a frieze showing a procession of Bactrian camels, bordered by geometric bands, with square fields in the corners each with a bird figure. Abi Mansur Bugtekin served in Khurasan under the Samanid ruler 'Abd al-Malik ibn Nuh (r. 954–61), who had him executed in 961. The Suaire de St Josse was probably brought to France during or after the First Crusade (1096–99) by Stephen Henry, Count of Blois, a Norman who had married into the family of William the Conqueror.[28] It was his son Stephen (*c.* 1092–1154), later King of England, who donated the textile to the abbey, where during a ceremony held in his presence in 1134, it was placed in a sumptuous reliquary in which it was used to cover the remains of St Josse. How it reached the Levant and where Stephen Henry of Blois acquired the fabric is not clear. It could have been a diplomatic gift to either the Byzantine court of Constantinople or the Fatimid court of Cairo. The fact that it was such a magnificent textile ensured that it survived not only the journey from Khurasan, but also that from the Holy Land to France, where it was treasured as a wrap for the remains of a Christian saint.

Several inscribed *tiraz* textile fragments in The al-Sabah Collection shed light on the legacy of the *tiraz* system in the eastern Iranian world, particularly Khurasan and Transoxiana, in the mid- to late twelfth century (figs I.5.F–I). In the preceding 150 years (for much of the late tenth to the early twelfth centuries) the leadership of the caliphate in Baghdad had been threatened and challenged, first by the Shi'ite Buyids and then the Seljuq Turks (see chapter 1).

Seljuq domination of the caliphate saw the establishment of the sultanate as an office of political and military leadership, while the caliphate as an institution came to exercise only religious authority.[29] The Seljuq chieftain and military leader Tughril Beg (r. 1037–63), who conquered Baghdad in 1055 and ended Buyid domination over the caliphate, reduced the Abbasid caliphs to mere figureheads and was the first to hold the epithet or title of 'al-sultan al-mu'azzam' ('the exalted sultan') as is

documented by surviving coins.[30] The title *al-sultan*, awarded by the Abbasid caliph as more or less an honorific (*laqab*), but not formalised, had been used before by some of the Buyid emirs. Following Seljuq precedent, the Ghaznavids, who ruled over much of Iran, Khurasan, Transoxiana and also parts of north India, began to use the title extensively.[31] Khurasan, a key province politically and economically for much of the Abbasid caliphate, owing to its rich resources in silver, had always had secessionist tendencies, even when the Abbasids were still in full control of the province (see chapter 2, pp. 60–62).

The establishment of the Samanid dynasty in Khurasan and Transoxiana in the tenth century had seen a decisive break with control from Baghdad, then controlled by the Buyids. While nominally acknowledging the Abbasid caliphs, the Samanids developed a confidence that led to a revival of Iranian culture, and is also manifested in the use of monumental inscriptions such as the *tiraz* in the name of the Samanid governor Abi Mansur Bugtekin on the Suaire de St Josse, discussed above (fig. I.5.E). Founded by a former Turkish *mamluk* ('military slave') named Sabuktigin (r. 977–997), son-in-law of a former Samanid general Alp Tigin, the Ghaznavids became a major military force under Mahmud of Ghazna (r. 998–1030), who extended Ghaznavid control well into south Asia. Perhaps the most important surviving Ghaznavid monuments are those built at their winter retreat at Lashkari Bazar under Mas'ud I of Ghazna (r. 1030–40), which are decorated extensively with stucco and marble wall decorations, as well as fresco paintings depicting courtiers (see fig. 1.39), and in the capital at Ghazna under Mahmud's great-grandson Mas'ud III (r. 1099–1115), a minaret and an extensive palace complex, from which inscriptions bearing Mas'ud's title, *al-sultan al-'azam*, have survived.[32]

While the Abbasids in Baghdad were experiencing a brief renaissance of independence and artistic patronage under the caliphs al-Muqtafi (r. 1136–60) and al-Nasir (r. 1180–1225), the Ghurids, a Persianate dynasty of Tajik origin, with their capital at Firuzkuh in Ghur province in central Afghanistan, rose to power.[33] Originally vassals of the Ghaznavids, they benefited from the rivalry between the latter and the Seljuqs, and eventually eclipsed the Ghaznavids, establishing themselves as an imperial power between the Hindukush and north India. Around 1150 they assumed the title of *al-sultan al-mu'azzam*.[34]

In 1174 CE the city of Ghazna finally fell to the Ghurids and became a base for the conquest of India, where the

I.5.F   Fragments of a *tiraz* textile, with inscriptions naming the Ghurid sultan Ghiyath al-Din Abu al-Fath Muhammad ibn Sam (r. 1163–1203), eastern Iran or Khurasan, late 12th – early 13th century CE. Silk lampas with gilded metal thread, piece (a) (right) 15.5 × 31 cm, piece (b) (left) 15.5 × 15 cm. The al-Sabah Collection, Kuwait, inv. no. LNS 1216 T a, b.

I.5.G   Fragment of a *tiraz* textile, with an inscription naming the Ghurid sultan Ghiyath al-Din Abu al-Fath Muhammad ibn Sam (r. 1163–1203), eastern Iran or Khurasan, late 12th – early 13th century CE. Silk samite with supplementary weft and gilded metal thread, 4 × 12 cm. The al-Sabah Collection, Kuwait, inv. no. LNS 702 T b.

I.5.H   Fragment of a *tiraz* textile, with an inscription naming the Ghurid sultan Ghiyath al-Din Abu al-Fath Muhammad ibn Sam (r. 1163–1203), eastern Iran or Khurasan, late 12th – early 13th century CE. Silk samite with supplementary weft and gilded metal thread, 8 × 17 cm. The al-Sabah Collection, Kuwait, inv. no. LNS 702 T a.

I.5.I   Fragment of a *tiraz* textile, with an inscription naming the Ghurid sultan Muʻizz al-Din Abu al-Muzaffar Muhammad ibn Sam (r. 1173–1206), eastern Iran or Khurasan, late 12th – early 13th century CE. Silk lampas with supplementary weft and gilded metal thread, 6.5 × 7 cm. The al-Sabah Collection, Kuwait, inv. no. LNS 655 T.

Turkic *mamluk* general of the Ghurids, Qutb al-Din Aybak (in office 1192–1206 as general and 1206–10 as Sultan of Delhi), founded the sultanate of Delhi in 1206, which ultimately lasted until 1290. The Ghurid Empire reached its zenith, stretching from Khurasan to north India, under the Ghurid sultans Shams al-Din ('the sun of religion') Abu al-Fath Muhammad ibn Sam of Ghur (r. 1163–1203) and his brother Shihab al-Din ('the flame of religion') Abu al-Muzaffar Muhammad ibn Sam of Ghazna (r. jointly with his brother 1173–1203, and as sole ruler 1203–06).[35] Shams al-Din Abu al-Fath Muhammad ibn Sam changed his *laqab* to 'Ghiyath al-Din' ('succourer of religion') in 1163, bearing the title *al-sultan al-'azam* ('the most mighty sultan').[36] Shihab al-Din Abu al-Muzaffar Muhammad ibn Sam changed his *laqab* to 'Mu'izz al-Din' ('honourer of religion') about 1174, and was awarded the title *al-sultan al-mu'azzam*, replacing his earlier titles *al-malik al-mu'azzam* ('the exalted king') and *al-malik al-'azam* ('the most mighty king'). From then on both carried the title *al-sultan*, with Ghiyath al-Din carrying the more elevated one as the more senior of the two brothers, and worked together.[37] While Ghiyath al-Din established a friendly relationship with the Abbasid caliph al-Nasir (r. 1180–1225 CE), supported by the exchange of several embassies between Firuzkuh and Baghdad and defending the Ghurid realms against the Khwarazm-Shahs on the borders of Khurasan, Mu'izz al-Din campaigned in India from his base in Ghazna. Ghiyath al-Din died in Herat in 1203 and Mu'izz al-Din was assassinated in 1206 during one of his campaigns in the Indus valley. After their deaths the Ghurid Empire began to decline and eventually fall apart. Their names and titles are documented in a number of *tiraz* textile fragments preserved in The al-Sabah Collection (figs I.5.F–I).

The Ghurids were great patrons of the arts. Ghiyath al-Din commissioned a number of mosques, madrasas and caravanserais in Khurasan; he was also a patron of the arts of the book, as is documented by a magnificent four-volume Quran, now at the Iran Bastan Museum, Tehran, executed by master calligraphers and illuminators and completed in 584 AH / 1189 CE, which contains a colophon documenting Ghiyath al-Din's full name with perhaps the most extensive set of his titles that have survived from before the conquest of north India.[38] Perhaps the most iconic and studied of all Ghurid monuments is the minaret of Jam in modern Afghanistan, probably the location of the Ghurid capital Firuzkuh (fig. I.5.J). It comprises an

extensive programme of Quranic inscriptions (fig. I.5.K), which have been interpreted as symbolizing a military victory either by Ghiyath al-Din against the Khwarazm-Shahs or by his brother Mu'izz al-Din against the Indian Rajput ruler Prithviraja III (r. 1177–92 CE) in 1192 CE in the second Battle of Tara'in.[39] Ghiyath al-Din's names and titles are recorded in inscriptions below the minaret's first and second balcony and as a fragment on the octagonal base.[40]

The inscription below the first balcony, rendered in a monumental style of Kufic executed in turquoise tile mosaic (fig. I.5.L), is of particular interest here. The names and titles of Ghiyath al-Din are documented in a *tiraz* fragment in two pieces in The al-Sabah Collection (LNS 1216 T a, b), in two thin inscription bands above and below a more prominent band between the two (fig. I.5.F) in a form and use of titulature almost identical with those inscribed on the minaret, except for a reversal of *al-din wa al-dunya*.[41] This is the most complete rendering of his titles, including his name Muhammad ibn Sam, among these fragments. Two further fragments, LNS 702 T a (fig. I.5.H) and LNS 702 T b (fig. I.5.G) provide evidence only for the titles, the name having presumably been lost.[42] More importantly the style of the inscription in the central band of LNS 1216 T a, b, a mirrored repetition of the title *al-sultan*, is characterised by a bold and solid line of evenly thick and proportioned letters linked by curved joints below the baseline and terminating in elaborately split palmette foliations and floriations. A very similar calligraphic style is found in the turquoise tile mosaic inscription on the minaret which also comprises foliated letters terminating in elegantly split palmettes (see fig. I.5.L).

If the minaret of Jam was a symbol of victory over the Rajputs in north India, it is indeed curious why the names and titles of Ghiyath al-Din's brother, Mu'izz al-Din, are not mentioned there. Instead, both are recorded in the inscriptions of the Qutb Minar, a minaret commissioned near the Quwwat-ul-Islam mosque in south Delhi by the Ghurid general Qutb al-Din Aybak.[43] While Ghiyath al-Din is commemorated in the fourth band above the base, that of Mu'izz al-Din is found in the second band above the base.[44] There he is referred to with a lengthy assemblage of titles and honorifics that eclipse those of his brother Ghiyath al-Din and culminate in his *kunya*, Abu al-Muzaffar, and *ism*, Muhammad ibn Sam.[45] The inscription documented in the textile LNS 655 T at The al-Sabah Collection is fragmented and preserves the second

I.5.J   Minaret of Jam, Ghor Province, Afghanistan, from the reign of the Ghurid sultan Ghiyath al-Din Abu al-Fath Muhammad ibn Sam (r. 1163–1203), dated 570 AH / 1174–75 CE.

I.5.K   Kufic inscriptions (Surah Maryam, Quran 19) in unglazed brick, minaret of Jam, Ghor Province, Afghanistan, from the reign of the Ghurid sultan Ghiyath al-Din Abu al-Fath Muhammad ibn Sam (r. 1163–1203), dated 570 AH / 1174–75 CE

I.5.L   Kufic inscriptions in glazed brick, minaret of Jam, Ghor Province, Afghanistan, naming the Ghurid sultan Ghiyath al-Din Abu al-Fath Muhammad ibn Sam (r. 1163–1203), dated 570 AH / 1174–75 CE.

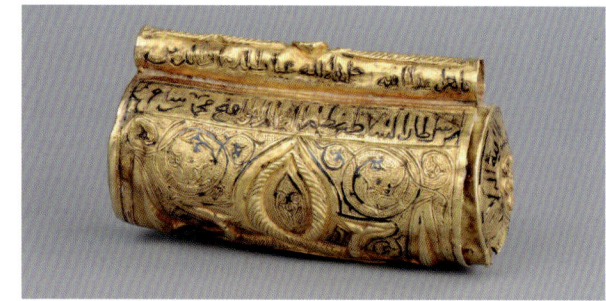

I.5.M   Pair of pendants inscribed with the titles of the Ghurid sultan Ghiyath al-Din Abu al-Fath Muhammad ibn Sam (r. 1163–1203), Khurasan, Ghurid dynasty, late 12th century CE. Gold sheet, repoussé with niello, 3.18 × 5.61 × 2.65 cm. The Al-Sabah Collection, Kuwait, inv. no. LNS 1890 J a, b.

part of Muʿizz al-Din's title, *al-sultan al-ʿazam*, and his *kunya*, Abu al-Muzaffar (fig. I.5.I), suggesting that the fragment must date from the period after Ghiyath al-Din's death in 1203 CE, when Muʿizz al-Din took this title from his brother, holding it until he himself died in 1206 CE.[46] It is curious, though, that Ghiyath al-Din is referred to only as *al-sultan al-muʿazam* in the fragments discussed here, rather than the more elevated *al-sultan al-ʿazam*.

A pair of identical engraved and niello-inlaid gold pendants of a kind known as *tawidh* ('amulet case') in The al-Sabah Collection can be added to the small corpus of works that document the patronage of sultan Ghiyath al-Din and record his elaborate titulature (LNS 1890 J a, b; fig. I.5.M).[47] They are worked in high-relief repoussé, with full-length cylindrical lugs and removable domical ends. The repoussé work at the top centre of each lug comprises a classical-type scallop shell motif, flanked by ribbed and fan-shaped split-palmettes; just below the lug, a pair of crowned, seated sphinxes flank a cusped arch, beneath which is a large, rectangular four-clawed bezel, which has now lost its stone. A pair of addorsed harpies are located on the central section of the body, their tails interlacing and forming a cusped teardrop-shaped motif, the latter flanked on either side by a spiralling half-palmette scroll. The harpies are surmounted by an inscribed band just below the lug at the back of the pendant.

The repoussé decoration links these small ornaments to the larger body of metalwork that has survived from the eastern Iranian world. But what is striking are the extensive inscriptions in Naskh script, engraved and niello-inlaid, running in bands along the pendants in a number of places, including the lug, below the bezel, the upper body and around the perimeter of the end pieces. They comprise an elaborate sequence of titles that relate to the sultan Ghiyath al-Din Abu al-Fath Muhammad ibn Sam,[48]

which complement the evidence for the titles used in the textile fragments discussed here. However, the inscriptions on the pendants refer to Ghiyath al-Din *as al-sultan al-muʿazzam shahanshah* ('the exalted sultan, king of kings'), *sultan al-salatin* ('sultan of sultans'), *malik al-raqab al-am mawla muluk al-ʿarab wa al-ajam* ('master of the fate of nations, master of the kings of the Arab and non-Arab nations'), all attributes that are part of Ghiyath al-Din's titulature in the inscriptions on the Qutb Minar, mentioned above.[49] In contrast to the inscriptions on the minaret of Jam, as well as those documented in the textile fragments, the inscriptions on the pendants are rendered in cursive Naskh script, which is also the case with the four-volume Ghurid Quran mentioned above, and most importantly the inscriptions on the Qutb Minar. Although still common in the twelfth century, Kufic was at that time in the process of being replaced by Naskh in public inscriptions, the former perhaps regarded as a more traditional choice. This was not a process limited to the eastern Iranian world, but happened also across the central Islamic lands. Here the change is evident if we consider the inscriptions on the minaret of Jam and the textile fragments discussed above, all from the late twelfth century, beside the inscriptions of the Qutb Minar and the gold pendants. By the later thirteenth century Naskh had eclipsed Kufic entirely.

The textile fragments discussed above, which were reportedly found in the province of Samangan with a large cache of other magnificent textile fragments, are very rare survivals of what were once magnificent robes; these were made in court workshops that executed the orders of the Ghurid administration and must have been tightly controlled as they produced *tiraz* inscriptions that contained the names and titles of the Ghurid sultans. In terms of materials and weaving techniques, the Ghurid *tiraz* fragments document the continuity of craft traditions in the eastern Iranian world. The fact that they are made of silk and gold and silver thread, in complicated lampas and samite compound weaves, shows that the Ghurid workshops were building on weaving traditions that had existed in the eastern Iranian world since pre-Islamic times and continued well into the early Islamic period under the Buyid and Samanid dynasties and then the Seljuqs.[50] Examples of extant robes in related compound weaves are discussed in chapter 1 (see figs 1.12, 1.36–1.38). A collection of small fragments comprising lozenge-shaped cartouches with vegetal borders, which seem to have come from the same fabric as the tripartite inscription band discussed above (see fig. I.5.F), provides no more than a glimpse of how sumptuously decorated the robe they once adorned must have been (fig. I.5.N).[51] While such inscribed robes would have been worn by the Ghurid sultans themselves, it is likely that they were also gifted as robes of honour to courtiers as well as foreign dignitaries and embassies.

What makes these Ghurid fragments stand out is the personalised nature of their inscriptions, which focus less on administrative process – as was the case in the *tiraz* inscriptions of the caliphates – and more on the glorification of the sultan who ultimately commissioned them and whose name lent an aura of status and exclusivity. At the same time, the titles were a way to confer legitimacy on incumbents who held military might, and by extension political power, but lacked the dynastic pedigree of the Abbasid caliphs and their connection with the origins of Islam itself. With the sack of Baghdad by the Mongols in 1258 and the exile of the last survivor of the Abbasid family to Egypt, we see a similar development under the Mamluks of Egypt, who developed an industry producing highly luxurious compound-woven silk textiles inscribed with the names and titles of their sultanate patrons; these textiles were later often gifted as robes of honour or traded with the European merchants of early modern Europe.[52] In the eastern Iranian world, western and central Asia, the Mongol Ilkhans developed an industry of compound-woven silk textiles that were also gifted as part of diplomatic exchanges with European allies, and also traded along the long Silk Road between central Asia and southern Europe, where they became known as 'Cloth of Gold' or *panni tartarici* ('Tartar textiles') owing to their extensive use of gold thread.[53]

Particularly interesting in the context of *tiraz* inscriptions are textiles that contain the names and titles of Ilkhanid rulers such as Sultan Abu Sa'id (r. 1319–35 CE). His name and titles are recorded in bands comprising an elegant Naskh inscription on the famous burial outfit of Duke Rudolf IV of the house of Habsburg in the Dommuseum, Vienna, as well as that of his distant relative Cangrande della Scala of Verona.[54] The inscriptions read: 'Praise to our lord, the glorious sultan, most glorious king of kings (*shahanshah*) highness of the world and religion (*'ala' al-dunya wa al-din*) (A)bu Sa'id Bahadur Khan, may God perpetuate his rule.'[55] The titulature relates in some detail to earlier precedents, as discussed above, and represents the continuity in the post-caliphal world of inscribing the rulers' name on textiles that were far more luxurious and precious in terms of materials and more complicated in terms of manufacture than those *tiraz* textiles that have survived in Egyptian graves.

I.5.N   Textile fragments (probably from the same cloth as fig. I.5.G), comprising small lozenge-shaped cartouches with vegetal borders, Eastern Iran or Khurasan, late 12th – early 13th century CE. Silk lampas with gilded metal thread, diam. (each piece) *c.* 1 cm. The Al-Sabah Collection, Kuwait, inv. no. LNS 1216 T.

Cat. 107 *TIRAZ* FRAGMENT FROM
THE ABBASID DYNASTY
**Eastern Iran or Khurasan,
10th century CE**

Description: Fragment of undyed *mulham*
(cotton weft on silk warp) with
a single line of Kufic inscription
embroidered in red silk chain stitch

Materials: cotton and silk: plain weave
and embroidery

Dimensions: h. 3.6 cm, w. 10.1 cm;
max. letter height 2.5 cm

Ground fabric: silk warp and cotton weft
(*mulham*), undyed, weft-faced
plain weave; very good–good
quality (1–2)

Thread count: warp 18 Z-spun, weft 25 Z-spun

Thread thickness: warp 0.05 mm tight twist, weft
0.3–0.5 mm medium–tight twist

Embroidery: silk, dyed (red), chain stitch

Provenance: art market, 1970s–1980s

Inv. no. LNS 94 T

Related works: See page 509

Inscription: undecipherable

The particular style of script seen here is found on several *mulham* fragments,
where it is likewise embroidered in red or blue silk floss in chain stitch (Related
works 1–5). These span a period between the late ninth and early tenth century.
The inscription on a fragment in the Textile Museum, Washington, DC,
records its manufacture in Merw during the reign of the Abbasid caliph al-

Muktafi (r. 902–08) (Related works 3). Because of the homogeneity of the
group listed here, in terms of materials, technical detail and epigraphic
style, a tentative attribution to a Khurasani workshop can be suggested
for the present piece. It is noteworthy that the inscriptions in these similar
fragments are composed of letters of a lesser height than those in this textile,
with the exception of the piece in Berlin, where the inscription is *c.* 2.0–
2.5 cm high.

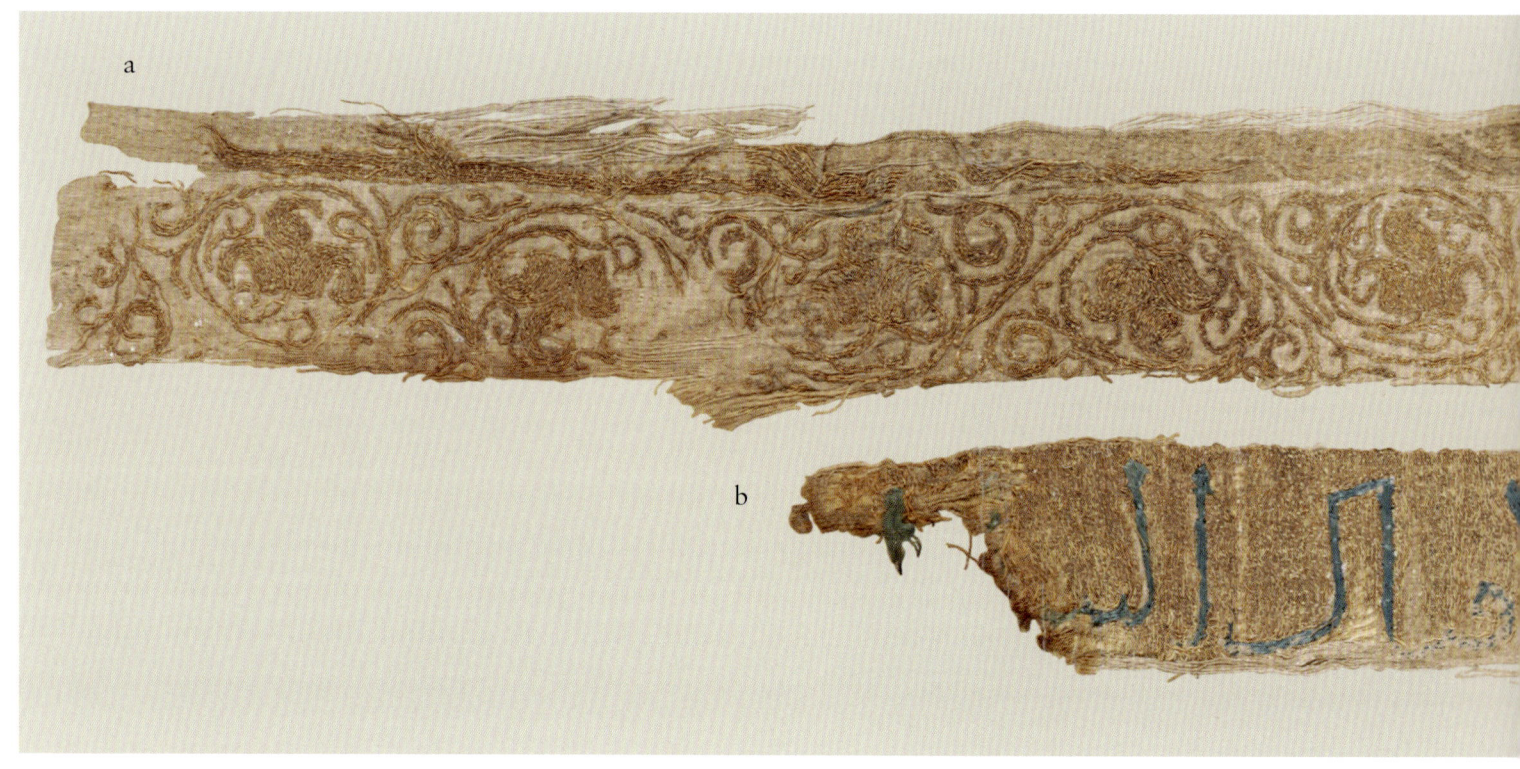

a

b

Cat. 108 *TIRAZ* FRAGMENT FROM
THE GHAZNAVID OR
GHURID DYNASTIES
**Eastern Iran or Khurasan,
12th century CE**

Description: Fragment (two pieces) of undyed
mulham, one (a) decorated with
an elaborate palmette scroll
embroidered in gold thread, and
the other (b) inscribed with a
repeated benedictory phrase in
Naskh script, embroidered in
blue silk against a background
embroidered in gold thread.

Materials: cotton, silk and gold thread:
plain weave and embroidery

Dimensions: (a) h 5.2 cm, w 50 cm
(b) h 3.9 cm, w 37.7 cm;
max. letter height 3.7 cm

Ground fabric: mulham (silk warp, cotton weft),
undyed, regular plain weave, tight
texture; very good quality (1)

Thread count: warp 33 Z-spun, weft 30 Z-spun

Thread thickness: warp 0.1 mm medium twist,
weft 0.1–0.2 mm medium twist

Embroidery: silk floss, dyed (blue), gold thread
composed of undyed silk core
wrapped with strips of gilded
animal substrate; gold thread
couched to the ground fabric
with paired stitched in silk floss;
inscription embroidered in blue silk
floss couched to the ground fabric

Provenance: art market

Inv. no. LNS 423 T a, b

Inscription: repetition of

[…] glory and prosperity […]

العز و الاقبال [...] [...]

The use of *mulham* indicates an eastern Iranian origin, possibly Khurasan.
Mulham was one of the most esteemed fabric types in the medieval period,
and the best qualities were produced in Khurasan. Several dated *tiraz* textile
inscriptions stating their manufacture in Merw or Nishapur have been discussed
earlier (see pp. 322–25). Three *mulham* fragments with elaborate zoomorphic
motifs embroidered in silk and gold thread, using chain stitch, are in the Textile
Museum, Washington, DC, and Boston Museum of Fine Arts (see figs 3.17–3.19).
While these have traditionally been attributed to tenth- or eleventh-century
Baghdad, the surviving *tiraz* inscriptions on *mulham* documenting a place of
production refer only to Merw or Nishapur.[56] All surviving *tiraz* textiles from
Baghdad are embroidered on cotton ground fabrics, rather than *mulham*.
There are some hybrid examples, however, where the style and execution of

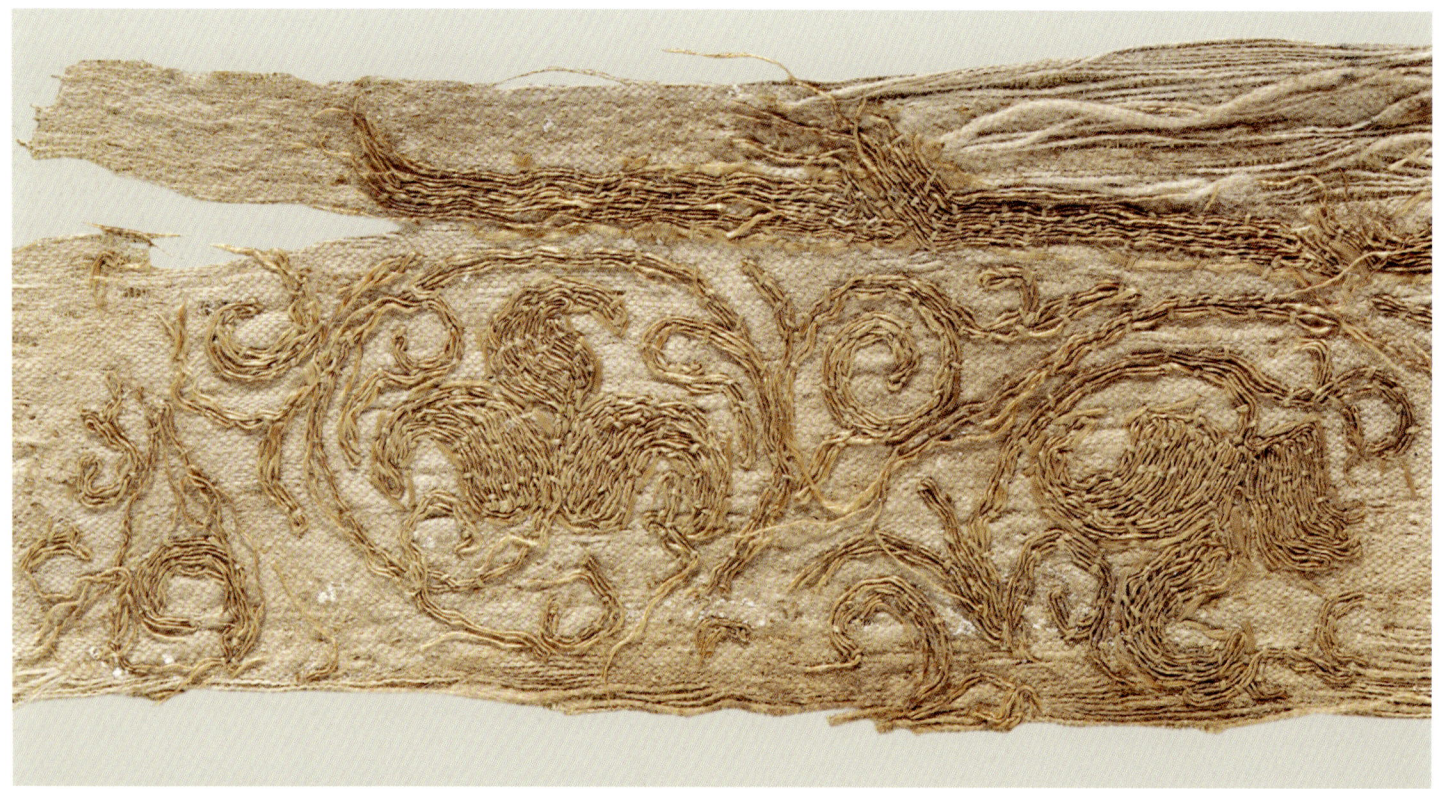

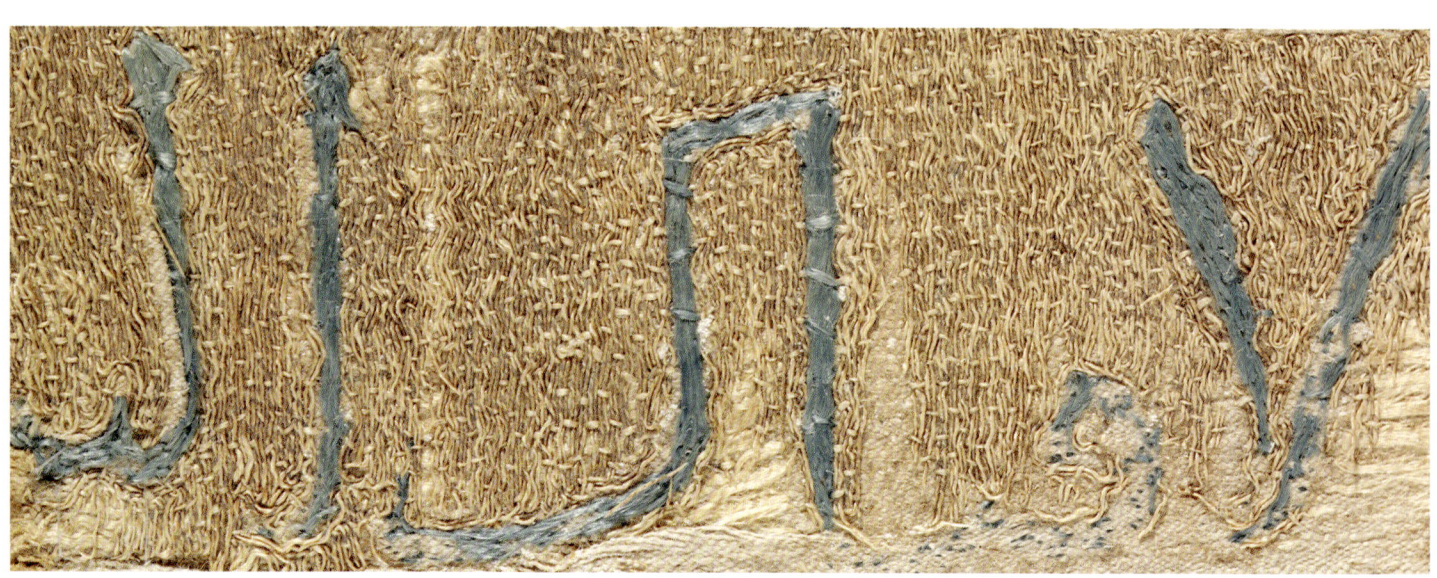

the inscription conforms with Iraqi prototypes, but which are embroidered on *mulham* (see fig. 3.15, and cat. nos 95 and 105 for a discussion). It is, of course, possible that *mulham* fabrics that had been imported from Khurasan were later inscribed in Baghdad, using styles of epigraphy in chain stitch embroidery that are documented in historical inscriptions.

The cursive inscription found on fragment (b) here points to a twelfth-century date as it is comparable in style to similar short benedictory inscriptions on Khurasanian metalwork attributed to the Ghurid sultanate. A very close comparison for the inscription can be found on a brass flask in the British Museum, London (fig. 108.1).[57] It was acquired in Rawalpindi; its unusual combination of elements consisting of a flattened bulbous body with a long neck and two prominent goat-shaped handles on its shoulders, the body mounted on a square foot, has been explained as a consequence of south Asian influence.[58] It is decorated with incised and inlaid palmette scrolls and knots, and has cursive and Kufic inscriptions. The cursive inscription set against a scroll background on both flattened sides of the body, with elongated thickening hastae set against a palmette scroll, relates very closely to that on the present textile fragment in terms of design; common elements are the trefoil palmettes on fragment (a), and the benedictory content of the inscription, which, like that of the *tiraz* fragment, comprises short phrases with good wishes to the owner. Particularly striking are the similarities with regard to the word *al-iqbal* (prosperity) in both inscriptions and the shape of the *lam–alif.*

108.1   Pilgrim flask with goat-shaped handles, Khurasan or Punjab, and detail of the benedictory inscription with the word *al-iqbal*, attributed to the Ghurid dynasty, 12th century CE, cast brass engraved and inlaid with silver, 32 × 22 × 6 cm. The British Museum, London, inv. no. 1883, 1019.7.

6

YEMEN

Yemen (Arabic: al-Yaman) is a region located in the south-west the Arabian peninsula, bordering on both the Red Sea and the Arabian Sea (see map, pp. 12–13). It played an important role in ancient times as a commercial hub from where incense was traded. It was divided into distinct states: Saba', Qataban, Ma'in and Hadramawt. Its main urban centres were Aden and San'a'. By the fourth century, Judaism and Christianity had replaced polytheism, and the two religions were in conflict with each other after an influx of Abyssinian Christian settlers. From the sixth century, a Persian presence was established in Yemen under the governor Badham, which curbed Abyssinian influence and lasted until the coming of Islam.[1] During the Islamic conquests, Yemenis made up a vast majority of the Arab armies. The early caliphates established governorships in San'a' to exert tighter control of this important province. But the course of Yemeni history is dominated by dynasties that ruled in a semi-independent manner reflecting the complicated tribal make-up of the country and diverging religious affiliations; they often only nominally acknowledged greater external powers. Foremost were the Ziyadids, or Banu Ziyad (203–409 AH / 818–1018 CE), who took their name from Muhammad bin Ziyad, a protégé of the Abbasid caliph al-Ma'mun's minister al-Fadl bin Sahl. The Yu'firids, or Banu Yu'fir (232–387 AH / 847–997 CE) were the first local Yemeni dynasty to emerge in Islamic times. The Sulayhids, the Banu al-Sulayhi (439–532 AH / 1047–1138 CE), a Shi'ite dynasty, acknowledged the Fatimids. And the Sulaymanids, sharifs, originally from Mecca (c. 462–569 AH / c. 1069–1173 CE), were instrumental in urging the Ayyubids to conquer Yemen in 569 AH / 1173 CE.

The importance of Yemen and its products for the pre-Islamic trader is illustrated by a passage from Qalqashandi, who writes about the seasonal trade fairs of the Arabian merchants which took them throughout the Arabian peninsula, including Bahrain and Oman:

Thence they would go, to encamp at Iram and the villages of Shihr of the Yemen, where fairs would be set up for some days. They would next go and stop at Aden of the Yemen from which they bought perfumes (latima) and various sorts of scent (tib). After this they would take their way to visit Hadramaut of the land of the Yemen. Some, on the other hand, used to omit (calling) there, and go (straight) to San'a' to hold fairs where they traded for its kharaz (beads, gems, or shells of the type called wada', 'cowries'), leatherware (adam), and striped cloaks (burud) which were exported to San'a from Ma'afir.[2]

The text speaks of striped cloaks (burud). A burda was a very popular type of cloak in Arabia and is frequently mentioned in sources discussing the pre-Islamic period, such as an account relating to al-Nu'man of Hira (c. 580–602) in the Kitab al-aghani ('Book of songs'); it mentions 'perfume which the lord of Mudar allowed him. This was sold and the proceeds spent on skins, silk (harir) … and striped material (burd) of 'asb-cloth, washi-silk, and striped cloth of Aden (musaiyar 'Adani)'.[3] 'Asb cloth was a type of fabric in which individual yarns are tie-dyed, similar to the south-east Asian ikat (see chapter 3). In pre-Islamic times, the Kaaba in Mecca is said to have been covered in 'asb cloth,[4] and the Prophet Muhammad is said to have covered the Kaaba with Yemeni cloth.[5] An account of the enshrouding of the Prophet Muhammad mentions that his body was wrapped in three white Yemeni cotton cloths, until his companion 'Abdallah Abu Bakr took one sheet for himself as he wanted to use it as his own shroud.[6]

There are many references relating to Yemeni fabrics in sources discussing the early caliphates.[7] For example Hisham ibn 'Abd al-Malik had a 'pavilion (suradik) set up for himself, made of striped stuff (hibra) which Yusuf ibn 'Omar had made for him in the Yemen'.[8] A list compiled by an Abbasid administrator of special products of the provinces, brought to the treasury during the reign of Harun al-Rashid (r. 786–809), mentions that his physician, Bakhtishu' ibn Jibra'il, obtained annually, along with other perquisites, three robes of figured material from the Yemen ('al-washi al-yamani').[9]

Yemeni fabrics were frequently compared with those of Egypt or Iraq in terms of quality and luxuriousness, and Yemeni cloth in this case seemed more valuable than silk:

The best kinds of figured *washi*-stuffs are the *sabiri* kind, the Kufan variety, the *ibrism*-silk kind (probably embroidered with silk), the type which is embroidered with gold and woven (*al-mudhahhab al-mansuj*), then the Alexandrine figured *washi* stuff of pure linen, then that which is woven with gold, then the spun figured cloth (*al-washi al-ghazli*), then that which has in it *ibrism* silk, but contains no gold; that is the Yemeni kind, because in this fashion it is more valuable than the spun (*ghazli*) stuff. The *ibrism*-silk kind does not fetch the price that the Yemen type does, for a spun (*ghazli*) garment sometimes fetches a thousand dinars.[10]

The chronicler al-Mas'udi mentioned that the Umayyad caliph Sulayman (r. 715–17) had a very discernible sense of fashion for *washi*, a type of cloth also produced in Yemen. He said of Sulayman:

[He] used to wear fine robes, and robes of variegated silk (*washi*). In his day excellent *washi* was made in Yemen, Kufa, and Alexandria. All the people used to wear *washi* for their mantles (*djubba*), cloaks (*ardiya*), trousers (*sarawil*), turbans (*'ama'im*), and caps (*kalansuwa*). Nobody of his household used to enter his presence except in *washi*; thus it was with his friends, governors, and household. He used to wear it while riding, or in the pulpit (*mimbar*). None of his servants, even the cook, entered his presence except in *washi*; for the latter used to come before him wearing *washi* on his breast, and a long hat (*tawila*) of *washi* on his head. He (Sulaiman) even ordered that his shroud should be made of *washi*.[11]

The evidence of *tiraz* textiles can to some extent support what historical sources tell us about Yemeni textiles. For one thing, several cotton *tiraz* textiles have survived that were manufactured in San'a'.[12] Except for one, all of them are inscribed with the names of Abbasid caliphs, the earliest dated 250 AH / 864–65 CE during the reign of al-Musta'in (r. 862–66) and the latest 311 AH / 923–24 CE during the reign of al-Muqtadir (r. 908–32). They all feature embroidered inscriptions. The embroidered textiles in The al-Sabah Collection discussed below add to the existing corpus of these Abbasid textiles from Yemen.

A piece at the Metropolitan Museum of Art, New York, which was manufactured in a *tiraz* workshop in San'a', contrasts significantly with this group, in that its inscription is tapestry-woven in wool on cotton, and features a benedictory text, without mention of a particular patron, accompanied by an embroidered geometric band (p. 347, figs 110.1 and 110.2).[13] The epigraphic style of the inscription is indicative of a late Umayyad or early Abbasid date, and relates quite closely to that found on an ivory pyxis in the treasury of the church of Sankt Gereon in Cologne, which was made in Aden in the name of the amir 'Abdallah ibn Rabi', governor of Mecca between 762 and 764 under the Abbasids.[14]

From the late tenth century, cotton *ikat*s survive that have gilded inscriptions in the name of amirs of the Zaydi imamate.[15] These inscriptions all feature a very bold, angular style of script that contrasts with other painted, heavily ornamented scripts on Yemeni *ikat*s, but also the very thin and subtle styles of embroidered inscriptions. The *ikat* discussed below (cat. no 111) differs from these, in that its inscription was embroidered, rather than painted.

Cat. 109 *TIRAZ* FRAGMENT FROM
THE ABBASID DYNASTY
Yemen, probably San'a', second
half of the 9th century CE

Description: Fragment of undyed cotton,
with one line of Kufic inscription
embroidered in brownish cotton;
the lower edge has a twisted fringe.

Materials: cotton: plain weave and
embroidery

Dimensions: h. 16.0 cm, w. 15.0 cm;
max. letter height 0.8 cm

Ground fabric: cotton, undyed, balanced plain
weave, tight texture, very regular;
very good quality (1)

Thread count: warp 29 Z-spun, weft 30 Z-spun

Thread thickness: warp 0.1–0.25 mm tight twist,
weft 0.1–0.15 mm tight twist

Embroidery: cotton, dyed (brownish), Z-spun,
two-plied S-spun, back stitch;
twisted fringe two-plied

Provenance: Ex H.P. Kraus collection, no. 37

Inv. no. LNS 161 T

Related works: See page 509

Inscription:

[...] ايّده الله مما امر الامير جعفر بن امير المؤمنين (اطال الله) [...]

[...] may God support him, of what ordered the amir Ja'far son of the
Commander of the Believers (may God prolong his life) [...]

This fragment has previously been attributed to ninth-century Misr in Egypt, an
attribution that must, however, be reconsidered. Apart from its cotton ground
fabric, its inscription shares details of manufacture and epigraphic style with
two other fragments, one in the Metropolitan Museum of Art, New York,
and another in the Benaki Museum in Athens (Related works 2, 3). These two
fragments have inscriptions embroidered in dyed multi-ply cotton on a cotton
ground fabric, a feature found here as well. The Metropolitan Museum piece was
made in a *tiraz* workshop in San'a' as its inscription records. Microscopic analysis
of the textile at the Metropolitan Museum can confirm the similarity (figs
109.1–109.3). This and the Benaki Museum fragment comprise Z-spun cotton
fabric with blue, brown and reddish stripes. Obviously, the present textile differs
from these in that it is made of undyed cotton, but it resembles them in that all
three have fringes made up of carefully twisted multi-ply yarns. The letterforms
of the inscriptions are squarish and comprise letter stems with small hook-like
and pointed terminals. Circular letterforms appear pointed (such as *mim* and *fa*),
and the terminals of letters below the baseline are squared rather than rounded.
The fragments in the Metropolitan and Benaki museums are both from the
period of the Abbasid caliph al-Musta'in (r. 862–66), the former bearing the date
250 AH / 864–65 CE. On the basis of the inscription of the Metropolitan Museum
piece (Related work 2), the al-Sabah piece can also be attributed to a workshop
in San'a' in the second half of the ninth century. Another piece that documents
San'a', but can be rather dated to the late Umayyad or early Abbasid dynasties
based on the style of epigraphy, is in the Metropolitan Museum (Related
works 1). Several later textiles with inscriptions documenting manufacture in

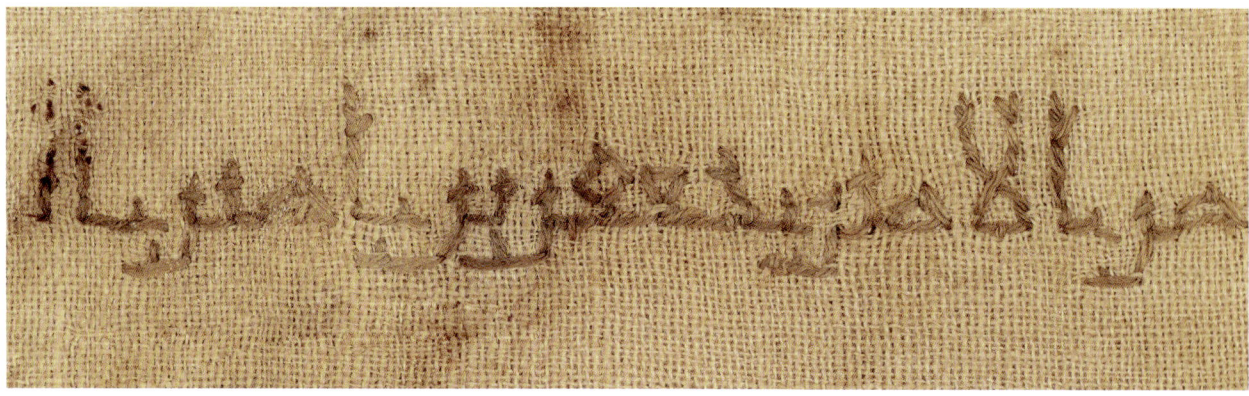

tiraz workshops in San'a' from the reign of the Abbasid caliph al-Mu'tadid are discussed below (pp. 345–47).

The present inscription mentions that the textile was among 'what [was] ordered [by] the amir Ja'far', who is referred to as *ibn amir al-mu'minin* – that is, the son of the ruling caliph. Given the tentative dating of the piece in the period around 250 AH / 864–65 CE, based on the comparison with the Metropolitan Museum fragment mentioned above, the amir Ja'far's identity would have to be sought in the environment of the caliphs roughly contemporary with that date. In fact, an Egyptian *tiraz* fragment has survived from the reign of the Abbasid caliph al-Mu'tamid (r. 870–92), which was ordered by an amir of the same name, Ja'far, who is also referred to as *ibn*; the now fragmentary inscription must have once read *ibn amir al-mu'minin* (Related works 4). One of caliph al-Mu'tamid's sons, Ja'far al-Mufawwad, was appointed in 261 AH / 875–76 CE as al-Mu'tamid's first successor and viceroy

109.1   Fragment of a *tiraz* textile, San'a', Yemen, dated 250 AH / 864–65 CE. Cotton, with cotton embroidery, 42 × 28 cm. Metropolitan Museum of Art, New York, inv. no. 31.106.46.

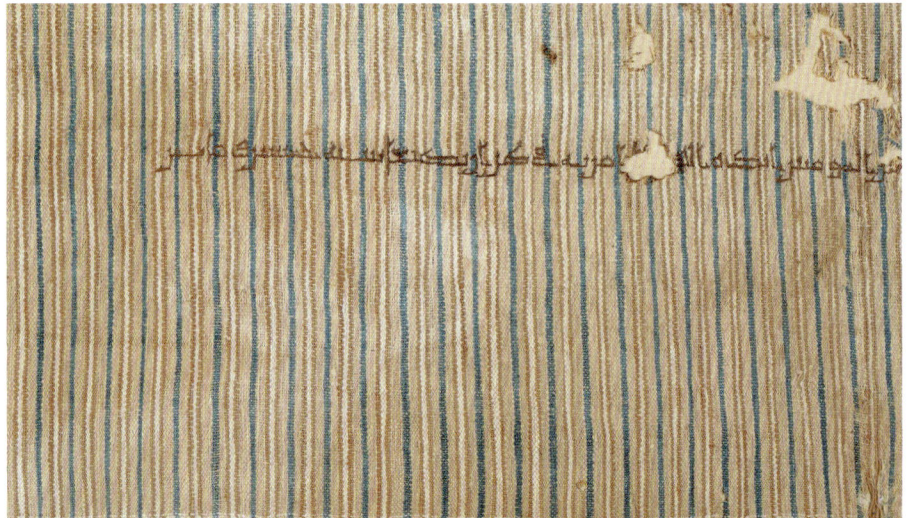

109.2   Detail of figure 109.1, showing the inscription embroidered in couching stitch. Metropolitan Museum of Art, New York, inv. no. 31.106.46.

109.3   Detail of figure 109.1, showing the inscription embroidered in couching stitch. Metropolitan Museum of Art, New York, inv. no. 31.106.46.

of the west. At the same time Ja'far's brother al-Muwaffaq was appointed as viceroy of the east.[16] It is therefore very likely that the amir Ja'far referred to here is identical with Ja'far al-Mufawwad.

Viceroys or heirs designate are documented on a number of *tiraz* inscriptions in an ordering capacity. They were sometimes appointed by caliphs to share the responsibility of rulership over certain geographical areas of key importance to Abbasid politics. They were not strictly speaking regional governors, since the areas assigned to a viceroy contained several provinces, and they were often not resident in the area assigned to them. Viceroys were usually in direct line of succession to the caliphate. For example, during his pilgrimage to Mecca in 802, the Abbasid caliph Harun al-Rashid assigned vice-regencies to his sons and proclaimed their succession. His son Muhammad al-Amin, residing in Baghdad, was appointed as his first heir. Harun's sons 'Abdallah al-Ma'mun, who was assigned a vice-regency over Khurasan, and al-Qasim al-Mu'tamin, who was to rule over the areas bordering the Byzantine empire, the Jazira and northern Syria, became al-Amin's heirs.[17] According to the ninth-century historian al-Azraqi, al-Ma'mun's influence in Khurasan included the mint and the *tiraz* workshops.[18]

No extant textiles document the involvement of Harun al-Rashid's viceroys in ordering textiles, but there are several extant *tiraz* textile inscriptions from the reigns of later caliphs that document the involvement of their viceroys, whose names are recorded as part of the ordering credit. From the reign of al-Mutawakkil (r. 847–61) two items have survived that were ordered by his son, the amir Abu 'Abdallah, who in 252 AH / 866–67 CE was enthroned as the caliph al-Mu'tazz (r. 866–69) (Related works 5, 6). In 235 AH / 849–50 CE al-Mutawakkil appointed his sons as vice-regents over vast parts of his empire: Abu 'Abdallah over Khurasan, al-Muntasir over Egypt and al-Mu'ayyad over Syria and Palestine.[19] Although neither inscription mentions the place of production, both textiles must be of Egyptian production, as both are made of the typical linen ground fabric and use Egyptian embroidery stitches, which is significant in view of the fact that Abu 'Abdallah controlled Khurasan. This implies that although Abu 'Abdallah was regent over Khurasan he was still able to place an order for textiles in Egypt and have his name mentioned in the *tiraz* inscription. Considering all this, the present textile is of considerable importance as it provides further material evidence for Ja'far al-Mufawwad's regency over the west, which obviously must have included Yemen.

Cat. 110 *TIRAZ* FRAGMENT FROM THE REIGN OF THE ABBASID CALIPH AL-MU'TADID
(r. 892–902)
Yemen, 287 AH / 900 CE

Description: Fragment of undyed cotton, with one of Kufic inscription embroidered in brown cotton, accompanied by an in-woven band (0.7 cm) in ochre cotton with interspersed dashes of indigo cotton; there is a second short line of embroidered Kufic inscription in brown cotton just above the twisted fringe.

Dimensions: h. 14.5 cm, w. 35.0 cm; max. letter height 1.1 cm

Materials: cotton: plain weave and embroidery

Ground fabric: cotton warp and weft, undyed, balanced plain weave, close texture; good quality (2); decorative band: cotton weft, dyed (ochre) with supplementary weft filling of indigo-dyed cotton at set intervals; twisted fringe six-plied

Thread count: warp 19 Z-spun, weft 18 Z-spun

Thread thickness: warp 0.15–0.25 mm medium–tight twist, weft 0.25–0.3 mm medium–tight twist

Embroidery: cotton, dyed (brown), couching stitch

Provenance: Ex H.P. Kraus collection, no. 39

Inv. no. LNS 163 T

Related works: See page 509

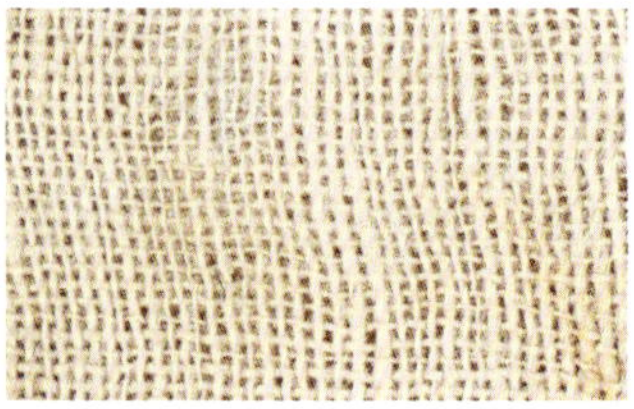

Inscription:

Line 1:   [...] [من] الله لعبد الله الخليفة ابي العباس المعت-(ضد بالله ام-)ـير المؤمنين ايده (الله) [...] (عا؟) سنة سبع و [...]

[...] [from] God to the servant of God the caliph Abi al-'Abbas al-Mu'ta(did bi-llah the Com)mander of the Faithful, may (God) strengthen him. [...] ('a) in the year seven and [...]

Line 2:   لله اسحق (؟) نصر (؟) لله

For God. Ishaq(?) victory(?) God

The date contained in the inscription is fragmentary. Only the third digit is still extant and reads *sab'a* (seven). The caliph mentioned in the inscription whose *kunya* was Abu al-'Abbas is al-Mu'tadid (r. 279–89 AH / 892–902 CE). The textile must, therefore, date from 287 AH / 900–01 CE. In terms of manufacture and epigraphy, the inscription relates to those found on a group of Yemeni cotton fabrics, all of which date from al-Mu'tadid's reign and which also were made in *tiraz* workshops in San'a' (Related works 4–6). Like the present piece, some of these are plain undyed cotton fabrics (Related works 4, 6). Others comprise *ikat*

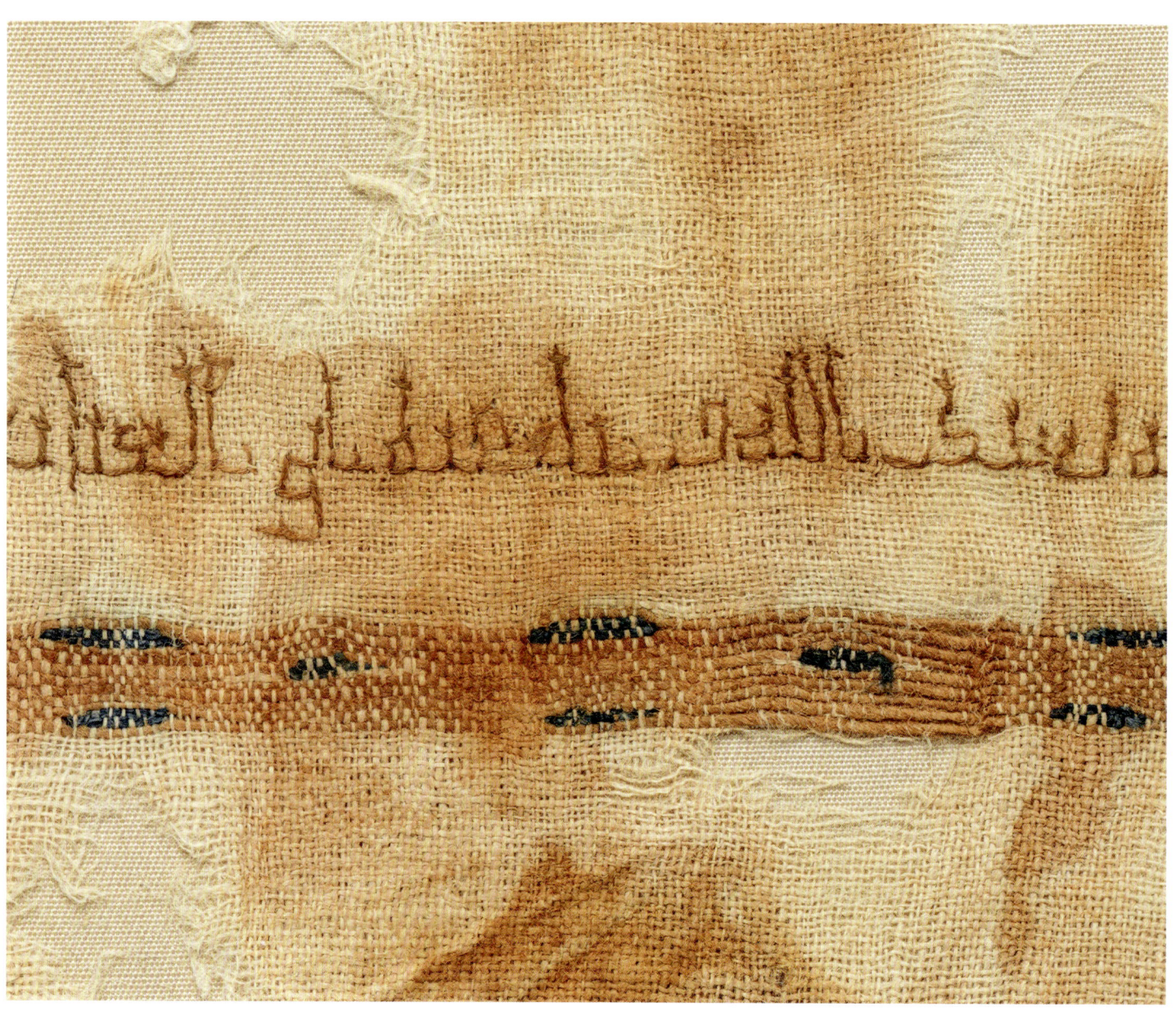

(tie-dyed) ground fabrics (Related works 5). These fragments relate to others made in San'a', albeit during the reigns of the Abbasid caliphs al-Musta'in and al-Mu'tamid (Related works 2, 3). Like those, the present fragment is embroidered in cotton, using couching stitches on a cotton ground fabric.

Interesting here is the addition of a decorative band in dyed ochre cotton, with dashes of indigo-dyed cotton yarn inserted into the weft as a supplementary weft filling, which is reminiscent of the aesthetic of *ikat*s. Brocading is found in a number of Yemeni textiles.[20] The decorative band on a Yemeni textile from the early Abbasid period in the Metropolitan Museum of Art, New York, which was made in San'a' in the late Umayyad or early Abbasid period (Related works 1, fig. 110.1), features brocaded lozenges and an inscription; the lozenges (fig. 110.2) were executed in a technique that resembles the insertion of the blue yarns into the decorative band in the present piece. Below the inscription in the Metropolitan Museum piece is a coloured band with small fields of teal and ochre yarns inserted into the weft, similar to what is found here. The carefully twisted fringe on our example is perhaps another trademark of Yemeni manufacture, as this feature is found in many examples from Yemen. An *ikat* textile in the Museum of Islamic Art, Cairo, with an embroidered inscription, documents the *tiraz al-khassa* in San'a' as late as 311 AH / 923–24 CE during the first reign of the caliph al-Muqtadir (Related works 7).

110.1   Fragment of a shawl with *tiraz* inscription, San'a', Yemen, 8th–9th century CE. Cotton, with cotton brocade, 35.6 × 63.5 cm. Metropolitan Museum of Art, New York, Gift of George D. Pratt, 1931, inv. no. 31.106.23.

110.2   Detail of figure 110.1, showing the brocaded decorative band. Metropolitan Museum of Art, New York, inv. no. 31.106.23.

Cat. 111   *TIRAZ* FRAGMENT FROM
THE ABBASID DYNASTY
Yemen, probably San'a',
10th century CE

Description: Fragment of cotton *ikat* in
dark sand colour and medium-
light blue, decorated with
embroidered bands: one runs
perpendicular to the warp
comprising a sequence of fields
with a variety of diamond and
lozenge shapes, between two
bands of embroidered inscriptions
in Kufic; another consists of an
embroidered Kufic inscription
along the tie-dyed warps. A smaller
inscription runs along the edge
where there was once a fringe,
and an epigraphic repeat frames
what appears to have formed a
decorative square.

Materials: cotton *ikat*: plain weave
and embroidery

Dimensions: h. 55.2 cm, w. 84.3 cm;
max. letter height 2.0 cm

Ground fabric: cotton warp and weft, warp-faced
plain weave, dense texture, regular
structure; very good quality (1)

Thread count: warp 20 Z-spun, weft 7 Z-spun

Thread thickness: warp 0.3–0.5 mm tight twist,
weft 0.2 mm tight twist

Embroidery: cotton, undyed, Z-spun two-plied,
couching stitch

Published: Curatola et al. 2010, no. 40.

Inv. no. LNS 29 T

Related works: See page 509

Inscription:

بسم الله الرحمن الرحيم [...]

In the name of God, the Most Merciful, the Most Compassionate [...]

Upper left corner:

بركة من الله لعبد الله [...] هيد الله

Blessing from God to the servant of God [...] Hayd Allah (?)

Within the decorative square: epigraphic repetition of

الا

This piece is typical of the *ikat*s produced in Yemen. The technique, which
involves tie-dyeing individual cotton threads for the warp, is known in Arabic
as *'asb*, the root of which means to bind or tie. An *ikat* fabric in the Museum of
Islamic Art, Cairo, with an embroidered inscription dated 284 AH / 897–98 CE,
during the reign of the caliph al-Mu'tadid, was made in San'a' (Related works 1).
An undated *ikat* in the Textile Museum, Washington, DC, attributed by Ernst
Kühnel to the tenth century, relates very closely to the present piece in terms
of the decoration, its arrangement, the style of script, and the nature of the
ground fabric (Related works 2). Its fragmentary inscription contains text from
Quran 1 (Surah al-Fatiha) and Quran 62 (Surah al-Ikhlas); Kühnel suggested
that this might have once mentioned the name of an imam at the end, and
attributed the piece to the San'a' workshops based on a close comparison with
other embroidered textiles from San'a'. Several surviving *ikat*s with painted
inscriptions carry names and titles of Zaydi imams.[21] In comparison with the
present piece, these, with their bold golden lettering, are very ostentatious, and
are characterized by a very different underlying aesthetic.

Cat. 112   **TEXTILE FRAGMENT WITH GEOMETRIC PATTERN FROM THE ABBASID DYNASTY**
Yemen, 10th century CE

Description: Fragment of plain-weave cotton, with bands composed of ochre and white yarn on an indigo blue ground, separated at regular intervals by warp-less stripes; the bands are chequered and have a coordinated colour scheme with small diamond shapes composed of supplementary weft in white, ochre and light blue, creating a sequence of chevrons and brocaded lozenges, which alternate with a stripe two checks wide comprising crenellated decoration perpendicular to the warp, executed in cream-coloured cotton brocaded on the ground fabric. The warp-less stripes are seven checks wide, and there is an undecorated border at one side of the fabric.

Materials: plain weave, brocading and embroidery

Dimensions: h. 23.7 cm, w. 90.0 cm

Ground fabric: cotton warp and weft, undyed, and dyed (blue and ochre), warp-faced plain weave, balanced, dense texture; very good quality (1)

Thread count: warp 23 Z-spun, weft 18 Z-spun

Thread thickness: warp 0.2–0.4 mm tight twist, 0.2–0.3 mm tight twist

Decoration: brocading: cotton, undyed, and dyed (light blue, ochre), Z-spun, tight twist

Inv. no. LNS 103 T

Related works: See pages 509–10

This fragment belongs to a group of textiles attributed by Georgette Cornu to Abbasid Yemen, based on their similarity in design and manufacture to a fragment in the Metropolitan Museum of Art, New York, made in San'a' (Related works 1).[22] This comprises a cotton ground fabric with a single band of tapestry-woven lozenge decoration accentuated with supplementary wefts, accompanied below by an early Kufic inscription datable to the eighth or ninth century on the basis of its epigraphic style; the inscription documents the textile's manufacture in a *tiraz* workshop in San'a'. Two items very closely related in aesthetic and method of manufacture to the present piece are in the Musée des Tissus, Lyon, and Dumbarton Oaks, Washington, DC (Related works 2, 3). On both, the overall decoration is arranged in vertical registers or stripes separated from each other by warp-less stripes. In both cases the decoration within the broad registers comprises a diagonal arrangement of lozenges and dots arranged alternately. As it is very difficult to date these pieces on the basis of their decoration alone, it is significant that both the Dumbarton Oaks and Lyon pieces carry embroidered benedictory inscriptions which are comparable in style and execution to those found on textiles from San'a' (Related works 4–9).[23] The group of textiles discussed by Cornu, to which the present piece belongs, have as a key characteristic brocaded designs that resemble crenellations, often surrounding small lozenges executed in supplementary weft, applied after the ground fabric had been woven.[24]

Cat. 113   TEXTILE FRAGMENT WITH GEOMETRIC PATTERNS FROM THE ABBASID DYNASTY

Yemen, 10th century CE

Description: Fragment of cotton, dyed light brown, decorated with several stripes of coloured warps in blue, cream and brown and tie-dyed (*ikat*); the two stripes with brown base colour are embroidered in satin stitch stepped designs, which in the broader stripe form an overall pattern of diamond shapes with a small oval in cream-coloured thread at their centre; the *ikat* stripe forms a large lozenge pattern.

Materials: cotton *ikat*: plain weave and embroidery

Dimensions: h. 13.2 cm, w. 17.8 cm

Ground fabric: cotton warp and weft, undyed, monochrome dyed and tie-dyed (*ikat*) (light brown, blue, greenish-blue), predominant-warp plain weave, close texture, regular structure; very good quality (1)

Thread count: warp 31 Z-spun, weft 17 Z-spun

Thread thickness: warp 0.1–0.3 mm medium–tight twist, weft 0.1–0.3 mm tight twist

Embroidery: cotton, undyed, and dyed (blue and brown), Z-spun, satin stitch in a continuous stepped motion crossing two or three warp and weft threads at a time

Inv. no. LNS 102 T

Related works: See page 510

This is a very fine example of Yemeni cotton fabric with an in-woven *ikat* stripe and embroidered pattern. The embroidery forms a large lozenge pattern very similar to one seen on the textile discussed above (cat. no. 112). These fragments belong to a small group of cotton textiles, which are all embroidered in the same technique and share basic features of design. The embroidery is similar to brocading, as the thread is not stitched through the fabric, but crosses over and under a succession of warp and weft threads as if it was woven. Yet it is worked onto the finished fabric and strictly speaking is not woven. Typical of the designs found in this group are overall patterns composed of individual diamond shapes with a small oval at the centre. These are achieved by embroidering a succession of stepped perpendicular lines which cross each other, giving the impression of smaller individual motifs.

Georgette Cornu has observed this technique on a number of items in the Musée des Tissus in Lyon (Related works 1–4). All of these share basic features, such as the use of cotton as a ground fabric, a colour scheme comprising tones of brown, blue and earth colours, as well as embroidered (or brocaded) designs. Cornu attributed these items to Yemen and speculated that they might be the *washi* cloths for which Yemen was so renowned in medieval literature.[25] Since most of these items are not inscribed, the attribution to Yemen must rely on the observation of the decorative technique on pieces that can be securely attributed to Yemen. Cornu, however, stressed similarities between the embroidery seen on the fragments in Lyon and two items that could be dated and were both made in San'a'. One, discussed above, in the Metropolitan Museum of Art, New York, was made in the eighth or ninth century and features similarly brocaded designs (Related works 6). The other textile, in the Museum of Islamic Art, Cairo, dates from the reign of the Abbasid caliph al-Mu'tamid (Related works 7).

Cat. 114 *TIRAZ* FRAGMENT FROM
THE ABBASID DYNASTY
Yemen or Iraq, 10th century CE

Description: Fragment of undyed cotton,
comprising a corner of a square
or rectangular field, bordered
by an intertwined cable pattern
containing four lines of Kufic
inscription, the characters outlined
in red and then gilded; there is
a selvedge on the left side of the
inscription field.

Materials: cotton, painted and gilded

Dimensions: h. 13.4 cm, w. 6.7 cm;
max. letter height 1.7 cm

Ground fabric: cotton warp and weft, undyed,
warp-faced plain weave, loose
weave (*sharb*); medium quality (3)

Thread count: warp 20 Z-spun, weft 12 Z-spun

Thread thickness: warp 0.15–0.3 mm loose–medium
twist, weft 0.15–0.3 mm loose–
medium twist

Decoration: outlines in ink, traces of animal(?)
glue or resin, gold paint

Provenance: Ex H.P. Kraus collection, no. 245

Inv. no. LNS 75 T

Related works: See page 510

Inscription:
Line 1: undecipherable

Line 2: [...] ‫عادة[س]‬ (...)
[...] Happiness (...)

Line 3: [...] ‫و (بـ)ـركة)‬ (...)
[...] (B)lessing (...)

Line 4: [...] ‫سلامة‬ (...)
[...] Peace (...)

A fragment with an almost identical arrangement of text in three lines forming a square bordered by a cable pattern on two sides is in the Biblioteca Apostolica Vaticana (Related works 1). It comprises, as here, benedictory phrases, albeit in that case repetition of a single one. Both fragments feature text applied to a cotton ground fabric by applying gold – a technique considered in detail below. In terms of epigraphy, the letters are characterized by pronounced hook-like letter terminals, a *lam–alif* that swings upwards, and letters such as *ra* and *waw* with pronounced swan-necks. Overall the volume of the letters is bold, with variations in thickness to emphasize dynamic movement.

A very close comparison with both pieces is a fragment in the Textile Museum, Washington, DC, which has three lines of text bordered by almost the same type of intertwined cable pattern (Related works 2). Unlike the inscription on the present piece, its benedictory text is personalized, asking for God's blessing and protection for a certain ‘Abd al-Salam; Kühnel observed the content of its inscription in another gold-painted cotton textile in the Museum of Islamic Art, Cairo, but here for a certain Husayn ibn ‘Abd al-‘Aziz (Related works 3). The same ‘Abd al-‘Aziz is mentioned in another piece in Washington (Related works 4). A further example in the Textile Museum, Washington, comprises two lines of text in a similar style of epigraphy documenting the order of a certain Bin Abi Shuja’ (Related works 5); Kühnel speculated that Bin Abi Shuja’ was connected to one of the Buyid rulers, but could not substantiate this claim.[26] Both Kühnel and Cornu attribute all these examples to a single centre in Iraq and date them to the late tenth or early eleventh century. Kühnel made this case by linking the aesthetic of gold-thread embroidery on cotton, associated with Iraq, to that of gold painting.[27]

While an Iraqi attribution is plausible, an attribution to Yemen should at least be considered. The technique of painting inscriptions in gold onto a cotton ground is found on a number of Yemeni *ikat*s, a group that Kühnel did not consider in understanding the nature of these fragments. In addition to several

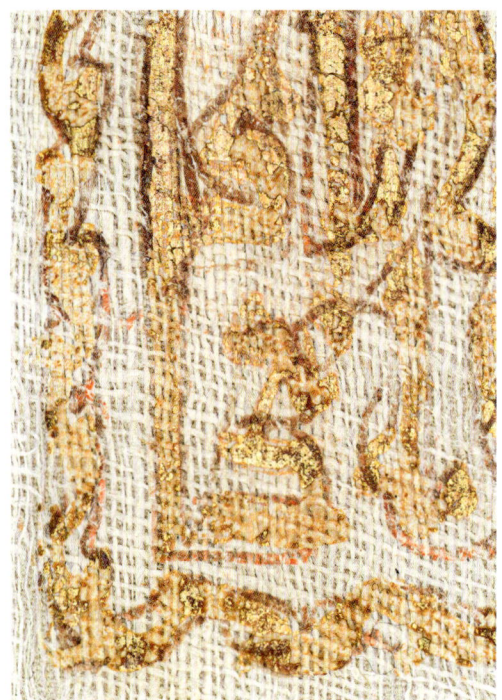

examples with purely benedictory inscriptions, at least three cotton *ikat*s have survived that are inscribed with the names of amirs of the Zaydi dynasty.[28] One at Dumbarton Oaks documents an order of Abu Ibrahim bin al-Muntasir bi-llah al-Jamr bin Muhammad (Related works 6). Another textile at the Biblioteca Apostolica Vaticana mentions the same individual (Related works 7). Sheila Blair suggested that in both inscriptions the *laqab* al-Muntasir bi-llah refers to the Zaydi amir 'Abdallah ibn Muhammad al-Muntasir, who took the title amir in San'a' in 369 AH / 980 CE, thus providing a date *post quem* for the textiles.[29] A third gold-painted *ikat*, at the Cleveland Museum of Art, is inscribed with the name of the Zaydi imam referred to as *amir al-mu'minin* ('Commander of the Believers'), Yusuf ibn Yahya ibn Nasir (r. 980–1003), a second cousin once removed of 'Abdallah ibn Muhammad al-Muntasir (Related works 8).[30]

The epigraphic style used in these Zaydi inscriptions differs in some respects from that of the present example. They are larger and often comprise knotted letters with pronounced hook-like terminals and are much more refined in terms of execution. One could argue that these were prominent inscriptions referring to members of the ruling elite, and therefore required a more prominent refined style, while the small inscription seen here was placed close to the selvedge, therefore not in a prominent position, and was perhaps intended to mark ownership or to personalize the textile. However, on closer inspection certain letterforms found in the Zaydi inscriptions mentioned above also appear in the smaller inscriptions discussed here. Particularly obvious is the letter *'ayn*, which looks like a small trefoil flower. It appears both in one of the inscriptions from the Textile Museum in Washington and that at Dumbarton Oaks (Related works 5, 6). Another feature is the stepped approach to lettering, with pronounced differentiation of higher and lower letter terminals.

A Yemeni connection is perhaps also suggested by the way the inscriptions are executed. The Zaydi inscriptions, as well as most non-personalized benedictory ones, were outlined in ink or black pigment first with what appears to be the nib of a pen, given the fine lines, and then filled in with gum ammoniac, to which was then applied gold leaf, rather than shell gold.[31] The calligraphy of the famous Blue Quran was executed in a similar way.[32] The execution of the script on the present fragment conforms with this.[33] The preparation of the cloth was necessary in order to provide the gold leaf with a base, as it would not have fused with the textile ground in the same way a pigment would have done. For this reason, cotton or linen was sometimes glazed, but there seems no evidence of glazing here.

7

PALESTINE

The province of Palestine (Arabic: Filastin) was central to the early Islamic caliphates, because of the centrality of Jerusalem as the second most important holy site after Mecca and the location of the Dome of the Rock and the al-Aqsa mosque; simultaneously, it was (and is) the home of the other two great traditions of People of the Book, Judaism and Christianity. While, under the Umayyads, Palestine was in the heartland of the caliphate, under the Abbasids it became a province, with the city of Ramla as its capital (see map, pp. 12–13).[1] Both the Tulunids and the Ikhshidids were active in Palestine, which they ruled as an extension of their stronghold in Egypt. The Ikhshidids minted coins in Palestine, as is documented by surviving examples.[2] After the Fatimids had conquered Egypt in 969, they also swiftly occupied Palestine and drove out the remaining Ikhshidid governor, al-Hasan ibn 'Ubaydallah ibn Tughj, thus ending Abbasid influence there. It was, of course, the interference of the Fatimids under al-Hakim which began a process of political power struggles over Jerusalem that culminated in the First Crusade in 1096–99.

In the north of Palestine, located on the western shore of the Sea of Galilee, Tabariyya (Tiberias) was a well-known centre for the manufacture of grass mats. Tabariyya had been founded c. 87 by Herod Antipas and named in honour of the Roman emperor Tiberius. After the Islamic conquest of Palestine in 635, Tabariyya served as regional capital of the province of al-Urdunn (Jordan). The Umayyads built a palace on the shores of the lake, called Khirbat al-Minya, as well as a large congregational mosque similar to that at Damascus. Well into the Abbasid period, Tabariyya was an important centre of learning, particularly of Hebrew scholarship. Both the historian al-Muqaddasi in 985 and the eleventh-century traveller Nasir-e Khosraw described the city. Al-Muqaddasi, writing before 985–86, stated that the merchants of Tabariyya exported long pieces of matting.[3] In his *Sefer nameh*, Nasir-e Khosrow mentions the making of prayer mats from grass and rushes: 'In the town of Tiberias they make reed prayer mats, sold for five dinars.[4] In the twelfth century, the geographer al-Idrisi stated that Tabariyya produced mats called 'al-samaniyya', which were highly praised and, according to him, not produced anywhere else than in Palestine.[5]

Grass and rushes have been excluded from most studies of *tiraz* textiles. Although they are not orthodox textile materials, they can be woven on a loom in much the same way as textile yarns. A few surviving examples show that grasses and reeds were woven to a high standard of craftsmanship (see pp. 88–91).[6] The inscriptions on these items are comparable in epigraphic aesthetic to a number of *tiraz* textile inscriptions from the tenth century. It is likely that the *tiraz* workshops in which these mats were manufactured were part of the same institutional set-up as those producing linen and silk tapestry *tiraz* textiles.

The only evidence for the manufacture of grass woven mats in a *tiraz* workshop is an almost intact example of such a mat at the Benaki Museum, Athens. Its inscription, which contains benedictory phrases dedicated to an unnamed owner (*li-sahibihi*), documents its manufacture in a *tiraz al-khassa* in Tabariyya (fig. 3.1).[7] Based on its monumental style of script it has been attributed to the mid-tenth century.[8] Another mat, this one intact and of similar composition and workmanship, is at the Metropolitan Museum of Art, New York; it has a benedictory inscription dedicated to an unnamed patron but no mention of a workshop (fig. 3.3).[9] A fragment of a grass woven mat at the Museum für Islamische Kunst, Berlin, also features an inscription in a monumental style of script, documenting its manufacture in a *tiraz al-khassa*, albeit without a location (fig. 3.2).[10]

That prayer mats were produced not only in Palestine is indicated by a passage in the biography of the Fatimid court secretary Jawdhar, describing how al-Mu'izz's secretary Jawdhar was asked by his master to order inscribed prayer mats from Mahdia in north Africa; al-Mu'izz had thought out the inscriptions very carefully.[11] The use of such mats under the Fatimids is further documented in al-Maqrizi's account of the contents of the Fatimid *khaza'in al-farsh* ('treasury of furnishings'), where mats (*husur*s) were listed among the tents and their contents.[12]

Cat. 115   **FRAGMENT OF A FLOOR
MAT WITH A *TIRAZ*
INSCRIPTION FROM THE
ABBASID OR EARLY
FATIMID DYNASTY**
**Greater Syria, probably Tabariyya
(Tiberias), 10th century CE**

Description: Fragment of a floor mat, made
of esparto grass (or reed) in
three shades of brown, woven
on a hemp warp, with a selvedge
on the right side. It has a base
of light brown, on which are
arranged three registers: in the
lower portion of the piece are the
remains of a main central field,
once compirising a probably
formulaic Kufic inscription,
framed by an undulating split-
palmette scroll (3.5 cm), both in
mid-brown; above the central
field is a broad band in dark
brown against which is set a Kufic
inscription in reserve (7.5 cm);
another tripartite inscription band,
on a strip of matting above (6 cm)
in dark brown, is set against the
light-brown ground fabric with
the remnant of a smaller Kufic
inscription (2 cm).

Materials: hemp and esparto grass:
plain weave

Dimensions: h. 46.5 cm, w. 40.3 cm;
max. letter height 7.5 cm

Ground fabric: hemp warp (undyed) and esparto
grass weft, weft-faced plain weave,
dense texture; very good quality
(1); selvedge on the right side of
the inscription

Thread count: paired warp 3 S-spun two-plied
Z-spun, weft 17 halved stalks

Thread thickness: warp 0.5 mm tight twist,
weft 1.0 mm

Inv. no. LNS 54 T

Related works: See page 510

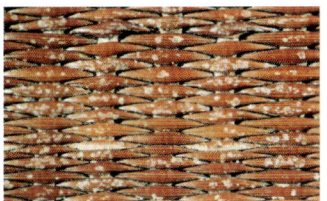

Inscription (main line):

سعاد[ة] وسلام والدوام على(...) بركة (منه؟) وسعادة

Happin[ess] and peace and permanence to (...) blessing (from him ?) and
happiness

This fragment was once part of a large mat that was probably used for prayer.
Probably the most important surviving example of an early Islamic mat is at the
Benaki Museum, Athens (Related works 1; see fig. 3.1). The inscription on the
Athens mat contains a number of benedictions conferred on its owner (*li-sahibihi*)
and records that it had been ordered in the *tiraz al-khassa* in Tabariyya. Its
ground fabric consists of hemp warps into which a double weft of fine flattened
grass strands has been woven. The use of spun textile yarns, rather than grass,
for the warp suggests that this mat was woven on a conventional loom. It is of
very high quality.[13] Not only are the materials used very fine, but the layout must
have involved careful planning: both fringes are carefully knotted, a couple of
weft bands are placed in exact order at each end, and an intricately woven lattice-
shaped band frames the main field, which itself contains the carefully spaced
inscriptions on either end. Aesthetically, and perhaps technically, this piece is
comparable with the large linen sheets woven in Egypt during the same period.
Also its dimensions, its sparing use of ornament and its unornamented single lines
of inscription may resemble those of linen shawls or large turban-cloths, of which
only fragments have survived; the dimensions – 115 cm from selvedge to selvedge
– conform with those of many contemporary linen textiles made in Egypt.

Another complete mat, albeit one that carries only a benedictory formula,
without mentioning a workshop, is in the Metropolitan Museum of Art in New
York (Related works 2; see fig. 3.3). A fragment of a larger mat, comparable
with the present piece, is in the Museum für Islamische Kunst, Berlin (Related
works 3; see fig. 3.2). Like the Benaki Museum mat, it too bears an inscription
documenting its manufacture at a *tiraz al-khassa*, the location of which is lost.

Two further fragments are in the Bouvier Collection (Related works 4, 5). One of them preserves the phrase '[mimm]a umira' ('[of what was] ordered'), inscribed in a style of script comparable with that on the Athens mat (Related works 4). The other, a fragment in the Pfister Collection at the Biblioteca Apostolica Vaticana (Related works 6), also features remnants of what was probably once a benedictory text in its border and, interestingly, a figure of a stag with ostentatious antlers within what remains of the main field. Fibre analysis performed at the Musée National d'Histoire Naturelle, Paris, on one of the fragments in the Bouvier Collection (Related works 4) has shown that the material used for the warp was hemp and that for the weft the grass *Andropogon*, often erroneously referred to as reed or rushes in the literature; the grass is recorded in the flora of Palestine.[14] These materials may also have been used in the other examples mentioned here, a matter that could be clarified only by further examination of the fibres. Several supplementary examples in the Bouvier Collection and the Textile Museum, Washington, DC, are made of date-palm leaves, plaited rather than woven, and have thus been attributed to Egypt, rather than Palestine.[15]

The epigraphic style of the inscriptions in these mats is characterized by a rather angular script with wedge-shaped upper letter-stem terminals, unfoliated, with the *ya* and terminal *'ayn* reversing and curving below the baseline, box-shaped letters such *kaf* or *ta*, and upright rather than curved *alif* and upper terminals. In a way, the script has its roots in the ninth century, when a style of script was used that was not yet foliated. Examples of this style are found in the inscriptions of the Nilometer in Cairo.[16] A *tiraz* textile inscription that conforms to this style of epigraphy is in the Textile Museum, Washington, DC (Related works 7). It was made in the *tiraz al-khassa* in Damietta in 334 AH / 945–46 CE, during the reign of the Abbasid caliph al-Mustakfi (r. 944–46). In another *tiraz* textile from al-Mustakfi's reign, at the Textile Museum, Washington, the link between *lam* or *mim* and *ha* is noteworthy (Related works 8). The preceding letter joins the *ha* above the baseline in mid-section. The same can be observed in the way the *lam* joins the *kha* in the word *al-khassa* on the mats in the Metropolitan Museum and the Museum für Islamische Kunst. The style of epigraphy used in Egyptian *tiraz* inscriptions from the reign of al-Muti' (r. 946–74), al-Mustakfi's successor, changes. As can be seen from a sequence of inscriptions at the Textile Museum, Washington, upper letter terminals start to be foliated, with pronounced swan-necks for *kaf*, *ta*, terminal *nun* and *ra*, a feature not seen in the mats discussed here. Therefore, based on the evidence of epigraphy, one should consider an attribution to the first half of the tenth century for the group. Considering the quality of the present piece, its execution and materials, and the elegant style of the inscription, which is comparable with that of the mats discussed above, there is little doubt that this, too, was a product of the workshops of Tabariyya.

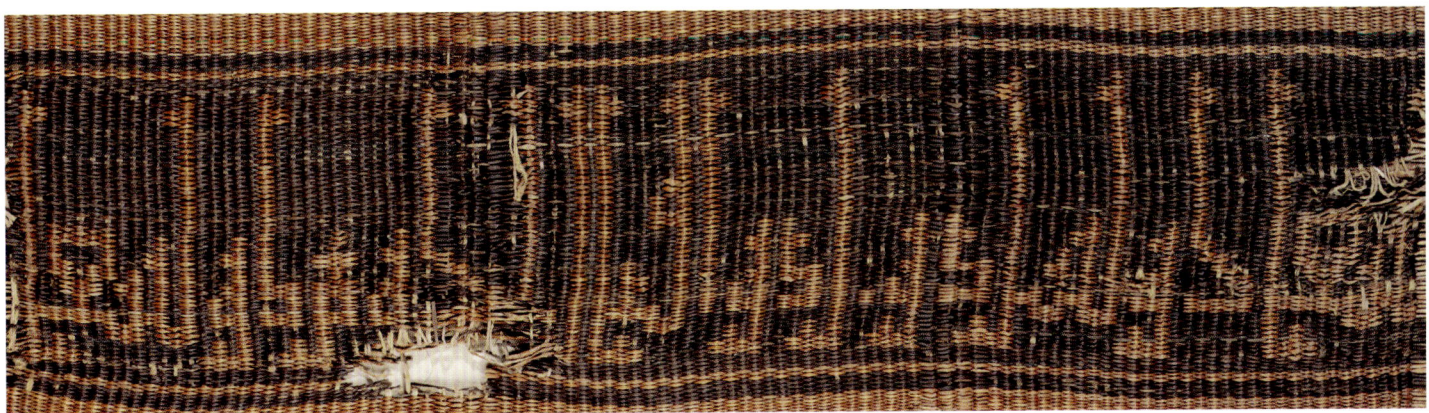

The *Sirat al-ustadh jawdhar* ('The life of the master Jawdhar), an account of the life of one of the most of the most trusted secretaries of the Fatimid caliph al-Muʿizz, allows an insight into how highly esteemed grass mats were as objects within the court context.[17] It describes how al-Muʿizz asked Jawdhar to order inscribed reed prayer mats from Mahdia, the former heartland of the Fatimids before the conquest of Egypt, which were to be inscribed with a text chosen by al-Muʿizz himself. Recent controlled excavations of the Fatimid funerary complex at Istabl ʿAntar in the Southern Cemetery of Cairo have shown that mats were used in several tombs in order to cover an enshrouded corpse and also provide a supplementary layer between corpse and ground.[18] This may explain the rather fragmentary nature of most surviving examples. The Benaki Museum piece shows traces of what are perhaps the results of human decomposition. Like the Benaki piece, the finds at Istabl ʿAntar seem to have survived almost completely. They were, however, undecorated and of far inferior quality. The Shafiʿite theologian al-Ghazali describes, in his *Kitab dhikr al-mawt wa-ma baʿdahu* ('Book of the remembrance of death and the afterlife'), how the Prophet Muhammad was laid on a mat covered with some of his garments from life before his interment (see chapter 2, p. 79).[19] While it may be difficult to deduce from such accounts alone that there existed a tradition in Islam to deposit the dead on a mat, it may be significant that such mats were sometimes used by the living for prayer, as the account of Jawdhar tells us. They might have been thought to carry *baraka* ('blessing') that would extend to the deceased in their grave.

8

THE INDIAN SUBCONTINENT

The history of Islam on the Indian subcontinent goes back to the expansion of the Umayyad empire under the Arab military commander Muhammad ibn Qasim al-Thaqafi, who, while still only a teenager, led an expedition ordered by the governor of Iraq, al-Hajjaj ibn Yusuf (in office 692–714), to Sind in western India in 89–92 AH / 708–11 CE.[1] Instead of taking the route across the Arabian Sea, he arrived overland via the Makran Desert and had support troops brought in by ship. He conquered the port city of Daybul at the mouth of the Indus river, massacred many of the inhabitants and established a settlement there. From there, he took several other cities north-east, including Multan (see map, pp. 12–13). He exerted great influence, first on the Umayyad caliph 'Abd al-Malik (r. 685–705) and then on his successor, the caliph al-Walid bin 'Abd al-Malik (r. 705–15). What followed was a period of coexistence among Muslims, Buddhists and Hindus, the Muslim population, though not the majority, emerging as the dominant force. Muhammad bin Qasim's son 'Amr founded the city of Mansura (Brahmanabad), not far from modern Hyderabad in Sind province. Direct rule of Sind as part of the Abbasid empire lasted until the ninth century, after which local Arab–Muslim families took over power. By the tenth century, the northern parts of the province around Multan had become an Isma'ili stronghold that proclaimed allegiance to the Fatimids. Mahmud of Ghazna, who was a defender of Sunni orthodoxy, took Multan in 1006. The seaports of Sind had already been adherents of Sunnism and, while Upper Sind remained Ghaznavid, they came under the control of the Sumeras (or Sumras), a Rajput dynasty. It was only under the Ghurid sultan Mu'izz al-Din Abu al-Muzaffar Muhammad ibn Sam (r. jointly with his brother Ghiyath al-Din 1173–1203, and as sole ruler 1203–06) that the whole of Sind became part of the growing Ghurid Empire, which stretched all the way to north India and the sultanate of Delhi.

Another region important for the history of interactions between the Indian subcontinent and the early Islamic world is Gujarat. The region was ruled by Hindu rulers until the takeover by the Delhi sultans at the end of the thirteenth century. In 1298 the last Vaghela ruler was defeated by the generals of 'Ala' al-Din Khalji.[2] Islam had a presence in Gujarat before the conquest by the Delhi sultans – Kafur, the eunuch general and minister of 'Ala' al-Din Khalji, was captured during the conquest of Cambay (Kambhat), where he had been the slave of a wealthy *khoja*, a Nizari Isma'ili.[3] Early Islamic travellers and geographers knew much about Gujarat, particularly its ports, from which precious materials such as gold, silver, pearls, animals (horses and camels), wood (teak, bamboo and aloe wood) and betelnut were traded.

That the west coast of India engaged in trade with western Asia and the Mediterranean region in antiquity is documented by a first-century account entitled the *Periplus of the Erythraean Sea*.[4] It is, however, the trade letters and notes of Jewish merchants found in the synagogue of Old Cairo – the so-called Geniza documents – and other locations such as the Red Sea port of Qusayr al-Qadim that contain the most numerous and informative references to Indian trade during the early Islamic period.[5] They speak of Yemeni traders from Aden, who functioned as dealers out of the ports of Egypt with connections into the heart of the Mediterranean and the Indian Ocean. Whole families engaged in the trade in commercial goods, which included precious and non-precious metals, spices and pharmaceuticals. Textiles appear to have been traded only if they were of some rarity or considered a luxury, as they took up a lot of space in the holds of ships; cotton textiles appear in the letters and were traded in quite large quantities, but were not considered of prime importance, unlike Indian silk muslin, for example.[6] One merchant, Jekuthiel, is expressly mentioned as entrusting expensive textiles, destined for a firm in Aden, to another trader, named Joseph Lebdi, in Nahrwara in Gujarat. Instead of taking the textiles to Aden as instructed, Lebdi sold them all in the Red Sea port of Dahlak. His son Abu al-Barakat also came back from India with textiles as the most precious part of his cargo.[7]

While the luxury textiles referred to in the Cairo Geniza documents are rather elusive – most have probably vanished – a group of block-printed resist-dyed cotton textiles have traditionally been associated with Fustat, where many were allegedly found. Many of these were probably sold to European and American collectors in much the same way as the inscribed textiles discussed in this book. In a study of the Newberry collection at the Ashmolean Museum in Oxford, probably the largest such collection, the historian of south-east Asia Ruth Barnes covered more than a thousand fragments, categorizing them and attempting for the first time to provide a historical context for this material.[8] She related the textiles to others, found in more recent excavations, such as at the Red Sea port of Qusayr al-Qadim and Fustat (Old Cairo). Carbon dating carried out on a selection of fragments provided interesting and unexpected results.[9] She dated most textiles between the thirteenth and sixteenth centuries, when Egypt was ruled by the Mamluks, who had strong transoceanic trade with the Indian Ocean and China beyond, but there were two that did not fall into this chronological schema. A fragment with the remnant of an epigraphic border, decorated with a lotus vine motif that resembles two similar ones on a fragment from Qusayr al-Qadim, was carbon dated to CE 1010+/–55 years;[10] one of its borders contains a Kufic inscription alluding to the textile's owner.[11] An uninscribed fragment in the Newberry collection was also tested, giving a result of CE 1060+/–40.[12] A third indigo-dyed fragment at the Ashmolean Museum, featuring registers with striding elephants, was tested after the publication of Ruth Barnes's book and could be dated to CE 895+/–75 years, a date that pushes the chronology even further back.[13] More circumstantial evidence is provided by the find of a resist-dyed cotton fragment during the excavations at Fustat-C, carried out by George Scanlon and Władysław Kubiak.[14] It has been claimed that the layer in which this textile was found dates from the eleventh century, on the basis of archaeological stratigraphy, and the fact that its archaeological context was relatively undisturbed.

Although most of the excavations at Fustat produced hardly any stratigraphic evidence, Barnes suggested that, together with the evidence from radiocarbon dating, the possibility exists of an earlier chronology than hitherto thought. Already in the 1950s, Ernst Kühnel identified as Indian two fragments at the Textile Museum in Washington, DC, and on the basis of their inscriptions, which he compared with those found on Abbasid ceramics from Samarra, dated them to the tenth century.[15] He reasoned that these pieces are therefore some of the earliest types of imported printed cotton found in Islamic Egypt. The inscription on one contains a benedictory repetition alluding to the textile's owner, 'baraka wa tawfiq li-sahibihi'.[16] The textiles discussed below also relate to the style of script found in the Washington fragments, particularly at the word 'li-sahibihi', also found in cat. no. 118.

The Newberry collection in the Ashmolean Museum also contains a number of cotton fragments with early inscriptions, mostly short benedictory phrases.[17] Barnes suggested that some of these textiles were made in India and that the script was copied from Fatimid inscriptions, implying dates in the eleventh and twelfth centuries, allowing for a lapse in time. Several resist-dyed cotton fragments with short benedictory Kufic inscriptions are also found in the Bouvier Collection. While Georgette Cornu attributes these fragments to fourteenth- and fifteenth-century India, comparing their style with inscriptions found in provincial centres during the Mamluk period, the inscription on one indigo-dyed fragment is very close to the textiles in the Textile Museum, Washington, mentioned above.[18] The treatment of the word 'li-sahibihi' is almost identical, suggesting that the piece may in fact be much earlier than Cornu proposed, following Kühnel's dating. Two further fragments in blue with Kufic inscriptions also employ a style that appears early medieval, rather than later.[19]

While scholars have sought various origins for the use of early scripts in Gujarati printed and resist-dyed textiles – adducing, particularly, the idea of external influence from a foreign aesthetic – no one has so far considered the evidence of surviving pre-Sultanate inscriptions in

I.8.A   Foundation inscription from the Great Mosque in Banbhore, dated 239 AH / 853–54 CE.
Carved stone. Archaeological Museum, Banbhore, Sindh, Pakistan.

the coastal regions of north India, where Islam was established for many centuries from the time of the conquest in the early eighth century. While Ernst Kühnel saw similarities with the inscriptions on ceramics from Samarra, Ruth Barnes made many analogies with Fatimid inscriptions.

One of the earliest inscriptions from Sind is a foundation inscription from the Great Mosque in Banbhore (c. 65 km south-east of Karachi in Pakistan), dated 239 AH / 853–54 CE; it documents the order for the construction of the mosque by the governor Harun ibn Muhammad through the agency of ʿAli ibn ʿIsa, both of whom bear the title *mawla amir al-muʾminin* (fig. I.8.A).[20] It has been suggested that Banbhore is in fact the city of Daybul, an important seaport and a critical location in the history of the early Islamic settlement of Sind, the seat of a governor under the Umayyads and Abbasids.[21] According to Arabic sources the Abbasid caliph al-Muʿtasim (r. 833–42) had ʿAnbisa ibn Ishaq al-Dhabbi appointed as governor of Sind. He demolished the ruined structures of an earlier Hindu temple in the city of Daybul, work that continued under the patronage

of the caliph al-Wathiq (r. 842–47) until the caliph al-Mutawakkil (r. 847–61) appointed Harun ibn Muhammad as the new governor of the province, who completed the work.[22] The palaeography of the inscription has been described in great detail: the *alif* is slanted towards the right, *jim* and *ha* are archaic, the *dal* is cursive, *nun* and *ra* are curved upwards, and *mim* and *ha* as well as *lam–alif* are triangular.[23] Letters are ornamented with arrowhead or hook-like terminals, particularly projecting out from the *alif*.

Another significant group of early inscriptions can be found on a set of four massive bronze door knockers from the *dar al-imara* at Mansura, the historic capital of the province of Sind under the Umayyads and Abbasids, where they probably decorated the entrance (fig. I.8.B).[24] Each inscription, executed in an elegant form of foliated Kufic, encircles a central sculpted face of mask-like anthropomorphic or zoomorphic head (in the latter case, perhaps a mythical creature) from which a multi-lobed handle is suspended. The text of the inscriptions names the Habbarid amir ʿAbdallah ibn ʿUmar, known from the silver coinage of Mansura and from a reference in

I.8.B   Door-knocker with Kufic inscription round the edge of the plate, from the mosque of Mansura, *c.* 10th century CE. Cast and engraved bronze, diam *c.* 56 cm. National Museum of Pakistan, Islamabad.

the *Akhbar al-sind wa al-hind* ('The history of Sind and India') to have been in office *c.* 270 AH / 883–84 CE.[25] These inscriptions display many of the features of the one from the Great Mosque discussed above, particularly the prominent arrowhead terminals, but they are also foliated in letters such as *'ayn*. A similar type of script can be seen in the block-printed and embroidered fragment cat. no. 119, which also features foliations and floriations in some of the letters.

Another foundation inscription on a stone slab from the Great Mosque in Banbhore is dated 294 AH / 906–07 CE and documents the building's construction by the amir Muhammad ibn 'Abdallah (fig. I.8.C).[26] Muhammad ibn 'Abdallah was probably the son of the governor Muhammad ibn 'Umar, who is mentioned on the Mansura bronze door knockers.[27] The inscriptions are very similar indeed and one can see a connection between them, which is borne out aesthetically. Upper letter terminals are characterized by hook-like protrusions, the final *nun*, *ra* and *waw* curl upwards, and the *'ayn* is open.[28] Interestingly, a similar aesthetic can be found on a series of coins struck in Iraq for the Abbasid caliph al-Muqtadir (r. 908–32), which conform to a type that had its origins in India, the so-called Hindu–Shahi model.[29] Because these coins are such an anomaly, Flood suggested that they were perhaps minted to be distributed among the tribes of the Kabul Valley to underpin their allegiance to the Abbasids.[30] There might well be a connection to Khurasan with regard to epigraphic styles, as is suggested by a group of *tiraz* textiles with inscriptions that relate to the particular aesthetic of the inscriptions discussed here. One of them, a *mulham* with a silk-embroidered inscription in the name of the caliph al-Mu'tadid (r. 892–902), also features elegant upward-bending and slightly slanted letter stems with hook-like terminals, triangular and circular *mim*s, triangular *'ayn* and stepped *sin* (fig. I.8.D).[31] Its

I.8.C   Floriated Kufic foundation inscription from the Great Mosque of Banbhore, dated 294 AH / 906–07 CE. Carved stone. Archaeological Museum, Banbhore, Sindh, Pakistan.

I.8.D   Detail of a fragment of a *tiraz* textile, from the reign of the Abbasid caliph al-Muʿtadid (r. 892–902), eastern Iran or Khurasan. *Mulham* (cotton and silk plain weave), with silk embroidery, 37.5 × 35.6 cm. Metropolitan Museum of Art, New York, Gift of George D. Pratt, 1931, inv. no. 31.19.2.

I.8.E   Rubbing of part of a floriated Kufic dedicatory inscription, epitaph from the Shrine of Ibrahim, Bhadreshwar, Gujarat, dated 554 AH / 1159–60 CE. Carved stone. Reproduced from Z.A. Desai, 'Kufi Epitaphs from Bhadreswar in Gujarat', *Epigraphia Indica: Arabic and Persian Supplement* (1965), pl. Ii.

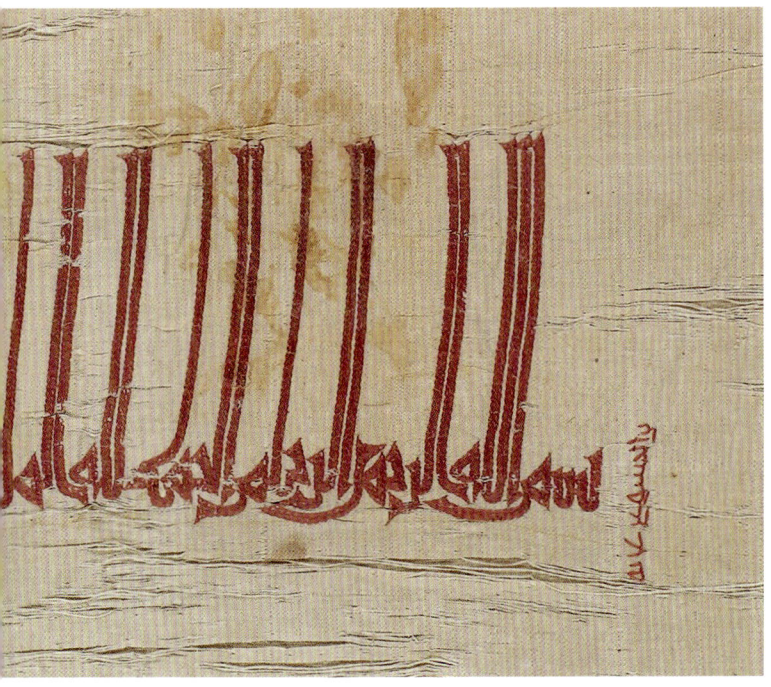

into the Red Sea and the Persian Gulf.[34] A series of epitaphs found in the Gujarati port city of Bhadreshwar provides evidence for the existence of very developed floriated inscriptions in the period before Gujarat was conquered by the Ghurids at the end of the thirteenth century, and when the Hindu Chalukya dynasty was still in power.[35] The earliest, still *in situ* at the Dargah of La'l Shahbaz, mentions an individual tentatively identified as Ibrahim ibn Abu al-'Azm 'Abdallah ibn Bakr and is dated 554 AH / 1159–60 CE (fig. I.8.E).[36] One of the inscriptions is dated Sha'ban 569 AH / March 1174 CE and comprises a complicated net of knotted and plaited letter stems. Rather than looking for transoceanic influence in these inscriptions, it might be useful to consider connections closer to home in eastern Iran and Afghanistan, from where much of the pressure to invade Gujarat came. Knotted or plaited Kufic can, for example, be observed on the Samanid pottery of eastern Iran, traditionally dated to the late tenth century.[37] It still appears in the twelfth century on the so-called 'Bobrinski bucket', a bronze cauldron dated 1163 and made in Herat just before the city was captured by the Ghurids in 1175.[38]

A serious evaluation of the Arabic epigraphy found on Gujarati textiles has never been undertaken. Nevertheless, the preceding discussion shows that these inscriptions existed in a context of a highly developed use of Arabic script, even in areas that were considered peripheral from the point of view of the great Islamic empires. What seems clear when looking at formal aspects is that the western parts of the Indian subcontinent were perhaps influenced by what was happening not only beyond the sea, but also further north in eastern Iran and Khurasan, long before the Ghurid sultanate of Delhi was established, which created a political connection with these regions that lasted many hundreds of years. Carbon dating has shown that it can provide a useful tool to shake up an accepted chronology, and perhaps in the future epigraphic resist-dyed textiles, such as the ones discussed here, should be tested to a lager extent, so that one can begin to establish a chronology of scripts based on scientific analysis.

date, between 892 and 902, is within the period between the bronze door knockers and the foundation inscription from 294 AH / 906–07 CE. Several other *mulham* textiles with related inscriptions are known. One is in the Textile Museum, Washington, DC, dated to 283 AH / 896–97 CE.[32] Another is in the Museum für Islamische Kunst, Berlin, with an inscription documenting its manufacture in Merw in 287 AH / 900–01 CE, therefore linking the group to Khurasan.[33]

The origin of floriated inscriptions is also a matter of debate. Although they are found on many so-called epigraphic Fustat textiles, they are quite distinct from the early styles of the fragments discussed here. As mentioned earlier, Ruth Barnes seeks an external source in Fatimid Egypt. Flood seems to follow this line of thought with respect to foliated scripts, referring to the diffusion of tradesmen and pilgrims across the Indian Ocean region

Cat. 116   INSCRIBED TEXTILE FRAGMENT FROM THE PRE-SULTANATE PERIOD
West India, Gujarat, 10th to 11th century CE

Description: Fragment of cotton, resist-dyed and block-printed in indigo blue, with a pattern of octagons each containing a circular medallion that encloses a multi-lobed rosette, from which emanate four flowering stems with three palmettes on either side; between the octagons are lozenge-shaped fillers with a circular motif at the centre; below the main field of decoration is a band of Kufic inscription bordered on both sides by a band of lozenges.

Materials: cotton and indigo: plain weave, block-printed and resist-dyed

Dimensions: h. 29 cm, w. 12.6 cm; max. letter height 4.6 cm (including elements below the baseline; letter height from baseline 2.8 cm)

Ground fabric: cotton warp and weft, resist-dyed (blue), balanced plain weave, regular, dense texture (*dabiqi*), coarse; good–medium quality (2–3)

Thread count: warp 12 Z-spun, weft 13 Z-spun

Thread thickness: warp 0.25–0.5 mm tight twist, weft 0.3–0.5 mm tight twist

Decoration: indigo, block-printed and resist-dyed

Provenance: Ex H.P. Kraus collection, no. 205

Published: Curatola et al. 2010, p. 71, no. 38

Inv. no. LNS 84 T

Related works: See page 510

Inscription:

[...] and from him blessing [...]

[...] ومنه بركة [...]

Cat. 117   **INSCRIBED TEXTILE
FRAGMENT FROM THE
PRE-SULTANATE PERIOD**
**West India, Gujarat, 10th
to 11th century CE**

Description: Fragment of cotton, resist-dyed
and block-printed in indigo blue,
comprising an inscription band
in Kufic framed by a border of
small crescents below and a dotted
border above, with a frieze of
small arches topped by arrowhead
motifs; sewn on its right side to
a cloth of the same material and
technique, comprising multiple
rows of small heart-shaped flowers.

Materials: cotton and indigo: plain weave,
block-printed and resist-dyed

Dimensions: h. 11.3 cm, w. 23.7 cm;
max. letter height 2.0 cm

Ground fabric: cotton warp and weft, resist-dyed
(blue), plain weave (warp-faced?),
dense texture; good quality (2);
seam on the right side, attaching
another fragment

Thread count: warp 30 Z-spun, weft 13 Z-spun

Thread thickness: warp 0.25–0.3 mm tight twist,
weft 0.3 mm tight twist

Decoration: indigo, resist-dyed with printing
blocks; seam on the right side,
attaching another fragment

Provenance: Ex H.P. Kraus collection,
New York or Vienna, no. 206

Inv. no. LNS 85 T

Related works: See page 510

Inscription: repetition of

[بر]كة من عمل محمد بركة مــن (عمل محمد)

[Bles]sing, made by Muhammad, blessing, of what (was made by Muhammad)

A fragment in the Bouvier Collection comprises an epigraphic band and an
almost identical arched frieze very close in style to the present piece. However,
the rest of the decoration seems to differ (Related works 1). It is unusual to find
the maker's name, but he is mentioned on this example as Muhammad. No other
textile in this group, it seems, includes the maker's name in the inscription.

Cat. 118   **INSCRIBED TEXTILE FRAGMENT FROM THE PRE-SULTANATE PERIOD**
West India, Gujarat, 10th to 11th century CE

Description: Fragment of undyed cotton fabric, of near triangular form marked by a border, block-printed and resist-dyed, with three lines of Kufic inscription of benedictory content referring to the owner; three rectangular cuts have been made into the main field along the shortest edge.

Materials: cotton and indigo: plain weave, block-printed and resist-dyed

Dimensions: h. 17 cm, w. 15 cm; max. letter height *c.* 5.0 cm

Ground fabric: cotton warp and weft, undyed, balanced plain weave, close texture (*dabiqi*), regular structure; good–medium quality (2–3)

Thread count: warp 29 Z-spun, weft 23 Z-spun

Thread thickness: warp 0.1–0.3 mm medium twist, weft 0.15 mm medium twist

Decoration: block-printed and resist-dyed

Provenance: Ex H.P. Kraus collection, no. 264

Inv. no. LNS 80 T

Related works: See page 510

Inscription:

[…] from God to its owner

[...] من الله لصاحبه [...]

The text, block-printed and probably resist-dyed, was once part of a longer phrase conferring God's blessings on its owner – the word 'baraka' ('blessing'), found in a number of other epigraphic resist-dyed textiles (Related works 1–3), is obviously missing. It may well have been contained in another compartment once attached to a larger piece, but now lost. The script used here, with its distinctive letterforms, points to a tenth- or eleventh-century date for the fragment. Indicative are the upwardly curved terminal *nun* in *min*, the hook-like terminals of *alif* and *lam*, and the rectangular shape of the *sad*.

Cat. 119   **INSCRIBED TEXTILE FRAGMENT FROM THE PRE-SULTANATE PERIOD**
West India, Sind or Gujarat, 10th to 11th century CE

Description: Fragment of undyed linen, with three decorative bands, block-printed in black ink and then embroidered: the uppermost one comprises a frieze of split palmettes (height 1 cm); the central band (height 3.7 cm) has an inscription in floriated Kufic characters embroidered in red silk; and the lowermost band consists of a sequence of octagonal cartouches (height 4.3 cm) with small palmettes in the spandrels between, each cartouche containing a circular inscription embroidered in brown silk against an embroidered yellow silk background, which encloses a central field containing a pair of birds to either side of a tree of life motif, also embroidered in brown silk against a yellow silk background.

Materials: cotton, silk and ink: plain weave, block-print and embroidery

Dimensions: h. 9.4 cm, w. 10.0 cm; max. letter height 2.9 cm

Ground fabric: cotton warp and weft, undyed, balanced plain weave (tabby), dense weave (*dabiqi*), mostly regular; medium quality (3)

Thread count: warp 23 Z-spun, weft 20 Z-spun

Thread thickness: warp 0.15–0.5 mm slight–medium twist, weft 0.25–0.5 mm slight–medium twist

Embroidery: silk (*c.* 0.5–1.0 mm), dyed (yellowish-green), chain stitch

Published: Curatola et al. 2010, p. 72, cat. no. 39; Spuhler 2020, pp. 232–33, cat. no. 197

Inv. no. LNS 18 T

Inscription: undecipherable

This is an interesting fragment, as the design was marked first by block-printing it onto the fabric and then embroidering over and around the printed designs. Since the block-printed designs eliminated the need for the embroiderer to count threads, he was able to use chain stitch, an embroidery technique used mostly in Iraqi and Khurasani *tiraz* textiles. Furthermore, chain stitching allowed the embroiderer to cover larger areas with silk floss than did any of the stitches that involved counting threads. So here both the decorative areas and the background are embroidered, whereas in most Egyptian *tiraz* textiles only the inscription or decoration was embroidered and the background was left blank.

The combination of cotton ground fabric with its Z-spun warp and weft, the block-printed design and the epigraphic style of the inscription suggests a non-Egyptian, probably Indian, origin for this piece. In terms of material and technique, it relates to resist-dyed cottons imported from India in the early medieval period. As in resist-dyed textiles, the decoration of the present piece was block-printed, albeit in black pigment rather than wax. A very close comparison for the particular style of floriated Kufic calligraphy seen here can be found in a foundation inscription on a stone slab from the Great Mosque in Banbhore, Pakistan, dated 294 AH / 906–07 CE (discussed above; see fig. I.8.C).[39] Its particular style of calligraphy is characterized by hook-like letter terminals, the final *nun*, *ra* and *waw* curling upwards, and the open form of *'ayn*, which are also found here. Another close comparison is the inscription on the bronze door knockers from the mosque of Mansura, also in Sind (see fig. I.8.B). For a discussion of the style of these inscriptions see pp. 364–67.

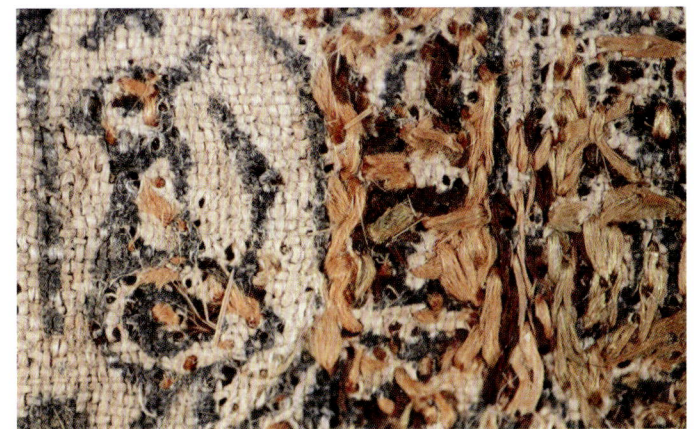

PART II

THE FATIMID CALIPHATE
IN EGYPT

The Fatimids are perhaps the most enigmatic of all the dynasties of the medieval Islamic world. This is partly because of their turbulent history – they established a Shi'ite counter-caliphate from their north African stronghold in Mahdia, from where they conquered Egypt in 973 – and partly because we know quite a lot about them through historical sources, particularly about the great disaster for the dynasty, the dispersal of the Fatimid treasury under the caliph al-Mustansir (r. 1036–94) at the end of the eleventh century. Perhaps the best sources are the Mamluk historian al-Maqrizi, who relied on much earlier sources contemporary with the Fatimid dynasty, and the biography of the Fatimid court secretary Jawdhar, active under the caliph al-Mu'izz (r. 953–75). The Fatimid dynasty was full of figures larger than life. While al-Mu'izz and al-'Aziz (r. 975–96) were astute statesmen, the caliph al-Hakim (r. 996–1021) proved to be a very unstable personality. His reign came to an abrupt end one night when he disappeared, never to be seen again. It was during his time that power struggles with the family began a downward spiral against the backdrop of the rise of Sunni orthodoxy under the central Asian Seljuqs and their successors the Ayyubids, and then the First Crusade; all these factors eventually led to to the dynasty's demise in 1171 under the last Fatimid vizier and later Ayyubid sultan, Salah al-Din (Saladin; r. 1174–93).[1]

FATIMID TEXTILE INSTITUTIONS

It is probably because of the Fatimids that so many Abbasid textiles were excavated in Fatimid cemeteries. Reflecting back to the time of the Fatimids, the Mamluk historian Ibn Taghribirdi tells us that the Fatimids had kept many Abbasid textiles, which had come to Egypt after the Buyid takeover of Baghdad in 991, as a token of their hatred for them.[2] It is, of course, also possible that the Fatimids were in possession of many Abbasid textiles, because they took over the treasury of the Ikhshidids, who had ruled Egypt

PAGE 374: Detail, Cat. 147 (LNS 259 T)

before them. The accumulated wealth of these treasuries must have been immense.[3] Even the descriptions of the dresses of the Fatimid caliphs and the princesses of the dynasty are staggering (see chapters 1 and 2). When the treasury was dispersed, all of this wealth poured onto the open market. Some items reached Europe as the prized possessions of returning crusader knights, and survived in church treasuries all over the continent.

Concerning the origin of the Fatimid textile institutions in Cairo, al-Maqrizi tells us, on the authority of a certain Ibn Abi Taiy, that al-Mu'izz founded the institution of the *dar al-kiswa* ('house of cloth'), where all kinds of government-requisitioned garments and cloth used to be cut. According to their various ranks, the caliph invested his courtiers and their families with summer and winter clothing (*kiswa*), a custom that continued under his successors. A register was created for this purpose and called the *khizanat al-kiswa* ('treasury of cloth').[4] It was from there that robes of investiture and the annual dispersal of clothes to the courtiers and staff were organized:

> Another interesting item of historical information … is that, from the *Khaza'in al-Kiswa*, they used to bring forth to all their servants, retainers, and dependents, both great and small, high and low, robes for summer and winter, from the turban to the trousers, and other clothing of less importance, and the napkins (*mindil*) of splendid cloth and precious stuffs for apparel … I have heard a certain person say that he was present at the 'Investiture' at *al-Kasr* which used to take place in summer and winter, the value (of the stuffs given away) then being more than six hundred thousand dinars. The emirs used to be invested with garments of *Dabiki*, and turbans with gold *tiraz* borders, these two items being worth five hundred dinars. The greatest emirs were invested with necklaces (*tawk*), bracelets (*siwar*), and ornamented swords … In 516 AH.

(CE 1122) the various articles upon which money was spent, came to 14,305 pieces. The largest sum of money ever expended on such a thing as that in the days of al-Afdal (*c*. 500 AH.) throughout the whole of his administration, in the year 513 AH. (1119 CE) was 8,775 pieces.[5]

On the authority of the late Fatimid author Ibn Tuwayr, al-Maqrizi describes the annual presentation of clothing and furnishings to the caliph by the *sahib al-tiraz*:

When he arrives with the royal requisitions (*al-isti'malat al-khassa*) which include the umbrella (*mizalla*), the *badla* (a kind of garment), the *badana* (a garment especially for the caliph) and the royal apparel for the Friday prayer (*al-libas al-khass al-Djuma'i*), etc., he is greeted with great honour, and a beast assigned to him from the caliph's stables, which remains at his service until he returns to his charge. He stays at al-Ghazzala on the bank of the river. It used to be one of the royal belvederes, and Shu'a ibn Shawar renovated it. If the manager of the *tiraz* factories (*sahib al-tiraz*) had ten houses in Cairo, still he would only be allowed to stay in al-Ghazzala. Hospitality is dispensed to him as to strangers arriving (as ambassador) to the state. He comes before the caliph after bringing all the chests (*safat*) which enclose these precious robes. All he has is displayed while he draws attention to one thing after another in the hands of the royal *farrashes* ['porters or attendants'] in the palace of the caliph, wherever the monarch happens to be in residence. Great honour is shown to his personage, especially when the materials ordered suit the requirements. When this is completed, it is compared with the account which he has with him, and they are delivered to the master of the robes, and he is invested publicly before the caliph, nobody else apart from him being

invested in this fashion. After this he returns to his own place. Sometimes, when he is not able to come away, he sends a lieutenant, somebody related to him, who must be no less than a son or a brother of his, for the office is highly important. The sum assigned to him each month is seventy *dinar*s. The lieutenant is assigned twenty *dinar*s because he takes over his charge when the manager of the *tiraz* comes (to court) in person and takes his place when he is absent at his work.[6]

These passages give us an interesting insight into the working of the Fatimid administration regarding textiles, in many ways more detailed than what we know about the Abbasids in that respect. From this passage it is clear that the royal wardrobe was ordered through an institution of which the *sahib al-tiraz* was the head. The position of the *sahib* was connected with a certain degree of prestige as becomes evident from the text. Serjeant, whose translation is quoted here, calls the *sahib al-tiraz* 'manager of the *tiraz* factories'. This might not automatically imply, however, that he was the head of the production himself. Since he resided in Cairo his position seems to have been more that of an intermediary between the court and the institution he presided over, rather than being directly involved in the many stages of the production and transmission. What exactly this institution was is not explicitly revealed by the text. It may in reality have been either the *diwan al-tiraz*, the government office overseeing the requisition of inscribed textiles, or the *khizanat al-kiswat*, the treasury or storehouse in which the court wardrobe and all cloth requisitioned by the court were kept and accounted for.

TEXTILE PRODUCTION
The *Qawanin al-dawanin* ('Rules of the government offices') by the late Fatimid author and government official Ibn Mammati describes the way official orders sent to the workshops were carried out:

The *tiraz*. This service (*mu'amala*) has an inspector (*nazir*), an overseer (*musharif*), a controller (*mutwalli*), and two accountants (*shahid*). Now if any sort of article is required to be manufactured, a list is made out by the *Diwan al-Khizana* ('Office of the Wardrobe'), and sent to them along with the required (or computed) money, and gold thread (*dhahab maghzul*) for their expenses. When the chests (*safat*) are brought back, they are compared with the chits which went with them, and checked. If the value comes to more than has been spent on it, the excellent nature of the workmen is inferred from that, but they derive no benefit from it all – that is to say the surplus. If the value is less than the expenditure, the extent of the deficiency is elucidated and requisition is made from the *Diwan*, and the employees are required to pay it. The employees take the responsibility of payment on themselves, and extract it from the gold embroiderers (*rakkam*). A series of happenings of this kind in what they bring, indicates the dishonesty of their characters.[7]

This shows clearly that in function and intention the *diwan al-tiraz* and the *diwan al-khizana* were separate units, but closely connected. The *diwan al-khizana* issued requests for textiles and supplied the necessary funding, and then the *diwan al-tiraz* ordered them. Since the *khizana* took care of the storage and upkeep of the state wardrobe, it was best able to assess what needed to be ordered. It seems that the *diwan al-tiraz* carried out the physical transaction and was, therefore, mainly a financial institution, both for the generating of taxes and the handling of entrusted funds. We may assume that this *diwan* had offices in the relevant centres of textile production and was able to contact the necessary middlemen and brokers locally. These middlemen would then have arranged for the acquisition of the necessary raw material and placed the orders with certain weavers. This, at least, is the impression given in the passage by al-Muqaddasi, who tells us that weavers could sell only through appointed brokers.[8]

A well-known passage by the Persian traveller Nasir-e Khosrow not only describes the highly desirable varieties of cloth produced in the Nile Delta, but also relates information on the interaction between brokers and manufacturers:

> Tinnis makes coloured *kasab* (*rangin*) used for turbans, headdresses (*wikaya*), and women's clothing. Nowhere else is such fine *kasab* made as in Tinnis. White *kasab* is made at Damietta; the *kasab* woven in the sultan's workshop (*kargah*) is neither sold nor given to anyone. I have heard that the ruler of Fars (one of the Buwayhids) had sent 20,000 *dinars* to Tinnīs to buy a complete set of royal robes (*yek-dast djama-yi-khass*). His agents stayed several years in the town without being able to manage this transaction. There are famous weavers there who weave the royal robes. I was told that one of them had woven a piece of cloth designed for the turban of the sultan (*dastar*). He received for this piece of work the sum of 500 Maghribi *dinars*. I have seen this turban. It is estimated to be worth 4,000 Maghribi *dinars*.[9]

How involved the upper ranks of the Fatimid administration were in the ordering of textiles is illustrated by an incident described in the biography of al-Mu'izz's private secretary Jawdhar. The caliph al-Mu'izz issues an order for a prayer mat and requests Jawdhar to write to the governor of Mahdia, detailing the protocol of the inscription to be inscribed on it, which is to mention Jawdhar's involvement as intermediary. Jawdhar was far too reserved about this and ordered the governor Nusair to refer only to the order of the caliph in the inscription.

> The order of the Imam arrived with the *ustadh* to write to Nusair, his governor in al-Mahdiya,

to order the matmakers to make a prayer mat for the Slave taken prisoner by al-Hasan bin 'Ammar bin Abi 'l-Husain in the battle known as al-Hufra. He prescribed for them what to write on the embroidered band. It was customary that in the bands made by embroiderers and weavers, it was inscribed: 'Made through Jawdhar, freedman (*mawla*) of the Commander of the Believers'. But the Imam ordered only to inscribe Jawdhar's name on the embroidery if sufficient space to do so was available, and that is why he (Jawdhar) confined himself to what was strictly necessary in the embroidered band. When the order reached Nusair, as prescribed in the *ustadh*'s letter not to mention his name in the embroidery and not to go beyond what the Imam had ordered, he gave the slaves the orders accordingly. When they had spread the fabric out in front of them, they saw that they had enough space to write the name on it as they used to do, and hence they embroidered it.[10]

This passage sheds light on two issues: the intentional choice of formulas and the importance of the chain of delegation expressed. The fact that al-Mu'izz himself was involved in choosing the right formulaic content of the inscription shows that components of *tiraz* inscriptions indicating the commissioning were not arbitrarily worded, but were a matter of highest concern. The passage also clearly shows that, because the order had been issued by the caliph, his secretary was mentioned as the executive regardless of whether he had actually dispatched the order to the provincial governor. Jawdhar was merely passing on the caliph's order.

Just as in the Abbasid administration, Fatimid viziers were closely engaged with the requisition of textiles, as is documented by numerous examples of inscriptions listing the names of viziers and their titles. The earliest mention of a Fatimid vizier in a *tiraz* inscription is that of al-'Aziz's vizier Abu al-Faraj Ya'qub ibn Yusuf ibn Killis (in office 975–84), an illustrious figure, discussed in more detail

later.[11] Only one of al-Hakim's viziers is recorded: Abu Muhammad al-Hasan ibn 'Ammar ibn Abi al-Husayn.[12] All of al-Hakim's viziers were appointed to an office called *wasata* ('intermediary vizierate'), an administrative office similar to that of the *wizarat al-tanfidh* ('vizier of execution'), which according to the Iraqi Shafi'ite scholar al-Mawardi served to mediate between the ruler and his subjects and to enforce his rules and regulations, but was not as highly positioned in the court and government hierarchy as the vizier.[13] Usually, al-Hakim's viziers were in office only for short periods. The absence of ordering credits for viziers during almost all of al-Hakim's reign is likely to reflect the restricted status of his viziers, who would not have been able to issue orders for *tiraz* textiles on their own.[14]

After this hiatus, al-Zahir's vizier Abu al-Hasan 'Ammar ibn Muhammad (in office 1020–21, also under al-'Aziz in 995–96) seems to be the first one, recorded in a *tiraz* inscription now at the Royal Ontario Museum.[15] From then on it seems that viziers were back in the driving seat of power – so much so that their titles became ever more inflated. From al-Zahir's later years and the reign of his successor al-Mustansir, textiles inscribed with the names of Abu al-Qasim 'Ali ibn Ahmad al-Jarjara'i survive (see cat. nos 142, 143, 145).[16] His title *al-wazir al-awhid safi amir al-mu'minin wa khalisatuhu* ('the most illustrious vizier, the true and chosen friend of the Commander of the Faithful') and its variant, *al-'awhad al-safi amir al-mu'minin wa khalisatuhu* ('the unique, the true and chosen comrade of the Commander of the Faithful'), are indicative of the growing self-confidence of the Fatimid vizierate under the later caliphs. Al-Mustansir's viziers Abu al-Barakat al-Husayn ibn *imad al-dawla* Muhammad (in office 1048–50),[17] Abu Muhammad al-Hasan ibn 'Ali ibn 'Abd al-Rahman al-Yazuri (in office 1050–51 and 1058–59)[18] and Abu al-Faraj Muhammad ibn Ja'far ibn Muhammad ibn 'Ali ibn al-Hasan al-Maghribi (in office 1059–61)[19] are all recorded by surviving *tiraz* inscriptions carrying ever more elaborate titles. The famous vizier of al-Mustansir, Badr al-Jamali (in office 1073–95), who reorganized the

Fatimid state after a near financial disaster, carried the title *al-sayyid al-ʾajal amir al-juyush* ('the most exalted lord, commander of the armies').[20] His son, Abu al-Qasim Shahanshah al-Afdal ibn Badr al-Jamali *amir al-juyush* (in office 1094–1102 under the caliph al-Mustaʿli), carried like his father the lengthy title *al-sayyid al-ʾajal al-Afdal amir al-juyush sayf al-islam nasir al-imam kafil al-qudat al-muslimin* ('the most exalted lord al-Afdal, commander of the armies, sword of Islam, protector of the Imam, protector of the judges of the Muslims').[21] The exponential growth of titles that went hand in hand with the demise of the power of the caliphate was also an issue in the eastern Islamic lands, where the titles of the Buyid amirs reflected their de facto rulership, but also the fact that they needed the formal recognition of the caliph, who was by that point a mere figurehead. The Seljuqs later ruled along similar lines.[22] The titles of the Ghurid sultan Ghiyath al-Din, discussed earlier, are testimony to this arrangement (see pp. 326–31).

FATIMID *TIRAZ* TEXTILES

Tiraz textiles of the Fatimid dynasty seem to continue the aesthetic and epigraphy of those produced in Egypt just before the Fatimid conquest under the Ikhshidids. Although embroidered *tiraz* inscriptions do not completely disappear, there nevertheless seems to be a focus on tapestry weaving in caliphal inscriptions. One magnificent large linen loom-width fragment from the reign of al-Muʿizz (r. 953–75), with an inscription tapestry-woven in silk in a monumental style of foliated script used in the

early period of Fatimid rule in Egypt, is now in the Aga Khan Museum, Toronto; another fragment of sheer linen, dyed indigo blue with yellow lettering, from the reign of al-ʿAziz (r. 975–96) is in the Metropolitan Museum of Art in New York.[23] *Tiraz* textiles from the time of al-ʿAziz begin to include more and more decorative bands with intricately woven floral and zoomorphic designs. An example of outstanding quality is in the Museum of Islamic Art, Cairo. This has two bands of inscription: one comprises an addorsed foliated caliphal inscription in yellow silk, set against a red silk background, which contains a protocol in the name of al-ʿAziz; the other has a smaller benedictory inscription on both sides of decoration that features small confronted birds.[24] The textiles in The al-Sabah Collection from the reigns of al-Zahir and al-Mustansir are examples of the latter aesthetic. Several other purely decorative fragments, which can be attributed to the later Fatimid period, document more complicated composite decorative schemes as they are found in *tiraz* textiles from the reigns of the caliphs al-Mustaʿli (r. 1094–1101),[25] al-Amir (r. 1101–30)[26] and al-Hafiz (r. 1131–49).[27]

There seems generally to have been a strong element of Coptic workmanship in the *tiraz* textiles of the Fatimid period. For example, a technique such as the crossing and pairing of warps on which tapestry was executed (discussed in chapter 3) had its origins in pre-Islamic Egypt, where it can be observed in Coptic wool tapestry on linen. In Fatimid *tiraz*, it was adapted to silk tapestry on linen. Many Fatimid textiles in The al-Sabah Collection adhere to this craft detail.

Cat. 120 *TIRAZ* **FRAGMENT ATTRIBUTED TO THE REIGN OF THE FATIMID CALIPH AL-'AZIZ (r. 975–96)**
Egypt, late 10th century CE

Description: Fragment of undyed linen, with one line of Kufic inscription embroidered in dark blue silk, accompanied by three monochrome ochre bands below.

Materials: linen and silk: plain weave and embroidery

Dimensions: h. 9.4 cm, w. 13.2 cm; max. letter height 1.5 cm

Ground fabric: linen warp and weft, undyed, balanced plain weave, dense texture (*dabiqi*); good quality (2)

Thread count: warp 25 S-spun, weft 23 S-spun

Thread thickness: warp 0.3–0.5 mm medium twist, weft 0.3–0.5 mm medium twist

Embroidery: silk, dyed (dark blue), couching (above the baseline) and chain stitch (lower letter terminals)

Provenance: Ex H.P. Kraus collection, no. 57

Inv. no. LNS 176 T

Related works: See page 510

Inscription: [...] امير ال[م]ؤمنين صلوات الله عليه مما أمر الوزير بعـ[ـمـ]ـلـه [...]

[...] [Commander of the] Faithful, God's blessings be upon him. Of what has been ordered by the vizier to be m[ad]e [...]

This fragment is significant as it relates closely to a dated piece at the Royal Ontario Museum, Toronto, from the reign of the caliph al-'Aziz (r. 975–96), which also has an embroidered inscription, in a comparable epigraphic style, and documents its order by a vizier (Related works 1). Both pieces are executed in dark blue silk. The letter stems are couched while the lower terminals are chain stitched. In both pieces, the inscription is embroidered on weft threads pulled out from the ground fabric to enable a proper horizontal alignment of the inscription. As in the present piece, the Royal Ontario Museum *tiraz* comprises

horizontal bars linking groups of letter stems. The epigraphy of the two pieces is very closely related. Striking similarities are found in the angularity of the letters below the baseline and in the proportion between horizontal and vertical extensions of the letters. Both letter stems and lower letters have wedge-shaped terminals. The *waw* in *mu'minin* is curled upwards. The *sad* in *salawat* differs: one is curled upwards, one is not, but the final *ta* is the same. The *mim*s are round and are placed directly on the baseline. The introductory *'ayn* in *'alayhi* is curled inward in both inscriptions.

At least fifteen Fatimid textiles made in Egypt with embroidered inscriptions have survived, ranging chronologically from the time of al-Mu'izz (r. 953–75) to the reign of al-Hakim (r. 996–1021).[28] Only two of these textiles record their place of production: Tuna and possibly Misr.[29] Although it is very tempting to assume that embroidery disappeared under the Fatimids, a theory that sees embroidery as a foreign craft, which ceases when the foreign power ceases, the textile evidence suggests that this was not the case. Also, the literary sources would seem to support the latter view. In the Fatimid treasury lists, recorded by al-Maqrizi in his *Khitat* (discussed in chapter 1), embroidered costumes are listed on several occasions, indicating that they were not a rare commodity.

Another area of common ground is the content of the inscription. The Royal Ontario Museum *tiraz* inscription has survived completely. It reads: 'Bismillah al-rahman al-rahim 'izz min Allah wa ni'ma al-i(mam) [*sic*] amir al-mu'minin salawatu Allah 'alayhi mimma amara al-wazir bi-'amalihi sanat khams wa sab'in wa thulth m'ia'. The inscription on the al-Sabah example has survived

only fragmentarily. It follows the wording of the Royal Ontario piece from 'al-mu'minin' to 'bi-'amalihi' word for word. Identical are the blessing upon the *amir al-mu'minin* ('salawatu Allah 'alayhi'), the ordering formula ('mimma amara bi-'amalihi'), the ordering individual ('al-wazir') and the fact that this person is referred to only in the capacity of his office and not by name. It is an interesting detail that the Royal Ontario Museum inscription does not mention the name of the caliph, to whom it refers as *amir al-mu'minin*. However, it carries a date of 375 AH / 985–86 CE, which links it to the reign of the Fatimid caliph al-'Aziz (r. 975–96). Given the number of similarities described above, the present piece must also date from that period.

The first to hold the office and title of vizier under the Fatimids officially was Abu al-Faraj Ya'qub ibn Yusuf ibn Killis (lived 930–991), who was born in Baghdad to a Jewish family that then moved to Syria and finally to Egypt.[30] At 13 he entered the household of the Ikhshidid regent Kafur and progressed steadily in various administrative positions. In 967 he converted to Islam and after Kafur's death fell out with the vizier Abu al-Fadl Ja'far bin al-Furat, who had him imprisoned. Upon his release he fled to Ifriqiya, where he allied himself with the Fatimid caliph al-Mu'izz, with whom he returned to Egypt upon the Fatimid conquest in 969. Under al-Mu'izz, Ibn Killis reorganized the financial affairs of the state and it was under al-'Aziz in 977 that Ibn Killis was appointed as the first Fatimid vizier, carrying the title *al-wazir al-'ajal* ('the illustrious vizier'), which later viziers also used. It was at this period that the Fatimid state was at its most prosperous. Ibn Killis was a man of letters and promoted learning and study. It was he who suggested turning al-Azhar into a university. When Ibn Killis died in 991, the caliph al-'Aziz himself led the funerary procession and organized the enshrouding of his body (see chapter 2).

Al-Maqrizi recorded in his *Khitat* that viziers were first mentioned in *tiraz* inscriptions under the caliph al-'Aziz.[31] However, at least two *tiraz* inscriptions exist from the reign of al-Mu'izz that seem to contradict this. One, with a tapestry-woven inscription, in the Benaki Museum, Athens, is dated 365 AH / 975–76 CE and documents its order by an unnamed vizier and its manufacture in Misr in a *tiraz al-khassa*.[32] Another, with a fragmentary inscription, also in tapestry, is in the Textile Museum, Washington, DC.[33] It is, however, from the reign of al-'Aziz that a number of textiles have survived with mostly tapestry-woven inscriptions relating to Ibn Killis directly.[34] In these he is mentioned by his full name and also with the titles that he had received as an honour. In some he is referred to as *'abd amir al-mu'minin* ('slave of the Commander of the Faithful'), *wazir amir al-mu'minin* ('vizier of the Commander of the Faithful') and *al-wazir al-'ajal* ('the illustrious vizier'). These inscriptions record the high esteem that Ibn Killis enjoyed from al-'Aziz, but also reflect the high level of influence that he wielded at court and in the administration, which led to the inclusion of his name in these public texts, along with that of the caliph.

Cat. 121   *TIRAZ* FRAGMENT FROM
THE FATIMID DYNASTY
**Egypt, late 10th to early
11th century CE**

Description: Fragment of undyed linen, with
two lines of Kufic inscription,
embroidered in red silk.
Materials: linen and silk: plain weave
and embroidery
Dimensions: h. 7.5 cm, w. 10.0 cm;
max. letter height 2.0 cm
Ground fabric: linen warp and weft, undyed,
balanced plain weave, dense
texture (*dabiqi*); good quality (2)
Thread count: warp 22 Z-spun, weft 19 Z-spun
Thread thickness: warp 0.2–0.5 mm loose-medium
twist, weft 0.2–0.4 mm medium–
tight twist
Embroidery: silk, dyed (red), chain stitch
Provenance: Ex H.P. Kraus collection, no. 136

Inv. no. LNS 244 T

Inscription: repetition of

The kingdom is God's

الملك لله

Cat. 122 *TIRAZ* FRAGMENT FROM
THE FATIMID DYNASTY
**Egypt, late 10th to early
11th century CE**

Description: Fragment of linen dyed dark blue,
with two lines of Kufic inscription
embroidered in ochre and reddish
silk.

Materials: linen and silk: plain weave
and embroidery

Dimensions: h. 20.0 cm, w. 18.0 cm;
max. letter height 1.7 cm

Ground fabric: linen warp and weft, dyed (dark
blue), predominant-warp plain
weave, gauzy texture (*sharb*),
irregularities; medium quality (3);
selvedge on the right side of the
inscription

Thread count: warp 20 S-spun, weft 12 S-spun

Thread thickness: warp 0.15–0.2 mm tight twist,
weft 0.15 mm tight twist

Embroidery: silk, dyed (ochre and reddish),
chain stitch

Provenance: Ex H.P. Kraus collection, no. 25

Inv. no. LNS 150 T

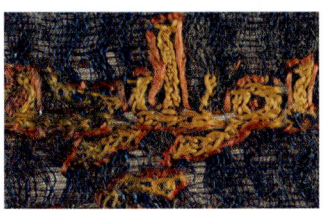

Inscription:

Line 1:

[...] [الـ]ـرحيم بركة من الله [...]

[...] [the] Merciful, blessing from God [...]

Line 2: undecipherable

The present inscription is of an epigraphic type that would normally be found tapestry-woven, rather than embroidered. The letters are of a bold angular shape, and the chain stitch embroidery used here does not have to rely on counted stitches, which would be difficult on a gauzy base fabric. The bold angular Kufic used here suggests a date in the early Fatimid period, perhaps in the late tenth or early eleventh century.

Cat. 123 *TIRAZ* FRAGMENT FROM
THE REIGN OF THE FATIMID
CALIPH AL-'AZIZ (r. 975–96)
Egypt, late 10th century CE

Description: Fragment of undyed linen, with one
line of foliated Kufic inscription
tapestry-woven in dark brown silk.

Materials: linen and silk: plain weave and
tapestry

Dimensions: h. 10.5 cm, w. 11.5 cm;
max. letter height 5.4 cm

Ground fabric: linen warp and weft, undyed,
warp-faced plain weave, gauzy
texture (*sharb*); good quality (2)

Thread count: warp 19 S-spun, weft 15 S-spun

Thread thickness: warp 0.15–0.3 mm tight twist,
weft 0.15–0.2 mm tight twist

Tapestry: silk, dyed (dark brown); slit and
toothed; hastae woven on warps
lifted up from the base fabric;
discontinuous supplementary
weft filling between the letters

Provenance: Ex H.P. Kraus collection, no. 63

Inv. no. LNS 182 T

Related works: See page 510

Inscription:

[...] [al-Mans]u[r] al-'Aziz [...]

[...] [المنص]و [ر] (!) العزيز [...]

This *tiraz* fragment records part of the *laqab* and the *kunya* of the Fatimid caliph al-'Aziz (r. 975–96). Its epigraphic style is typical of larger tapestry-woven inscriptions from the period of his reign. However, several points distinguish this particular inscription. In terms of content, the *kunya* and *laqab* follow each other immediately without the insertion of the term *al-imam*, which would normally introduce the caliph's *laqab*. Furthermore, it appears that al-'Aziz's *kunya* 'al-Mansur' is written incorrectly, as the final *ra* is omitted. The upcurving letter preceding the introductory *alif* in 'al-'Aziz' is clearly a *waw*, as its beginning comprises a loop. Furthermore, the final *za* in 'al-'Aziz' is curved upwards above the baseline rather than, like a *senna*, with a short appendage below the baseline. The latter feature is very common in *tiraz* inscriptions from al-'Aziz's reign. The combination of all these characteristics can be found in a *tiraz* textile inscription in the Royal Ontario Museum, Toronto (Related works 1), which comprises more surviving text than the present piece. This inscription, too, is executed in dark brown silk, its letters are of medium height (3.0 cm) and the ground fabric on which it is woven is of gauzy texture.

The epigraphic style of this inscription, with its elegant swan-neck and foliated letter terminals, continues a style that was already used during the Ikhshidid dynasty in Egypt under the caliph al-Muti', before the Fatimid conquest in 969 (see cat. no. 38). A prominent example from the reign of al-Mu'izz in the Textile Museum, Washington, DC, shows that this style continued under the Fatimids after the conquest.[35] One textile, in the Aga Khan Museum, Toronto, displays very monumental letters *c.* 10 cm high.[36] Another, in the Textile Museum, Washington, DC, dates from the reign of al-'Aziz, and mentions his vizier Ibn Killis.[37] A shawl fragment dated 373 AH / 983–84 CE, in sheer bluish-green linen of full-loom width, is in the Metropolitan Museum of Art, New York (Related works 2). Its inscription documents its manufacture in the *tiraz al-khassa* in Tinnis, a location that had already produced textiles during the Abbasid caliphate.

Cat. 124 *TIRAZ* **FRAGMENT FROM THE REIGN OF THE FATIMID CALIPH AL-'AZIZ** (r. 975–96)
Egypt, late 10th century CE

Description: Fragment of undyed linen, with one line of Kufic inscription tapestry-woven in ochre silk.

Materials: linen and silk: plain weave and tapestry

Dimensions: h. 29.5 cm, w. 36.0 cm; max. letter height 1.0 cm

Ground fabric: linen warp and weft, undyed, predominant-warp plain weave, close texture (*sharb*); good quality (2)

Thread count: warp 21 S-spun, weft 17 S-spun

Thread thickness: warp 0.15–0.2 mm medium–tight twist, weft 0.15 mm medium–tight twist

Tapestry: silk, dyed (ochre); slit and toothed; discontinuous supplementary paired linen weft filling

Provenance: Ex H.P. Kraus collection, no. 68

Inv. no. LNS 187 T

Related works: See page 510

Inscription:

بسم الله الرحمن الرحيم نصر من الله لعبد الله نزار ابي المنصور الإمام العزيز بالله أمير المؤمنين صلوات الله عليه سنة خمس [...]

In the name of God, the Most Merciful, the Most Compassionate. Assistance from God to God's servant Nizar Abi al-Mansur al-imam al-'Aziz bi-llah the Commander of the Faithful. May God's blessings be upon him. In the year five [...]

This inscription belongs to the same category as cat. no. 125, which is also in the name of the Fatimid caliph al-'Aziz. The two textiles share details of epigraphic style and manufacture. Two further *tiraz* inscriptions from al-'Aziz's reign should be added here. One is in the Textile Museum, Washington, DC (Related works 1). The other is in the Royal Ontario Museum, Toronto (Related works 2). Both have inscriptions tapestry-woven in red silk in letters of a small size, comparable with this example (respectively, 0.7 cm and 1.0 cm). Furthermore, looking at details such as the execution of the *kunya* Abi al-Mansur with its upwardly curved *waw*, common to all three inscriptions, one may assume that they are all the products of the same craft environment, if not the same workshop. The date of the present piece, of which only the first digit, five, has survived, is not clear and could be any of three possible dates in the two decades of al-'Aziz's reign.

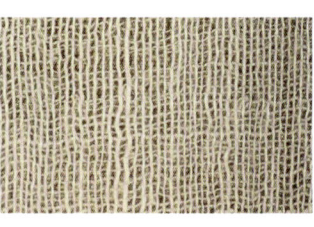

Cat. 125 *TIRAZ* FRAGMENT FROM
THE REIGN OF THE FATIMID
CALIPH AL-ʿAZIZ (r. 975–96)
Egypt, late 10th century CE

Description: Fragment of undyed linen, with
one line of Kufic inscription
tapestry-woven in ochre silk.

Materials: linen and silk: plain weave
and tapestry

Dimensions: h. 29.9 cm, w. 39.2 cm;
max. letter height 1.7 cm

Ground fabric: linen warp and weft, undyed,
predominant-warp plain weave,
close texture (*dabiqi*), very regular;
very good quality (1)

Thread count: warp 27 S-spun, weft 20 S-spun

Thread thickness: warp 0.2–0.3 mm medium–tight
twist, weft 0.15–0.2 mm medium–
tight twist

Tapestry: silk, dyed (ochre); slit; densely
woven supplementary linen weft
filling

Provenance: Ex H.P. Kraus collection, no. 68

Inv. no. LNS 156 T

Related works: See page 510

Inscription: بسم الله (؟) الرحمن الرحيم نصر من الله لعبد الله نزار أبي المنصـ[ور] [...]

In the name of God (?) the Most Merciful, the Most Compassionate. Assistance
from God to God's servant Nizar Abi al-Mans[ur] [...]

The benedictory wishes contained in the inscription are conferred on 'God's
servant' (*li-ʿabd Allah*), a phrase that usually introduces the *ism* and *kunya* of the
ruling caliph. This is what seems to be the case here, though the correct reading
of the wording after *ʿabd Allah* poses some difficulty. The last word reads *alif,
lam, mim, nun, sad*, and could read 'al-Mansur', part of the *kunya* 'Abu al-
Mansur' of the Fatimid caliph al-ʿAziz (r. 975–96). Consequently, the preceding
words should be his *ism* ('given name'): *Nizar*. After the word *ʿabd Allah*, a *nun,
za* and *alif* are clearly visible; then there is a lacuna, followed by the remains of
a hasta, and what could be a *ba* and a terminal *ya*. Although the *ism* and *kunya*
of the caliph al-ʿAziz, like that of most Fatimid caliphs, are usually introduced
by the peculiarly Fatimid phrase 'li-ʿabd Allah wa wali'ihi' ('to the servant and
friend of God'), it is not uncommon to find that the term *wali'ihi* is actually left
out, as is the case here and in the *tiraz* inscriptions from the same caliph's reign |
in Related works 1–4.

The epigraphic style of the inscription is characterized by a rather angular
treatment of the letters, including normally rounded ones, such as *mim*.
The size of the letters is small and the tapestry inscription is embedded in a
band of tightly woven linen. The hastae go beyond this band and are woven
separately. This style is not unique to the Fatimid period and has its roots in
earlier inscriptions from the Abbasid period, as dated examples from the reigns
of the caliphs al-Radi and al-Mutiʿ show.[38] Many of these were made in Delta
locations, such as Shata and Tuna, but also in Misr. This seems to continue
under the Fatimids, as there is an inscription in a comparable style from the reign
of al-Muʿizz, which was also produced in Shata.[39] Examples in this epigraphic
style from al-ʿAziz's reign also mention Shata and Tuna as places of production
(Related works 1, 7, 8).

Cat. 126 *TIRAZ* FRAGMENT FROM THE REIGN OF THE FATIMID CALIPH AL-ʿAZIZ (r. 975–96)
Egypt, late 10th century CE

Description: Fragment of undyed linen, with one line of Kufic inscription tapestry-woven in red silk.

Materials: linen and silk: plain weave and tapestry

Dimensions: h. 15.5 cm, w. 48.1 cm; max. letter height 0.9 cm

Ground fabric: linen warp and weft, undyed, balanced plain weave, close texture (*sharb*); good quality (2); selvedge on the right side of the inscription, with signs of stitching

Thread count: warp 22 S-spun, weft 18 S-spun

Thread thickness: warp 0.15–0.25 mm tight twist, weft 0.2 mm tight twist

Tapestry: silk, dyed (red); slit and toothed; discontinuous supplementary paired weft filling between the letters

Provenance: Ex H.P. Kraus collection, no. 61

Inv. no. LNS 180 T

Related works: See page 510

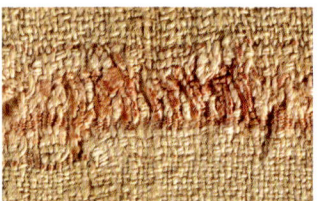

Inscription:

بسم الله الرحمن الرحيم نص[ر] [...] (... ؟ ...) نظار الاما[م] العزيز بالله أمير المؤمنين صلوات الله (عليه نصر من الله)

In the name of God, the Most Merciful, the Most Compassionate. Hel[p] [...] (... ? ...) Nizar the ima[m] al-ʿAziz bi-llah the Commander of the Faithful. God's blessings be (upon him, assistance from God)

This piece belongs to a group of *tiraz* textiles that show certain recurring characteristics in terms of manufacture, the size of the letters and the epigraphic style. They are all tapestry-woven within a band reserved from the ground fabric, where the background is also executed in tapestry around the inscription. The reason for this seems to be the small size of the inscriptions. While in larger inscriptions it was plausible to weave the letters above and below the baseline on warps lifted up from the base fabric, the wefts continuing behind, in a small inscription this was too difficult. Epigraphically the present inscription comprises a juxtaposition of narrowly placed letters such as *alif* and *lam* (and final letters),

elongated letters such as *sad* and *za*, and letters placed widely apart from others such as *mim* and *lam–alif*. The same characteristics are found particularly in Related works 5 and 6.

This textile seems to be the only one from al-ʿAziz's reign in which the sequence of the caliph's *kunya* ends with 'Nizar', actually his *ism* ('given name'). It normally reads 'Nizar Abu al-Mansur', followed by the term *al-imam* and then the caliph's *laqab*. Here 'Nizar' is placed directly before 'al-imam'. Unfortunately, the inscription immediately preceding 'Nizar' is no longer decipherable.

The epigraphic style seen here already exists under al-Muʿizz and continues later under al-Hakim and was common in textiles produced in workshops in the Delta, as documented by a number of surviving inscriptions. Two locations that occur frequently are Shata and Tuna. A textile in the name of the Fatimid caliph al-Muʿizz from this group was made in Shata.[40] Two textiles that relate closely to the present piece and date from the reign of al-ʿAziz were made in the Delta as well – one in Shata, one in Tuna (Related works 2, 3).

Cat. 127 *TIRAZ* FRAGMENT
ATTRIBUTED TO THE
REIGN OF THE FATIMID
CALIPH AL-ʿAZIZ (r. 975–96)
Egypt, late 10th century CE

Description: Fragment of undyed linen, with
one line of Kufic inscription
tapestry-woven in dark brown silk.

Materials: linen and silk: plain weave
and tapestry

Dimensions: h. 8 cm, w. 5.6 cm;
max. letter height 0.8 cm

Ground fabric: linen warp and weft, undyed,
predominant-warp plain weave,
gauzy texture (*sharb*); good
quality (2)

Thread count: warp 24 S-spun, weft 17 S-spun

Thread thickness: warp 0.1–0.15 mm tight twist,
weft 0.1 mm tight twist

Tapestry: silk, dyed (dark brown); slit
and toothed; discontinuous
supplementary paired linen weft
filling, S-spun (0.1 mm), tight
twist, between the letters

Provenance: Ex H.P. Kraus collection, no. 67

Inv. no. LNS 186 T

Inscription:

[...] الله و بالله العلي لعبدالله الـ[...] (؟)

[...] God, and through God the high is achieved to the servant of God the [...] (?)

The present inscription records the introductory phrase *li-ʿabd Allah*, which should be followed by the caliphal *ism* and *kunya*. However, only a very fragmented portion of this part of the inscription has survived, which does not allow a conclusive attribution on this basis alone. It comprises *al-* followed by a void, then what seems to be the remains of a *mim*, then a *senna*, followed by the upper portion of a long rounded letter. The epigraphic style was already used under the Ikhshidids, and then the Fatimid caliphs al-Muʿizz (r. 953–75), al-ʿAziz (975–96) and later al-Hakim (r. 996–1021), as discussed in the preceding catalogue entries. However, the style used here is very close to that found in cat. no. 126 which dates from the reign of al-ʿAziz.

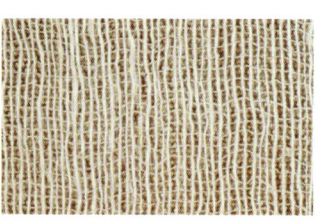

Cat. 128 *TIRAZ* FRAGMENT FROM
THE REIGN OF THE
FATIMID CALIPH AL-HAKIM
(r. 996–1021)
Egypt, 403 AH / 1012–13 CE

Description: Fragment of undyed linen, with
three registers tapestry-woven in
coloured silk: two have addorsed
Kufic inscriptions in cream on a
dark blue ground, and between
these two is a band (3.0 cm)
containing a continuous sequence
of cartouches, each with a griffin
in light greenish-blue with dark
brown outlines, set against a
beige ground.

Materials: linen and silk: plain weave
and tapestry

Dimensions: h. 8.7 cm, w. 20.2 cm;
max. letter height 2.2 cm

Ground fabric: linen warp and weft, undyed,
plain weave

Thread count: warp 31 S-spun (weft lost)

Thread thickness: warp 0.15–0.25 mm medium–tight
twist, weft not extant

Tapestry: silk (dark blue, greenish-blue,
brown, beige); inscription: paired
linen yarn S-spun; slit and toothed

Provenance: Ex H.P. Kraus collection, no. 69

Inv. no. LNS 73 T

Related works: See pages 510–11

Inscription:

Line 1:

[...] أمر بعمله في طراز العامة بدمياط سنة ثلث و اربع ما[ئة]

[...] ordered its fabrication in *tiraz al-'amma* in Damietta, in the year four
hund[red] and three

Line 2:

[...] [و]حده لا شريك له محمد رسول الله صلى الله عليه {و} عـ[لي آله] [...]

[...] [a]lone and has no partner, Muhammad is the prophet of God, may God's
blessings be upon him {and} up[on his family [...]

One other fragment dated 403 AH / 1012–13 CE has been published (Related
works 1). This also is a tapestry-woven fragment with a Kufic inscription, but
stating that the piece was made in Dabqu (Dabiq) at a *tiraz al-'amma*. Five
textiles dating from al-Hakim's reign are known from Damietta, three of which
were made at a *tiraz al-'amma* (Related works 2–4) and two at a *tiraz al-khassa*
(Related works 5, 6).

The epigraphic style of the inscription on the present piece is an example of a
type that dates from the latter part of al-Hakim's reign. It is stylistically related
to textiles from the reign of al-Hakim's predecessor, al-'Aziz (r. 975–96). This is
particularly evident from the use of the foliated and elegantly upturned terminal
letters, such as *waw*, *nun* and *mim*, which are almost S-shaped. The hastae are
all straight and the curve in *waw* or *nun* appears on the baseline, where it forms
a curl. One of the closest comparisons with this inscription is one at the Museum
of Islamic Art, Cairo, which mentions the name of the heir to the throne of al-
Hakim, 'Abd al-Rahim ibn Ilyas, and can thus be dated 404–11 AH / 1013–21 CE,
only shortly after the date of our piece (Related works 7). That this particular
style of calligraphy continued into the period of al-Mustansir is suggested by
another piece at the Museum of Islamic Art, Cairo, which also features an
inscription in cream on a dark blue ground (Related works 8).

The present piece shares with these not only features of epigraphic style,
but also details of arrangement, decorative repertoire and colour schemes.
The inscriptions on the related works are addorsed against a decorative band
containing a continuous sequence of animals, pairs of confronted birds, or
cartouches containing alternating pairs of confronted birds and single griffins; in
this case there are cartouches containing single griffins, with small palmettes in
the spandrels between the cartouches. On all pieces in this group, the counter-
balance between the cream-coloured inscriptions against a darker background
is quite prominent. As the textile in Cairo with the name of 'Abd al-Rahim ibn
Ilyas suggests (Related works 7), the present fragment is only a portion of a
larger piece which might have comprised several bands with addorsed, probably
larger, inscriptions.

Cat. 129 *TIRAZ* FRAGMENT FROM
THE REIGN OF THE
FATIMID CALIPH AL-
HAKIM (r. 996–1021)
**Egypt, late 10th to early
11th century CE**

Description: Fragment of undyed linen,
with one line of foliated Kufic
inscription tapestry-woven in
red silk.

Materials: linen and silk: plain weave
and tapestry

Dimensions: h. 20 cm, w. 52.2 cm;
max. letter height 1.1 cm

Ground fabric: linen warp and weft, warp-
faced plain weave, gauzy texture
(*sharb*), regular structure; very
good quality (1); loom width
with selvedges right and left

Thread count: warp 19 S-spun, weft 11 S-spun

Thread thickness: warp 0.1–0.25 mm tight twist,
weft 0.05–0.15 mm tight twist

Tapestry: silk, dyed (red); slit; locked in
by supplementary linen weft
filling

Provenance: art market, 1970s–1980s

Inv. no. LNS 53 T

Related works: See page 511

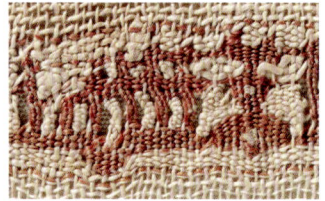

Inscription:

بسم (!) الملك لله (ا) لحمد لله الرحمن الرحيم نصر من الله لـ[صنور] ابي علي الامام الحاكم (م) (ا) بامر الله امير المؤمنين (ابن) العزيز بالله صلي الله (...) لاله الا الله الخير مقبل انشا[ء] الله.

In the name (!). Sovereignty belongs to God. (P)raise be to God, the Most Merciful, the Most Compassionate. Help from God to Mans[ur] Abi 'Ali the Imam al-Hakim (*mim*) (*alif*) bi-'Amr Allah the Commander of the Faithful (son of) al-'Aziz bi-llah, may God's blessings (…) there is no god except God, the good is coming if God wi[lls] it

The inscription, preserved in its entirety, mentions the *ism*, *kunya* and *laqab* of the Fatimid caliph al-Hakim (r. 996–1021), 'al-Mansur Abu 'Ali al-Hakim bi-'Amr Allah'. A date is not included in the inscription, which ends with a phrase of pious content: 'al-khayr muqbal insha'allah'. The style seen here is characterized by its small size, its stout appearance, and an emphasis on groups of hastae that terminate in a sharp pointed tip. The area surrounding the inscription is always densely woven with linen wefts. Several *tiraz* textiles with similar inscriptions have survived, which may help to place the present piece in context. The dates

on two items from al-Hakim's reign, one in the Museum für Islamische Kunst, Berlin, the other at Dumbarton Oaks, suggest that this type of inscription might date from the beginning of al-Hakim's reign (Related works 1, 2).

This inscription contains a number of mistakes, either missing or superfluous letters. After the *laqab* of al-Hakim there is a *mim* and what appears to be an *alif* before the *laqab* continues with 'bi-'Amr Allah'. Furthermore the 'ibn' before 'al-'Aziz bi-llah' is missing or merged with the end of 'al-mu'minin'. After 'al-'Aziz bi-llah salla Allahu' and before the *shahada* there is a sequence of letters that does not seem to make sense. There should be a preposition, such as "alayhuma', referring back to the two caliphs. As here, in the inscription on a textile at Dumbarton Oaks, Washington, DC, the father of al-Hakim, al-'Aziz, is mentioned and so is the phrase 'salla Allahu 'alayhuma' (Related works 2). This style of rather small-scale inscription (0.6–1.2 cm in height) is already found during al-'Aziz's reign, as documented by several comparable examples.[41] Textiles like these may have been produced in workshops in the Delta, as is suggested by one from al-Hakim's reign, made in the *tiraz al-'amma* in Tuna (Related works 3). Already under al-'Aziz inscriptions of this type were made in several Delta locations, as discussed above (pp. 391–93).

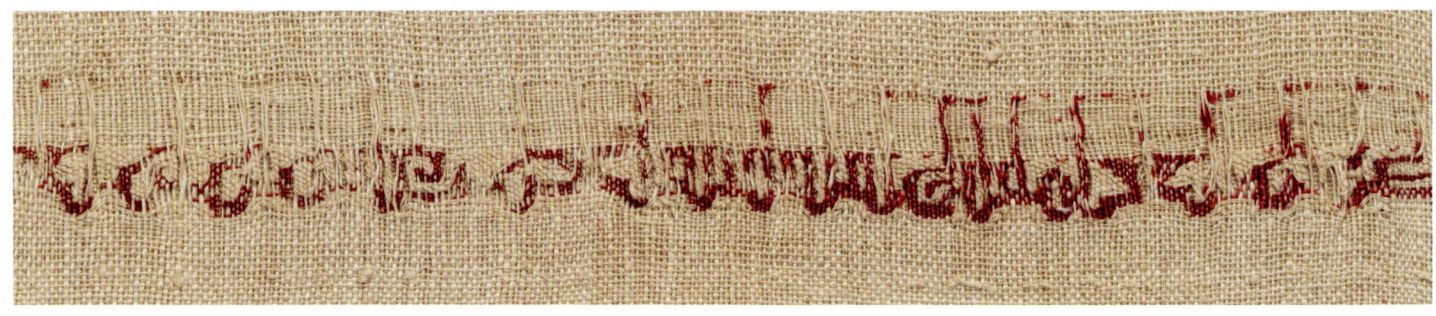

Cat. 130   *TIRAZ* FRAGMENT FROM
THE FATIMID DYNASTY
**Egypt, late 10th to
11th century CE**

Description: Fragment of undyed linen, with
one line of Kufic inscription
tapestry-woven in red silk.

Materials: linen and silk: plain weave
and tapestry

Dimensions: h. 31 cm, w. 33 cm;
max. letter height 0.9 cm

Ground fabric: linen warp and weft, undyed,
predominant-warp plain weave,
close texture (*sharb*); very good
quality (1)

Thread count: warp 29 S-spun, weft 22 S-spun

Thread thickness: warp 0.15–0.3 mm medium twist,
weft 0.15 mm tight twist

Tapestry: silk, dyed (red); slit and toothed;
hastae woven on warps lifted up
from the base fabric, silk yarns
carried from one hasta to the
next as supplementary weft;
discontinuous supplementary
linen weft filling

Provenance: Ex H.P. Kraus collection, no. 66

Inv. no. LNS 184 T

Inscription:

(…) the worlds (…)

(…) العلمين (…)

Cat. 131 *TIRAZ* FRAGMENT
ATTRIBUTED TO THE
REIGN OF THE FATIMID
CALIPH AL-HAKIM
(r. 996–1021)
**Egypt, late 10th to early
11th century CE**

Description: Fragment of undyed linen, with
one line of Kufic inscription
tapestry-woven in red silk.

Materials: linen and silk: plain weave
and tapestry

Dimensions: h. 20.5 cm, w. 34 cm;
max. letter height 1.0 cm

Ground fabric: linen warp and weft, undyed,
balanced plain weave, close texture
(*sharb*); very good quality (1)

Thread count: warp 21 S-spun, weft 23 S-spun

Thread thickness: warp 0.15–0.2 mm medium–tight
twist, weft 0.1–0.15 mm tight twist

Tapestry: silk, dyed (red); slit and toothed;
hastae woven on warps lifted up
from the base fabric; tapestry yarns
carried forward as a floating weft

Provenance: Ex H.P. Kraus collection, no. 65

Inv. no. LNS 183 T

Related works: See page 511

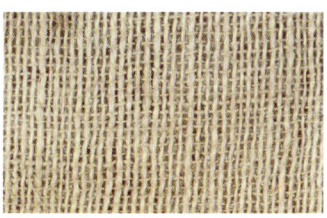

Inscription:

[...] [نص]ـر من الله و فتح قريب لعبد الله له (!) [ا]مرلله امير المؤمنين صلوات الله عليه وعلى آبائه الائمة الطاهريـ[ـن] و أبنائه الائمة [...]

[…] [assistance] from God and an imminent victory to the servant of God, to him (!) ’[A]mr Allah Commander of the Faithful, blessings of God be upon him and his ancestors the immaculate Imams and upon his descendants the Imams […]

Both the *ism* and *laqab* in this inscription are incomplete, not allowing a conclusive attribution. The phrase in the present inscription introducing the caliphal *ism*, *li-'abd Allah*, lacks the actual *ism* and *kunya*. Furthermore, the caliphal *laqab* contains only part of the caliphal title, in this case '[’A]mr Allah', but lacking 'al-Hakim' which should have preceded it.

The epigraphic style of the inscription is characterized by a very dense arrangement of the letters. Almost all terminal letters that would normally descend below the baseline are curved upwards above the baseline. The connections between letters, such as *lam–alif* and sometimes the *senna*, are in some cases extended in a curve below the baseline. The *mim* is frequently rounded, whereas the *ha* is square-shaped. The medial *'ayn* is triangular in shape with a void in the centre and a vertical extension. Two *tiraz* textiles which comprise inscriptions in the name of the caliph al-Hakim in a comparable epigraphic style are in the Royal Ontario Museum, Toronto (Related works 1, 2). The first of these also has floating weft threads between the hastae to carry the thread forward for the tapestry. Both inscriptions are woven, like the present piece, in dyed silk directly into the ground fabric, albeit one is in blue rather than red. They also share the small size of the letters (respectively, 1.1 cm and 0.7 cm). Another related inscription from the reign of al-Hakim is in the Biblioteca Apostolica Vaticana, Vatican City (Related works 3). Although its inscription is of a comparable epigraphic style, it differs from the previous examples in its execution of the inscription in cream-coloured linen set within a band of green silk.

Cat. 132   *TIRAZ* FRAGMENT FROM
THE REIGN OF THE
FATIMID CALIPH AL-HAKIM
(r. 996–1021)
**Egypt, late 10th to early
11th century CE**

Description: Fragment of undyed linen, with
one line of Kufic inscription
tapestry-woven in dark brown silk.

Materials: linen and silk: plain weave
and tapestry

Dimensions: h. 10.0 cm, w. 54.5 cm;
max. letter height 1.6 cm

Ground fabric: linen warp and weft, undyed,
balanced plain-weave, close
texture (*dabiqi*); good quality (2)

Thread count: warp 26 S-spun, weft 18 S-spun

Thread thickness: warp 0.3–0.4 mm medium twist,
weft 0.25–0.3 mm tight twist

Tapestry: silk, dyed (dark brown); slit;
hastae woven on warps lifted
up from the base fabric;
supplementary linen weft filling
between the letters on the baseline

Provenance: Ex H.P. Kraus collection, no. 33

Inv. no. LNS 157 T

Related works: See page 511

Inscription:

[...] (...؟...) صلى الله عليه وعلى آله (...) الاخيار الاتقياء الطيبيين (...؟...) لا اله الا الله (...) نصر من الله لعبدالله و وليه المنصور أبي علي الإمام الحاكم بأمر الله امـ[ـير] [...]

[...] (...?...) God's blessings be upon him and his family (...) the excellent, the pious, the good (...?...) there is no God but God (...) assistance from God to the servant of God and his ally al-Mansur Abi 'Ali al-imam al-Hakim bi-'Amr Allah the Comm[ander] [...]

Although the beginning of the surviving line of inscription is difficult to decipher, the end is legible and contains the *ism* and *kunya* 'al-Mansur Abi 'Ali' and the *laqab* 'al-Hakim bi-'Amr Allah' of the Fatimid caliph al-Hakim (r. 996–1021).

The epigraphic style of the inscription fits in with a number of *tiraz* inscriptions of relatively small size – compared with the monumental floriated ones from al-Hakim's reign – with quite angular, densely placed letterforms, hastae that are woven set apart from the ground and connected by two thin lines of inwoven silk at the top. Two comparable items have survived that were made in Tuna (Related works 7, 9). Others, as discussed above (see cat. nos 125, 126, 129), were made in Shata; like those, the present textile was probably made in a Delta location, though it is not possible to be more precise about a specific textile centre.

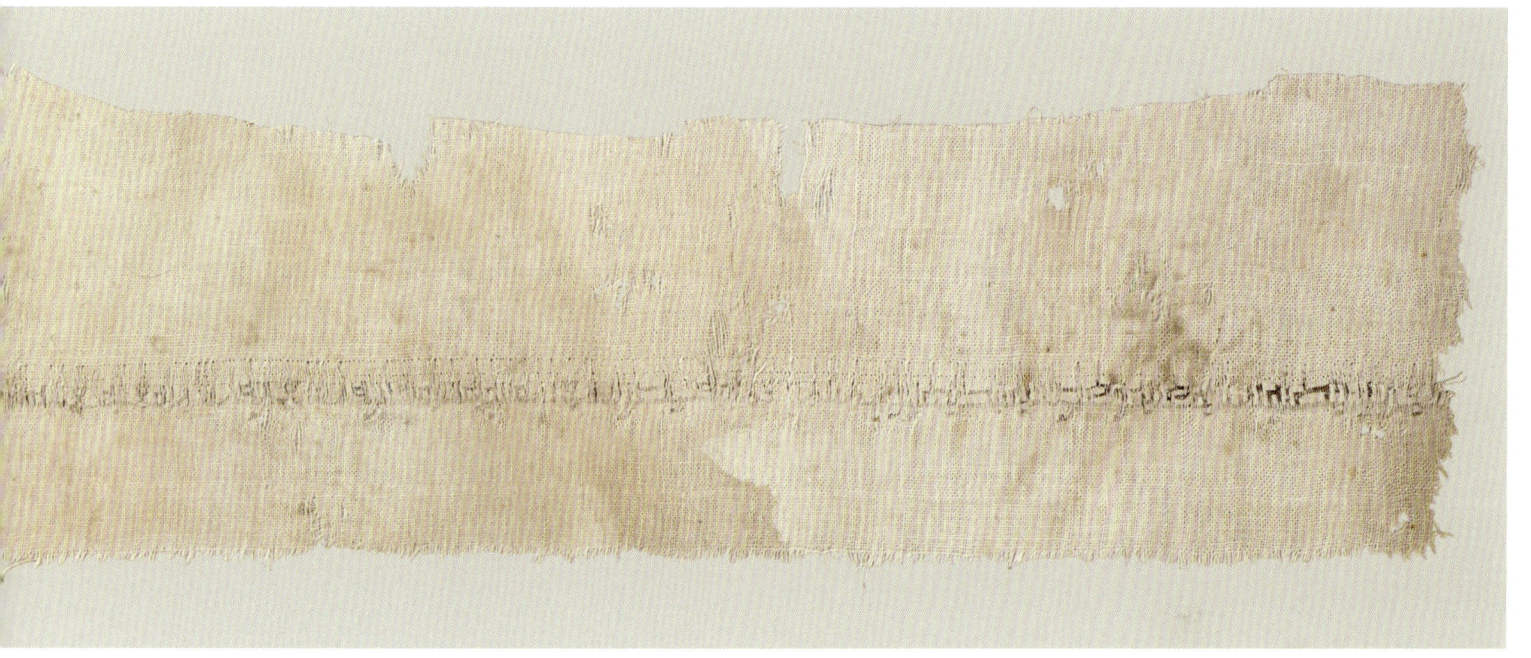

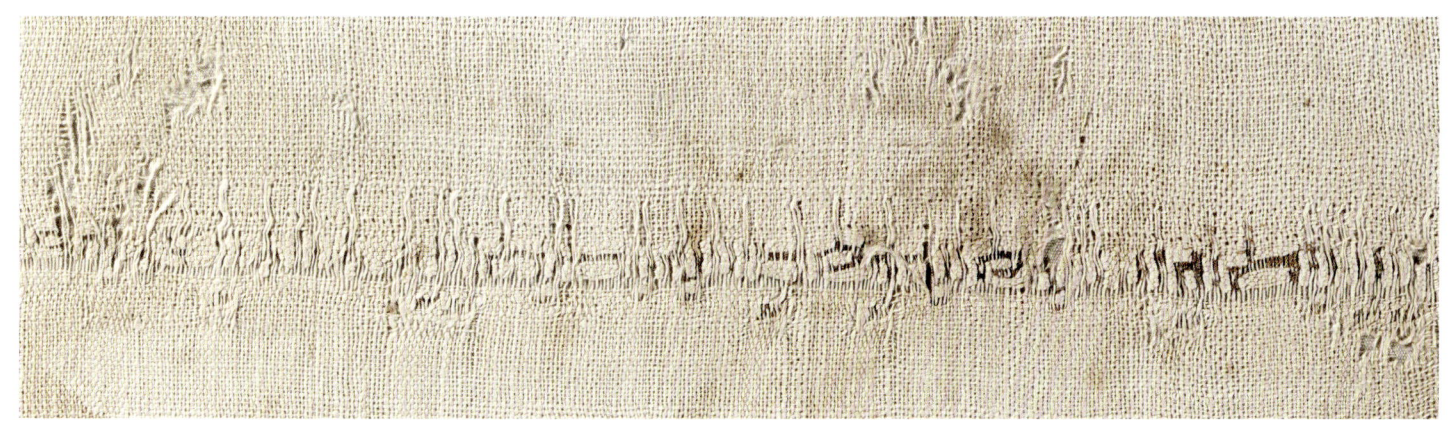

Cat. 133   *TIRAZ* FRAGMENT
ATTRIBUTED TO THE
REIGN OF THE FATIMID
CALIPH AL-HAKIM
(r. 996–1021)
**Egypt, late 10th to early
11th century CE**

Description: Fragment of undyed linen, with
one line of Kufic inscription
tapestry-woven in dark brown silk.

Materials: linen and silk: plain weave and
tapestry

Dimensions: h. 14 cm, w. 42.7 cm;
max. letter height 1.8 cm

Ground fabric: linen warp and weft, undyed,
balanced plain weave, close texture
(*sharb*); very good quality (1)

Thread count: warp 27 S-spun, weft 22 S-spun

Thread thickness: warp 0.2 mm medium twist,
weft 0.2 mm medium–tight twist

Tapestry: silk, dyed (dark brown); slit; hastae
woven on warps lifted up from the
base fabric; supplementary linen
weft filling above the baseline
between the lower letters

Provenance: Ex H.P. Kraus collection, no. 34

Inv. no. LNS 158 T

Inscription: بسم الله الرحمن الرحيم لا اله الا الله وحده لا شريك له (...؟...)

In the name of God the Most Merciful, the Most Compassionate. There is no
God but God alone and has no partner (… ? …)

This piece appears once to have been connected to cat. no. 132, which features
the same type of Kufic inscription and was also scissor cut into the same
format. That textile bears an inscription mentioning the *ism*, *kunya* and *laqab*
'al-Mansur Abu 'Ali al-Hakim bi-'Amr Allah' of the Fatimid caliph al-Hakim
(r. 996–1021).

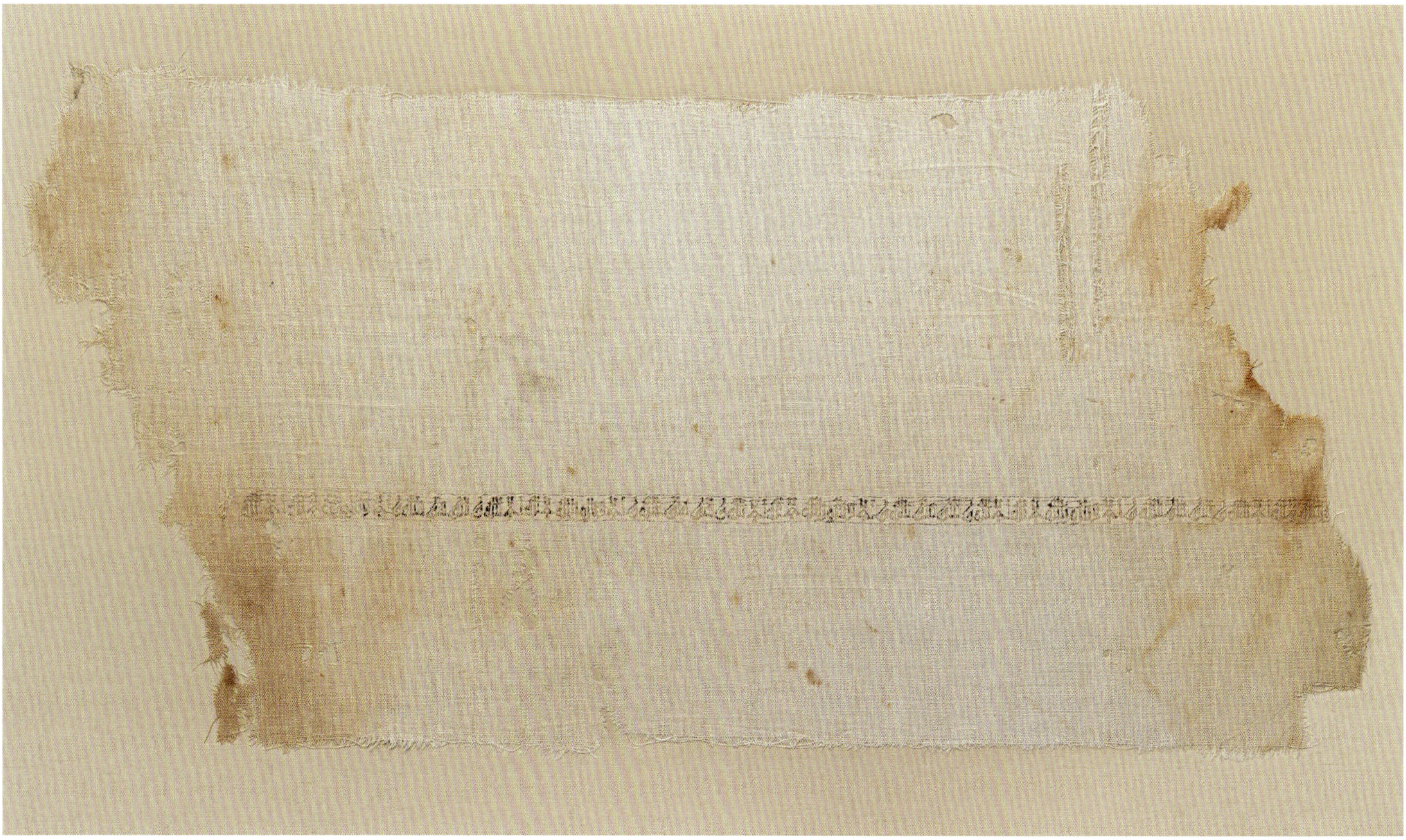

Cat. 134 *TIRAZ* FRAGMENT FROM
THE FATIMID DYNASTY
Egypt, late 10th to
11th century CE

Description: Fragment of undyed linen, with
a band of Kufic inscription
tapestry-woven in brown silk.

Materials: linen and silk: plain weave and
tapestry

Dimensions: h. 25.7 cm, w. 45.3 cm;
max. letter height 1.0 cm

Ground fabric: linen warp and weft, undyed, warp-
faced plain weave, dense texture
(*dabiqi*); very good quality (1)

Thread count: warp 28 S-spun, weft 16 S-spun

Thread thickness: warp 0.15–0.2 mm medium twist,
weft 0.2 mm medium twist

Tapestry: silk, dyed (dark brown); slit
and toothed; discontinuous
supplementary paired linen weft
filling between the letters

Provenance: Ex H.P. Kraus collection, no. 73

Inv. no. LNS 191 T

Related works: See page 511

Inscription: repetition of

There is no God but God, the Manifest Truth. For God

لا اله الا الله الحق المبين لله

This piece relates in terms of epigraphy to a textile from the reign of al-Hakim in the Textile Museum, Washington, DC (Related works 1). They share the small size of the letters (*c*. 0.9–1.0 cm), which were tapestry-woven, embedded within a silk background forming a band distinctive from the linen ground fabric. The letters are characterized by pronounced swan-neck upper and lower terminals, something also found in monumental inscriptions of that period. The inscription here does not contain a caliphal protocol, but rather a benedictory repeat of the *shahada*. A piece in the Bouvier Collection, which is closely related in epigraphy and execution to the present piece and the textile in Washington, also features a benedictory repetition, and has been attributed to the reign of al-Hakim (r. 996–1021) (Related works 2).

In terms of quality of the material, as well as the tapestry weaving, all three pieces are very close. It is very likely that the workshops producing textiles for the Fatimid court in the great centres of the Delta also manufactured for the open market, though on these the inscriptions were limited to non-caliphal content, as seen here.

Cat. 135 *TIRAZ* FRAGMENT FROM
THE FATIMID DYNASTY
**Egypt, late 10th to
11th century CE**

Description: Fragment (two pieces) of undyed
linen, roughly rectangular, with
one line of Kufic inscription
tapestry-woven in blue silk; the
larger fragment conserves part
of the untwisted fringe.

Materials: linen and silk: plain weave
and tapestry

Dimensions: piece (a) (right): h. 15.5 cm,
w. 18.4 cm; max. letter height
0.7 cm
piece (b) (left): h. 37.2 cm,
w. 28.5 cm; max. letter height
0.7 cm

Ground fabric: linen warp and weft, undyed,
predominant-warp plain weave,
loose texture (*sharb*); very good
quality (1); untwisted fringe

Thread count: warp 22 S-spun, weft 19 S-spun

Thread thickness: warp 0.15–0.2 mm slight–medium
twist, weft 0.15 mm tight twist

Tapestry: silk, dyed (dark blue); slit
and toothed; discontinuous
supplementary linen weft

Provenance: Ex H.P. Kraus collection,
nos 75–76

Inv. no. LNS 193 T a, b

Inscription: corrupted repetition of
Blessing from God?

بركة من الله؟

Cat. 136 *TIRAZ* **FRAGMENT FROM THE FATIMID DYNASTY**
Egypt, late 10th to 11th century CE

Description: Fragment (three pieces) of undyed linen, roughly rectangular, with one line of Kufic inscription tapestry-woven in red silk.

Materials: linen and silk: plain weave and tapestry

Dimensions: piece (a) (right): h. 15.7 cm, w. 44.7 cm; max. letter height 1.0 cm
piece (b) (center): h. 17.4 cm, w. 24.7 cm; max. letter height 1.0 cm
piece (c) (left): h. 18.3 cm, w. 29.6 cm; max. letter height 1.0 cm

Ground fabric: linen warp and weft, undyed, predominant-warp plain weave, close texture (*dabiqi*); very good quality (1)

Thread count: warp 30 S-spun, weft 22 S-spun

Thread thickness: warp 0.1–0.25 mm slight–medium twist, weft 0.15 mm tight twist

Tapestry: silk, dyed (red); slit and toothed; hastae woven on warps lifted up from the base fabric; discontinuous supplementary linen weft

Provenance: Ex H.P. Kraus collection, nos 77–79

Inv. no. LNS 194 T a–c

Inscription: repetition of

And success is granted by God

والتوفيق بالله

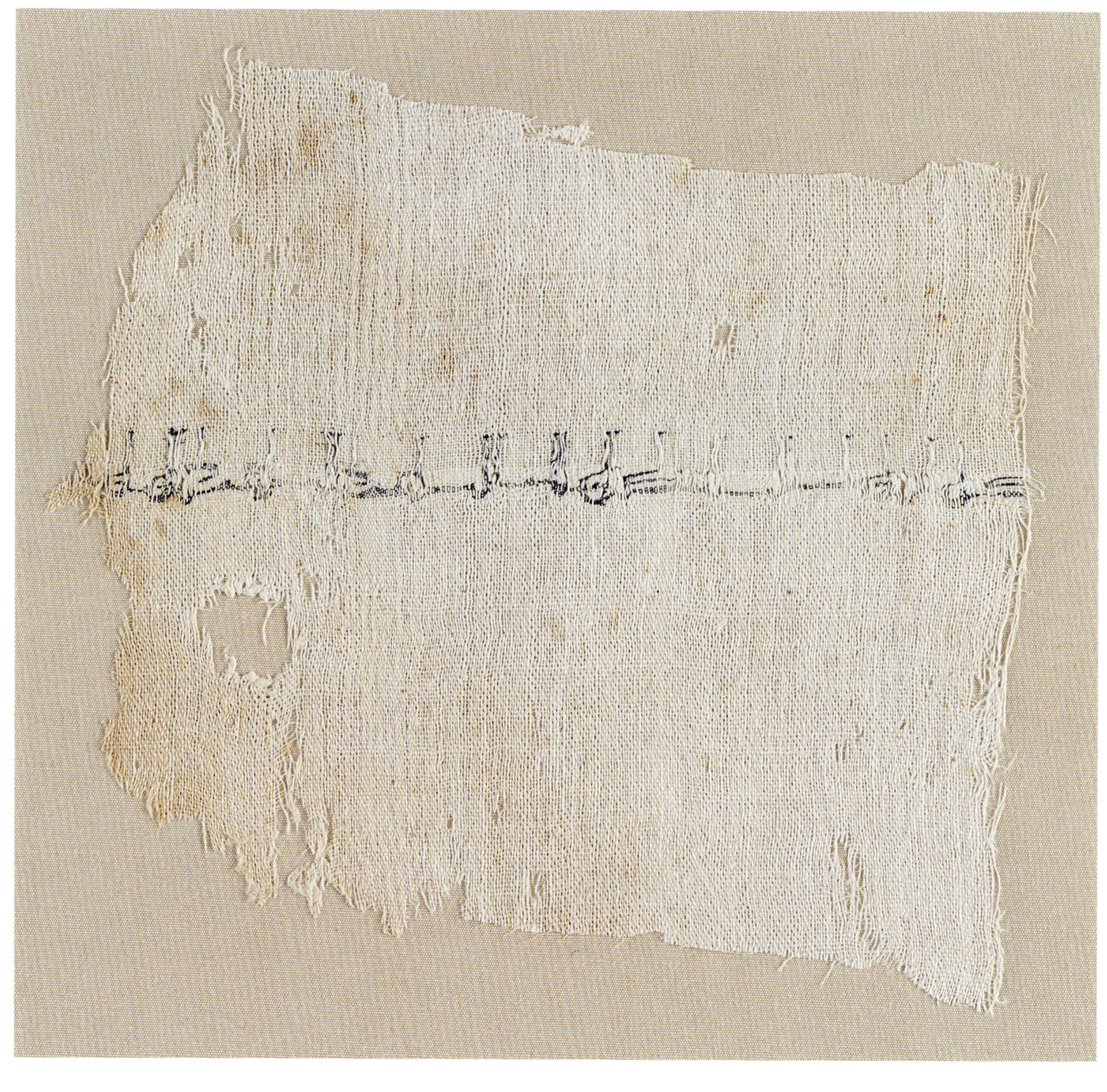

Cat. 137 *TIRAZ* FRAGMENT FROM
THE FATIMID DYNASTY
**Egypt, late 10th to
11th century CE**

Description: Fragment of undyed linen, with
one line of Kufic inscription
tapestry-woven in blue silk.

Materials: linen and silk: plain weave
and tapestry

Dimensions: h. 10.5 cm, w. 12.5 cm;
max. letter height 1 cm

Ground fabric: linen warp and weft, undyed,
predominant-warp plain weave,
close texture (*dabiqi*), very regular;
very good–good quality (1–2)

Thread count: warp 28 S-spun, weft 18 S-spun

Thread thickness: warp 0.2–0.3 mm slight–medium
twist, weft 0.15 mm tight twist

Tapestry: silk, dyed (dark blue); hastae
woven on warps lifted up from
the base fabric; discontinuous
supplementary paired linen weft
filling above and partly below the
baseline

Provenance: Ex H.P. Kraus collection, no. 156

Inv. no. LNS 262 T

Inscription: repetition of

Assistance from God (?)

نصر من الله (؟)

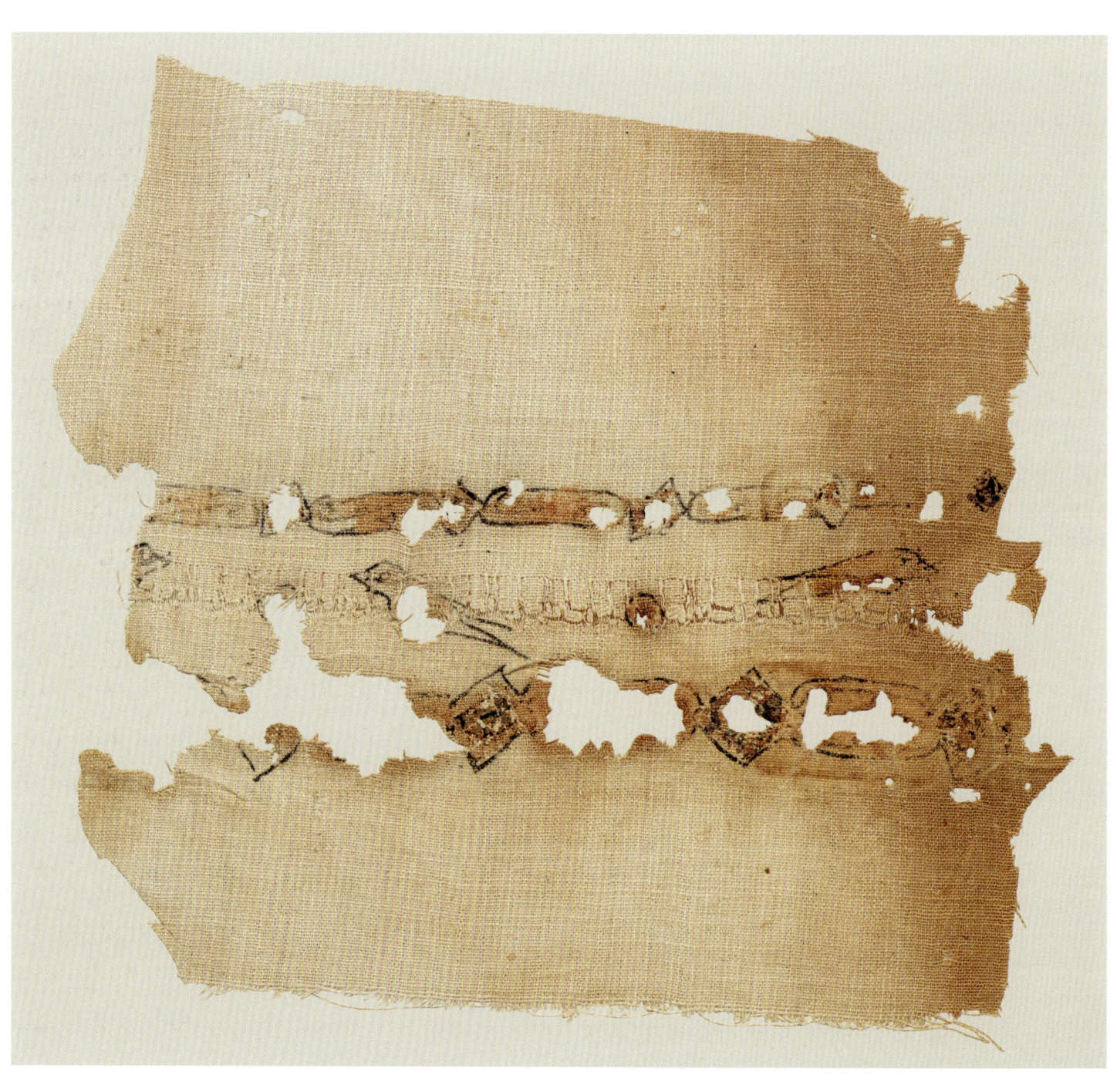

Cat. 138 *TIRAZ* FRAGMENT FROM
THE FATIMID DYNASTY
Egypt, late 10th to
12th century CE

Description: Fragment of undyed linen, with
one line of Kufic inscription
tapestry-woven in red silk, most
of it gone, with a decorative band,
bearing birds, painted and gilded
across the inscription; above and
below are two further bands of
painted decoration in faded red
and dark brown.

Materials: linen, silk, ink, pigments and
gilding: plain weave, tapestry
and painting

Dimensions: h. 15.0 cm, w. 16.0 cm;
max. letter height 0.8 cm

Ground fabric: linen warp and weft, undyed,
predominant-warp plain weave,
dense texture (*dabiqi*);
good quality (2)

Thread count: warp 31 S-spun, weft 20 S-spun

Thread thickness: warp 0.15–0.4 mm medium twist,
weft 0.15–0.4 mm medium twist

Tapestry: silk, dyed (red); slit and toothed;
hastae woven on warps lifted up
from the base fabric; additional
design outlined over the tapestried
inscription with ink and filled in
with applied coloured pigments
(faded red, dark brown) and
gilding

Provenance: Ex H.P. Kraus collection, no. 155

Inv. no. LNS 261 T

Related works: See page 511

Inscription: repetition of

Sovereignty is God's

الملك لله

It is interesting that here a tapestry-woven band of benedictory text is accompanied by zoomorphic and geometric designs painted onto the fabric at a later stage, perhaps to embellish an otherwise rather monotonous textile. The designs, and particularly the birds, are executed with great skill and fluidity. Three very closely related fragments with birds of a similar tactility are at the Biblioteca Apostolica Vaticana, Vatican City (Related works 1–3). The strokes seem to have been executed with the nib of a pen or stylus, as they are very fine. As textiles were expensive items, re-use of fabrics was common in the early Islamic period. Painting a textile could give an old fabric a new lease on life and also allow the owner to personalize a fabric. It was also an inexpensive method of emulating the caliphal fashion of *tiraz* inscriptions for segments of the population that would normally never have had access to these prized inscribed fabrics.

Cornu attributed the fragments in the Vatican to either Egypt or Iraq. The same ambiguous attribution was given to two fragments in the Bouvier Collection (Related works 5, 6). However, the evidence of the present piece reinforces an Egyptian attribution on account of the material and the tapestry-woven inscription underneath the painted figures. A fragment of *mulham* embroidered with an inscription in silk at the Benaki Museum, Athens, features a very similar arrangement of painted birds accompanying a decorative band. Here too the painted decoration would seem to constitute a secondary embellishment of a previously imported fabric (Related works 4). The fact that the decoration was applied to a *mulham* ground fabric would suggest an Iranian or Iraqi origin. Another *mulham*, attributed to Seljuq Iran or Iraq, with painted and gilded inscription and decoration, is in the Cleveland Museum of Art (Related works 8). What distinguishes the piece in the Benaki Museum from the others in the group is the use of gilding to highlight the designs. The birds seen here are also very close in their naturalism to those depicted on a Fatimid tapestry-woven fragment of silk on linen at the Metropolitan Museum of Art, New York, attributed to the eleventh century, where details of the wings, the beaks and the eyes are clearly visible.[42]

Cat. 139 *TIRAZ* **FRAGMENT FROM THE REIGN OF THE FATIMID CALIPH AL-HAKIM** (r. 996–1021)
Egypt, late 10th to early 11th century CE

Description: Fragment of undyed linen, with one line of Kufic inscription tapestry-woven in dark brown and ochre silk.

Materials: linen and silk: plain weave and tapestry

Dimensions: h. 26.5 cm, w. 39.5 cm; max. letter height 3.6 cm

Ground fabric: linen warp and weft, undyed, predominant-warp plain weave, gauzy texture (*sharb*), regular structure; good quality (2)

Thread count: warp 22 S-spun, weft 11 S-spun

Thread thickness: warp 0.15–0.2 mm slight–medium twist, weft 0.15 mm tight twist

Tapestry: silk, dyed (dark brown and ochre); slit and toothed; woven against supplementary linen weft

Provenance: Ex H.P. Kraus collection, no. 58

Inv. no. LNS 177 T

Related works: See page 511

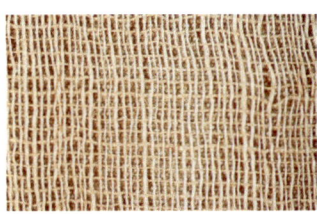

Inscription:

[بسـ]م اللـه الرحمن الرحيم نصر من الله وفتح {قريب} لعبد الله و (وليه) علي (...) الإمام الحاكـم بأمر[لله] [...]

[…] [In the nam]e of God the Most Merciful, the Most Compassionate. Assistance from God and an [imminent] victory to the servant and ally of God 'Ali (…) the imam al-Hakim bi-'Amr Allah […]

This piece has previously been attributed to the reign of the Abbasid caliph al-Muti' (r. 946–74) by comparison with a number of textiles inscribed in floriated Kufic that date from his reign.[43] Although the inscription here falls broadly within the category of floriated Kufic, certain aspects of the textile's manufacture and epigraphy link it to a specific group of inscribed textiles that date mainly from the reign of the Fatimid caliph al-Hakim (r. 996–1021), supported by its reading here. The inscriptions are condensed, with letters placed very close together, so that there is more stress on the vertical than the horizontal extent of the inscription. Furthermore, the tapestry of the letters above the baseline is not executed on warps lifted up from the warps of the base fabric, but the whole inscription and its background, in each case, is woven in tapestry, the inscription in silk and the background in linen.[44] In this way the areas around the inscription are very densely textured and keep the inscription in place. A further trademark of these inscriptions is the presence of horizontal lines linking the hastae, probably to carry the thread from one to the next. It seems that this style carried on under al-Zahir (r. 1021–36), perhaps during his early reign, as one surviving specimen suggests.[45]

The choice of religious text in this inscription also relects a Fatimid context. The text comprises two phrases which are found only in Fatimid inscriptions. One, 'al-fath qarib', alludes to the ongoing power struggles between the Fatimids and the Abbasids and expresses a hope for a future victory over the Holy Places of Mecca and Medina. The other, 'wa wali'ihi', accompanies the phrase 'li-'abd Allah' in Fatimid inscriptions and refers to the person of the caliph as an ally of God. The wording of the present inscription seems to be incorrect with regard to the *kunya* of the caliph al-Hakim. It should read 'al-Mansur Abu 'Ali', but in fact reads only "Ali' followed by a lacuna, then after 'al-imam' the *laqab* is identifiable as 'al-Hakim'. Comparable inscriptions of the same type frequently contain mistakes and omissions, so that it is not surprising to find such an error in the present piece.

Cat. 140 *TIRAZ* FRAGMENT FROM THE FATIMID DYNASTY
Egypt, 11th century CE

Description: Fragment of undyed linen, with a decorative calligraphic band tapestry-woven in red silk.

Materials: linen and silk: plain weave and tapestry

Dimensions: h. 26.6 cm, w. 14 cm; max. letter height 5.7 cm

Ground fabric: linen warp and weft, undyed, warp-faced plain weave, gauzy texture (*sharb*); good quality (2)

Thread count: warp 15 S-spun, weft 7 S-spun

Thread thickness: warp 0.25–0.3 mm tight twist, weft 0.15–0.2 mm tight twist

Tapestry: silk, dyed (red, blue); 54 picks per cm; slit; supplementary linen weft filling between the letters

Provenance: Ex H.P. Kraus collection, New York, no. 159

Inv. no. LNS 265 T

Related works: See page 511

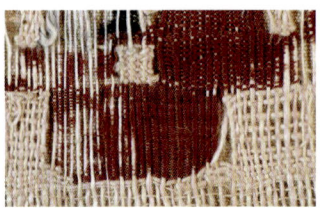

Inscription:

In the name of God, the Most Merciful (?) [...]

بسم الله الرحم (؟) [...]

Cat. 141 *TIRAZ* FRAGMENT FROM
THE REIGN OF THE
FATIMID CALIPH AL-ZAHIR
(r. 1021–36)
Egypt, 11th century CE

Description: Fragment of undyed linen, with
a line of Kufic inscription
tapestry-woven in blue silk.

Materials: linen and silk: tapestry weave

Dimensions: h. 23.0 cm, w. 26.0 cm;
max. letter height 1.0 cm

Ground fabric: linen warp and weft, undyed,
balanced plain weave, gauzy
texture (*sharb*); very good–good
quality (1–2)

Thread count: warp 24 S-spun, weft 22 S-spun

Thread thickness: warp 0.15–0.2 mm medium twist,
weft 0.15 mm tight twist

Tapestry: linen, undyed, S-spun, set against
discontinuous dark blue tram silk
weft; selvedge on the right side of
the inscription; untwisted fringe
with weftless band

Provenance: Ex H.P. Kraus collection,
New York, no. 86

Inv. no. LNS 200 T

Related works: See page 511

Inscription: بسم الله الرحمن الرحيم الامام علي ابو الحسن الظاهر لإعزاز [دين الله] [...]

In the name of God, the Most Merciful, the Most Compassionate. The Imam 'Ali
Abu al-Hasan al-Zahir li-I'zaz [din Allah] [...]

This fragment is inscribed with the beginning of a longer text mentioning the
Fatimid caliph al-Zahir (r. 1021–36). A comparable epigraphic style can be found
in a tiraz inscription from al-Zahir's reign at the Textile Museum, Washington,
DC (Related works 1). Although the inscription on that piece consists of an
addorsed band, it shares with the present inscription letter terminals that are
sometimes curled inwards and sometimes wedge-shaped. In both cases, the
inscription is woven in linen against a dark blue silk background.

Cat. 142 *TIRAZ* FRAGMENT FROM THE REIGN OF THE FATIMID CALIPH AL-ZAHIR (r. 1021–36)
Egypt, 11th century CE

Description: Fragment (two pieces) of undyed linen, with two lines of inscription in floriated Kufic tapestry-woven in dark blue silk each set against a decorative band: the first (1.0 cm) contains a sequence of running foxes executed in undyed linen outlined in dark blue silk and dark blue silk outlined in undyed linen, set against a rusty brown background; the other (1.0 cm) is set above the first and is of the same type.

Materials: linen and silk: plain weave and tapestry

Dimensions: piece (a) (left): h. 10.5 cm, w. 11.5 cm; max. letter height 1.0 cm
piece (b) (right): h. 13.0 cm, w. 20.5 cm; max. letter height 1.0 cm

Ground fabric: linen warp and weft, undyed, balanced plain weave, close texture (*sharb*); good quality (2)

Thread count: warp 27 S-spun, weft 20 S-spun

Thread thickness: warp 0.15–0.3 mm medium–tight twist, weft 0.15–0.3 mm medium–tight twist

Tapestry: silk, dyed (blue, rusty brown), and linen, undyed; slit and toothed; supplementary linen weft filling between the letters

Provenance: Ex H.P. Kraus collection, nos 62, 85

Inv. no. LNS 181 T a, b

Related works: See pages 511–12

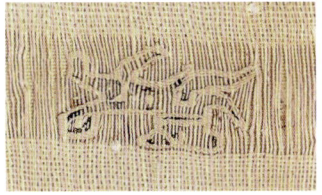

Inscription:
Line 1:

[...] الله علي ولي الله صلى الله عليهما نصر من الله وفتح قريب لعبد الله ووليه [...] حسن الإمام الظاهر لإعزاز دين الله امير المؤ[منين] [...]

[...] God. 'Ali ally of God. Blessings from God be upon them. Assistance from God and an imminent victory to the servant and ally of God [...] Hasan the Imam al-Zahir li-I'zaz din Allah the Commander of the Faith[ful] [...]

Line 2:

[...] آبائه الائمة الطاهرين مما أمر بعمله الوزير الأجل صفي أمير المؤمنين و خليصته ابي القاسم علي بن احمد امتع (الله به و الدين)
[...]

[...] his ancestors, the immaculate Imams. Of what has been ordered to be made by the vizier, the most illustrious, the true and chosen comrade of the Commander of the Faithful Abi al-Qasim 'Ali the son of Ahmad. May God (benefit the religion through him)

This inscription mentions the name of the Fatimid caliph al-Zahir (r. 1021–36) and records an order by his vizier Abu al-Qasim 'Ali ibn Ahmad al-Jarjara'i

(d. 1045). Originally from Iraq, Abu al-Qasim came to Egypt as a *katib* under the caliph al-Hakim (r. 996–1021). In 406 AH / 1013–14 CE he became director of the *diwan al-nafaqat*, an office that managed the expenditure on the administration of the royal court, and in 412 AH / 1021–22 CE was installed as *wasata*. Abu al-Qasim became vizier in 418 AH / 1027–28 CE, an office he also held under al-Zahir's successor, al-Mustansir (r. 1036–94), until his death in Ramadan 436 AH / March 1045 CE .[46] The textile can thus be attributed to the period 418–27 AH / 1027–36 CE . Fifteen surviving *tiraz* inscriptions document an order by Abu al-Qasim during his tenure under al-Zahir (Related works 1–15). Of these, ten inscriptions record his title *wazir al-ʾajal safi amir al-muʾminin wa khalisatuhu* ('the most illustrious vizier, the true and chosen comrade of the Commander of the Faithful') (Related works 3–7, 10, 11, 13–15). Five inscriptions still record the exact dates of manufacture, ranging between 420 AH / 1029–30 CE and 427 AH / 1035–36 CE (Related works 11–15). Several inscriptions provide evidence concerning workshops and places of manufacture: one for an unidentified *tiraz al-ʿamma* (Related works 10), two for a *tiraz al-ʿamma* in Tinnis (Related works 11, 12), two for a *tiraz al-ʿamma* in Tuna (Related works 14, 15), and one for a *tiraz al-khassa* in Tinnis (Related works 13).

Cat. 143 *TIRAZ* FRAGMENT FROM THE REIGN OF THE FATIMID CALIPH AL-ZAHIR (r. 1021–36)
Egypt, 11th century CE

Description: Fragment of linen, dyed light blue, with two lines of inscription in foliated Kufic and two decorative bands tapestry-woven in coloured silk; the inscriptions are in dark blue accompanied by ochre floriations and are addorsed against a decorative band (1.5 cm) consisting of lozenges in brown, blue and ochre, which probably once contained floral motifs; the second decorative band (1.5 cm), set apart from this tripartite arrangement, follows the other in colour and design.

Materials: linen and silk: plain weave and tapestry

Dimensions: h. 40.5 cm, w. 34.2 cm; max. letter height 1.5 cm

Ground fabric: linen warp and weft, dyed (light blue), predominant-warp plain weave, dense texture (*dabiqi*); very good quality (1)

Thread count: warp 45 S-spun, weft 28 S-spun

Thread thickness: warp 0.15 mm medium twist, weft 0.15 mm medium–tight twist

Tapestry: silk, dyed (dark blue, ochre, brown), and linen, dyed (blue); slit and toothed; inscription woven within a separate band of discontinuous densified paired linen weft, with occasionally crossed warps marking the transition between ground fabric and tapestried areas

Provenance: Ex H.P. Kraus collection, no. 70

Inv. no. LNS 188 T

Related works: See page 512

Inscription:

Line 1:

[...] عـ[ـ]لي ولي الله صلىٰ الله عليه نصر من الله {لـ}عـ(ـبد الله) [...]

[...] ['A]li the ally of God. Blessings of God be upon him. Help from God (to) the s(ervant of God) [...]

Line 2:

[...] مما امر بعمله الوزير الاجـ[ـلـ]ل [...]

[...] of what was ordered by the illustrious vizier [...]

This piece can be attributed to the reign of the Fatimid caliph al-Zahir. The title *al-wazir al-'ajal* ('the illustrious vizier') of the ordering vizier mentioned in the inscription does not of itself allow a conclusive attribution of the piece, as several viziers of Fatimid caliphs carried that title. However, a comparison of the epigraphic style of the inscription and its aesthetic with that of pieces conclusively datable to al-Zahir's reign shows that the piece must date from his reign. In consequence, the title mentioned here must refer to al-Zahir's vizier Abu al-Qasim 'Ali ibn Ahmad al-Jarjara'i (in office 1027–45). He is mentioned with this title in several *tiraz* inscriptions from the reign of al-Zahir (Related works 1–8). For a biography and further references, see cat. no. 142.

Several features characterize the particular epigraphic style used here, which is representative of the period of al-Zahir. The letters are generally of an even thickness. Hastae usually comprise a wedge-shaped terminal, while the terminals of letters curving up above the baseline tend to be elongated foliate trumpet-shapes. The *mim* is round, while *ha* and *ta marbuta* are square-shaped. The *'ayn* is in the shape of a trefoil. The whole inscription is set against a floriated background of in-curling stems terminating in small fleurs-de-lis.

A number of *tiraz* inscriptions can be related to the present piece visually. While all of these share epigraphic details, some of them also display the same aesthetic of the tripartite arrangement of inscriptions and decorative band accompanied by a separate decorative band. A piece in the Royal Ontario Museum made in a *tiraz al-'amma* in Damietta is a particularly close comparison (Related works 1). While many of the other comparative pieces feature decorative bands containing zoomorphic cartouches, the Toronto example features floral content, like the present piece. It is likely that the present piece was also produced in a Delta location, if not in Damietta itself. It is rare to find dyed ground fabrics among the surviving *tiraz* corpus. This may reflect the high cost of dyeing linen, as suggested by surviving accounts among the Geniza documents. It is more likely, however, that the overwhelming prevalence of undyed materials is due to the fact that most *tiraz* textiles survived because they were used as burial shrouds. White was a preferred choice for shrouds. The only other example of a caliphal *tiraz* textile with dyed ground fabric from the reign of al-Zahir so far known is in the Benaki Museum, Athens (Related works 2). Its ground fabric is dyed green. It was made in a *tiraz al-'amma* in Tinnis and, like the present piece, was ordered by the vizier Abu al-Qasim 'Ali ibn Ahmad.

Cat. 144 *TIRAZ* FRAGMENT FROM
THE REIGN OF THE FATIMID
CALIPH AL-MUSTANSIR
(r. 1036–94)
Egypt, mid- to late
11th century CE

Description: Fragment of undyed linen
(remnant at upper right corner),
with two lines of confronted
foliated Kufic inscription tapestry-
woven in dark blue characters
with dark red streaks on a cream
linen ground; a decorative band
(1.2 cm) between the lines of the
inscription is composed of two
registers of confronted and paired
S-shaped motifs in cream linen on
a dark blue ground with dark red
streaks.

Materials: linen and silk: plain weave and
tapestry

Dimensions: h. 10 cm, w. 31 cm;
max. letter height 1.1 cm

Ground fabric: linen warp and weft, undyed,
balanced plain weave, loose
regular texture (*sharb*); very
good quality (1)

Thread count: warp 34 S-spun (some paired),
weft *c.* 22 per 0.5 cm S-spun

Thread thickness: warp 0.05–0.1 mm tight twist,
weft 0.05–0.1 mm tight twist

Tapestry: inscription: silk, dyed (dark
blue and red); slit and toothed;
weft-faced, 52 paired wefts on
single warps, very dense texture;
discontinuous undyed linen weft
filling around the inscription

Decorative band: silk, dyed (dark blue and red),
and undyed linen; slit and toothed;
threads carried over from the end
of one design to the beginning
of the next; transition from the
ground fabric to tapestried areas
characterized by crossed warps

Inv. no. LNS 17 T

Related works: See page 512

Inscription:

Line 1: [...] معد وله و الله لعبد قريب فتح و الله من نصر [و عليه] عـ[ليه و] آلـ[لـ] [صـ]ـلى [...]

[...] May the blessings of [Go]d be [upon him and] assistance from God and an imminent victory for the servant and ally of God Ma'ad [...]

Line 2: [...] وابنائه الطاهرين الائمة ابائه علي و عليه الله صاوات [مومنين...]

[...] believers, may God's blessings be upon him and his forefathers the immaculate imams and upon his descendants [...]

The inscription states the beginning of the caliph's given name (*ism*) 'Ma'ad', which in this case does not refer to Ma'ad Abu Tamim al-Mu'izz (r. 953–75), but his descendant Ma'ad Abu Tamim al-Mustansir (r. 1036–94). The attribution to al-Mustansir rests on the comparison with a textile in the Metropolitan Museum of Art, New York, which resembles the present fragment in the arrangement of the inscription and decoration, colour scheme, the content of the inscription and the epigraphy of the foliated characters (Related works 1). The Metropolitan Museum textile states in its inscription the full names and titles of al-Mustansir, "abd Allah Ma'ad Abu Tamim al-imam al-Mustansir bi-llah amir al-mu'(minin)'; the decoration between the lines of inscription comprises a vegetal scroll with small multi-leaf buds, but both the inscription and the decorative band are set against a background of gold-thread tapestry, which makes this a very luxurious textile, unlike the al-Sabah example. The S-shaped motifs on our piece can be compared with those on an item in the Textile Museum, Washington, DC (Related works 2), where paired S-shapes serve as the background for the inscription. S-shaped motifs such as these are also found on other Fatimid works of art. A tin mirror attributed to Fatimid Egypt at the Benaki Museum, Athens, features a prominent band of confronted S-shapes, for example.[47]

Cat. 145 *TIRAZ* **FRAGMENT ATTRIBUTED TO THE REIGN OF THE FATIMID CALIPH AL-MUSTANSIR**
(r. 1036–94)
Egypt, 1036–45 CE

Description: Fragment of undyed linen, with two lines of inscription in floriated Kufic tapestry-woven in coloured silk – greenish blue and mustard on a red ground – either side of a sequence of greenish-blue and red cartouches containing the figure of a hare and the word 'al-mulk' alternating; a second band (1.5 cm) comprises the same decorative arrangement of alternating hare and text.

Materials: linen and silk: plain weave and tapestry

Dimensions: h. 14.9 cm, w. 14.5 cm; max. letter height 2.0 cm

Ground fabric: linen warp and weft, predominant-warp plain weave, close texture (*dabiqi*), regular; superior quality (1+); selvedge on the left side

Thread count: warp 41 S-spun, weft 32 S-spun

Thread thickness: warp 0.05–0.15 mm tight twist, weft 0.05–0.1 mm tight twist

Tapestry: undyed linen, and silk, dyed (red, greenish-blue, mustard; 84 picks per cm; slit and toothed

Inv. no. LNS 46 T

Related works: See page 512

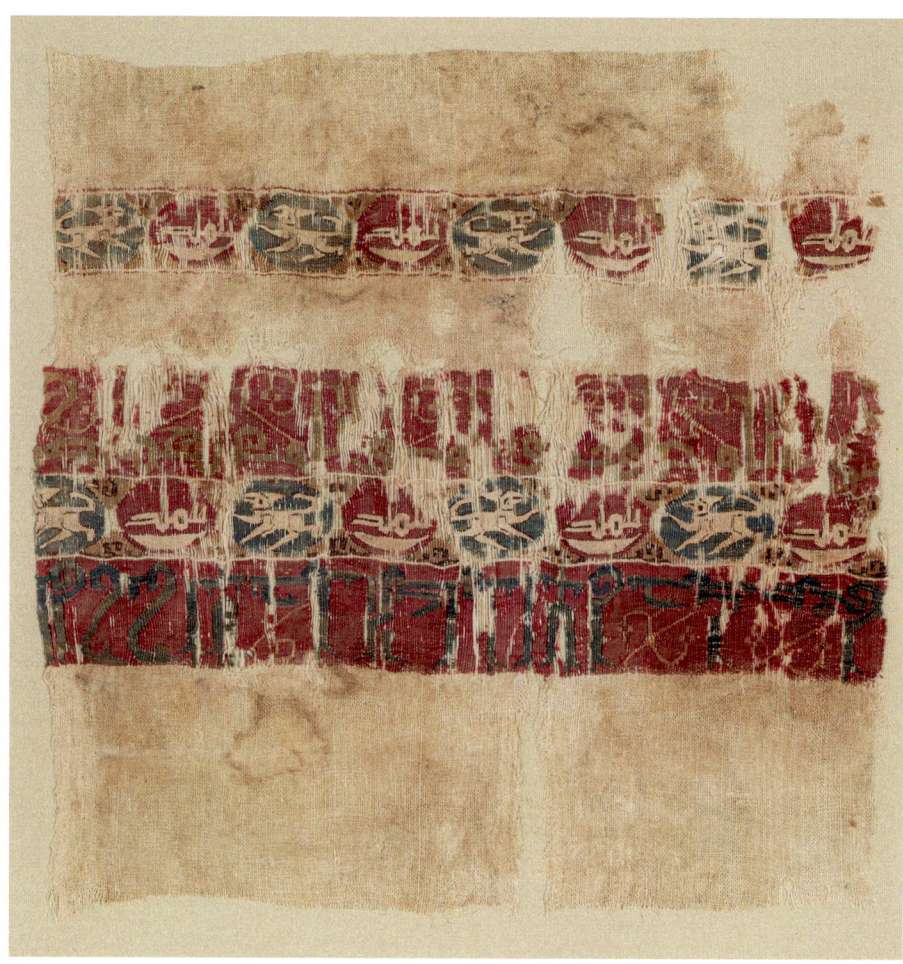

Inscription:

Line 1: [...] لأجلّ الكامل الأوحد صفى امير المؤمنين ً [آ]الوزير [...]

[...] the illustrious vizier, the unique, comrade [of the Commander of the Faithful] [...]

Line 2: [...] ر]سول الله علي ولي الله صلي الله عليهما نصر [...]

[...] Prophet of God, 'Ali the ally of God. Blessings from God be upon them. Victory [...]

Within the cartouches: الملك

Sovereignty

The arrangement of inscriptions and decorative bands, plus the particular style of the floriated inscription on this piece, can be found throughout the period of al-Zahir (r. 1021–36) and al-Mustansir (r. 1036–94). Hence an attribution on the epigraphic style of the inscription alone would be imprecise. The inscribed text of the present fragment alludes to a vizier whose titles are mentioned as *al-wazir al-ʾajal al-kamil al-ʾawhad*. It is on the basis of these titles that an attribution to al-Mustansir's reign can be made. The title belonged to al-Mustansir's first vizier Abu al-Qasim ʿAli ibn Ahmad al-Jarjaraʾi (for his biography, see pp. 379–80 and cat. nos 142–43). Abu al-Qasim had already been vizier in 418–27 AH / 1027–36CE under al-Mustansir's predecessor, al-Zahir, and was documented in *tiraz* inscriptions with the titles *al-wazir al-ʾajal safi amir al-muʾminin wa khalisatuhu*. It is only under al-Mustansir that the titles *al-kamil al-ʾawhad* were added, as is documented by a complete *tiraz* inscription at the Metropolitan Museum of Art, New York (Related works 1). Further inscriptions with this title, albeit incomplete, have been documented (Related works 2, 3, 5).

A small fragment from al-Mustansir's reign in the Metropolitan Museum, New York, relates very closely to the present fragment in terms of epigraphic style and the arrangement of both the addorsed inscriptions and the decoration comprising a main band and a supplementary band, albeit with all administrative data lost (Related works 16). Another closely related fragment at the Metropolitan Museum from the reign of al-Zahir illustrates the difficulty of dating the present piece on aesthetics alone;[48] it closely resembles the al-Sabah fragment as well as Related works 16, but its inscription mentions the name of al-Zahir, and the beginning of Abu al-Qasim ʿAli ibn Ahmad's titles. This makes it clear that the vizier's titles are critical in attributing our piece to al-Mustansir's reign. Matters are further complicated by the fact that many inscriptions exist from al-Mustansir's reign where Abu al-Qasim ʿAli ibn Ahmad al-Jarjaraʾi is not referred to with the titles *al-ʾajal al-kamil al-ʾawhad*, but with the set of titles that are also found in inscriptions from al-Zahir's reign (Related works 4, 6–15). Since none of the inscriptions can be dated to particular years it is difficult to build a chronological sequence to see at which point Abu al-Qasim started using additional titles under al-Mustansir.

Cat. 146   *TIRAZ* FRAGMENT FROM THE FATIMID DYNASTY
Egypt, mid-11th century CE

Description: Fragment of undyed linen, with tapestry-woven decoration in black and brown silk organized in two registers: the more substantial one consists of two lines of Kufic inscription enclosing a central band of palmette motifs in a diamond-shaped trellis; the other, a single thin band, repeats this non-epigraphic decoration. The inscription is particularly delicate, being set against a fine background of tendrils with three-pointed terminals.

Materials: linen and silk: plain weave and tapestry

Dimensions: h. 16.8 cm, w. 28.5 cm; max. letter height 1.0 cm

Ground fabric: linen warp and weft, undyed, balanced plain weave, close texture (*dabiqi*), glazed and polished; very good quality (1); seam on one side

Thread count: warp 35 S-spun, weft 33 S-spun

Thread thickness: warp 0.1–0.25 mm slight twist, weft 0.1–0.2 mm slight twist

Tapestry: silk, dyed (dark brown, purplish-red, mustard); slit and toothed; discontinuous supplementary linen weft filling

Inv. no. LNS 772 T

Related works: See page 512

Inscription: undecipherable

The composition and script of this *tiraz* may be compared with a number of dated *tiraz* fragments produced during the reign of the Fatimid caliph al-Mustansir (r. 1036–94), especially during the middle years of his reign. A closely related example that mentions al-Mustansir's vizier al-Hasan ibn 'imad al-dawla Muhammad ibn Ahmad (in office 1048–49) is in the Textile Museum, Washington, DC (Related works 1). Another similar piece, inscribed with the titles of the vizier Abu al-Faraj Muhammad ibn Ja'far (in office 1058–60), is in the Museum für Islamische Kunst, Berlin (Related works 2). A third that mentions the latter vizier by name is in the Textile Museum in Washington (Related works 3). A fourth is in the Boston Museum of Fine Arts (Related works 4). The inscriptions on these fragments have in common that they comprise a squarish style of script, itself unfoliated, set against a floriated background of what appear to be vine scrolls bending upwards in a swan-neck fashion, a feature that can be observed on the present fragment as well. In all of these, the two bands of script are juxtaposed against a band made up of a sequence of small lozenges filled with quatrefoil designs, not too dissimilar to what is found here. This fragment formed part of a sleeve – a seam is visible on one side. The inscription band was cut out of a larger piece and inserted into a sleeve; such bands are represented in painting and sculpture of the early Islamic period, and the Fatimid dynasty in particular, as discussed in chapter 1.

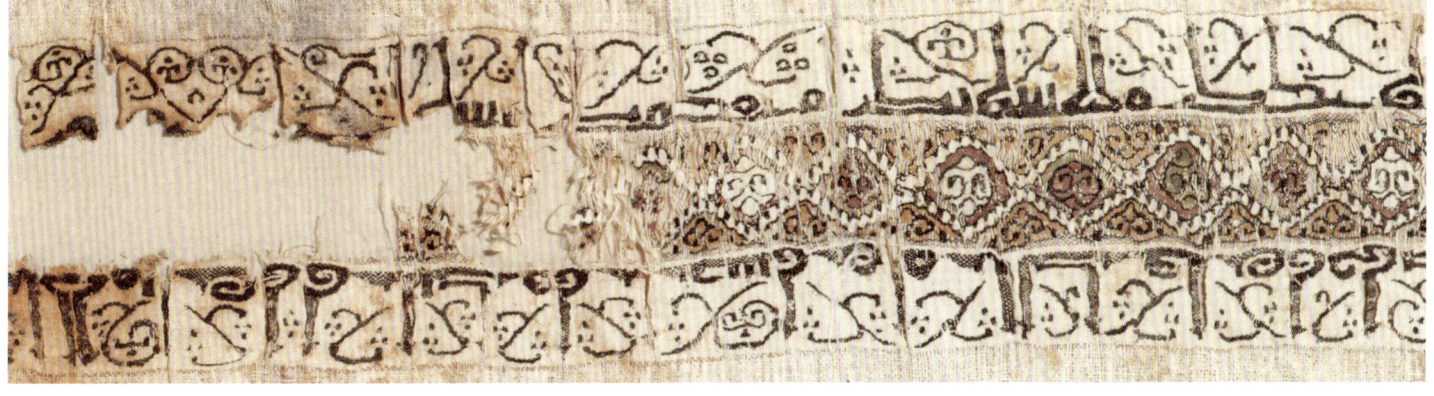

Cat. 147 *TIRAZ* **FRAGMENT FROM THE FATIMID DYNASTY**
Egypt, 11th century CE

Description: Fragment of linen dyed dark blue, with a silk tapestry-woven tripartite band consisting of a decorative band (4.5 cm) having a yellow ground with a series of striding quadrupeds in blue, beige, ochre and red silk, which is bordered by two lines of foliated Kufic inscription executed in yellow over a red ground.

Materials: linen and silk: plain wave and tapestry

Dimensions: h. 14.0 cm, w. 20.2 cm; max. letter height 2.2 cm

Ground fabric: linen warp and weft, dyed (dark blue), balanced plain weave, dense texture; very good quality (1)

Thread count: warp 24 Z-spun, weft 26 Z-spun

Thread thickness: warp 0.3 mm tight twist, weft 0.2 mm tight twist

Tapestry: silk, dyed (red, ochre, light blue, beige); slit and toothed; woven on paired warps

Provenance: Ex H.P. Kraus collection, no. 153

Inv. no. LNS 259 T

Inscription: repetition of

[…] and assistance from God […]

[…] و نصر من الله [...]

Cat. 148 *TIRAZ* **FRAGMENT FROM THE FATIMID DYNASTY**
Egypt, 11th to 12th century CE

Description: Fragment of undyed linen, with a complex central frieze tapestry-woven in dark brown and light brown silk. The frieze is composed of a central band with medallions, bordered above and below by two highly ornamented Kufic inscriptions; on either side, it has smaller bands with dark wavy patterns over a light brown background.

Materials: linen and silk: plain weave and tapestry

Dimensions: h. 10.8 cm, w. 26.7 cm; max. letter height 1.0 cm

Ground fabric: linen warp and weft, undyed, predominant-warp plain weave, close texture (*dabiqi*); good quality (2); selvedge on the right side

Thread count: warp 31 S-spun, weft 20 S-spun

Thread thickness: warp 0.2 mm slight–medium twist, weft 0.15–0.2 mm medium twist

Tapestry: silk, dyed (dark brown, reddish-brown), and linen, undyed; slit and toothed; woven on crossed and paired warps; discontinuous supplementary linen weft filling between the letters

Provenance: Ex H.P. Kraus collection, no. 168

Inv. no. LNS 268 T

Related works: See pages 512–13

Inscription: undecipherable

This fragment relates closely to the one discussed in cat. no. 146 and the examples discussed there, but is perhaps not as fine as those.

Cat. 149 *TIRAZ* FRAGMENT FROM
THE REIGN OF THE FATIMID
CALIPH AL-MUSTANSIR
(r. 1036–94)
Egypt, mid- to late
11th century CE

Description: Large fragment of undyed linen,
with one line of small Kufic
inscription highly decorated and
tapestry-woven in dark purple silk.

Materials: linen and silk: plain weave and
tapestry

Dimensions: h. 27.9 cm, w. 64 cm;
max. letter height 0.5 cm

Ground fabric: linen warp and weft, undyed,
predominant-weft plain weave,
dense texture (*dabiqi*); very good
quality (1)

Thread count: warp 18 Z-spun, weft 22 S-spun

Thread thickness: warp 0.2–0.4 mm medium twist,
weft 0.2–0.5 mm medium twist

Tapestry: silk, dyed (dark purple), and linen,
undyed; slit and toothed

Provenance: Ex H.P. Kraus collection, no. 89

Inv. no. LNS 203 T

Related works: See page 513

Inscription:

بسم الله الرحمن الرحيم لا اله الا الله نصر من الله وفتح قريب لعبد الله و وليه الإمام المستنصر بالله أمير المؤمنين و نصر من الله
و نعمة من الله [...]

In the name of God, the Most Merciful, the Most Compassionate. There is no
God but God. Help from God and an imminent victory to the servant and ally
of God al-imam al-Mustansir bi-llah the Commander of the Faithful and help
from God and prosperity from God [...]

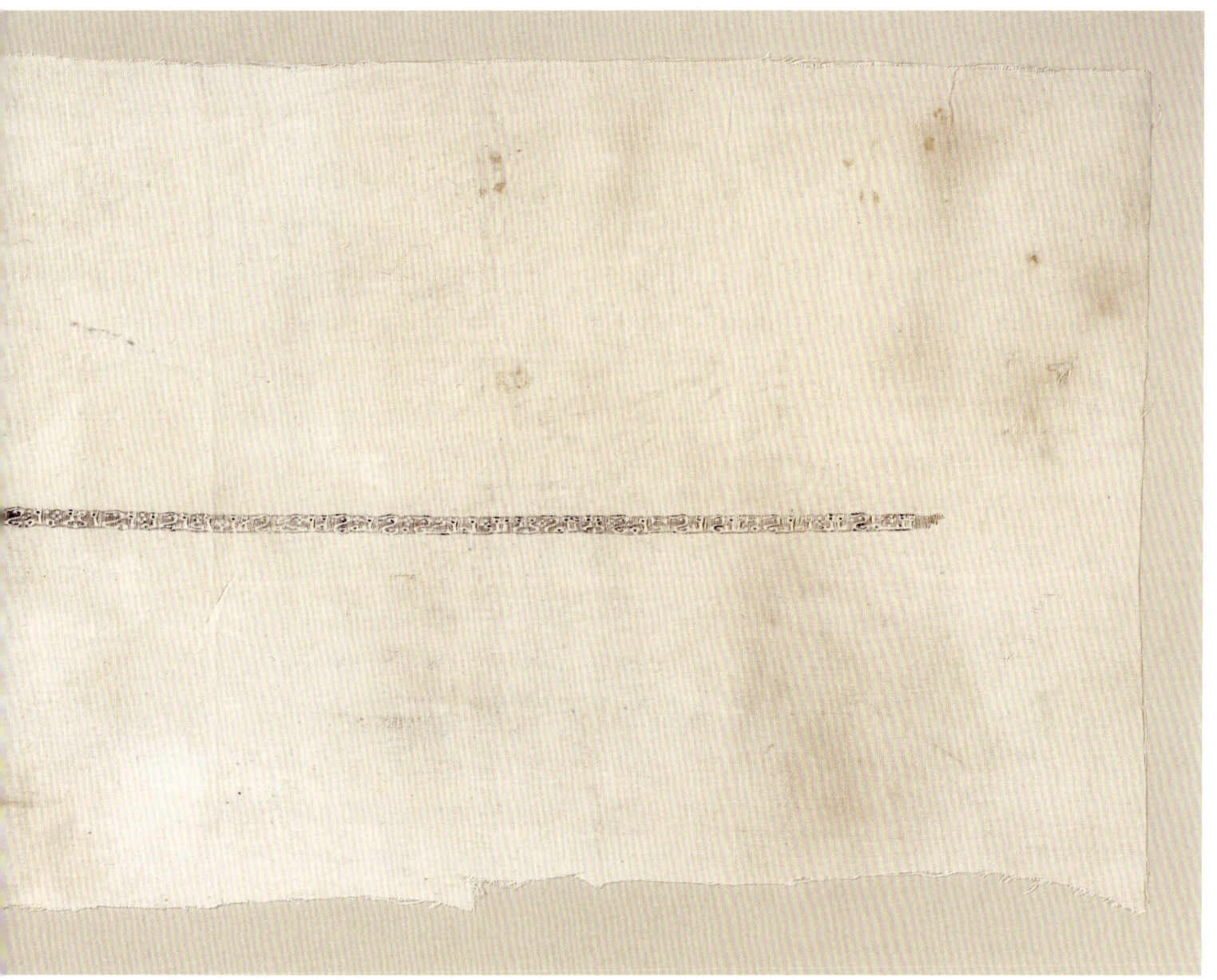

The style of script seen here in a single line, woven in linen against a silk background, relates to that on a textile at the Textile Museum, Washington, DC, which is inscribed with the name and titles of one of al-Mustansir's vizers, Abu Muhammad al-Husayn bin 'Ali bin 'Abd al-Rahman al-Yazuri (in office 1050–51 and 1058–59) (Related works 1). The letters are floriated with split palmettes growing out of the upper letter stems and curving elegantly above the baseline. Interspersed are small quatrefoils.

Cat. 150 *TIRAZ* FRAGMENT FROM
THE REIGN OF THE FATIMID
CALIPH AL-MUSTANSIR
(r. 1036–94)
**Egypt, mid- to late
11th century CE**

Description: Fragment of undyed linen, with one
line of Kufic inscription tapestry-
woven in blue silk with vine
decoration between the uprights.

Materials: linen and silk: plain weave and
tapestry

Dimensions: h. 14.5 cm, w. 34.5 cm;
max. letter height 1.3 cm

Ground fabric: linen warp and weft, undyed,
predominant-warp plain weave,
dense texture (*dabiqi*); very good–
good quality (1–2)

Thread count: warp 36 S-spun, weft 23 S-spun

Thread thickness: warp 0.2–0.25 mm slight–medium
twist, weft 0.15 mm medium–tight
twist

Tapestry: silk, dyed (dark blue); slit
and toothed; discontinuous
supplementary paired linen weft
between the letters

Provenance: Ex H.P. Kraus collection, no. 87

Inv. no. LNS 201 T

Related works: See page 513

Inscription:

بسم الله الرحمن الرحيم ولي الله نصر من الله لعبد الله و وليه معد أبي تميم الإمام المستنصر بالله أمير المؤمنين [...]

In the name of God, the Most Merciful, the Most Compassionate. The ally of
God. Assistance from God to the servant and ally of God Maʿad Abi Tamim al-
imam al-Mustansir bi-llah the Commander of the Faithful [...]

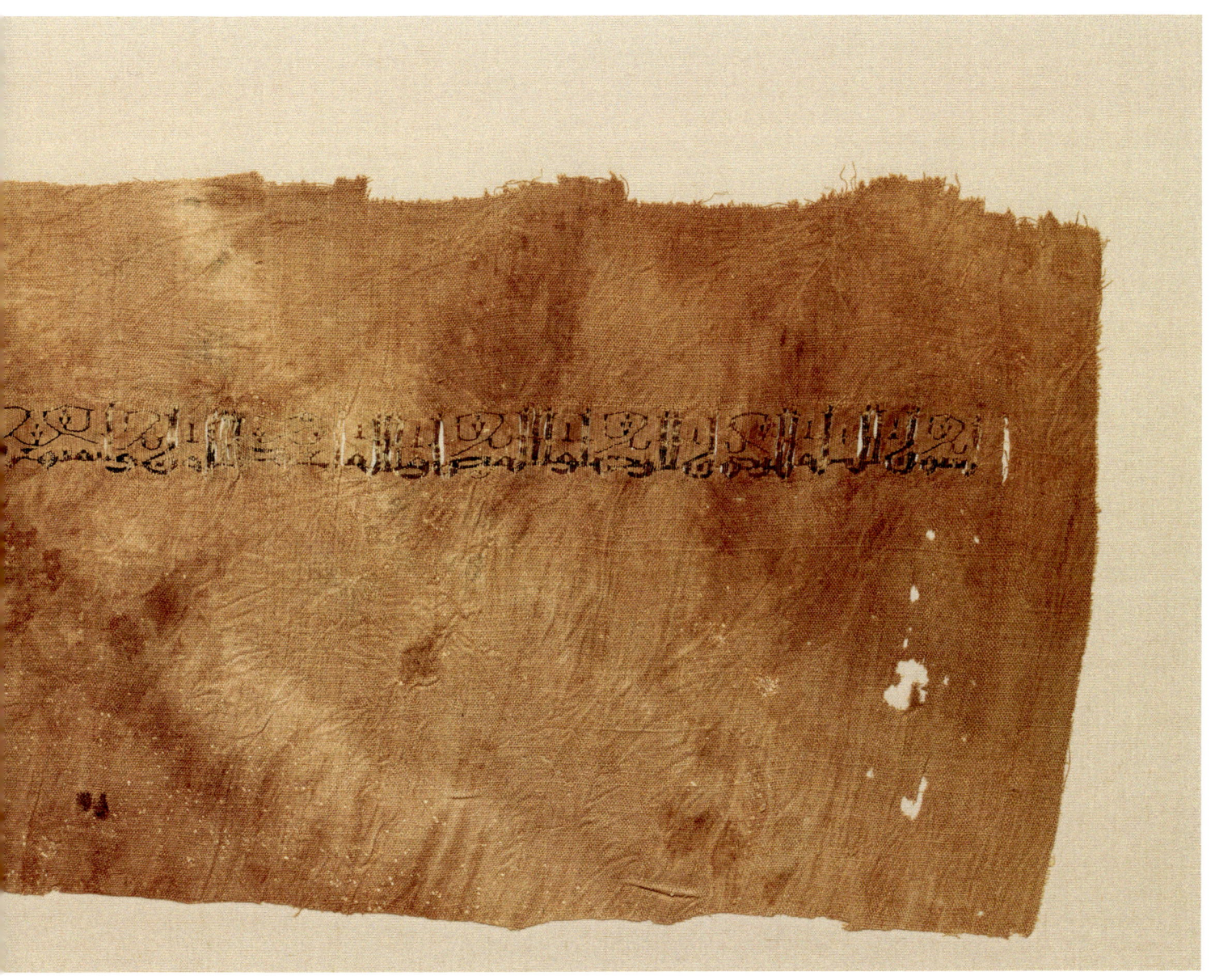

The style of inscription seen here has its origins in the time of al-Zahir (r. 1021–36), where it can be found on a fragment in the Vatican (Related works 1). As in that piece, the inscription here also features unfoliated letters set against a backdrop of floriations that look like vine scrolls. A similar approach has been observed in fragments discussed earlier (see cat. nos 145, 146, 148, 149). However, here letters such as *waw* or *ra* have pronounced sickle-shaped terminals below the baseline, rather than curling upwards as observed in those pieces.

Cat. 151   *TIRAZ* FRAGMENT FROM
THE FATIMID DYNASTY
Egypt, 11th century CE

Description: Large fragment of undyed linen,
with one line of floriated Kufic
inscription tapestry-woven in
dark blue silk.

Materials: linen and silk: plain weave
and tapestry

Dimensions: h. 18.2 cm, w. 50.8 cm;
max. letter height 1.5 cm

Ground fabric: linen warp and weft, predominant-
warp plain weave, loose texture
(*sharb*); very good quality (1+);
untwisted fringe

Thread count: warp 30 S-spun, weft 25 S-spun

Thread thickness: warp 0.1–0.15 mm medium twist,
weft 0.15 mm medium–tight twist

Tapestry: silk (only traces remaining), dyed
(dark blue); slit and toothed;
supplementary paired linen weft
filling between the letters

Provenance: Ex H.P. Kraus collection, no. 10

Inv. no. LNS 204 T

Related works: See page 513

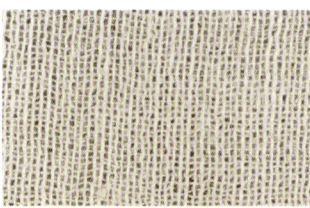

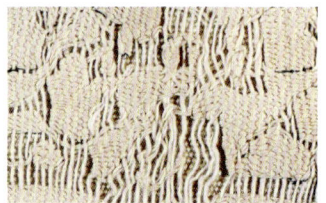

Inscription: undecipherable

Cat. 152   *TIRAZ* FRAGMENT FROM
THE REIGN OF THE FATIMID
CALIPH AL-MUSTANSIR
(r. 1036–94)
Egypt, mid- to late
11th century CE

Description: Large fragment of undyed linen,
with one line of Kufic inscription,
tapestry-woven in dark blue silk.

Materials: linen and silk: plain weave and
tapestry

Dimensions: h. 36.2 cm, w. 87.4 cm;
max. letter height 1.5 cm

Ground fabric: linen warp and weft, undyed,
predominant-warp plain weave,
dense texture (*dabiqi*); very good
quality (1); selvedge on the right
side of inscription; untwisted fringe

Thread count: warp 31 S-spun, weft 22 S-spun

Thread thickness: warp 0.2–0.3 mm medium twist,
weft 0.1–0.25 mm medium twist

Tapestry: silk, dyed (dark blue); slit and
toothed; supplementary paired
linen weft between the letters

Provenance: Ex H.P. Kraus collection, no. 88

Inv. no. LNS 202 T

Inscription:

بسم الله الرحمن الرحيم نصر من الله لعبد الله ووليه معد أبي تميم الإمام المستنصر بالله أمير المؤمنين صلوات الله عليه وعلى ابائه و
ابنائه الطاهرين (؟) نصر من الله لعبد الله و وليه [...]

In the name of God the Most Merciful, the Most Compassionate. Assistance
from God to the servant and ally of God Maʿad Abi Tamim al-imam al-
Mustansir bi-llah the Commander of the Faithful. God's blessings be upon him
and his immaculate ancestors and descendants (?). Assistance from God to the
servant and ally of God [...]

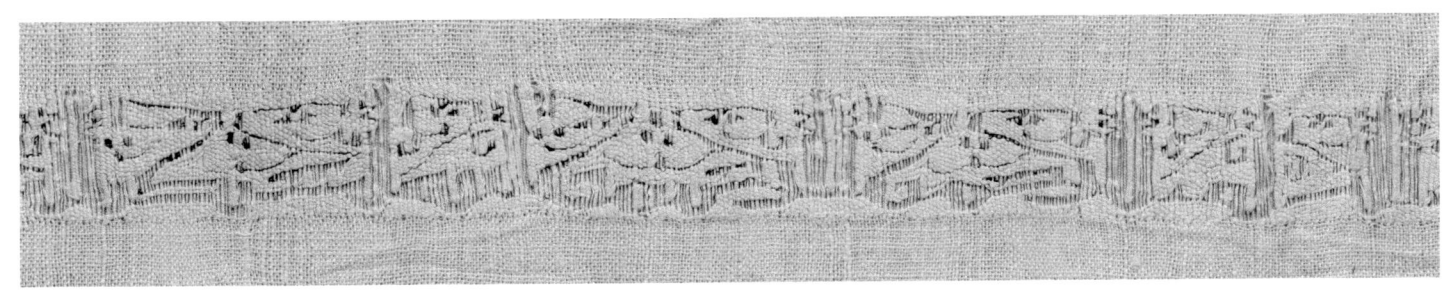

Cat. 153   *TIRAZ* FRAGMENT FROM
THE FATIMID DYNASTY
Egypt, 11th century CE

Description: Fragment of undyed linen, with one
line of Kufic inscription tapestry-
woven in red silk, with floriated
decoration between the uprights.

Materials: linen and silk: plain weave and
tapestry

Dimensions: h. 16.5 cm, w. 19.5 cm;
max. letter height 0.9 cm

Ground fabric: linen warp and weft, balanced
plain weave, dense texture (*dabiqi*);
very good–good quality (1–2)

Thread count: warp 28 S-spun, weft 23 S-spun

Thread thickness: warp 0.1–0.3 mm medium twist,
weft 0.15–0.25 mm medium–tight
twist

Tapestry: silk, dyed (faded red); slit and
toothed; supplementary linen weft
filling between the letters

Provenance: Ex H.P. Kraus collection, no. 91

Inv. no. LNS 205 T

Inscription: undecipherable

Cat. 154 *TIRAZ* **FRAGMENT FROM THE FATIMID DYNASTY**
Egypt, 11th century CE

Description: Fragment of undyed linen, with an inscription in floriated Kufic characters embroidered in dark brown and ochre silk.

Materials: linen and silk: plain weave and embroidery

Dimensions: h. 12.0 cm, w. 19.5 cm; max. letter height 1.3 cm

Ground fabric: linen warp and weft, undyed, balanced plain weave, close texture (*dabiqi*); medium quality (3)

Thread count: warp 19 S-spun, weft 17 S-spun

Thread thickness: warp 0.25–0.5 mm medium twist, weft 0.25–0.5 mm medium twist

Embroidery: silk, dyed (dark brown, ochre), couching and chain stitch

Provenance: Ex H.P. Kraus collection, no. 92

Inv. no. LNS 206 T

Inscription: repetition of (possibly)

Sovereignty

كلملا

This fragment copies in embroidery the style of tapestry-woven inscriptions that would have often contained a caliphal protocol.

Cat. 155   *TIRAZ* FRAGMENT FROM
THE FATIMID DYNASTY
Egypt, 11th century CE

Description: Fragment of undyed linen, with
two bands tapestry-woven in
dark blue, red and beige silk; the
lower band (2.0 cm) consists of a
Kufic inscription with floriated
decoration between the uprights;
the upper, decorative band (1.2 cm)
is mostly gone.

Materials: linen and silk: plain weave
and tapestry

Dimensions: h. 14.0 cm, w. 17 cm;
max. letter height 1.2 cm

Ground fabric: linen warp and weft, undyed,
predominant-warp plain weave,
gauzy texture (*sharb*), regular
structure; very good–good
quality (1–2)

Thread count: warp 28 S-spun, weft 15 S-spun

Thread thickness: warp 0.1 mm tight twist,
weft 0.05–0.1 mm tight twist

Tapestry: silk, dyed (dark blue, red, beige);
slit and toothed

Provenance: Ex H.P. Kraus collection, no. 93

Inv. no. LNS 207 T

Related works: See page 513

Inscription: undecipherable

This piece is interesting, since the inscription turns upside down part way through, as if the weaver stopped and picked up again incorrectly. A similar occurrence of an abrupt change in an inscription can be observed in an unpublished fragment from the reign of al-Hakim in the Benaki Museum, Athens (Related works 1; discussed in chapter 3, see fig. 3.43).[49]

Cat. 156 *TIRAZ* FRAGMENT FROM
THE FATIMID DYNASTY
Egypt, 11th century CE

Description: Fragment of undyed linen, with
one line of Kufic inscription
tapestry-woven in red silk,
decorated with floriated stems
between the upright letters.

Materials: linen and silk: plain weave
and tapestry

Dimensions: h. 10.0 cm, w. 12.5 cm;
max. letter height 1.6 cm

Ground fabric: linen warp and weft, undyed,
predominant-warp plain weave,
close texture (*dabiqi*); very good
quality (1); selvedge on the left side
of the inscription

Thread count: warp 27 S-spun, weft 20 S-spun

Thread thickness: warp 0.25 mm medium twist,
weft 0.15–0.2 mm tight twist

Tapestry: silk, dyed (red); discontinuous
supplementary paired linen weft
filling between the letters

Provenance: Ex H.P. Kraus collection, no. 94

Inv. no. LNS 208 T

Related works: See page 513

Inscription: undecipherable

The text on this fragment cannot be deciphered, even though some of the letters are clearly identifiable and follow the epigraphic style common in inscriptions from al-Mustansir's reign.[50] The inscription constitutes the remaining part of a larger inscription, which ended at the selvedge on the left side. From an epigraphic perspective, the script is close to examples from the reign of al-Mustansir. Two examples from al-Mustansir's reign in the Bouvier Collection relate to the present piece very closely (Related works 1, 2). Both mention the names and titles of al-Mustansir. Looking at particular letterforms, the inward and upward curling *waw* is very prominent, as are the circular *mim* and the flower-shaped *'ayn*. All of these characteristics are also present in the al-Sabah fragment. Furthermore, inscriptions from this period feature prominent floriated scrolls that seem to grow out of the letter stems, usually bent and curled upwards in a swan-neck fashion, terminating with small trefoil buds; these, too, are present here.

Cat. 157 **_TIRAZ_ FRAGMENT FROM THE FATIMID DYNASTY**
Egypt, 11th century CE

Description: Fragment of undyed linen, with a band of floriated Kufic inscription tapestry-woven in red silk, consisting of one line repeated in mirror image.

Materials: linen and silk: plain weave and tapestry

Dimensions: h. 8.5 cm, w. 16.0 cm; max. letter height 1.5 cm

Ground fabric: linen warp and weft, undyed, predominant-warp plain weave, close texture (_dabiqi_); good quality (2)

Thread count: warp 24 S-spun, weft 16 S-spun

Thread thickness: warp 0.3 mm slight–medium twist, weft 0.15–0.2 mm tight twist

Tapestry: silk, dyed (red); discontinuous supplementary paired linen weft filling between the letters

Provenance: Ex H.P. Kraus collection, no. 95

Inv. no. LNS 209 T

Inscription:

Line 1: undecipherable

Line 2: (possibly)

[…] ordered to be made in the _tiraz al-khassa_ […]

[…] امر بعمله بطراز الخاصة […]

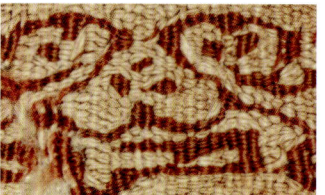

Cat. 158 *TIRAZ* **FRAGMENT FROM THE FATIMID DYNASTY**
Egypt, 11th century CE

Description: Fragment of undyed linen, with two lines of Kufic inscription in mirror image tapestry-woven in blue silk, having floral decorations between the uprights.

Materials: linen and silk: plain weave and tapestry

Dimensions: h. 9.5 cm, w. 23.0 cm; max. letter height 0.9 cm

Ground fabric: linen warp and weft, undyed, predominant-warp plain weave, close texture (*dabiqi*); very good quality (1)

Thread count: warp 33 S-spun, weft 29 S-spun

Thread thickness: warp 0.15–0.25 mm medium twist, weft 0.15–0.2 mm medium twist

Tapestry: silk, dyed (dark blue); discontinuous supplementary paired linen weft filling between the letters

Provenance: Ex H.P. Kraus collection, New York, no. 84

Inv. no. LNS 199 T

Inscription:

Line 1:

[...] [لا] شريك له محمد رسول الله صلى الله عليه نصر من الله و [...]

[...] He [has no] partner / associate, Muhammad is the Prophet of God, may God's blessings be upon him [...]

Line 2:

[...] علي ولي الله صلى الله عليه نصر من الله و فتح قريب لعبد [...]

[...] 'Ali is God's ally, God's blessing upon him and an imminent victory to the servant [...]

Cat. 159   *TIRAZ* FRAGMENT FROM
THE FATIMID DYNASTY
Egypt, 11th to 12th century CE

Description: Fragment (two pieces) of undyed
linen, with an ornamental band
embroidered in red, green and
black silk, with two bands of
S-scrolls lining the central frieze.

Materials: linen and silk: plain weave and
embroidery

Dimensions: piece (a) (right): h. 37.6 cm,
w. 16.5 cm; max. letter height
1.8 cm
piece (b) (left): h. 39.2 cm,
w. 11.1 cm; max. letter height
1.8 cm

Ground fabric: linen warp and weft, undyed,
predominant-warp plain weave,
close texture (*dabiqi*); medium
quality (3); selvedge on the right
side of the inscription

Thread count: warp 13 S-spun, weft 12 S-spun

Thread thickness: warp 0.3–1.0 mm medium twist,
weft 0.3–0.4 mm medium twist

Embroidery: silk, dyed (red, greenish-blue,
black), couching and chain stitch

Provenance: Ex H.P. Kraus collection,
nos 163–64

Inv. no. LNS 267 T a, b

Inscription: undecipherable

This fragment is interesting as it copies the style of inscription in the textiles described above from the period of al-Mustansir, albeit in embroidery and hardly legible. Perhaps this was a cheaper and more readily available way of adapting a *tiraz* aesthetic for the general consumer, as the quality of the work does not reach that of caliphal *tiraz* textiles. A textile like this would have been suitable for general consumption outside the court environment. The selvedge here indicates that this fragment was once part of a larger garment.

Cat. 160 *TIRAZ* **FRAGMENT FROM THE FATIMID DYNASTY**
Egypt, 11th century CE

Description: Fragment of light beige linen, with one line of floriated Kufic inscription of benedictory content tapestry-woven in red silk with occasional insertions of blue, and a thin red band woven in red silk along the fringe.

Materials: linen and silk: plain weave and tapestry

Dimensions: h. 25.7 cm, w. 59.1 cm; max. letter height 1.4 cm

Ground fabric: linen warp and weft, undyed, balanced plain weave, close texture (*sharb*), very regular structure; very good quality (1); untwisted fringe

Thread count: warp 23 S-spun, weft 20 S-spun

Thread thickness: warp 0.15–0.2 mm tight twist, weft 0.2 mm tight twist

Tapestry: silk, dyed (red and blue), and linen, undyed; slit and toothed

Inv. no. LNS 116 T

Related works: See page 513

Inscription: repetition of an abbreviated version of Sovereignty الملك

This is a fine example of its kind. The ground fabric is made of high-quality material with regard to the regularity of the yarn, its texture and colour, the regularity of the weaving and its careful execution. The epigraphic style of the inscription is characterized by a rather stout style of Kufic with floriation growing out of the hastae and significantly thickened terminals of the low letters below the baseline, which look like a festoon. This feature can be found for the first time in inscriptions from the early reign of al-Zahir (r. 1021–36) (Related works 1), and continues until the end of the reign of al-Mustansir (r. 1036–94) (Related works 2–6).

Cat. 161 *TIRAZ* FRAGMENT FROM THE FATIMID DYNASTY
Egypt, 11th century CE

Description: Large fragment of undyed linen, with two tapestry-woven bands of decoration, the first an ornate Kufic inscription in brown silk, and the second a smaller band (0.7 cm) with oval shapes on a brown silk background; the fringe, set apart from the decoration, has survived.

Materials: linen and silk: plain weave and tapestry

Dimensions: h. 30.9 cm, w. 42 cm; max. letter height 1.5 cm

Ground fabric: linen warp and weft, undyed, predominant-warp plain weave, gauzy texture (*sharb*); good quality (2); untwisted fringe

Thread count: warp 23 S-spun, weft 13 S-spun

Thread thickness: warp 0.1–0.3 mm slight–tight twist, weft 0.1–0.15 mm tight twist

Tapestry: silk, dyed (dark brown), and undyed linen, S-spun, paired; slit and toothed

Provenance: Ex H.P. Kraus collection, no. 152

Inv. no. LNS 258 T

Inscription: repetition of

Success is through God

التوفيق بالله

As on cat. no. 160, the inscription here is characterized by a floriated background and prominent sickle-like terminals of the letters below the baseline, forming a festoon. Relevant comparative examples date from the reign of the caliph al-Mustansir, as discussed above.

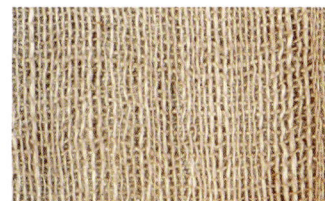

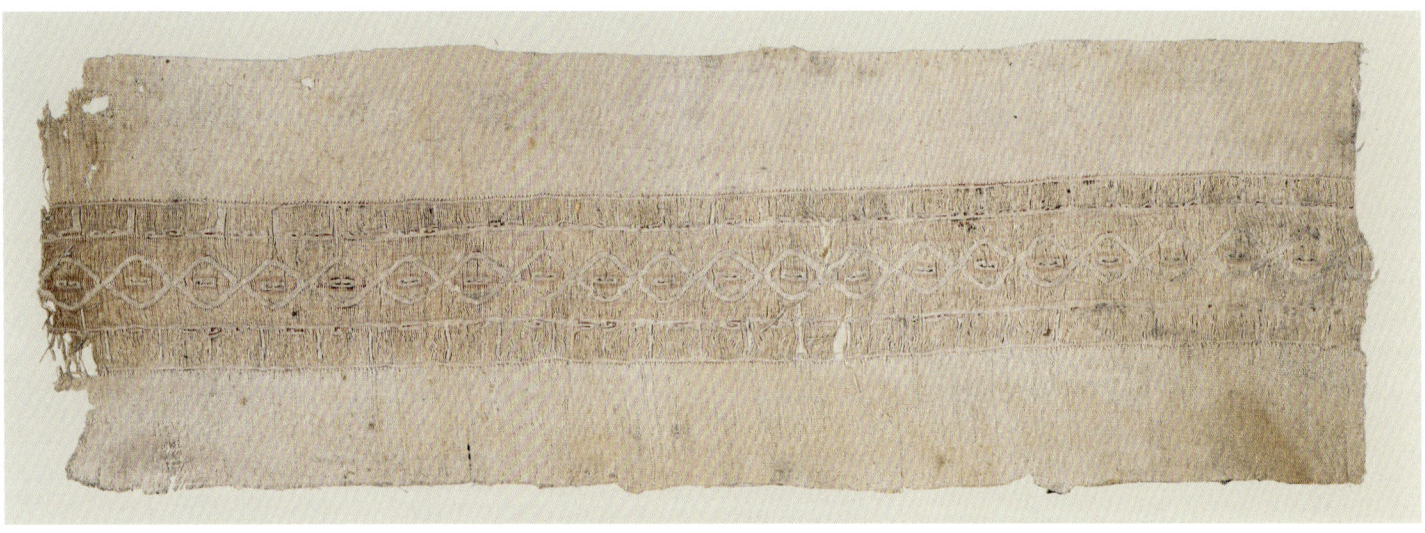

Cat. 162 **_TIRAZ_ FRAGMENT FROM THE FATIMID DYNASTY**
Egypt, mid-11th to 12th century CE

Description: Fragment of undyed linen, with a band (5.5 cm) tapestry-woven in red and dark brown silk (remnants in the central and the lower left section), comprising two registers, one with a Kufic inscription and one with a sequence of lozenges containing a geometric motif between them.

Materials: linen and silk: plain weave and tapestry

Dimensions: h. 14.5 cm, w. 42.7 cm; max. letter height 1.5 cm

Ground fabric: linen warp and weft, undyed, warp-faced plain weave, very regular, dense texture (_dabiqi_); very good quality (1)

Thread count: warp 37 S-spun, weft 14 S-spun

Thread thickness: warp 0.2 mm medium twist, weft 0.2 mm medium twist

Tapestry: silk, dyed (traces of red, dark brown), and linen, undyed; woven on crossed and paired warps

Inv. no. LNS 416 T

Related works: See page 513

Inscription: undecipherable

The style of script used here, with its squat and flattened baseline, is reminiscent of that used on caliphal _tiraz_ textiles during the reign of al-Mustansir (1036–94 CE), as are the particular lozenge-shaped motifs in the centre of the inscription band. An example is in the Bouvier Collection (Related works 1).

Cat. 163   *TIRAZ* FRAGMENT FROM
THE FATIMID DYNASTY
Egypt, 12th century CE

Description: Fragment of undyed linen,
decorated with two bands
(*c.* 3.9 cm) tapestry-woven
in coloured silk floss; each is
bordered above and below with
a plain blue decorative band
comprising a sequence of lozenge-
shaped cartouches containing
alternately a single bird and a pair
of confronted birds, the spandrels
in between filled with small
palmettes.

Materials: linen and silk: plain weave
and tapestry

Dimensions: h. 12 cm, w. 26.2 cm

Ground fabric: linen warp and weft, undyed,
balanced plain weave, loose texture
(*sharb*), slightly coarse structure;
medium quality (3); selvedge on
the right side

Thread count: warp 17 S-spun, weft 14 S-spun

Thread thickness: warp 0.3–0.5 mm medium twist,
weft 0.1–0.5 mm medium twist

Tapestry: silk, dyed (blue, green, yellow,
brown, black); slit and toothed

Inv. no. LNS 420 T

Cat. 164 *TIRAZ* FRAGMENT FROM
THE FATIMID DYNASTY
Egypt, 11th century CE

Description: Fragment of light blue linen, with
one band (2.4 cm) containing
an inscription in floriated Kufic
tapestry-woven in blue linen set
against a background of dark
brown silk, bordered above and
below by narrow decorative
bands of a rope-pattern design.

Materials: linen and silk: plain weave
and tapestry

Dimensions: h. 11.5 cm, w. 34.7 cm;
max. letter height 1.4 cm

Ground fabric: linen warp and weft, dyed (light
blue), balanced plain weave,
close texture (*dabiqi*); medium
quality (3)

Thread count: warp 19 S-spun, weft 18 S-spun

Thread thickness: warp 0.3 mm medium–tight twist,
weft 0.3 mm medium–tight twist

Tapestry: silk, dyed (red, brown), and linen,
dyed (blue); slit and toothed

Inv. no. LNS 1093 T

Inscription: undecipherable

The epigraphic style used here, with rather angular letterforms below the
baseline with festoon-like terminals, is typical for inscriptions dating from
the time of al-Mustansir.

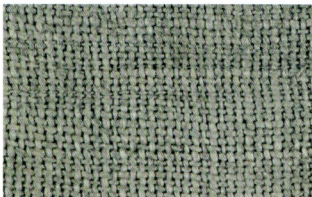

**Cat. 165   *TIRAZ* FRAGMENT FROM
THE FATIMID DYNASTY**
Egypt, mid-11th to mid-
12th century CE

Description: Fragment of undyed linen, on
which two bands have been sewn:
the first (4.0 cm), set against a
yellow stylized floral background,
is tapestry-woven comprising a
sequence of cartouches with a red
ground, containing quadrupeds,
beneath an inscription in Kufic
with pronounced letter terminals
below the baseline; the second,
located below the first, comprises
a chequered motif in blue, red
and yellow.

Materials: linen and silk: plain weave
and tapestry

Dimensions: h. 9.2 cm, w. 29 cm

LINEN GROUND

Ground fabric: undyed linen warp and weft,
plain weave, predominant
warp, regular; coarse medium
quality (3)

Thread count: warp 23 Z-spun, weft 19 Z-spun

Thread thickness: warp 0.2 mm medium twist,
weft 0.3 mm medium twist

TAPESTRY BAND

Ground fabric: undyed linen warp
(no weft remaining)

Thread count: warp 25 S-spun

Thread thickness: warp 0.2 mm tight twist

Decoration: tram silk floss, dyed (red, blue,
mustard, brown), and undyed
linen, weft-faced plain weave;
c. 58 picks per cm (0.1 mm);
slit and toothed

CHEQUERED BAND

Ground fabric: warp linen dyed blue and undyed,
weft silk dyed yellow and red,
regular, warp faced; medium
quality (3)

Thread count: per cm: warp 16 S-spun, weft *c.* 32
silk floss

Thread thickness: warp 0.2–0.5 mm medium–tight
twist, weft silk floss 0.3 mm

Inv. no. LNS 49 T

Related works: See page 513

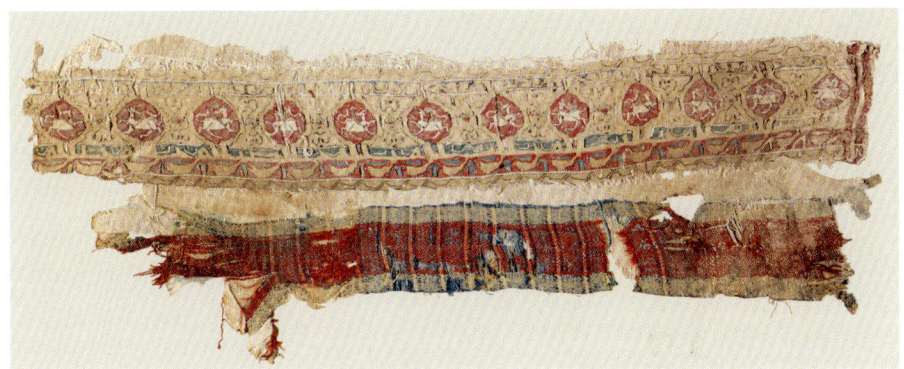

Inscription: repetition of   نصر من الله

Assistance from God

This is a composite fragment stitched together in the medieval period, probably
in order to re-use the silk bands, which would have been held in high esteem for
their decoration and material. The technical details of the linen base and the
other two fragments are different. The linen of all three pieces is of a different
character. While it is impossible to date the time when the three fragments became
attached, a date for the tapestry-woven fragment can be proposed. Its frieze of
quadrupeds contained within cartouches and the pronounced letter terminals
below the baseline of the inscription conform with dated pieces from the reign
of al-Mustansir (r. 1036–94). A very close comparison for the quadrupeds can be
found on a piece in the Victoria and Albert Museum, London (Related works 1),
which is dated to al-Mustansir's reign. The particular letterform seen here
conforms with that on a textile in the Textile Museum, Washington, DC, which is
datable to the tenure of his vizier Badr al-Jamali (d. 1094) during the latter part of
al-Mustansir's reign, *c.* 466–87 AH / 1073–94 CE (Related works 2).

Cat. 166 *TIRAZ* **FRAGMENT FROM THE FATIMID DYNASTY**
Egypt, 11th to 12th century CE

Description: Fragment (three pieces) of undyed linen, with a symmetrical arrangement of multicoloured silk tapestry-woven bands. The central band consists of five registers: a medial band with a sequence of lozenge-shaped cartouches filled with an alternating sequence of a small bird and a palmette, bordered above and below with an addorsed Kufic inscription in yellow on a brownish floriated background repeating the phrase 'al-mulk', finished on either side with a rope pattern in yellow and red; the medial band is accompanied on either side by a floriated Kufic inscription in red, again repeating the phrase 'al-mulk', and a decorative band with intertwined cartouches containing a small flower.

Materials: linen and silk: plain weave and tapestry

Dimensions: piece (a) (opposite): h. 17.0 cm, w. 16.4 cm; max. letter height 1.2 cm
piece (b) (p. 460): h. 22.0 cm, w. 20.0 cm; max. letter height 1.2 cm
piece (c) (p. 461): h. 19.4 cm, w. 17.3 cm; max. letter height 1.2 cm

Ground fabric: linen warp and weft, undyed, predominant-warp plain weave, loose texture (*sharb*), regular structure; two seams on the left (piece (b)) and right (piece (c)) side of the inscription bands; good quality (2)

Thread count: warp 21 S-spun, weft 18 S-spun

Thread thickness: warp 0.15–0.25 mm tight twist, weft 0.1–0.15 mm tight twist

Tapestry: silk, dyed (red, greenish blue, brown), and undyed linen; slit and toothed; discontinuous linen weft filling

Provenance: Ex H.P. Kraus collection, New York, nos 165–167

Inv. no. LNS 78 T a–c

Related works: See page 513

Inscription: repetition of (possibly)   الملك

Sovereignty

The script seen here is typical of the epigraphic style used under the Fatimid caliphs al-Zahir (r. 1021–36) (Related works 1) and al-Mustansir (r. 1036–94) (Related works 2–7), but also al-Musta'li (r. 1094–1101) (Related works 8). It is characterized by squat, squarish letters with floriations and a festoon of boat-shaped letter terminals below the baseline. While those inscriptions are all in a single line, the style was also used in more complex and decorative compositions, as seen here.

Details of LNS 78 T a

LNS 78 T b

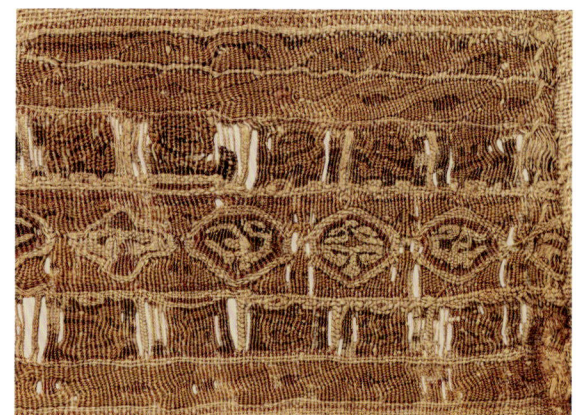

Details of LNS 78 T b

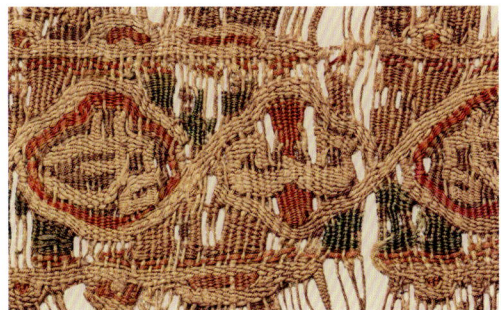

Details of LNS 78 T C

LNS 78 T C

The overall aesthetic comprising multi-layered bands with an addorsed inscription enclosing a band of sequential lozenges filled with small birds, woven in a multitude of colours, finds a close comparison in a piece in the Bouvier Collection (Related works 7). It comprises a floriated Kufic inscription similar to that on the present piece, albeit without the prominent festoon below the baseline. Another comparative piece in the Boston Museum of Fine Arts comprises a multi-layered arrangement with several inscription bands similar to ones seen here (Related works 9). The present fragment shows signs of tailoring on two of the pieces (pieces (b), (c)) clearly visible. Perhaps they once formed part of a sleeve. Sleeve bands with *tiraz* inscriptions as a feature of medieval dress are described in contemporary texts and depicted in ceramics and miniatures. It is noteworthy here that on piece (b) the inscription in the lowermost band suddenly stops, and the band is continued with a sequence of half-cartouches or arch-like designs containing a confronted pair of birds, with a small tri-lobed flower in the spandrel between.

Cat. 167 *TIRAZ* **FRAGMENT FROM THE FATIMID DYNASTY**
Egypt, 11th to 12th century CE

Description: Fragment of undyed line with two decorative bands of a different textile sewn in; this second textile consists of a linen ground fabric with tapestry-woven decoration in ochre, red, blue and brown silk. Both bands (7.1 cm) are complex in their decoration: a central frieze is formed by series of medallions containing hares over a blue background, separated by floral motifs; to either side of this central band are two thin ochre bands with wavy motifs; above and below these are two bands of meaningless Kufic inscription on a dark background, with scroll motifs between the uprights. The whole frieze is then bordered by an additional band in ochre with wavy motifs.

Materials: linen and silk: plain weave and tapestry, sewn in

Dimensions: h. 40.9 cm, w. 63.6 cm; max. letter height 1.1 cm

TEXTILE 1

Ground fabric: linen warp and weft, undyed, predominant-warp plain weave, close texture (*dabiqi*); medium quality (3); selvedge on the left side

Thread count: warp 22 Z-spun, weft 14 Z-spun

Thread thickness: warp 0.25–0.3 mm medium twist, weft 0.3 mm medium twist

TEXTILE 2

Ground fabric: linen warp (weft lost), undyed; good quality (2)

Thread count: warp 25 S-spun

Thread thickness: warp 0.25 mm tight twist

Tapestry: silk, dyed (ochre, red, greenish-blue, dark brown), woven on paired linen warps; slit and toothed

Provenance: Ex H.P. Kraus collection, no. 175

Inv. no. LNS 275 T

Inscription: epigraphic repetition of لهل

This textile is interesting as it comprises pieces from a once larger tapestry-woven decorative *tiraz* band that were cut out of their original ground fabric and inserted into a new ground fabric of different make-up. It appears that the pieces might have been inserted as decorative bands for a shawl, as one side of the fragment has a selvedge, suggesting that the *tiraz* bands once might have extended from selvedge to selvedge. The fact that, in making the new hybrid textile, care was taken to insert these pieces shows how valuable and desirable *tiraz* bands like these were. It also shows that they could have a number of life cycles, before the textiles they formed part of were eventually used as shrouds.

Cat. 168 *TIRAZ* FRAGMENT FROM
THE FATIMID DYNASTY
Egypt, 11th to 12th century CE

Description: Fragment (three pieces) of undyed
linen, with two decorative bands
tapestry-woven in red, ochre, blue
and brown silk. The main tripartite
band (10.4 cm) consists of a central
frieze with a series of animals
alternating in undyed linen and
brown silk inside red medallions;
on either side of the central frieze
is an epigraphic band (2.1 cm)
with a meaningless repetition of
the letters *mim* and *nun* in undyed
linen with red background and
dark scroll decoration between the
uprights; the third element of this
main band is a border in plain blue
on either side. The other decorative
band consists of alternating white
and brown medallions over a blue
background.

Materials: linen and silk: plain weave
and tapestry

Dimensions: piece (a) (right): h. 29.9 cm,
w. 17.4 cm
piece (b) (lower left): h. 19.2 cm,
w. 8.4 cm
piece (c) (upper left): h. 2.8 cm,
w. 2.4 cm

Ground fabric: linen warp and weft, undyed,
predominant-warp plain weave,
close texture (*dabiqi*); good
quality (2)

Thread count: warp 28 S-spun, weft 16 S-spun

Thread thickness: warp 0.2–0.3 mm medium twist,
weft 0.2–0.3 mm medium–tight
twist

Tapestry: silk, dyed (red, ochre, greenish-
blue, dark brown), and undyed
linen; *c.* 74 picks per cm; slit and
toothed

Provenance: Ex H.P. Kraus collection, no. 183

Inv. no. LNS 282 T

Inscription: epigraphic repetition of ‌من

**Cat. 169   *TIRAZ* FRAGMENT FROM
THE FATIMID DYNASTY**
Egypt, 11th to 12th century CE

Description: Fragment (three pieces) of linen,
composed of stripes of blue and
undyed linen with a decorative
band tapestry-woven in ochre, red,
green and dark brown silk, the
centre of which consists of a frieze
of animals inscribed in medallions;
the central frieze is bordered by
two lines of inscription in ochre
on a red background.

Materials: linen and silk: plain weave
and tapestry

Dimensions: piece (a) (right): h. 11.5 cm,
w. 20.4 cm
piece (b) (centre): h. 8.5 cm,
w. 12.8 cm
piece (c) (left): h. 8.4 cm,
w. 12.5 cm

Ground fabric: linen warp and weft, undyed
and dyed (dark blue), warp-faced
plain weave, close texture (*dabiqi*);
good quality (2)

Thread count: warp 26 Z-spun, weft 13 per 0.5 cm
Z-spun

Thread thickness: warp 0.2–0.4 mm medium–tight
twist, weft 0.1–0.15 mm medium–
tight twist

Tapestry: silk, dyed (ochre, red, green, dark
brown), and linen, undyed; slit
and toothed

Provenance: Ex H.P. Kraus collection, no. 226

Inv. no. LNS 311 T

Related works: See page 513

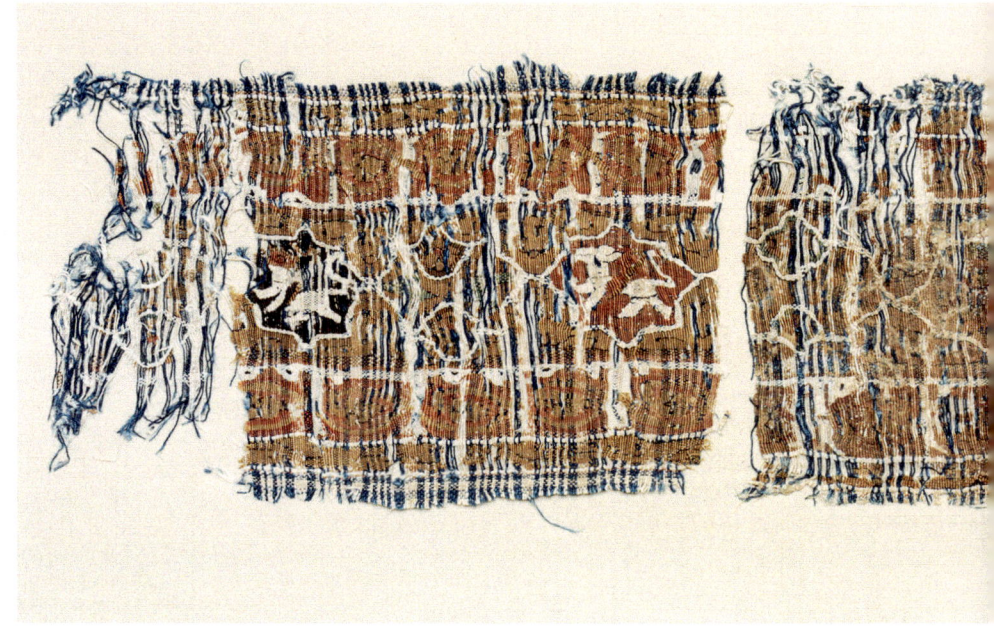

Inscription: repetition of (possibly)   الله

God

This fragment is interesting as it comprises a striped base fabric into which
the tapestried decoration was woven. Very few striped textiles have survived,
suggesting that early Islamic Egyptian textiles were much more diverse than the
cream or white linen aesthetic of most surviving *tiraz* textiles might suggest.
A piece in the Boston Museum of Fine Arts (Related works 1) comprises a
chequered base fabric composed of both undyed linen warp and weft and blue
silk warp and weft. It is, furthermore, embroidered with an inscription in Naskh
in gold-thread (membrane wound on yellow silk) and red silk (couched and
outlined in stem stitch). On the basis of the Naskh inscription and its epigraphic
style it has been attributed to the Ayyubid dynasty (1169–1250). For another
chequered example, see cat. no. 165.

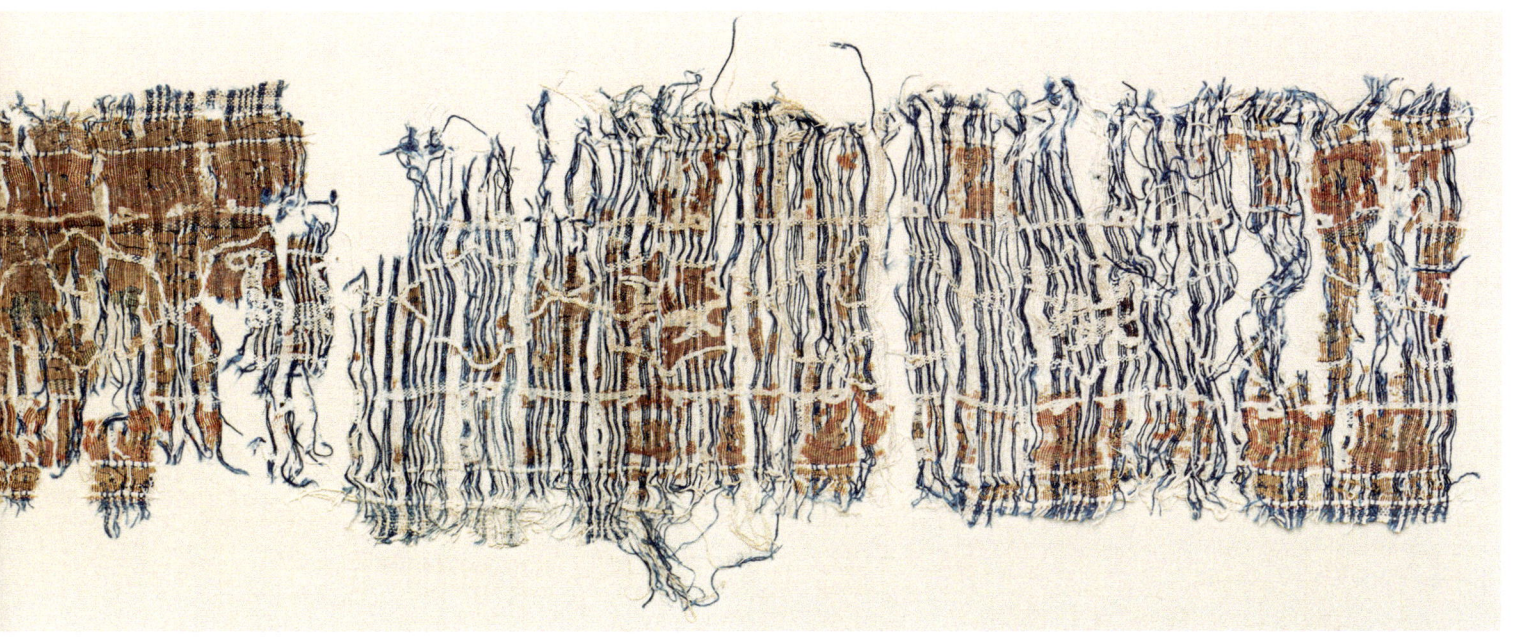

Cat. 170 *TIRAZ* **FRAGMENT FROM THE FATIMID DYNASTY**
Egypt, 11th century CE

Description: Fragment of undyed linen, decorated with two bands (5.0 cm) tapestry-woven in coloured silk floss, each band consisting of five registers: the two outermost registers are yellow and consist of a thin wavy line inwoven; the two bordering the central band comprise a repetition in floriated Kufic, possibly reading 'al-mulk li-llah' in yellow on a red ground; the central band is a repeating sequence of three cartouches, two with hares in yellow against a red or brown background flanking one containing a stylized flower or tree motif, with decoration in blue or green in the spandrels between.

Materials: linen and silk: plain weave and tapestry

Dimensions: h. 21.9 cm, w. 44 cm; max. letter height 1.3 cm

Ground fabric: undyed linen warp and weft, predominant-warp plain weave, loose texture (*sharb*), some irregularities; medium quality (3)

Thread count: warp 23 S-spun, weft 15 S-spun

Thread thickness: warp 0.2 mm tight twist, weft 0.1–0.15 mm tight twist

Tapestry: silk, dyed (red, mustard, green, light blue, dark blue, dark brown); 54 picks per cm; slit and toothed

Inv. no. LNS 32 T

Related works: See page 513

Inscription: repetition of (possibly)   الملك لله
Sovereignty belongs to God

Tiraz textiles with inscriptions in a similar subdued style, with floriated background addorsed against a frieze of hares contained within small cartouches, are found during the reign of the Fatimid caliphs al-Zahir (r. 1021–36) and al-Mustansir (r. 1036–94). A related fragment from the reign of al-Zahir is in the Kelsey Museum of Archaeology in Ann Arbor (Related works 1). A fragment with a similar style of calligraphy from al-Mustansir's reign is in the Bouvier Collection (Related works 2), and another related piece is in the Cleveland Museum of Art (Related works 3).

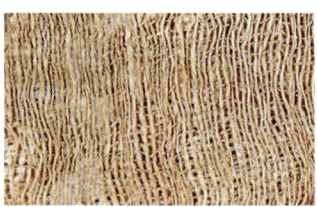

Cat. 171   **TEXTILE FRAGMENT FROM THE FATIMID DYNASTY**
Egypt, mid-11th to mid-12th century CE

Description: Fragment of a tapestry-woven *tiraz* band in silk weft on a linen warp comprising three main registers of decoration: the central register has a sequence of cartouches in red containing hares, set within intertwined bands of stylized floral scrolls in yellow and brown; the two outer registers each consist of bands containing a sequence of hares on a green background, bordered above and below by an arrangement of intertwined yellow bands with floral motifs enclosing small triangular shapes in red and green.

Materials: linen and silk: plain weave and tapestry

Dimensions: h. 13.6 cm, w. 20.8 cm

Ground fabric: linen warp (weft lost), undyed, very fine; very good quality (1)

Thread count: warp 23 S-spun

Thread thickness: 0.1 mm tight twist

Tapestry: silk floss; *c.* 74 picks per cm (0.1 mm); slit and toothed

Inv. no. LNS 45 T

Related works: See page 513

A close comparison for the present piece in terms of decorative elements, such as the hares contained within cartouches and the colour scheme, is in the Abegg-Stiftung (Related works 1). This has been dated to the beginning of the twelfth century.

Cat. 172 **TEXTILE FRAGMENT FROM THE FATIMID DYNASTY**
Egypt, 11th to 12th century CE

Description: Fragment of undyed linen, onto which has been sewn, on its lower edge, a tapestry-woven band comprising several registers of decoration, three of which comprise a wave-like rope-patterned scroll in mustard against a red ground; these frame two wider registers, one of which features a sequence of alternating cartouches with a quadruped and a flower, bordered by two narrower registers with palmette scrolls, the other consisting of a pattern of confronted S-shapes in red with floriated terminals in green and mustard.

Materials: linen and silk

Dimensions: h. 16.2 cm, w. 23.7 cm

TEXTILE 1

Ground fabric: linen warp and weft, undyed, predominant-warp plain weave, dense, regular structure; good quality (2)

Thread count: warp 16 Z-spun, weft 18 S-spun

Thread thickness: warp 0.3–0.5 mm medium–tight twist, weft 0.25 mm medium twist

TEXTILE 2

Ground fabric: linen warp (weft lost), undyed

Thread count: warp 22 S-spun

Thread thickness: warp 0.4 mm slight–medium twist

Tapestry: silk, dyed (ochre, dark red, dark blue, dark brown, green), and undyed linen; slit and toothed; stitched to textile 1; two further seams, above and below the band with S-shapes

Inv. no. LNS 48 T

Related works: See page 513

The type of decoration seen here, with its rather crowded arrangement, suggests an attribution to, perhaps, the reign of the caliph al-Mustansir bi-llah (r. 1036–94) or possibly his successors. The frieze of confronted S-shapes appears quite frequently on *tiraz* textiles during al-Mustansir's reign, where they form the floriated background to the caliphal inscriptions., as seen in an example in the Textile Museum, Washington, DC (Related works 1). An undated *tiraz* fragment in the Abegg-Stiftung, Riggisberg (Related works 2), which has been attributed to the period of the caliph al-Musta'li or that of al-Amir, comprises a band that is very close to the present one. It, too, is part of a larger composition and appears on its own, without accompanying inscription. The same design can be found on a knitted fragment in the Bouvier Collection (Related works 3) where the colours (cream against a red background) are reversed from the present piece. A mirror with a repoussé decorated silver face on a cast-iron base in the Benaki Museum, Athens, which is probably eleventh or twelfth century and Egyptian, has the same pattern.[51] The connection with the floriated background of *tiraz* inscriptions suggests that this type of motif originated as a floriation and became stylized once it had been transferred to other contexts.

Cat. 173   *TIRAZ* FRAGMENT FROM
THE FATIMID DYNASTY
Egypt, 11th to 12th century CE

Description: Fragment of undyed linen with
bands of decoration tapestry-
woven in ochre, red, blue, black
and green silk; a central band of
floral decoration (5.0 cm) in ochre
and blue is lined above and below
by symmetrical friezes formed by
a central band of facing birds in
medallions, bordered by bands
of Kufic inscription on a red silk
background.

Materials: linen and silk: plain weave
and tapestry

Dimensions: h. 18.0 cm, w. 29.0 cm;
max. letter height 0.7 cm

Ground fabric: linen warp and weft, undyed,
balanced plain weave, close texture
(*dabiqi*); very good–good quality
(1–2); seams on both sides of the
decorative band

Thread count: warp 26 S-spun, weft 27 S-spun

Thread thickness: warp 0.15–0.2 mm slight–medium
twist, weft 0.1–0.15 mm medium–
tight twist

Tapestry: silk, dyed (ochre, red, light blue,
black, green); discontinuous linen
weft filling between the letters

Provenance: Ex H.P. Kraus collection, no. 96

Inv. no. LNS 210 T

Inscription: repetition of

Victory will be attained by the help of God

نصر من الله

This fragment relates to cat. no. 172 in terms of its decorative scheme. It was
once part of a sleeve, into which a portion of a *tiraz* band had been inserted, as
seams on both sides of the band indicate. It seems that the sleeve, and perhaps
the entire garment, was made from one length of fabric, which would have been
decorated with bands at both ends. The inscriptions were then cut up to fit into
the tailored garment. A fragment such as this is evidence for the re-use of *tiraz*
textiles over time. The tailored garment could well have been made long after
the original length of cloth had been produced.

Cat. 174 *TIRAZ* **FRAGMENTS FROM THE FATIMID DYNASTY**
Egypt, 11th to 12th century CE

Description: Two fragments of undyed linen, with two bands of decoration (6.5 cm) tapestry-woven in red, ochre, blue and black silk, both having the same pattern of animals in medallions with a calligraphic band below, over a red background; this central decoration is lined above and below with bands of red vines and two plain ochre bands.

Materials: linen and silk: plain weave and tapestry

Dimensions: piece (a) (right): h. 34.7 cm, w. 26.2 cm; max. letter height 3.5 cm
piece (b) (left): h. 9.9 cm, w. 11.2 cm; max. letter height 3.5 cm

Ground fabric: linen warp and weft, undyed, predominant-warp plain weave, loose texture (*sharb*); very good quality (1)

Thread count: warp 30 S-spun, weft 29 S-spun

Thread thickness: warp 0.15–0.3 mm slight–medium twist, weft 0.1 mm medium twist

Tapestry: silk, dyed (red, ochre, mid-blue, black), and undyed linen, S-spun, paired; slit and toothed; paired wefts woven on crossed and paired warps

Provenance: Ex H.P. Kraus collection, no. 119

Inv. no. LNS 230 T

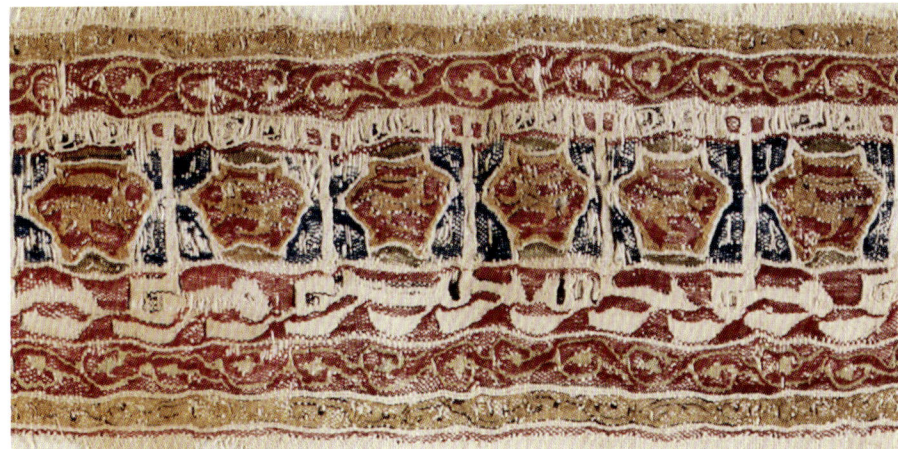

Inscription: corrupted repetition of

Blessing from God

بركة من الله

Cat. 175 *TIRAZ* FRAGMENT FROM
THE FATIMID DYNASTY
Egypt, 11th to 12th century CE

Description: Fragment of undyed linen (piece
b) onto which has been sewn a
band (5.5 cm), comprising linen
with tapestry-woven decoration in
green, brown and red silk (piece
a); the decoration is divided into
three registers, the central one with
calligraphic and floral decoration,
and the two outer ones having
Kufic text on a green background.

Materials: linen and silk: plain weave and
tapestry

Dimensions: piece (a): h. 10.1 cm, w. 14.2 cm;
max. letter height 1.0 cm
piece (b): h. 28.2 cm, w. 24.7 cm

TEXTILE 1

Ground fabric: linen warp and weft, undyed,
predominant-warp plain weave,
loose texture (*sharb*); good
quality (2)

Thread count: warp 20 S-spun, weft 21 S-spun

Thread thickness: warp 0.3 mm slight twist, weft 0.1–
0.2 mm slight twist; tailored with
two parallel seams

TEXTILE 2

Ground fabric: linen warp (weft lost), undyed

Thread count: warp 20 S-spun

Thread thickness: warp 0.1–0.2 mm medium twist

Tapestry: silk, dyed (dark brown, green, red),
and linen, undyed, S-spun paired;
slit and toothed; paired wefts
woven on paired warps

Provenance: Ex H.P. Kraus collection, no. 120

Inv. no. LNS 231 T

Inscription: epigraphic repetition of

Victory will be attained by the help of God

نصر من الله

The decorative band in this fragment represents a re-use of a longer and more
elaborate decorative band of quite complex composition and high quality of
execution. The band would have been far too valuable to discard, hence its
re-use. For other examples of re-used tiraz bands, see cat. nos 167, 172, 173.

Cat. 176   *TIRAZ* FRAGMENT FROM
THE FATIMID DYNASTY
Egypt, 11th to 12th century CE

Description: Fragment (three pieces) of undyed
linen, with decorative and
calligraphic bands, tapestry-woven
in blue, brown, red, green and
ochre silk; two calligraphic bands
in blue silk, with floral decoration
between the uprights, are separated
by additional bands formed by
medallions bordered by pseudo-
epigraphic figuration.

Materials: linen and silk: plain weave
and tapestry

Dimensions: piece (a) (right): h. 10.7 cm,
w. 6.5 cm; max. letter height 3.5 cm
piece (b) (centre): h. 15.2 cm,
w. 5.3 cm; max. letter height 3.5 cm
piece (c) (left): h. 13.3 cm,
w. 5.4 cm; max. letter height 3.5 cm

Ground fabric: linen warp and weft, undyed,
warp-faced plain weave, dense;
good–medium quality (2–3);
selvedge on the right side of the
inscription in fragment (a),
and the left side in fragment (c)

Thread count: warp 32 S-spun, weft 14 S-spun

Thread thickness: warp 0.3–0.5 mm slight–medium
twist, weft 0.3 mm slight–medium
twist

Tapestry: silk, dyed (dark blue, dark
brown, red, green, ochre), and
undyed linen; slit and toothed;
discontinuous supplementary
linen weft filling

Provenance: Ex H.P. Kraus collection, nos
121–122

Inv. no. LNS 232 T a–c

Inscription: corrupted epigraphic repetition of   نصر من [الله]
Victory will be attained by [the help of God]

Cat. 177 *TIRAZ* **FRAGMENT FROM THE FATIMID DYNASTY**
Egypt, 11th to 12th century CE

Description: Fragment (two pieces) of undyed linen with two bands of inscription (2.5 cm) consisting of repeated formulas, tapestry-woven in yellow, dark brown and red silk. On the upper band, the non-meaningful inscription is in Kufic characters, in red silk over a yellow silk background, bordered by two smaller bands of foliated decoration; on the lower band the inscription is in *naskhi*, in yellow silk over a red background, and bordered too by two smaller bands of foliated decoration over a dark background.

Materials: linen and silk: plain weave and tapestry

Dimensions: piece (a) (right): h. 12.7 cm, w. 20.5 cm; max. letter height (Kufic) 0.9 cm, (*naskhi*) 0.7 cm piece (b) (left): h. 13.1 cm, w. 9 cm

Ground fabric: linen warp and weft, undyed, predominant-warp plain weave, dense texture (*dabiqi*); good–medium quality (2–3)

Thread count: warp 25 S-spun, weft 13 S-spun

Thread thickness: warp 0.3 mm slight–medium twist, weft 0.3 mm slight–medium twist

Tapestry: silk, dyed (red, dark brown, yellow), and undyed linen; slit and toothed

Provenance: Ex H.P. Kraus collection, no. 203

Inv. no. LNS 300 T

Inscription:
Line 1: repetition of   لعا

Line 2:   نصر من الله
Victory will be attained by the help of God

Cat. 178 *TIRAZ* FRAGMENT FROM THE FATIMID DYNASTY
Egypt, first half of the 12th century CE

Description: Fragment of undyed linen, (remnant at upper left corner) with decoration tapestry-woven in crimson, brown and mustard silk, comprising two bands with stylized palmette scrolls enclosing a Naskh inscription, accompanied by a sequence of quadrupeds or hares chasing each other and a confronted pair of hares on the right side.

Materials: linen and silk: plain weave and tapestry

Dimensions: h. 4.5 cm, w. 27.5 cm; max. letter height 2.0 cm

Ground fabric: linen warp and weft, undyed, balanced plain weave, regular, close texture (*dabiqi*); very good (1)

Thread count: warp 27 S-spun, weft 24 Z-spun

Thread thickness: warp 0.15 mm medium–tight twist, weft 0.1–0.15 mm medium–tight twist

Tapestry: silk 0.1 mm, dyed (mustard, crimson, brown), and undyed linen; 88 picks per cm; slit and toothed; weft-faced, dense texture; woven on crossed and paired warps.

Inv. no. LNS 47 T

Related works: See page 513

Inscription: repetition of

نصر من الله

Victory will be attained by the help of God

The religious phrase used in this *tiraz* is a repetition of the standard invocation 'nasr min Allah' ('Victory will be attained by the help of God'). Interestingly, the inscription here is executed in a cursive style, rather than the angular Kufic favoured by the Fatimids in the earlier part of their caliphate. The use of cursive (Naskh) is normally associated with the revival of Sunnism under the Seljuqs and Ghaznavids, and it was first used in public text in the eastern Islamic world during the early eleventh century, from where it spread to Iraq and the Levant. In Egypt it appeared in *tiraz* textile inscriptions by the early twelfth century, long before the Fatimid dynasty came to an end in 1171.[52] It is possible that in Egypt this was not necessarily connected to a change of the religious climate, but instead reflected changes in how the government was run. By the late eleventh century, when internal power struggles within the caliphal family and revolts by the Turkish and Berber military weakened the authority of the Fatimid caliphs, power was increasingly exercised by viziers on behalf of the ruling caliph. Perhaps Kufic script was seen as more conservative, reflecting an older, more orthodox order, while cursive script possibly allowed viziers to express themselves more prominently, and symbolized political change.

A significant *tiraz* textile inscription at the Textile Museum, Washington, DC, features a line of text in cursive script documenting the name and inflated titles of Abu al-Qasim Shahanshah bin Badr al-Jamali al-Malik al-Afdal, son of the famous Armenian-born vizier Badr al-Jamali (Related works 1). Abu al-Qasim was in office from 487 AH / 1094 CE until he was assassinated in

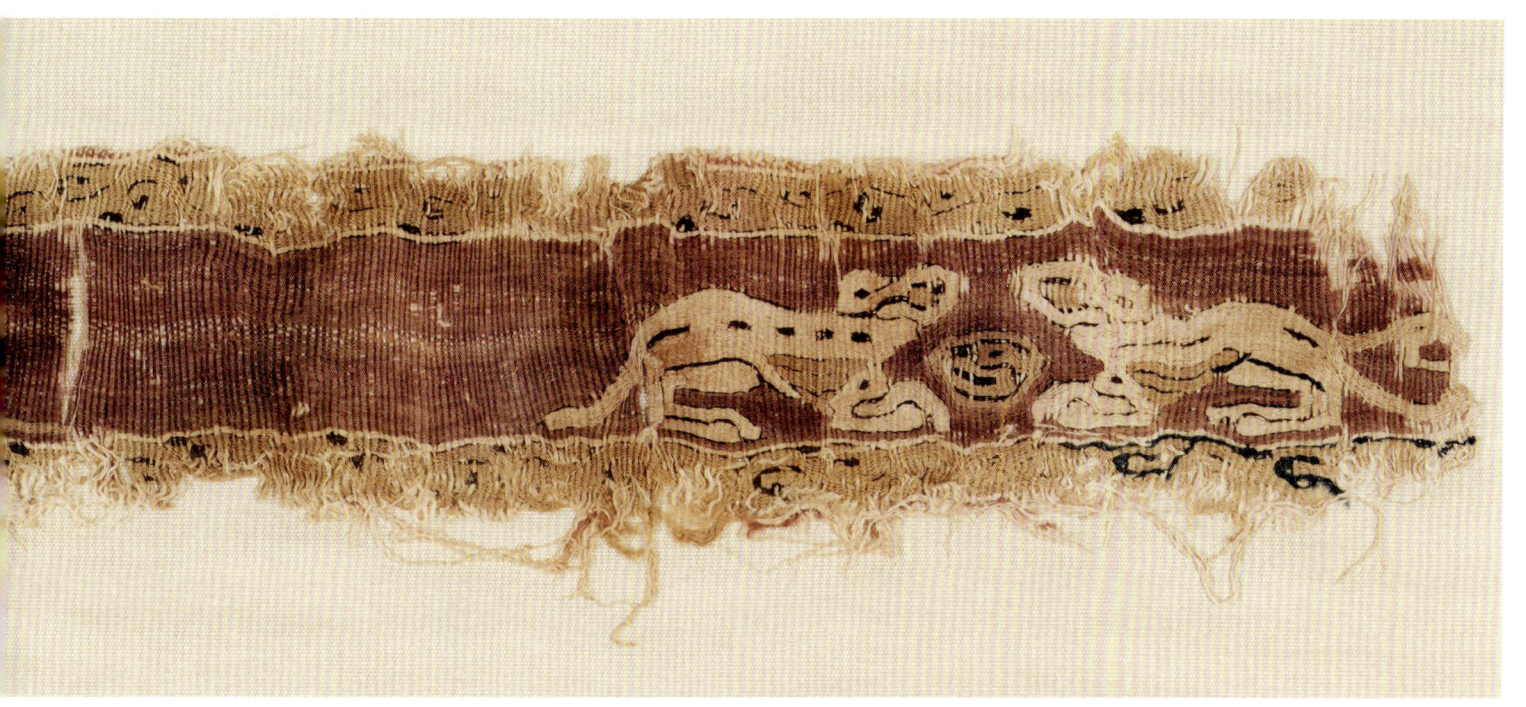

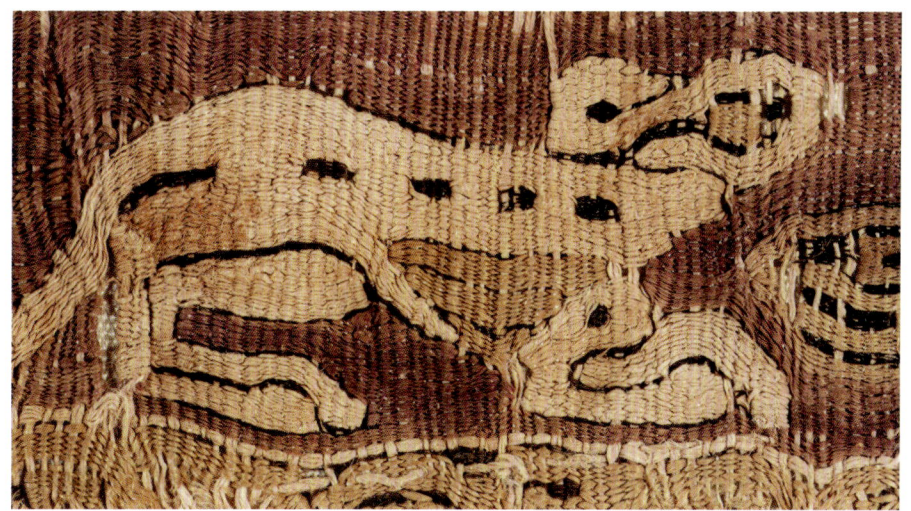

515 AH / 1121 CE, serving under the Fatimid caliphs al-Mustansir (r. 1036–94), al-Musta'li (r. 1094–1101) and al-Amir (r. 1101–30). Abu al-Qasim brought al-Musta'li to the throne when the latter was only five years old. Another closely related inscription, albeit undated, is in the Cleveland Museum of Art (Related works 2); both this and the other example have an inscription that is uncoloured and set against a dark red band interspersed with floral designs. The same is true of the present fragment, but here there are also two confronted quadrupeds that form part of the same band, preceding the inscription, perhaps originally meant to divide the text, or mark the beginning of the band of text. Following the reign of al-Amir, cursive *tiraz* inscriptions became more common until the end of the Fatimid caliphate, as is documented by another textile at the Textile Museum, Washington, DC, with an inscription mentioning the caliph al-Hafiz (r. 1131–49) (Related works 3). This piece comprises a very prominent display of text in five lines that probably once contained invocations on al-Hafiz's predecessors, and content relating to Isma'ili doctrine.

Interestingly, while *tiraz* inscriptions featured cursive text more and more, architectural inscriptions remained conservative in a continued use of floriated Kufic. Both the dome added by al-Hafiz at the al-Azhar mosque, as well as the mihrab added to the mosque of Ibn Tulun by the vizier al-Afdal Shahanshah, carry inscriptions in floriated Kufic.[53] Also the mosque constructed for the vizier of the caliph al-Fa'iz, Abu al-Gharat Faris al-Muslimin al-Malik al-Salih Tala'i' ibn Ruzzik al-Ghassani al-Armani, known as al-Salih Tala'i' (in office 1154–61), still comprises prominent displays of floriated Kufic.[54] The change from Kufic to cursive in public inscriptions in Egypt comes to full fruition with the overthrow of the Fatimid caliphate by the last Fatimid vizier and later Ayyubid sultan, Salah al-Din. Once Salah al-Din had taken the reins of power, the first time a cursive inscription was used in an architectural setting was on the madrasa that he had constructed next to the shrine of the imam al-Shaf'i, dated 575 AH / 1179 CE.[55] Four years later a cursive foundation inscription commemorates the construction of the Ayyubid citadel of Cairo.[56]

Cat. 179   *TIRAZ* **FRAGMENT FROM THE FATIMID DYNASTY**
Egypt, 11th to 12th century CE

Description: Fragment of linen with alternating stripes undyed and dyed blue, with a band of repititious Naskh inscription, tapestry-woven in undyed silk; selvedge in red silk on the right.

Materials: linen and silk: plain wave and tapestry

Dimensions: h. 17.0 cm, w. 10.0 cm; max. letter height 1.0 cm

Ground fabric: linen warp and weft, undyed, and dyed (blue), predominant-warp plain weave, close texture (*dabiqi*); good quality (2); selvedge on the right side of the inscription

Thread count: warp 23 S-spun, weft 12 S-spun

Thread thickness: warp 0.3 mm medium–tight twist, weft 0.3 mm medium–tight twist

Tapestry: silk, dyed (yellow, red); slit and toothed; discontinuous linen weft filling

Provenance: Ex H.P. Kraus collection, no. 142

Inv. no. LNS 250 T

Inscription:

[...] [Victory will be attained by the help] of God

[...]ـر من الله

Cat. 180 *TIRAZ* FRAGMENT FROM
THE FATIMID DYNASTY
**Egypt, late 11th to
12th century CE**

Description: Fragment of undyed linen, with
two bands of decoration tapestry-
woven in blue and dark brown
silk: the lower one consists of
a wide frieze of plain blue silk
(3.3 cm), bordered above and
below by epigraphic bands in
dark brown silk; the upper one
is a tripartite band (2.5 cm) with
a Kufic inscription executed in
undyed linen over a brown silk
background, bordered above and
below by two narrower bands
with scroll motifs.

Materials: linen and silk: plain wave
and tapestry

Dimensions: h. 12.5 cm, w. 7.5 cm;
max. letter height 0.6 cm

Ground fabric: linen warp and weft, undyed,
warp-faced plain weave, dense
texture (*dabiqi*); good–medium
quality (2–3)

Thread count: warp 34 S-spun, weft 14 S-spun

Thread thickness: warp 0.3 mm medium–tight twist,
weft 0.3 mm medium–tight twist

Tapestry: silk, dyed (dark brown, dark
blue); blue band 58 picks per cm;
discontinuous linen weft filling
between the letters of the
inscription,

Provenance: Ex H.P. Kraus collection, no. 149

Inv. no. LNS 255 T

Inscription: repetition of

Victory will be attained by the help of God

نصر من الله

Cat. 181 *TIRAZ* FRAGMENT FROM
THE FATIMID DYNASTY
**Egypt, late 11th to
12th century CE**

Description: Fragment of undyed linen, with
lines of Naskh inscription tapestry-
woven in dark brown silk on either
side of a central band in blue silk
with red borders (2.5 cm); below
is a fragmented ornamental band
(2.5 cm), the silk of which has
almost gone.

Materials: linen and silk: plain wave
and tapestry

Dimensions: h. 10.0 cm, w. 10.5 cm;
max. letter height 0.8 cm

Ground fabric: linen warp and weft (mostly lost),
undyed, warp-faced plain weave,
close texture (*dabiqi*); good quality
(2); selvedge on the left side of the
inscription

Thread count: warp 26 S-spun, weft 8 per 0.5 cm
S-spun

Thread thickness: warp 0.25 mm medium twist,
weft 0.25 mm medium twist

Tapestry: silk, dyed (dark brown); slit and
toothed; discontinuous linen weft
filling; continuous silk weft band,
dyed (dark blue, red), 98 picks
per cm

Provenance: Ex H.P. Kraus collection, no. 140

Inv. no. LNS 248 T

Inscription: repetition of
Assistance from God

نصر من الله

Cat. 182   *TIRAZ* FRAGMENT FROM
THE FATIMID DYNASTY
**Egypt, late 11th to
12th century CE**

Description: Fragment of linen dyed blue with
repetitious inscriptions in Naskh
tapestry-woven in red silk over an
ochre silk background, bordered
by two lines of script woven in
red silk.

Materials: linen and silk: plain wave
and tapestry

Dimensions: h. 17.0 cm, w. 9.0 cm;
max. letter height 1.2 cm, 2.1 cm

Ground fabric: linen warp and weft, dyed (light
blue), predominant-warp plain
weave, close texture (*dabiqi*);
good quality (2)

Thread count: warp 30 S-spun, weft 18 S-spun

Thread thickness: warp 0.15–0.2 mm medium–tight
twist, weft 0.1–0.15 mm tight twist

Tapestry: silk, dyed (red, ochre); slit and
toothed; outer inscriptions woven
against discontinuous linen weft
filling

Provenance: Ex H.P. Kraus collection,
New York, no. 139

Inv. no. LNS 247 T

Inscription: repetition of

Assistance from God

نصر من الله

Cat. 183 *TIRAZ* FRAGMENT FROM
THE FATIMID DYNASTY
**Egypt, late 11th to
12th century CE**

Description: Fragment of undyed linen with
calligraphic bands tapestry-woven
in red, ochre and black silk, and
undyed linen: a large red band,
bearing a Naskh inscription in
undyed linen, is framed by two
smaller ochre bands. Above are
two additional bands of Naskh
inscription in red and black silk,
both on undyed linen background;
both are separated by a thin band
of red silk.

Materials: linen and silk: plain weave
and tapestry

Dimensions: h. 5.4 cm, w. 26.3 cm;
max. letter height 0.9 cm, 0.5 cm

Ground fabric: undyed linen warp (weft lost),
undyed

Thread count: warp 18 Z-spun

Thread thickness: warp 0.2 mm tight twist

Tapestry: silk, dyed (red, ochre, black), and
undyed linen; slit and toothed,
discontinuous linen weft filling;
area with red background woven
on crossed and paired warps;
74 picks per cm

Provenance: Ex H.P. Kraus collection, no. 153

Inv. no. LNS 301 T

Inscription: repetition of
Assistance from God

نصر من الله

Cat. 184 *TIRAZ* FRAGMENT FROM THE FATIMID DYNASTY
Egypt, 11th century CE

Description: Fragment of undyed linen, with a tripartite band of decoration tapestry-woven in undyed linen and coloured silk, comprising an addorsed foliated Kufic inscription in red against a cream-coloured ground, and a central band with a series of interlinked cartouches containing figures of hares, in blue and mustard against a red ground and in undyed linen against a brown silk ground.

Materials: linen and silk: plain weave and tapestry

Dimensions: h. 19.2 cm, w. 26.7 cm; max. letter height 4.3 cm

Ground fabric: undyed linen warp and weft, balanced plain weave, dense texture (*dabiqi*), some irregularities; medium quality (3)

Thread count: warp 19 S-spun, weft 21 S-spun

Thread thickness: warp 0.15–0.5 medium–tight twist, weft 0.25–0.5 medium–tight twist

Tapestry: silk floss, dyed (red, brown, blue, mustard, greenish); slit and toothed; discontinuous supplementary linen weft filling; the linen contours appear to have been woven first and the voids filled later with coloured silk floss wefts, as the linen is quite densely woven, whereas in places the silk is not

Provenance: Ex H.P. Kraus collection, no. 146

Inv. no. LNS 76 T

Related works: See page 513

Inscription: repetition of (possibly)

Prosperity and power?

نعمة و عز؟

The epigraphic style seen in this fragment is characterized by its emphasis on the terminals of letters such as *waw*, which curl upwards from the baseline in a reverse S-shape. They end in halved split palmettes fanning out. Here they are disproportionately broad in comparison with the rest of the inscription – a feature also seen on cat. no. 185. This feature is seen in a number of related textiles (Related works 1, 2). Normally these inscriptions are either pseudo-epigraphic or they comprise short benedictory phrases, as in the present piece. Another noteworthy characteristic is the high degree of stylization of the script and the decorative details. In the fragment at the Victoria and Albert Museum, London, the script is itself almost a decorative design (Related works 1). Another piece, in the Bouvier Collection, has pronounced upper hastae (Related works 2). Cornu attributes these textiles to the last quarter of the eleventh century and suggests that they were produced in the Fayyum, as they show a certain degree of archaism not found in the caliphal workshops of the Delta.[57]

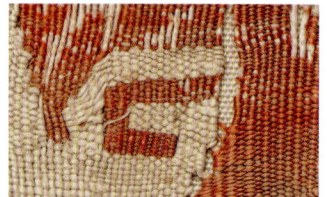

Cat. 185   *TIRAZ* FRAGMENT FROM THE FATIMID DYNASTY
Egypt, 11th century CE

Description: Fragment of linen, dyed blue, with tapestry-woven decoration in undyed linen and mustard-coloured silk (remnants seen in the lower left section) comprising an epigraphic band with a meaningless repetition of the letters *lam–mim–alif*, terminal letters in foliated Kufic; below is a star-shaped motif within a larger cartouche.

Materials: linen and silk: tapestry weave

Dimensions: h. 12 cm, w. 26.2 cm; max. letter height 5.5 cm

Ground fabric: linen warp (weft lost), dyed (light blue)

Thread count: warp 24 S-spun

Thread thickness: warp 0.15–0.2 mm tight twist

Tapestry: undyed linen, S-spun, 0.3–0.5 mm medium twist; *c.* 38 picks per cm; silk, dyed (ochre); *c.* 79 picks per cm; woven on paired warps

Inv. no. LNS 417 T

Related works: See page 513

Inscription: epigraphic repetition of ٱلماك

The style of the script in this fragment is very close to that on one in the Victoria and Albert Museum, London (Related works 1), with which it shares, in particular, the mirroring of the terminal *nun* with its pronounced foliations. Another fragment, in the Bouvier Collection, is also tapestry-woven in a similar style on a blue linen warp (Related works 2). All three pieces seem to owe more to traditional Coptic traditions, with their rather unrefined details, than to the fine products of the caliphal *tiraz* workshops. Yet in the use of pseudo-

calligraphic bands they certainly attempt to imitate those products. Cornu suggested that the type of foliated script they display relates to that found in the official *tiraz* inscriptions of al-'Aziz up to the reign of al-Mustansir, and hence suggested an eleventh-century date for them.[58]

Cat. 186 *TIRAZ* FRAGMENT FROM
THE FATIMID DYNASTY
Egypt, 11th to 12th century CE

Description: Fragment of undyed linen, with
five bands of decoration tapestry-
woven in ochre, beige, blue, green
and black silk. The central band
(5.7 cm) consists of pairs of birds
facing each other, with ochre and
beige rosettes between, bordered
by scroll designs in blue silk,
undyed linen and green silk; above
and below are single bands of Kufic
inscription (2.3 cm) on an ochre
background, with outer borders
either side of floral decoration on a
blue, green and ochre background
(1.7 cm).

Materials: linen and silk: plain weave
and tapestry

Dimensions: h. 28.8 cm, w. 33.2 cm;
max. letter height 2.3 cm

Ground fabric: linen warp and weft, undyed,
predominant-warp plain weave,
gauzy texture (*sharb*); very good
quality (1)

Thread count: warp 24 S-spun, weft 15 S-spun

Thread thickness: warp 0.15 mm tight twist,
weft 0.15 mm tight twist

Tapestry: silk, dyed (ochre, dark beige, light
blue, green, black) and undyed
linen; *c.* 68 picks per cm; slit and
toothed

Provenance: Ex H.P. Kraus collection, no. 123

Inv. no. LNS 233 T

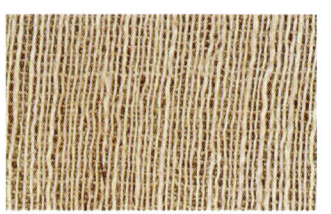

Inscription: repetition of (possibly)

عز من الله يمن من الله نصر من الله

Glory from God. Fortune from God. Victory by the help of God

Cat. 187 *TIRAZ* **FRAGMENT FROM THE FATIMID DYNASTY**
Egypt, 11th to 12th century CE

Description: Fragment of linen with blue stripes, comprising a central band (8.3 cm) tapestry-woven in undyed silk paired with undyed and dyed linen, decorated with a quadruped and birds within two medallions.

Materials: linen and silk: plain weave and tapestry

Dimensions: h. 13.1 cm, w. 38.8 cm

Ground fabric: linen warp, dyed (blue), and undyed, and weft, undyed; warp-faced plain weave, dense texture (*dabiqi*), regular; good–medium quality (2–3); selvedge to the left of the decorative band

Thread count: warp 28 S-spun, weft 18 S-spun

Thread thickness: warp 0.3–0.4 mm slight–medium twist, weft 0.3–0.4 mm slight–medium twist

Tapestry: silk, undyed, paired with linen, dyed (blue), and undyed, S-spun; *c*. 44 picks per cm; slit and toothed; woven on crossed and paired warps

Inv. no. LNS 405 T

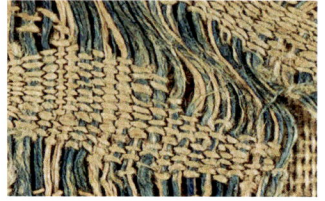

Cat. 188 *TIRAZ* **FRAGMENT FROM THE FATIMID DYNASTY**
Egypt, late 11th to 12th century CE

Description: Fragment of undyed linen (remnants on the upper edge and lower left corner), with a broad tapestry-woven band in yellow and red silk floss sewn on (stitches visible on the edge of the tapestry), comprising six epigraphic bands: a larger and a smaller Naskh inscription alternate with five bands (4.9–5.9 cm) of a complicated geometric interlace with small bird and floral motifs filling the compartments in between.

Materials: linen and silk: plain weave and tapestry

Dimensions: h. 31.2 cm, w. 17.0 cm; max. letter height 1.5 cm and 0.9 cm

TEXTILE 1
Ground fabric: linen warp (weft lost), undyed
Thread count: warp 21 S-spun
Thread thickness: warp 0.3 mm medium twist

TEXTILE 2
Ground fabric: linen warp and weft, undyed, balanced plain weave, dense texture (*dabiqi*), very regular; very good quality (1)
Thread count: warp 28 Z-spun, weft 29 Z-spun
Thread thickness: 2 warp 0.1–0.3mm medium twist, weft 0.1–0.3 medium twist
Tapestry: silk, dyed (red yellow), 58 picks per cm; discontinuous supplementary linen weft filling; sewn above and below to fabric 2

Provenance: art market

Inv. no. LNS 421 T

Inscription: possibly repetition of (...) in (...) good fortune?

الاقبال؟ (...) في (...)

The *tiraz* tapestry fragment in this textile was re-used, cut out from an originally larger piece and then attached to another plain-weave ground fabric, possibly to adorn a sleeve or any prominent part of a tunic, as, for example, with those discussed in chapter 1 (pp. 46–49; figs 1.54–1.56).

Cat. 189   *TIRAZ* FRAGMENT FROM
THE FATIMID DYNASTY
**Egypt, late 11th to
12th century CE**

Description: Fragment of undyed linen, with a
tapestry-woven decorative band
(6.5 cm) in yellow and red silk
floss, comprising three registers:
the two outer ones contain a
repetition of benedictory phrases,
and the central one has interlaced
cartouches with representations
of hares and palmettes in the
spandrels between.

Materials: linen and silk: plain weave
and tapestry

Dimensions: h. 18.1 cm, w. 66.8 cm;
max. letter height 1.1 cm

Ground fabric: linen warp and weft, undyed,
predominant-warp plain weave,
dense texture (*dabiqi*), regular–
coarse structure; medium quality
(3); loom width (66.8 cm) with
selvedges on the right and left sides

Thread count: warp 17 S-spun, weft 16 S-spun

Thread thickness: warp 0.5 mm medium twist,
weft 0.5 mm medium twist

Tapestry: silk, dyed (yellow and red), *c.* 44
picks per cm

Provenance: art market

Inv. no. LNS 422 T

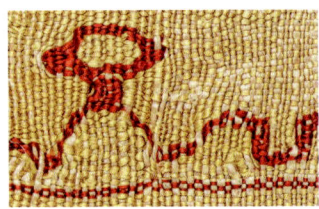

Inscription: possibly repetition of
Perfection and prosperity

الكامله و الاقبال

This textile is interesting as it constitutes a complete loom width, in this case almost 70 cm. This is comparatively narrow compared with textiles such as the Veil of St Anne, discussed in chapter 1 (see fig. 1.49), which is 150 cm wide. It is very likely that the textile here was once the end piece or sash of a turban-cloth, a long narrow textile that would have been wound around a cap in order to sit on the top of the wearer's head. The textile's untwisted fringe is well preserved.

RELATED WORKS

Cat. 1

1 Museum für Islamische Kunst, Berlin, inv. no. 4504: Kühnel 1925, pp. 85–86, fig. 2 (date not mentioned, or lost, place of production not mentioned, made by Marwan bin Mari)
2 Textile Museum, Washington, DC, inv. no. 73.447: Kühnel and Bellinger 1952, pp. 83–84, pl. XLIII (no caliph mentioned, date lost, *tiraz al-khassa* in Misr)
3 Keir Collection, inv. no. 74: Spuhler 1978, p. 144, no. 74 (administrative data not mentioned, or lost)
4 Museum of Islamic Art, Cairo, inv. no. 9023: Maher 1977, p. 164, no. 436 (date not mentioned, or lost, *tiraz al-khassa* in Misr)
5 Museum of Islamic Art, Cairo, inv. no. 12298: Lamm 1937, pp. 109–11, fig. 59; Sokoly 2002, no. 83 (dated 278 AH / 891–92 CE, *tiraz al-khassa* in Merw, by order of the governor of Khurasan and heir designate, al-Mu'tadid bi-llah)
6 Kelsey Museum of Archaeology, Ann Arbor, MI, inv. no. 22504: Day 1937, pp. 424–26, no. 4, fig. 4 (dated 289 AH / 901–02 CE, San'a')

Cat. 2

1 Textile Museum, Washington, DC, inv. no. 73.658: Kühnel and Bellinger 1952, p. 7, pl. II; Sokoly 2002, no. 38.5 (dated 245 AH / 859–60 CE, Misr)

Cat. 3

1 Textile Museum, Washington, DC, inv. no. 73.652: Kühnel and Bellinger 1952, p. 8, pl. II; Sokoly 2002, no. 37 (date lost, place of production lost, ordered by the amir Abu 'Abdallah, later caliph al-Mu'tazz)
2 Textile Museum, Washington, DC, inv. no. 73.645: Kühnel and Bellinger 1952, p. 6, pl. II; Sokoly 2002, no. 38.2 (dated 240 AH / 854–55 CE, Misr)
3 Textile Museum, Washington, DC, inv. no. 73.658: Kühnel and Bellinger 1952, pp. 7–8, pl. II; Sokoly 2002, no. 38.5 (dated 245 AH / 859–60 CE, Misr)
4 Kelsey Museum of Archaeology, Ann Arbor, MI, inv. no. 22.501: Day 1937, pp. 420–23, no. 1, fig. 1; Sokoly 2002, no. 38.3 (dated 241 AH / 855–56 CE, ordered by Abu 'Abdallah)
5 Museum of Islamic Art, Cairo, inv. no. 12550: Wiet 1935b, p. 7, no. 20; Sokoly 2002, no. 38 (dated 239 AH / 853–54 CE, Misr)
6 Museum of Islamic Art, Cairo, inv. no. 12264: Wiet 1935b, p. 8, no. 21; Sokoly 2002, no. 38.1 (dated 239 AH / 853–54 CE, administrative data not mentioned, or lost)
7 Museum of Islamic Art, Cairo, inv. no. 9458: Wiet 1935b, p. 8, no. 22; Sokoly 2002, no. 38.7 (date and administrative data lost or not mentioned)
8 Ex Tano Collection: *RCEA* 1931–91, vol. II, 1932, p. 275, inv. no. 476A:

Sokoly 2002, no. 38.6 (date lost, Misr)
9 Museum of Islamic Art, Cairo, inv. no. 10848: Wiet 1935b, p. 7, no. 19; Sokoly 2002, no. 35 (dated 230 AH / 844–45 CE, Tuna)
10 Cleveland Museum of Art, inv. no. 32.25: Sokoly 2002, no. 36 (date lost, Tuna)
11 Textile Museum, Washington, DC, inv. no. 73.650: Kühnel and Bellinger 1952, pp. 8–9, pl. III; Sokoly 2002, no. 41 (dated 248 AH / 862–63 CE, Tinnis, by order of the vizier)

Cat. 4

1 Textile Museum, Washington, DC, inv. no. 73.658: Kühnel and Bellinger 1952, p. 7, pl. II; Sokoly 2002, no. 38.5 (dated 245 AH / 859–60 CE, Misr)
2 Textile Museum, Washington, DC, inv. no. 73.664: Kühnel and Bellinger 1952, p. 12, pl. IV; Sokoly 2002, no. 77 (dated 273 AH / 886–87 CE, Misr)

Cat. 5

1 Textile Museum, Washington, DC, inv. no. 73.634: Kühnel and Bellinger 1952, p. 11, pl. IV; Sokoly 2002, no. 74 (dated 272 AH / 885–86 CE, Alexandria)
2 Textile Museum, Washington, DC, inv. no. 73.664: Kühnel and Bellinger 1952, p. 12, pl. IV; Sokoly 2002, no. 77 (dated 273 AH / 886–87 CE, Misr)
3 Royal Ontario Museum, Toronto, inv. no. 978.76.331: Sokoly 2002, no. 87 (possibly dated 270 AH / 883–84 CE, *tiraz* workshop in an unnamed location)
4 Textile Museum, Washington, DC, inv. no. 73.23: Kühnel and Bellinger 1952, pp. 16–17, pl. VII; Sokoly 2002, no. 96 (date and administrative data lost)
5 Völkerkunde-Museum, Basel, inv. no. 9470: Marzouk 1959, pp. 283–84, fig. 1; Sokoly 2002, no. 101 (dated 280 AH / 893–94 CE, Misr)
6 Textile Museum, Washington, DC, inv. no. 73.446: Kühnel and Bellinger 1952, pp. 13, pl. VII; Sokoly, no. 105 (dated 281 AH / 894–95 CE, Misr)
7 Textile Museum, Washington, DC, inv. no. 73.653: Kühnel and Bellinger 1952, pp. 13–14, pl. VII; Sokoly 108 (dated 282 AH / 895–96 CE, Alexandria)

Cat. 6

1 Textile Museum, Washington, DC, inv. no. 73.634: Kühnel and Bellinger 1952, p. 11, pl. IV; Sokoly 2002, no. 74 (dated 272 AH / 885–86 CE, Alexandria, ordering officer not mentioned)
2 Textile Museum, Washington, DC, inv. no. 73.664: Kühnel and Bellinger 1952, p. 10, pl. IV; Sokoly 2002, no. 77 (dated 273 AH / 886–87 CE, Misr, ordering officer not mentioned)

Cat. 7

1 Textile Museum, Washington, DC, inv. no. 73.13: Kühnel and Bellinger 1952, p. 21, pl. X; Sokoly 2002, no. 259 (dated 300 AH / 912–13 CE, *tiraz al-'amma* in Misr, by order of the vizier by intermediation of Shafi')
2 Textile Museum, Washington, DC, inv. no. 73.189: Kühnel and Bellinger 1952, p. 24, pl. XI; Sokoly 2002, no. 301 (dated 303 AH / 915–16 CE, Misr, by order of the vizier 'Ali ibn 'Isa by intermediation of Shafi' al-Muqtadiri)
3 Ashmolean Museum, Oxford, inv. no. 1988.31: Sokoly 2002, no. 467 (datable to 308 AH / 920–21 or 318 AH / 930–31 CE, place of production lost, by intermediation of Shafi')
4 Cleveland Museum of Art, inv. no. 32.19: Sokoly 2002, no. 414 (dated 310 AH / 922–23 CE, Misr, by order of the vizier by intermediation of Shafi' *mawla amir al-mu'minin*)
5 Keir Collection on loan to the Dallas Museum of Art, inv. no. K.1.2014.597: Spuhler 1978, pp. 141–42, no. 71; Sokoly 2002, no. 454 (dated 318 AH / 930–31 CE, Misr, by order of the vizier 'Ali ibn 'Isa, by intermediation of Shafi' *mawla amir al-mu'minin*; max. letter height 0.7 cm)
6 Royal Ontario Museum, Toronto, inv. no. 978.76.49: Sokoly 2002, no. 197 (dated 295 AH / 908–09 CE, *tiraz al-khassa* in Tinnis, by order of the vizier by intermediation of Shafi' *mawla amir al-mu'minin*)
7 Royal Ontario Museum, Toronto, inv. no. 978.76.3: Sokoly 2002, no. 215 (datable to 295–96 AH / 907–09 CE, *tiraz al-'amma* in Tinnis, by order of the vizier al-'Abbas [Hamid ibn al-'Abbas or Abu Ahmad al-'Abbas] by intermediation of Shafi')
8 Royal Ontario Museum, Toronto, inv. no. 978.76.318: Sokoly 2002, no. 195 (dated 306 AH / 918–19 CE, Misr, by order of the amir)
9 Erzherzog Rainer Collection, Österreichische Nationalbibliothek, Vienna, no. 849: Karabacek et al. 1894, pp. 227–28, no. 849; Sokoly 2002, no. 214 (datable to 295–96 AH / 907–09 CE, place of production lost, by order of the vizier Abu Ahmad al-'Abbas bin al-Hasan)
10 Kelsey Museum of Archaeology, Ann Arbor, MI, inv. no. 22.507: Day 1937, pp. 427–28, no. 7, fig. 7; Sokoly 2002, no. 241 (dated 298 AH / 910–11 CE, *tiraz al-'amma* in Misr, by order of the vizier Abu al-Hasan 'Ali Muhammad by intermediation of Bishr *mawla amir al-mu'minin*)
11 Royal Ontario Museum, Toronto, inv. no. 978.76.789: Sokoly 2002, no. 262 (dated 300 AH / 912–13 CE, Misr, by order of the vizier)
12 Royal Ontario Museum, Toronto, inv. no. 978.76.330: Sokoly 2002, no. 267 (administrative data lost)
13 Bouvier Collection, inv. no. JFB I 131: Geneva 1993, pp. 172–74,

no. 98; Sokoly 2002, no. 290 (datable to 301–04 AH / 913–17 CE or 314–16 AH / 926–29 CE, place of production lost, by order of the vizier 'Ali ibn 'Isa *mawla amir al-mu'minin*)
14 Textile Museum, Washington, DC, inv. no. 73.189: Kühnel and Bellinger 1952, p. 24, pl. XI; Sokoly 2002, no. 301 (dated 303 AH / 915–16 CE, by order of the vizier 'Ali ibn 'Isa, by intermediation of Shafi' al-Muqtadiri)
15 Royal Ontario Museum, Toronto, inv. no. 978.76.29: Sokoly 2002, no. 302 (dated 303 AH / 915–16 CE, by order of the vizier 'Ali ibn 'Isa by intermediation of Shafi' al-Muqtadiri *mawla amir al-mu'minin*)
16 Textile Museum, Washington, DC, inv. no. 73.444: Kühnel and Bellinger 1952, pp. 25–26, pl. XI; Sokoly 2002, no. 337 (dated 306 AH / 918–19 CE)
17 Cleveland Museum of Art, inv. no. 32.19: Sokoly 2002, no. 414 (dated 310 AH / 922–23 CE, by order of the vizier Hamid ibn al-'Abbas by intermediation of Shafi' *mawla amir al-mu'minin*)
18 Keir Collection, inv. no. 71: Spuhler 1978, pp. 141–42, no. 71; Sokoly 2002, no. 454 (dated 318 AH / 930–31 CE, by order of the vizier 'Ali ibn 'Isa by intermedition of Shafi' *mawla amir al-mu'minin*)
19 Ashmolean Museum, Oxford, inv. no. 1988.31: Sokoly 2002, no. 467 (datable to 308 AH / 920–21 or 318 AH / 930–31 CE, place of production and ordering officer lost, by intermediation of Shafi')
20 Textile Museum, Washington, DC, inv. no. 73.649: Kühnel and Bellinger 1952, p. 23, pl. IX; Sokoly 2002, no. 555 (date and administrative data lost, made by Muhammad ibn Mu'alla)

Cat. 8

1 Royal Ontario Museum, Toronto, inv. no. 978.76.71: Sokoly 2002, no. 199 (dated 299–301 AH / 911–14 CE, or 312–13 AH / 924–26 CE, *tiraz al-khassa* in Tinnis, by order of the vizier Muhammad ibn 'Ubaydallah)
2 Islamic Museum, Cairo, inv. no. 9783: *RCEA* 1931–91, vol. III, 1932, p. 62, no. 905; Sokoly 2002, no. 243 (dated 299 AH / 911–12 CE, by order of the vizier 'Ali ibn Muhammad)
3 Islamic Museum, Cairo, inv. no. 8205: *RCEA* 1931–91, vol. III, 1932, pp. 62–63, no. 906; Sokoly 2002, no. 244 (dated 299 AH / 911–12 CE, by order of the vizier Abu al-Hasan 'Ali ibn Muhammad)
4 Islamic Museum, Cairo, inv. no. 11483: *RCEA* 1931–91, vol. III, 1932, p. 219, no. 906B; Sokoly 2002, no. 245 (dated 299 AH / 911–12 CE, *tiraz* workshop in an unnamed location, by order of

the vizier Abu al-Hasan ʿAli ibn Muhammad)

5 Royal Ontario Museum, Toronto, inv. no. 978.76.18: Sokoly 2002, no. 246 (dated 299 AH / 911–12 CE, Tinnis, by order of the vizier Abu al-Hasan ʿAli ibn Muhammad by intermediation of Shafiʿ *mawla amir al-muʾminin*)

6 Islamic Museum, Cairo, inv. no. 10605: *RCEA* 1931–91, vol. III, 1932, p. 68, no. 917; Sokoly 2002, no. 247 (dated 299–301 AH / 911–14 CE, Misr, by order of the vizier Muhammad ibn ʿUbaydallah)

7 Bouvier Collection, inv. no. JFB I 11: Geneva 1993, pp. 168–69, no. 95; Sokoly 2002, no. 218 (dated 296 AH / 908–09 CE, *tiraz al-ʿamma* in Misr, by order of the vizier Abu al-Hasan ʿAli bin Muhammad by intermediation of Bishr *mawla amir al-muʾminin*)

8 Royal Ontario Museum, Toronto, inv. no. 978.76.36: Sokoly 2002, no. 219 (dated 296 AH / 908–09 CE, *tiraz al-ʿamma* in Misr, by intermediation of Shafiʿ *mawla amir al-muʾminin*)

9 Royal Ontario Museum, Toronto, inv. no. 978.76.2: Sokoly 2002, no. 229 (dated 296–99 AH / 908–12 CE, or 304–06 AH / 916–19 CE, Misr, by intermediation of Shafiʿ *mawla amir al-muʾminin*)

10 Metropolitan Museum of Art, New York, inv. no. 31.19.8: Upton 1930–31, p. 162, no. 1, fig. 1; Sokoly 2002, no. 230 (dated 296–99 AH / 908–12 CE, or 304–06 AH / 916–19 CE, *tiraz al-ʿamma* in Misr)

11 Ex Nahman Collection: *RCEA* 1931–91, vol. III, 1932, pp. 58–59, no. 899; Sokoly 2002, no. 236 (dated 298 AH / 910–11 CE, *tiraz al-ʿamma* in an unnamed location, by intermediation of ʿAbd al-Malik *mawla amir al-muʾminin*)

12 Textile Museum, Washington, DC, inv. no. 73.448: Kühnel and Bellinger 1952, p. 25, pl. X, detail pl. XL; Sokoly 2002, no. 308 (dated 304 AH / 916–17 CE (?), *tiraz al-ʿamma* in Misr, by intermediation of Shafiʿ *mawla amir al-muʾminin*)

13 Islamic Museum, Cairo, inv. no. 3950: *RCEA* 1931–91, vol. III, 1932, p. 105, no. 981 (dated 305 AH / 917–18 CE, Misr, by intermediation of Shafiʿ *mawla amir al-muʾminin*)

14 Islamic Museum, Cairo, no. 10387: *RCEA* 1931–91, vol. III, 1932, pp. 48–49, no. 883; Sokoly 2002, no. 217 (dated 296 AH / 908–09 CE, *tiraz al-ʿamma* in Damietta, by order of the vizier Abu al-Hasan ʿAli ibn Muhammad)

15 Ex Tano Collection: *RCEA* 1931–91, vol. III, 1932, p. 59, no. 900; Sokoly 2002, no. 237 (dated 298 AH / 910–11 CE, *tiraz al-ʿamma* in Misr, by order of the vizier Abu al-Hasan ʿAli ibn Muhammad)

16 Kelsey Museum of Archaeology, Ann Arbor, MI, inv. no. 22.507: Day 1937, pp. 427–28, no. 7, fig. 7;

Sokoly 2002, no. 241 (dated 298 AH / 910–11 CE, by order of the vizier Abu al-Hasan ʿAli ibn Muhammad)

17 Islamic Museum, Cairo, inv. no. 9595: *RCEA* 1931–91, vol. III, 1932, pp. 91–92, no. 958; Sokoly 2002, no. 272 (dated 301 AH / 913–14 CE, Misr, by order of the vizier Al-Hasan ibn Muhammad)

18 Textile Museum, Washington, DC, inv. no. 73.449: Kühnel and Bellinger 1952, pp. 21–22, 25, pl. XI (datable to 301–04 AH / 913–17, or 314–16 AH / 926–29 CE, *tiraz al-ʿamma* in an unnamed location, by order of the vizier ʿAli ibn ʿIsa by intermediation of Shafiʿ *mawla amir al-muʾminin*)

Cat. 9

1 Royal Ontario Museum, Toronto, inv. no. 978.76.49: Sokoly 2002, no. 197 (dated 295 AH / 907–08 CE, *tiraz al-khassa* in Tinnis, by order of the vizier by intermediation of Shafiʿ *mawla amir al-muʾminin*)

Cat. 10

1 Royal Ontario Museum, Toronto, inv. no. 978.76.935: Sokoly 2002, no. 206 (possibly datable to 316 AH / 928–29 CE, administrative data not mentioned)

2 Royal Ontario Museum, Toronto, inv. no. 978.76.167: Sokoly 2002, no. 207 (administrative data lost)

3 Royal Ontario Museum, Toronto, inv. no. 978.76.320: Sokoly 2002, no. 208 (possibly dated 320 AH / 932–33 CE, administrative data not mentioned, or lost)

4 Museum of Islamic Art, Cairo, inv. no. 10387: *RCEA* 1931–91, vol. III, 1932, pp. 48–49, no. 883; Sokoly 2002, no. 256 (dated 296 AH / 908–09 CE, *tiraz al-ʿamma* in Damietta, by order of the vizier Abu al-Hasan ʿAli ibn Muhammad by intermediation of Bishr al-khadim *mawla amir al-muʾminin*)

5 Benaki Museum, Athens, inv. no. 14828: *RCEA* 1931–91, vol. III, 1932, p. 70, no. 921; Sokoly 2002, no. 256 (dated 300 AH / 912–13 CE)

6 Royal Ontario Museum, Toronto, inv. no. 978.76.948: Sokoly 2002, no. 268 (dated 300 AH / 912–13 CE)

7 Benaki Museum, Athens, inv. no. 14802: *RCEA* 1931–91, vol. III, 1932, pp. 92–93, no. 960; Sokoly 2002, no. 274 (dated 301 AH / 913–14 CE, Misr, by order of the vizier Abu al-Husayn ʿAli ibn ʿIsa *mawla amir al-muʾminin*)

8 Ex Nahman Collection, Cairo: *RCEA* 1931–91, vol. III, 1932, p. 177, no. 1120; Sokoly 2002, no. 285 (datable to 301–04 AH / 913–17 CE, or 314–16 AH / 926–29 CE, *tiraz al-ʿamma* in Tinnis, by order of the vizier ʿAli ibn ʿIsa by intermediation of Shafiʿ *mawla amir al-muʾminin*)

9 Royal Ontario Museum, Toronto, inv. no. 978.76.985: Sokoly 2002, no. 292 (datable to 301–04 AH / 913–17 CE or 314–16 AH / 926–29 CE,

tiraz al-khassa in Misr(?), by order of the vizier ʿAli ibn ʿIsa by intermediation of Muhammad)

10 Ex Nahman Collection: *RCEA* 1931–91, vol. III, 1932, pp. 97–98, no. 968; Sokoly 2002, no. 299 (dated 303 AH / 915–16 CE, by order of the vizier ʿAli ibn ʿIsa)

11 Ex Nahman Collection: *RCEA* 1931–91, vol. III, 1932, p. 118, no. 1006; Sokoly 2002, no. 334 (dated 306 AH / 918–19 CE, by order of the vizier Hamid ibn al-ʿAbbas)

12 Ex Nahman Collection: *RCEA* 1931–91, vol. III, 1932, p. 150, no. 1070; Sokoly 2002, no. 348 (datable to 306–11 AH / 918–24 CE, *tiraz al-ʿamma* in Tinnis, by order of the vizier Hamid ibn al-ʿAbbas by intermediation of Shafiʿ *mawla amir al-muʾminin*)

13 Benaki Museum, Athens, inv. no. 14830: *RCEA* 1931–91, vol. III, 1932, p. 129, no. 1026; Sokoly 2002, no. 373 (dated 308 AH / 920–21 CE, *tiraz al-khassa* in Misr, by order of the vizier Hamid ibn al-ʿAbbas)

14 Kelsey Museum of Archeology, Ann Arbor, MI, inv. no. 22.509: Day 1937, pp. 429–30, fig. 9; Sokoly 2002, no. 382 (dated 308 AH / 920–21 CE)

15 Ex Nahman Collection: *RCEA* 1931–91, vol. III, 1932, p. 143, no. 1055; Sokoly 2002, no. 409 (dated 310 AH / 922–23 CE, by order of the vizier)

16 Museum of Islamic Art, Cairo, inv. no. 8717: *RCEA* 1931–91, vol. III, 1932, p. 171, no. 1107; Sokoly 2002, no. 441 (dated 316 AH / 928–29 CE, Misr, other administrative data lost)

17 Museum of Islamic Art, Cairo, inv. no. 8717: *RCEA* 1931–91, vol. III, 1932, p. 178, no. 1122; Sokoly 2002, no. 445 (dated 316 AH / 928–29, *tiraz* workshop in Misr, by order of the vizier Muhammad ibn ʿAli by intermediation of Shafiʿ al-Muqtadiri)

18 Brooklyn Museum, inv. no. 38.839: Sokoly 2002, no. 450 (datable to 316–18 AH / 928–31 CE, Damietta, by order of the vizier Muhammad ibn ʿAli by intermediation of Shafiʿ)

19 Royal Ontario Museum, Toronto, inv. no. 978.76.351: Sokoly 2002, no. 465 (administrative data lost)

20 Museum of Islamic Art, Cairo, inv. no. 8428: *RCEA* 1931–91, vol. III, 1932, p. 182, no. 1128; Maher 1977, p. 165, no. 46; Sokoly 2002, no. 472 (datable to 309 AH / 921–22 CE or 319 AH / 931–32 CE, place and ordering officer lost, by intermediation of Shafiʿ al-Muqtadiri *mawla amir al-muʾminin*)

21 Museum of Islamic Art, Cairo, inv. no. 8081: *RCEA* 1931–91, vol. III, 1932, p. 193, no. 1147; Sokoly 2002, no. 479 (administrative data lost)

22 Museum of Islamic Art, Cairo, inv. no. 8128: *RCEA* 1931–91,

vol. III, 1932, pp. 193–94, no. 1148; Sokoly 2002, no. 480 (date lost, *tiraz al-ʿamma*, place and ordering officer lost)

23 Museum of Islamic Art, Cairo, inv. no. 8166: *RCEA* 1931–91, vol. III, 1932, p. 194, no. 1149; Sokoly 2002, no. 481 (administrative data lost)

24 Museum of Islamic Art, Cairo, inv. no. 10295: *RCEA* 1931–91, vol. III, 1932, p. 203, no. 1174; Sokoly 2002, no. 503 (administrative data lost)

25 Museum of Islamic Art, Cairo, inv. no. 10347: *RCEA* 1931–91, vol. III, 1932, pp. 204–05, no. 1179; Sokoly 2002, no. 507 (administrative data lost)

26 Museum of Islamic Art, Cairo, inv. no. 10561: *RCEA* 1931–91, vol. III, 1932, p. 208, no. 1188; Sokoly 2002, no. 514 (administrative data lost)

27 Museum of Islamic Art, Cairo, inv. no. 10671: *RCEA* 1931–91, vol. III, 1932, p. 210, no. 1192; Sokoly 2002, no. 517 (administrative data lost)

28 Museum of Islamic Art, Cairo, inv. no. 11241: *RCEA* 1931–91, vol. III, 1932, p. 212, no. 1197; Sokoly 2002, no. 522 (administrative data lost)

29 Benaki Museum, Athens, inv. no. 14859: *RCEA* 1931–91, vol. III, 1932, p. 212, no. 1200; Sokoly 2002, no. 525 (administrative data lost)

30 Benaki Museum, Athens, inv. no. 14857: *RCEA* 1931–91, vol. IV, 1933, p. 2, no. 1205; Sokoly 2002, no. 530 (administrative data lost)

31 Benaki Museum, Athens, inv. no. 14833: *RCEA* 1931–91, vol. IV, 1933, p. 3, no. 1206; Sokoly 2002, no. 531 (administrative data lost)

32 Benaki Museum, Athens, 14812: *RCEA* 1931–91, vol. IV, 1933, p. 3, no. 1207; Sokoly 2002, no. 532 (administrative data lost)

33 Benaki Museum, Athens, inv. no. unknown: *RCEA* 1931–91, vol. IV, 1933, p. 6, no. 1215; Sokoly 2002, no. 539 (administrative data lost)

34 Ex Nahman Collection: *RCEA* 1931–91, vol. IV, 1933, p. 8, no. 1219; Sokoly 2002, no. 542 (administrative data lost)

35 Ex Nahman Collection: *RCEA* 1931–91, vol. IV, 1933, pp. 8–9, no. 1221; Sokoly 2002, no. 544 (administrative data lost)

36 Ex Nahman Collection: *RCEA* 1931–91, vol. IV, 1933, p. 9, no. 1222; Sokoly 2002, no. 545 (administrative data lost)

37 Ex Tano Collection: *RCEA* 1931–91, vol. IV, 1933, p. 10, no. 1225; Sokoly 2002, no. 548 (date lost, by order of the vizier, place of production and workshop lost)

38 Ex Tano Collection: *RCEA* 1931–91, vol. IV, 1933, pp. 11–12,

no. 1228; Sokoly 2002, no. 550 (administrative data lost)

39   Private collection: *RCEA* 1931–91, vol. IV, 1933, p. 12, no. 1229; Sokoly 2002, no. 551 (administrative data lost)

40   Bernisches Historisches Museum, Bern, inv. no. 962: Combe 1950, pp. 93–94; Sokoly 2002, no. 570 (administrative data lost)

41   Private collection: François de Ricqlès 1996, p. 59, lot 290; Sokoly 2002, no. 574.2 (administrative data lost)

42   Museum of Islamic Art, Cairo, inv. no. 12192: *RCEA* 1931–91, vol. IV, 1933, p. 205, no. 1204A; Wiet 1935b, p. 26, no. 89; Marzouk 1942, no. 4; Maher 1977, pp. 164–65, no. 44; Sokoly 2002, no. 577 (administrative data not mentioned)

43   Museum of Islamic Art, Cairo, inv. no. 10326: *RCEA* 1931–91, vol. III, 1932, p. 204, no. 1177; Sokoly 2002, no. 581 (administrative data not mentioned)

44   Museum of Islamic Art, Cairo, inv. no. 10458: *RCEA* 1931–91, vol. III, 1932, p. 207, no. 1185; Sokoly 2002, no. 582 (administrative data not mentioned)

45   Metropolitan Museum of Art, New York, inv. no. 29.179.1: Upton 1930–31, p. 166, no. 10, fig. 10; Sokoly 2002, no. 586 (administrative data not mentioned)

46   Museum of Islamic Art, Cairo, inv. no. 9388: *RCEA* 1931–91, vol. III, 1932, p. 178, no. 1122; Sokoly 2002, no. 445 (dated 316 AH / 928–29 CE, *tiraz* workshop in Misr, by order of the vizier Muhammad ibn 'Ali by intermediation of Shafi' al-Muqtadiri)

Cat. 11

1   Royal Ontario Museum, Toronto, inv. no. 978.76.351: Sokoly 2002, no. 465 (administrative data not mentioned; max. letter height 1.9 cm)

2   Royal Ontario Museum, Toronto, inv. no. 978.76.320: Sokoly 2002, no. 208 (dated 320 AH / 932–33 CE, place of production and ordering officer not mentioned, or lost)

3   Royal Ontario Museum, Toronto, inv. no. 978.76.948: Sokoly 2002, no. 268 (dated 300 AH / 912–13 CE, other administrative data not mentioned)

Cat. 12

1   Textile Museum, Washington, DC, inv. no. 73.449: Kühnel and Bellinger 1952, pp. 21–22, pl. XI; Sokoly 2002, no. 289 (dated 301–04 AH / 913–17 CE, or 314–16 AH / 926–29 CE, *tiraz al-'amma* in an unnamed location, by order of the vizier 'Ali ibn 'Isa by intermediation of Shafi' *mawla amir al-mu'minin*)

2   Textile Museum, Washington, DC, inv. no. 73.13: Kühnel and Bellinger 1952, p. 21, pl. X; Sokoly 2002, no. 259 (dated 300 AH / 912–13 CE, *tiraz al-'amma* in Misr, by order of the vizier by intermediation of Shafi')

3   Museum of Islamic Art, Cairo, inv. no. 10369: *RCEA* 1931–91, vol. III, 1932, p. 67, no. 914; Sokoly 2002, no. 250 (dated 300 AH / 912–13 CE, *tiraz al-'amma* in Misr, by intermediation of Shafi' *mawla amir al-mu'minin*)

4   Museum für Islamische Kunst, Berlin, inv. no. 5560: Kühnel 1933, p. 60, no. 1, pl. II, fig. 2; Sokoly 2002, no. 575 (*tiraz al-'amma* in Misr, by order of the vizier 'Ali ibn 'Isa by intermediation of Shafi' *mawla amir al-mu'minin*)

5   Museum für Islamische Kunst, Berlin, inv. no. 6417: Kühnel, 1952, pp. 166–67, no. IIIa, fig. 4; Sokoly 2002, no. 296 (dated 303 AH / 915–16 CE, *tiraz al-'amma* in Misr, by order of the vizier ['Ali ibn 'Isa] by intermediation of Shafi' *mawla amir al-mu'minin*)

6   Museum of Islamic Art, Cairo, inv. no. 10369: *RCEA* 1931–91, vol. III, 1932, p. 67, no. 914; Sokoly 2002, no. 250 (dated 300 AH / 912–13 CE)

7   Museum of Islamic Art, Cairo, inv. no. 10758: *RCEA* 1931–91, vol. III, 1932, p. 69, no. 919; Sokoly 2002, no. 254 (dated 300 AH / 912–13 CE, *tiraz al-khassa* in Misr, by intermediation of Shafi' al-Muqtadiri *mawla amir al-mu'minin*)

8   Textile Museum, Washington, DC, inv. no. 73.13: Kühnel and Bellinger 1952, p. 21, pl. X, detail pl. XL; Sokoly 2002, no. 259 (dated 300 AH / 912–13 CE, *tiraz al-'amma* in Misr, by order of the vizier by intermediation of Shafi')

9   Royal Ontario Museum, Toronto, inv. no. 978.76.789: Sokoly 2002, no. 262 (dated 300 AH / 912–13 CE, Misr, by order of the vizier)

10 Royal Ontario Museum, Toronto, inv. no. 978.76.388: Sokoly 2002, no. 266 (dated 300 AH / 912–13 CE, Misr?, by order of the vizier)

11 Los Angeles County Museum of Art, inv. no. M.73.5.620: Pal 1973, p. 197, no. 400; Sokoly 2002, no. 261 (probably dated 300 AH / 912–13 CE, probably *tiraz* workshop in Tinnis)

12 Museum of Islamic Art, Cairo, inv. no. 9791: *RCEA* 1931–91, vol. III, 1932, pp. 89–90, no. 954; Sokoly 2002, no. 257 (dated 300 AH / 912–13 CE, *tiraz al-khassa* in Madinat al-Salam)

13 Royal Ontario Museum, Toronto, inv. no. 978.76.400: Sokoly 2002, no. 264 (dated 300 AH / 912–13 CE, *tiraz al-khassa* in Madinat al-Salam)

14 Museum of Islamic Art, Cairo, inv. no. 10122: *RCEA* 1931–91, vol. 1932, p. 66, no. 912; Sokoly 2002, no. 249 (dated 300 AH / 912–13 CE, place of production and ordering officer not mentioned)

15 Museum of Islamic Art, Cairo, inv. no. 10472: *RCEA* 1931–91, vol. III, 1932, p. 67, no. 915; Sokoly 2002, no. 251 (dated 300 AH / 912–13 CE, by order of the vizier)

16 Museum of Islamic Art, Cairo, inv. no. 10475: *RCEA* 1931–91, vol. III, 1932, p. 68, no. 916; Sokoly 2002, no. 252 (dated 300 AH / 912–13 CE, place of production and ordering officer not mentioned)

17 Museum of Islamic Art, Cairo, inv. no. 10623: *RCEA* 1931–91, vol. III, 1932, pp. 68–69, no. 918; Sokoly 2002, no. 253 (dated 300 AH / 912–13 CE, place of production and ordering officer not mentioned)

18 Benaki Museum, Athens, inv. no. 14829: *RCEA* 1931–91, vol. III, 1932, pp. 69–70, no. 920; Sokoly 2002, no. 255 (dated 300 AH / 912–13 CE, place of production and ordering officer not mentioned)

19 Benaki Museum, Athens, inv. no. 14828: *RCEA* 1931–91, vol. III, 1932, p. 70, no. 921; Sokoly 2002, no. 256 (dated 300 AH / 912–13 CE, place of production and ordering officer not mentioned)

20 Museum of Islamic Art, Cairo, inv. no. 10447: *RCEA* 1931–91, vol. III, 1932, p. 207, no. 1184; Sokoly 2002, no. 270 (dated 300 AH / 912–13 CE, by order of the vizier by intermediation of [...] *mawla amir al-mu'minin*)

21 Museum of Islamic Art, Cairo, inv. no. 10461: *RCEA* 1931–91, vol. III, 1932, p. 220, no. 919A; Sokoly 2002, no. 258 (dated 300 AH / 912–13 CE, place of production and ordering officer not mentioned)

22 Textile Museum, Washington, DC, inv. no. 73.635: Kühnel and Bellinger 1952, p. 22, pl. IX; Sokoly 2002, no. 260 (dated 300 AH / 912–13 CE, place of production and ordering officer not mentioned)

23 Cleveland Museum of Art, inv. no. 32.29: Sokoly 2002, no. 585 (probably dated 300 AH / 912–13 CE, place of production and ordering officer not mentioned)

24 Royal Ontario Museum, Toronto, inv. no. 978.76.418: Sokoly 2002, no. 263 (dated 300 AH / 912–13 CE, place of production and ordering officer not mentioned)

25 Royal Ontario Museum, Toronto, inv. no. 978.76.84: Sokoly 2002, no. 265 (dated 300 AH / 912–13 CE, place of production and ordering officer not mentioned)

26 Royal Ontario Museum, Toronto, inv. no. 978.76.948: Sokoly 2002, no. 268 (dated 300 AH / 912–13 CE, place of production and ordering officer not mentioned)

Cat. 13

1   Dumbarton Oaks, Washington, DC, inv. no. 33.35: Glidden and Thompson, 1988, pp. 122–23, no. 2, fig. 2; Sokoly 2002, no. 338 (dated 306 AH / 918–19 CE, *tiraz* workshop in Tinnis, by order of the vizier Hamid ibn al-'Abbas by

intermediation of Shafi' *mawla amir al-mu'minin*)

2   Biblioteca Apostolica Vaticana, Vatican City, inv. no. 6788: Cornu 1992, pp. 137–39; Sokoly 2002, no. 353 (datable to 306–311 AH / 918–24 CE, *tiraz al-'amma* in Tinnis, by order of the vizier Hamid bin al-'Abbas by intermediation of Shafi' *mawla amir al-mu'minin*)

3   Textile Museum, Washington, DC, inv. no. 73.530: Kühnel and Bellinger 1952, p. 26, pl. IX, detail pl. XXXIX; Sokoly 2002, no. 366 (dated 307 AH / 919–20 CE, *tiraz* workshop in Tinnis, by intermediation of Shafi' *mawla amir al-mu'minin*)

4   Biblioteca Apostolica Vaticana, Vatican City, inv. no. 6786: Cornu 1992, pp. 134–36; Sokoly 2002, no. 369 (dated 307 AH / 919–20 CE, Tinnis, by order of the vizier Hamid ibn al-'Abbas by intermediation of Shafi' *mawla amir al-mu'minin*)

5   Biblioteca Apostolica Vaticana, Vatican City, inv. no. 6789: Cornu 1992, pp. 136–37; Sokoly 2002, no. 379 (dated 308 AH / 920–21 CE, Misr, by order of the vizier)

6   Cleveland Museum of Art, inv. no. 32.28: Sokoly 2002, no. 563 (administrative data lost)

Cat. 14

1   Benaki Museum, Athens, inv. no. 14810: *RCEA* 1931–91, vol. III, 1932, p. 95, no. 964; Sokoly 2002, no. 295 (dated 302 AH / 914–15 CE, by order of the vizier Abu al-Hasan 'Ali ibn 'Isa)

2   Royal Ontario Museum, Toronto, inv. no. 978.76.3: Sokoly 2002, no. 215 (datable to 295–96 AH / 907–09, *tiraz al-'amma* in Misr, by order of the vizier [...] al-'Abbas)

3   Royal Ontario Museum, Toronto, inv. no. 978.76.36: Sokoly 2002, no. 219 (dated 296 AH / 908–09 CE, *tiraz al-'amma* in Misr, by order of the vizier Abu [Ahmad(?)] bin 'Ali bin Muhammad by intermediation of Shafi' *mawla amir al-mu'minin*)

4   Royal Ontario Museum, Toronto, inv. no. 978.76.2: Sokoly 2002, no. 229 (datable to 296–99 AH / 908–12 CE, or 304–06 AH / 916–19 CE, Misr, by order of the vizier by intermediation of Shafi' *mawla amir al-mu'minin*)

5   Textile Museum, Washington, DC, inv. no. 73.13: Kühnel and Bellinger 1952, p. 21, pl. X; Sokoly 2002, no. 259 (dated 300 AH / 912–13 CE, *tiraz al-'amma* in Misr, by order of the vizier by intermediation of Shafi')

6   Metropolitan Museum of Art, New York, inv. no. 29.179.18: Upton 1930–31, p. 163, no. 3, fig. 3; Sokoly 2002, no. 293 (dated 301–04 AH / 913–17 CE or 314–16 AH / 926–29 CE, *tiraz al-'amma* in Misr, by order of the vizier 'Ali ibn 'Isa by intermediation of Shafi' al-Muqtadiri *mawla amir al-mu'minin*)

7 Textile Museum, Washington, DC, inv. no. 73.189: Kühnel and Bellinger 1952, p. 24, pl. XI; Sokoly 2002, no. 301 (dated 303 AH / 915–16 CE; Misr, by order of the vizier 'Ali ibn 'Isa by intermediation of Shafi' al-Muqtadiri)

8 Textile Museum, Washington, DC, inv. no. 73.448: Kühnel and Bellinger 1952, p. 25, pl. X; Sokoly 2002, no. 308 (possibly dated 304 AH / 916–17 CE, *tiraz al-'amma* in Misr, by order of the vizier 'Ali ibn Muhammad by intermediation of Shafi' *mawla amir al-mu'minin*)

9 Biblioteca Apostolica Vaticana, Vatican City, inv. no. 6787: Cornu 1992, pp. 131–32; Sokoly 2002, no. 368 (dated 307 AH / 919–20 CE, Misr, by order of the vizier Hamid ibn al-'Abbas by intermediation of Shafi' *mawla amir al-mu'minin*)

10 Metropolitan Museum of Art, New York, inv. no. 31.19.10: Upton 1930–31, p. 164, no. 6, fig. 6; Sokoly 2002, no. 383 (dated 308 AH / 920–21 CE, *tiraz al-'amma* in Misr, by order of the vizier Hamid ibn al-'Abbas by intermediation of Shafi' al-Muqtadiri *mawla amir al-mu'minin*)

11 Cleveland Museum of Art, inv. no. 32.19: Sokoly 2002, no. 414 (dated 310 AH / 922 CE, Misr, by order of the vizier Hamid ibn al-'Abbas by intermediation of Shafi' *mawla amir al-mu'minin*)

12 Royal Ontario Museum, Toronto, inv. no. 978.76.298: Sokoly 2002, no. 439 (dated 312 AH / 924–25 CE, *tiraz al-khassa* in Misr, by order of the vizier 'Ali ibn Muhammad by intermediation of Shafi' al-Muqtadiri *mawla amir al-mu'minin*)

13 Keir Collection of Islamic Art, on loan to the Dallas Museum of Art, inv. no. 71: Spuhler 1978, pp. 141–42, no. 71; Sokoly 2002, no. 454 (dated 318 AH / 930–31 CE, Misr, by order of the vizier 'Ali ibn 'Isa by intermediation of Shafi' *mawla amir al-mu'minin*)

14 Museum für Islamische Kunst, Berlin, inv. no. 5560: Kühnel 1933, p. 60, no. 1, pl. II, fig. 2; Sokoly 2002, no. 575 (date not mentioned, *tiraz al-'amma* in Misr, by order of vizier 'Ali ibn 'Isa by intermediation of Shafi' *mawla amir al-mu'minin*)

Cat. 15

1 Cleveland Museum of Art, inv. no. 32.19: Sokoly 2002, no. 414 (dated 310 AH / 922–23 CE, Misr, by order of the vizier Hamid ibn al-'Abbas by intermediation of Shafi' *mawla amir al-mu'minin*)

2 Royal Ontario Museum, Toronto, inv. no. 978.76.318: Sokoly 2002, no. 195 (dated 306 AH / 918–19 CE, Misr, by order of the amir)

3 Erzherzog Rainer Collection, Österreichische Nationalbibliothek, Vienna, inv. no. Ar. L. Nr. 19: Karabacek et al. 1894, pp. 227–28, no. 849; Sokoly 2002, no. 214 (datable to 295–96 AH / 907–09 CE,

by order of the vizier Abu Ahmad al-'Abbas bin al-Hasan)

4 Royal Ontario Museum, Toronto, inv. no. 978.76.36: Sokoly 2002, no. 219 (dated 296 AH / 908–09 CE, *tiraz al-'amma* in Misr, by order of the vizier Abu [Ahmad] bin 'Ali bin Muhammad)

5 Kelsey Museum of Archaeology, Ann Arbor, MI, inv. no. 22.507: Day 1937, pp. 427–28, no. 7, fig. 7; Sokoly 2002, no. 241 (dated 298 AH / 910–11 CE, *tiraz al-'amma* in Misr, by order of the vizier Abu al-Hasan 'Ali Muhammad by intermediation of Bishr *mawla amir al-mu'minin*)

6 Textile Museum, Washington, DC, inv. no. 73.13: Kühnel and Bellinger 1952, p. 21, pl. X, detail pl. XL; Sokoly 2002, no. 259 (dated 300 AH / 912–13 CE, *tiraz al-'amma* in Misr, by order of the vizier by intermediation of Shafi')

7 Royal Ontario Museum, Toronto, inv. no. 978.76.789: Sokoly 2002, no. 262 (by order of the vizier)

8 Royal Ontario Museum, Toronto, inv. no. 978.76.330: Sokoly 2002, no. 267 (administrative data lost)

9 Bouvier Collection, inv. no. JFB I 131: Geneva 1993, pp. 172–74, no. 98; Sokoly 2002, no. 290 (datable to 301–04 AH / 913–17 CE or 314–16 AH / 926–29 CE, by order of the vizier 'Ali ibn 'Isa *mawla amir al-mu'minin*)

10 Royal Ontario Museum, Toronto, inv. no. 978.76.42: Sokoly 2002, no. 309 (dated 304 AH / 916–17 CE, by order of the vizier 'Ali ibn 'Isa by intermediation of Shafi' *mawla amir al-mu'minin*)

11 Textile Museum, Washington, DC, inv. no. 73.444: Kühnel and Bellinger 1952, p. 21, pl. XI; Sokoly 2002, no. 337 (dated 306 AH / 918–19 CE, Misr, ordering officer not mentioned)

12 Royal Ontario Museum, Toronto, inv. no. 978.76.70: Sokoly 2002, no. 391.1 (dated 309 AH / 921–22 CE, Misr, by order of the vizier Hamid ibn al-'Abbas)

13 Ashmolean Museum, Oxford, inv. no. 1988.31: Sokoly 2002, no. 467 (datable to 308 AH / 920–21 CE or 318 AH / 930–31 CE, place of production and ordering officer lost, by intermediation of Shafi')

14 Textile Museum, Washington, DC, inv. no. 59.17.5: Sokoly 2002, no. 471 (date lost, Misr, ordering officer not mentioned, or lost)

Cat. 16

1 Bouvier Collection, inv. no. JFB I 1: Geneva 1993, pp. 171–72, no. 97; Sokoly 2002, no. 557 (administrative data lost)

2 Royal Ontario Museum, Toronto, inv. no. 978.76.789: Sokoly 2002, no. 262 (dated 300 AH / 912–13 CE, Misr, by order of the vizier; max. letter height 1.6 cm)

3 Textile Museum, Washington, DC, inv. no. 73.449: Kühnel and Bellinger 1952, pp. 21–22, pl. XI;

Sokoly 2002, no. 289 (datable to 301–04 AH / 913–17 CE, or 314–16 AH / 926–29 CE, *tiraz al-'amma* in an unnamed location, by order of the vizier 'Ali ibn 'Isa by intermediation of Shafi' *mawla amir al-mu'minin*; max. letter height 1.6 cm)

4 Textile Museum, Washington, DC, inv. no. 73.448: Kühnel and Bellinger 1952, p. 25, pl. X; Sokoly 2002, no. 308 (probably datable to 304 AH / 916–17 CE, *tiraz al-'amma* in Misr, by order of the vizier 'Ali ibn Muhammad by intermediation of Shafi' *mawla amir al-mu'minin*; max. letter height 1.8 cm)

5 Biblioteca Apostolica Vaticana, Vatican City, inv. no. 6787: Cornu 1992, pp. 131–32; Sokoly 2002, no. 368 (dated 307 AH / 919–20 CE, Misr, by order of the vizier Hamid ibn al-'Abbas by intermediation of Shafi' *mawla amir al-mu'minin*; max. letter height 3.0 cm)

6 Metropolitan Museum of Art, New York, inv. no. 31.19.10: Upton 1930–31, p. 164, no. 6, fig. 6; Sokoly 2002, no. 383 (dated 308 AH / 920–21 CE, *tiraz al-'amma* in Misr, by order of the vizier Hamid ibn al-'Abbas by intermediation of Shafi' Al-Muqtadiri *mawla amir al-mu'minin*; max. letter height 1.8 cm)

7 Royal Ontario Museum, Toronto, inv. no. 978.76.70: Sokoly 2002, no. 391.1 (dated 309 AH / 921–22 CE, Misr, by order of the vizier Hamid ibn al-'Abbas; max. letter height 1.9 cm)

8 Royal Ontario Museum, Toronto, inv. no. 978.76.787: Sokoly 2002, no. 416 (date not mentioned, or lost, by order of the vizier Hamid ibn al-'Abbas; max. letter height 2.0 cm)

9 Royal Ontario Museum, Toronto, inv. no. 978.76.787: Sokoly 2002, no. 416.1 (dated 310 AH / 922–23 CE, Misr, by order of the vizier Hamid ibn al-'Abbas by intermediation of Shafi' *mawla amir al-mu'minin*; max. letter height 2.0 cm)

10 Royal Ontario Museum, Toronto, inv. no. 978.76.298: Sokoly 2002, no. 439 (dated 312 AH / 924–25 CE, *tiraz al-khassa* in Misr, by order of the vizier 'Ali ibn Muhammad by intermediation of Shafi' *mawla amir al-mu'minin*; max. letter height 1.9 cm)

Cat. 17

1 Bouvier Collection, inv. no. JFB I 11: Geneva 1993, pp. 168–69, no. 95; Sokoly 2002, no. 218 (dated 296 AH / 908–09 CE, *tiraz al-'amma* in Misr, by order of the vizier; max. letter height 0.6 cm)

2 Royal Ontario Museum, Toronto, inv. no. 978.76.2: Sokoly 2002, no. 229 (datable to 296–99 AH / 908–12 CE, or 304–06 AH / 916–19 CE, Misr, by order of the vizier 'Ali ibn Muhammad by intermediation of Shafi' *mawla amir al-mu'minin*; max. letter height 0.6 cm)

3 Textile Museum, Washington, DC, inv. no. 73.443: Kühnel and

Bellinger 1952, pp. 19–20, pl. X; Sokoly 2002, no. 234 (dated 297 AH / 909–10 CE, *tiraz al-'amma* in Misr; max. letter height 0.5 cm)

4 Textile Museum, Washington, DC, inv. no. 73.31: Kühnel and Bellinger 1952, pp. 23–24, pl. X; Sokoly, no. 275 (dated 301 AH / 913–14 CE, *tiraz al-'amma* in Misr, by order of the vizier 'Ali bin 'Isa *mawla amir al-mu'minin*; max. letter height 0.5 cm)

5 Royal Ontario Museum, Toronto, inv. no. 978.76.29: Sokoly 2002, no. 302 (datable to 303 AH / 915–16 CE, by order of the vizier 'Ali ibn 'Isa by intermediation of Shafi' al-Muqtadiri *mawla amir al-mu'minin*; max. letter height 0.6 cm)

6 Textile Museum, Washington, DC, inv. no. 59.17.3: Sokoly 2002, no. 394 (dated 310 AH / 922–23 CE, Misr, by order of the vizier Abu (Muhammad?); max. letter height 0.8 cm)

7 Metropolitan Museum of Art, New York, inv. no. 31.106.34: Sokoly 2002, no. 420 (dated 310 AH / 922–23 CE, *tiraz al-khassa* in Misr, by order of the vizier 'Abdallah bin Muhammad by intermediation of Shafi' *mawla amir al-mu'minin*; max. letter height 0.5 cm)

8 Keir Collection of Islamic Art, on loan to the Dallas Museum of Art, inv. no. K.1.2014.597: Spuhler 1978, pp. 141–42, no. 71; Sokoly 2002, no. 454 (dated 318 AH / 930–31 CE, Misr, by order of the vizier 'Ali ibn 'Isa, by intermediation of Shafi' *mawla amir al-mu'minin*; max. letter height 0.7 cm)

Cat. 18

1 Royal Ontario Museum, Toronto, inv. no. 978.76.2: Sokoly 2002, no. 229 (datable to 296–99 AH / 908–12 CE or 304–06 AH / 916–19 CE, Misr, by order of the vizier 'Ali ibn Muhammad by intermediation by Shafi' *mawla amir al-mu'minin*; max. letter height 0.6 cm)

2 Textile Museum, Washington, DC, inv. no. 73.13: Kühnel and Bellinger 1952, p. 21, pl. X, detail pl. XL; Sokoly 2002, no. 259 (dated 300 AH / 912–13 CE, *tiraz al-'amma* in Misr, by order of the vizier by intermediation of Shafi'; max. letter height 0.8 cm)

3 Royal Ontario Museum, Toronto, inv. no. 978.76.388: Sokoly 2002, no. 266 (dated 300 AH / 912–13 CE, Misr(?), by order of the vizier; max. letter height 1.5 cm)

4 Royal Ontario Museum, Toronto, inv. no. 978.76.330: Sokoly 2002, no. 267 (administrative data lost; max. letter height 1.3 cm)

5 Royal Ontario Museum, Toronto, inv. no. 978.76.29: Sokoly 2002, no. 302 (dated 303 AH / 915–16 CE, by order of the vizier 'Ali ibn 'Isa by intermediation of Shafi' al-Muqtadiri *mawla amir al-mu'minin*; max. letter height 0.6 cm)

6 Cleveland Museum of Art, inv. no. 32.18: Sokoly 2002, no. 351

(datable to 306–11 AH / 918–24 CE, Misr, by order of the vizier Hamid bin al-'Abbas; max. letter height 0.9 cm)

7 Cleveland Museum of Art, inv. no. 32.19: Sokoly 2002, no. 414 (dated 310 AH / 922–23 CE, Misr, by order of the vizier Hamid ibn al-'Abbas by intermediation of Shafi' *mawla amir al-mu'minin*; max. letter height 1.0 cm)

8 Keir Collection of Islamic Art, on loan to the Dallas Museum of Art, inv. no. 71: Spuhler 1978, pp. 141–42, no. 71; Sokoly 2002, no. 454 (dated 318 AH / 930–31 CE, Misr, by order of the vizier 'Ali ibn 'Isa by intermediation of Shafi' *mawla amir al-mu'minin*; max. letter height 0.7 cm)

9 Cleveland Museum of Art, inv. no. 32.26: Sokoly 2002, no. 584 (by order of the vizier by intermediation of a *mawla amir al-mu'minin*; max. letter height 0.7 cm)

10 Textile Museum, Washington, DC, inv. no. 73.12: Kühnel and Bellinger 1952, pp. 36–37, pl. XVI; Sokoly 2002, no. 635 (dated 322 AH / 933–34 CE, Misr, by order of the vizier 'Ali ibn Muhammad by intermediation of Shafi' *mawla amir al-mu'minin*; max. letter height 0.9 cm)

11 Textile Museum, Washington, DC, inv. no. 73.630: Kühnel and Bellinger 1952, pp. 37–38, pl. XVI; Sokoly 2002, no. 648 (datable to 322–24 AH / 933–36 CE or 326–27 AH / 937–39 CE, *tiraz al-khassa* in Misr, by order of the vizier Muhammad ibn 'Ali by intermediation of 'Ubayyid *mawla amir al-mu'minin*; max. letter height 0.9 cm)

Cat. 19

1 Royal Ontario Museum, Toronto, inv. no. 978.76.49: Sokoly 2002, no. 197 (dated 295 AH / 907–08 CE, *tiraz al-khassa* Tinnis, by order of the vizier by intermediation of Shafi' *mawla amir al-mu'minin*; max. letter height 1.6 cm)

2 Royal Ontario Museum, Toronto, inv. no. 978.76.71: Sokoly 2002, no. 199 (datable to 299–301 AH / 911–14 CE, or 312–13 AH / 924–26 CE, *tiraz al-khassa* in Tinnis, by order of the vizier Muhammad ibn 'Ubaydallah; max. letter height 1.8 cm)

3 Royal Ontario Museum, Toronto, inv. no. 978.76.321: Sokoly 2002, no. 202 (reign of al-Muqtadir, administrative data lost; max. letter height 1.4 cm)

4 Metropolitan Museum of Art, New York, inv. no. 31.106.52: Schimmel 1992, p. 13, fig. d; Sokoly 2002, no. 269 (dated 300 AH / 912–13 CE, administrative data not mentioned)

5 Textile Museum, Washington, DC, inv. no. 73.15: Kühnel and Bellinger 1952, p. 30, pl. XIV; Sokoly 2002, no. 291 (datable to 301–04 AH / 913–17 CE, or 314–16 AH / 926–29 CE, by order of the wazir 'Ali ibn 'Isa; max. letter height 2.3 cm)

6 Royal Ontario Museum, Toronto, inv. no. 978.76.416: Sokoly 2002, no. 312.1 (dated 305 AH / 917–18 CE, administrative data not mentioned, or lost; max. letter height 2.0 cm)

7 Royal Ontario Museum, Toronto, inv. no. 978.76.934: Sokoly, no. 339 (dated 306 AH / 918–19 CE, *tiraz* workshop in Tinnis, by order of the vizier Hamid ibn al-'Abbas by intermediation of Shafi' *mawla amir al-mu'minin*; max. letter height 2.2 cm)

8 Royal Ontario Museum, Toronto, inv. no. 978.76.417: Sokoly 2002, no. 355 (datable to 306–11 AH / 918–24 CE, by order of the vizier 'Ali ibn 'Isa; max. letter height 1.3 cm)

9 Metropolitan Museum of Art, New York, inv. no. 31.19.12: Upton 1930–31, p. 164, no. 5, fig 5; Walker and Froom 1992, pp. 35–6, no. 24; Sokoly 2002, no. 357 (datable to 306–11 AH / 918–24 CE, by order of the vizier Hamid bin al-'Abbas; max. letter height 2.6 cm)

10 Royal Ontario Museum, Toronto, inv. no. 978.76.56: Sokoly 2002, no. 357.1 (dated 306–11 AH / 918–24 CE, by order of the vizier Hamid bin al-'Abbas; max. letter height 3.3 cm)

11 Cooper-Hewitt Museum, New York, inv. no. 1972.81.40: Sokoly 2002, no. 380 (dated 308 AH / 920–21 CE, Misr, administrative data not mentioned, or lost; max. letter height 2.1 cm)

12 Metropolitan Museum of Art, New York, inv. no. 31.19.9: Upton 1930–31, p. 164, no. 7, fig. 7; Sokoly 2002, no. 381 (dated 308 AH / 920–21, administrative data not mentioned; max. letter height 2.4 cm)

13 Textile Museum, Washington, DC, inv. no. 73.660: Kühnel and Bellinger 1952, p. 28, pl. XIV; Sokoly 2002, no. 391 (dated 309 AH / 921–22 CE, *tiraz* workshop in Tinnis?, by order of the vizier Hamid ibn al-'Abbas by intermediation of Shafi' *mawla amir al-mu'minin*; max. letter height 2.5 cm)

14 Kelsey Museum of Archeology, Ann Arbor, MI, inv. no. 22.510: Day 1937, p. 430, fig. 10; Sokoly 2002, no. 431 (dated 314 AH / 926–27 CE, by order of the vizier 'Abdallah bin Muhammad; max. letter height 4.9 cm)

15 Bouvier Collection, inv. no. JFB I 3: Geneva 1993, p. 170, no. 96; Sokoly 2002, no. 556 (reign of al-Muqtadir, administrative data lost; max. letter height 1.5 cm)

16 Textile Museum, Washington, DC, inv. no. 73.648: Kühnel and Bellinger 1952, pp. 29–30, pl. XIV; Sokoly 2002, no. 556 (reign of al-Muqtadir, administrative data lost; max. letter height 2.0 cm)

17 Biblioteca Apostolica Vaticana, Vatican City, inv. no. 6790: Cornu 1992, pp. 138–40; Sokoly 2002, no. 564 (reign of al-Muqtadir, administrative data lost; max. letter height 2.0 cm)

18 Biblioteca Apostolica Vaticana, Vatican City, inv. no. 6904: Cornu 1992, pp. 140–41; Sokoly 2002, no. 565 (reign of al-Muqtadir, administrative data lost; max. letter height 2.0 cm)

19 Cooper-Hewitt Museum, New York, inv. no. 1938.83.1: Sokoly 2002, no. 574.1 (reign of al-Muqtadir, administrative data lost)

20. Metropolitan Museum of Art, New York, inv. no. 29.179.30: Sokoly 2002. no. 621 (datable to 320–22 AH / 932–34 CE, administrative data lost; max. letter height 1.1 cm)

21 Royal Ontario Museum, Toronto, inv. no. 978.76.414: Sokoly 2002, no. 627 (datable to 322–29 AH / 934–41 CE, administrative data lost; max. letter height unknown)

22 Royal Ontario Museum, Toronto, inv. no. 978.76.389: Sokoly 2002, no. 630 (datable to 322–29 AH / 934–41 CE, administrative data lost; max. letter height 1.6 cm)

23 Textile Museum, Washington, DC, inv. no. 73.454: Kühnel and Bellinger 1952, pp. 41–42, pl. XVII; Sokoly 2002, no. 633 (datable 322–29 AH / 934–40 CE, administrative data not mentioned; max. letter height 1.4 cm)

24 Royal Ontario Museum, Toronto, inv. no. 978.76.69: Sokoly 2002, no. 676 (dated 327 AH / 939–40 CE, administrative data not mentioned; max. letter height 1.6 cm)

25 Cleveland Museum of Art, inv. no. 32.20: Sokoly 2002, no. 715 (datable to 322–29 AH / 934–41 CE, administrative data lost; max. letter height 2.0 cm)

26 Royal Ontario Museum, Toronto, inv. no. 978.76.10: Sokoly 2002, no. 723 (datable to 322–29 AH / 934–41 CE, ordered by the wazir 'Ali [ibn Muhammad?]; max. letter height 1.5 cm)

Cat. 20

1 Metropolitan Museum of Art, New York, inv. no. 31.106.52: Schimmel 1992, p. 13, fig. d; Sokoly 2002, no. 269 (dated 310 AH / 922–23 CE, administrative data lost)

2 Royal Ontario Museum, Toronto, inv. no. 978.76.416: Sokoly 2002, no. 312.1 (dated 305 AH / 917–18 CE, administrative data lost)

Cat. 21

1 Royal Ontario Museum, Toronto, inv. no. 978.76.416: Sokoly 2002, no. 312.1 (dated 305 AH / 917–18 CE, administrative data lost)

2 Royal Ontario Museum, Toronto, inv. no. 978.76.417: Sokoly 2002, no. 355 (datable to 306–311 AH / 918–24 CE, by order of the vizier 'Ali ibn 'Isa)

3 Metropolitan Museum of Art, New York, inv. no. 31.19.12: Upton 1930–31, p. 164, no. 5, fig. 5; Sokoly 2002, no. 357 (datable to 306–311 AH / 918–24 CE, by order of the vizier Hamid ibn al-'Abbas)

4 Royal Ontario Museum, Toronto, inv. no. 978.76.56: Sokoly 2002, no. 357.1 (datable to 306–311 AH / 918–24 CE, by order of the vizier Hamid ibn al-'Abbas)

5 Metropolitan Museum of Art, New York, inv. no. 31.19.9: Upton 1930–31, p. 164, no. 7, fig. 7; Sokoly 2002, no. 381 (dated 308 AH / 920–21 CE, administrative data not mentioned)

6 Royal Ontario Museum, Toronto, inv. no. 978.76.70: Sokoly 2002, no. 391.1 (dated 309 AH / 921–22 CE, Misr, by order of the vizier Hamid ibn al-'Abbas)

7 Royal Ontario Museum, Toronto, inv. no. 978.76.402: Sokoly 2002, no. 392 (possibly dated 309 AH / 921–22 CE, administrative data not mentioned)

8 Royal Ontario Museum, Toronto, inv. no. 978.76.6: Sokoly 2002, no. 417 (dated 310 AH / 922–23 CE, by order of the vizier 'Ali ibn 'Isa)

9 Royal Ontario Museum, Toronto, inv. no. 978.76.390: Sokoly 2002, no. 419 (dated 310 AH / 922–23 CE, administrative data lost or not mentioned)

10 Kelsey Museum of Archaeology, Ann Arbor, MI, inv. no. 22.510: Day 1937, p. 430, no. 10, fig. 10; Sokoly 2002, no. 431 (dated 314 AH / 926–27 CE, by order of the vizier 'Abdallah bin Muhammad)

11 Kelsey Museum of Archaeology, Ann Arbor, MI, inv. no. 22.511: Day 1937, p. 431, no. 11, fig. 11; Sokoly 2002, no. 447 (dated 316 AH / 928–29 CE, by order of the vizier 'Ali ibn 'Isa)

12 Bouvier Collection, inv. no. JFB I 3: Geneva 1993, p. 170, no. 96; Sokoly 2002, no. 556 (date and administrative data lost)

13 Textile Museum, Washington, DC, inv. no. 73.648: Kühnel and Bellinger 1952, pp. 29–30, pl. XIV; Sokoly 2002, no. 558 (date and administrative data lost)

14 Biblioteca Apostolica Vaticana, Vatican City, inv. no. 6790: Cornu 1992, pp. 138–40; Sokoly 2002, no. 564 (date and administrative data lost)

15 Biblioteca Apostolica Vaticana, Vatican City, inv. no. 6904: Cornu 1992, pp. 140–41; Sokoly 2002, no. 565 (date and administrative data lost)

16 Cooper-Hewitt Museum, New York, inv. no. 1938.83.1: Sokoly 2002, no. 574.1 (date and administrative data lost)

Cat. 23

1 Royal Ontario Museum, Toronto, inv. no. 978.76: Sokoly 2002, no. 591 (by intermediation of Shafi')

2 Royal Ontario Museum, Toronto, inv. no. 978.76.52: Sokoly 2002, no. 592 (administrative data lost)

3 Royal Ontario Museum, Toronto, inv. no. 978.76.452: Sokoly 2002, no. 593 (administrative data lost)

4 Museum of Islamic Art, Cairo, inv. no. 10202: *RCEA* 1931–91,

vol. IV, 1933, p. 13, no. 1231; Sokoly 2002, no. 595 (possibly dated 320 AH / 932–33 CE, by order of the vizier Muhammad ibn 'Ali *mawla amir al-mu'minin*)

5　Textile Museum, Washington, DC, inv. no. 73.647: Kühnel and Bellinger 1952, pp. 34–35, pl. XV; Sokoly 2002, no. 596 (dated 320 AH / 932–33 CE, Misr?, by order of the vizier 'Ali Muhammad by intermediation of 'Ubayyid *mawla amir al-mu'minin*)

6　Royal Ontario Museum, Toronto, inv. no. 978.76.1140: Sokoly 2002, no. 597 (datable to 320 AH / 932–33 CE, Misr, by order of the vizier Muhammad ibn 'Ali by intermediation of Fa'iz *mawla amir al-mu'minin*)

7　Kelsey Museum of Archaeology, Ann Arbor, MI, inv. no. 22.512: Day 1937, pp. 431–32, no. 12, fig. 12; Sokoly 2002, 598 (possibly dated 320 AH / 932–33 CE, *tiraz al-'amma* in Misr, by order of the vizier 'Ali ibn 'Isa by intermediation of Shafi' *mawla amir al-mu'minin*)

8　Metropolitan Museum of Art, New York, inv. no. 31.19.11: Upton 1930–31, p. 166, no. 11, fig. 11; Sokoly 2002, no. 599 (dated 320 AH / 932–33 CE, Misr, by order of the vizier Muhammad ibn 'Ali by intermediation of 'Ubayyid *mawla amir al-mu'minin*)

9　Bouvier Collection, inv. no. JFB I 109: Geneva 1993, p. 176, no. 100 (dated 320 AH / 932–33 CE, Misr?, by order of the vizier 'Ali Muhammad by intermediation of 'Ubayyid *mawla amir al-mu'minin*)

10　Museum of Islamic Art, Cairo, inv. no. 8164: *RCEA* 1931–91, vol. IV, 1933, pp. 19–20, no. 1242; Sokoly 2002, no. 600 (datable to 320–21 AH / 932–33 CE, by order of the vizier Muhammad)

11　Museum of Islamic Art, Cairo, inv. no. 11490: *RCEA* 1931–91, vol. IV, 1933, p. 21, no. 1246; Sokoly 2002, no. 601 (datable to 320–21 AH / 932–33 CE, Misr, by order of the vizier 'Ali ibn Muhammad 'Ali, by intermediation of [...] *mawla amir al-mu'minin*)

12　Benaki Museum, Athens, inv. no. 14864: *RCEA* 1931–91, vol. IV, 1933, pp. 22–23, no. 1249; Sokoly 2002, no. 602 (datable to 320–21 AH / 932–33 CE, by order of the vizier 'Ali Muhammad by intermediation of Shafi'(?) *mawla amir al-mu'minin*)

13　Ex Abemayor Collection: *RCEA* 1931–91, vol. IV, 1933, p. 24, no. 1252; Sokoly 2002, no. 603 (datable to 320–21 AH / 932–33 CE, by order of the vizier Abu 'Ali Muhammad ibn 'Ali by intermediation of [...] *mawla amir al-mu'minin*)

14　Ex Tano Collection: *RCEA* 1931–91, vol. IV, 1933, pp. 24–25, no. 1253; Sokoly 2002, no. 604 (datable

to 320–21 AH / 932–33 CE, *tiraz* workshop in Misr, by order of the vizier Muhammad ibn 'Ali, by intermediation of [...] *mawla amir al-mu'minin*)

15　Textile Museum, Washington, DC, inv. no. 73.629: Kühnel and Bellinger 1952, pp. 35–36, pl. XV; *RCEA* 1931–91, vol. IV, 1933, no. 1254; Sokoly 2002, no. 605 (datable to 320–21 AH / 932–33 CE, *tiraz* workshop in Misr, by order of the vizier Abu 'Ali Muhammad ibn 'Ali by intermediation of Shafi' *mawla amir al-mu'minin*)

16　Royal Ontario Museum, Toronto, inv. no. 978.76.43: Sokoly 2002, no. 606 (datable to 320–21 AH / 932–33 CE, by order of the vizier Muhammad ibn 'Ali by intermediation of [...] *mawla amir al-mu'minin*)

17　Ex Tano Collection: *RCEA* 1931–91, vol. IV, 1933, pp. 16–17, no. 1237 (dated 321 AH / 933 CE, Misr, by order of the vizier by intermediation of Shafi' *mawla amir al-mu'minin*)

18　Bouvier Collection, inv. no. JFB I 7: Geneva 1993, pp. 177–78, no. 101; Sokoly 2002, no. 610 (dated 321 AH / 933 CE, *tiraz al-khassa*, by order of the vizier 'Ali ibn Muhammad by intermediation of Shafi' *mawla amir al-mu'minin*)

19　Museum of Islamic Art, Cairo, inv. no. 10086: *RCEA* 1931–91, vol. IV, 1933, p. 20, no. 1243; Sokoly 2002, no. 611 (dated 322 AH / 933–34 CE, by order of the vizier by intermediation of [...] *mawla amir al-mu'minin*)

20　Museum of Islamic Art, Cairo, inv. no. 10704: *RCEA* 1931–91, vol. IV, 1933, pp. 25–26, no. 1255; Sokoly 2002, no. 612 (dated 322 AH / 933–34 CE, Misr, by order of the vizier Muhammad ibn 'Ali)

21　Museum of Islamic Art, Cairo, inv. no. 12183: *RCEA* 1931–91, vol. IV, 1933, p. 206, no. 1248A; Sokoly 2002, no. 613 (by order of the vizier)

22　Ex Abemayor Collection: *RCEA* 1931–91, vol. IV, 1933, p. 206, no. 1252A; Sokoly 2002, no. 614 (*tiraz al-'amma* in an unnamed location, ordered by 'Ali ibn 'Isa)

23　Museum of Islamic Art, Cairo, inv. no. 11528: *RCEA* 1931–91, vol. IV, 1933, pp. 21–22, no. 1247; Sokoly 2002, no. 615 (administrative data lost)

24　Museum of Islamic Art, Cairo, inv. no. 11588: *RCEA* 1931–91, vol. IV, 1933, p. 22, no. 1248; Sokoly 2002, no. 616 (administrative data lost)

25　Metropolitan Museum of Art, New York, inv. no. 29.179.30: Sokoly 2002, no. 621 (administrative data lost)

26　Museum of Islamic Art, Cairo, inv. no. 10184: *RCEA* 1931–91, vol. IV, 1933, pp. 20–21, no. 1244; Sokoly 2002, no. 622 (administrative data lost)

Cat. 24

1　Metropolitan Museum of Art, New York, inv. no. 29.179.30: Sokoly 2002, no. 621 (administrative data lost)

Cat. 25

1　Textile Museum, Washington, DC, inv. no. 73.214: Kühnel and Bellinger 1952, pp. 39–40, pl. XVIII; Sokoly 2002, no. 670 (dated 325 AH / 936–37 CE, Shata, by order of the vizier Sulayman ibn al-Hasan by intermediation of Jabir)

2　Royal Ontario Museum, Toronto, inv. no. 978.76.421: Sokoly 2002, no. 628 (administrative data lost)

Cat. 26

1　Museum of Islamic Art, Cairo, inv. no. 10709: *RCEA* 1931–91, vol. IV, 1933, p. 64, no. 1331; Sokoly 2002, no. 739 (reign of al-Radi, Misr, by order of the vizier 'Ali ibn 'Isa by intermediation of [...] *mawla amir al-mu'minin*)

2　Ex Tano Collection: *RCEA* 1931–91, vol. IV, 1933, p. 45, no. 1290; Sokoly 2002, no. 644 (datable to 322–24 AH / 933–36 CE or 326–27 AH / 937–39 CE, Misr, by order of the vizier Abu 'Ali Muhammad ibn 'Ali by intermediation of 'Ubayyid *mawla amir al-mu'minin*)

3　Royal Ontario Museum, Toronto, inv. no. 978.76.51: Sokoly 2002, no. 651 (datable to 322–24 AH / 933–36 CE or 326–27 AH / 937–39 CE, *tiraz al-khassa* in Misr, by order of the vizier Muhammad ibn 'Ali by intermediation of 'Ubayyid)

4　Royal Ontario Museum, Toronto, inv. no. 978.76.33: Sokoly 2002, no. 653 (datable to 322–24 AH / 933–36 CE or 326–27 AH / 937–39 CE, by order of the vizier Muhammad ibn 'Ali by intermediation of 'Ubayyid *mawla amir al-mu'minin*)

5　Museum für Islamische Kunst, Berlin, inv. no. 5565: *RCEA* 1931–91, vol. IV, 1933, pp. 206–07, no. 1260A; Sokoly 2002, no. 655 (dated 323 AH / 934–35 CE, *tiraz al-khassa* in Misr, by order of the vizier al-Fadl ibn Ja'far by intermediation of 'Ubayyid *mawla amir al-mu'minin*)

Cat. 27

1　Museum der Kulturen, Basel, inv. no. 9461: Marzouk 1959, p. 286, p. 284, fig. 2; Sokoly 2002, no. 709 (administrative data lost)

2　Royal Ontario Museum, Toronto, inv. no. 978.76.22: Sokoly 2002, no. 732 (datable to 322–24 AH / 933–36 CE, or 326–27 AH / 937–39 CE, by order of the vizier Muhammad ibn 'Ali)

3　Royal Ontario Museum, Toronto, inv. no. 978.76.24: Sokoly 2002, no. 650 (datable to 322–24 AH / 933–36 CE, or 326–27 AH / 937–39 CE, by order of the vizier Muhammad ibn 'Ali)

4　Kelsey Museum of Archeology, Ann Arbor, MI, inv. no. 22.515:

Day 1937, p. 437, no. 15, fig. 15; Sokoly 2002, no. 654 (datable to 322–24 AH / 933–36 CE, or 326–27 AH / 937–39 CE, by order of the vizier Muhammad ibn 'Ali by intermediation of [...] *al-khadim*)

5　Textile Museum, Washington, DC, inv. no. 73.371: Kühnel and Bellinger 1952, p. 39, pl. XVI, detail pl. XL; Sokoly 2002, no. 658 (dated 323 AH / 934–35 CE, by order of the vizier Muhammad ibn 'Ali)

6　Royal Ontario Museum, Toronto, inv. no. 978.76.51: Sokoly 2002, no. 651 (datable to 322–24 AH / 933–36 CE, or 326–27 AH / 937–39 CE, *tiraz al-khassa* in Misr, by order of the vizier Muhammad ibn 'Ali by intermediation of 'Ubayyid)

Cat. 28

1　Textile Museum, Washington, DC, inv. no. 73.214: Kühnel and Bellinger 1952, pp. 39–40, pl. XVIII; Sokoly 2002, no. 670 (dated 325 AH / 936–37 CE, Shata, by order of the vizier Sulayman ibn al-Hasan by intermediation of Jabir)

2　Royal Ontario Museum, Toronto, inv. no. 978.76.421: Sokoly 2002, no. 628 (administrative data lost)

3　Royal Ontario Museum, Toronto, inv. no. 978.76.396: Sokoly 2002, no. 629 (administrative data lost)

4　Royal Ontario Museum, Toronto, inv. no. 978.76.37: Sokoly 2002, no. 631 (administrative data lost)

5　Cleveland Museum of Art, inv. no. 32.23: Sokoly 2002, no. 714 (administrative data lost)

Cat. 29

1　Stockholm, National Museum, inv. no. 140 / 1939: Lamm 1938, pp. 109–10, no. 7, pl. II; Sokoly 2002, no. 656 (dated 323 AH / 934–35 CE, *tiraz al-khassa* in Misr, by intermediation of Jabir)

2　Benaki Museum, Athens, inv. no. 15108: *RCEA* 1931–91, vol. IV, 1933, p. 32, no. 1266; Sokoly 2002, no. 659 (dated 324 AH / 935–36 CE, *tiraz al-khassa* in Misr, by order of the two viziers (*wazirayn*) Abu 'Ali Muhammad ibn 'Ali and 'Ali ibn Abu 'Ali by intermediation of Jabir *mawla amir al-mu'minin*)

3　Benaki Museum, Athens, inv. no. 14876: *RCEA* 1931–91, vol. IV, 1933, p. 47, no. 1294; Sokoly 2002, no. 663 (datable to 324–26 AH / 935–38 CE, *tiraz al-khassa* in Misr, by order of the vizier Abu al-Fath al-Fadl ibn Ja'far by intermediation of Jabir *mawla amir al-mu'minin*)

4　Benaki Museum, Athens, inv. no. 14869; *RCEA* 1931–91, vol. IV, 1933, pp. 47–48, no. 1295; Sokoly 2002, no. 664 (datable to 324–26 AH / 935–38 CE, *tiraz al-khassa* in Misr, by order of the vizier Abu al-Fath al-Fadl ibn Ja'far by intermediation of Jabir [*mawla amir al-mu'minin*?])

5　Metropolitan Museum of Art, New York, inv. no. 29.179.5ab:

Upton 1930–31, p. 167, no. 12, fig. 12; Sokoly 2002, no. 667 (datable to 324–26 AH / 935–38 CE, probably by order of the vizier Abu al-Fath al-Fadl ibn al-Furat)

6 Benaki Museum, Athens, inv. no. 14880: *RCEA* 1931–91, vol. IV, 1933, p. 39, no. 1278; Sokoly 2002, no. 673 (dated 326 AH / 937–38 CE, by order of the vizier Muhammad ibn ʿAli)

7 Textile Museum, Washington, DC, inv. no. 73.453: Kühnel and Bellinger 1952, p. 43, pl. XVIII; Sokoly 2002, no. 712 (administrative data lost)

8 Detroit Institute of Art, inv. no. 32.60: https://dia.org/collection/fragment-tiraz-textile-49332; Sokoly 2002, no. 718 (administrative data lost)

9 Ex Tano Collection: *RCEA* 1931–91, vol. IV, 1933, p. 45, no. 1290; Sokoly 2002, no. 644 (datable to 322–24 AH / 933–36 CE, or 326–27 AH / 937–39 CE, *tiraz al-khassa* in Misr, by order of the vizier Abu ʿAli Muhammad ibn ʿAli by intermediation of ʿUbayyid *mawla amir al-muʾminin*)

10 Museum für Islamische Kunst, Berlin, inv. no. 5565: Kühnel 1933, pp. 61–62, no. 2, pl. II, fig 3; *RCEA* 1931–91, vol. IV, 1933, pp. 206–07, no. 1260A; Sokoly 2002, no. 655 (dated 323 AH / 934–35 CE, *tiraz al-khassa* in Misr, by order of the vizier al-Fadl Jaʿfar by intermediation of ʿUbayyid *mawla amir al-muʾminin*)

11 Textile Museum, Washington, DC, inv. no. 73.214: Kühnel and Bellinger 1952, pp. 39–40, pl. XVIII; Sokoly 2002, no. 670 (dated 325 AH / 936–37 CE, Shata, by order of the vizier Sulayman ibn al-Hasan by intermediation of Jabir)

12 Royal Ontario Museum, Toronto, inv. no. 978.76.429: Sokoly 2002, no. 683 (dated 329 AH / 940–41 CE, *tiraz al-khassa* in Damietta, by order of the vizier Ahmad ibn Muhammad)

13 Metropolitan Museum of Art, New York, inv. no. 29.179.14: Upton 1930–31, pp. 167–68, no. 13, fig. 13; Sokoly 2002, no. 684 (dated 329 AH / 940–41 CE, *tiraz al-khassa* in Damietta, by order of the vizier Fadl ibn Jaʿfar)

14 Ex Tano Collection: *RCEA* 1931–91, vol. IV, 1933, p. 71, no. 1349; Sokoly 2002, no. 744 (*tiraz al-khassa* in Damietta)

Cat. 30

1 Textile Museum, Washington, DC, inv. no. 73.214: Kühnel and Bellinger 1952, pp. 39–40, pl. XVIII; Sokoly 2002, no. 670 (dated 325 AH / 936–37 CE, Shata, by order of the vizier Sulayman ibn al-Hasan by intermediation of Jabir)

2 Royal Ontario Museum, Toronto, inv. no. 978.76.421: Sokoly 2002, no. 628 (administrative data lost)

Cat. 32

1 Textile Museum, Washington, DC, inv. no. 73.452: Kühnel and Bellinger 1952, pp. 42–43, no. 73.452, pl. XVIII; Sokoly 2002, no. 711 (by order of the vizier)

2 Benaki Museum, Athens, inv. no. 14880: *RCEA* 1931–91, vol. IV, 1933, p. 39, no. 1278; Sokoly 2002, no. 673 (dated 326 AH / 937–38 CE, by order of the vizier Muhammad ibn ʿAli)

3 Benaki Museum, Athens, inv. no. 14876: *RCEA* 1931–91, vol. IV, 1933, p. 47, no. 1294; Sokoly 2002, no. 663 (datable to 324–26 AH / 935–38 CE, *tiraz al-khassa* in Misr, by order of the vizier Abu al-Fath al-Fadl ibn Jaʿfar by intermediation of Jabir *mawla amir al-muʾminin*)

4 Benaki Museum, Athens, inv. no. 14869; *RCEA* 1931–91, vol. IV, 1933, pp. 47–48, no. 1295; Sokoly 2002, no. 664 (datable to 324–26 AH / 935–38 CE, *tiraz al-khassa* in Misr, by order of the vizier Abu al-Fath al-Fadl ibn Jaʿfar by intermediation of Jabir [*mawla amir al-muʾminin*?])

5 Metropolitan Museum of Art, New York, inv. no. 29.179.5ab: Upton 1930–31, p. 167, no. 12, fig. 12; Sokoly 2002, no. 667 (datable to 324–26 AH / 936–39 CE, by order of the vizier Abu al-Fath al-Fadl ibn al-Furat)

6 Royal Ontario Museum, Toronto, inv. no. 978.76.429: Sokoly 2002, no. 683 (dated 329 AH / 940–41 CE, *tiraz al-khassa* in Damietta, by order of the vizier Ahmad ibn Muhammad)

Cat. 36

1 Royal Ontario Museum, Toronto, inv. no. 978.76.31: Sokoly 2002, no. 755 (datable to 329 AH / 940–41 CE, [Mi]sr, by order of the vizier Sulayman ibn al-Hasan)

2 Textile Museum, Washington, DC, inv. no. 73.372: Kühnel and Bellinger 1952, pp. 44–45, pl. XIX; Sokoly 2002, no. 771 (dated 330 AH / 941–42 CE, *tiraz* workshop in Misr, by order of the vizier Sulayman ibn al-Hasan)

3 Museum of Islamic Art, Doha (found in Dabro Dammo): Mordini 1957, p. 36, fig. 40; Wiet 1959, pl. XV g; Sokoly 2002, no. 773 (dated 330 AH / 941–42 CE, *tiraz* workshop in Misr, by order of the vizier Sulayman ibn al-Hasan)

4 Boston Museum of Fine Arts, inv. no. 32.29: Britton 1938, p. 47, fig. 26; Sokoly 2002, no. 791 (administrative data lost)

5 Royal Ontario Museum, Toronto, inv. no. 978.76.34: Sokoly 2002, no. 792 (date lost, Misr, by order of the vizier Sulayman ibn al-Hasan ?)

6 Royal Ontario Museum, Toronto, inv. no. 978.76.51: Sokoly 2002, no. 651 (datable to 322–24 AH / 933–36 CE or 326–27 AH / 937–39 CE, *tiraz al-khassa* in Misr, by order of the vizier Muhammad ibn ʿAli)

7 Textile Museum, Washington, DC, inv. no. 73.13: Kühnel and Bellinger 1952, p. 21, pls X, XL; Sokoly 2002, no. 259 (dated 300 AH / 912–13 CE, *tiraz al-ʿamma* in Misr, by order of the vizier by intermediation of Shafiʿ)

Cat. 37

1 Textile Museum, Washington, DC, inv. no. 73.215: Kühnel and Bellinger 1952, pp. 49–50, pl. XXII; Sokoly 2002, no. 879 (dated 345 AH / 956–57 CE, no administrative data mentioned)

2 Private collection: Sokoly 2002, no. 915 (dated 359 AH / 970–71 CE, no administrative data mentioned)

3 Museum für Islamische Kunst, Berlin, inv. no. 5559: Kühnel 1933, pp. 62–63, no. 3, pl. II, fig. 4; Sokoly 2002, no. 802 (date lost, *tiraz al-ʿamma* in Shata)

4 Royal Ontario Museum, Toronto, inv. no. 978.76.353: Sokoly 2002, no. 808 (no administrative data mentioned)

5 Royal Ontario Museum, Toronto, inv. no. 978.76.72: Sokoly 2002, no. 810 (administrative data lost)

6 Royal Ontario Museum, Toronto, inv. no. 978.76.405: Sokoly 2002, no. 815 (administrative data lost)

7 Textile Museum, Washington, DC, inv. no. 73.638: Kühnel and Bellinger 1952, pp. 47–48, pl. XXI, detail pl. XLI; Sokoly 2002, no. 852 (dated 338 AH / 949–50 CE, Shata, by order of the vizier by intermediation of Faʾiz)

8 Royal Ontario Museum, Toronto, inv. no. 978.76.325: Sokoly 2002, no. 865 (dated 340 AH / 951–52 CE, no administrative data mentioned)

9 Royal Ontario Museum, Toronto, inv. no. 978.76.422: Sokoly 2002, no. 866 (dated 340 AH / 951–52 CE, no administrative data mentioned)

10 Royal Ontario Museum, Toronto, inv. no. 978.76.60: Sokoly 2002, no. 868 (dated 341 AH / 952–53 CE, no administrative data mentioned)

11 Textile Museum, Washington, DC, inv. no. 73.27: Kühnel and Bellinger 1952, p. 51, pl. XXII; Sokoly 2002, no. 889 (dated 350 AH / 961–62 CE, no administrative data mentioned)

12 Royal Ontario Museum, Toronto, inv. no. 978.76.61: Sokoly 2002, no. 893 (dated 350 AH / 961–62 CE, no administrative data mentioned)

13 Bouvier Collection, inv. no. JFB I 8: Geneva 1993, pp. 181–82, no. 104; Sokoly 2002, no. 1037 (administrative data lost)

14 Museum der Kulturen, Basel, inv. no. 9465: Marzouk 1959, p. 289, p. 285, fig. 4; Sokoly 2002, no. 1039 (date lost, no administrative data mentioned)

15 Keir Collection of Islamic Art, on loan to the Dallas Museum of Art, inv. no. 75c: Spuhler 1978, p. 145, no. 75c; Sokoly 2002, no. 1048 (administrative data lost)

16 Metropolitan Museum of Art, New York, inv. no. 29.179.40: Sokoly 2002, no. 1116 (administrative data not mentioned, or lost)

17 Textile Museum, Washington, DC, inv. no. 73.662: Kühnel and Bellinger 1952, p. 46, pl. XX; Sokoly 2002, no. 799 (dated 334 AH / 945–46 CE, *tiraz al-khassa* in Damietta, by order of the vizier Muhammad ibn ʿAli)

Cat. 38

1 Royal Ontario Museum, Toronto, inv. no. 978.76.955: Sokoly 2002, no. 811 (date lost, reign of al-Mutiʿ; administrative data not mentioned, or lost; max. letter height 7.3 cm)

2 Kelsey Museum of Archeology, Ann Arbor, MI, inv. no. 22.520: Day 1937, p. 441, no. 20, fig. 20; Sokoly 2002, no. 819 (datable to 334–54 AH / 945–65 CE, administrative data not mentioned; max. letter height 8.7 cm)

3 Textile Museum, Washington, DC, inv. no. 73.215: Kühnel and Bellinger 1952, pp. 49–50, pl. XXII; Sokoly 2002, no. 879 (dated 345 AH / 956–57 CE, administrative data not mentioned; max. letter height 7.0 cm)

4 Textile Museum, Washington, DC, inv. no. 73.400: Kühnel and Bellinger 1952, pp. 50–51, pl. XXII; Sokoly 2002, no. 888 (dated 350 AH / 961–62 CE, administrative data not mentioned; max. letter height 3.7 cm)

5 Textile Museum, Washington, DC, inv. no. 73.27: Kühnel and Bellinger 1952, p. 51, pl. XXII; Sokoly 2002, no. 889 (dated 350 AH / 961–62 CE, administrative data not mentioned; max. letter height 5.8 cm)

6 Biblioteca Apostolica Vaticana, Vatican City, inv. no. 6737: Cornu 1992, pp. 150–51; Sokoly 2002, no. 892 (dated 350 AH / 961–62 CE, administrative data not mentioned; max. letter height 7.0 cm)

7 Metropolitan Museum of Art, New York, inv. no. 31.106.44: Dimand 1930, p. 93, fig. 1; Sokoly 2002, no. 901 (dated 353 AH / 964 CE, administrative data not mentioned; max. letter height 8.0 cm)

8 Museum für Islamische Kunst, Berlin, inv. no. 5564: Kühnel 1933, p. 63, no. 3, pl. II; *RCEA* 1931–91, vol. V, 1934, pp. 19–20, no. 1638; Sokoly 2002, no. 911 (dated 357 AH / 967–68 CE, administrative data not mentioned; max. letter height 5.0 cm)

9 Textile Museum, Washington, DC, inv. no. 73.252: Kühnel and Bellinger 1952, pp. 52–53, pl. XXIII; Sokoly 2002, no. 1041 (date lost, *tiraz* workshop, place of production and ordering officer lost; max. letter height 11.0 cm)

10 Royal Ontario Museum, Toronto, inv. no. 963.95.4: Golombek and Gervers 1977, p. 100; Sokoly 2002, no. 1050 (date and administrative data lost; max. letter height 6.2 cm)

11 Royal Ontario Museum, Toronto, inv. no. 978.76.424: Sokoly 2002,

no. 1052 (date and administrative data lost; max. letter height 6.4 cm)

12 Royal Ontario Museum, Toronto, inv. no. 978.76.471: Sokoly 2002, no. 1053 (date and administrative data lost; max. letter height 8.4 cm)

13 Kelsey Museum of Archaeology, Ann Arbor, MI, inv. no. 22.522: Day 1937, p. 442, no. 22, fig. 22; Sokoly 2002, no. 1055 (date and administrative data lost; max. letter height 5.9 cm)

14 Kelsey Museum of Archaeology, Ann Arbor, MI, inv. no. 22.523: Day 1937, pp. 442–43, no. 23, fig. 23; Sokoly 2002, no. 1056 (date lost, administrative data not mentioned, or lost; max. letter height 11.7 cm)

15 Royal Ontario Museum, Toronto, inv. no. 970.364.16: Sokoly 2002, no. 1058 (date lost, administrative data not mentioned, or lost; max. letter height 14.8 cm)

16 Metropolitan Museum of Art, New York, inv. no. 31.106.45: Walker and Froom 1992, pp. 24–25, no. 14; *RCEA* 1931–91, vol. V, 1934, p. 74, no. 1773; Sokoly 2002, no. 1060 (date lost, administrative data not mentioned, or lost; max. letter height 12.7 cm)

17 The Nasser D. Khalili Collection of Islamic Art, inv. no. TXT 5: Cornu et al. 2023, pp. 56–57; Sokoly 2002, no. 1060.1 (date and administrative data lost; max. letter height unknown)

18 Museum für Islamische Kunst, Berlin, inv. no. 2631: Kühnel 1925, pp. 83–84, fig. 1; Sokoly 2002, no. 1075 (date and administrative data not mentioned; max. letter height 3.5 cm)

19 Textile Museum, Washington, DC, inv. no. 73.28: Kühnel and Bellinger 1952, p. 52, pl. XXIII; Sokoly 2002, no. 1084 (date and administrative data not mentioned; max. letter height 5.5 cm)

20 Biblioteca Apostolica Vaticana, Vatican City, inv. no. 6747: Cornu 1992, pp. 148–49; Sokoly 2002, no. 1087 (date and administrative data not mentioned, or lost; max. letter height 12.0 cm)

Cat. 39

1 Royal Ontario Museum, Toronto, inv. no. 978.76.985: Sokoly 2002, no. 292 (dated 301–04 AH / 913–17 CE, or 314–16 AH / 926–29 CE, *tiraz al-khassa* in Misr?, by order of the vizier ‘Ali ibn ‘Isa by intermediation of Muhammad; max. letter height 8.5 cm)

2 Kelsey Museum of Archaeology, Ann Arbor, MI, inv. no. 22.509: Day 1937, pp. 429–30, fig. 9; Sokoly 2002, no. 382 (dated 308 AH / 920–21 CE, administrative data not mentioned; max. letter height 4.2 cm)

3 Royal Ontario Museum, Toronto, inv. no. 978.76.421: Sokoly 2002, no. 628 (administrative data not mentioned, or lost; max. letter height 1.6 cm)

4 Royal Ontario Museum, Toronto, inv. no. 978.76.37: Sokoly 2002, no. 631 (date lost, administrative data not mentioned, or lost; letter height small)

5 Benaki Museum, inv. no. 15108: *RCEA* 1931–91, vol. IV, 1933, p. 32, no. 1266; Sokoly 2002, no. 659 (dated 324 AH / 935–36, *tiraz al-khassa* in Misr, by order of the viziers Abu ‘Ali Muhammad ibn ‘Ali and ‘Ali ibn Abu ‘Ali by intermediation of Jabir *mawla amir al-mu’minin*; letter height small)

6 Textile Museum, Washington, DC, inv. no. 73.452: Kühnel and Bellinger 1952, pp. 42–43, pl. XVIII; Sokoly 2002, no. 711 (date lost, by order of the vizier; max. letter height 2.9 cm)

7 Textile Museum, Washington, DC, inv. no. 73.453: Kühnel and Bellinger 1952, p. 43, pl. XVIII; Sokoly 2002, no. 712 (date lost, administrative data lost; max. letter height 3.2 cm)

8 Kelsey Museum of Archaeology, Ann Arbor, MI, inv. no. 26.743: Guest 1931, pp. 132–33, no. 4, pl. I, no. 4; Sokoly 2002, no. 1115 (date and administrative data not mentioned, or lost; max. letter height 1.2 cm)

9 Royal Ontario Museum, Toronto, inv. no. 978.76.333: Sokoly 2002, no. 745 (date lost, administrative data not mentioned, or lost; max. letter height 2.2 cm)

10 Textile Museum, Washington, DC, inv. no. 73.662: Kühnel and Bellinger 1952, p. 46, pl. XX; Sokoly 2002, no. 799 (dated 334 AH / 945–46 CE, *tiraz al-khassa* in Damietta, by order of the vizier Muhammad ibn ‘Ali; max. letter height 4.0 cm)

11 Royal Ontario Museum, Toronto, inv. no. 978.76.353: Sokoly 2002, no. 808 (date and administrative data not mentioned, or lost; max. letter height 2.5 cm)

12 Royal Ontario Museum, Toronto, inv. no. 978.76.422: Sokoly 2002, no. 866 (dated 340 AH / 951–52 CE, administrative data not mentioned, or lost; max. letter height 2.2 cm)

13 Textile Museum, Washington, DC, inv. no. 73.27: Kühnel and Bellinger 1952, p. 51, pl. XXII; Sokoly 2002, no. 889 (dated 350 AH / 961–62 CE, administraive data not mentioned; max. letter height 5.8 cm)

14 Royal Ontario Museum, Toronto, inv. no. 978.76.61: Sokoly 2002, no. 893 (dated 350 AH / 961–62 CE, administrative data not mentioned; max. letter height 3.4 cm)

15 Metropolitan Museum of Art, New York, inv. no. 29.179.40: Sokoly 2002, no. 1116 (date and administrative data not mentioned, or lost; max. letter height 2.0 cm)

16 Textile Museum, Washington, DC, inv. no. 73.666: Kühnel and Bellinger 1952, p. 56, pl. XXV; Sokoly 2002, no. 1167 (date lost, by order of the vizier; max. letter height 7.5 cm)

Cat. 40

1 Textile Museum, Washington, DC, inv. no. 73.214: Kühnel and Bellinger 1952, pp. 39–40, pl. XVIII; Sokoly 2002, no. 670 (dated 325 AH / 936–37, Shata, by order of the vizier Sulayman ibn al-Hasan by intermediation of Jabir)

Cat. 41

1 Textile Museum, Washington, DC, inv. no. 73.214: Kühnel and Bellinger 1952, pp. 39–40, pl. XVIII; Sokoly 2002, no. 670 (dated 325 AH / 936–37 CE, Shata, by order of the vizier Sulayman ibn al-Hasan by intermediation of Jabir)

Cat. 42

1 Textile Museum, Washington, DC, inv. no. 73.664: Kühnel and Bellinger 1952, p. 11, pl. IV; Sokoly 2002, no. 77 (dated 273 AH / 886–87 CE, Misr, ordering officer not mentioned)

Cat. 43

1 Textile Museum, Washington, DC, inv. no. 73.8: Kühnel and Bellinger 1952, p. 95, pl. LI

2 Textile Museum, Washington, DC, inv. no. 73.37: Kühnel and Bellinger 1952, p. 96, pl. LI

Cat. 44

1 Textile Museum, Washington, DC, inv. no. 73.8: Kühnel and Bellinger 1952, p. 95, pl. LI

2 Textile Museum, Washington, DC, inv. no. 73.37: Kühnel and Bellinger 1952, p. 96, pl. LI

Cat. 51

1 Ex Elsberg Collection (current whereabouts unknown): Merlange 1928, pp. 15–16, no. 6

Cat. 52

1 Ex Elsberg Collection (current whereabouts unknown): Merlange 1928, pp. 15–16, no. 6

Cat. 54

1 Ashmolean Museum, Oxford, inv. no. EA1984.353: Barnes 1999; https://jameelcentre.ashmolean.org/object/EA1984.353

2 Textile Museum, Washington, DC, inv. no. 73.444: Kühnel and Bellinger 1952, pp. 25–26, pl. XI; Mackie 1996, p. 83, fig. 58; Sokoly 2002, no. 337 (dated 306 AH / 918–19 CE, Misr)

Cat. 55

1 Museum of Islamic Art, Cairo, inv. no. 14473: Marzouk 1942, pl. 1; Grohmann 1957, pl. 2, fig. 4; Maher 1977, p. 161, no. 31; Yusuf 1995, p. 325, pl. 5; Sokoly 2002, no. 14 (dated 168 AH / 784–85 CE, reign of al-Mahdi, Qays)

2 Bouvier Collection, inv. no. JFB I 101: Geneva 1993, pp. 55–58, no. 10; Sokoly 2002, no. 15 (by order of the amir Isma‘il)

3 Bouvier Collection, inv. no. JFB M 91: Geneva 1993, pp. 61–64, no. 14

4 Bouvier Collection, inv. no. JFB I 72: Geneva 1993, pp. 64–65, no. 16

5 Bouvier Collection, inv. no. JFB I 73: Geneva 1993, pp. 66, no. 17

6 Bouvier Collection, inv. no. JFB I 62: Geneva 1993, pp. 67–68, no. 18

Cat. 56

1 Museum of Islamic Art, Cairo, inv. no. 14473: Marzouk 1942, pl. 1; Grohmann 1957, pl. 2, fig. 4; Maher 1977, p. 161, no. 31; Yusuf 1995, p. 325, pl. 5; Sokoly 2002, no. 14 (dated 168 AH / 784–85 CE, reign of al-Mahdi, Qays)

Cat. 57

1 Bouvier Collection, inv. no. JFB I 62: Geneva 1993, pp. 67–68, no. 18

Cat. 59

1 Museum of Islamic Art, Cairo, inv. no. 14473: Marzouk 1942, pl. 1; Grohmann 1957, pl. 2, fig. 4; Maher 1977, p. 161, no. 31; Yusuf 1995, p. 325, pl. 5; Sokoly 2002, no. 14 (dated 168 AH / 784–85 CE, reign of al-Mahdi, Qays)

2 Bouvier Collection, inv. no. JFB I 101: Geneva 1993, pp. 55–58, no. 10; Sokoly 2002, no. 15 (by order of the amir Isma‘il)

3 Bouvier Collection, inv. no. JFB I 30: Geneva 1993, pp. 58–59, no. 11

Cat. 60

1 Bouvier Collection, inv. no. JFB I 82: Geneva 1993, pp. 161–62, no. 89

2 Museum of Islamic Art, Cairo, inv. no. 13425: Maher 1977, p. 163, no. 40; Sokoly 2002, no. 10 (inscribed: ‘Bismillah baraka min Allah mimma ‘umila fi tiraz al-khassa bi-Madinat al-Bahnasa […]’)

3 Museum of Islamic Art, Cairo, inv. no. 7120: Grohmann 1971, p. 102 n. 1, pl. XIX, no. 2; Sokoly 2002, no. 26 (inscribed: ‘[…] [A]llah mimma ‘umila fi tiraz al-khassa bi-Madinat al-Bahnasa […]’)

4 Museum of Islamic Art, Cairo, inv. no. 15017: Grohmann 1971, pl. XXVII, fig. 2; Maher 1977, p. 159, no. 23; Sokoly 2002, no. 27 (inscribed: line 1, ‘[Bismilla]h al-rahman al-rahi[m] […]’; line 2, ‘[…] [tira]z(?) Bahnasa sanat […]’)

5 Museum of Islamic Art, Cairo, inv. no. 13143: Maher 1977, p. 161, no. 33; Sokoly 2002, no. 28 (inscribed: ‘[…] bi-Bahnasa […]’)

6 Museum of Islamic Art, Cairo, inv. no. 4827: Maher 1977, p. 159, no. 24; Sokoly 2002, no. 30 (inscribed: ‘[…] Bahnasa […]’)

7 Museum of Islamic Art, Cairo, inv. no. 15720: Sokoly 2002, no. 31 (inscribed: ‘[…] Bahnasa […]’)

8 Museum of Islamic Art, Cairo, inv. no. unknown: Yusuf 1995, pp. 319–20, p. 327, pl. 9; Sokoly 2002, no. 35.1 (possibly dated 230 AH / 844–45 CE, inscribed: line 1, ‘[…] [A]llah yumn wa baraka li-[…]’; line 2, ‘[…]a bi-Bahnasa sanat wa thalathin wa [mi’atan]’)

9   Abegg-Stiftung, Riggisberg
   (Bern), inv. no. 1391: Otavsky and
   Muhammad Salim 1995, pp. 36–37,
   no. 8

Cat. 61
1   Bouvier Collection, inv. no. JFB I
   85: Geneva 1993, pp. 158–59,
   no. 86; Sokoly 2002, no. 34
   (inscribed: '[…] [a]l-khassa bi-
   mad[inat] […]')
2   Bouvier Collection, inv. no. JFB I
   84: Geneva 1993, pp. 159–60, no. 87
   (inscribed: '[…] li-sahibihi mimma
   […]')
3   Museum of Islamic Art, Cairo,
   inv. no. 13425: Maher 1977,
   p. 163, no. 40; Sokoly 2002, no. 10
   (inscribed: 'Bismillah baraka min
   Allah mimma 'umila fi tiraz al-
   khassa bi-Madinat al-Bahnasa […]')
4   Museum of Islamic Art, Cairo,
   inv. no. 7120: Grohmann 1971,
   p. 102 n. 1, pl. XIX, no. 2; Sokoly
   2002, no. 26 (inscribed: '[…] [A]llah
   mimma 'umila fi tiraz al-khassa bi-
   Madinat al-Bahnasa […]')

Cat. 62
1   Museum of Islamic Art, Cairo,
   inv. no. unknown: Yusuf 1995,
   pp. 319–20, p. 327, pl. 9; Sokoly
   2002, no. 35.1 (possibly dated
   230 AH / 844–45 CE, inscribed: line 1,
   '[…] [A]llah yumn wa baraka li-
   […]'; line 2, '[…]a bi-Bahnasa sanat
   wa thalathin wa [mi'atan]')
2   Museum of Islamic Art, Cairo,
   inv. no. 15720: Sokoly 2002, no. 31
   (inscribed: '[…] Bahnasa […]')

Cat. 63
1   Museum of Islamic Art, Cairo,
   inv. no. unknown: Yusuf 1995,
   pp. 319–20 and p. 327, pl. 9; Sokoly
   2002, no. 35.1 (dated 230 AH /
   844–45 CE, inscribed: 1. '[…] [A]
   llah yumn wa baraka li-[…]' 2. '[…]
   a bi-Bahnasa sanat thalathin wa
   [mi'atan]')
2   Museum of Islamic Art, Cairo,
   inv. no. 15720: Sokoly 2002, no. 31
   (inscribed: '[…] Bahnasa […]')

Cat. 66
1   Bouvier Collection, inv. no. JFB M
   1: Geneva 1993, pp. 45–46, no. 2
2   Textile Museum, Washington,
   DC, inv. no. 73.524: Kühnel and
   Bellinger 1952, pp. 5–6, pl. I; Sokoly
   2002, no. 5 (inscribed: '[…] (amir
   al-m)u'minin M(arwan) amara bihi
   […]')
3   Cleveland Museum of Art,
   inv. no. 1959.48: Shepherd 1960,
   pp. 7–14; Baker 1995, p. 55; Sokoly
   2002, no. 25; McWilliams and
   Sokoly 2021, pp. 132–33, no. 34
   (inscribed: 'Bismillah baraka min
   Allah li-sahibihi mimma 'umila fi
   tiraz […]')
4   Bouvier Collection, inv. no. JFB I 88:
   Geneva 1993, pp. 70–71, no. 20
5   Metropolitan Museum of Art, New
   York, inv. no. 2001.420: Dospěl
   Williams 2019, fig. 13 (inscribed:
   '(…) mimma ama[ra] […]')

Cat. 67
1   Textile Museum, Washington,
   DC, inv. no. 73.524: Kühnel and
   Bellinger 1952, pp. 5–6, pl. I; Sokoly
   2002, no. 5 (inscribed: '[…] (amir
   al-m)u'minin M(arwan) amara bihi
   […]')
2   Cleveland Museum of Art,
   inv. no. 1959.48: Shepherd 1960,
   pp. 7–14; Baker 1995, p. 55; Sokoly
   2002, no. 25; McWilliams and
   Sokoly 2021, pp. 132–33, no. 34
   (inscribed: 'Bismillah baraka min
   Allah li-sahibihi mimma 'umila fi
   tiraz […]')
3   Bouvier Collection, inv. no. JFB M
   59: Geneva 1993, pp. 48–49, no. 4
4   Bouvier Collection, inv. no. JFB M
   2: Geneva 1993, pp. 50–51, no. 5
5   Metropolitan Museum of Art,
   New York, inv. no. 2001.420:
   Dospěl Williams 2019, fig. 13
   (inscribed: '(…) mimma ama[ra]
   […]')
6   Metropolitan Museum of Art, New
   York, inv. no. 50.83: Canepa 2010,
   pp. 137–38, fig. 7 b/w; Ekhtiar et al.
   2011, no. 25, pp. 47–48, ill. p. 47

Cat. 69
1   Cleveland Museum of Art,
   inv. no. 1959.48: Shepherd 1960,
   pp. 7–14; Baker 1995, p. 55; Sokoly
   2002, no. 25; McWilliams and
   Sokoly 2021, pp. 132–33, no. 34
   (inscribed: 'Bismillah baraka min
   Allah li-sahibihi mimma 'umila fi
   tiraz […]')
2   Bouvier Collection, inv. no. JFB I 88:
   Geneva 1993, pp. 85–88, no. 34
3   Bouvier Collection, inv. no. JFB I
   92: Geneva 1993, pp. 89–90, no. 35

Cat. 70
1   Textile Museum, Washington, DC,
   inv. no. 73.581: Kühnel and Bellinger
   1952, p. 83, pl. XLII
2   Bouvier Collection, inv. no. JFB
   M 39: Geneva 1993, pp. 74–76, no. 24
3   Bouvier Collection, inv. no. JFB
   M 65: Geneva 1993, pp. 76–77, no. 25
4   Bouvier Collection, inv. no. JFB
   M 35: Geneva 1993, p. 78, no. 26
5   Private collection: Rogers 1983,
   pp. 13–15, figs 9, 10

Cat. 72
1   Bouvier Collection, inv. no. JFB M
   47: Geneva 1993, pp. 105–06, no. 49
2   Bouvier Collection, inv. no. JFB M
   46: Geneva 1993, p. 104, no. 48

Cat. 73
1   Brooklyn Museum, New York,
   inv. no. 86.227.97: Ferber et al. 1987,
   p. 200, no. 141
2   Bouvier Collection, inv. no. JFB M
   12: Geneva 1993, pp. 92–95, no. 38
3   Bouvier Collection, inv. no. JFB M
   9: Geneva 1993, pp. 92–95, no. 53

Cat. 74
1   Boston Museum of Fine Arts,
   inv. no. 11.1398: Britton 1938, p. 42,
   fig. 18
2   Musée du Louvre, Paris, inv. no. E
   25405: David-Weill 1957, pp. 73–76

3   Brooklyn Museum of Art,
   New York, inv. no. 57.120.3:
   Thompson 1971, pp. 88–89, no. 38

Cat. 75
1   Museum of Islamic Art, Cairo,
   inv. no. 9061: Grohmann 1971,
   p. 112b n. 1, pl. XXIII, fig. 1
2   Biblioteca Apostolica Vaticana,
   Vatican City, inv. no. 6856: Cornu
   1992, pp. 94–96, 101–03
3   Biblioteca Apostolica Vaticana,
   Vatican City, inv. no. 6870: Cornu
   1992, pp. 94–96, 101–03
4   Bouvier Collection, inv. no. JFB I
   120: Geneva 1993, pp. 151–53, no. 81

Cat. 76
1   Biblioteca Apostolica Vaticana,
   Vatican City, inv. no. 6867: Cornu
   1992, pp. 122–24, illus. p. 498

Cat. 77
1   Biblioteca Apostolica Vaticana,
   Vatican City, inv. no. 6856: Cornu
   1992, pp. 94–96, illus. p. 491 (date
   lost, *tiraz al-khassa* in an unknown
   location)

Cat. 79
1   Textile Museum, Washington, DC,
   inv. no. 71.3: Kühnel and Bellinger
   1952, p. 85, pl. XLII
2   Bouvier Collection, inv. no. JFB I
   94: Geneva 1993, pp. 140–41, no. 71
3   Bouvier Collection, inv. no. JFB I
   69: Geneva 1993, p. 141, no. 72

Cat. 80
1   Bouvier Collection, inv. no. JFB I
   60: Geneva 1993, pp. 138–39, no. 69

Cat. 81
1   Bardo Museum, Tunis: Fendri
   1967–68

Cat. 82
1   Museum of Islamic Art, Cairo,
   inv. no. 9052: Wiet 1935a, p. 286,
   pl. XLVII; Wiet 1935b, p. 19, no. 64
2   Bouvier Collection, inv. no. JFB I
   134: Geneva 1993, p. 142, no. 73
3   Biblioteca Apostolica Vaticana,
   Vatican City, inv. no. 6724: Cornu
   1992, pp. 127–30, illus. p. 499

Cat. 83
1   Museum of Islamic Art, Cairo,
   inv. no. 9052: Wiet 1935a, p. 286,
   pl. XLVII; Wiet 1935b, p. 19, no. 64

Cat. 84
1   Bouvier Collection, inv. no. JFB I 55:
   Geneva 1993, pp. 138–39, no. 69

Cat. 86
1   Textile Museum, Washington, DC,
   inv. no. 721.3: Kühnel and Bellinger
   1952, pl. XLII, p. 85
2   Bouvier Collection, inv. no. JFB I
   94: Geneva 1993, p. 140, no. 73
3   Bouvier Collection, inv. no. JFB I
   69: Geneva 1993, p. 141, no. 74

Cat. 87
1   Katoen Natie Collection,
   inv. no. 711/DM159B: De Moor et

al. 2006, pp. 224–26, figs 74–75;
   Dospěl Williams 2022, p. 37,
   fig. 9a, b.
2   Bouvier Collection, inv. no. JFB I
   60: Geneva 1993, pp. 153–54, no. 82
3   Bouvier Collection, inv. no. JFB I
   123: Geneva 1993, p. 155, no. 83

Cat. 88
1   Katoen Natie Collection,
   inv. no. 711/DM159B: De Moor
   et al. 2006, pp. 224–26, figs
   74–75; Dospěl Williams 2022, p. 37,
   fig. 9a, b.
2   Bouvier Collection, inv. no. JFB I
   60: Geneva 1993, pp. 153–54, no. 82
3   Bouvier Collection, inv. no. JFB I
   123: Geneva 1993, p. 155, no. 83

Cat. 89
1   Katoen Natie Collection,
   inv. no. 711/DM159B: De Moor
   et al. 2006, pp. 224–26, figs
   74–75; Dospěl Williams 2022, p. 37,
   fig. 9a, b
2   Bouvier Collection, inv. no. JFB I
   120: Geneva 1993, p. 152, no. 81

Cat. 90
1   Katoen Natie Collection,
   inv. no. 711/DM159B: De Moor
   et al. 2006, pp. 224–26, figs
   74–75; Dospěl Williams 2022, p. 37,
   fig. 9a, b

Cat. 91
1   Katoen Natie Collection,
   inv. no. 711/DM159B: De Moor
   et al. 2006, pp. 224–26, figs
   74–75; Dospěl Williams 2022, p. 37,
   fig. 9a, b
2   Bouvier Collection, inv. no. JFB I
   123: Geneva 1993, p. 155, no. 83

Cat. 92
1   Katoen Natie Collection,
   inv. no. 711/DM159B: De Moor
   et al. 2006, pp. 224–26, figs
   74–75; Dospěl Williams 2022, p. 37,
   fig. 9a, b
2   Bouvier Collection, inv. no. JFB I
   120: Geneva 1993, p. 152, no. 81
3   Bouvier Collection, inv. no. JFB I
   60: Geneva 1993, p. 154, no. 82

Cat. 93
1   Katoen Natie Collection,
   inv. no. 711/DM159B: De Moor
   et al. 2006, pp. 224–26, figs
   74–75; Dospěl Williams 2022, p. 37,
   fig. 9a, b

Cat. 95
1   Royal Ontario Museum, Toronto,
   inv. no. 978.76.400: Sokoly 2002,
   no. 264 (dated 300 AH / 912–13 CE,
   tiraz al-khassa in Madinat al-Salam)
2   Royal Ontario Museum, Toronto,
   inv. no. 978.76.84: Sokoly 2002,
   no. 265 (dated 300 AH / 912–13 CE,
   administrative data not mentioned)
3   Ashmolean Museum, Oxford,
   inv. no. 1988.43: Sokoly 2002,
   no. 468 (date and administrative
   data not mentioned, or lost)
4   Textile Museum, Washington, DC,
   inv. no. 73.33: Kühnel and Bellinger,

1952, pp. 33–34, pl. IX; Sokoly 2002, no. 560 (date and administrative data not mentioned, or lost)

Cat. 96

1 Royal Ontario Museum, Toronto, inv. no. 978.76.76: Sokoly 2002, no. 319 (dated 305 AH / 917–18 CE, *tiraz al-khassa* in Madinat al-Salam, by order of the vizier 'Ali ibn Muhammad)

2 Textile Museum, Washington, DC, inv. no. 73.17: Kühnel and Bellinger, 1952, pp. 28–29, pl. XII; Sokoly 2002, no. 413 (dated 310 AH / 922–23 CE, *tiraz al-khassa* in Madinat al-Salam, by intermediation of the vizier Hamid bin al-'Abbas)

3 Textile Museum, Washington, DC, inv. no. 73.557: Kühnel and Bellinger, 1952, pp. 31–32, pl. XII; Sokoly 2002, no. 453 (dated 318 AH / 930–31 CE, by intermediation of Hasan ibn al-Husayn ibn *al-amir al-mu'minin*)

4 Textile Museum, Washington, DC, inv. no. 73.369: Kühnel and Bellinger, 1952, p. 34, pl. XIII; Sokoly 2002, no. 561 (reign of al-Muqtadir, administrative data lost)

5 Royal Ontario Museum, Toronto, inv. no. 978.76.315: Sokoly 2002, no. 233 (dated 297 AH / 909–10 CE, administrative data lost)

6 Biblioteca Apostolica Vaticana, Vatican City, inv. no. 6788: Cornu 1992, pp. 137–39; Sokoly 2002, no. 353: datable 306–311 AH / 918–23 CE, *tiraz al-'amma* in Tinnis, by order of the vizier Hamid bin al-'Abbas by intermediation of Shafi' *mawla amir al-mu'minin*)

7 Textile Museum, Washington, DC, inv. no. 73.530: Kühnel and Bellinger 1952, p. 26, pl. IX; Sokoly 2002, no. 366 (dated 307 AH / 919–20 CE, *tiraz* workshop in Tinnis, by intermediation of Shafi' *mawla amir al-mu'minin*)

Cat. 97

1 Ashmolean Museum, Oxford, inv. no. 1988.48: Britton 1942, p. 161, fig. 2; Sokoly 2002, no. 458 (dated 320 AH / 932–33 CE, administrative data not mentioned)

2 Museum of Islamic Art, Cairo, inv. no. 10569: *RCEA* 1931–91, vol. III, 1932, pp. 191–92, no. 1143; Pfister 1937, p. 169; Sokoly 2002, no. 459 (dated 320 AH / 932–33 CE, administrative data lost)

3 Museum of Islamic Art, Cairo, inv. no. 9787: *RCEA* 1931–91, vol. IV, 1933, pp. 13–14, no. 1232; Pfister 1937, p. 169; Sokoly 2002, no. 461 (dated 320 AH / 932–33 CE, *tiraz al-khassa* in Madinat al-Salam)

4 Museum of Fine Arts, Boston, inv. no. 32.109: *RCEA* 1931–91, vol. IV, 1933, p. 14, no. 1233; Britton 1938, pp. 30–31, no. 32.109, fig. 4; Sokoly 2002, no. 463 (dated 320 AH / 932–33 CE, *tiraz al-khassa* in Madinat al-Salam)

Cat. 98

1 Royal Ontario Museum Toronto, inv. no. 978.76.400: Sokoly 2002, no. 264 (dated 300 AH / 912–13 CE, *tiraz al-khassa* in Madinat al-Salam)

2 Museum of Fine Arts, Boston, inv. no. 32.109: *RCEA* 1931–91, vol. IV, 1933, p. 14, no. 1233; Britton 1938, pp. 30–31, no. 32.109, fig. 4; Sokoly 2002, no. 463 (dated 320 AH / 932–33 CE, *tiraz al-khassa* in Madinat al-Salam)

3 Biblioteca Apostolica Vaticana, Vatican City, inv. no. 6796: Cornu 1992, pp. 170–1; Sokoly 2002, no. 1128 (reign of Al-Qadir, made in the *tiraz al-khassa* in Madinat al-Salam, by intermediation of al-Fath *mawla amir al-mu'minin*)

Cat. 105

1 Textile Museum, Washington, DC, inv. no. 73.368: Kühnel and Bellinger 1952, p. 32, pl. XIII; Sokoly 2002, no. 562 (dated 320 AH / 932–33 CE, *tiraz al-khassa*, place of production and ordering officer lost)

2 Museum of Fine Arts, Boston, inv. no. 31.50: Britton, 1938, p. 31, no. 31.50, fig. 5; Sokoly 2002, no. 562 (date and administrative data lost)

3 Museum of Fine Arts, Boston, inv. no. 31.49: Britton 1938, p. 32, no. 31.49, fig. 6; Sokoly 2002, no. 713 (date and administrative data lost)

4 Biblioteca Apostolica Vaticana, Vatican City, inv. no. 6740: Cornu 1992, pp. 163–64; Sokoly 2002, no. 1120 (dated 382 AH / 992–93 CE, or 392 AH / 1001–02 CE, administrative data not mentioned)

5 Dumbarton Oaks, Washington, DC, inv. no. 33.22: Glidden and Thompson 1989, pp. 93–97, no. 15, fig. 15; Sokoly 2002, no. 1123 (dated 399 AH / 1008–09 CE, administrative data not mentioned)

Cat. 106

1 Biblioteca Apostolica Vaticana, Vatican City, inv. no. 6740: Cornu 1992, pp. 163–64; Sokoly 2002, no. 1120 (datable 381–422 AH / 991–1031 CE, administrative data not mentioned)

2 Biblioteca Apostolica Vaticana, Vatican City, inv. no. 6739: Cornu 1992, pp. 175–77 (datable 422–467 AH / 1031–75CE, administrative data not mentioned)

3 Bouvier Collection, inv. no. JFB I 52: Geneva 1993, pp. 186–87, no. 109 (non-historical)

4 Bouvier Collection, inv. no. JFB I 36: Geneva 1993, pp. 187–88, no. 110 (non-historical)

5 Textile Museum, Washington, DC, inv. no. 73.505: Kühnel and Bellinger 1952, pp. 93–94, pl. L (non-historical)

6 Textile Museum, Washington, DC, inv. no. 73.563: Kühnel and Bellinger 1952, p. 94, pl. L (non-historical)

7 Metropolitan Museum of Art, New York, inv. no. 31.106.32: Walker and Froom 1992, no. 20, pp. 31–32 (non-historical)

8 Metropolitan Museum of Art, New York, inv. no. 31.19.6 (non-historical)

9 Metropolitan Museum of Art, New York, inv. no. 31.106.24 (non-historical)

Cat. 107

1 Metropolitan Museum of Art, New York, inv. 31.19.2: Sokoly 2002, no. 53 (date lost, reign of al-Mu'tamid, administrative data lost)

2 Textile Museum, Washington, DC, inv. no. 73.366: Kühnel and Bellinger 1952, pp. 14–15, pl. VI; Sokoly 2002, no. 112 (dated 283 AH / 896–97 CE, by order of the amir, place of production lost)

3 Textile Museum, Washington, DC, inv. no. 73.657: Kühnel and Bellinger 1952, p. 19, pl. VIII; Sokoly 2002, no. 190 (date lost, Merw)

4 Kelsey Museum of Archaeology, Ann Arbor, MI, inv. no. 22.506: Day 1937, pp. 426–27, no. 6, fig. 6; Sokoly 2002, no. 170 (dated 293 AH / 906–07 CE, administrative data not mentioned)

5 Museum für Islamische Kunst, Berlin, inv. no. 5558: Kühnel 1933, p. 60, no. 1; *RCEA* 1931–91, vol. IV, 1933, p. 205, no. 1215A; Sokoly 2002, no. 576 (date not mentioned, reign of al-Muqtadir, administrative data not mentioned)

Cat. 109

1 Metropolitan Museum of Art, New York, inv. no. 31.106.23: Walker and Froom 1992, pp. 13–14, no. 2; Sokoly 2002, no. 3 (date lost, *tiraz* workshop in San'a')

2 Metropolitan Museum of Art, New York, inv. no. 31.106.46: Sokoly 2002, no. 43 (dated 250 AH / 864–65 CE, *tiraz* workshop in San'a')

3 Benaki Museum, Athens, inv. no. 15600: unpublished (date lost, reign of al-Musta'in)

4 Metropolitan Museum of Art, New York, inv. no. 31.106.47: Sokoly 2002, no. 52 (date lost, reign of al-Mu'tamid, by order of the amir Ja'far *ibn* [al-amir al-mu'minin])

5 Textile Museum, Washington, DC, inv. no. 73.652: Kühnel and Bellinger 1952, p. 8, pl. II; Sokoly 2002, no. 37 (date lost, reign of al-Mutawakkil, by order of the amir Abu 'Abdallah)

6 Textile Museum, Washington, DC, inv. no. 73.665: Kühnel and Bellinger 1952, pp. 7–8, pl. II; Sokoly 2002, no. 38.4 (dated 245 AH / 859–60 CE, by order of the amir Abu 'Abdallah *ibn amir al-mu'minin* by intermediation of 'Ubaydallah [ibn Yahya ibn Khaqan])

Cat. 110

1 Metropolitan Museum of Art, New York, inv. no. 31.106.23: Walker and Froom 1992, pp. 13–14, no. 2; Sokoly 2002, no. 3 (date lost, *tiraz* workshop in San'a')

2 Metropolitan Museum of Art, New York, inv. no. 31.106.46: Sokoly 2002, no. 43 (dated 250 AH / 864–65 CE, *tiraz* workshop in San'a')

3 Museum of Islamic Art, Cairo, inv. no. 13228: Lamm 1937, p. 145; Sokoly 2002, no. 70.1 (dated 270 AH / 883–84 CE, *tiraz* workshop in San'a')

4 Kulturen, Lund, inv. no. 37.702: Lamm 1938, pp. 106–07, no. 3, pl. I; Sokoly 2002, no. 79 (dated 276 AH / 889–90 CE, *tiraz al-khassa* in San'a')

5 Museum of Islamic Art, Cairo, inv. no. 13214: Lamm 1937, p. 145; Sokoly 2002, no. 116.1 (dated 284 AH / 897–98 CE, *tiraz [al-khassa]* in San'a')

6 Kelsey Museum of Archaeology, Ann Arbor, MI, inv. no. 22.504: Day 1937, pp. 424–26, no. 4, fig. 4; Sokoly 2002, no. 135 (dated 289 AH / 901–02 CE, *tiraz al-khassa* in San'a')

7 Museum of Islamic Art, Cairo, inv. no. 9053: *RCEA* 1931–91, vol. III, 1932, pp. 151–52, no. 1072; Pfister 1936, pp. 78–79; Lamm 1937, pp. 145–46; Sokoly 2002, no. 422 (dated 311 AH / 923–24 CE, *tiraz al-khassa* in San'a')

Cat. 111

1 Museum of Islamic Art, Cairo, inv. no. 13214: Lamm 1937, p. 145; Sokoly 2002, no. 116.1 (dated 284 AH / 897–98 CE, *tiraz [al-khassa]* in San'a')

2 Textile Museum, Washington, DC, inv. no. 73.494: Kühnel and Bellinger 1952, pp. 89–90, pl. XLVII

Cat. 112

1 Metropolitan Museum of Art, New York, inv. no. 31.106.23: Walker and Froom 1992, pp. 13–14, no. 2; Sokoly 2002, no. 3 (date lost, *tiraz* workshop in San'a')

2 Musée des Tissus, Lyon, inv. no. 36.659: Cornu 1991, pp. 50–55, figs 1–4 (not inscribed)

3 Dumbarton Oaks, Washington, DC, inv. no. 1933.42: Glidden and Thompson 1989, pp. 91–93, no. 14, fig. 14 (non-historical inscription)

4 Metropolitan Museum of Art, New York, inv. no. 31.106.46: Sokoly 2002, no. 43 (dated 250 AH / 864–65 CE, *tiraz* workshop in San'a')

5 Museum of Islamic Art, Cairo, inv. no. 13228: Lamm 1937, p. 145; Sokoly 2002, no. 70.1 (dated 270 AH / 883–84 CE, *tiraz* workshop in San'a')

6 Kulturen, Lund, inv. no. 37.702: Lamm 1938, pp. 106–07, no. 3, pl. I; Sokoly 2002, no. 79 (dated 276 AH / 889–90 CE, *tiraz al-khassa* in San'a')

7 Museum of Islamic Art, Cairo, inv. no. 13214: Lamm 1937, p. 145; Sokoly 2002, no. 116.1 (dated 284 AH / 897–98 CE, *tiraz [al-khassa]* in San'a')

8 Kelsey Museum of Archaeology, Ann Arbor, MI, inv. no. 22.504: Day 1937, pp. 424–26, no. 4, fig. 4; Sokoly 2002, no. 135 (dated 289 AH / 901–02 CE, *tiraz al-khassa* in San'a')

9 Museum of Islamic Art, Cairo, inv. no. 9053: *RCEA* 1931–91, vol. III, 1932, pp. 151–52, no. 1072; Pfister 1936, pp. 78–79; Lamm 1937, pp. 145–46; Sokoly 2002, no. 422 (dated 311 AH / 923–24, *tiraz al-khassa* in San'a')

Cat. 113

1 Musée des Tissus, Lyon, inv. no. 36.659: Cornu 1991, pp. 50–55, figs 1–4 (non-historical)
2 Musée des Tissus, Lyon, inv. no. 46.380: Cornu 1991, pp. 55–57, fig. 6 (non-historical)
3 Musée des Tissus, Lyon, inv. no. 24.569 / 8: Cornu 1991, pp. 58–61, figs 8, 9 (non-historical)
4 Musée des Tissus, Lyon, inv. no. 41.659: Cornu 1991, pp. 61–66, figs 10–11 (non-historical)
5 Textile Museum, Washington, DC, inv. no. 73.255: Cornu 1991, p. 56, fig. 5 (non-historical)
6 Metropolitan Museum of Art, New York, inv. no. 31.106.23: Walker and Froom 1992, pp. 13–14, no. 2; Sokoly 2002, no. 3 (date lost, *tiraz* workshop in San'a')
7 Museum of Islamic Art, Cairo, inv. no. 13228: Lamm 1937, p. 145; Sokoly 2002, no. 70.1 (dated 270 AH / 883–84, *tiraz* workshop in San'a')

Cat. 114

1 Biblioteca Apostolica Vaticana, Vatican City, inv. no. 6763: Pfister 1945–46, pp. 47–90, no. 36, pl. X; Cornu 1992, pp. 184–85, illus. p. 518
2 Textile Museum, Washington, DC, inv. no. 73.612: Kühnel and Bellinger 1952, pp. 97–98, pl. LI
3 Museum of Islamic Art, Cairo, inv. no. unknown: *RCEA* 1931–91, vol. VI, 1935, no. 2140
4 Textile Museum, Washington, DC, inv. no. 73.53: Kühnel and Bellinger 1952, pp. 97–98
5 Textile Museum, Washington, DC, inv. no. 73.52: Kühnel and Bellinger 1952, pp. 98–99, pl. LI
6 Dumbarton Oaks, Washington, DC, inv. no. BZ.1933.37: Glidden and Thompson 1989, pp. 89–91, no. 12, fig. 12; McWilliams and Sokoly 2021, pp. 82–83, cat. no. 11 (date not mentioned, by order of Abu Ibrahim bin al-Muntasir bi-llah al-Jamr bin Muhammad)
7 Biblioteca Apostolica Vaticana, Vatican City, inv. no. 6744: Cornu 1992, pp. 63–65, illus. p. 483 (date not mentioned, by order of Abu Ibrahim bin al-Muntasir bi-llah al-Jamr bin Muhammad)
8 Cleveland Museum of Art, inv. no. 1950.353; Mackie 2015, pp. 122–24, fig. 3.14 (date not mentioned, *al-da'i ila al-haqq, amir al-mu'minin* Yusuf ibn Yahya ibn Nasir li-Din Allah Ahmad)

Cat. 115

1 Benaki Museum, Athens, inv. no. 14735: *RCEA* 1931–91, vol. IV, 1933, pp. 173–74, no. 1542;

Combe 1939, pp. 841–44; Sokoly 2002, no. 588; Evans 2012, pp. 263–64, no. 185 (inscribed 'mimma umira bi-'amalihi fi tiraz al-khassa bi-Tabariyya')
2 Metropolitan Museum of Art, New York, inv. no. 39.113: Dimand 1942–43, pp. 76–79; Ekhtiar et al. 2011, pp. 50–51, no. 28
3 Museum für Islamische Kunst, Berlin, inv. no. I. 68/63: unpublished (inscribed 'tiraz al-khassa')
4 Bouvier Collection, inv. no. JFB I 45: Geneva 1993, pp. 130–31, no. 65 (inscribed '[mimm]a umira')
5 Bouvier Collection, inv. no. JFB I 46: Geneva 1993, p. 132, no. 66
6 Biblioteca Apostolica Vaticana, Vatican City, inv. no. 6940: Cornu 1992, pp. 59–62, illus. 480
7 Textile Museum, Washington, DC, inv. no. 73.662: Kühnel and Bellinger 1952, p. 46, pl. XX; Sokoly 2002, no. 799 (dated 334 AH / 945–46 CE, *tiraz al-khassa* in Damietta, by order of the vizier Muhammad bin 'Ali)
8 Textile Museum, Washington, DC, inv. no. 73.651: Kühnel and Bellinger 1952, p. 47, pl. XX; Sokoly 2002, no. 803 (date lost, reign of al-Mustakfi, administrative data not mentioned)

Cat. 116

1 Bouvier Collection, inv. no. JFB I 126: Geneva 1993, pp. 312–14, no. 208
2 Textile Museum Washington, DC, inv. no. 6.115: Kühnel and Bellinger 1952, pp. 99–100, pl. LII
3 Textile Museum Washington, DC, inv. no. 6.122, at https://collections-gwu.zetcom.net/en/collection/item/8267/: Kühnel and Bellinger 1952, p. 100

Cat. 117

1 Bouvier Collection, inv. no. JFB I 126: Geneva 1993, pp. 312–14, no. 208
2 Textile Museum, Washington, DC, inv. no. 6.115: Kühnel and Bellinger 1952, pp. 99–100, pl. LII
3 Textile Museum, Washington, DC, inv. no. 6.122, at https://collections-gwu.zetcom.net/en/collection/item/8267/: Kühnel and Bellinger 1952, p. 100

Cat. 118

1 Bouvier Collection, inv. no. JFB I 126: Geneva 1993, pp. 312–14, no. 208
2 Textile Museum, Washington, DC, inv. no. 6.115: Kühnel and Bellinger 1952, pp. 99–100, pl. LII
3 Textile Museum, Washington, DC, inv. no. 6.122, at https://collections-gwu.zetcom.net/en/collection/item/8267/: Kühnel and Bellinger 1952, p. 100

Cat. 120

1 Royal Ontario Museum, Toronto, inv. no. 978.76.302: Gervers 1979, p. 127; Sokoly 2002, no. 1207

(dated 375 AH / 985–86 CE, by order of the vizier)

Cat. 123

1 Royal Ontario Museum, Toronto, inv. no. 978.76.324: Sokoly 2002, no. 1181 (date lost, ordered from a *tiraz*)
2 Metropolitan Museum of Art, New York, inv. no. 1971.151: Ettinghausen et al. 2001, p. 209, fig. 336; Sokoly 2002, no. 1205.1 (dated 373 AH / 983–84 CE, *tiraz al-khassa* in Tinnis)

Cat. 124

1 Textile Museum, Washington, DC, inv. no. 73.32: Kühnel and Bellinger 1952, p. 61, pl. XXVII; Sokoly 2002, no. 1316 (administrative data not mentioned)
2 Royal Ontario Museum, Toronto, inv. no. 978.76.299: Sokoly 2002, no. 1323 (administrative data lost)

Cat. 125

1 Textile Museum, Washington, DC, inv. no. 73.38: Kühnel and Bellinger 1952, pp. 58–59, pl. XXVI; Sokoly 2002, no. 1220 (dated 378 AH / 988–89 CE, *tiraz al-'amma* in Tuna)
2 Royal Ontario Museum, Toronto, inv. no. 978.76.355: Sokoly 2002, no. 1324 (reign of al-'Aziz, administrative data lost)
3 Musée Nationale de l'Art d'Afrique et d'Océanie, Paris, inv. no. 1971–74/2: El-Habib 1973, pp. 299–302; Sokoly 2002, no. 1342 (reign of al-'Aziz, administrative data not mentioned, or lost)
4 Royal Ontario Museum, Toronto, inv. no. 978.76.354: Sokoly 2002, no. 1345 (reign of al-'Aziz, administrative data not mentioned, or lost)
5 Kulturen, Lund, inv. no. 37.679: Lamm 1938, p. 113, no. 14, pl. VI; Sokoly 2002, no. 1186 (datable 365–73 AH / 975–84 CE, by order of the vizier Abu al-Faraj Ya'qub bin Yusuf *'abd amir al-mu'minin*)
6 Textile Museum, Washington, DC, inv. no. 73.35: Kühnel and Bellinger 1952, p. 58, pl. XXVI; Sokoly 2002, no. 1206 (dated 374 AH / 984–85 CE, administrative data not mentioned)
7 Biblioteca Apostolica Vaticana, Vatican City, inv. no. 6896: Cornu 1992, pp. 200–02; Sokoly 2002, no. 1215 (dated 377 AH / 987–88 CE, Shata)
8 Textile Museum, Washington, DC, inv. no. 73.38: Kühnel and Bellinger 1952, pp. 58–59, pl. XXVI; Sokoly 2002, no. 1220 (dated 378 AH / 988–89 CE, *tiraz al-'amma* in Tuna)
9 Kelsey Museum of Archaeology, Ann Arbor, MI, inv. no. 94.182: Sokoly 2002, no. 1221 (dated 379 AH / 989–90 CE, administrative data not mentioned, or lost)
10 Metropolitan Museum of Art, New York, inv. no. 29.179.22: Upton 1930–31, p. 168, no. 15, fig. 15; Sokoly 2002, no. 1311

(reign of al-'Aziz, administrative data not mentioned, or lost)
11 Cooper-Hewitt Museum, New York, inv. no. 1939.11.3 ABC; Sokoly 2002, no. 1320 (dated 379 AH / 989–90 CE, administrative data not mentioned, or lost)
12 Royal Ontario Museum, Toronto, inv. no. 978.76.355: Sokoly 2002, no. 1324 (reign of al-'Aziz, administrative data not mentioned, or lost)

Cat. 126

1 Textile Museum, Washington, DC, inv. no. 73.35: Kühnel and Bellinger 1952, p. 58, pl. XXVI; Sokoly 2002, no. 1206 (dated 374 AH / 984–85 CE, administrative data not mentioned)
2 Biblioteca Apostolica Vaticana, Vatican City, inv. no. 6896: Cornu 1992, pp. 200–02; Sokoly 2002, no. 1215 (dated 377 AH / 987–88 CE, Shata)
3 Textile Museum, Washington, DC, inv. no. 73.38: Kühnel and Bellinger 1952, pp. 58–59, pl. XXVI; Sokoly 2002, no. 1220 (dated 378 AH / 988–89 CE, *tiraz al-'amma* in Tuna)
4 Metropolitan Museum of Art, New York, inv. no. 29.179.22: Upton 1930–31, p. 168, no. 15, fig. 15; Sokoly 2002, no. 1311 (reign of al-'Aziz, administrative data not mentioned, or lost)
5 Textile Museum, Washington, DC, inv. no. 73.32: Kühnel and Bellinger 1952, p. 61, pl. XXVII; Sokoly 2002, no. 1316 (reign of al-'Aziz, administrative data not mentioned)
6 Royal Ontario Museum, Toronto, inv. no. 978.76.299: Sokoly 2002, no. 1323 (reign of al-'Aziz, administrative data not mentioned)
7 Royal Ontario Museum, Toronto, inv. no. 978.76.355: Sokoly 2002, no. 1324 (reign of al-'Aziz, administrative data not mentioned)

Cat. 128

1 formerly Tano Collection: *RCEA* 1931–91, vol. VI, 1935, p. 95, no. 2175; Sokoly 2002, no. 1411 (dated 403 AH / 1012–13 CE, *tiraz al-'amma* in Dabqu [Dabiq])
2 Textile Museum, Washington, DC, inv. no. 73.672: Kühnel and Bellinger 1952, pp. 63–64, pl. XXVIII; Sokoly 2002, no. 1390 (dated 393 AH / 1002–03 CE, *tiraz al-'amma* in Damietta)
3 Royal Ontario Museum, Toronto, inv. no. 978.76.68, ex Abemayor Collection: *RCEA* 1931–91, vol. VI, 1935, pp. 126–27, no. 2223; Sokoly 2002, no. 1427 (dated 411 AH / 1020–21 CE, *tiraz al-'amma* in Damietta)
4 Museum of Islamic Art, Cairo, inv. no. 10123: *RCEA* 1931–91, vol. VI, 1935, pp. 182–83, no. 2338; Sokoly 2002, no. 1429 (dated 415 AH / 1024–25 CE, *tiraz al-'amma* in Damietta)
5 Museum of Islamic Art, Cairo, inv. no. 13015: *RCEA* 1931–91, vol. VI, 1935, pp. 226–27, no. 2056A;

Marzouk 1942, p. 103; Marzouk 1943, p. 164 n. 4, fig. 3; Paris 1998, p. 109, no. 31; Sokoly 2002, no. 1373 (dated 387 AH / 997–98 CE, *tiraz al-khassa* in Damietta)

6 Biblioteca Apostolica Vaticana, Vatican City, inv. no. 6902: Cornu 1992, pp. 207–09; Pfister 1945–46, p. 76, no. 57, pl. XV; Sokoly 2002, no. 1521 (reign of al-Hakim, date lost, *tiraz al-khassa* in Damietta)

7 Museum of Islamic Art, Cairo, inv. no. 8264: *RCEA* 1931–91, vol. VI, 1935, p. 119, no. 2213; Marzouk 1942, p. 107, p. 194, pl. 7 (detail); Marzouk 1943, p. 165 n. 6, fig. 7; Hassan 1948, p. 352; Sokoly 2002, no. 1416 (datable to 404–11 AH / 1013–21 CE, *wali ahd al-muslimin wa khalifa amir al-mu'minin* Abu al-Qasim 'Abd al-Rahim ibn Ilyas ibn Ahmad ibn Mahdi bi-llah *amir al-mu'minin*)

8 Museum of Islamic Art, Cairo, inv. no. 9751: Wiet 1935b, p. 52, no. 203; *RCEA* 1931–91, vol. VIII, 1937, pp. 8–9, no. 2812; Marzouk 1942, p. 107, no. 29; Sokoly 2002, no. 1747 (reign of al-Mustansir, administrative data not mentioned, or lost)

Cat. 129

1 Museum für Islamische Kunst, Berlin, inv. no. 5561: Kühnel 1933, p. 63, no. 4, pl. II, fig. 6; *RCEA* 1931–91, vol. VI, 1935, p. 19, no. 2046; Sokoly 2002, no. 1367 (dated 386 AH / 996–97 CE, administrative data not mentioned, letter height small)

2 Dumbarton Oaks, Washington, DC, inv. no. 33.10: *RCEA* 1931–91, vol. VI, 1935, pp. 40–41, no. 2084; Glidden and Thompson 1988, p. 129, no. 7, fig. 7; Sokoly 2002, no. 1381 (dated 390 AH / 999–1000 CE, administrative data not mentioned, max. letter height 0.7 cm)

3 Röhsska Museet, Gothenburg, inv. no. 235/1935: Lamm 1935, p. 7, fig. 4; Lamm 1938, p. 116, no. 19; Sokoly 2002, no. 1507 (reign of al-Hakim, date lost, *tiraz al-'amma* in Tuna; max. letter height 1.0 cm)

4 Biblioteca Apostolica Vaticana, Vatican City, inv. no. 6901: Pfister 1945–46, p. 75, no. 55, pl. XIV; Cornu 1992, pp. 202–03 (reign of al-Hakim, date lost, administrative data not mentioned; max. letter height 1.0 cm)

5 Textile Museum, Washington, DC, inv. no. 73.659: Kühnel and Bellinger 1952, pp. 62–63, pl. XXVIII; Sokoly 2002, no. 1545 (reign of al-Hakim, date and administrative data not mentioned; max. letter height 1.0 cm)

Cat. 131

1 Royal Ontario Museum, Toronto, inv. no. 978.76.62: Sokoly 2002, no. 1353 (administrative data not mentioned, or lost)

2 Royal Ontario Museum, Toronto, inv. no. 978.76.53: Sokoly 2002,

---

no. 1354 (administrative data not mentioned, or lost)

3 Biblioteca Apostolica Vaticana, Vatican City, inv. no. 6903: Cornu 1992, pp. 215–16; Sokoly 2002, no. 1547 (administrative data not mentioned, or lost)

Cat. 132

1 Royal Ontario Museum, Toronto, inv. no. 978.76.410: Sokoly 2002, no. 1352 (datable 399 AH / 1008–09 CE, administrative data not mentioned, or lost)

2 Royal Ontario Museum, Toronto, inv. no. 978.76.62: Sokoly 2002, no. 1353 (reign of al-Hakim, date lost, administrative data not mentioned, or lost)

3 Royal Ontario Museum, Toronto, inv. no. 978.76.45: Sokoly 2002, no. 1358 (reign of al-Hakim, date lost, administrative data not mentioned, or lost)

4 Royal Ontario Museum, Toronto, inv. no. 978.76.73: Sokoly 2002, no. 1360 (dated 388 AH / 998 CE, administrative data not mentioned, or lost)

5 Royal Ontario Museum, Toronto, inv. no. 978.76.352: Sokoly 2002, no. 1362 (reign of al-Hakim, date lost, administrative data not mentioned, or lost)

6 Museum für Islamische Kunst, Berlin, inv. no. 5561: Kühnel 1933, p. 63, no. 4, pl. II, fig. 6; Sokoly 2002, no. 1367 (dated 386 AH / 996–97 CE, administrative data not mentioned)

7 Textile Museum, Washington, DC, inv. no. 73.628: Kühnel and Bellinger 1952, p. 62, pl. XXVIII; Sokoly 2002, no. 1368 (dated 386 AH / 996–97 CE, *tiraz al-'amma* in Tuna, by order of the vizier Abu Muhammad al-Hasan 'Ammar *'abd amir al-mu'minin*)

8 Dumbarton Oaks, Washington, DC, inv. no. 33.10: Glidden and Thompson 1988, p. 129, no. 7, fig. 7; Sokoly 2002, no. 1381 (dated 390 AH / 999–1000 CE, administrative data not mentioned)

9 Röhsska Museet, Gothenburg, inv. no. 235/1935: Lamm 1938, p. 116, no. 19; Sokoly 2002, no. 1507 (reign of al-Hakim, date lost, *tiraz al-'amma* in Tuna)

10 Biblioteca Apostolica Vaticana, Vatican City, inv. no. 6901: Cornu 1992, pp. 202–03; Sokoly 2002, no. 1519 (reign of al-Hakim, date lost, administrative data not mentioned, or lost)

11 Textile Museum, Washington, DC, inv. no. 73.659: Kühnel and Bellinger 1952, pp. 62–63, pl. XXVIII; Sokoly 2002, no. 1545 (reign of al-Hakim, date and administrative data not mentioned, or lost)

Cat. 134

1 Textile Museum, Washington, DC, inv. no. 73.43: Kühnel and Bellinger 1952, pp. 67–69, pl. XXX; Sokoly 2002, no. 1512 (reign of al-Hakim,

---

administrative data not mentioned, or lost)

2 Bouvier Collection, inv. no. JFB I 133: Geneva 1993, pp. 206–08, no. 122 (non-historical inscription)

Cat. 138

1 Biblioteca Apostolica Vaticana, Vatican City, inv. no. 6783: Cornu 1992, pp. 187–88, illus. p. 520 (non-historical inscription)

2 Biblioteca Apostolica Vaticana, Vatican City, inv. no. 6782: Cornu 1992, pp. 188–90, illus. p. 520 (non-historical inscription)

3 Biblioteca Apostolica Vaticana, Vatican City, inv. no. 6784: Cornu 1992, pp. 190–91, illus. p. 521 (non-historical inscription)

4 Benaki Museum, Athens, inv. no. 15046: unpublished (non-historical inscription)

5 Bouvier Collection, inv. no. JFB I 91: Geneva 1993, pp. 188–90 (non-historical inscription)

6 Bouvier Collection, inv. no. JFB I 116: Geneva 1993, p. 191 (non-historical inscription)

7 Metropolitan Museum of Art, New York, inv. no. 32.129.3: unpublished (non-historical inscription)

8 Cleveland Museum of Art, inv. no. 1950.551: Mackie 2015, p. 158, p. 160, fig. 4.33 (non-historical inscription)

Cat. 139

1 Textile Museum, Washington, DC, inv. no. 73.627: Kühnel and Bellinger 1952, p. 70, pl. XXXI; Sokoly 2002, no. 1516 (reign of al-Hakim, date and administrative data not mentioned, or lost)

2 Boston Museum of Fine Arts, inv. no. 34.119: Britton 1938, p. 53, fig. 40; Sokoly 2002, no. 1517 (reign of al-Hakim, date and administrative data not mentioned, or lost)

3 Boston Museum of Fine Arts, inv. no. 32.31: Britton 1938, p. 54, fig. 42; Sokoly 2002, no. 1518 (reign of al-Hakim, date lost and administrative data not mentioned, or lost)

4 Dumbarton Oaks, Washington, DC, inv. no. 33.13: Glidden and Thompson 1988, pp. 129–31, no. 8, fig. 8; Sokoly 2002, no. 1525 (reign of al-Hakim, date and administrative data not mentioned, or lost)

5 Kelsey Museum of Archaeology, Ann Arbor, MI, inv. no. 22.526: Day 1937, p. 444, no. 26, fig. 26; Sokoly 2002, no. 1530 (reign of al-Hakim, date and administrative data not mentioned, or lost)

6 Museum of Islamic Art, Cairo, inv. no. 10847: *RCEA* 1931–91, vol. VI, 1935, p. 135, no. 2243; Kühnel 1986, fig. 9; Sokoly 2002, no. 1549 (reign of al-Hakim, date and administrative data not mentioned, or lost)

7 Boston Museum of Fine Arts, inv. no. 34.116: Britton 1938, p. 54,

---

fig. 41; Sokoly 2002, no. 1550 (reign of al-Hakim, date and administrative data not mentioned, or lost)

Cat. 140

1 Museum of Islamic Art, Cairo, inv. no. 10847: *RCEA* 1931–91, vol. VI, 1935, p. 135, no. 2243; Kühnel 1986, fig. 9; Sokoly 2002, no. 1549 (reign of al-Hakim, date and administrative data not mentioned, or lost)

2 Boston Museum of Fine Arts, inv. no. 34.119: Britton 1938, p. 53, fig. 40; Sokoly 2002, no. 1517 (reign of al-Hakim, date and administrative data mentioned, or lost)

3 Metropolitan Museum of Art, New York, inv. no. 31.106.54: Walker and Froom 1992, pp. 20–22, no. 10 (administrative data not mentioned or lost)

Cat. 141

1 Textile Museum, Washington, DC, inv. no. 73.57: Kühnel and Bellinger 1952, pp. 70–71, pl. XXXII; Sokoly 2002, no. 1628 (reign of al-Zahir, administrative data not mentioned, or lost)

Cat. 142

1 Cincinnati Art Museum, inv. no. 1986.187: Sokoly 2002, no. 1566 (datable 418–27 AH / 1027–36 CE, by order of the vizier *al-wazir al-'ajal*)

2 Musée de Cluny, Paris, inv. no. 21871: *RCEA* 1931–91, vol. VII, 1936, p. 19, no. 2433; Paris 1998, p. 209, no. 195; Sokoly 2002, no. 1568 (datable 418–27 AH / 1027–36 CE, by order of the vizier *al-wazir al-'ajal safi amir al-mu'minin* […])

3 Ex Abemayor Collection: *RCEA* 1931–91, vol. VII, 1936, pp. 23–24, no. 2440; Sokoly 2002, no. 1569 (datable 418–27 AH / 1027–36 CE, by order of the vizier *al-wazir al-'ajal safi amir al-mu'minin wa khalisatuhu* Abu al-Qasim 'Ali)

4 Walters Art Gallery, Baltimore, inv. no. 85.528: Sokoly 2002, no. 1570 (datable 418–27 AH / 1027–36 CE, by order of the vizier *al-wazir al-'ajal safi amir al-mu'minin wa khalisatuhu* Abu al-Qasim 'Ali)

5 Museum of Islamic Art, Cairo, inv. no. 7966: *RCEA* 1931–91, vol. VII, 1936, pp. 63–64, no. 2501; Marzouk 1955, pp. 46–47, fig. 2; Sokoly 2002, no. 1571 (datable 418–27 AH / 1027–36 CE, by order of the vizier *al-wazir al-'ajal safi amir al-mu'minin wa khalisatuhu* Abu al-Qasim 'Ali ibn Ahmad)

6 Museum of Islamic Art, Cairo, inv. no. 14039: Marzouk 1955, pp. 50–51, fig. 4; Sokoly 2002, no. 1572 (datable 418–27 AH / 1027–36 CE, by order of the vizier *al-wazir al-'ajal safi amir al-mu'minin wa khalisatuhu* 'Ali ibn Ahmad)

7 Cleveland Museum of Art, inv. no. 50.554: *RCEA* 1931–91,

vol. VII, 1936, pp. 23–24, no. 2440; Sokoly 2002, no. 1573 (datable 418–27 AH / 1027–36 CE, by order of the vizier *al-wazir al-'ajal saf[i amir al-mu'minin wa kha]lisatuhu* Abu al-Qasim 'A[li])

8   Detroit Institute of Art, inv. no. 32.27: https://dia.org/collection/fragment-tiraz-textile-49091; Sokoly 2002, no. 1574 (datable 418–27 AH / 1027–36 CE, by order of the vizier *al-wazir al-'ajal safi amir al-mu'minin […]*)

9   Metropolitan Museum of Art, New York, inv. no. 55.69.6: Sokoly 2002, no. 1575 (datable 418–27 AH / 1027–36 CE, by order of the vizier *al-wazir al-'ajal […]*)

10   Kelsey Museum of Archaeology, Ann Arbor, MI, inv. no. 26.735: Guest 1930, pp. 762–64, no. 2, pl. XII, no. 1383; RCEA 1931–91, vol. VII, 1936, pp. 24–25, no. 2442; Sokoly 2002, no. 1576 (datable 418–27 AH / 1027–36 CE, *tiraz al-'amma*, by order of the vizier *al-wazir al-'ajal safi amir al-mu'minin wa khalisatuhu* Abu al-Qasim 'Ali ibn Ahmad)

11   Benaki Museum, Athens, inv. no. D.11: Combe 1940, p. 267, no. 13, pl. III; Sokoly 2002, no. 1577 (dated 420 AH / 1029–30 CE, *tiraz al-'amma* in Tinnis, by order of the vizier *al-wazir al-'ajal safi amir al-mu'minin wa khalisatuhu* Abu al-Qasim 'Ali ibn Ahmad)

12   Cincinnati Art Museum, inv. no. 1986.188ab: Sokoly 2002, no. 1584 (dated 423 AH / 1031–32 CE, *tiraz al-'amma* in Tinnis, by order of the vizier *al-wazir al-'ajal [safi] amir al-mu'minin […]*)

13   Benaki Museum, Athens, inv. no. 15020: Combe 1940, pp. 268–69, no. 16; Sokoly 2002, no. 1587 (dated 424 AH / 1032–33 CE, *tiraz al-khassa* in Tinnis, by order of the vizier *al-wazir al-'ajal safi amir al-mu'minin wa khalisatuhu* Abu al-Qasim 'Ali ibn Ahmad)

14   Museum of Islamic Art, Cairo, inv. no. 12854: RCEA 1931–91, vol. VII, 1936, pp. 12–13, no. 2418; Sokoly 2002, no. 1592 (dated 427 AH / 1035–36 CE, *tiraz al-'amma* in Tuna, by order of the vizier *[al-wazir] al-'ajal safi amir al-mu'minin wa khalisatuhu* Abu al-Qasim 'Ali ibn Ahmad)

15   Museum of Islamic Art, Cairo, inv. no. 11472: RCEA 1931–91, vol. VII, 1936, p. 12, no. 2417; Marzouk 1942, pl. 11; Sokoly 2002, no. 1593 (dated 427 AH / 1035–36 CE, *tiraz al-'amma* in Tuna, by order of the vizier *al-wazir al-'ajal safi amir al-mu'minin wa khalisatuhu* Abu al-Qasim 'Ali ibn Ahmad)

Cat. 143

1   Royal Ontario Museum, Toronto, inv. no. 970.364.2a, b: Golombek and Gervers 1977, pp. 107–08; Sokoly 2002, no. 1564 (dated 412 AH / 1021–22, *tiraz al-'amma* in Damietta)

2   Benaki Museum, Athens, inv. no. 15020: Combe 1940, pp. 268–69, no. 16; Sokoly 2002, no. 1587 (dated 424 AH / 1032–33 CE, *tiraz al-khassa* in Tinnis, by order of the vizier *al-wazir al-'ajal safi amir al-mu'minin wa khalisatuhu* Abu al-Qasim 'Ali ibn Ahmad)

3   Royal Ontario Museum, Toronto, inv. no. 978.76.195: Sokoly 2002, no. 1561 (reign of al-Zahir, date and administrative data lost)

4   Biblioteca Apostolica Vaticana, Vatican City, inv. no. 6832: Cornu 1992, pp. 224–25; Sokoly 2002, no. 1567 (datable 418–27 AH / 1027–36 CE, by order of the vizier *al-wazir al-'ajal safi amir al-mu'minin wa khalisatuhu [Abu al-Qasim 'Ali]*)

5   Walters Art Gallery, Baltimore, inv. no. 83.528: Sokoly 2002, no. 1570 (datable 418–27 AH / 1027–36 CE, by order of the vizier *al-wazir al-'ajal safi amir al-mu'minin wa khalisatuhu* Abu al-Qasim 'Ali)

6   Cleveland Museum of Art, inv. no. 50.554: RCEA 1931–91, vol. VII, 1936, pp. 23–24, no. 2440; Sokoly 2002, no. 1573 (datable 418–27 AH / 1027–36 CE, by order of the vizier *al-wazir al-'ajal saf[i amir al-mu'minin wa kha]lisatuhu* Abu al-Qasim 'A[li])

7   Metropolitan Museum of Art, New York, inv. no. 55.69.6: RCEA 1931–91, vol. VII, 1936, pp. 20–21, no. 2435; Sokoly 2002, no. 1575 (datable 418–27 AH / 1027–36 CE, by order of the vizier *al-wazir al-'ajal […]*)

8   Kelsey Museum of Archaeology, Ann Arbor, MI, inv. no. 26.735: RCEA 1931–91, vol. VII, 1936, pp. 24–25, no. 2442; Sokoly 2002, no. 1576 (datable 418–27 AH / 1027–36 CE, by order of the vizier *al-wazir al-'ajal safi amir al-mu'minin wa khalisatuhu* Abu al-Qasim 'Ali ibn Ahmad)

Cat. 144

1   Metropolitan Museum of Art, New York, inv. no. 46.156.1: Sokoly 2002, no. 1769 (reign of al-Mustansir, date and administrative data not mentioned, or lost)

2   Textile Museum, Washington, DC, inv. no. 73.67: Kühnel and Bellinger 1952, p. 78, pl. XXXVI; Sokoly 2002, no. 1694 (date lost, by order of the vizier *al-wazir al-'ajal*)

Cat. 145

1   Metropolitan Museum of Art, New York, inv. no. unknown: RCEA 1931–91, vol. VII, 1936, pp. 67–68, no. 2508; Sokoly 2002, no. 1665 (datable 427–36 AH / 1036–45 CE, by order of the vizier *al-wazir al-'ajal al-kamil al-'awhad safi amir al-mu'minin wa khalisatuhu* Abu al-Qasim 'Ali ibn Ahmad)

2   Ex Tano Collection: RCEA 1931–91, vol. VII 1936, p. 69, no. 2510; Sokoly 2002, no. 1659 (datable 427–36 AH / 1036–45 CE, by order of the vizier *[al-wazir al-'ajal] al-kamil al-'awhad safi amir al-mu'minin wa khalisatuhu* Abu al-Qasim 'Ali ibn Ahmad)

3   Ex Tano Collection: RCEA 1931–91, vol. VII, 1936, pp. 69–70, no. 2511; Sokoly 2002, no. 1660 (datable 427–36 AH / 1036–45 CE, by order of the vizier *al-wazir al-'ajal al-kamil al-'awhad safi amir al-mu'minin wa khalisatuhu*)

4   Royal Ontario Museum, Toronto, inv. no. 978.76.323: Sokoly 2002, no. 1652 (datable 427–36 AH / 1036–45 CE, by order of the vizier *al-wazir al-'ajal safi amir al-mu'minin wa khalisatuhu [Abu al-Qasim 'Ali ibn Ahmad]*)

5   Ex Tano Collection: RCEA 1931–91, vol. VII, 1936, pp. 69–70, no. 2511; Sokoly 2002, no. 1660 (datable 427–36 AH / 1036–45 CE, by order of the vizier *al-wazir al-'ajal al-kamil al-'awhad safi amir al-mu'minin wa khalisatuhu […]*)

6   Metropolitan Museum of Art, New York, inv. no. 31.106.50: Sokoly 2002, no. 1655 (datable 427–36 AH / 1036–45 CE, by order of the vizier *al-wazir al-'ajal safi amir al-mu'minin wa khalisatuhu* Abu al-Qasim 'Ali ibn Ahmad)

7   Museum of Islamic Art, Cairo, inv. no. 8407: RCEA 1931–91, vol. VII, 1936, p. 64, no. 2502; Sokoly 2002, no. 1656 (datable 427–36 AH / 1036–45 CE, by order of the vizier *[al-wazir al-'ajal] safi amir al-mu'minin wa khalisatuhu* Abu al-Qasim 'Ali ibn Ahmad)

8   Museum of Islamic Art, Cairo, inv. no. 10998: RCEA 1931–91, vol. VII, 1936, p. 65, no. 2504; Sokoly 2002, no. 1657 (datable 427–36 AH / 1036–45 CE, by order of the vizier *[al-wazir] al-'ajal safi amir al-mu'minin wa khalisatuhu* Abu al-Qasim 'Ali ibn Ahmad)

9   Museum of Islamic Art, Cairo, inv. no. 11088: RCEA 1931–91, vol. VII, 1936, p. 65, no. 2505; Sokoly 2002, no. 1658 (datable 427–36 AH / 1036–45 CE, by order of the vizier *al-wazir al-'ajal safi amir al-mu'minin wa khalisatuhu* Abu al-Qasim 'Ali ibn Ahmad)

10   Ex Tano Collection: RCEA 1931–91, vol. VII, 1936, p. 69, no. 2510; Sokoly 2002, no. 1659 (datable 427–36 AH / 1036–45 CE, by order of the vizier *[al-wazir al-'ajal] safi amir al-mu'minin wa khalisatuhu* Abu al-Qasim 'Ali ibn Ahmad)

11   Ex Tano Collection: RCEA 1931–91, vol. VII, 1936, p. 70, no. 2512; Sokoly 2002, no. 1661 (datable 427–36 AH / 1036–45 CE, by order of the vizier *al-wazir al-'ajal safi amir al-mu'minin wa khalisatuhu* Abu al-Qasim 'Ali ibn Ahmad)

12   Museum of Islamic Art, Cairo, inv. no. 10465: RCEA 1931–91, vol. 1936, p. 64, no. 2503; Sokoly 2002, no. 1662 (datable 427–36 AH / 1036–45 CE, by order of the vizier *al-wazir al-'ajal safi amir al-mu'minin wa khalisatuhu […]*)

13   Metropolitan Museum of Art, New York, inv. no. unknown: RCEA 1931–91, vol. VII, 1936, p. 67, no. 2507; Sokoly 2002, no. 1664 (datable 427–36 AH / 1036–45 CE, by order of the vizier *al-wazir al-'ajal […]*)

14   Ex Abemayor Collection: RCEA 1931–91, vol. VII, 1936, pp. 68–69, no. 2509; Sokoly 2002, no. 1666 (datable 427–36 AH / 1036–45 CE, by order of the vizier *al-wazir al-'ajal safi amir al-mu'minin […]*)

15   Royal Ontario Museum, Toronto, inv. no. 978.76.943: Sokoly 2002, no. 1667 (datable 427–36 AH / 1036–45 CE, by order of the vizier *al-wazir al-'ajal safi amir al-mu'minin wa khalisatuhu […]*)

16   Metropolitan Museum of Art, New York, inv. no. 55.69.5: Sokoly 2002, no. 1767 (reign of al-Mustansir, date and administrative data not mentioned, or lost)

Cat. 146

1   Textile Museum, Washington, DC, inv. no. 73.491: Kühnel and Bellinger 1952, pp. 72–73, pl. XXXIII; Sokoly 2002, no. 1675 (datable 440–41 AH / 1048–49 CE, by order of the vizier *[al-Hasan ibn] 'imad al-dawla* Muhammad ibn Ahmad)

2   Museum für Islamische Kunst, Berlin, inv. no. 3132: Kühnel 1927, pp. 22–23, no. 3132, pl. 7; RCEA 1931–91, vol. VII, 1936, p. 184, no. 2691; Sokoly 2002, no. 1692 (datable 450–52 AH / 1058–60 CE, by order of the vizier *al-wazir al-'ajal* [Abu al-Faraj Muhammad ibn Ja'far])

3   Textile Museum, Washington, DC, inv. no. 73.455: Kühnel and Bellinger 1952, pp. 76–77, pl. XXXV; Sokoly 2002, no. 1693 (datable 450–52 AH / 1058–60 CE, by order of the vizier *al-wazir al-'ajal* Abu al-Faraj Muhammad ibn Ja'far)

4   Boston Museum of Fine Arts, inv. no. 15.1304: Britton 1938, pp. 58–59, no. 15.1304, fig. 50; Sokoly 2002, no. 1753 (reign of al-Mustansir, date and administrative data not mentioned, or lost)

Cat. 148

1   Textile Museum, Washington, DC, inv. no. 73.491: Kühnel and Bellinger 1952, pp. 72–73, pl. XXXIII; Sokoly 2002, no. 1675 (datable 440–41 AH / 1048–49 CE, by order of the vizier *[al-Hasan ibn] 'imad al-dawla* Muhammad ibn Ahmad)

2   Museum für Islamische Kunst, Berlin, inv. no. 3132: Kühnel 1927, pp. 22–23, no. 3132, pl. 7; RCEA 1931–91, vol. VII, 1936, p. 184, no. 2691; Sokoly 2002, no. 1692 (datable 450–52 AH / 1058–60 CE, by order of the vizier *al-wazir al-'ajal* [Abu al-Faraj Muhammad ibn Ja'far])

3   Textile Museum, Washington, DC, inv. no. 73.455: Kühnel and Bellinger 1952, pp. 76–77,

pl. XXXV; Sokoly 2002, no. 1693
(datable 450–52 AH / 1058–60 CE,
by order of the vizier *al-wazir al-
'ajal* Abu al-Faraj Muhammad ibn
Ja'far)

4 Boston Museum of Fine Arts,
   inv. no. 15.1304: Britton 1938,
   pp. 58–59, no. 15.1304, fig. 50;
   Sokoly 2002, no. 1753 (reign of al-
   Mustansir, date and administrative
   data not mentioned, or lost)

Cat. 149

1 Textile Museum, Washington,
   DC, inv. no. 73.375: Kühnel and
   Bellinger 1952, p. 75, pl. XXXIV;
   Sokoly 2002, no. 1681 (datable
   442 AH / 1050–51 CE, or 450 AH /
   1058–59 CE, by order of the vizier
   Abu Muhammad al-Husayn bin 'Ali
   bin 'Abd al-Rahman [al-Yazuri])

Cat. 150

1 Biblioteca Apostolica Vaticani,
   Vatican City, inv. no. 6832: Cornu
   1992, pp. 224–25, illus. p. 532;
   Sokoly 2002, no. 1567 (datable
   418–27 AH / 1027–36 CE, by order of
   the vizier *al-wazir al-'ajal safi amir
   al-mu'minin wa khalisatuhu* [Abu
   al-Qasim Ahmad ibn 'Ali]

Cat. 151

1 Victoria and Albert Museum,
   inv. no. 865: Kendrick 1924,
   pp. 11–12, pl. I; Contadini 1998,
   p. 68, pl. 25; Sokoly 2002, no. 1799
   (datable 544–49 AH / 1149–54 CE,
   reign of al-Zafir)

Cat. 155

1 Benaki Museum, Athens,
   inv. no. 15190: unpublished

Cat. 156

1 Bouvier Collection, inv. no. JFB I 61,
   I 61 bis: Geneva 1993, pp. 213–14,
   no. 127; Sokoly 2002, no. 1695
   (datable 450–52 AH / 1058–61 CE,
   by order of the vizier *al-wazir al-
   'ajal* [Abu al-Faraj Muhammad ibn
   Ja'far])

2 Bouvier Collection, inv. no. JFB
   I 14: Geneva 1993, pp. 215–18,
   no. 128; Sokoly 2002, no. 1762
   (reign of al-Mustansir, date and
   administrative data lost)

Cat. 160

1 Royal Ontario Museum, Toronto,
   inv. no. 978.76.55: Sokoly 2002,
   no. 1583 (dated 421 AH / 1030–31 CE,
   made in a *tiraz al-'amma*)

2 Textile Museum, Washington, DC,
   inv. no. 73.461: Kühnel and Bellinger
   1952, pp. 79–80, pl. XXXVII;
   Sokoly 2002, no. 1698 (datable
   466–87 AH / 1073–94 CE, by order
   of the vizier *al-sayyid al-'ajal amir
   al-juyush* [probably Badr al-Jamali
   (d. 1094)])

3 Cleveland Museum of Art,
   inv. no. 32.24: Sokoly 2002, no. 1746
   (reign of al-Mustansir, date and
   administrative data lost)

4 Biblioteca Apostolica Vaticani,
   Vatican City, inv. no. 6900: Cornu
   1992, pp. 225–26; Sokoly 2002,
   no. 1759 (reign of al-Mustansir,
   date and administrative data lost)

5 Royal Ontario Museum, Toronto,
   inv. no. 970.364.17: Golombek and
   Gervers 1977, p. 112; Sokoly 2002,
   no. 1763 (reign of al-Mustansir, date
   and administrative data lost)

6 Metropolitan Museum of Art,
   New York, inv. no. 31.106.36:
   Sokoly 2002, no. 1768 (reign of al-
   Mustansir, date and administrative
   data lost)

Cat. 162

1 Bouvier Collection, inv. no. JFB
   I 14: Geneva 1993, pp. 215–18,
   no. 128; Sokoly 2002, no. 1762
   (reign of al-Mustansir, date and
   administrative data lost)

Cat. 165

1 Victoria and Albert Museum,
   London, inv. no. 1381–1888:
   Kendrick 1924, p. 10, no. 861, pl. VI;
   Sokoly 2002, no. 1741 (reign of al-
   Mustansir, date and administrative
   data lost)

2 Textile Museum, Washington, DC,
   inv. no. 73.461: Kühnel and Bellinger
   1952, pp. 79–80, pl. XXXVII; Sokoly
   2002, no. 1698 (datable 466–87 AH
   / 1073–94 CE, by order of the vizier
   al-sayyid al-'ajal amir al-juyush
   [probably Badr al-Jamali (d. 1094)])

Cat. 166

1 Royal Ontario Museum, Toronto,
   inv. no. 978.76.55: Sokoly 2002,
   no. 1583 (dated 421 AH / 1030–31 CE,
   made in a *tiraz al-'amma*)

2 Textile Museum, Washington, DC,
   inv. no. 73.461: Kühnel and
   Bellinger 1952, pp. 79–80,
   pl. XXXVII; Sokoly 2002,
   no. 73.461 (datable 466–87 AH /
   1073–94 CE, by order of the vizier
   al-sayyid al-'ajal amir al-juyush
   [Badr al-Jamali (d. 1094)])

3 Cleveland Museum of Art,
   inv. no. 32.24: Sokoly 2002, no. 1746
   (reign of al-Mustansir, date and
   administrative data lost)

4 Biblioteca Apostolica Vaticani,
   Vatican City, inv. no. 6900: Cornu
   1992, pp. 225–26; Sokoly 2002,
   no. 1759 (reign of al-Mustansir,
   date and administrative data lost)

5 Royal Ontario Museum, Toronto,
   inv. no. 970.364.17: Golombek
   and Gervers 1977, p. 112; Sokoly
   2002, no. 1763 (reign of al-
   Mustansir, date and administrative
   data lost)

6 Metropolitan Museum of Art,
   New York, inv. no. 31.106.36:
   Sokoly 2002, no. 1768 (reign of al-
   Mustansir, date and administrative
   data lost)

7 Bouvier Collection, inv. no. JFB
   I 14: Geneva 1993, pp. 215–18;
   Sokoly 2002, no. 1762 (reign of al-
   Mustansir, date and administrative
   data lost)

8 Museum of Islamic Art, Cairo,
   inv. no. 9075/1: *RCEA* 1931–91,
   vol. VIII, p. 48, no. 2880;
   Marzouk 1943, p. 166 n. 12, fig. 11;
   Sokoly 2002, no. 1787 (datable 487–
   95 AH / 1094–1101 CE, ordered by
   the vizier *al-sayyid al-'ajal al-Afdal
   amir* [al-juyush])

9 Boston Museum of Fine Arts,
   inv. no. 30.676: Britton 1938, p. 67,
   fig. 81 (non-historical inscriptions)

Cat. 169

1 Boston Museum of Fine Arts,
   inv. no. 30.684: Britton 1938, p. 71,
   fig. 90; https://collections.mfa.
   org/objects/66610/linen-and-silk-
   embroidery?ctx=f26c62b0-ea2b-
   4392-92c5-8888f9bc67d2&idx=0
   (non-historical inscription)

Cat. 170

1 Kelsey Museum of Archaeology,
   Ann Arbor, MI, inv. no. 22.527:
   Day 1937, pp. 444–45, no. 27,
   fig. 27; Sokoly 2002, no. 1579
   (dated 420 AH / 1029–30 CE, *tiraz
   al-khassa*)

2 Bouvier Collection, inv. no. JFB I 61,
   I 61 bis: Geneva 1993, pp. 213–14,
   no. 127; Sokoly 2002, no. 1695
   (datable 450–52 AH / 1058–61 CE,
   by order of the vizier *al-wazir al-
   'ajal* [Abu al-Faraj Muhammad ibn
   Ja'far])

3 Cleveland Museum of Art,
   inv. no. 50.527: *RCEA* 1931–91,
   vol. VIII, 1937, p. 24, no. 2843;

Sokoly 2002, no. 1754 (reign of al-
Mustansir, date and administrative
data not mentioned, or lost)

Cat. 171

1 Abegg-Stiftung, Riggisberg (Bern):
   Otavsky and Muhammad Salim
   1995, p. 82, no. 44 (non-historical
   inscription)

Cat. 172

1 Textile Museum, Washington, DC,
   inv. no. 73.67: Kühnel and Bellinger
   1952, p. 78; Sokoly 2002, no. 1694
   (datable 450–52 AH / 1058–60 CE, by
   order of the vizier *al-wazir al-'ajal*
   [Abu al-Faraj Muhammad ibn Ja'far
   al-Yazuri])

2 Abegg-Stiftung, Riggisberg (Bern):
   Otavsky and Muhammad Salim
   1995, pp. 78–79, no. 41 (non-
   historical inscription)

3 Bouvier Collection, inv. no. JFB M
   144: Geneva 1993, p. 265, no. 163
   (not inscribed)

Cat. 178

1 Textile Museum, Washington,
   DC, inv. no. 73.680: Kühnel
   and Bellinger 1952, pp. 80–81,
   pl. XXXVIII; Sokoly 2002, no. 1793
   (datable 495–515 AH / 1102–21 CE,
   by order of the vizier *al-sayyid al-
   'ajal* al-Afdal *amir al-juyush sayf*
   [al-islam])

2 Cleveland Museum of Art,
   inv. no. 1982.291: Mackie 2015,
   pp. 117–18, fig. 3.36 (non-historical
   inscription)

3 Textile Museum, Washington, DC,
   inv. no. 73.199: Kühnel and Bellinger
   1952, pp. 81–82, pl. XXXVIII;
   Sokoly 2002, no. 1797 (reign of al-
   Hafiz, date and administrative
   data not mentioned, or lost)

Cat. 184

1 Victoria and Albert Museum,
   inv. no. unknown: Kendrick 1924,
   p. 14, no. 872, pl. V (non-historical
   inscription)

2 Bouvier Collection, inv. no. JFB I
   95: Geneva 1993, pp. 232–33, no. 138
   (non-historical inscription)

Cat. 185

1 Victoria and Albert Museum,
   inv. no. unknown: Kendrick 1924,
   p. 14, no. 872, pl. V (non-historical
   inscription)

2 Bouvier Collection, inv. no. JFB
   95: Geneva 1993, pp. 232–33, cat.
   no. 138 (non-historical inscription)

NOTES

PREFACE

1 For a comprehensive discussion and listing of published *tiraz* textiles with protocollary inscriptions, see Sokoly 2002.

CHAPTER 1

1 For a discussion of this topic, see Stillman and Stillman 2003, pp. 29–39.
2 Apart from inscribed textiles from the central Islamic lands, The al-Sabah Collection holds a large collection of textiles from the Iranian world and central Asia, which are discussed in Spuhler 2020.
3 Musei Vaticani, Vatican City, inv. no. MV.2290.0.0; for an image, see https://www.museivaticani.va/content/museivaticani/en/collezioni/musei/braccio-nuovo/Augusto-di-Prima-Porta.html (accessed 22 March 2024).
4 For an overview of Parthian clothing, see Kawami 2011.
5 Museo Archeologico Nazionale di Napoli, Farnese Collection, inv. nos 6115, 6117.
6 The British Museum, inv. no. 1972,0229.1.
7 Silver, with mercury gilding, diam. 23.3–23.4 cm, weight 713 g. Metropolitan Museum of Art, New York, Harris Brisbane Dick Fund, 1970, inv. no. 1970.6.
8 Marshak 1994.
9 Ibid.; Raspopova 2006.
10 Mackie 2015, pp. 66–67.
11 Ibid., pp. 65, 68–69.
12 For a comprehensive discussion on this topic, see Stillman and Stillman 2003, pp. 10–15.
13 Ibid., pp. 16–20.
14 Ibn al-Athir 1886, vol. II, pp. 133–34.
15 Mona al-Moadin, 'Fragment of a mural painting', Discover Islamic Art, at http://islamicart.museumwnf.org/database_item.php?id=object;ISL;sy;Mus01;3;en (accessed 16 September 2021).
16 For a detailed discussion of al-Walid II's personality and its connection to the architecture of Khirbat al-Mafjar, see Hamilton 1988.
17 Behrens-Abouseif 1997.
18 A gold *dinar* of the 'standing caliph' type, minted in Damascus in 77 AH / 696–97 CE under caliph 'Abd al-Malik, is in the Ashmolean Museum, Oxford, inv. no. HCR 6573.
19 Ettinghausen et al. 2001, p. 44, fig. 50.
20 For a detailed discussion of the painting, see Grabar 1954.
21 Ettinghausen et al. 2001, p. 45.
22 Stillman and Stillman 2003, pp. 39–40.
23 Ibid., p. 33.
24 Ibid., p. 35.
25 Ibid., p. 34.
26 Evans 2012, pp. 238–41, no. 173A–C.

27 Ibid., p. 238, attempts a digital reconstruction based on the evidence of the fragments.
28 Ibid.
29 Ibid., p. 240.
30 For a discussion of this topic from the point of view of historical literary sources, see Ahsan 1973, pp. 54–113.
31 Stillman and Stillman 2003, p. 44.
32 Ibid., p. 46.
33 Ibid., 2003 p. 47; see also Ahsan 1973, p. 113.
34 Ahsan 1973, p. 112.
35 Stillman and Stillman 2003, p. 47.
36 Qaddumi 1996.
37 Ibid., pp. 207–08; for a discussion, see Stillman and Stillman 2003, p. 43.
38 Qaddumi 1996, p. 207.
39 Ibid., pp. 204–05.
40 Serjeant 1972, p. 212. For the original Arabic text, see Azdi 1902, pp. 35–36.
41 It is significant to note that the obverse of the medal features a camel led by a man with a knee-length qamis, and headgear that suspends sideways, and a sword held in his left hand.
42 For a discussion of the site, see Northedge 1993. The painting is discussed in Ettinghausen 1962, pp. 42–43, who linked its style to an eastern or central Asian, rather than a Mediterranean, tradition.
43 Mackie 2015, pp. 76–77.
44 Examples are in the Metropolitan Museum of Art, New York, inv. no. 67.10a and b, and the Freer Gallery of Art, Washington, DC, inv. nos F1965.20 and F1966.1, where the female figures have been connected to the Hellenistic cult of Dionysus or the Iranian goddess of fertility, healing and wisdom, Anahita.
45 Herzfeld 1948, p. 274, no. 9; Kühnel 1925, p. 87, fig. 3; Sokoly 2002, no. 54.
46 Miles 1964, pl. XLVII, fig. 1.
47 For the figure of Auriga, see 'Abd al-Rahman al-Sufi, *Kitab suwar al-kawakib al-thabitah*, Bodleian Library, University of Oxford, MS Marsh 144, p. 120.
48 Pope and Ackerman 1938–39, vol. VI, p. 984; Krody 2015, pp. 26–29. For a comprehensive study of the garment and the textile from which it was made, see Winter 2020.
49 Winter 2020, p. 36.
50 See Amedroz et al. 1920, pp. 428–29, where in the year 1001 Abu Sa'd Zadanfarrukh ibn Azadmard is sent by Baha' al-Dawla to accompany a messenger of his general and governor Abu 'Ali Hasan ibn Ustadh-Hurmuz, also referred to as 'Amid al-Juyush.
51 Winter 2020, pp. 33–49.
52 Hilal al-Sabi' 1964, pp. 93–99; Hilal al-Sabi' 1977, pp. 75–78.
53 Hilal al-Sabi' 1964, p. 95; Hilal al-Sabi' 1977, p. 75.

54 Hilal al-Sabi' 1964, p. 94; Hilal al-Sabi' 1977, p. 75. Hilal relates that 'Adud al-Dawla received in his investiture jewelled armbands and collar, and also a studded crown with a jewelled tassel.
55 Hilal al-Sabi' 1964, p. 95; Hilal al-Sabi' 1977, p. 76. Because Hilal refers here to the investiture of 'Adud al-Dawla, the inscription is in the name of the Abbasid caliph al-Qa'im (r. 1030–75).
56 Hilal al-Sabi' 1964, p. 95; Hilal al-Sabi' 1977, p. 76.
57 Ibn Khaldun 1900, vol. I, pp. 214–15; Ibn Khaldun 1967, p. 213.
58 Winter 2020, p. 41, fig. 3.4.
59 Canby et al. 2016, pp. 95–96, no. 24.
60 Spuhler 2020, pp. 30–31, no. 5; see also fragments of coats on pp. 20–23, no. 1, pp. 24–25, no. 2.
61 Bosworth 1963, p. 136; for a discussion of this passage in the context of the *khassakiyya*, a military elite corps of slaves (*mamluks*), see Gibson 2012, p. 81.
62 Heidemann et al. 2014.
63 Ibid., p. 64.
64 The second figure at the Metropolitan Museum of Art, New York, is inv. no. 57.51.18.
65 LNS 2 ST; for an image, see Heidemann et al. 2014, p. 43, fig. 9.
66 Ibid., pp. 40–49.
67 Ibid., pp. 58–62.
68 Ibid., p. 64.
69 Hermitage Museum 1990, p. 14, p. 42, no. 19. For a discussion, see also Ettinghausen et al. 2001, pp. 122–23.
70 Ettinghausen 1962, pp. 61–65.
71 Ibid., pp. 104–24.
72 Bloom 2008, p. 67, fig. 38.
73 Golombek 1988, p. 29; see also Golombek and Gervers 1977, p. 85.
74 Romberg 1985, pp. 53–87, esp. tables 1–11, where all-silk costumes represent a good percentage of the items.
75 Maqrizi 1853–54, vol. I, pp. 409–20.
76 The contents of the *khizanat al-kiswa* are listed in ibid., pp. 409–13; Romberg 1985, pp. 53–87, tables 1–11. The *Kitab al-dhakha'ir* discusses the textiles found in the Fatimid treasury in far greater detail than the accounts of the *Kitab al-hadaya wa al-tuhaf*, a related work; see Qaddumi 1996, pp. 9–11, 229–41.
77 Romberg 1985, pp. 77–80, tables 1–4.
78 Ibid., p. 77, table 1.
79 Ibid., pp. 81–86, tables 5–10.
80 Ibid., p. 87, table 11.
81 Ibn Duqmaq 1893, vol. II, p. 79; trans. in Serjeant 1972, p. 147.
82 Nasir-e Khosraw 1881, vol. II, pp. 110–13; Serjeant 1972, p. 142. For a verbatim citation of the passage, see p. 378 of the present volume.

83 Nasir-e Khosraw 1881, vol. II, pp. 110–13; Serjeant 1972, p. 142.
84 Maqrizi 1853–54, vol. I, pp. 409–10; trans. in Serjeant 1972, pp. 157–58.
85 Romberg 1985, pp. 77–87.
86 Sokoly 2002, p. 63; of 1,821 recorded textiles with historical *tiraz* inscriptions, only 32 are decorated with gold thread, 3 from the Abbasid period, the rest Fatimid.
87 Cornu 1998; Elsberg and Guest 1936; see also Bloom 2008, p. 160.
88 D'Agnel 1904, pp. 333–34, pl. XXVIII; Marçais and Wiet 1934; Martiniani-Reber 1992, pp. 53–54. St Anne was the mother of Mary and the maternal grandmother of Jesus.
89 Marçais and Wiet 1934, p. 192.
90 Linen, silk (linen plain weave with in-woven polychrome silk tapestry), 72.4 × 74.9 cm. Metropolitan Museum of Art, New York, Rogers Fund, inv. no. 1932 32.96.
91 Cornu 1998; Cornu 1999; Durand and Saragoza 2002, p. 219, no. 182.
92 Textile Museum, Washington, DC, inv. no. 73.444; Mackie 1996, p. 83, no. 58. Its dimensions (96 × 64 cm) suggest that it was a child's tunic.
93 Museum of Cairo University, inv. no +17. I saw the piece in 1992 but was not permitted to photograph it; its measurements are c. 60 × 70 cm; for a drawing see Sokoly 2002, vol. II, pl. 33.
94 Royal Ontario Museum, Toronto, inv. no. 978.76.70, with an embroidered inscription dated to 309 AH / 921–22 CE; Sokoly 2002, no. 391.1.
95 Ashmolean Museum, Oxford, inv. no. 1998.270; Barnes 1999. For the tunic in Kuwait, see Jenkins 1983, p. 105.
96 Without further explanation, Marilyn Jenkins dated the Kuwait tunic to the sixteenth century CE; Jenkins 1983, p. 105.
97 Dolezalek 2017, pp. 4–10; Samman 1982, pp. 31–34.
98 For a study of imperial Byzantine dress of this period, see Piltz 1997.
99 Ettinghausen 1962, pp. 44–50.
100 Dolezalek 2017, pp. 10–18; Samman 1982, pp. 10–24.
101 Dolezalek 2017, pp. 7–9.

CHAPTER 2

1 Grohmann 1934, p. 785.
2 Micklewright 1991, p. 32; Walker and Froom 1992, pp. 1–2; Otavsky and Muhammad Salim 1995, p. 284; Blair 1996, p. 20.
3 Ibn Khaldun 1967, pp. 214–23, esp. pp. 219–21.
4 Karabacek 1908; coin formulas are discussed on pp. 29–34, *tiraz* textiles on pp. 35–40, and papyri protocols on pp. 41–60. Karabacek states (p. 28) that he is the first scholar to undertake such comparisons.

5   Ibid., p. 28; Karabacek called this common repertoire of formulas in official inscriptions 'der Parallelismus im staatlichen Formelwesen' ('parallelism in state protocols').

6   Karabacek 1881, p. 84 n. 56; Karabacek further remarks (p. 85) that *susanjird* and *tiraz* borders are not one and the same.

7   Bayhaqi 1902, pp. 498–503; see also Karabacek 1908, pp. 7–15, where in addition to the edited text a German translation is provided.

8   Bayhaqi 1902, p. 498. Serjeant 1972, pp. 12–13, translated the term *qaratis* as 'paper' rather than 'papyrus'; Khan 1993, p. 11 states, however, that paper was not used in the Middle East until it was introduced from China in the eighth century – during the Umayyad period only papyrus or vellum was used.

9   On the coinage reforms of 'Abd al-Malik, see Miles 1952; Grierson 1960; Miles 1967.

10 Bosworth 1996a, p. 592; Darley-Doran 1996, pp. 592–93.

11 Darley-Doran 1996, p. 593.

12 Khan 1993, pp. 11–22.

13 Ibid., p. 17.

14 Grohmann 1960, pp. 5–7, published part of an Arabic papyrus protocol in the name of the Umayyad caliph al-Mu'awiya II (r. 683–84).

15 The chronology of the introduction of Arabic into papyrus protocols is outlined in Khan 1993, p. 17.

16 Bosworth 1986; Kennedy 1998, p. 72; Abbott 1938.

17 Österreichische Nationalbibliothek, Vienna, inv. no. P.II. no. 2163; Karabacek 1908, p. 24; Österreichische Nationalbibliothek, Vienna, per. inv. no. Ar. P. 4057 (formerly P.III. no. 51); Grohmann 1924, vol. I, pt 3, pp. 199–200, ill. Tafel 30a; Karabacek 1908, p. 24. Karabacek dated these to the ninth century on the basis of the *ductus* of the script. Work on the epigraphy of papyri inscriptions in Khan 1992, pp. 37–38, however, suggests a date for these items in the seventh century or the first half of the eighth, when the final *ya* was extended backwards underneath the word, as seen here in the word *fi*.

18 Baer 1989, pp. 85–86, figs 4–5, 17. I am indebted to Manuel Keene, formerly at The al-Sabah Collection, for bringing this object to my attention.

19 Ibid., p. 85, fig. 3.

20 The inscription reads: 'baraka wa khayr li-sahibihi ... ishrab haniyan mari'an ... mimma 'amala Muhammad ... bi-tiraz Jurjan'; Baer 1989, p. 95 n. 14, provides only a partial translation.

21 Baer implies that 'Jurjan' lacks a long *alif* and assumes that it means the Iranian city of Jurjan (sometimes

also written 'Gurgan'), which lies at the south-eastern corner of the Caspian Sea; the name is written with a long *alif* before the final *nun*. Since early Islamic inscriptions often omitted the *alif* it is quite possible that Baer's assumption is correct. This is further supported by a search through Yaqut's geographical dictionary, which does not list any place name corresponding to the sequence of letters *kha*, or *jim – ra – kha*, or *jim – nun – ya*; see Yaqut 1866–73.

22 Her attributions to Jurjan in Iran and the eleventh to twelfth century go hand in hand, probably provoked by the fact that in the twelfth and thirteenth centuries Jurjan is believed to have had a large ceramic industry, on the evidence of a group of lustre-painted vessels found there during excavations in 1925; Bahrami 1949, pp. 15, 125–26.

23 Hamilton 1988, p. 56, fig. 23.

24 Ibid., p. 27, fig. 8, p. 58, fig. 25A–B.

25 See the papyri discussed above, but also the abundance of textile inscriptions listed below in the Catalogue and also in Sokoly 2002, Appendix 41.

26 The horizontal stroke of the initial *'ayn* in the word *'amal*, for instance, is extended to the right; the initial *kaf*, as in *baraka*, is extended horizontally with the upper stroke parallel with the lower horizontal; the *sad* in *sahibihi* is extended horizontally with straight parallel horizontal strokes; the *lam–alif* is formed by two straight strokes crossing each other at an angle of 45 degrees and linked at the base by a horizontal stroke.

27 Grohmann 1971, 'Schrifttafel II: Die arabische Schrift in der Zeit der rechtmäßigen Kalifen und Umayyaden'; Khan 1992, pp. 27–36.

28 Bahrami 1949, pp. 33–34.

29 Serjeant 1972, pp. 80–81.

30 Bahrami 1949, p. 35. Controlled excavations during the 1970s brought to light several kilns and a range of ceramics dating from the Sasano-Arab to the Timurid and Safavid periods, including unglazed wares which can be dated to the first centuries of Islam; Kiani 1984, pp. 37–42.

31 Karabacek 1908, pp. 9, 12.

32 Evans 2012, pp. 238–41, no. 173A–C; Sokoly 2002, no. 1. In Sokoly 2002, see nos 3–10 for several other textiles that can be dated to the Umayyad period on the evidence of the epigraphic style of their inscriptions.

33 Evans 2012, p. 238, attempts a digital reconstruction based on the evidence of the fragments.

34 Abbott 1938, pls I–IV.

35 Evans 2012, p. 238.

36 Micklewright 1991, p. 32.

37 Sokoly 2002, no. 588 (see fig. 3.4 in the present volume), no. 22.

38 For a brief discussion on this approach, see McWilliams and Sokoly 2021, pp. 4–5.

39 Blair 1992b has suggested that the construction of the building was begun rather than completed in 691–92.

40 Grabar 1973, pp. 61–64, identifies three basic themes contained in these inscriptions, all of which assert the fundamental principles of Islam and are missionary in character: (1) the special position of the Prophet Muhammad and the universality of his mission; (2) a definition of the position of Jesus and other prophets in Islamic terms; (3) a threat of divine punishment to Christians and Jews in the light of Islam as the final revelation

41 Surah 9:33; surah 61:9.

42 Grabar 1973, p. 63.

43 Of course, the craftsmen who embroidered or wove the inscriptions often made mistakes in spelling words or names; it is likely that inscriptions were planned in the central offices of the caliphal or provincial administration and then copied out on papyrus, parchment or paper cartoons as blueprints, which were then provided to the workshops; the practice of weaving from cartoons, for example, was common among Coptic weavers in Egypt.

44 Azraqi 1857–61, vol. I, p. 162.

45 Ibid., p. 166.

46 Balkhi 1899, pp. 106–09.

47 Ibid., p. 107.

48 Ibid., p. 108.

49 Bayhaqi 1862, p. 161; for 'Ali al-Rida's life, see Lewis 1960.

50 Balkhi 1899, p. 108.

51 Ibn al-Athir 1873–74, vol. VII, p. 143; trans. in Serjeant 1972, p. 19; see also Fida 1869–70, p. 56.

52 Wensinck 1986, p. 74.

53 Bierman 1980, pp. 18–19; for detailed analysis of how the coin record from Tulunid Egypt sheds light on this issue, see Grabar 1957, esp., with regard to *tiraz* textile inscriptions, pp. 63–65.

54 Lamm 1938, pp. 105–06, no. 1, pl. 1; Sokoly 2002, no. 56.

55 Sokoly 2002, nos 70–73, 75, 76, 80, 81, 84, 100, 102, 107.

56 Ibid., nos 73 (private collection; *RCEA* 1931–91, vol. II, p. 232, no. 731), 75 (Royal Ontario Museum, Toronto, inv. no. 978.76.41).

57 Ibn al-Athir 1873–74, vol. VII, pp. 161–62; trans. in Serjeant 1972, p. 19.

58 Sokoly 2002, nos 59, 82, 83, and Appendix 52; see also Bierman 1980, pp. 21–25.

59 Textile Museum Washington, DC, inv. no. 73.4; Kühnel and Bellinger 1952, p. 10, pl. V; Sokoly 2002, no. 59. Tano Collection, *RCEA* 1931–91, vol. II, p. 246, no. 753; Sokoly 2002, no. 82.

60 Museum of Islamic Art Cairo, inv. no. 12298; Hawary 1933–34, pp. 61–2, pl. I; Lamm 1937, pp. 109–11, fig. 59; Sokoly 2002, no. 83; Wiet 1935a, p. 24, no. 82.

61 Sokoly 2002, nos 110, 113, 116, 118, 119, 123, 125, 128, 130, 133, 145, 148, 150, 151, 158, 160.

62 Sokoly 2002 lists 427 known inscriptions mentioning viziers, spanning almost 350 years, from the reign of the Abbasid caliph Harun al-Rashid (r. 786–809), through the reign of the Fatimid caliph al-Amir (r. 1101–30); significantly, viziers are absent in inscriptions from Egypt between 862–63 and 901–02, during the interlude of the Tulunids in Egypt.

63 Sourdel 1960, pp. 388, 442.

64 Jawdhari 1954, p. 88; Jawdhari 1958, pp. 129–30.

65 Bierman 1980, pp. 65–66, argues that this change in protocol was also intended to project the Fatimids' legitimacy as caliphs to the largely Sunni, but also the Isma'ili public in Egypt.

66 Halm 1996, p. 414, adds an interesting historical detail: as the Friday preacher, a relative of the Abbasids, had gone into hiding, his deputy, clad in white rather than black as required previously, had to read the prayer, albeit from a slip of paper as he could not yet remember the correct formulas by heart.

67 *RCEA* 1931–91, vol. V, p. 95.

68 Darley-Doran 1996, p. 596.

69 Sokoly 2002, no. 1138; see also Lamm 1937, pp. 96–99, pl. XVIc; Marzouk 1957a; Marzouk 1957b.

70 Trans. in Marzouk 1957b, 38–39; the Arabic text reads:

بسم الله الملك الحق المبين و صلى الله على [محمّد] خاتم النبيّين و على آله الطيّـ[بـين] (الطيّبين) بركة من الله [و غبـ]طة (غبطة) و يمن و سرور (؟) و سلامة و سعادة و جلالة و عصمة و تأييد و توفيق لعبد الله و وليّه معد أبى تميم الـ[إمام (الإمام) المعزّ لدين الله] أمير المؤمنين صلوات الله عليه و على آبائه الطـ[يّبـ]ين (الطيّبين) [و] أبنائه الأكرمين و سلّم تسليما ممّا ... سنة خمس وأربعين ثلث مائة

71 Sokoly 2002, nos 1399, 1416, 1417, 1564, 1582, 1627, 1648.

72 Bierman 1980, pp. 19–20; see Gordon 2001 for a general overview of the practice of robing in the medieval world, but in particular the essays of Dominique Sourdel on the Abbasids (pp. 137–45) and Paula Sanders on the Fatimids (pp. 225–39).

73 Sokoly 2002, nos 12, 13, 16, 17, 23.

74 Hilal al-Sabi' 1964, pp. 93–99; Hilal al-Sabi' 1977, pp. 75–78. The Dar al-Khilafah was the name of the main palace of Abbasid at Samarra, which functioned as the primary residence of the Abbasid caliph al-Mu'tasim and several of his successors for a period of almost fifty years during the middle of the ninth century.

75 Ibn Abi Usaybi'ah 1882, vol. I, p. 136.

76 See also Sokoly 2002, nos 53, 59, 83, 88, 112, 122, 170, 171, 188,

190, 356, 449, 462, 559, 561, 562, 576, 713, 1120, 1122, 1123.

77 Qaddumi 1996, pp. 148–55.

78 Ibid., p. 151; this is, to my knowledge, the only text concerning Abbasid ceremonial that explicitly states the content of *tiraz* inscriptions.

79 Grabar 1973, p. 162.

80 Isfahani 1927–36, vol. V, p. 371; trans. in Serjeant 1972, p. 51. The protocol contained the following wording: 'mimma amara bi-sana'atihi Hammad 'Ajrad'.

81 Bierman 1980, pp. 78–79: 'properly marked clothing woven in the appropriate fiber, became insignia identifying the ranks in the strongly centralized, hierarchical administration formed by al-Mu'izz'.

82 Maqrizi 1853–54, vol. I, pp. 409–10, describes the investiture during the founding of the *dar al-kiswa* under al-Mu'izz; ibid., pp. 410–13, describes the investiture in 1122 of Ibn al-Ma'mun, son of the Fatimid vizier Abu 'Abdallah Muhammad bin Fatik al-Bata'ihi al-Ma'mun (in office 1122–25), and in 1141 of the head of the chancery 'Ali ibn Munjib ibn al-Sayrafi.

83 Romberg 1985, pp. 77–87; Bierman 1997, p. 112, also drew attention to the contrast between the copious descriptions of Fatimid textual sources of the luxuriousness of fabrics and materials and the scarcity of descriptions of textile inscriptions, concluding that the visual qualities of high-class materials were greater indications of high rank than inscriptions alone.

84 Maqrizi 1853–54, vol. I, pp. 409–10; trans. in Serjeant 1972, pp. 157–58.

85 Maqrizi 1853–54, vol. I, pp. 446–50.

86 Ibid., p. 448.

87 Brett and Forman 1980, p. 65.

88 Golvin 1957, pp. 169–74; see also Bierman 1980, pp. 82–87.

89 Bierman 1980, p. 14; for prominent examples, see Sokoly 2002, nos 1041, 1056, 1058, 1060.

90 Grohmann 1957, p. 206.

91 Ibid., p. 209.

92 Tabbaa 1994, p. 122.

93 Ibid., pp. 123–24.

94 Sokoly 2002, no. 1479, pl. 153; nos 1529, 1530, pl. 160; no. 1549, pl. 162.

95 Binyon et al. 1933, p. 45, no. 25f, pl. XX.

96 Lane 1863–77, book I, part I, p. 789.

97 Ibn al-Athir 1886, vol. II, pp. 133–34; for a short biography of Ka'b ibn Zuhayr, see Basset 1978. Paret 1928, pp. 10–11, suggests that this incident is likely to be apocryphal, since none of the other early biographers of Muhammad mentions it.

98 Basset 1960, pp. 1314–15.

99 Ibid., p. 1314.

100 Hamilton 1988, p. 123.

101 Ibid., p. 113.

102 Ibid., p. 119.

103 Jahshiyari 1938, p. 204: 'wa kana al-Rashid yusammi Ja'far li-akhi wa yudkhiluhu ma'ahu fi thawbihi'.

104 Bloom 1985, p. 37, n. 112; Jawdhari 1954, pp. 112–13; Jawdhari 1958, p. 169.

105 Jawdhari 1954, pp. 138, no. 81; Jawdhari 1958, pp. 211–12, no. 81: 'Il envoya un billet à Notre Seigneur pour lui demander un de ses vêtements propre à lui servir de linceul quand il mourrait, afin d'avoir la bénédiction qui s'y rattache.' See also Bloom 1985, p. 32, p. 37 n. 112.

106 Bloom 1985, p. 37 n. 112; Jawdhari 1954, pp. 138–39, no. 81. The caliphs here are listed in a chronologically descending order, except for al-Mu'izz who lists his own garment last, perhaps as a sign of respect to his predecessors.

107 Trans. in Bloom 1985, p. 37 n. 112.

108 For a general discussion, see Halevi 2007, pp. 106–13.

109 Ibn Sa'd 1967–72, vol. I, p. 538.

110 Eliash 1971, pp. 270–71.

111 Ibn Sa'd 1967–72, vol. 2, p. 351; for a more general discussion of the Prophet's shrouds, see Halevi 2007, pp. 85–87.

112 Ibn Sa'd 1967–72, vol. 2, p. 351.

113 Ibn Sa'd 1904–40, vol. VIII, p. 78, lines 13–16; Grütter 1954, p. 80. For the family connections of Zaynab bint Jahsh, see Watt 1960.

114 Maqrizi 1853–54, vol. II, p. 7; Wüstenfeld 1881, pp. 150–51. Al-Maqrizi or his source may well have exaggerated here to enhance or underline the elevated position of Ya'qub ibn Killis.

115 Maqrizi 1853–54, vol. II, p. 7; Wüstenfeld 1881, pp. 150–51.

116 Wüstenfeld 1881, p. 204. For his edition of the Arabic text, Wüstenfeld relies on a manuscript of the *Akbar al-Duwal* (*historia regnorum*) of Jamal al-Din 'Ali ibn Zafir al-Azdi, Forschungsbibliothek, University of Gotha, Ms. orient. A 1555 (old Cod. Ms. Gothan. Möll. 245).

117 Sokoly 2017, pp. 283–84; Sanders 1994, pp. 28–29, 76, suggests that even proximity to the Fatimid caliph or seeing him could transfer caliphal *baraka* to the believer, and that food distributed by the Fatimid caliph or his palace on the occasion of large festivities was regarded as a source of *baraka*.

118 Maqrizi 1853–54, vol. I, p. 441, lines 6–7.

119 Ibid., vol. I, p. 454, lines 20–23.

120 Stillman 1986, p. 6.

121 Golombek 1988, p. 29.

122 On the general role of textiles in the medieval reliquary cult, see Martiniani-Reber 1992.

123 Sokoly 2002, no. 1789; D'Agnel 1904, pp. 333–34, pl. XXVIII; Marçais and Wiet 1934; Martiniani-Reber 1992, pp. 53–54.

124 Sokoly 2002, no. 1783; Delluc and Delluc 1983; Martiniani-Reber 1992, p. 54; Prieur 1936.

125 Flury-Lemberg 1988, pp. 320–21, p. 494, no. 81.

126 Brigitte Schmedding (1978) has published an exhaustive account of medieval textiles in Swiss churches, one of which is an Egyptian tapestry-woven silk textile that, *pace* Schmedding's date of the thirteenth–fifteenth centuries, may be as early as the late Fatimid period; Schmedding 1978, p. 183, no. 155. Another example is the *pallium* of St Césaire in Arles, which contains a strip of a Fatimid gold-woven tapestry, datable to the eleventh or early twelfth century (Benoît 1945, p. 59, pl. VII, 1–3); another is the chasuble of St Ulrich in Lucerne, which contains stripes of gold-thread tapestry of the style common in Egypt under the caliph al-Mustansir (r. 1036–94), published in Flury-Lemberg 1981, p. 171, figs 11–12, p. 174, fig. 15.

127 Matthews and Mordini 1959.

128 Ibid., p. 53. While the Kushan coins could be dated to the first–third centuries, the Islamic coins dated from the reign of the Umayyad caliph 'Abd al-Malik (r. 685–705) to that of the Abbasid caliph al-Radi (r. 934–40).

129 Sokoly 2002, nos 86, 165, 763, 773; all textiles are now in the Museum of Islamic Art in Qatar.

130 Niewöhner-Eberhard 2005, pp. 47–49: the textile fragments are conserved in the Museum Lüneburg (formerly Museum für das Fürstentum Lüneburg), while the psalter is in the Museum August Kestner, Hanover, inv. no. WM XXI a 37. The marriage of Otto II and the Byzantine princess Theophanu in 972 linked the Holy Roman Empire with Byzantium on the one hand, and Otto's father, Otto I, had already had exchanges with the caliphate of Córdoba under the caliph Abd al-Rahman III in 954–56. Both points of contact could have provided a means of exchange that included these textiles.

131 Niewöhner-Eberhard 2005, p. 51.

132 See Ibn Miskawayh 1921, vol. I, pp. 56–60 for a translation of an account of the Byzantine embassy on Muharram 2, 305 AH / 25 June 917 CE to the court of al-Muqtadir in Baghdad as described by the Persian chancery official at the Buyid court, Abu 'Ali Ahmad ibn Muhammad ibn Ya'qub Miskawayh al-Razi (lived 932–1030) in his *Kitab tajarib al-umam* ('Book of the experiences of nations').

133 Karabacek et al. 1894, pp. 227–28, no. 849.

134 Baginski and Shamir 1995.

135 Shamir 1995.

136 Brogan and Smith 1984.

137 Mackie 1989.

138 Mackie 1989, p. 85, pp. 89–90, nos 1–2; Sokoly 2002, nos 574.3, 574.4. Misr al-Fustat had been the capital of Umayyad Egypt and continued to be the main urban settlement when the centre of administration was moved north of the city under the Abbasids and Fatimids. Because of its location, chronology and rich artifactual evidence, Fustat is the most relevant of the settlements excavated in recent decades. The excavation led by George Scanlon brought to light numerous townhouses and a large number of ceramics, glass and coins, all representative of a wealthy population involved in the trade and manufacture of artefacts.

139 Herzfeld 1923; Herzfeld 1927; Lamm 1928; Sarre 1925.

140 Herzfeld 1948, p. 274, no. 9; Sokoly 2002, no. 54.

141 Kühnel 1952, pp. 163–64.

142 Kühnel 1927, p. 9.

143 Marzouk 1959, p. 283.

144 Ashton 1935.

145 Conversation with the author, Cairo, summer 1991; the collection in Cairo is the largest in the world, yet remains largely unstudied and unpublished.

146 I am grateful to the late Layla 'Ali Ibrahim, who kindly permitted me to take a slide of this photograph from one of her albums.

147 Maher 1977, pls 190, 191.

148 One would think that more of these records might have survived, hitherto undiscovered, in Cairene archives.

149 Ragib 1974, p. 83. During a conversation in Cairo in 1991, Layla 'Ali Ibrahim told me that the textile disappeared overnight from the storage house on the site, but reappeared the following day. It was unknown to her who was responsible for this incident. Since it was thought that the burial was that of 'Abd al-Rahim himself, an allegation never verified, the textile find was a delicate matter as it potentially concerned a senior member of the Fatimid family and therefore could have raised a multitude of religious issues.

150 Sokoly 2002, no. 1741.

151 Ibid., no. 1529.

152 Ibid., nos 38.3, 152.

153 McWilliams 2021, pp. 39–49.

154 Abdulfattah 2020 provides the first in-depth study on this major figure of the Egyptian art trade.

155 Geneva 1993, pp. 12–13; see also Vassilika 1996 on dealers of Egyptian antiquities; other names found frequently are Paul Mallon and Dikran Kelekian; Phocion Tano also dealt with Antonis Benakis, as is evident from the inventory records at the Benaki Museum in Athens, and Michel Abemayor emigrated to

New York, perhaps shortly before the Egyptian revolution of 1953, taking his collection with him, of which nearly 1,000 textiles items were sold to a benefactor who bequeathed them to the Royal Ontario Museum, Toronto, under the auspices of the textile historian Veronica Gervers in 1978.

156 Otavsky and Muhammad Salim 1995, pp. 29–30, no. 2; Sokoly 2002, no. 356.

157 Sokoly 1997a, pp. 73–74, 76.

158 For a full account of the textile finds see Crowfoot 2011, pp. 14–16 and 27–32 regarding *tiraz* textiles in particular; see also Baker 1995, p. 56, who mentions a textile from Qasr Ibrim now in the British Museum, Department of Egyptian Antiquities, inv. no. EA72264; for a recent analysis of the finds published in Crowfoot 2011, see Winnik 2024.

159 Gayraud 1995.

160 Gayraud 1994, pp. 4–7.

161 Ibid., p. 27, fig. 26.

162 Ibid., p. 8.

163 Gayraud 1995, pp. 7–8, p. 19, figs 16–17.

164 Ragib 1974, pp. 67–69, pl. I, where a foundation stone in the name of al-'Aziz's mother, found in the complex, is discussed.

165 Personal email communication, 19 October 2023.

166 Ibid.

167 Conversation with the author, Cairo, September 1991.

168 Goitein 1983, p. 160, describes a man on his deathbed who wishes to have a simple burial: 'No wailing, please; and of garments in which I shall be buried I wish to have no more than these: two cloaks, three robes, a washed turban of fine linen – it is already wound up – new underpants of mine, and a new waistband of mine.' Another account is also given in ibid., p. 160, where the garments specified consist of a tunic, a robe of *dimyati*, another of green silk, a scarf, underpants, a turban and a cloak. Goitein (p. 399 n. 83) also mentions the possessions of a grocer, for whom only a few of his clothes were selected for the burial, among them the *sarawil* (underpants); and (p. 188) details the will of a successful businesswoman who ordered for her burial outfits worth 50 dinars, including a *dabiqi* robe, a *mula'a* (wrap), a *tali* (skullcap), a wimple, a *dabiqi* kerchief, a veil and a *tustari kisa'* ('cloak of cloth from Tustar'). A will of a young woman (ibid., p. 189) states: 'I am not pleased with the shrouds I have, and wish, therefore, that some should be bought for me. This I wish to be bought: a *dabiqi* robe, a wimple, a wrap, a *muklaf* cloak, a half and a half as bedding, and a braid'; see also Halevi 2007, pp. 90–91.

169 Mackie 1996, p. 83, no. 58; Sokoly 2002, no. 337; its dimensions (96 × 64 cm) suggest it was a child's tunic; see also McWilliams and Sokoly 2021, pp. 72–73, no. 6.

170 Museum of Cairo University, inv. no +17. Its measurements were approx. 60 × 70 cm. For a drawing see Sokoly 2002, vol. II, pl. 33.

171 Benaki Museum, Athens, inv. no. 15686. Louise Mackie brought this piece to my attention almost thirty years ago; it has never been properly documented, published or photographed owing to its very large size (at least 90 cm wide and almost 3 metres long) and its being conserved rolled up. The inscription, which remains to be read, conforms to an Abbasid epigraphic style common in the ninth century; Mackie 2015, pp. 94–95, fig. 3.9.

172 Department of Eastern Art, Ashmolean Museum, Oxford (inv. no. 1998.270); Barnes 1999 (viewed in March 1998). For the tunic in The al-Sabah Collection, inv. no. LNS 57 T, see Jenkins 1983, p. 105.

173 Godlewski 2002, pp. 100–04.

174 Helmecke 2005, p. 196, fig. 1, p. 197, fig. 2; Godlewski 2004, pp. 142–43, figs 1, 2.

175 Godlewski 2002, p. 102, fig. 9; Helmecke 2005, pp. 201–02, fig. 7.

176 Godlewski 2004, p. 145, fig. 4; Godlewski 2014, p. 186, fig. 15.

177 A recent essay by Elizabeth Dospěl Williams has looked at this issue in some detail from the point of view of textiles in particular; see Dospěl Williams 2022. Halevi 2007, pp. 91–92, also touches on the question of Christian burial. In her recent PhD dissertation, Arielle Winnik has studied the shared use of funerary objects by Christians and Muslims in early medieval Egypt and considered the complexity of funerary practices; see Winnik 2022.

178 Maher 1977, pls 187–89.

179 Metropolitan Museum, New York, inv. no. 39.113; Dimand 1942–43; Ekhtiar et al. 2011, pp. 50–51, no. 28; McWilliams and Sokoly 2021, pp. 140–41, no. 38.

180 Combe 1939; Evans 2012, p. 263, no. 185; Sokoly 2002, no. 588.

181 Jawdhari 1954, p. 88; Jawdhari 1958, pp. 129–30.

182 Ghazali 1989, pp. 73–74: 'Thus then was the demise of the Emissary of God (may God bless him and grant him peace). He did not leave anything save that which was buried with him. Abu Ja'far said, "His grave was floored with a mat, and then with the garments he used to wear when awake, and then he was set upon them in his shrouds." He left after his death no property, and never in his life had he laid one brick or piece of straw upon another. In his death

there lies a most perfect lesson, and in him the Muslims have an excellent example.'

183 Sokoly 2002, no. 1416.

184 Gayraud 1994; Gayraud 1995, p. 10.

185 Sokoly 1997a, p. 76, fig. 37, shows a textile from the Royal Ontario Museum, Toronto, inv. no. ROM 978.76.77, which has a large circular hole right above the inscription, bordered by brownish stains that result from the decomposition of a body; the decomposition pattern must have been caused by the weight of a body pressing on the fabric, consequently soaking it with bodily fluids and causing decomposition. The piece was probably laid over the head flat, then the sides tucked in underneath.

186 Bukhari 1862–1908, vol. I, p. 321, *bab* 28.

187 Gayraud 1995, pp. 8–9, p. 19, figs 16–17.

188 Winnik 2024, pp. 94–95.

189 Grütter 1957, pp. 86–87.

190 Goitein 1983, p. 160, p. 414 n. 287.

191 Halevi 2007, p. 96.

192 Grütter 1957, p. 86.

193 Goitein 1983, p. 160. Goitein suggests that the garments were bought ready made and had to be adjusted to the deceased's body; ibid. 1983, p. 398 n. 71.

194 Grütter 1957, p. 86; see also Halevi 2007, pp. 96–99.

195 Grütter 1957, p. 87. Perhaps the mats discussed earlier that were found in Muslim burials had been personal prayer mats of the kind mentioned in the anecdote between the Fatimid caliph al-Mu'izz and his private secretary Jawdhar from the beginning of this section.

196 Halevi 2007, p. 112.

197 Sokoly 2017, pp. 294–85.

198 Qadi al-Nu'man 1978, pp. 55, 72.

CHAPTER 3

1   Cook 1993, p. 4.

2   Goitein 1967, p. 224; Goitein 1983, p. 167.

3   Goitein 1967, p. 226. In many sales accounts, prices of complete loads of flax per *qintar* (100 pounds) of bales vary according to quality.

4   Ibid., p. 224.

5   Ibid., p. 105, p. 418 n. 30.

6   Wingate 1942, p. 261.

7   Baines 1985, p. 6; Cook 1993, p. 8.

8   Cook 1993, p. 8.

9   Goitein 1967, p. 105, p. 418 n. 31.

10 The impact of dyeing and the costs involved are discussed below.

11 Cook 1993, p. 39.

12 Goitein 1983, p. 170, mentions that, in Geniza trousseau lists, cotton garments are almost never mentioned. He explains that this might be because cotton was less durable than linen and hence may

have meant that a lower value was set on such garments and the social status of the owner was therefore also lower.

13 Watson 1983, p. 31.

14 Lombard 1978, pp. 63–79.

15 Lamm 1937, pp. 4–7; Pfister 1937, p. 172.

16 Goitein 1967, p. 418 n. 35.

17 Golombek and Gervers 1977, p. 83.

18 Lombard 1978, p. 70.

19 Marzouk 1957b.

20 Barnes 1993; Barnes 1997a; Barnes 1997b.

21 Barnes 1996, pp. 84–85, nos 12, 13. While most pieces conformed with the Mamluk dates of the archaeological environments in which many were found, two fragments in the Ashmolean Museum, Oxford, were significantly earlier. One, inv. no. Newberry 1990.247, was dated to 1010 +/– 55 years, and another similar piece, inv. no. Newberry 1990.320, to 1060 +/– 40 years; see also Barnes 1997a.

22 Baginski and Tidhar 1980; Thompson 1971, pp. 9–10.

23 Golombek and Gervers 1977, p. 87.

24 Pfister 1936, pp. 12–16, Group B, p. 84.

25 Ibid., pp. 73–78, Group C.

26 Lombard 1978, pp. 37–38.

27 Sokoly 2002, nos 26–28, 35.1.

28 Ibid., no. 22.

29 Ibid., no. 14.

30 Ibid., nos 2, 589, 590.

31 Ibid., nos 589, 590; David-Weill 1957.

32 Kühnel and Bellinger 1952, no. 73.524, pl. I; Sokoly 2002, no. 5.

33 Sokoly 2002, no. 1627.

34 Goitein 1967, p. 105.

35 *Hudud al-'alam* 1937, p. 151.

36 Bierman 1981; Mackie 1985.

37 Day 1952; Evans 2012, pp. 238–41, no. 173A–C.

38 Mackie 1984, p. 128.

39 See particularly Idrisi 1836–40, vol. I, pp. 352–53, trans. in Serjeant 1972, p. 117: 'The city of Damascus contains many excellent qualities and many types of manufactures and various kinds of garments of silk (*harir*) such as khazz silk, precious and costly brocade of wonderful manufacture, with no equal; this is taken thence to every country and province adjoining it, and to those at a distance from it. The factories (*masani'*) for all those are marvellous, and their brocade resembles the finest brocade of Rum (Byzantium), approximating to the garments of Dastuwa and vying with the manufactures of Isfahan, surpassing the manufactures of the *tiraz* factories of Nishapur consisting of silken garments of one colour (*thiyab al-harir al-musmata*) and the

wonderful garments of Tinnis. Its (Damascus) *tiraz* factories contain all kinds of manufactures of precious cloth.'

40   Combe 1939; see also Evans 2012, pp. 263–64, no. 15; Sokoly 2002, no. 588.
41   Sokoly 2002, nos 811, 819, 879, 888, 889, 892, 901, 911, 1041, 1050, 1052, 1053, 1056, 1058, 1060.1, 1075, 1084, 1087, 1168, 1170, 1171, 1173, 1180, 1196, 1198.
42   Museum für Islamische Kunst, Berlin, inv. no. I68/63.
43   Dimand 1942–43; Ekhtiar et al. 2011, pp. 50–51, no. 28.
44   Muqaddasi 1906, p. 180.
45   Nasir-e Khosraw 1881, p. 58.
46   Idrisi 1885, text p. 10, trans. p. 128; Le Strange 1890, p. 338.
47   Jawdhari 1954, p. 88; Mansur al-Kitab 1958, pp. 129–30.
48   Maqrizi 1853–54, vol. I, pp. 416–17; trans. in Serjeant 1972, p. 159.
49   I am grateful to Louise Mackie for bringing this to my attention.
50   On the status and uses of gold in Islamic society, see Ehrenkreutz 1965.
51   Isfahani 1927–36, vol. V, p. 371; trans. in Serjeant 1972, p. 51.
52   Romberg 1985, p. 56.
53   Ibid., p. 77, Table 1.
54   Ibn Duqmaq 1893, vol. II, p. 79; trans. in Serjeant 1972, p. 147.
55   Sokoly 2002, Appendix 4. Added to this can be a number of non-historical *tiraz* textiles decorated with gold thread.
56   Ibid., nos 535, 895, 1034.
57   Ibid., nos 1139, 1789.
58   Maqrizi 1853–54, vol. I, p. 226; see also Serjeant 1972, p. 146
59   Geneva 1993, pp. 125–27, no. B; see also Sokoly 2002, no. 1510. For a recent study on gold, see Wertz et al. 2021, pp. 54–56.
60   I am grateful to Anne Wardwell, former curator at the Cleveland Museum of Art, who explained this to me in some detail; see also Wardwell 1992, pp. 362–63, 371–72; Watt and Wardwell 1997, pp. 107–63.
61   Sokoly 1997b, figs 53–58; Sokoly 2002, Appendix 5.
62   Bellinger 1959, pp. 3–4; see also Pfister 1937 on the importation of cotton into Egypt under the Abbasids and Fatimids. Pfister notes three pieces which he claims are linen/cotton-mix ground fabric with an embroidered inscription of non-Iraqi origin (p. 168).
63   Bellinger 1950; Bellinger 1951; Bellinger 1952; Carroll 1985.
64   For a tabulation, see Sokoly 2002, vol. II, fig. 9.
65   Ibid.
66   Goitein 1983, p. 166.
67   Sokoly 2002, nos 1386, 1411.
68   Bakri 1911, p. 86; Ibn Hawqal 1938–39, pp. 152–53; Idrisi 1866, text p. 156, trans. p. 186; Yaqut 1866–73, vol. II, pp. 548.
69   Contadini 1998, p. 42, p. 56 n. 20.

70   This is confirmed by Goitein, who mentions that other varieties of Egyptian linen are only occasionally found in the Geniza archive; Goitein 1983, pp. 165–66.
71   Bakri 1911, p. 86.
72   Ya'qubi 1892, vol. VII, pp. 337–38; trans. in Serjeant 1972, p. 140.
73   Ibn Hawqal 1938–39, pp. 152–53.
74   Idrisi 1866, text. p. 156; cf. Serjeant 1972, pp. 143–44.
75   Yaqut 1866–73, vol. I, p. 272; Qazwini 1848–49, vol. II, p. 99; cf. Serjeant 1972, p. 156.
76   Tanukhi 1921–22, text p. 143, trans. pp. 156–57.
77   Ya'qubi 1892, vol. VII, pp. 337–38; trans. in Serjeant 1972, p. 140. Maqrizi 1853–54, vol. I, p. 416, describes the tent furnishings (*farsh*) made from *dabiqi* as *mukhmal*; cf. Serjeant 1972, p. 159.
78   Azdi 1902, p. 35; trans. in Serjeant 1972, p. 139.
79   I am grateful to Nobuko Kajitani, formerly Conservator in Charge, in the Department of Textile Conservation, Metropolitan Museum of Art, New York, for providing me with this information.
80   Mas'udi 1861–77, vol. II, pp. 45–46; cf. Serjeant 1972, p. 72.
81   Tha'alibi 1867, p. 129; trans. in Serjeant 1972, p. 105.
82   Tanukhi 1921–22, text p. 29, trans. p. 31; cf. Serjeant 1972, p. 43.
83   Romberg 1985, p. 77, Table 1, p. 78, Table 2, p. 80, Table 4; see also p. 73 n. 24 for a definition of *wasitani*.
84   Ibid., p. 77, Table 1, p. 78, Table 2, p. 79, Table 3.
85   Ibid., p. 79, Table 3, p. 80, Table 4.
86   Ibid., p. 80, Table 4.
87   Isfahani 1927–36, vol. V, p. 345; cf. Serjeant 1972, p. 138.
88   Tanukhi 1921–22, text p. 190, trans. p. 208; cf. Serjeant 1972, p. 139.
89   Goitein 1983, p. 166, p. 401 n. 115.
90   Baghdadi 1904, text p. 53, trans. p. 138; Serjeant 1972, p. 139.
91   Baghdadi 1904, text p. 55, trans. p. 140; Serjeant 1972, p. 139.
92   Romberg 1985, pp. 62–65, 69–71.
93   Maqrizi 1900, p. 507 (quoting from an unidentified source); trans. in Serjeant 1972, p. 146: 'At Tinnis they weave linen *sharb* cloths such as were woven nowhere else in the world, and they used to make for the caliph a garment called *badana* [a short sleeveless waistcoat; cf. Qaddumi 1996, p. 417] into the composition of which the only thread introduced for the warp and woof was two ounces (*uqiya*).' For references regarding turbans, see Goitein 1983, p. 166, p. 401 n. 118.
94   Ibn Hawqal 1938–39, pp. 152–53.
95   I am very grateful to Nobuko Kajitani, formerly Conservator in Charge, in the Department

of Textile Conservation, Metropolitan Museum of Art, New York, for providing me with this information.
96   Sokoly 2002, nos 1187, 1200, 1205, 1205.1, 1216, 1407, 1501, 1502, 1503, 1506, 1676, 1793.
97   Maqrizi 1900, p. 507. Speaking of a *sharb badana* (a light overcoat), Maqrizi says: 'the rest of the stuff was woven with gold, made with perfect workmanship, and with no need to be cut or sewn'; trans. in Serjeant 1972, p. 146; Goitein 1983, p. 401 n. 120, mentions an instance of 'a robe of fine linen decorated with silk' ('qajijat sharb bi-harir'); see also ibid., p. 403 n. 143.
98   Sokoly 2002, nos 1034, 1216, 1363, 1430, 1503, 1509, 1510, 1515, 1526, 1682, 1682.1, 1685, 1789; see also ibid., Appendix 4.
99   The Kufic inscription around the central drum of the Dome of the Rock in Jerusalem is executed in gold mosaic on a blue ground. Another example of golden script on blue is the well-known 'Blue Quran'; for a sample page and further references, see Déroche 1992, p. 58, no. 11.
100   Sokoly 2002, nos 1216, 1503.
101   Ibn Hawqal 1938–39, pp. 152–53; Maqrizi 1853–54, vol. I, p. 226, speaking about *sharb* turbans; trans. in Serjeant 1972, p. 146. Ya'qubi 1892, p. 338, speaks of 'thiyab al-shurub al-shafawiya'; trans. in Serjeant 1972, p. 140. Goitein 1983, p. 401 n. 118, lists an '*imamat sharb* of Damietta.
102   Sokoly 2002, nos 1187, 1205, 1205.1, 1216, 1225, 1226, 1227, 1347, 1581, 1584, 1588.
103   Ibid., nos 450, 1197, 1427, 1564, 1582, 1789.
104   Ibid., nos 1222, 1406, 1407, 1409, 1565, 1593.
105   Ibid., nos 802, 812, 814, 883, 890, 1044, 1198, 1374, 1394.
106   Ibid., no. 1426.
107   Ibid., nos 9, 19, 292, 655, 656, 754, 828, 882, 1034, 1035, 1169.
108   Yaqut 1866–73, vol. I, p. 101; cf. Serjeant 1972, p. 145.
109   Yaqut 1866–73, vol. I, p. 804; cf. Serjeant 1972, p. 145.
110   Idrisi 1866, text p. 159, trans. p. 189; cf. Serjeant 1972, p. 144.
111   In referring to the city of Dabiq, Maqrizi 1853–54, vol. I, p. 226, speaks about 'turbans of dyed sharb linen' ("imma'im al-sharb mulaqqana'); Goitein 1983, p. 401 n. 118, lists a Geniza document in which an '*imama sharb* costing 12 dinars is mentioned; another refers to a *sharb* headband ('isaba), and there is also an account for burial clothes comprising a laundered *sharb* turban.
112   Goitein 1983, p. 401 n. 117, lists a 'pearl coloured *ghilala sharb*, costing 5 dinars'.
113   Goitein 1983, p. 401 n. 119, lists a gala costume ('hulla wa-mi'jarha

sharb') and a *mula'a* cloak. Since *sharb* is such a fine material, these cloaks were perhaps similar to the present-day black *bisht* worn by dignitaries on the Arabian peninsula.
114   Sokoly 2002, nos 618, 629, 659, 694, 795, 808, 1053, 1312, 1321.
115   Ibid., no. 1789.
116   I am grateful to Bruno Motin at the French Ministry of Culture for the opportunity to study the 'Veil of St Anne' *in situ* at the conservator's studio of Mme Girot-Kurtzemann in Orange, near Avignon, in December 1997; because of the prominent central inscribed roundels linked by a large decorative band, the first possibility seems more likely, rather than that it was a turban-cloth.
117   For a more detailed description and illustration of the technique, see Bühler 1972, vol. I, p. 3, p. 5, fig. 8.
118   Lamm 1937, pp. 150–56, 235–37; Lane 1863–77, vol. III, p. 2058; Serjeant 1972, pp. 93, 123–24, 128, 132.
119   Bühler 1972, pp. 25–27.
120   Pfister 1936, p. 79; see also Balfour-Paul 1997, pp. 20, 27–28, 62–68.
121   Sokoly 2002, nos 70.1, 116.1, 422.
122   Ibid., nos 39, 40, 788, 895.
123   Bühler 1972, vol. III, illustrates several inscribed examples (no. 3, Museum der Kulturen, Basel, inv. no. III 9189; no. 7, Textile Museum, Washington, DC, inv. no. 73.377; no. 8, Museum der Kulturen, inv. no. III 16922) and several undecorated ones (no. 1, inv. no. III 11957; no. 2, inv. no. III 11957; no. 5, inv. no. III 14094; no. 6, Metropolitan Museum of Art, New York, inv. no. 29.179.34; no. 9, Textile Museum, inv. no. 73.255; no. 10, Metropolitan Museum of Art, inv. no. 90.5.24); Lamm 1937, pp. 147–48, pl. XVIIID: Nationalmuseum Stockholm, inv. no. 249/1932; Museum of Islamic Art, Cairo, inv. nos 13014, 10764; Metropolitan Museum of Art, inv. no. 29.179.25; Pfister 1945–46, pp. 70–71, nos 47–50. See also two inscribed pieces, in the Cleveland Museum of Art, inv. no. 50.363, and Museum of Islamic Art, inv. no. 14470.
124   Bühler 1972, vol. III, fig. 12, Museum der Kulturen, Basel, inv. no. III 11973; fig. 14, Detroit Institute of Art, inv. no. 31.18; fig. 15, Museum der Kulturen, inv. no. III 11874; fig. 17, Museum der Kulturen, inv. no. III 15492.
125   Detroit Institute of Art, inv. no. 31.18.
126   Bühler 1972, vol. I, pp. 27.
127   Sokoly 2002, nos 1752, 1767, 1768, 1769.
128   Metropolitan Museum of Art, New York, inv. no. 27.170.28.

129 Metropolitan Museum of Art, New York, inv. no. 27.170.4.
130 Golombek and Gervers 1977, p. 121 n. 23, provides a list of Yemeni *ikat*s, but also adds several that the authors suggest might be considered Egyptian imitations.
131 Dozy 1845, p. 113 n. 9.
132 Lamm 1937, p. 104.
133 Ibid., pp. 105–06; Serjeant 1972, pp. 89–92, p. 15 n. 32.
134 Ibn al-Faqih 1885, p. 254.
135 Tha'alibi 1867, p. 132.
136 'Arib 1897, p. 116; Ibn al-Faqih 1885, p. 254; Muqaddasi 1877, pp. 323–25; Tha'alibi 1908, p. 429.
137 Ibn al-Faqih 1885, p. 267.
138 Muqaddasi 1877, pp. 324–25.
139 Ibn Rusta 1892, pp. 123–24; Lamm 1937, p. 198.
140 Sokoly 2002, Appendix 9.
141 Ibid., nos 83, 122, 171, 190.
142 Lamm 1937, p. 104.
143 My observations contradict those of Lamm. It is an interesting detail that in many archaeological *mulham* fabrics the silk warps have decomposed before the cotton wefts, resulting in breaks exposing the cotton wefts, which hang loose horizontally. See Sokoly 2002, pl. 14, no. 53; pl. 15, no. 59; pl. 21, no. 112; pl. 26, no. 170; pl. 27, no. 188; pl. 28, no. 190; pl. 35, no. 233; pl. 62, no. 449; pl. 66, nos 559 and 561; pl. 67, no. 562; pl. 70, no. 576; pl. 89, no. 713; pl. 120, nos 1120, 1123.
144 Lamm 1937, p. 125, fig. 61.
145 Wiet 1937, figs 1–3. Wiet thought that these textiles were composed of linen warps and silk wefts, an unlikely combination of materials, but one that would make sense in terms of Lamm's definition of *mulham* consisting of a silk weft. However, until a textile with a selvedge can be identified, the question of silk warp or weft remains unclear.
146 Lamm 1937, p. 126; Britton 1938, figs 11–12.
147 Mackie 2015, p. 95, is a rare example of the discussion of quality.
148 Azdi 1902, p. 42; trans. in Serjeant 1972, p. 19.
149 Mas'udi 1861–77, vol. VII, pp. 190–91; cf. Serjeant 1972, p. 18. It is an interesting detail that Abu Mutahhar, quoted above, refers to a *mutawakkili dabiqi* while the present author refers to a *mutawakkili mulham*. Although there can be little doubt about the difference between *dabiqi* and *mulham*, the question arises as to what distinguished the *mutawakkili* versions from ordinary cloth. It is possible that *mutawakkili* distinguished cloth of a superior quality, which would have been fit for a caliph, as the detailed descriptions of the luxurious fabric quality in the two texts suggest.

150 Yaqut 1866–73, vol. I, p. 890; trans. in Serjeant 1972, p. 53.
151 Although this passage concerns only *dabiqi*, it nevertheless contains diagnostic factors that can be applied to other textile types as well.
152 Dimashqi 1977, p. 46; cf. Serjeant 1972, p. 140; see also Mackie 2015, p. 95.
153 Sokoly 2002, pp. 71, 74.
154 Goitein 1967, p. 106.
155 Ibid., p. 107.
156 Ibid., p. 420 n. 46.
157 Since the majority of *tiraz* textiles recorded here were not accessible for personal inspection, and were not illustrated, I had to rely on the descriptions given by previous authors. The information concerning the colour of the ground fabric was usually unambiguous, except in the *Répertoire chronologique d'épigraphie arabe* (RCEA 1931–91), where the colour of the ground fabric was mentioned only if it was dyed.
158 Sokoly 2002, nos 21, 70.1, 116.1, 788, 895.
159 Ibid., nos 18, 32, for the reddish examples; nos 21, 589, 590, for the blue examples.
160 Ibid., nos 1187, 1200, 1205, 1205.1, 1216, 1407, 1480, 1501–03, 1506, 1752, 1793.
161 Ibid., no. 1587.
162 Ibid., no. 1480.
163 Ibid., no. 1676.
164 An exception is a blue *dabiqi* textile inscribed in the name of the caliph al-Mustansir (r. 1036–94); ibid., no. 1752.
165 Goitein 1983, p. 401 n. 114.
166 Ibid., p. 166.
167 Ibid., p. 174.
168 Lamm 1937, p. 105; see also Sokoly 2002, pp. 244–52.
169 Grütter 1957, p. 85.
170 Fyzee 1969, p. 149.
171 Ibid., pp. 147–48. It was, however, permissible for women to wear all-silk costumes.
172 Goitein 1983, p. 174.
173 Sokoly 2002, Appendices 11–18.
174 Pfister 1936, pp. 1–2, 7–8. On the variety of red dyes used in the Islamic world, see Lombard 1978, pp. 118–29, where some of the relevant literary sources are given.
175 Pfister 1936, pp. 10–16.
176 Ibid., pp. 76–78, nos 26–33.
177 Ibid., p. 74, no. 9, p. 76, no. 28; Sokoly 2002, nos 2, 666. There is some controversy on the date of 88 AH / 707–08 CE, as the hundred digit may have been omitted, thus opening the possibility of the date 188 AH / 804–05 CE.
178 Owing to the early date of one of the items examined by Pfister, the question arises if lac dye had not already been imported to Egypt before the Muslim invasion; in this case, some of the Coptic material would indeed be pre-Islamic. However, a more recent study has

confirmed Pfister's findings, in that earlier pre-Islamic material was mostly dyed with madder, a plant-based red, while from the eighth century onwards lac became quite common; Wertz et al. 2021, pp. 56–60.
179 Lombard 1978, pp. 139–43.
180 On the etymology of the Arabic term, see Dietrich 1995.
181 Lombard 1978, p. 140, quotes two later medieval accounts, one by a Chinese source, the other a description by Marco Polo.
182 Ibid., p. 141.
183 Ibid., pp. 141–42, where the relevant literary sources are mentioned.
184 For a summary and listing of sources on this subject see Balfour-Paul 1997, p. 20.
185 Muqaddasi 1877, p. 98.
186 Déroche 1992, p. 58, no. 11, pp. 92–95, no. 42; Grohmann 1967, p. 111.
187 Karabaceck 1887, pp. 148–49.
188 Ibid., p. 150.
189 Karabacek 1888, pp. 113–16. That the same colourants used to dye paper were also used in textile manufacture is an interesting detail, since both are made of raw fibrous plant material – in Egypt this tended to be flax, whereas in other parts of the Islamic world it could be hemp, cotton or bast; Karabacek 1887, pp. 128–36. A later manuscript of Ahmad ibn Muhammad Nahhas's text is in the Bodleian Library, Oxford, MS Marsh 338; Nahhas 1999 provides a facsimile of this manuscript.
190 I was able, in 2018, to examine a folio of the Blue Quran at the Harvard Art Museums and compare this with a textile from Yemen. The folios have been discussed extensively – see McWilliams and Sokoly 2021, pp. 84–85; for the most recent scholarship, see George 2009 and Bloom 2015. Bloom found that the vellum was coloured superficially rather than dyed, and that the lettering was executed by the application of gold leaf on resin rather than in gold ink, or shell gold, which I can confirm from my own independent observation.
191 Wertz et al. 2021, p. 56, fig. 9.
192 Sokoly 2002, nos 39, 40, 895.
193 Several tapestry-woven textiles from the tomb of Thutmosis IV are in the Egyptian Museum, Cairo; Carter and Newberry 1904, pp. 143–44, nos 46526–29, pl. XXVIII.
194 Karabaceck 1881.
195 Kühnel and Bellinger 1952, pp. 101–02.
196 For a description, see ibid., p. 104, fig. 4: 'Stem stitch tends to pull together the threads over which it is worked, separating them from their neighbors. Back stitch … is the reverse of stem stitch, the face of one being the reverse of

the other. It, therefore, also pulls the threads on which it is worked, and whenever the ground fabric is pulled out of the line there is strain on the embroidery thread also.' In both stitches, the thread is inserted into the fabric, drawn backwards in a diagonal movement, then pulled out again and brought forward diagonally.
197 Ibid., p. 104, fig. 5: 'Flat stitch … has a diagonal pull on the face of the fabric and a straight pull on the back.' In flat stitch the thread is inserted, drawn horizontally on the back, pulled out and then drawn lower diagonally.
198 Ibid., p. 104, fig. 7: 'In braiding the thread is brought through the material at the base of the stem and is laid up one side of the stem and down again, darned under one or two wefts to hold it in place. It then repeats the course on the other side of the stem. On the third journey up, the first two courses are laced together, and the thread then goes to the back and is floated down to the bottom of the next stem.'
199 Ibid., p. 104, fig. 6: 'The thread is brought through the material, laid in the desired position on the face and carried through to the back again. From the back, couching stitches are taken over the thread on the face only often enough to hold it in place. As the thread on the face was anchored where it came through the fabric, the thread on the back never returns to the original starting point, but is carried directly from the last couching stitch to the beginning of the new figure. As the thread from the two sides only coincides in certain places the tension is apt to be quite uneven.'
200 Ibid., p. 105.
201 Ibid., pp. 14–15, pl. VI, and discussion of the technique p. 104.
202 Ibid.
203 Ibid.
204 Ibid., p. 106.
205 Textile Museum Washington, DC, inv. no. 73.30: Kühnel and Bellinger 1952, p. 102.
206 Sokoly 2002, nos 1139, 1141, 1145, 1146, 1150, 1177, 1207, 1219, 1280, 1308, 1334, 1498, 1499. These range chronologically from the time of al-Mu'izz (r. 953–75) to the reign of al-Hakim (r. 996–1021); only two record their place of production: Tuna (no. 1219) and possibly Misr al-Fustat (no. 1145).
207 Romberg 1985, pp. 81–82, tables 5–6, lists several instances of outfits embroidered with gold.
208 Yaqut 1866–73, vol. II, p. 602; cf. Serjeant 1972, p. 145.
209 Kühnel and Bellinger 1952, p. 106.
210 Sokoly 2002, nos 4, 11.1. Another example, albeit non-historical, is an unpublished textile in the Royal Ontario Museum, Toronto

Encyclopaedia of Islam, 2nd edn, ed.
P. Bearman et al.; online at https://
referenceworks.brillonline.com/
browse/encyclopaedia-of-islam-1,
2012 (accessed 3 February 2024)

Bosworth 2012c
Bosworth, C.E., 'Khurāsān', in
Encyclopaedia of Islam, 2nd edn,
ed. P. Bearman et al.; online at
https://referenceworks.brillonline.
com/browse/encyclopaedia-
of-islam-1, 2012 (accessed 30
November 2021)

Bosworth 2012d
Bosworth, C.E., 'Saldjūḳids', in
Encyclopaedia of Islam, 2nd edn,
ed. P. Bearman et al.; online at
https://referenceworks.brillonline.
com/browse/encyclopaedia-of-
islam-1, 2012 (accessed 3 February
2024)

Bosworth 2012e
Bosworth, C.E., 'Sulṭān', in
Encyclopaedia of Islam, 2nd edn,
ed. P. Bearman et al.; online at
https://referenceworks.brillonline.
com/browse/encyclopaedia-of-
islam-1, 2012 (accessed 3 February
2024)

Bowen 1960
Bowen, H., ''Alī b. 'Īsā', in
Encyclopaedia of Islam, 2nd edn,
ed. P. Bearman et al., vol. I, Leiden,
1960, pp. 386–88

Brett and Forman 1980
Brett, M., and W. Forman, *The
Moors: Islam in the West*, London,
1980

Britton 1938
Britton, N.P., *A Study of Some Early
Islamic Textiles in the Museum of
Fine Arts Boston*, Boston, 1938

Britton 1942
Britton, N.P., 'Pre-Mameluke Tiraz
in the Newberry Collection', *Ars
Islamica* 9 (1942), 158–66

Brockelmann 2012
Brockelmann, C., 'al-Washshā', in
Encyclopaedia of Islam, ed. M.Th.
Houtsma et al.; online at https://
referenceworks.brillonline.com/
browse/encyclopaedia-of-islam-1,
2012 (accessed 5 December 2021)

Brogan and Smith 1984
Brogan, O., and D.J. Smith, *Ghirza:
A Libyan Settlement in the Roman
Period*, Tripoli, 1984

Bühler 1972
Bühler, A., *Ikat, Batik, Plangi:
Reservemusterungen auf Garn und
Stoff aus Vorderasien, Zentralasien,
Südosteuropa und Nordafrika*, 3
vols, Basel, 1972

Bukhari 1862–1908
Abu 'Abdallah Muhammad ibn
Isma'il al-Bukhari, *Kitab al-jami'
al-sahih*, vols I–III, ed. M. Ludolf
Krehl, Leiden, 1862–68, vol. IV, ed.
T.W. Juynboll, Leiden, 1907–08

Burton Page 2012
Burton Page, J., 'Gudjarāt', in
Encyclopaedia of Islam, 2nd edn,
ed. P. Bearman et al.; online at
https://referenceworks.brillonline.
com/browse/encyclopaedia-of-
islam-2, 2012 (accessed 5 December
2021)

Canard 2012
Canard, M., 'Ibn Killis', in
Encyclopaedia of Islam, 2nd edn,
ed. P. Bearman et al.; online at
https://referenceworks.brillonline.
com/browse/encyclopaedia-
of-islam-2, 2012 (accessed 23
November 2021)

Canby et al. 2016
Canby, S.R., D. Beyazit, M. Rugiadi
and A.C.S. Peacock, *Court and
Cosmos: The Great Age of the
Seljuqs*, New York and New Haven,
2016

Canepa 2010
Canepa, M.P., 'Distant Displays
of Power: Understanding Cross-
Cultural Interaction among the
Elites of Rome, Sasanian Iran, and
Sui-Tang China', *Ars Orientalis* 38
(2010), 121–54

Carboni 2007
Carboni, S., *Venice and the Islamic
World, 828–1797*, New York, 2007

Carroll 1985
Carroll, D.L., 'Dating the Foot-
Powered Loom: The Coptic
Evidence', *American Journal of
Archaeology* 89 (1985), 168–73

Carroll 1986
Carroll, D.L., *Looms and Textiles
of the Copts: First Millennium
Egyptian Textiles in the Carl Austin
Rietz Collection of the California
Academy of Sciences*, Seattle and
London, 1986

Carter and Newberry 1904
Carter, H., and P.E. Newberry,
*Catalogue général des antiquités
égyptiennes du Musée du Caire,
nos. 46001–46529: The Tomb of
Thoutmôsis IV*, London, 1904

Chakravarti 2015
Chakravarti, R., 'Indian Trade
through Jewish Geniza Letters
(1000–1300)', *Studies in People's
History* 2 (2015), 27–40

Combe 1939
Combe, E., 'Natte de Tibériade
au Musée Benaki à Athènes',
in *Mélanges Syriens offerts à
Monsieur René Dussaud*, Paris,
1939, pp. 841–44

Combe 1940
Combe, E., 'Tissus fatimides du
Musée Benaki', *Mélanges Maspero*,
vol. III: *Orient Islamique*, Cairo,
1940, pp. 259–72

Combe 1950
Combe, E., 'Tissus musulmans à
inscriptions historiques', *Jahrbuch
des Bernischen Historischen
Museums in Bern* 30 (1950),
pp. 92–98

Contadini 1998
Contadini, A., *Fatimid Art at the
Victoria and Albert Museum*,
London, 1998

Cook 1993
Cook, J.G., *Handbook of Textile
Fibres*, vol. I: *Natural Fibres*,
Durham, 1993

Cornu 1982
Cornu, G., 'La tradition des textiles
au Yémen', *Bulletin de Liaison du
Centre International d'Étude des
Textiles Anciens* 55-6 (1982), 74–88

Cornu 1991
Cornu, G., 'Wasī yéménite des
IXe-Xe siècles au Musée Historique
des Tissus de Lyon', *Archéologie
Islamique* 2 (1991), 47–70

Cornu 1992
Cornu, G., *Tissus islamiques de la
collection Pfister*, Vatican City, 1992

Cornu 1998
Cornu, G., 'Les tissus d'apparat
fatimides', in *L'Égypte fatimide:
son art et son histoire*, ed. M.
Barrucand, Paris, 1998, pp. 331–37

Cornu 1999
Cornu, G., 'Le "Suaire" de Cadouin,
pièce de tiraz fatimide', *Archéologie
Islamique* 8-9 (1999), 29–36

Cornu et al. 2023
Cornu, G., et al., *Textiles, Carpets
and Costumes*, pt 1, Nasser D.
Khalili Collection of Islamic Art,
vol. XIV, Buckland Newton, Dorset,
2023

Creswell 1932–40
Creswell, K.A.C., *Early Muslim
Architecture: Umayyads, Early
Abbasids & Tulunids*, 2 vols,
Oxford, 1932–40

Creswell 1989
Creswell, K.A.C., *A Short Account
of Early Muslim Architecture*,
rev. and supplemented J.W. Allan,
Cairo, 1989

Crowfoot 2011
Crowfoot, E.G., *Qasr Ibrim:
The Textiles from the Cathedral
Cemetary*, London, 2011

Curatola et al. 2010
Curatola, G., M. Keene and S.
Kaoukji, *Art from the Islamic
Civilisation: From The al-Sabah
Collection, Kuwait*, Milan, 2010

D'Agnel 1904
D'Agnel, A., 'Le trésor de l'église
d'Apt (Vaucluse)', *Bulletin
Archéologique* (1904), 329–35

Darley-Doran 1996
Darley-Doran, R.E., 'Sikka, 2.
Coinage Practice', in *Encyclopaedia
of Islam*, 2nd edn, ed. P. Bearman
et al., vol. IX, Leiden, 1996,
pp. 592–99

David-Weill 1931–36
David-Weill J., *Les bois à
épigraphes*, 2 vols, Cairo, 1931–36

David-Weill 1957
David-Weill, J., 'Emendanda',
Arabica 4 (1957), 73–76

Day 1937
Day, F.D., 'Dated Tiraz in the
Collection of the University of
Michigan', *Ars Islamica* 4 (1937),
421–46

Day 1952
Day, F.D., 'The Tiraz Silk of
Marwan', in *Archaeologica
orientalia in memoriam Ernst
Herzfeld*, ed. G.C. Miles, Locust
Valley, NY, 1952, pp. 39–61, pl. VI

Delluc and Delluc 1983
Delluc, B., and G. Delluc, 'Le Suaire
de Cadouin: une toile brodée',
*Bulletin de la Société Historique
et Archéologique du Périgord* 110
(1983), 3–19

Déroche 1992
Déroche, F., *The Abbasid Tradition:
Qur'ans of the 8th to the 10th
centuries AD*, London, 1992

Desai 1965
Desai, Z.A., 'Kufi Epitaphs from
Bhadreswar in Gujarat', *Epigraphia
Indica: Arabic and Persian
Supplement* (1965), 1–8, pls I–V

Dhahabi 1996
Dhahabi, Shams al-Din, *Siyar a'lam
al-nubala*, vol. XV, Beirut, 1996

Dietrich 1995
Dietrich, A., 'Nil', in *Encyclopaedia
of Islam*, 2nd edn, ed. P. Bearman et
al., vol. VIII, Leiden, 1995, p. 37

Digby 2012
Digby, S., 'Kāfūr', in *Encyclopaedia
of Islam*, 2nd edn, ed. P. Bearman et
al.; online at https://referenceworks.
brillonline.com/browse/
encyclopaedia-of-islam-2, 2012
(accessed 5 December 2021)

Dimand 1932
Dimand, M.S., 'A Recent Gift of
Egypto-Arabic Textiles', *Bulletin of
the Metropolitan Museum of Art* 27
(1932), 92–96

Dimand 1942–43
Dimand, M.S., 'Two Abbasid
Straw Mats Made in Palestine',
*Metropolitan Museum of Art
Bulletin* new ser., 1 (1942–43), 76–79

Dimand 1944
Dimand, Maurice S., *A Handbook
of Muhammadan Art*, 2nd, rev. and
enlarged, edn, New York, 1944

Dimashqi 1977
Ja'far ibn 'Ali al-Dimashqi,
Al-ishara ila mahasin al-tijara,
Cairo, 1977

Dolezalek 2017
Dolezalek, I., *Arabic Script
on Christian Kings: Textile
Inscriptions on Royal Garments
from Norman Sicily*, Berlin and
Boston, 2017

Dospěl Williams 2019
Dospěl Williams, E., 'A Taste for
Textiles: Designing Umayyad and
'Abbasid Interiors', in *Catalogue
of the Textiles in the Dumbarton
Oaks Byzantine Collection*, ed.
G. Bühl and E. Dospěl Williams,
Washington, DC, 2019; online at
https://www.doaks.org/resources/
textiles/essays/williams

Dospěl Williams 2022
Dospěl Williams, E., 'Adoption,
Adaptation, Reinterpretation:
Inscribed Textiles in Medieval
Egypt's Christian and Jewish
Communities', in *Social
Fabrics: Inscribed Textiles from
Medieval Egyptian Tombs*, ed.
M. McWilliams and J. Sokoly,
Cambridge, MA, New Haven
and London, 2021, pp. 30–37

Dozy 1845
Dozy, R.P.A., *Dictionnaire détaillée
des noms des vêtements chez les
Arabes*, Amsterdam, 1845

Drouot Richelieu 1993
Drouot Richelieu, *Archéologie, arts
d'orient*, Paris, 2 July 1993 [sale
catalogue]

Durand and Rettig 2002
Durand, M., and S. Rettig, 'Un
atelier sous controle califal identifié

dans le Fayoum: Le tiraz privé de Tutun', in *Égypte, la trame de l'histoire: textiles pharaoniques, coptes et islamiques*, ed. M. Durand and F. Saragoza, Paris, 2002

Durand and Saragoza 2002
Durand, M., and F. Saragoza (eds), *Égypte, la trame de l'histoire: textiles pharaoniques, coptes et islamiques*, Paris, 2002

Ehrenkreutz 1965
Ehrenkreutz, A.S., '<u>D</u>hahab', in *Encyclopaedia of Islam*, 2nd edn, ed. P. Bearman et al., vol. II, Leiden, 1965, p. 214

Ekhtiar et al. 2011
Ekhtiar, M.D., P.P. Soucek, S.R. Canby and N.N. Haidar (eds), *Masterpieces from the Department of Islamic Art in the Metropolitan Museum of Art*, New York, 2011

El-Habib 1973
El-Habib, M., 'Notes sur un *tiraz* au nom de Abi'l Mansur al-Aziz bi-llah, le Fatimide (365–386 H. / 975–996 ap. J.-C.)', *Revue du Louvre et des Musées de France* 13 (1973), 299–302

Eliash 1971
Eliash, J., 'On the Genesis and Development of the Twelver-Shi'i Three-Tenet Shahadah', *Der Islam* 47 (1971), 265–72

Ellis 2001
Ellis, M., *Embroideries and Samplers from Islamic Egypt*, Oxford, 2001

Elsberg and Guest 1936
Elsberg, H.A., and R. Guest, 'The Veil of Saint Anne', *Burlington Magazine for Connoisseurs* 68 (1936), 140–47

Enlart 1920
Enlart, C.,'Un tissu persan du Xe siècle découvert à Saint-Josse (Pas-de-Calais)', *Monuments et Mémoires de la Fondation Eugène Piot* 24, nos 1–2 (1920), 129–48

Ettinghausen 1943
Ettinghausen, R., 'The Bobrinski "Kettle": Patron and Style of an Islamic Bronze', *Gazette des Beaux-Arts* 6th ser., 24 (1943), 193–208

Ettinghausen 1962
Ettinghausen, R., *Treasures of Asia: Arab Painting*, Geneva, 1962

Ettinghausen et al. 2001
Ettinghausen, R., O. Grabar and M. Jenkins, *Islamic Art and Architecture, 650–1250*, New Haven, 2001

Evans 2012
Evans, H.C., *Byzantium and Islam: Age of Transition, 7th–9th Century*, New Haven and London, 2012

Fendri 1967–68
Fendri, M., 'Un vêtement islamique ancien au Musée du Bardo', *Africa: Revue des Études de Recherches Préhistoriques, Antiques, Islamiques et Ethnographiques*, 2 (1967–68), 241–68 [Institut National d'Archéologie et d'Art, Tunis]

Ferber et al. 1987
Ferber, L.S., and Brooklyn Museum, *The Collector's Eye: The Ernest Erickson Collections at the Brooklyn Museum*, New York, 1987

Fida 1869–70
Abu al-Fida, *Mukhtasar fi akhbar al-bashar*, vol. II, Istanbul, 1869–70

Flood 2009
Flood, F.B., *Objects of Translation: Material Culture and Medieval 'Hindu–Muslim' Encounter*, Princeton, 2009

Flury-Lemberg 1981
Flury-Lemberg, M., 'Das "Ulrichsgewand" aus dem Kloster St Urban', in *Documenta textilia: Festschrift für Sigrid Müller-Christensen*, ed. M. Flury-Lemberg and K. Stolleis, Munich, 1981, pp. 163–77

Flury-Lemberg 1988
Flury-Lemberg, M., *Textile Conservation and Research: A Documentation of the Textile Department on the Occasion of the Twentieth Anniversary of the Abegg Foundation*, Bern, 1988

François de Ricqlès 1996
François de Ricqlès, *Archéologie, Arts d'Orient*, Drouot-Richelieu, Paris, 21 March 1996 [sale catalogue]

Friedman 2006
Friedman, M.A., and M. Friedman. 'Qusayr and Geniza Documents on the Indian Ocean Trade', *Journal of the American Oriental Society* 126 (2006), 401–09

Friedmann 2012
Friedmann, Y., 'Muḥammad b. al-Ḳāsim', in *Encyclopaedia of Islam*, 2nd edn, ed. P. Bearman et al.; online at https://referenceworks. brillonline.com/browse/ encyclopaedia-of-islam-2, 2012 (accessed 5 December 2021)

Fyzee 1969
Fyzee, A.A.A., *Compendium of Fatimid Law*, Simla, 1969

Galtier and Bakri 1909
Galtier, E., and Ahhmad ibn 'Abd Allah Bakri, *Foutouh al bahnasa*, Cairo, 1909

Gayraud 1994
Gayraud, R.-P., 'Istabl 'Antar (Fostat) 1992: rapport de fouilles', *Annales Islamologiques* 28 (1994), 1–27

Gayraud 1995
Gayraud, R.-P., 'Istabl 'Antar (Fostat) 1994: rapport de fouilles', *Annales Islamologiques* 29 (1995), 1–24

Geneva 1993
Geneva, Collection Bouvier, *Tissus d'Égypte: témoins du monde arabe, VIIIe–XVe siècles*, Geneva and Paris, 1993

Geneva 1994
Geneva, Musée d'Art et d'Histoire, *L'œuvre d'art sous le regard des sciences*, Geneva, 1994

George 2009
George, A., 'Calligraphy, Colour and Light in the Blue Qur'an', *Journal of Qur'anic Studies* 11 (2009), 75–125

Gervers 1979
Gervers, V., 'Weavers, Tailors and Traders: A New Collection of Medieval Islamic Textiles in the Royal Ontario Museum, Toronto', *Hali* 2 (1979), pp. 125–32

Ghafur 1966
Ghafur, M.A., 'Fourteen Kufic Inscriptions of Banbhore, the Site of Daybul', *Pakistan Archaeology* 3 (1966), 65–90

Ghazali 1989
al-Ghazali, Abu Hamid Muhammad ibn Muhammad, *The Remembrance of Death and the Afterlife / Kitab dhikr al-mawt wa-ma ba'dahu*, trans. T.J. Winter, Cambridge, 1989

Gibson 2012
Gibson, M., 'A Symbolic Khassakiyya: Representations of the Palace Guard in Murals and Stucco Sculpture', in *Islamic Art, Architecture and Material Culture: New Perspectives*, ed. M.S. Graves, Oxford, 2012, pp. 81–91

Glidden and Thompson 1988
Glidden, H.W., and Thompson, D., '"Tiraz" Fabrics in the Byzantine Collection, Dumbarton Oaks', pt 1: '"Tiraz" from Egypt', *Bulletin of the Asia Institute* new ser., 2 (1988), 119–39

Glidden and Thompson 1989
Glidden, H.W., and Thompson, D., '"Tiraz" in the Byzantine Collection, Dumbarton Oaks', pts 2–3: 'Tiraz from the Yemen, Iraq, Iran and an Unknown Place', *Bulletin of the Asia Institute* new ser., 3 (1989), 89–105

Godlewski 2002
Godlewski, W., 'Les textiles issus des fouilles récentes de Naqlun', in *Égypte, la trame de l'histoire: textiles pharaoniques, coptes et islamiques*, ed. M. Durand and F. Saragoza, Paris, 2002, pp. 100–04

Godlewski 2004
Godlewski, W., 'Season 2003', *Polish Archaeology in the Mediterranean* 15 (2004), 141–51

Godlewski 2014
Godlewski, W., with Barbara Czaja, 'Excavations in 2010–2011', *Polish Archaeology in the Mediterranean* 23 (2014), 173–91

Goitein 1954
Goitein, S.D., 'From the Mediterranean to India: Documents on the Trade to India, South Arabia, and East Africa from the Eleventh and Twelfth Centuries', *Speculum* 29 (1954), 181–97

Goitein 1967
Goitein, S.D., *A Mediterranean Society: The Jewish Communities of the Arab World as Portrayed in the Documents of the Cairo Geniza*, vol. I: *Economic Foundations*, Berkeley and Los Angeles, 1967

Goitein 1980
Goitein, S.D., 'From Aden to India: Specimens of the Correspondence of India Traders of the Twelfth Century', *Journal of the Economic and Social History of the Orient* 23, nos 1–2 (1980), 43–66

Goitein 1983
Goitein, S.D., *A Mediterranean Society: The Jewish Communities of the Arab World as Portrayed in the Documents of the Cairo Geniza*, vol. IV: *Daily Life*, Berkeley, Los Angeles and London, 1983

Goitein 1987
Goitein, S.D., 'Portrait of a Medieval India Trader: Three Letters from the Cairo Geniza', *Bulletin of the School of Oriental and African Studies* 50 (1987), 449–64

Goitein 1988
Goitein, S.D., *A Mediterranean Society: The Jewish Communities of the Arab World as Portrayed in the Documents of the Cairo Geniza*, vol. V: *The Individual: Portrait of a Mediterranean Personality of the High Middle Ages as Reflected in the Cairo Geniza*, Berkeley, Los Angeles and London, 1988

Goitein and Friedman 2008
Goitein, S.D., and M.A. Friedman, *India Traders of the Middle Ages: Documents from the Cairo Geniza: India Book*, pt 1, Leiden, 2008

Golombek 1988
Golombek, L., 'The Draped Universe of Islam', in *Content and Context of Visual Arts in the Islamic World*, ed. P.P. Soucek, University Park, PA, and London, 1988, pp. 25–49

Golombek and Gervers 1977
Golombek, L., and V. Gervers, 'Tiraz Fabrics in the Royal Ontario Museum', in *Studies in Textile History in Memory of Harold B. Burnham*, ed. V. Gervers, Toronto, 1977, pp. 82–125

Golvin 1957
Golvin, L., *Le Magrib central à l'époque des Zirides: recherches d'archéologie et d'histoire*, Paris, 1957

Gordon 2001
Gordon, S., *Robes and Honor: The Medieval World of Investiture*, New York, 2001

Grabar 1954
Grabar, O., 'The Painting of the Six Kings at Qusayr 'Amrah', *Ars Orientalis* 1 (1954), 185–87

Grabar 1957
Grabar, O., 'The Coinage of the Tulunids', *Numismatic Notes and Monographs* 139 (1957), pp. iii, v, vii–x, 1–78

Grabar 1973
Grabar, O., *The Formation of Islamic Art*, New Haven, 1973

Grierson 1960
Grierson, P., 'The Monetary Reforms of 'Abd al-Malik', *Journal of the Economic and Social History of the Orient* 3 (1960), 241–64

Grohmann 1924
Grohmann, A., *Corpus papyrorum Raineri, Archiducis Austriae*, III: *Series Arabica*, vol. I, *Allgemeine Einführung in die arabischen Papyri*, pt 1: Einführung; pt 2: *Einleitung und Texte*; pt 3: Tafeln, Vienna, 1923–24

Grohmann 1934
Grohmann, A., 'Ṭirāz', in *Encyclopaedia of Islam*, ed. M.Th. Houtsma et al., vol. IV, Leiden, 1934, pp. 785–93

Grohmann 1957
Grohmann, A., 'The Origin and

Development of Floriated Kufic', *Ars Orientalis* 2 (1957), 183–213

Grohmann 1960
Grohmann, A., 'Zum Papyrusprotokoll in früharabischer Zeit', *Jahrbücher der Österreichischen Byzantinischen Gesellschaft* 9 (1960), 1–19

Grohmann 1967
Grohmann, A., *Arabische Paläographie*, vol. I, Vienna, 1967

Grohmann 1971
Grohmann, A., *Arabische Paläographie*, vol. II, Vienna, 1971

Grohmann et al. 2012
Grohmann, A., et al., 'al-Yaman', in *Encyclopaedia of Islam*, 2nd edn, ed. P. Bearman et al.; online at https://referenceworks.brillonline.com/browse/encyclopaedia-of-islam-1, 2012 (accessed 8 December 2021)

Grütter 1954
Grütter, I., 'Arabische Bestattungsbräuche in frühislamischer Zeit', *Der Islam* 31 (1954), 147–73

Grütter 1957
Grütter, I., 'Arabische Bestattungsbräuche in frühislamischer Zeit (Fortsetzung)', *Der Islam* 32 (1957), 79–104

Guest 1930
Guest, A.R., 'Further Arabic Inscriptions on Textiles (III)', *Journal of the Royal Asiatic Society* (1930), pp. 761–66

Guest, 1931
Guest, A.R., 'Further Arabic Inscriptions on Textiles (IV)', *Journal of the Royal Asiatic Society* (1931), pp. 129–34

Haig et al. 2012
Haig, T.W., C.E. Bosworth, S. Ansari, C. Shackle and Y. Crowe, 'Sind', in *Encyclopaedia of Islam*, 2nd edn, ed. P. Bearman et al.; online at https://referenceworks.brillonline.com/browse/encyclopaedia-of-islam-2, 2012 (accessed 5 December 2021)

Halevi 2007
Halevi, L., *Muḥammad's Grave: Death Rites and the Making of Islamic Society*, New York, 2007

Halm 1996
Halm, H., *The Empire of the Mahdi: The Rise of the Fatimids*, Leiden, 1996

Hamilton 1988
Hamilton, R., *Walid and his Friends: An Umayyad Tragedy*, Oxford, 1988

Harris 2004
Harris, J., *5000 Years of Textiles*, London, 2004

Hassan 1948
Hassan, Z.M., *Funun al-islam*, Cairo, 1948

Hawary 1933–34
El-Hawary, M.H.M., 'Un tissu abbaside de Perse', *Bulletin de l'Institut d'Égypte* 16 (1933–34), 61–71

Heidemann et al. 2014
Heidemann, S., J.-F. de Lapérouse and V. Parry, 'The Large Audience:

Life-Sized Stucco Figures of Royal Princes from the Seljuq Period', *Muqarnas* 31 (2014), 35–71

Helmecke 2005
Helmecke, G., 'Textiles with Arabic Inscriptions Excavated in Naqlun, 1999–2003', *Polish Archaeology in the Mediterranean* 16 (2005), 195–202

Hermitage Museum 1990
Masterpieces of Islamic Art in the Hermitage Museum, Kuwait, 1990

Herodotus 1921
Herodotus, trans. A.D. Godley, 4 vols, London and New York, 1921

Herzfeld 1923
Herzfeld, E., *Der Wandschmuck der Bauten von Samarra und ihre Ornamentik*, Berlin, 1923

Herzfeld 1927
Herzfeld, E., *Die Malereien von Samarra*, Berlin, 1927

Herzfeld 1948
Herzfeld, E., *Geschichte der Stadt Samarra*, Berlin, 1948

Hilal al-Sabi' 1904
Hilal al-Sabi', *Kitab al-wuzara*, ed. H.F. Amedroz, Leiden, 1904

Hilal al-Sabi' 1964
Hilal al-Sabi', *Rusum dar al-khilafah: The Etiquette, Protocol and Diplomacy of the 'Abbasid Caliphate in Baghdad*, ed. Mikha'il 'Awad, Baghdad, 1964

Hilal al-Sabi' 1977
Hilal al-Sabi', *Rusum dar al-khilafah / The Rules and Regulations of the 'Abbasid Court*, trans. Elie A. Salem, Beirut, 1977

Holt 2012
Holt, P.M., 'al-Fayyūm', in *Encyclopaedia of Islam*, 2nd edn, ed. P. Bearman et al.; online at https://referenceworks.brillonline.com/browse/encyclopaedia-of-islam-2, 2012 (accessed 9 November 2021)

Hudud al-'alam 1937
Hudud al-'alam / 'The Regions of the World': A Persian Geography, 372 AH / 982 AD, trans. V. Minorsky, London, 1937

Ibn Abi Usaybi'ah 1882
Ahmad ibn al-Qasim Ibn Abi Usaybi'ah, *'Uyun al-anba' fi tabaqat al-atibba'*, 2 vols, Königsberg, 1882

Ibn al-Athir 1873–74
'Izz al-Din 'Ali bin Muhammad Ibn al-Athir, *Al-kamil fi al-tarikh*, 12 vols, Cairo, 1873–74

Ibn al-Athir 1886
'Izz al-Din 'Ali bin Muhammad Ibn al-Athir, *Al-kamil fi al-tarikh*, 12 vols, Cairo, 1886

Ibn Duqmaq 1893
Ibrahim ibn Muhammad Ibn Duqmaq, *Kitab al-intisar li wasita 'aqad al-amsar / Description de l'Égypte*, 2 vols, ed. C. Vollers, Cairo, 1893

Ibn al-Faqih 1885
Ibn al-Faqih al-Hamadhani, *Compendium libri Kitab al-boldan*, ed. M.J. de Goeje, Leiden, 1885

Ibn Hawqal 1938–39
Abu al-Qasim Ibn Hawqal al-Nasibi, *Opus geographicum: liber imaginis*

terrae, ed. J.H. Kramers, 2nd edn, 2 vols in 1, Leiden, 1938–39

Ibn Khaldun 1900
'Abd al-Rahman ibn Muhammad Ibn Khaldun, *Al-muqaddima*, 7 vols, Beirut, 1900

Ibn Khaldun 1967
Ibn Khaldun, *An Introduction to History: The Muqqadimah*, trans. F. Rosenthal, London, 1967

Ibn Mammati 1943
As'ad ibn al-Muhadhdhab Ibn Mammati, *Kitab qawanin al-dawawin*, ed. A.S. Atiya, Cairo, 1943

Ibn Miskawayh 1921
Abu 'Ali Ahmad ibn Muhammad ibn Ya'qub Miskawayh al-Razi, *The Experiences of the Nations by Miskawaihi, Office-holder at the Courts of the Buwaihid Sultans, Mu'izz al-daulah, Rukn al-daulah, and 'Adud al-daulah*, ed. and trans. D.S. Margoliouth, 2 vols, Oxford, 1921

Ibn Rusta 1892
Abu 'Ali Ahmad ibn 'Umar Ibn Rusta, *Kitab al-'alak al-nafisa VII*, ed. M.J. de Goeje, Leiden, 1892

Ibn Sa'd 1904–40
Muhammad Ibn Sa'd, *Kitab al-tabaqat al-kabir*, 9 vols, ed. E. Sachau, Leiden, 1904–40

Ibn Sa'd 1967–72
Muhammad Ibn Sa'd, *Ibn Sa'd's Kitab tabaqat al-kabir*, 2 vols, trans. S. Moinul Haq with H.K. Ghazanfar, Karachi, 1967–72

Ibn Taghribirdi 1855–61
Yusuf Ibn Taghribirdi, *Al-nujum al-zahira fi muluki misr wa al-qahira*, 2 vols, ed. T.W.J. Juynboll and B.F. Matthes, Leiden, 1855–61

Ibn Taghribirdi 1909–30
Ibn Taghribirdi, *Abu 'l-Mahasin ibn Taghri Birdi's Annals entitled Annujum az-zahira fi muluk misr wal-kahira*, ed. W. Popper, University of California Publications in Semitic Philology, Berkeley, 1909–30

Idrisi 1836–40
Abu 'Abdallah Muhammad al-Idrisi, *Géographie d'Édrisi traduite de l'arabe en français d'après deux manuscrits de la Bibliothèque du Roi et accompagnée de notes*, trans. and ed. P.A. Jaubert, Paris, 1836–40

Idrisi 1866
Abu 'Abdallah Muhammad al-Idrisi, *Al-maghrib wa ard al-sudan wa misr wa al-andalus, makhuda min kitab nuzhat al-mushtaq fi ikhteraq al-ifaq / Description de l'Afrique et de l'Espagne*, ed. and trans. R.P.A. Dozy and M.J. de Goeje, Leiden, 1866

Idrisi 1885
Gildemeister, J., 'Beiträge zur Palästinakunde aus arabischen Quellen, 5. Idrisi', *Zeitschrift des Deutschen Palaestina-Vereins* 8 (1885), 117–45 [incl. original Arabic text of al-Idrisi's Geography, 'Idrisi's Palaestina und Syrien im arabischen Text', ed. J. Gildemeister, appendix ('Beilage'), pp. 1–28]

Imad 1990
al-Imad, L.S., *The Fatimid Vizirate, 969–1172*, Berlin, 1990

Isfahani 1868
Abu al-Faraj al-Isfahani, *Kitab al-aghani*, ed. R.-E. Brünnow, 20 vols, Cairo, 1868

Isfahani 1927–36
Abu al-Faraj al-Isfahani, *Kitab al-aghani*, 16 vols, Cairo, 1927–36

Istakhri 1870
Abu Ishak al-Farisi al-Istakhri, *Viae regnorum: descriptio ditionis moslemicae*, ed. M.J. de Goeje, Bibliotheca Geographorum Arabicum 1, Leiden, 1870

Jahiz 1932
Abu 'Uthman 'Amr ibn Bahr al-Kinani al-Basri al-Jahiz, *Al-Tabassur bi al-Tidjara*, ed. Hasan Husni 'Abd al-Wahhab, Damascus, 1351 AH/ 1932 CE (Revue de l'académie arabe de Damas, XII)

Jahshihyari 1938
Abu 'Abdallah Muhammad ibn 'Abdus al-Jahshiyari, *Kitab al-wuzara wa al-kuttab*, Cairo, 1938

Jawdhari 1954
Abu 'Ali Mansur al-'Azizi al-Jawdhari, *Sirat al-ustadh jawdhar wa bihi tawqi'at al-a'imma al-fatimiyin*, ed. Muhammad Kamil Husayn and Muhammad 'Abd al-Hadi Shu'aira, Cairo, 1954

Jawdhari 1958
Abu 'Ali Mansur al-'Azizi al-Jawdhari, *Vie de l'Ustadh Jaudhar (contenant sermons, lettres et rescrits des premiers califes fâtimides) écrite par Mansûr le secrétaire à l'époque du calife al-'Azîz billâh (365–386/975–996), traduite de l'arabe sur l'édition de M. Kâmil Husain et M. 'Abd al-Hâdi Cha'ira*, trans. M. Canard, Algiers, 1958

Jenkins 1983
Jenkins, M. (ed.), *The al-Sabah Collection: Islamic Art in the Kuwait National Museum*, London, 1983

Jonghe and Tavernier 1983
Jonghe, D. de, and M. Tavernier, 'Le phénomène du croisage des fils de chaîne dans les tapisseries coptes', *Bulletin de Liaison du Centre International d'Étude des Textiles Anciens* 57–58 (1983), 174–86

Kahle 1935
Kahle, P., 'Die Schätze der Fatimiden', *Zeitschrift der Deutschen Morgenländischen Gesellschaft* 89 new ser., 14 (1935), 329–62

Karabacek 1881
Karabacek, J. von, *Die Persische Nadelmalerei Susandschird: ein Beitrag zur Entwicklungsgeschichte der Tapisserie de Haute Lisse*, Leipzig, 1881

Karabacek 1887
Karabacek, J. von, 'Das arabische Papier', *Mittheilungen aus der Sammlung der Papyrus Erzherzog Rainer* 2–3 (1887), 87–178

Karabacek 1888
Karabacek, J. von, 'Neue Quellen

zur Papiergeschichte', *Mittheilungen aus der Sammlung der Papyrus Erzherzog Rainer* 4 (1888), 75–122

Karabacek 1908
Karabacek, J. von, *Zur orientalischen Altertumskunde*, vol. II: *Die arabischen Papyrusprotokolle*, Vienna, 1908

Karabacek et al. 1894
Karabacek, J., J. Krall and K. Wessely, *Papyrus Erzherzog Rainer: Führer durch die Ausstellung*, Vienna, 1894

Kawami 2011
Kawami, Trudi, 'Clothing, iii', *Encyclopaedia Iranica*, vol. V/7, 2011, pp. 737–39; available online at http://www.iranicaonline.org/articles/clothing-iii (accessed 26 June 2021)

Kendrick 1924
Kendrick, A.F., *Catalogue of Muhammadan Textiles of the Medieval Period*, London, 1924

Kennedy 1986
Kennedy, H., *The Prophet and the Age of the Caliphates: The Islamic Near East from the Sixth to the Eleventh Century*, London and New York, 1986

Kennedy 1993a
Kennedy, H., 'al-Mu'tamid 'Alā'llāh', in *Encyclopaedia of Islam*, 2nd edn, ed. P. Bearman et al., vol. VII, Leiden, 1993, pp. 765–66

Kennedy 1993b
Kennedy, H., 'al-Mutawakkil 'Alā'llāh', in *Encyclopaedia of Islam*, 2nd edn, ed. P. Bearman et al., vol. VII, Leiden, 1993, pp. 777–78

Kennedy 1998
Kennedy, H., 'Egypt as a Province in the Islamic Caliphate, 641–868', in *The Cambridge History of Egypt*, ed. C.F. Petry and M.W. Daly, Cambridge, 1998, pp. 62–85

Khan 1992
Khan, G., *Arabic Papyri: Selected Material from the Khalili Collection*, Oxford and London, 1992

Khan 1993
Khan, G., *Bills, Letters and Deeds: Arabic Papyri of the 7th to 11th Centuries*, London, 1993

Khan 2002
Khan, M.I., 'The Grand Mosque of Banbhore: A Reappraisal', *Ancient Pakistan* 15 (2002), 1–9

Kiani 1984
Kiani, M.Y., *The Islamic City of Gurgan*, Berlin, 1984

Kraus n.d.
Kraus, H.P., *Islamic Textiles*, New York, n.d. [typescript sale catalogue]

Kraus 1978
Kraus, H. P., *A Rare Book Saga: The Autobiography of H. P. Kraus*, New York, 1978

Krody 2015
Krody, S. (ed.), *Unraveling Identity: Our Textiles, our Stories*, Washington, DC, 2015

Kühnel 1925
Kühnel, E., 'Tirazstoffe der

Abbasiden', *Der Islam* 14 (1925), pp. 82–88

Kühnel 1927
Kühnel, E., *Islamische Stoffe aus ägyptischen Gräbern in der islamischen Kunstabteilung und in der Stoffsammlung des Schlossmuseums*, Berlin, 1927

Kühnel 1933
Kühnel, E., 'Zur Tiraz-Epigraphik der Abbasiden und Fatimiden', *Aus fünf Jahrtausenden Morgenländischer Kultur: Festschrift Max Freiherrn von Oppenheim zum 70. Geburtstage*, Berlin, 1933, pp. 59–65

Kühnel 1952
Kühnel, E., 'Neue Beiträge zur Tiraz-Epigraphik', in *Documenta islamica inedita: Festschrift für Richard Hartmann*, Berlin, 1952, pp. 163–71

Kühnel 1960
Kühnel, E., *The Rug Tiraz of Akhmim*, Workshop Notes, the Textile Museum Washington, Paper 22, Washington, DC, 1960

Kühnel 1986
Kühnel, E., *Islamische Schriftkunst*, Graz, 1986

Kühnel and Bellinger 1952
Kühnel, E., and L. Bellinger, *Catalogue of Dated Tiraz Fabrics: Umayyad, Abbasid, Fatimid*, Washington, DC, 1952

Lamm 1928
Lamm, C.J., *Das Glas von Samarra*, Berlin, 1928

Lamm 1935
Lamm, C.J., 'Arabiska inskrifter pa nagra textilfragment fran Egypten', *Röhsska Konstslöjdmuseets Arstryck* (1935), 3–11

Lamm 1937
Lamm, C.J., *Cotton in Medieval Textiles in the Near East*, Paris, 1937

Lamm 1938
Lamm, C.J., 'Dated or Datable Tiraz in Sweden', *Le Monde Oriental* 32 (1938), 103–25

Lane 1863–77
Lane, E.W., *An Arabic–English Lexicon*, 2 vols, London, 1863–77

Le Strange 1890
Le Strange, G. (trans.), *Palestine under the Moslems: A Description of Syria and the Holy Land from A.D. 650 to 1500, Translated from the Works of the Arab Geographers*, London, 1890

Lev 1991
Lev, Y., *State and Society in Fatimid Egypt*, Leiden, 1991

Lewis 1960
Lewis, B., ''Ali al-Rida', in *Encyclopaedia of Islam*, 2nd edn, ed. P. Bearman et al., vol. I, Leiden, 1960, pp. 399–400

Lombard 1978
Lombard, M., *Études d'économie médiévale*, vol. III: *Les textiles dans le monde musulman du VIIe au XIIe siècle*, Paris, 1978

Mackie 1984
Mackie, L.W., 'Toward an Understanding of Mamluk Silks:

National and International Considerations', *Muqarnas* 2 (1984), 127–46

Mackie 1985
Mackie, L.W., 'Covered with Flowers: Medieval Floor Coverings Excavated at Fustat in 1980', in *Oriental Carpet and Textiles Studies*, ed. I.R. Pinner and W.B. Denny, London, 1985, pp. 23–35

Mackie 1989
Mackie, L.W., 'Textiles', in *Fustat Expedition Final Report*, ed. W. Kubiak and G. Scanlon, Winona Lake, IN, 1989, pp. 81–101

Mackie 1996
Mackie, L.W., 'Increase the Prestige: Islamic Textiles', *Arts of Asia* 26, no. 1 (1996), 82–93

Mackie 2015
Mackie, L.W., *Symbols of Power: Luxury Textiles from Islamic Lands, 7th to 21st Century*, Cleveland, 2015

Madelung 1965
Madelung, W., *Der Imam al-Qasim ibn Ibrahim und die Glaubenslehre der Zaiditen*, Berlin, 1965

Maher 1977
Maher, S., *Al-nasij al-islami*, Cairo, 1977

Makariou 2012
Makariou, S., *Islamic Art at the Musée du Louvre*, Paris, 2012

Maqrizi 1853–54
Abu al-'Abbas Ahmad b. 'Ali b. 'Abd al-Qadir al-Husayni Taqi al-Din Ahmad al-Maqrizi, *Kitab al-mawa'iz wa al-'itibar fi dhikr al-khitat wa al-athar*, 2 vols, Bulaq, 1853–54

Maqrizi 1900
Abu al-'Abbas Ahmad b. 'Ali b. 'Abd al-Qadir al-Husayni Taqi al-Din Ahmad al-Maqrizi, *Kitab al-mawa'iz wa al-'itibar fi dhikr al-khitat wa al-athar / Description topographique et historique de l'Égypte*, trans. U. Bouriant, Cairo, 1900

Marçais and Wiet 1934
Marçais, G., and G. Wiet, 'Le "Voile de Sainte Anne" d'Apt', *Monuments et Mémoires de la Fondation Piot* 34 (1934), 177–94

Maricq and Wiet 1959
Maricq, A., and G. Wiet, *Le minaret de Djam: la découverte de la capitale des sultans ghorides, XIIe–XIIIe siècles*, Paris, 1959

Marshak 1994
Marshak, B., 'Le programme iconographique des peintures de la "Salle des ambassadeurs" à Afrasiab (Samarkand)', *Arts Asiatiques* 49 (1994), 5–20

Martiniani-Reber 1992
Martiniani-Reber, M., 'Le rôle des étoffes dans le culte des reliques au Moyen Âge', *Bulletin du CIETA* 70 (1992), 53–58

Marzouk 1942
Marzouk, M.A.A., *Al-zakhrafat al-mansujat fi al-aqmisat al-fatimiyya*, Cairo, 1942

Marzouk 1943
Marzouk, M.A.A., 'The Evolution

of Inscriptions on Fatimid Textiles', *Ars Islamica* 10 (1943), 164–66

Marzouk 1948–49
Marzouk, M.A.A., 'Alexandria as a Textile Centre, 331 B.C.–1517 A.D.', *Bulletin de la Société d'Archéologie Copte* 13 (1948–49), 111–35

Marzouk 1954
Marzouk, M.A.A., 'The Turban of Samuel Ibn Musa: The Earliest Dated Islamic Textile', *Bulletin of the Faculty of Arts Cairo University* 16 (1954), 143–51

Marzouk 1955
Marzouk, M.A.A., 'Four Dated Tiraz Fabrics of the Fatimid Khalif az-Zahir', *Kunst des Orients* 2 (1955), 45–51

Marzouk 1957a
Marzouk, M.A.A., 'The Earliest Fatimid Textile', in *Akten des Vierundzwanzigsten Internationalen Orientalisten-Kongresses München, 28. August bis 4. September 1957*, ed. H. Franke, Wiesbaden, 1957, pp. 356–57

Marzouk 1957b
Marzouk, M.A.A., 'The Earliest Fatimid Textile (Tiraz al-Mansuriya)', *Bulletin of the Faculty of Arts Alexandria University* 11 (1957), 37–44

Marzouk 1959
Marzouk, M.A.A., 'Five Tiraz Fabrics in the Völkerkunde-Museum of Basel', in *Aus der Welt des islamischen Kunst: Festschrift für Ernst Kühnel zum 75. Geburtstag am 26.10.1957*, ed. R. Ettinghausen, Berlin, 1959, pp. 283–89

Mas'udi 1861–77
'Ali ibn al-Husayn al-Mas'udi, *Muruj al-dhahab wa ma'adin al-jawhar / Livre des Prairies d'Or*, ed. and trans. C.B. de Meynard and P. de Courteille, 9 vols, Paris, 1861–77

Mas'udi 1894
'Ali ibn al-Husayn al-Mas'udi, *Kitab at-tanbih wa'l-ishraf*, ed. M. J. de Goeje, Leiden, 1894

Matthews and Mordini 1959
Matthews, D., and A. Mordini, 'The Monastery of Debra Damo, Ethiopia', *Archaeologia* 97 (1959), 1–58, pls I–XV

Mawardi 1909
Abu al-Hasan 'Ali ibn Muhammad al-Mawardi, *Al-ahkam al-sultaniyya wa al-wilayat al-diniyya*, ed. Muhammad Badr al-Din Na'sani, Cairo, 1909

Mawardi 1929
Abu al-Hasan 'Ali ibn Muhammad al-Mawardi, *Kitab qawanin al-wizara wa siyasat al-mulk*, Cairo, 1929

Mawardi 1996
Abu al-Hasan 'Ali ibn Muhammad al-Mawardi, *Al-ahkam al-sultaniyya wa al-wilayat al-diniyya / The Ordinances of Government*, trans. W. H. Wahba, Reading, 1996

McWilliams 2021
McWilliams, M., 'Interwoven Motives: Collections of Tiraz Textiles in American Museums, c. 1890–1950', in *Social Fabrics:*

Inscribed Textiles from Medieval Egyptian Tombs, ed. M. McWilliams and J. Sokoly, Cambridge, MA, New Haven and London, 2021, pp. 39–49

McWilliams and Sokoly 2021
McWilliams, M., and J. Sokoly (eds), *Social Fabrics: Inscribed Textiles from Medieval Egyptian Tombs*, Cambridge, MA, New Haven and London, 2021

Merlange 1928
Merlange, G., 'Catalogue of the Elsberg Collection', *Bulletin of the Needle and Bobbin Club* 12, no. 1 (1928), 8–28

Micklewright 1991
Micklewright, N., '*Tiraz* Fragments: Unanswered Questions about Medieval Islamic Textiles', in *Brocade of the Pen: The Art of Islamic Writing*, ed. C.G. Fisher, East Lansing, MI, 1991, pp. 31–43

Miles 1952
Miles, G.C., 'Mihrab and 'Anazah: A Study in Early Islamic Iconography', in *Archaeologica orientalia in memoriam Ernst Herzfeld*, ed. G.C. Miles, Locust Valley, NY, 1952, pp. 156–71

Miles 1964
Miles, G.C., 'A Portrait of the Buyid Prince Rukn Al-Dawlah', *American Numismatic Society Museum Notes* 11 (1964), 283–93

Miles 1967
Miles, G.C., 'The Earliest Arab Gold Coinage', *American Numismatic Society Museum Notes* 13 (1967), 205–29

Monneret de Villard 1955
Monneret de Villard, U., 'Tessuti e ricami mesopotamici ai tempi degli Abbasidi e dei Selguqidi', *Atti della Accademia Nazionale dei Lincei: Memorie, Classe di Scienze Morali, Storiche e Filologiche* 8th ser., 7 (1955), 183–234

Moor et al. 2006
Moor, A. de, C. Verhecken-Lammens and M. Van Strydonk, 'Relevance and Irrelevance of Radiocarbon Dating of Inscribed Textiles', in *Textile Messages: Inscribed Fabrics from Roman to Abbasid Egypt*, ed. C. Fluck and G. Helmecke, Leiden, 2006, pp. 223–31

Mordini 1957
Mordini, A., 'Tre *tiraz* Abbasidi provenienti dal convento di Dabra Dammo', *Istituto di Studi Etiopici, Bollettino* 2 (1957), 33–38.

Mughal 1992
Mughal, M.R., 'Early Muslim Cities in Sindh and Patterns of International Trade', *Islamic Studies* 31 (1992), 267–86 [Islamic Research Institute, International Islamic University, Islamabad]

Muhammad Salim 1997
Muhammad Salim, Muhhammad 'Abbas, 'The Function of some Woven Fabrics in Riggisberg', in *Islamische Textilkunst des Mittelalters: aktuelle Probleme*, ed. K. Otavsky, Riggisberger Berichte 5, Riggisberg, 1997, pp. 65–69

Muqaddasi 1877
Shams al-din Abu 'Abdallah Muhammad ibn Ahmad ibn Abi Bakr al-Banna' al-Shami al-Muqaddasi al-Ma'ruf bi al-Bashari, *Descriptio imperii moslemici*, ed. M.J. de Goeje, Leiden, 1877

Muqaddasi 1906
Shams al-din Abu 'Abdallah Muhammad ibn Ahmad ibn Abi Bakr al-Banna' al-Shami al-Muqaddasi al-Ma'ruf bi al-Bashari, *Shiqqaq al-matari*, ed. G. Le Strange, Leiden, 1906

Nahhas 1999
Ahmad ibn Muhammad Nahhas, *'Umdat al-kuttab*, Frankfurt, 1999 [facs. edn of Oxford, Bodleian Library, MS Marsh 338]

Nasir-e Khosraw 1881
Nasir-e Khosraw, *Sefer nameh / Relation du voyage de Nassiri Khosrau en Syrie, en Palestine, en Égypte, en Arabie et en Perse, pendant les années de l'Hégire 437–444 (1035–1042)*, ed. and trans. C. Schefer, 2 vols, Paris, 1881

Nasir-e Khosraw 1986
Nasir-e Khosraw, *The Book of Travels / Safarnama*, ed. and trans. W.M. Thackston, Albany, NY, 1986

Niewöhner-Eberhard 2005
Niewöhner-Eberhard, E., 'Schutzstreifen in einem Bremer Evangeliar: zwei Stofffragmente mit arabischer Inschrift aus dem Lüneburger Schatz der Goldenen Tafel', *Codices Manuscripti: Zeitschrift für Handschriftenkunde* 52–53 (2005), 47–58

Northedge 1993
Northedge, A., 'An Interpretation of the Palace of the Caliph at Samarra (Dar al-Khilafa or Jawsaq al-Khaqani)', *Ars Orientalis* 23 (1993), 143–70

O'Kane 2018
O'Kane, B., 'The Egyptian Art of the Tiraz in Fatimid Times', in *The World of the Fatimids*, ed. A. S. Melikian-Chirvani, Toronto, 2018, pp. 178–89

Otavsky and Muhammad Salim 1995
Otavsky, K., and M.'A. Muhammad Salim, *Mittelalterliche Textilien*, vol. I: *Ägypten, Persien und Mesopotamien, Spanien und Nordafrika*, Riggisberg, 1995

Pal 1973
Pal, P. (ed.), *Islamic Art: The Nasli M. Heeramaneck Collection*, Los Angeles, 1973

Paret 1928
Paret, R., 'Die Legende von der Verleihung des Prophetenmantels (*burda*) an Ka'b ibn Zuhair', *Der Islam* 17 (1928), 9–14

Paris 1998
Trésors fatimides du Caire, Paris, 1998 [Institut du Monde Arabe]

Peck 1969
Peck, E.H., 'The Representation of Costumes in the Reliefs of Taq-i-Bustan', *Artibus Asiae* 31 (1969), 101–46

Pfister 1936
Pfister, R., 'Matériaux pour servir au classement des textiles égyptiens postérieurs à la Conquête Arabe', *Revue des Arts Asiatiques* 10 (1936), 1–16, 73–85

Pfister 1937
Pfister, R., 'L'introduction du coton en Égypte musulmane', *Revue des Arts Asiatiques* 11 (1937), 167–72

Pfister 1945–46
Pfister, R., 'Toiles à inscriptions abbasides et fatimides', *Bulletin d'Études Orientales* 11 (1945–46), 47–90

Piltz 1997
Piltz, E., 'Middle Byzantine Court Costume', in *Byzantine Court Culture from 829 to 1204*, ed. H. Maguire, Washington, DC, 1997, pp. 39–51

Pinder-Wilson 2001
Pinder-Wilson, Ralph, 'Ghaznavid and Ghurid Minarets', *Iran* 39 (2001), 155–86

Pope and Ackerman 1938–39
Pope, A.U., and Phyllis Ackerman, *A Survey of Persian Art from Prehistoric Times to the Present*, 7 vols, 1938–39

Prieur 1936
Prieur, C., 'À propos du Suaire de Cadouin', *La Semaine Religieuse du Diocèse de Périgueux et de Sarlat* 70 (1936), 405–10

Qaddumi 1996
al-Hijjawi al-Qaddumi, G. (trans.), *Book of Gifts and Rarities / Kitab-al-hadaya wa al-tuhaf: Selections Compiled in the Fifteenth Century from an Eleventh-Century Manuscript on Gifts and Treasures*, Cambridge, MA, 1996

Qadi al-Nu'man 1978
Qadi al-Nu'man ibn Muhammad, *Kitab al-majalis wa al-musayarat*, ed. al-Habib al-Faqi, Ibrahim Shabbuh and Muhammad al-Ya'alawi, Tunis, 1978

Qalqashandi 1913–19
al-Qalqashandi, Ahmad, *Subh al-a'sha fi sina'at al-insha'*, 14 vols, Cairo, 1913–19

Qazwini 1848–49
Zakariya' ibn Muhammad ibn Mahmud al-Qazwini, *Kitab 'aja'ib al-makhluqat wa ghara'ib al-mawjudat / Zakarija ben Muhammed ben Muhammed el-Cazwini's Kosmographie*, ed. F. Wüstenfeld, 2 vols, Göttingen, 1848–49; repr. Wiesbaden, 1967

Ragib 1974
Ragib, Y., 'Sur deux monuments funéraires du cimitière d'al-Qarafa al-Kubra au Caire', *Annales Islamologiques* 12 (1974), 67–83

Ragib 1982
Ragib, Y., *Marchands d'étoffes du Fayyoum au IIIe/IXe siècle d'après leurs archives*, vol. I: *Les actes des Banu 'Abd al-Mu'min*, Cairo, 1982

Raspopova 2006
Raspopova, V., 'Textiles Represented in the Sogdian Murals', in *Central Asian Textiles and their Contexts in the Early Middle Ages*, ed. R. Schorta, Riggisberger Berichte 9, Riggisberg, 2006, pp. 61–74

RCEA 1931–91
Répertoire chronologique d'épigraphie arabe, 18 vols, Cairo, 1931–91

Rekaya 1991
Rekaya, M., 'al-Ma'mūn, Abu 'l-'Abbās 'Abd Allāh b. Hārūn al-Rashīd', in *Encyclopaedia of Islam*, ed. P. Bearman et al., vol. VI, Leiden, 1991, pp. 331–39

Ritter 2016
Ritter, M., 'Cloth of Gold from West Asia in a Late Medieval European Context. The Abu Sa'id Textile in Vienna: Princely Funeral and Cultural Transfer', in *Oriental Silks in Medieval Europe*, ed. J. von Fircks and R. Schorta, Riggisberger Berichte 21, Riggisberg, 2016, pp. 231–51

Rogers 1983
Rogers, C. (ed.), *Early Islamic Textiles*, Brighton, 1983

Rogers 2010
Rogers, J.M., *The Arts of Islam: Masterpieces from the Khalili Collection*, London, 2010

Romberg 1985
Romberg, H., 'The Fatimid Treasury', M.Phil. thesis, University of Oxford, 1985

Roth 1951
Roth, H.L., *Ancient Egyptian and Greek Looms*, Halifax, 1951

Rump 2003
Rump, J.H., 'Skriften på væggen: om Koranfriser i islamisk arkitektur', *Carsten Niebuhr Biblioteket* 2 (2003), 4–10

Samman 1982
Samman, Tarif Al, 'Arabische Inschriften auf Krönungsgewändern des Heiligen Römischen Reiches', *Jahrbuch der Kunsthistorischen Sammlungen in Wien* 78 (1982), 7–34

Sanders 1994
Sanders, P., *Ritual, Politics, and the City in Fatimid Cairo*, Albany, NY, 1994

Sarre 1925
Sarre, F., *Die Keramik von Samarra*, Berlin, 1925

Schimmel 1992
Schimmel, A., and B. Rivolta, 'Islamic Calligraphy', *Metropolitan Museum of Art Bulletin* 50/1 (1992), 1–56

Schmedding 1978
Schmedding, B., *Mittelalterliche Textilien in Kirchen und Klöstern der Schweiz*, Bern, 1978

Serjeant 1972
Serjeant, R.B., *Islamic Textiles: Material for a History up to the Mongol Conquest*, Beirut, 1972

Shamir 1995
Shamir, O., 'Textiles from the Nahal Shahaq Site', *'Atiqot* 26 (1995), 42–48

Shepherd 1960
Shepherd, D., 'An Early Tiraz from Egypt', *Bulletin of the Cleveland Museum of Art* 47 (1960), 7–14

Shurinova 1967
Shurinova, R.D., *Koptskie tkani:*

sobranie Gosudarstvennogo muzeja izobrazitel'nych iskusstv imeni A. S. Puškina, Moskva / Coptic Textiles: Collection of Coptic Textiles, State Pushkin Museum of Fine Arts, Moscow, Leningrad, 1967

Sokoly 1997a
Sokoly, J., 'Between Life and Death: The Funerary Context of Tiraz Textiles', in *Islamische Textilkunst des Mittelalters: aktuelle Probleme*, ed. K. Otavsky, Riggisberger Berichte 5, Riggisberg, 1997, pp. 71–78

Sokoly 1997b
Sokoly, J., 'Towards a Model of Early Islamic Textile Institutions in Egypt', in *Islamische Textilkunst des Mittelalters: aktuelle Probleme*, ed. K. Otavsky, Riggisberger Berichte 5, Riggisberg, 1997, pp. 115–22

Sokoly 2002
Sokoly, J., 'Tiraz Textiles from Egypt: Production, Administration and Uses of Tiraz Textiles from Egypt under the 'Umayyad, 'Abbasid and Fatimid Dynasties', 6 vols, D.Phil. diss., University of Oxford, 2002

Sokoly 2006
Sokoly, J., 'Textiles', in *Medieval Islamic Civilization: An Encyclopedia*, 2 vols, ed. Josef W. Meri, New York, 2006, vol. 2, pp. 801–5

Sokoly 2017
Sokoly, J., 'Textiles and Identity', in *A Companion to Islamic Art and Architecture*, ed. G. Necipoglu and F.B. Flood, Hoboken, NJ, 2017, pp. 275–99

Sokoly 2021
Sokoly, J., 'Social Fabrics: Early Islamic Egypt through the Lens of Inscribed Tiraz Textiles', in *Social Fabrics: Inscribed Textiles from Medieval Egyptian Tombs*, ed. M. McWilliams and J. Sokoly, Cambridge, MA, New Haven and London, 2021, pp. 18–29

Sourdel 1960
Sourdel, D., 'Questions de cérémonial 'Abbasside', *Revue des Études Islamiques* 28 (1960), 121–48

Sourdel 1965
Sourdel, D., 'al-Djardjarāʾī', in *Encyclopaedia of Islam*, 2nd edn, ed. P. Bearman et al., vol. II, Leiden, 1965, pp. 461–62

Sourdel 1971
Sourdel, D., 'Hilāl b. al-Muḥassin b. Ibrāhīm al-Ṣābiʾ', *The Encyclopaedia of Islam*, 2nd edn, ed. P. Bearman et al., vol. III, Leiden, 1971, pp. 387–88

Sourdel 2012
Sourdel, D., 'Ibn Muḳla', in *Encyclopaedia of Islam*, 2nd edn, ed. P. Bearman et al.; online at https://referenceworks.brillonline.com/browse/encyclopaedia-of-islam-2, 2012 (accessed 6 November 2021)

Sourdel and Minganti 2012
Sourdel, D., and P. Minganti, 'Filasṭīn', in *Encyclopaedia of Islam*, 2nd edn, ed. P. Bearman et al.; online at https://referenceworks.brillonline.com/browse/encyclopaedia-of-islam-2, 2012 (accessed 30 November 2021)

Spuhler 1978
Spuhler, F., *Islamic Carpets and Textiles in the Keir Collection*, London, 1978

Spuhler 2020
Spuhler, F., *Early Islamic Textiles from along the Silk Road*, London, 2020

Stauffer 1995
Stauffer, A., M. Hill, H.C. Evans and D. Walker, *Textiles of Late Antiquity*, New York, 1995

Stillman 1986
Stillman, N.A., 'Khil'a', *Encyclopaedia of Islam*, 2nd edn, ed. P. Bearman et al., vol. V, Leiden, 1986, pp. 6–7

Stillman and Stillman 2003
Stillman, Y.K., and N.A Stillman, *Arab Dress: A Short History from the Dawn of Islam to Modern Times*, Leiden and Boston, 2003

Tabbaa 1994
Tabbaa, Y., 'The Transformation of Arabic Writing', pt 2: 'The Public Text', *Ars Orientalis* 24 (1994), 119–47

Tanukhi 1921–22
Abu 'Ali al-Muhassin al-Tanukhi, *Nishwar al-muhadara / The Tabletalk of a Mesopotamian Judge*, ed. and trans. D.S. Margoliouth, 2 vols, London, 1921–22

Thaʿalibi 1867
'Abd al-Malik ibn Muhammad al-Thaʿalibi, *Lataʾif wa al-maʿarif*, ed. P. de Jong, Leiden, 1867

Thaʿalibi 1908
'Abd al-Malik ibn Muhammad al-Thaʿalibi, *Kitab thimar al-qulub fi al-muadaf wa al-mansub*, Cairo, 1908

Thompson 1971
Thompson, D., *Coptic Textiles in the Brooklyn Museum of Art*, New York, 1971

Udovitch 1984
Udovitch, A.L., review of Y. Ragib, *Marchands d'étoffes du Fayyoum au IIIe/IXe siècle d'après leurs archives*, vol. I: *Les actes des Banu 'Abd al-Mu'min*, Cairo, 1982, in *Studia Islamica* 59 (1984), 187–88

Upton 1930–31
Upton, J.M., 'Dated Egypto-Arabic Textiles in the Metropolitan Museum of Art', *Metropolitan Museum Studies* 3 (1930–31), 158–73

Vassilika 1996
Vassilika, E., 'Egypt, ancient. XX. Collectors and dealers. 2. Dealers', *The Dictionary of Art*, ed. J. Turner, London and New York, 1996, vol. X, pp. 91–92

Van der Vliet 2006
Van der Vliet, Jacques, '"In a robe of gold": Status, Magic and Politics on Inscribed Christian Textiles from Egypt', in *Textile Messages: Inscribed Fabrics from Roman to Abbasid Egypt*, ed. C. Fluck and G. Helmecke, Leiden, 2006, pp. 23–67

Vogelsang-Eastwood 1990
Vogelsang-Eastwood, G., *Resist Dyed Textiles from Quseir al-Qadim, Egypt*, Paris, 1990 [Association pour l'Étude et la Documentation des Textiles d'Asie]

Volbach 1969
Volbach, W.F., *Early Decorative Textiles*, trans. Y. Gabriel, London, 1969

Volbach and Kühnel 1926
Volbach, W.F., and E. Kühnel, *Late Antique Coptic and Islamic Textiles of Egypt*, New York, 1926

Volov 1966
Volov, L., 'Plaited Kufic on Samanid Epigraphic Pottery', *Ars Orientalis* 6 (1966), 107–33

Walker and Froom 1992
Walker, D., and A. Froom, *Tiraz: Inscribed Textiles from Islamic Workshops*, exhibition notebook, Metropolitan Museum of Art, New York, 1992 [typescript]

Ward 1993
Ward, R.M., *Islamic Metalwork*, London, 1993

Wardwell 1992
Wardwell, A.E., 'Two Silk and Gold Textiles of the Early Mongol Period', *Bulletin of the Cleveland Museum of Art* 79 (1992), 354–78

Watson 1983
Watson, A.M., *Agricultural Innovation in the Early Islamic World: The Diffusion of Crops and Farming Techniques, 700–1100*, Cambridge, 1983

Watt 1960
Watt, W.M., '"Abd Allāh b. Djaḥsh', in *Encyclopaedia of Islam*, 2nd edn, ed. P. Bearman et al., vol. I, Leiden, 1960, p. 44

Watt and Wardwell 1997
Watt, J.C.Y., and A.E. Wardwell, *When Silk was Gold: Central Asian and Chinese Textiles*, New York, 1997

Wensinck 1986
Wensinck, A.J., 'Khuṭba', in *Encyclopaedia of Islam*, 2nd edn, ed. P. Bearman et al., vol. V, Leiden, 1986, pp. 74–75

Wertz et al. 2021
Wertz, J.H., M.L. Winter, R. Hanson and M. Montague, 'Beyond the Surface: Technical Analysis of Egyptian Textiles, *c.* 4th–12th Century', in *Social Fabrics: Inscribed Textiles from Medieval Egyptian Tombs*, ed. M. McWilliams and J. Sokoly, Cambridge, MA, New Haven and London, 2021

Wiet 1930
Wiet, G., *Album du Museé Arabe du Caire*, Cairo, 1930

Wiet 1935a
Wiet, G., 'Tissus et tapisseries du Musée Arabe du Caire', *Syria* 16 (1935), 278–90

Wiet 1935b
Wiet, G., *Exposition des tapisseries et tissus du Musée Arabe du Caire (du VIIe au XVIIe siècle), période musulmane*, Paris, 1935

Wiet 1937
Wiet, G., 'Tissus brodés de Mésopotamie', *Ars Islamica* 4 (1937), 54–63

Wiet 1959
Wiet, G., 'Note on the Cloths found at Debra Damo', *Archaeologia* 97 (1959), 58

Wingate 1942
Wingate, I.B., *Textile Fabrics and their Selection*, Englewood Cliffs, NJ, 1942

Winlock and Crum 1926
Winlock, H.E., and W.E. Crum, *The Monastery of Epiphanius at Thebes*, pt 1, New York, 1926

Winnik 2022
Winnik, A., 'The Art of Burial in the Medieval Nile Valley: Christian and Islamic Interchange in Religious Funerary Contexts', PhD diss., Bryn Mawr College, 2022

Winnik 2024
Winnik, A., 'Dress and Identity in Christian Nubia', *Convivium* 11, no. 1 (2024), pp. 90–101

Winter 2020
Winter, M.L., 'When Curtains Fall: A Shape-Shifting Silk of the Late Abbasid Period', *Medieval Globe* 6, no. 1 (2020), 31–55

Wüstenfeld 1881
Wüstenfeld, F., *Geschichte der Fatimiden-Chalifen, nach arabischen Quellen*, Göttingen, 1881

Yaʿqubi 1892
Abu al-ʿAbbas Ahmad bin Abi Yaʿqub bin Jaʿfar bin Wahb bin Wadih al-Yaʿqubi, *Kitab al-buldan*, ed. M.J. de Goeje, Leiden, 1892 (Bibliotheca Geographorum Arabicarum, vol. 7)

Yaqut 1866–73
Yaqut ibn 'Abdallah al-Hamawi, *Jacut's Geographisches Wörterbuch aus den Handschriften zu Berlin, St Petersburg, Paris, London and Oxford*, 6 vols, ed. F. Wüstenfeld, Leipzig, 1866–73

Yusuf 1995
Yusuf, Abd al-Raʾuf, *Darasat athar islamiyyah, al-majlis al-khamis*, Cairo, 1995

Zambaur 1927
Zambaur, E. de, *Manuel de généalogie et de chronologie pour l'histoire de l'Islam*, Hanover, 1927

SELECT LIST OF ISLAMIC DYNASTIES

The dynastic tables below, based on those published in Bosworth 1996b, list the Rightly Guided ('Rashidun') caliphs, as well as the caliphs of the three major dynasties discussed in this book: the Umayyads, the Abbasids and the Fatimids. They provide a key to the names and titles of caliphs referred to in the text and in the inscriptions.

The Rightly Guided or 'Patriarchal' or 'Orthodox' ('Rashidun') caliphs (11–40 AH / 632–61 CE)

Short form used in this book	Full form in Bosworth 1996b	AH	CE
Abu Bakr	Abu Bakr 'Atiq, Ibn Abi Quhafa, al-Siddiq	11	632
'Umar ibn al-Khattab	Abu Hafs 'Umar (I) ibn al-Khattab, al-Faruq	13	634
	Abu 'Amr or Abu 'Abdallah or Abu Layla 'Uthman ibn 'Affan, Dhu'l-Nurayn	23	644
'Ali	Abu al-Hasan 'Ali ibn Abi Talib, al-Imam al-Murtada	35–40	656–61

Umayyad dynasty (41–132 AH / 661–750 CE)

The Sufyanids

Short form used in this book	Full form in Bosworth 1996b	AH	CE
	Abu 'Abd al-Rahman Mu'awiya I ibn Abi Sufyan	41–60	661–680
	Abu Khalid Yazid I ibn Mu'awiya	60–64	680–683
Mu'awiya II	Mu'awiya II ibn Yazid I	64	683–684

The Marwanids

Short form used in this book	Full form in Bosworth 1996b	AH	CE
Marwan ibn al-Hakam	Abu 'Abd al-Malik Marwan I ibn al-Hakam	64–65	684–685
'Abd al-Malik ibn Marwan	Abu al-Walid 'Abd al-Malik ibn Marwan I, Abu 'l-Muluk	65–86	685–705
al-Walid I	Abu al-'Abbas al-Walid I ibn 'Abd al-Malik	86–96	705–715
Sulayman ibn 'Abd al-Malik	Abu Ayyub Sulayman ibn 'Abd al-Malik	96–99	715–717
	Abu Hafs 'Umar (II) ibn 'Abd al-'Aziz	99–101	717–720
	Abu Khalid Yazid II ibn 'Abd al-Malik	101–105	720–724

Hisham ibn ʿAbd al-Malik	Abu al-Walid Hisham ibn ʿAbd al-Malik	105–125	724–743
al-Walid II ibn Yazid	Abu al-ʿAbbas al-Walid II ibn Yazid II	125–126	743–744
	Abu Khalid Yazid III ibn al-Walid I	126	744
	Ibrahim ibn al-Walid I	126	744
Marwan II ibn Muhammad al-Himar	Abu ʿAbd al-Malik Marwan II ibn Muhammad, al-Jaʿdi al-Himar	127–132	744–750

The extent of the Umayyad dynasty, c. 750 CE

Abbasid dynasty (132–923 AH / 749–1517 CE)

The Abbasid caliphs in Iran and Baghdad, 132–656 AH / 749–1258 CE

Short form used in this book	Full form in Bosworth 1996b	AH	CE
al-Saffah	'Abdallah ibn Muhammad al-Imam, Abu al-'Abbas al-Saffah	132–136	749–754
al-Mansur	'Abdallah ibn Muhammad al-Imam, Abu Ja'far al-Mansur	136–158	754–775
al-Mahdi	Muhammad ibn al-Mansur, Abu 'Abdallah al-Mahdi	158–169	775–785
	Musa ibn al-Mahdi, Abu Muhammad al-Hadi	169–170	785–786
Harun al-Rashid	Harun ibn al-Mahdi, Abu Ja'far al-Rashid	170–193	786–809
al-Amin	Muhammad ibn al-Rashid, Abu Musa al-Amin	193–196	809–813
al-Ma'mun	'Abdallah ibn al-Rashid, Abu Ja'far al-Ma'mun	196–218	813–833
	Ibrahim ibn al-Mahdi (in Baghdad)	201–203	817–819
al-Mu'tasim	Muhammad ibn al-Rashid, Abu Ishaq al-Mu'tasim	218–227	833–842
al-Wathiq	Harun ibn al-Mu'tasim, Abu Ja'far al-Wathiq	227–232	842–847
al-Mutawakkil	Ja'far ibn al-Mu'tasim, Abu al-Fadl al-Mutawakkil	232–247	847–861
	Muhammad ibn al-Mutawakkil, Abu Ja'far al-Muntasir	247–248	861–862
al-Musta'in	Ahmad ibn Muhammad, Abu al-'Abbas al-Musta'in	248–252	862–866
al-Mu'tazz	Muhammad ibn al-Mutawakkil, Abu 'Abdallah al-Mu'tazz	252–255	866–869
	Muhammad ibn al-Wathiq, Abu Ishaq al-Muhtadi	255–256	869–870
al-Mu'tamid	Ahmad ibn al-Mutawakkil, Abu al-'Abbas al-Mu'tamid	256–279	870–892
al-Mu'tadid	Ahmad ibn al-Muwaffaq, Abu al-'Abbas al-Mu'tadid	279–289	892–902
al-Muktafi	'Ali ibn al-Mu'tadid, Abu Muhammad al-Muktafi	289–295	902–908
al-Muqtadir	Ja'far ibn al-Mu'tadid, Abu al-Fadl al-Muqtadir (first reign)	295	908
	Ibn al-Mu'tazz al-Murtada al-Muntasif (in Baghdad)	296	908
al-Muqtadir	Ja'far al-Muqtadir (second reign)	296–317	908–929
	Muhammad ibn al-Mu'tadid, Abu Mansur al-Qahir (first reign, in Baghdad)	317	929
al-Muqtadir	Ja'far al-Muqtadir (third reign)	317–320	929–932

al-Qahir	Muhammad al-Qahir (second reign)	320–322	932–934
al-Radi	Ahmad ibn al-Muqtadir, Abu al-ʿAbbas al-Radi	322–329	934–940
al-Muttaqi	Ibrahim ibn al-Muqtadir, Abu Ishaq al-Muttaqi	329–333	940–944
al-Mustakfi	ʿAbdallah ibn al-Muktafi, Abu al-Qasim al-Mustakfi	333–334	944–946
al-Mutiʿ	al-Fadl ibn al-Muqtadir, Abu al-Qasim al-Mutiʿ	334–363	946–74
al-Taʾiʿ	ʿAbd al-Karim ibn al-Mutiʿ, Abu al-Fadl al-Taʾiʿ	363–381	974–991
al-Qadir	Ahmad ibn Ishaq, Abu al-ʿAbbas al-Qadir	381–422	991–1031
	ʿAbdallah ibn al-Qadir, Abu Jaʿfar al-Qaʾim	422–467	1031–1075

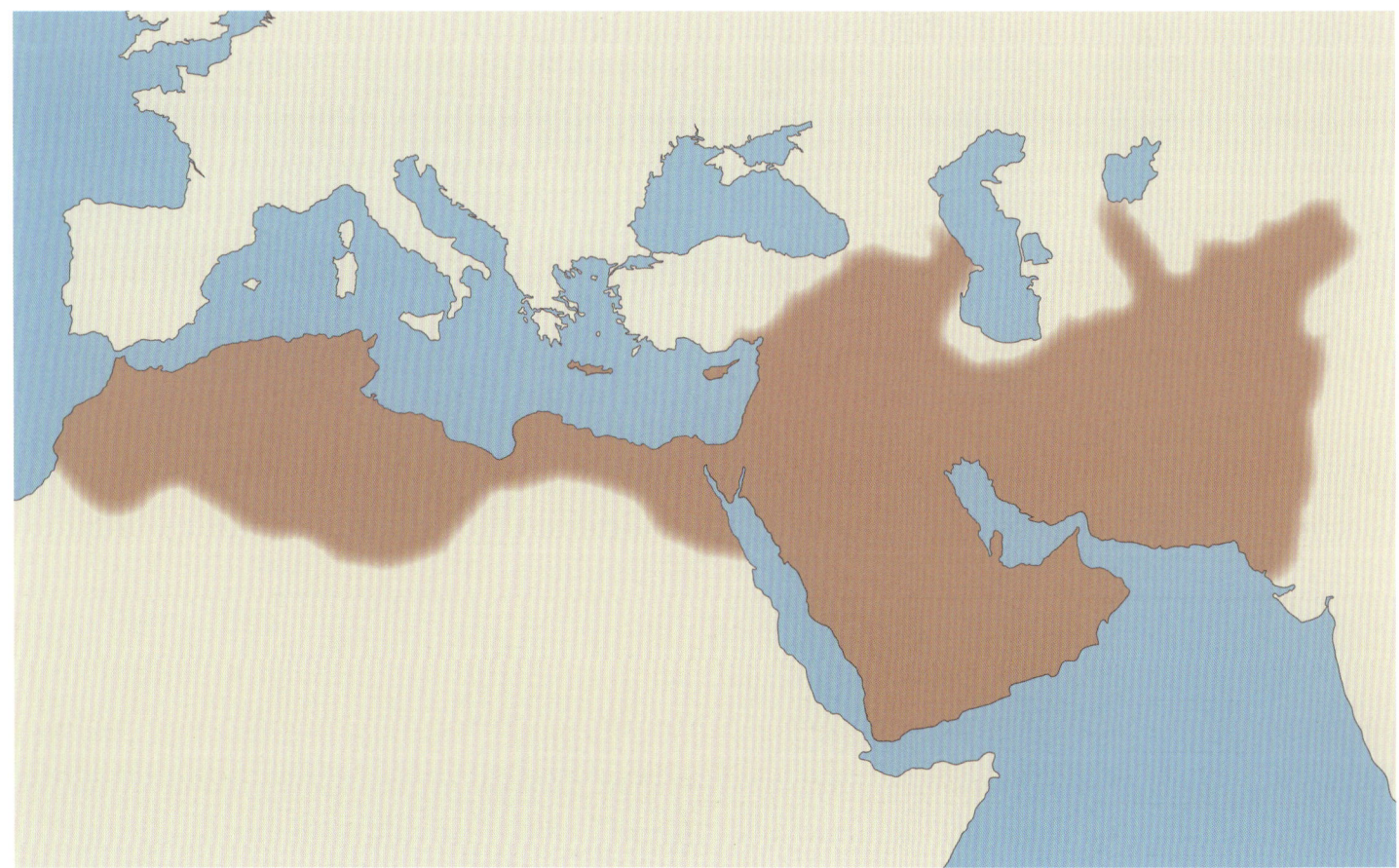

The extent of the Abbasid dynasty, *c*. 850 CE

al-Muqtadi	'Abdallah ibn Muhammad, Abu al-Qasim al-Muqtadi	467–487	1075–1094
	Ahmad ibn al-Muqtadi, Abu al-'Abbas al-Mustazhir	487–512	1094–1118
	al-Fadl ibn al-Mustazhir, Abu Mansur al-Mustarshid	512–529	1118–1135
	al-Mansur ibn al-Mustarshid, Abu Ja'far al-Rashid	529–530	1135–1136
al-Muqtafi	Muhammad ibn al-Mustazhir, Abu 'Abdallah al-Muqtafi	530–555	1136–1160
	Yusuf ibn al-Muqtafi, Abu 'l-Muzaffar al-Mustanjid	555–566	1160–1170
	al-Hasan ibn al-Mustanjid, Abu Muhammad al-Mustadi'	566–575	1170–1180
al-Nasir	Ahmad ibn al-Mustadi', Abu al-'Abbas al-Nasir	575–622	1180–1225
	Muhammad ibn al-Nasir, Abu Nasr al-Zahir	622–623	1225–1226
al-Mustansir	al-Mansur ibn al-Zahir, Abu Ja'far al-Mustansir	623–640	1226–1242
	'Abdallah ibn al-Mustansir, Abu Ahmad al-Musta'sim	640–656	1242–1258

Fatimid dynasty (297–567 AH / 909–1171 CE)

Short form used in this book	Full form in Bosworth 1996b (diacriticals removed)	AH	CE
al-Mahdi	'Abdallah (or 'Ubaydallah) ibn Husayn, Abu Muhammad al-Mahdi	297–322	909–934
	Muhammad ibn (?) al-Mahdi, Abu al-Qasim al-Qa'im	322–334	934–946
al-Mansur	Isma'il ibn al-Qa'im, Abu Tahir al-Mansur	334–341	946–953
al-Mu'izz	Ma'add ibn al-Mansur, Abu Tamim al-Mu'izz	341–365	953–975
al-'Aziz	Nizar ibn al-Mu'izz, Abu Mansur al-'Aziz	365–386	975–996
al-Hakim	al-Mansur ibn al-'Aziz, Abu 'Ali al-Hakim	386–411	996–1021
al-Zahir	'Ali ibn al-Hakim, Abu al-Hasan al-Zahir	411–427	1021–1036
al-Mustansir	Ma'add ibn al-Zahir, Abu Tamim al-Mustansir	427–487	1036–1094
al-Musta'li	Ahmad ibn al-Mustansir, Abu al-Qasim al-Musta'li	487–495	1094–1101
al-Amir	al-Mansur ibn al-Musta'li, Abu 'Ali al-Amir	495–524	1101–1130

	Interregnum; rule by al-Hafiz as regent but not yet as caliph; coins in the name of al-Muntazar 'the Expected One'	524–525	1130–1131
al-Hafiz	'Abd al-Majid ibn Muhammad, Abu al-Maymun al-Hafiz	525–544	1131–1149
al-Zafir	Isma'il ibn al-Hafiz, Abu al-Mansur al-Zafir	544–549	1149–1154
	'Isa ibn al-Zafir, Abu al-Qasim al-Fa'iz	549–555	1154–1160
	'Abdallah ibn Yusuf, Abu Muhammad al-'Adid	555–567	1160–1171

The extent of the Fatimid dynasty, *c.* 1000 CE

TABLE OF CONCORDANCE OF INVENTORY NUMBERS AND CATALOGUE NUMBERS

Inventory number	Catalogue number	Pages (main entry)
LNS 1 T	Cat. 75	270–71
LNS 17 T	Cat. 144	428–29
LNS 18 T	Cat. 119	372–73
LNS 19 T	Cat. 95	302–03
LNS 22 T	Cat. 69	258–59
LNS 23 T	Cat. 71	261
LNS 24 T a, b	Cat. 70	260
LNS 29 T	Cat. 111	348–49
LNS 30 T a, b	Cat. 97	306–07
LNS 31 T a–e	Cat. 68	256–57
LNS 32 T	Cat. 170	468
LNS 44 T	Cat. 67	254–55
LNS 45 T	Cat. 171	469
LNS 46 T	Cat. 145	430–31
LNS 47 T	Cat. 178	480–82
LNS 48 T	Cat. 172	470–71
LNS 49 T	Cat. 165	457
LNS 50 T a, b	Cat. 84	285
LNS 51 T	Cat. 53	227
LNS 52 T	Cat. 9	150–51
LNS 53 T	Cat. 129	398–99
LNS 54 T	Cat. 115	358–61
LNS 56 T	Cat. 66	252–53
LNS 57 T	Cat. 54	228–29
LNS 58 T	Cat. 62	246–47
LNS 60 T	Cat. 59	240–41
LNS 61 T	Cat. 106	320–21
LNS 63 T	Cat. 32	196–97
LNS 64 T	Cat. 28	191
LNS 65 T a–e	Cat. 74	266–69
LNS 66 T a–c	Cat. 77	274–75
LNS 67 T	Cat. 87	290–91

Inventory number	Catalogue number	Pages (main entry)
LNS 68 T	Cat. 55	232–33
LNS 69 T	Cat. 38	206–07
LNS 73 T	Cat. 128	396–97
LNS 75 T	Cat. 114	354–56
LNS 76 T	Cat. 184	488–89
LNS 78 T a–c	Cat. 166	458–61
LNS 80 T	Cat. 118	371
LNS 84 T	Cat. 116	368–69
LNS 85 T	Cat. 117	370
LNS 91 T	Cat. 41	212–13
LNS 92 T	Cat. 72	261
LNS 94 T	Cat. 107	332–33
LNS 102 T	Cat. 113	352–53
LNS 103 T	Cat. 112	350–51
LNS 110 T	Cat. 60	242–43
LNS 113 T	Cat. 61	244–45
LNS 116 T	Cat. 160	452
LNS 129 T	Cat. 8	146–49
LNS 130 T	Cat. 12	156–59
LNS 131 T	Cat. 14	162–63
LNS 132 T	Cat. 16	166–67
LNS 133 T	Cat. 22	178–79
LNS 134 T	Cat. 17	168–69
LNS 135 T	Cat. 18	170–71
LNS 136 T	Cat. 7	144–45
LNS 137 T	Cat. 15	164–65
LNS 138 T	Cat. 13	160–61
LNS 139 T	Cat. 20	174–75
LNS 140 T	Cat. 19	172–73
LNS 141 T	Cat. 1	132–33
LNS 142 T	Cat. 21	176–77
LNS 143 T	Cat. 105	318–19

Inventory number	Catalogue number	Pages (main entry)
LNS 144 T	Cat. 102	314–15
LNS 145 T a, b	Cat. 101	312–13
LNS 146 T	Cat. 100	311
LNS 147 T	Cat. 99	310
LNS 148 T	Cat. 98	308–09
LNS 149 T a, b	Cat. 96	304–05
LNS 150 T	Cat. 122	385
LNS 151 T	Cat. 39	208–09
LNS 152 T	Cat. 10	152–53
LNS 153 T	Cat. 30	193
LNS 154 T	Cat. 11	154–55
LNS 155 T	Cat. 25	184–85
LNS 156 T	Cat. 125	390–91
LNS 157 T	Cat. 132	404–05
LNS 158 T	Cat. 133	406–07
LNS 159 T	Cat. 3	136–37
LNS 160 T	Cat. 2	134–35
LNS 161 T	Cat. 109	340–43
LNS 162 T	Cat. 4	138–39
LNS 163 T	Cat. 110	344–47
LNS 164 T	Cat. 5	140–41
LNS 165 T	Cat. 23	180–81
LNS 166 T	Cat. 24	182–83
LNS 167 T	Cat. 27	189–90
LNS 168 T	Cat. 26	186–88
LNS 169 T	Cat. 29	192
LNS 170 T	Cat. 35	200–01
LNS 171 T	Cat. 33	198
LNS 172 T	Cat. 34	199
LNS 173 T	Cat. 36	202–03
LNS 174 T	Cat. 37	204–05
LNS 176 T	Cat. 120	381–83

Inventory number	Catalogue number	Pages (main entry)
LNS 177 T	Cat. 139	418–19
LNS 179 T	Cat. 31	194–195
LNS 180 T	Cat. 126	392–93
LNS 181 T a, b	Cat. 142	424–25
LNS 182 T	Cat. 123	386–87
LNS 183 T	Cat. 131	402–03
LNS 184 T	Cat. 130	400–01
LNS 186 T	Cat. 127	394–95
LNS 187 T	Cat. 124	388–89
LNS 188 T	Cat. 143	426–27
LNS 191 T	Cat. 134	408–09
LNS 193 T a, b	Cat. 135	410–11
LNS 194 T a–c	Cat. 136	412–13
LNS 199 T	Cat. 158	449
LNS 200 T	Cat. 141	422–23
LNS 201 T	Cat. 150	438–39
LNS 202 T	Cat. 152	442–43
LNS 203 T	Cat. 149	436–37
LNS 204 T	Cat. 151	440–41
LNS 205 T	Cat. 153	444
LNS 206 T	Cat. 154	445
LNS 207 T	Cat. 155	446
LNS 208 T	Cat. 156	447
LNS 209 T	Cat. 157	448
LNS 210 T	Cat. 173	472
LNS 219 T	Cat. 103	316
LNS 220 T	Cat. 104	317
LNS 221 T	Cat. 80	280–81
LNS 222 T	Cat. 79	278–79
LNS 223 T	Cat. 78	276–77
LNS 224 T	Cat. 81	282
LNS 225 T	Cat. 82	283

Inventory number	Catalogue number	Pages (main entry)
LNS 226 T a–c	Cat. 85	286–87
LNS 227 T	Cat. 86	288–89
LNS 228 T	Cat. 58	238–39
LNS 229 T	Cat. 83	284
LNS 230 T	Cat. 174	473
LNS 231 T	Cat. 175	474–75
LNS 232 T a–c	Cat. 176	476–77
LNS 233 T	Cat. 186	492–93
LNS 244 T	Cat. 121	384
LNS 247 T	Cat. 182	486
LNS 248 T	Cat. 181	485
LNS 250 T	Cat. 179	483
LNS 252 T	Cat. 45	219
LNS 255 T	Cat. 180	484
LNS 258 T	Cat. 161	453
LNS 259 T	Cat. 147	434
LNS 261 T	Cat. 138	416–17
LNS 262 T	Cat. 137	414–15
LNS 263 T	Cat. 6	142–43
LNS 265 T	Cat. 140	420–21
LNS 267 T a, b	Cat. 159	450–51
LNS 268 T	Cat. 148	435
LNS 275 T	Cat. 167	462–63
LNS 282 T	Cat. 168	464–65
LNS 286 T	Cat. 48	223
LNS 291 T	Cat. 47	222
LNS 292 T	Cat. 46	220–21
LNS 294 T	Cat. 49	224
LNS 295 T	Cat. 52	227
LNS 296 T	Cat. 51	226
LNS 297 T	Cat. 50	225
LNS 300 T	Cat. 177	478–79

Inventory number	Catalogue number	Pages (main entry)
LNS 301 T	Cat. 183	487
LNS 302 T	Cat. 63	248
LNS 303 T	Cat. 65	250–51
LNS 304 T	Cat. 64	249
LNS 306 T	Cat. 57	236–37
LNS 308 T	Cat. 56	234–35
LNS 309 T	Cat. 76	272–73
LNS 310 T a, b	Cat. 89	293
LNS 311 T	Cat. 169	466–67
LNS 312 T	Cat. 88	292
LNS 313 T	Cat. 90	294–95
LNS 314 T	Cat. 91	296–97
LNS 322 T	Cat. 92	298
LNS 323 T	Cat. 93	299
LNS 324 T	Cat. 43	216–17
LNS 325 T	Cat. 44	218
LNS 326 T	Cat. 42	214–15
LNS 331 T	Cat. 94	300
LNS 354 T	Cat. 40	210–11
LNS 404 T	Cat. 73	262
LNS 405 T	Cat. 187	494–95
LNS 416 T	Cat. 162	454
LNS 417 T	Cat. 185	490–491
LNS 420 T	Cat. 163	455
LNS 421 T	Cat. 188	496–97
LNS 422 T	Cat. 189	498–99
LNS 423 T a, b	Cat. 108	334–37
LNS 772 T	Cat. 146	432–33
LNS 1093 T	Cat. 164	456

LIST OF *TIRAZ* INSCRIPTIONS
COMPRISING HISTORICAL DATA

I. Abbasid Caliphate

Egypt

Cat. no.	Caliph	Date	Ordered by	Executive	Workshop	Location
Cat. 1	Harun al-Rashid (r. 786–809)					
Cat. 2	Al-Mutawakkil (r. 847–61)	240 AH / 854–55 CE				
Cat. 3	Al-Mutawakkil (r. 847–61)				*tiraz*	Alexandria
Cat. 5	Al-Muʿtadid (r. 892–902)	282 AH / 895–96 CE				Alexandria
Cat. 7	Al-Muqtadir (r. 908–32)	295 AH / 907–08 CE		Shafiʿ *m[awla] amir al-muʾminin*		
Cat. 8	Al-Muqtadir (r. 908–32)	299 AH / 911–12 CE	*al-wazir* ʿAli bin Muhammad	Bishr *mawla*	*tiraz*	Misr
Cat. 9	Al-Muqtadir (r. 908–32)	300 AH / 912–13 CE	*al-wazir* (?)		*tiraz*	
Cat. 10	Al-Muqtadir (r. 908–32)	300 AH / 912–13 CE		Shafiʿ *mawla amir al-muʾminin*	*[tiraz] al-khassa*	Misr
Cat. 11	Al-Muqtadir (r. 908–32)					
Cat. 12	Al-Muqtadir (r. 908–32)	300 AH / 912–13 CE	*al-wazir* ʿAli bin ʿIsa	Shafiʿ *mawla amir al-muʾminin*	*tiraz al-ʿamma*	Misr
Cat. 13	Al-Muqtadir (r. 908–32)					
Cat. 14	Al-Muqtadir (r. 908–32)	302(?) AH / 915–16(?) CE	*al-wazir* ʿAli bin ʿIsa	Shafiʿ		Misr
Cat. 15	Al-Muqtadir (r. 908–32)	310 AH / 922–23 CE	*al-wazir*			
Cat. 16	Al-Muqtadir (r. 908–32)					
Cat. 17	Al-Muqtadir (r. 908–32)		*al-wazir*		*tiraz al-ʿamma*	
Cat. 18	Al-Muqtadir (r. 908–32)					
Cat. 19	Al-Muqtadir (r. 908–32)					
Cat. 21	Al-Muqtadir (r. 908–32)					
Cat. 23	Al-Qahir (r. 932–34)					
Cat. 24	Al-Qahir (r. 932–34)					
Cat. 25	Al-Radi (r. 934–40)					
Cat. 26	Al-Radi (r. 934–40)	310 AH / 922–23(!) CE	*al-wazir* ʿAli bin ʿIsa	ʿUbayyid *mawla amir al-muʾminin*		
Cat. 27	Al-Radi (r. 934–40)	302(!) AH / 915–16(!) CE; datable 934–36 or 937–39	*al-wazir* Muhammad ibn ʿAli			
Cat. 28	Al-Radi (r. 934–40)					
Cat. 29	Al-Radi (r. 934–40)					
Cat. 32	Al-Radi (r. 934–40)		*al-wazir*			
Cat. 36	Al-Muttaqi (r. 940–44)					
Cat. 37	Al-Mutiʿ (r. 946–74)					
Cat. 38	Al-Mutiʿ (r. 946–74)					
Cat. 56	unknown				*tiraz*	

Iraq

Cat. no.	Caliph	Date	Ordered by	Executive	Workshop	Location
Cat. 95	Al-Muqtadir (r. 908–32)	300 AH / 912–13 CE				
Cat. 96	Al-Muqtadir (r. 908–32)	308 AH / 920–21 CE		[...] *mawla amir al-mu'minin*	*tiraz al-khassa*	Madinat al-Salam
Cat. 97	Al-Muqtadir (r. 908–32)	320 AH / 932–33 CE				
Cat. 98	Al-Muqtadir (r. 908–32)	3[...] / 9[...]			*tiraz al-khassa*	Madinat al-Salam

Yemen

Cat. no.	Caliph	Date	Ordered by	Executive	Workshop	Location
Cat. 109		Datable after 261 AH / 875–76 CE	*amir* Ja'far ibn *amir al-mu'minin* (Ja'far al-Mufawwad, al-Mu'tamid's first successor and viceroy)			
Cat. 110	Al-Mu'tadid (r. 892–902)	287 AH / 900 CE				

II. Fatimid Caliphate in Egypt

Cat. no.	Caliph	Date	Ordered by	Executive	Workshop	Location
Cat. 120	Al-'Aziz (r. 975–96)		*al-wazir*			
Cat. 123	Al-'Aziz (r. 975–96)					
Cat. 124	Al-'Aziz (r. 975–96)					
Cat. 125	Al-'Aziz (r. 975–96)					
Cat. 126	Al-'Aziz (r. 975–96)					
Cat. 128	Al-Hakim (996–1021)	403 AH / 1012–13 CE			*tiraz al-'amma*	Damietta
Cat. 129	Al-Hakim (996–1021)					
Cat. 131	Al-Hakim (996–1021) (attributed)					
Cat. 132	Al-Hakim (996–1021)					
Cat. 139	Al-Hakim (996–1021)					
Cat. 141	Al-Zahir (r. 1021–36)					
Cat. 142	Al-Zahir (r. 1021–36)		*al-wazir al-'ajal safi amir al-mu'minin* Abi al-Qasim ibn Ahmad			
Cat. 143	Al-Zahir (r. 1021–36)		*al-wazir al-'ajal*			
Cat. 144	Al-Mustansir (r. 1036–94)					
Cat. 145	Al-Mustansir (r. 1036–94)	Datable 1036–45 CE	*al-wazir al-'ajal al-'awhad safi [amir al-mu'minin]*			
Cat. 149	Al-Mustansir (r. 1036–94)					
Cat. 150	Al-Mustansir (r. 1036–94)					
Cat. 152	Al-Mustansir (r. 1036–94)					

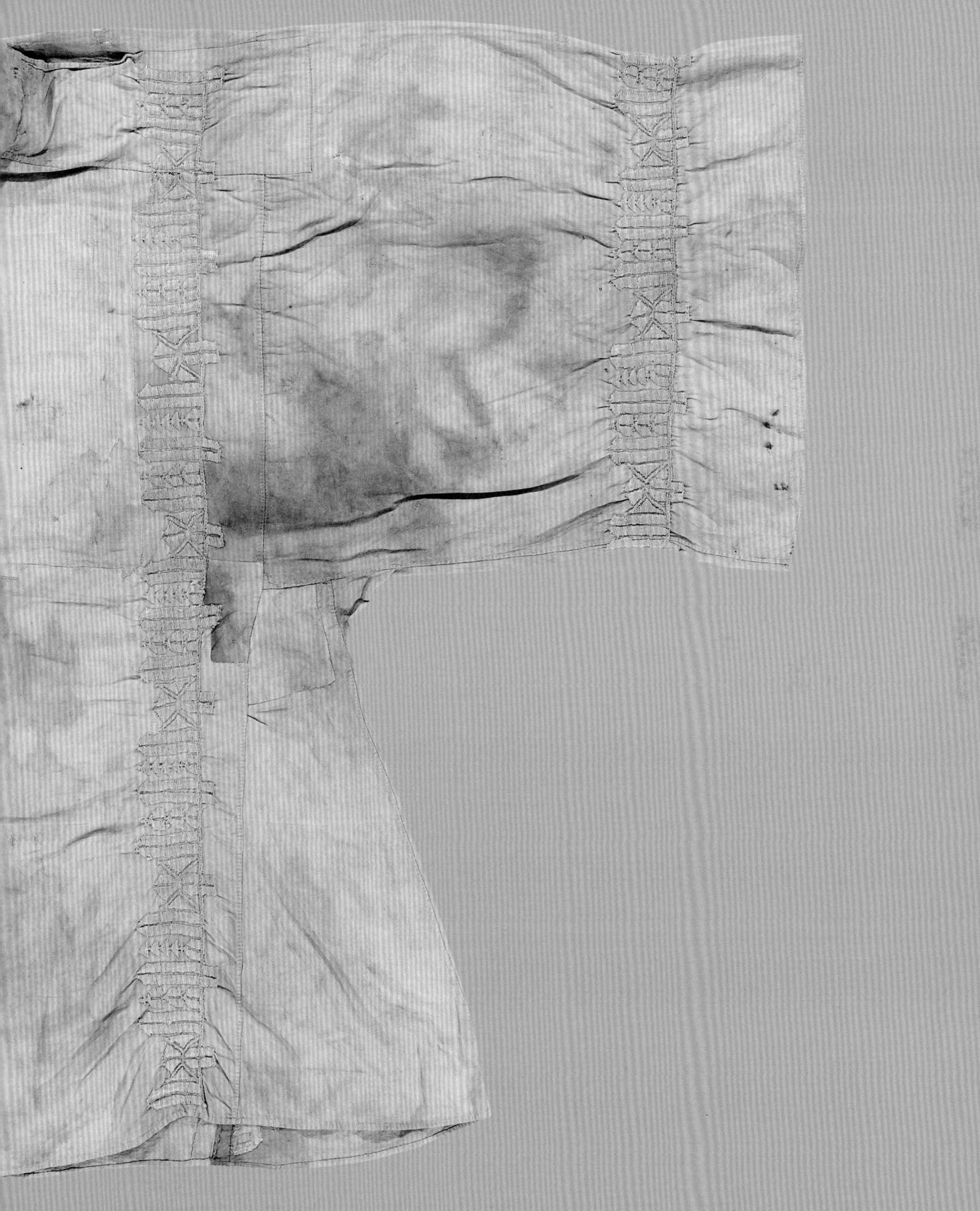

PICTURE CREDITS

INDEX

Page references in *italic* are to illustrations